S0-BEC-526

FLORIDA STATE
UNIVERSITY LIBRARIES

MAY 23 2001

TALLAHASSEE, FLORIDA

ECONOMIC THEORY AND PUBLIC DECISIONS

ECONOMISTS OF THE TWENTIETH CENTURY

General Editors: Mark Perlman, *University Professor of Economics, Emeritus, University of Pittsburgh* and Mark Blaug, *Professor Emeritus, University of London, Professor Emeritus, University of Buckingham and Visiting Professor, University of Exeter*

This innovative series comprises specially invited collections of articles and papers by economists whose work has made an important contribution to economics in the late twentieth century.

The proliferation of new journals and the ever-increasing number of new articles make it difficult for even the most assiduous economist to keep track of all the important recent advances. By focusing on those economists whose work is generally recognized to be at the forefront of the discipline, the series will be an essential reference point for the different specialisms included. Wherever possible, the articles in these volumes have been reproduced as originally published using facsimile reproduction, inclusive of footnotes and pagination to facilitate ease of reference.

A list of published and future titles in this series is printed at the end of this volume.

Economic Theory and Public Decisions

Selected Essays of Robert Dorfman

Robert Dorfman

David A. Wells Professor of Political Economy, Emeritus, Harvard University

ECONOMISTS OF THE TWENTIETH CENTURY SERIES

Edward Elgar
Cheltenham, UK • Brookfield, US

© Robert Dorfman, 1997

All rights reserved. No part of this publication may be reproduced, stored in a retrieval system, or transmitted in any form or by any means, electronic, mechanical, photocopying, recording, or otherwise without the prior permission of the publisher.

Published by
Edward Elgar Publishing Limited
8 Lansdown Place
Cheltenham
Glos GL50 2HU
UK

Edward Elgar Publishing Company
Old Post Road
Brookfield
Vermont 05036
US

A catalogue record for this book is available from the British Library

Library of Congress Cataloging-in-Publication Data
Dorfman, Robert.
    Economic theory and public decisions: selected essays of
Robert Dorfman/Robert Dorfman.
        (Economists of the 20th century series)
        Includes bibliographical references.
        1. Economic policy—Decision making. 2. Economics, Mathematical.
    3. Economics. I. Title. II. Series: Economists of the twentieth
    century.
    HD87.D67   1997
    338.9–dc20   96–35153
                                                                    CIP

ISBN 1 85898 212 X

Printed and bound in Great Britain by
Hartnolls Limited, Bodmin, Cornwall

To my wife, Nancy Shelling Dorfman, who suffered through my career twice: once living through it, and again reviewing it.

Contents

Acknowledgements

The author and publisher wish to thank the following who have kindly given permission for the use of copyright material.

Academic Press Inc. for article: 'On Optimal Congestion', *Journal of Environmental Economics and Management*, **11**, 1984, pp. 91–106.

American Economic Association for articles: 'Mathematical, or "Linear," Programming: A Nonmathematical Exposition', *American Economic Review*, **XLIII** (5), Part 1, December 1953, pp. 797–825; 'Operations Research', *American Economic Review*, **L**, September 1960, pp. 575–86, 602–7, 613–23; 'An Economic Interpretation of Optimal Control Theory', *American Economic Review*, **LIX** (5), December 1969, pp. 817–31; 'Optimal Advertising and Optimal Quality', *American Economic Review* (with Peter O. Steiner), **XLIV** (5), December 1954, pp. 826–36; 'Incidence of the Benefits and Costs of Environmental Programs', *American Economic Review*, **67** (1), February 1977, pp. 333–40; 'Comment: P.A. Samuelson, "Thünen at Two Hundred"', *Journal of Economic Literature*, **XXIV**, December 1986, pp. 1773–6; 'Thomas Robert Malthus and David Ricardo', *Journal of Economic Perspectives*, **3** (3), Summer 1989, pp. 153–64.

American Finance Association for article: 'The Meaning of Internal Rates of Return', *The Journal of Finance*, **XXXVI** (5), December 1981, pp. 1011–21.

Blackwell Publishers for article: 'Wassily Leontief's Contribution to Economics', *Swedish Journal of Economics*, **75**, 1973, pp. 430–49.

Elsevier Science Publishers for articles: 'A Catechism: Mathematics in Social Science', *The Review of Economics and Statistics*, **XXXVI**, 1954, pp. 374–77; 'The Nature and Significance of Input-Output', *The Review of Economics and Statistics*, **XXXVI** (2), May 1954, pp. 121–33; 'A Formula for the Gini Co-efficient', *The Review of Economics and Statistics*, **LXI** (1), February 1979, pp. 146–9; 'Protecting the Global Environment: An Immodest Proposal', *World Development*, **19** (1), 1991, pp. 103–10; 'Towards a Social Index of Environmental Quality', in *Economic Progress, Private Values, and Public Policy* (eds Bela Belassa and Richard Nelson), 1977, North-Holland Publishing Co., pp. 121–35.

HarperCollins Publishers for articles: 'Transition Costs of Changing Regulations', in *Attacking Regulatory Problems* (ed. Allen R. Ferguson), 1981, Ballinger Publishing Co., pp. 39–54; 'The Lessons of Pesticide Regulation', in *Reform of Environmental Regulation* (ed. Wesley A. Magat), 1982, Ballinger Publishing Co., pp. 13–29.

Institute of Management Sciences for article: 'Why Benefit–Cost Analysis is Widely Disregarded and What To Do About It', *Interfaces*, **16** (5), Sep.–Oct. 1996, pp. 1–6.

Institute of Mathematical Statistics for article: 'The Detection of Defective Members of Large Populations', *The Annals of Mathematical Statistics*, **XIV** (4), December 1943, pp. 436–40.

Iowa State University Press for article: 'Ethics, Economics, and the Environment', in *Economic Decision Making: Private and Public Decisions* (ed. Sisay Asefa), 1985, pp. 65–79.

John Wiley & Sons Ltd for article: 'Food for a Developing World' (with W.P. Falcon), in *Resources and World Development* (eds D.J. McLaren and B.J. Skinner), 1987, pp. 767–85.

Journal of the History of Economic Thought for article: 'Austrian and American Capital Theories: A Contrast of Cultures', **17**, Spring 1995, pp. 21–34.

Macmillan Press Ltd for articles: 'General Equilibrium with Public Goods', in *Public Economics* (eds J. Margolis and H. Guitton), 1969, pp. 247–75; 'Social Decisions without Social Preferences', in *Planning and Market Relations* (eds Michael Kaser and Richard Portes), 1971, pp. 117–29; 'Forty Years of Cost–Benefit Analysis', in *Econometric Contributions to Public Policy* (eds Richard Stone and William Peterson), 1978, pp. 268–84.

The *New York Times* for article: 'A Nobel Quest for the Invisible Hand', *New York Times*, October 23 1983, Business Section 3, p. 15.

Resources for the Future for article: 'The Technical Basis for Decision Making', in *The Governance of Common Property Resources* (ed. Edwin T. Haefele), 1974, The Johns Hopkins University Press for Resources for the Future, pp. 5–25.

Review of Economic Studies Ltd for article: 'A Graphical Exposition of Böhm-Bawerk's Interest Theory', *Review of Economic Studies*, **26**, February 1959, pp. 153–9.

Yale University Press for article: 'An Economist's View of Natural Resource and Environmental Problems', in *The Global Possible: Resources, Development and the New Century* (ed. Robert Repetto), 1985, pp. 67–95.

Every effort has been made to trace all the copyright holders but if any have been inadvertently overlooked the publishers will be pleased to make the necessary arrangements at the first opportunity.

Introduction

Ontogeny of an economist

My central concern during most of my career has been social decisions: how to reach them and how to judge them. This may seem to be a strange preoccupation for an economist until you pause to consider that social decision-making and welfare economics have such extensive overlaps that they cannot be disentangled. That central concern, though, does not imply that social decisions have been the explicit topic of most of my research and writing. On the contrary. Social decision-making is much too broad and inclusive a topic to be tackled bluntly and in its entirety. Instead, I have approached it piecemeal and somewhat deviously. But social deciding, by which I mean taking decisions that affect two or more people and take all their interests into account, has been lurking in the background and motivating nearly all my work. Obviously this circuitous approach to my central topic needs some explaining, so I shall provide it, beginning at the beginning.[1]

When I was an undergraduate in Columbia University in the 1930s, my field of concentration was mathematical statistics under the tutelage of Harold Hotelling, the leading theoretical statistician in the country at that time. When I graduated, in the midst of the Great Depression, there were practically no jobs for recent graduates with so little training, so I stayed on at Columbia for an MA degree in economics. (In those ancient days, few, if any, American universities offered advanced degrees in statistics; Columbia was not one.)

With this modest credential in my CV, and with Hotelling's help, I tried my hand at a number of statistical jobs that proved unsatisfactory for various reasons. Finally, I answered a 'help wanted' ad. placed by a commercial night school that gave cram courses for people preparing for Federal civil service examinations. They needed someone to teach the material for the Junior Statistican exam. I fitted that description and so, every Wednesday night for the following two months, I

---

1. In the interest of spinning a reasonably coherent narrative, I have tolerated some tension between the order in which papers are listed in the table of contents and the order in which they are discussed in this introduction.

   The table of contents is divided into six parts, each devoted to a very wide area. These parts are listed in about the order in which they rose to the top of my areas of interest. In each part the papers are listed in strict chronological order.

   On several occasions, I began publishing papers in one of these broad areas before I stopped writing papers that belonged to its chronological predecessor. In those instances, I violated the rules of chronology by continuing the list of papers belonging to the earlier topic until I had completed it.

   When I came to write the introduction, I found that I would be forced to separate the discussions of some closely related papers if I adhered to the partitioning according to the broad areas to which the papers were assigned in the table of contents. The two principles of organization turned out to conflict. I therefore chose to take up each paper where the logical connections seemed to call for it, even when that violated the chronological rules followed in arranging the table of contents.

   I believe that that policy revealed how and why my interests moved from subject to subject more effectively than would be possible if the papers were introduced in strict chronological order.

expounded the basic facts about means, medians, bar charts, and so on to about 50 hopeful students. I don't know how the students made out, but when the course was over I felt highly prepared for the examination, so why shouldn't I take it myself? I did, and I earned the second highest score in New York State. About a month later, I was offered a position in the Bureau of Labor Statistics (BLS) in Washington. The salary, though not munificent, was about 50 per cent higher than my current earnings at the time. I accepted, and worked at the BLS for about two years, receiving several promotions while there.

Meanwhile, the Depression had ended and the United States was moving rapidly towards a wartime footing. In particular the Office of Price Administration (OPA) had been established, was growing rapidly, and needed economic statisticians. They offered me an impressive-sounding job as a section chief in the Research Division. I accepted, and worked there for the next two years. While working for the OPA, I wrote a short note on a subject entirely unrelated to price administration. It was accepted by the *Annals of Mathematical Statistics*, and was fairly influential. I have included it in the present collection as Chapter 1, and hope you read it.

The summer of 1943 found me still at the OPA, concerned with repressing retail price inflation. World War II was being waged in full violence on three continents. I was eager to find a role more directly related to the fighting, but was strongly averse to trusting my fate to the punch-card machines that, in those days, assigned recruits to the wide variety of tasks that constitute modern warfare. (My brother, for example, fought his war as the mess sergeant in an infantry officers' mess.) I felt that I could make war more effectively at a task that utilized my training and experience in statistics. Just then the new field of operations research, recently invented by the Royal Air Force, was being introduced in the American armed forces. I heard of it, applied, was accepted, and was shipped off, after two or three weeks of preparation, to be an operations analyst with the Thirteenth Air Force in the South Pacific. My speciality was bombing tactics, though I had never actually seen a bomb or been aboard a military aircraft of any kind.

I remained in the South Pacific for a bit more than a year, analysing and comparing the results of a variety of bombing tactics used in that theatre. I was then transferred to Air Force Headquarters in the Pentagon. This seemingly routine move changed the direction of my career. In the Pentagon, I met George Dantzig, a young statistician who was also working in Air Force Headquarters. Though his work was entirely unrelated to mine, we had many interests in common and became friendly.

When the atomic bombs were dropped on Hiroshima and Nagasaki, bringing World War II to an abrupt end, I was still in the Pentagon. I had no connection with the Manhattan District project or any of its work. Nevertheless, I was asked to participate in planning and conducting the mammoth experiment of exploding two atomic bombs in Bikini Atoll to observe and measure their effects under controlled conditions. After the experiment it was time for me to reconvert to a less warlike occupation.

To this end, I applied for admission to the PhD programme in economics in the University of California at Berkeley, and was admitted. I chose economics because my work in the BLS and OPA gave me a head start in that field, and because economics seemed to embrace the critical social problems then confronting the country and the world. I chose Berkeley because I had visited San Francisco several times during the war and was charmed, and because I had been greatly impressed by several people I had met, mostly statisticians, connected with that campus. Admittedly, these were not good reasons for choosing a lifetime career, but it worked out well enough.

I spent two years in Berkeley studying economics, then was lured back to the Air Force by the prospect of earning a living wage. When I returned, I found my old friend Dantzig there, in a state of great excitement and frantic activity. In the interim, he had been engaged in an important and challenging project that bears some description.

Basically, his task was to develop an improved system for planning and budgeting the Air Force's long-run procurement and training programmes. At that time, the amount of paperwork and calculation needed to develop a long-run programme, complete with budgetary implications, for a large military organization was truly daunting. A small army of officers was required to labour with pencils and paper for most of a year to calculate the details of a plan, its implications and its costs. By the time they had constructed a plan in which the numerous details of purchasing, construction, training, and so on were reasonably consistent with each other, the assumptions and data used at the beginning would be out of date.

Danzig's project was motivated by the thought that the time and manpower required to elaborate a plan could be reduced greatly if the mass of considerations that the staff officers had to take into account could be expressed as a set of equations solvable by punch-card machines. Using punch-card machines for more than routine bookkeeping was novel at the time. The proposed approach to military planning had never been taken before, and many of the experienced staff officers regarded it as impracticable. That is why the job was turned over to a mathematical statistician.

Dantzig struggled with this ill-defined task for more than a year. At first he groped almost blindly, but gradually pieces of a solution fell into place. He built upon Leontief's input–output economic model, which had to be generalized substantially, tried numerous devices for solving the resulting equations, became acquainted with the first electronic computers and saw that they, rather than punch-card machines, were needed to perform the requisite calculations. Finally, in the summer of 1947, the pieces fitted together. In that September he solved the first pitifully small linear programming problem, using a mechanical desk calculator. Later that fall, the 'diet problem', consisting of finding the least expensive combination of 77 foods that met the Bureau of Home Economics's daily requirements for nine nutrients, was solved by his method, again using desk calculators. Since then Dantzig had been subjecting his discovery to a series of increasingly demanding tests. It performed beautifully every time, and he was becoming more and more confident that it could do the job specified by the Air Force. He reported all this to me in a state of high excitement.

By then, I had learned enough economics to appreciate the importance of this discovery, not only for business and economic planning, but for economic theory. In fact, I put it to work almost immediately, and used a mild generalization of

Dantzig's findings as a basis for my doctoral dissertation. Along with Tjalling Koopmans and one or two others, I thus became one of the first economists to learn of linear programming and its implications for economics.

I remained in the Pentagon for about a year, during which time Dantzig and I had many excited discussions about linear programming and its potential impact on economics. Then the doctoral dissertation that I had submitted was accepted and I was qualified to be invited back to Berkeley as an assistant professor.

Mathematical economist

I could not have embarked on the profession of professor of economics at a more propitious time. Graduate study in universities was a boom industry fed by demand accumulated during the war years and accentuated by the GI Bill of Rights. In particular, interest in applying mathematics in the social sciences, especially economics, was at an unprecedented level, possibly because of spectacular wartime successes in applying mathematics outside its traditional fields. And, closest to my personal interests, the hottest areas for applying mathematics in economics were linear programming and its close relative, game theory. I couldn't have planned my debut as a professor of economics better if I had the power to do so. Naturally, my principal responsibility when I joined the Berkeley faculty was to introduce instruction in mathematical methods in economics.

Here, perhaps, is the place to record some of my personal reservations. I did offer instruction in mathematical economics in Berkeley for five years, and then moved with my courses to Harvard. But I was always disturbed by the need to reduce the amount of instruction in the social science side of economics to make way for the mathematics. I remain ambivalent about the costs and benefits of the change, though I don't doubt that it was an inevitable part of the 'mathematization' that our culture has been experiencing since World War II. I shall return later to these worries.

1950 was a wonderful time to embark on a career of university teaching and research, and especially wonderful at the University of California, Berkeley. The Depression and the war were safely behind us. We appeared to be on the way to solving many of the world's most urgent problems. The Marshall Plan was reinvigorating Europe. The Agency for International Development (then called The International Cooperation Administration) was achieving some spectacular results by introducing the 'green revolution' in the so-called 'third world'. Here in the US, the post-war depression that many economists anticipated failed to appear. Instead, the transition from a wartime to a peacetime economy went smoothly and prosperously.

The universities enjoyed a boom during the 1950s and early 1960s, fed largely by the GI Bill of Rights and a variety of Federal research grants. In California, the university acquired a dynamic president in Clark Kerr, who busily set about realizing his vision of a truly state-wide university with university-scale campuses spanning California from Sacramento to San Diego. Everything seemed on its way to becoming bigger and better.

There were, however, some blemishes in this latter-day Eden, just as in the original one. In Washington, there were Rep. Martin Dies, Sen. Joe McCarthy and their epigones, who were threatening everyone who believed in free speech, faculty members and Federal government workers especially. Locally, there was the chronic academic ailment of splits of departments into more-or-less hostile factions. Members of any of these factions were (and, I suspect, are) not only unfriendly towards members of opposing factions, but worse, contemptuous of them on the grounds that they were unfeeling, or ignorant, or both.

The economics department at Berkeley was split into two factions along doctrinal and generational lines, which coincided. It is pretty accurate to call them the institutional and theoretical factions. The institutional faction had joined the department, typically, during the deepest years of the Great Depression. They were strongly motivated by sympathy with the sufferings of workers, the unemployed, the tenant farmers and the propertyless in general, under a callous capitalist regime. Probably the only name that might still be remembered is Dorothea Lange, the classic photographer of impoverished and dispossessed farmers, who was wife of a member of the institutional wing.

The theoretical faction was younger. Its members were recruited mostly during the heyday of the New Deal, after the publication of Keynes's *General Theory* and during or immediately after World War II. They believed that the free markets that flourished under capitalism were the essential force of a productive economic system, that they understood that force and that they knew how to correct the socially disruptive side-effects that it engendered. The reader should have no trouble conjecturing to which faction I belonged.

The split in the department not only breached collegiality, but generated both open and covert conflicts over every proposal to change an academic requirement or, most important, every proposed tenure appointment or promotion. Some time after I joined the department, I found out that the proposal to invite me had created a lively brouhaha, and that the then chairman, an institutionalist, had tried to avert the appointment by 'losing' some essential documents. That sort of unpleasantness seems to be an inevitable part of the cost of faculty self-government. A physicist once told me that physics advances funeral by funeral.

In spite of these blemishes, teaching at Berkeley, with its alert students, stimulating colleagues and amenities of the Berkeley–San Francisco environment, was an enjoyable privilege. It ended for me after five years, when I was invited to join the faculty at Harvard. Once again, a member of the institutionalist faction was chairman of the Berkeley department. I was at loggerheads with him for reasons, doubtless adequate, but now long since forgotten. I reported the invitation to the chairman, in the hope of obtaining some sort of concession. Instead, he simply congratulated me and wished me godspeed. And so ended my sojourn at Berkeley.

As my list of publications reflects, my principal concern during my years at Berkeley, 1950–55, was to convey both to my students and to the economics profession the remarkable strides in the use of mathematics in economics that emerged from World War II. My missionary zeal in this cause was expressed in both teaching and writing, and continued for several years after I transferred to Harvard. In this regard, I must recount one episode from those years, because it perhaps has a moral.

My doctoral dissertation concerned the applicability of linear programming to the behaviour of monopolistic and quasi-monopolistic firms. It was not entirely successful because the profit that such firms are presumed to maximize is not a linear function of their production and marketing choices. At best it can be represented as a quadratic function. How to apply the programming approach to problems involving nonlinear functions was then still unsolved. It was clearly an important problem for economics, since nearly all economic maximization problems turn out to have nonlinear objective functions.

So I teamed up with Edward Barankin, a professor in the mathematics department, to solve this problem. We struggled with it for several years and produced a monograph, 'On quadratic programming' (Barankin and Dorfman, 1958), with several interesting theorems but no practicable solution. Whereupon a student of George Dantzig's, Philip Wolfe, using our theorems and his own good sense, produced the definitive solution (Wolfe, 1959). It is clear now how this happened. Both Wolfe and ourselves were strongly influenced by the iterative approach embodied in Dantzig's simplex method for solving linear problems. But we followed Danzig almost slavishly by first finding a starting solution that satisfied the constraints of the problem and then seeking an iterative procedure that produced a succession of approximate solutions, each yielding a greater value of the objective (for example, the profit) than any before and never violating any of the constraints. Wolfe's strategy, on the other hand, was to find an iterative procedure that began by violating some constraints and continued by finding a succession of approximate solutions in which the extent of constraint violations was steadily reduced while the value attained by the objective function never fell (and often rose). This apparently simple shift in strategy was the key that unlocked the problem. We never even considered the possibility of iterating while some of the constraints were still violated. Moral: The greatest obstacle to solving a scientific problem is often self-imposed blinders.

As I said, while at Berkeley I zealously expounded the virtues of using any expedient mathematics to tackle problems in economics. I expressed my beliefs in a brief note, 'A catechism: Mathematics in social science', which is reprinted here as Chapter 3, and acted on them in the four expository papers (Chapters 2, 4, 5 and 6) also reprinted in Part One.

My opinions have not changed but, as I indicated a few pages ago, I have become uncomfortably aware of the cost of mathematizing economics. The only solution I can see is for economics, like physics, engineering, medicine and law, to expect students to equip themselves with the necessary knowledge of mathematics and statistics before enrolling for graduate study in economics. This, too, is unpleasant. It is likely to squeeze out valuable preparation in philosophy, history and social sciences during the student's undergraduate years. But it has become essential.

Fledgling Political Economist

I began to act on my concern with public decision-making shortly after I moved to Harvard, where applied economics enjoyed more attention and prestige than it received at Berkeley. During my second year at Harvard, I joined a seminar organized by Gordon M. Fair, a distinguished and dignified professor of sanitary engineering (accordingly known, behind his back, as 'Flush Gordon'), and Arthur

Maass, a young political scientist, to study the design and operation of complex water supply systems. The seminar met for seven or eight years. It pioneered in applying mathematical model-building and digital simulations on large main-frame computers to the analysis of complex systems of rivers, reservoirs, multipurpose dams and hydro-electric power plants. The major accomplishment was *Design of Water Resource Systems* (Maass et al, 1962), which remained the leading treatise on analysis of large-scale water resource systems for more than a decade. A few years later, the seminar published *Models for Managing Regional Water Quality* (Dorfman et al., 1972), but it was not as original or influential as *Design*.

Around this time, I published two papers dealing with public decisions on a more theoretical plane: 'General equilibrium with public goods' and 'Social decisions without social preferences'. Both are included in this collection (Chapters 9 and 18, respectively), and both express my long-standing conviction that it is not profitable to conceive of public decisions as the results of coherent maximization processes. Rather, I believe, public decisions should be regarded as outputs of pulls, pushes, trades and compromises among amorphous and rather ill-defined groups in the body politic all trying to influence public decisions in directions favourable to their interests and aspirations. Voting and elections are best understood as formalized procedures in the chiefly informal processes by which the groups that compose the body politic deal with each other and with the government decision-making apparatus. This is a theme that will appear repeatedly in my intellectual itinerary from here on. To be sure, it is alien territory for an economist, but necessary for him or her to explore if economics is to comprehend the important decisions that governments make. It would be helpful to consider the paper entitled, 'Incidence of the benefits and costs of environmental programs' (Chapter 21) along with the aforementioned, although it was published somewhat later, since it is essentially a continuation of the same concerns.

When I wrote 'General equilibrium with public goods', the welfare properties of perfectly competitive economies were well established, but there were no comparable theories for economies in which nonmarket goods or public goods were important. 'General equilibrium with public goods' was written to fill the gap. It studies the characteristics of equilibrium in a closed economy divided into two broad sectors: a private sector and a public or government sector. The private sector is just an Arrow–Debreu perfectly competitive economy. The government sector purchases inputs from the private sector and uses them to produce public goods and services which it donates to the private sector. It finances these activities by taxes on the private sector.

The chief contribution and difficulties of the paper concern the properties of the public sector equilibrium. This is by no means unexplored territory. On the contrary, it bulks large in the literature of political science and is the subject of more previous papers in economics than I can list. The problem is that there have been too many explorers returning with maps that contradict each other. The view of governmental decisions that seems most helpful to me is derived from A.F. Bentley's (1908) scheme of interest groups' manoeuvering and compromising to form (and sometimes to desert) coalitions large enough to have the policies they advocate adopted or the ones they oppose rejected.

The first half of the paper is devoted mostly to setting forth my view of this complex process. The remainder works out the prices and quantities in an equilibrium of such a two-sector (public and private) system, if an equilibrium is reached.

I think the exposition is unnecessarily difficult, partly because the notation is over-elaborate and partly because the approach is formal and mathematical rather than intuitive. Approached intuitively, the study of the equilibrium of a two-sector economy breaks up into three relatively straightforward sub-problems: the equilibrium of the public sector, that of the private sector, and the interaction between the two. All take the equilibrium vector of prices of private goods as the point of departure.

In equilibrium, the public sector produces the quantities of public goods that the interest groups have agreed on, as discussed above, by using the least costly vector of private goods inputs possible, so that the cost of producing the agreed-on vector of public goods, measured by the equilibrium price vector for private goods, will be minimized. The result will be a point on the government's transformation frontier at which the marginal rate of transformation of any two public goods produced will equal the ratio of their costs of production, in accordance with the government's production function.

The equilibrium of the private sector is determined similarly. Each interest group consists of similar and similarly situated households who choose input vectors (with outputs, as of labour, counted as negative outputs) on the highest indifference surfaces they can reach without violating their budget constraints. At the points so chosen, the marginal rates of substitution between the members of each pair of private goods consumed equals the slope of the budget constraint, that is, the ratio of the prices of the goods.

The third and final sub-problem is to determine the scale of economic activity so that the sum of the input vectors to all the sectors, the government sector and all the interest groups, is a point on the outer boundary of the community's feasible production set. Careful equation counting will show that, at least for production sets that are convex with constant returns to scale, the numbers of disposable variables and constraining equations just balance, as required for unique solvability of such a system of conditions. The first two sub-problems are standard problems in nonlinear programming. The third sub-problem concerns a single scaling parameter which can be found by trial and error.

But we should not let ourselves be misled by reaching a tidy result that confirms our hopes and expectations. The whole argument depends on the ability of the jockeying by interest groups to reach conclusions consistent with the public's considered preferences. I'm not sure that such confidence in the process has ever been well founded. Certainly, the writers of the US Constitution did not evince much faith in the wisdom of the public. That is why they provided for indirect election of the president and senators. For this reason also, restrictions on the privilege of voting used to be quite prevalent. Not only was the female half of the population disenfranchised, but some states used to have property qualifications for voters, and I remember from my childhood in New York when prospective voters had to pass literacy tests. In recent years, the introduction of expensive modern merchandizing methods into political campaigns has created further reasons to doubt the likelihood that contests among interest groups can guide governments to compromises that reconcile the different interests optimally. All in all, I now regard 'General equilibrium with public goods' as an exercise in optimism.

The 'Incidence of benefits and costs' paper consists of two loosely connected parts. The first concentrates attention on the distributional implications of governmental programmes, including provision of public goods, taking as its example the American programmes for reducing polluting emissions into the air and public waters. It found that the effects of those programmes on families with different incomes differed dramatically. The costs of those programmes to families in the lowest income strata were substantially greater than the amounts those families would have paid voluntarily for the benefits they received from them. But those programmes provided substantial consumer surpluses to families in the highest strata, while families in the intermediate strata received benefits that they regarded as worth just about their share of the costs.

That finding called attention to the concept that I called 'exactions', which was already implicit in the 'General equilibrium' paper. A governmental programme imposed an 'exaction' on a family to the extent that that family's share of the costs exceeded the amount that it would pay voluntarily to have the programme. Moreover, there is an asymmetry between imposing an exaction and providing a citizens' surplus. Citizens tend to resent bearing exactions, but to regard surpluses as more or less due to them. Thus, even aside from ethical considerations, it is politically unwise to impose exactions on any more citizens than necessary, and it is often possible to adjust the financing of public programmes so as to minimize the amount of exactions entailed.

The 'General equilibrium' paper assumed, unrealistically, that exactions were altogether forbidden; the 'Incidence' paper weakened that restriction to saying only that experienced politicians could and would adjust programmes so as to reduce the level of exactions, even at the cost of increasing the total costs of the programmes. One should therefore not take it for granted that the goal of public decisions is to achieve the intended results at minimum possible social cost.

The third member of this triad on the economic theory of public decisions, 'Social decisions without social preferences', attempted to apply the formation of n-person game theory to the interest-group depiction of public decisions. I think it was basically inconclusive because the most successful aspects of game theory depend on the rôle of side-payments in forming and cementing coalitions. But the use of side-payments presupposes some form of transferable utility, which most instances of interest-group politics lack.

There is a second theme in my professional work that, like the second theme in the sonata form, underlies and interacts with the main theme. It is capital theory, which I like to view as the theory of time, since capital is merely wealth that yields its services over substantial periods of time. The connection with the main theme is that the effects of most important public decisions extend over substantial lengths of time.

In my case, the second theme was announced actually before the main theme. When I was a graduate student, capital theory was covered in the basic microeconomics course. (This is usually no longer the case, to the intellectual impoverishment of the students.) I was fascinated by it, particularly by the Austrian school exemplified by Böhm-Bawerk, who disposed of as sharp an intellect as anyone who every practised economics. Böhm-Bawerk presents difficulties, however, especially to anyone who, like me, has a mathematical turn of mind. In order to follow his chain of reasoning, I translated it into mathematics (a method of reading, I learned much later, that Alfred Marshall often used), thereby discovering a significant flaw in the logic. I did not see how to correct the error at that time. I published my exposition some dozen years later in, 'A graphical exposition of Böhm-Bawerk's interest theory', with Böhm-Bawerk's mistake uncorrected and some of my own errors added to it. That essay is included in the present collection as Chapter 8.

Some years after publishing 'A graphical exposition', I discovered an elegant and revealing way to correct Böhm-Bawerk's error, and taught it in my course in the history of economics. I have yet to publish the correction because interest in capital theory had waned so completely by then that I didn't and don't know of any journal that would be likely to publish it. My own interest in capital theory has not waned, and capital-theoretic papers, for instance 'The meaning of internal rates of return' and 'Austrian and American capital theories' (both reprinted herein, Chapters 11 and 31, respectively), have continued to dribble out.

Along the way, I published several disconnected theoretical papers. Two of them, 'Optimal advertising and optimal quality' (with Peter O. Steiner) and 'A formula for the Gini coefficient', were merely transcripts, with some refinements, of sessions of the microeconomics course that I was giving at the time. They are reprinted here as Chapters 7 and 10.

Resource and environmental economist

Occasionally, I closed my books and looked at 'the real world', and practically all of those applications dealt with resource or environmental problems. For the most part, they did not result in journal articles. The work on *Design of Water Resource Systems* is a case in point. But three papers dealing with practical problems in natural resource or environmental economics are included in the section on natural resource and environmental economics in this volume to represent this phase of my work.

The earliest of these papers was 'Forty years of cost–benefit analysis', published in 1978 (here, Chapter 22). Almost twenty additional years of experience with benefit–cost analysis have accumulated since then. It might be supposed that later developments, including the recent 'Why benefit–cost analysis is widely disregarded and what to do about it' (Chapter 25), have superseded the 1978 paper, but that is not entirely so. The 'Forty years' paper includes a careful examination of the logical underpinnings of benefit–cost analysis, which is generally lacking in the extensive literature on the method, including my own subsequent papers. In consequence, benefit–cost analysis is frequently misapplied, the results are misinterpreted and unjustified conclusions are drawn. The first 40 years of experience with benefit–cost analysis exhibited these defects in application; the subsequent 20 years have confirmed them.

The most recent of the papers in the group is 'Why benefit–cost analysis is widely disregarded and what to do about it', just mentioned. The one-sentence answer it gives to the rhetorical question is, 'Because it doesn't answer the right questions'. For one thing, benefit–cost analysis carefully evades the critical question of who enjoys the benefits and who sustains the costs. In a democracy made up of diverse groups pursuing divergent interests, that question is of dominating concern to decision-makers. The paper calls attention to this and several other grave shortcomings in the way benefit–cost analysis is practised and used.

'The lessons of pesticide regulation' (Chapter 23) is a digest of what I learned as chair of a National Research Council committee charged with investigating why the enforcement of the Federal Insecticide, Fungicide, and Rodenticide Act (FIFRA) had been at a virtual standstill for the 30 years since the act was passed. The investigation turned into a case study in the daily nitty-gritty of trying to implement many of the regulations that Congress promulgates so blithely. Working on the study was a sobering experience for me. I hope that this digest of it conveys at least a faint whiff of the stresses and frustrations encountered in trying to comply with far-reaching, and apparently reasonable, governmental mandates. Although all the evidence and examples mentioned in the paper related to the implementation of FIFRA, they exemplify problems encountered throughout the Environmental Protection Agency (EPA) and beyond.

The earlier paper, 'Transition costs of changing regulations' (Chapter 12), pursues a similar theme. By and large, benefit–cost analyses compare the costs and benefits generated when the economy has attained equilibrium in response to alternative governmental policies. But the authors of those analyses, including myself, are well aware that the economy is rarely in equilibrium and that the economy's responses to being out of equilibrium are always costly. This paper assumes, for the sake of the argument, that new policies or regulations are imposed on an economy already in equilibrium, and considers the costs of moving to an equilibrium consistent with the changed state of affairs. These adjustment costs should be added to the costs included in conventional benefit–cost analyses.

'An economist's view of natural resource and environmental problems' (Chapter 14) is a rapid survey of the economic issues that arise in formulating policies for managing the country's natural resources and protecting its environment. It does not take a stand on any concrete issue, but is content with pointing out the main questions of principle that have to be faced. The paper that follows, 'Food for a developing world' (Chapter 15), written with Walter P. Falcon of Stanford's Food Research Institute, is quite different. It was written for an interdisciplinary conference on 'Resources and World Development' at a time when there was considerable concern about the ability of the planet to meet the requirements and depredations of a population that might well grow to 12 billion or so in the next 50 years. Several scientists made estimates of the size of the population that the planet could feed, taking account of the amount of arable land available, the average amount of solar energy received per arable hectare, the efficiency of plants at converting solar energy into biomass, and related considerations. A typical estimate, made by Roger Revelle (1974), director of the Harvard Center for Population Studies, found that the planet could provide subsistence diets (about 2000 calories per day for adults) for 76 billion people, plus or minus a few billion. At a more varied and adequate diet of, say, 3000 calories per day, about 50 billion people could be supported. Revelle, like most of the other scientists, was aware that actual dietary requirements depend on more than simple physiological calculations but did not venture into this more complicated terrain.

Falcon and I, being social scientists, took a more empirical approach. We were impressed by the persistently paradoxical behaviour of markets for farm products in most countries. On the one hand, when the paper was written as well as today, about half of the world's population suffered from chronic undernourishment and occasional famines, while farmers were glutting their markets with so much produce that farm prices would fall to less than the costs of production but for drastic governmental interferences. Millions lived on the verge of starvation while farmers could produce more food than people could buy!

Thus the physical limits to agriculture could not explain the worldwide under-nutrition. The paper presents several charts and tables to drive home the point that the world could produce plenty of food for its population when the paper was written, and still can, while about half the world's population doesn't earn enough to buy the food they need.

Since most of the undernourished people are farmers and peasants, increasing their productivity (despite the apparent glut) will provide the income they need to buy the food they need and simultaneously provide the food. This analysis leads to four major recommendations: (1) improve both the physical infrastructure in agricultural areas (for example, farm-to-market roads) and the organizational support for farming (such as agricultural extension service and farm credit facilities); (2) promote modernized technology (for example, high-yield varieties, chemical pesticides); (3) permit market prices that encourage rather than inhibit agriculture, particularly by terminating forced requisitions of agricultural products at admin-istrative prices; and (4) follow macroeconomic policies that promote exports and hinder inflation. We concede that the transition to the farm economy that these four recommendations would create would impose painful sacrifices on some people, but we see no other way to foster a farm economy that can attract and support an adequate work force and provide a significant market for urban products.

Like our predecessors, we refrain from guessing how large a population the world can support at a comfortable standard of living. We rest content with the finding that physical productivity does not set the limit; the distribution of income does. Undernutrition and its attendant evils are economic problems, not agronomic ones.

'Protecting the global environment' (Chapter 16) is another of the papers that oversteps the boundaries within which an economist speaks with some authority. It was inspired by a major achievement in the effort to protect the global en-vironment, the 'Montreal Protocol' for limiting the production and use of chemicals that deplete the protective ozone layer in the upper atmosphere. The ozone layer shields all terrestrial life from excessive exposure to ultraviolet solar radiation. In 1974, two scientists discovered that a family of industrial chemicals, the chlorofluorocarbons or CFCs, once released into the atmosphere, rise to the protective layer and destroy much of the ozone through chemical reactions. By then, the ozone layer had been noticeably thinned in several places. What then happened is instructive. The scientific findings were never called into question. The chemicals involved are not essential to important industries in any nations, though manufacturing and distributing them is profitable to several companies, notably Dupont in the United States and ICI in England. Nevertheless, it took 14 years of persistent effort by scientists and environmental advocates to persuade some 45 countries to agree to regulate the manufacture and use of CFCs about half as stringently as the scientists estimated was needed to arrest the erosion of the ozone layer. The resultant Montreal Protocol, of which we are so proud, appears to have retarded the destruction of the protective layer but has by no means halted it. Accordingly, the Protocol had to be renegotiated after about five years.

'On optimal congestion' (Chapter 13) is included in this group, although congestion is not a resource or environmental problem strictly speaking, because it is formally similar to environmental problems. Congestion arises, as do many environmental malfunctions, in situations where each individual makes choices he or she judges to be in his or her own best interest, without much incentive to take into account the effects of such actions on other users of the same facilities. In the case of congestible facilities (highways, public libraries, public beaches, and so on) these interpersonal effects give rise to a peculiar type of demand curve in which the total usage of the facility enters each user's demand function.

This type of demand function has been dubbed 'a ccdd' (constant crowding demand function) because it consists of a family of ordinary demand curves, each of which tells how much of a commodity consumers will demand at each price in some range, always on the apparently contradictory assumption that the level of market demand remains unchanged. The apparent self-contradiction lies in the implicit question: How much of a commodity will consumers demand if the price is p and each consumer believes that the total demand will be Q? Except for the one price, p, at which the total demand actually is Q, the consumers' beliefs will be falsified, the expectation will be revised and a new ccdd curve will become effective. Equilibrium will not be attained until the price and expectations are such that the expectations will be confirmed.

The paper works through the algebra of this sort of self-fulfilment and comes to a surprising conclusion. Ever since the days of the classic Pigou–Knight controversy over socially optimal toll road charges, economists have believed that the optimal toll would be the one that maximized the toll-operators' net profit. Not so in general. Things would work out that neatly only in a special group of cases to which the Pigou–Knight roads, Garrett Hardin's commons and Scott Gordon's fishery all belong.

Social decisions

My continuing concern with public decisions is most explicit in the group of papers, dated from 1970 to 1985, identified as dealing with 'Social decisions'. In some of them, I ventured far from an economist's legitimate turf into the areas of sociology and political theory. For those infractions, I apologize to the authorized practitioners, but feel no remorse. An economist cannot get on with his or her own task if he or she ignores the spillovers into the domains of neighbouring disciplines.

'Social decisions without social preferences' and 'Incidence of the benefits and costs' have already been discussed. 'The functions of the city' (Chapter 17) reverts to my thesis that a modern community consists of a number of diverse groups with divergent interests, beliefs and values, who must somehow adjust to living in close proximity and sharing opportunities and resources. This paper argues that these groups fulfill a deep-seated, ineradicable human need, and that one of a city's principal tasks is to maintain reasonably harmonious working relationships among the groups that comprise it.

The argument smacks of E.O. Wilson's 'sociobiology' (1975), and there is more than a faint hint of it in Adam Smith's *Theory of Moral Sentiments* (1759). For nearly all of the million or two years that humans have inhabited the Earth, the species consisted of fairly small hunting-gathering tribes, clans, bands, and so on, each deriving its sustenance from a limited turf that it guarded jealously from the incursions of neighbouring tribes, while invading neighbouring territory when circumstances permitted. The survival of any tribe and its members depended heavily on the dedication of its members to protecting its territory and each other. Macauley expressed the essential spirit eloquently:

> And how can a man die better
> Than facing fearful odds
> For the ashes of his fathers
> And the temples of his gods?

Thus was bred into us the virtues of loyalty and patriotism, and the need to be a respected member of a tightly knit group of individuals distinguished in some manner from all other members of the species. Other social animals acquire similarly the need and ability to identify, even unto death, with some close-knit group of kith or kin.

The age of the primitive clan ended only 10,000 or 20,000 years ago with the discovery and spread of settled agriculture, but the need to affiliate with a group of loyal allies remained and evolved, somewhat sublimated, into loyalty to medieval barons, to patriotism to the modern state, to the clannishness of ethnic groups in modern American cities, and so on. The paper describes how this vestigial human tendency affects the economics and social structures of modern cities, particularly in the United States.

'The technical basis for decision making' (Chapter 19) was a hard paper to write, and may be almost as hard to read. The problem with writing it was that it describes work very much in progress and, therefore, far from well digested and organized. A description from the perspective of 20 years may therefore be helpful.

The paper was written to set the stage for a 'Resources for the Future' conference on how decisions about the use of common property resources should be analysed, a topic dear to my heart and about which I had (and have) strong opinions. The result was a paper with a strong didactic flavour and, I'm afraid, a somewhat patronizing style.

The first four pages are devoted to the dull but often necessary task of clarifying terminology. The bulk of the paper is a conscientious survey of a variety of methods for sorting out and ranking alternative policies and projects, ranging from benefit-cost analysis to applying game-theoretic models, with numerous way-stations. The basic logic and also the shortcomings of all the methods are pointed out. Finally, the last five pages describe and cautiously advocate an analytic approach that is immune to the objections raised against the others.

The recommended approach is one developed by the Environmental Systems Program at Harvard. We called it 'Paretian Environmental Analysis', despite the unfortunate acronym. It faced frankly the problem that has come up so many times in my narrative, of making judgments that would be binding on population groups with conflicting interests. The basic idea is to think of a matrix with a row for each alternative considered and a column for each population group concerned. Each cell in the matrix contains a ranking or rating of the alternative corresponding to its row judged from the point of view of the group designated by its column. If it should happen when any pair of alternatives is compared that the rating of one of them is higher than that of the other in every column, then the alternative with the lower ratings is 'dominated' and can be dropped from further consideration. More sensitive measures of rating than comparative ranks and some methods for comparing the political significances of political groups are required to proceed beyond merely eliminating dominated choices, but such measures are often more practical in practice than in theory.

As far as I know, this approach has been carried through only once, but the result was spectacular. The application concerned a project known as the Cross-Florida Barge Canal. The canal would cross the Florida Peninsula from Jacksonville on the Atlantic coast to near Yankeetown on the Gulf of Mexico, slicing some 700 miles off the barge journey between Atlantic ports and Gulf ports in Louisiana, Texas, and so on. This canal had been debated for generations. Construction was even started in the 1930s, but abandoned during World War II. Jacksonville businessmen, the barge canal commpanies and the US Corps of Engineers favoured the canal; sportsmen, environmentalists, some farmers, and others opposed it. In the 1970s Congress authorized a fresh study which was carried out under the supervision of the Corps of Engineers according to the principles of PEA analysis, somewhat impeded by legal requirements and limited financing. The results were surprisingly clear cut. The groups that historically had opposed the canal continued to do so, as expected. But no group, not even the barge operators, expressed more than mild support for building it. Apparently, shipping freight by barge is so cheap that even the large saving in mileage per shipment is not enough to offset the construction and disruption costs of building and operating the canal. When even the shippers were shown to recognize how modest the saving would be, support for the canal project vanished. It has not been heard from since.

A single success cannot establish the primacy of PEA as a method for resolving political conflicts of interest, though it may establish a presumption of usefulness. The Environmental Systems Program ran out of steam and money years ago, but further trials of the approach seem to be worthwhile.

The motive for the paper on environmental quality indexes (Chapter 20) was entirely different. Since as far back as I remember, people have been proposing measures of overall environmental quality intended to be useful for comparing the quality of the environments in different localities, for following trends in environmental quality, and the like. None of them has gained wide acceptance. I could not help noticing that, whereas the public was concerned about the effects of environmental conditions on human health and welfare, none of the proposed indexes measured those effects; the indexes are simply averages of selected environmental descriptors, such as the coliform count in public waters or the concentration of sulphur dioxide in the atmosphere, without considering the descriptors' importance to human well-being. I therefore proposed an index that went directly to the effects of the environment on humans. Though my proposal was received with the same apathy as the others, I am including it in this collection because I believe that it has considerable merit.

The 'social index' measures the effects of environmental conditions on human activities and welfare from the outset. Since the paper explains its construction in some detail, here I need mention only that it has three components: economic effects, health effects and effects on amenities. The economic effects are measured by comparing the actual value of economic output in the relevant region with what that value would be under pristine conditions. The health effects are similarly measured by comparing actual mortality and morbidity indicators with what they would be under pristine conditions. The amenity effects are fussier. Essentially they are measured by the amount the communities concerned would be willing to pay to have various natural, historical and aesthetic amenities improved to defined standards.

The advantage of the social index is that it measures the conditions that are of direct concern to people and government officials. Its drawback, a serious one, is that it is a good deal more demanding, and therefore expensive, than merely describing physical and ecological conditions as the other indexes do. Still, that expensive step is necessary to make an environmental indicator suitable for establishing priorities for environmental protection and improvement.

Professor Peter Rogers (1996) has suggested a compromise that might be useful. It is to measure environmental quality by the cost of bringing the environmental conditions included in a conventional index up to a target standard. This would be substantially cheaper and easier than the type of measure that I suggest, and, though not quite what is needed, could serve as a helpful guide to environmental policy.

The paper on ethics, economics and the environment (Chapter 24) is my only excursion into applied philosophy. I was lured into it by observing the contortions forced upon the EPA by contradictions in the laws that Congress instructed it to enforce. It didn't take much study to perceive that Congress did not invent the contradictions; it inherited them from the philosophers, who had been struggling with them since the 18th century at least.

The contradictions in question reflect the views of two broad schools of ethical philosophy. One, traceable back to Aristotle, is based on the concepts of natural rights and duties. In the trade, these theories are called deontological. The other school, that perhaps emerged as recently as the Enlightenment, holds that the moral value of any act or policy depends only on its consequences. It is therefore called consequentialist. Bentham is a leading exponent.

The practical problem is that these two schools of thought are often contradictory. Further, not only are both deeply embedded in American laws and traditions, as my paper emphasizes, but, I have come to realize, many people (including myself) subscribe to both of them. Clearly, this circumstance is bound to lead to the kind of confusions that afflict Congress and the EPA.

After the essay was published, I was delighted to learn that some redoubtable philosophers, including Alasdair MacIntyre (1981) and Amartya Sen (1987) were bothered enough by this same contradiction to treat it at length. Neither, however, considered its legislative implications, as I did. Nor do I find in either of them a satisfying way to resolve the contradictions, or to deny them. We must, I conclude, live with inconsistency.

Historian of economics

It is recorded that Billy Rose once held the title of World's Fastest Typist, but was a professional typist for only a short time. In fact, for almost his entire career he did not type even his own correspondence. Why? He soon discovered that his comparative advantage lay in promoting musical extravaganzas. Billy Rose is a dramatic example, but perhaps is a poor place to start a discussion of comparative advantage. 'Comparative advantage' is very likely the most democratic of all economic concepts. Everybody has some, although few have Billy Rose's problem of having to ignore one remarkable talent to free time for exercising a different one.

This brings me to my point: professors of economics emeritus often have a comparative advantage in pursuing the history of economics. In the first place, we have longer memories than our younger colleagues. We have experienced how much economics (and, indeed, the world) has changed in just a few decades. We have seen fashions come and go and still bring us no closer to equilibrium (though perhaps an excessive amount of economics is devoted to analysing equilibrium). We are acutely aware that change is what matters; equilibrium stasis is evanescent. Our memories even include some episodes in which economics changed particularly swiftly. We may know first-hand how those changes came about, what forces promoted or resisted them, what and how lasting their consequences were. I, for one, don't have to read about the confusion into which Keynes's *General Theory* (1936) plunged the profession. Economists born, say, ten years after me will never grasp it; from the perspective of 60 years the impassioned controversies it generated are much too boring, and even silly, to read about.

My memory is scarred also by other significant changes – though none as important as the introduction of Keynesianism – and the daunting obstacles that had to be surmounted to bring them about. All of which gives us professors emeritus much more than a verbal appreciation of the stresses and tensions of change and of the accompanying threats to practising economists as their stock of knowledge becomes obsolete.

We emeriti also lose the ability to internalize the new developments that constitute change. (By 'new' I mean since we passed our final exams.) I, for one, despite considerable effort, am still not entirely at home with rational expectations or the capital asset pricing model, let alone alternative economics. In short, the area on which our competence is focused recedes inexorably into the past. So it is that many of us turn to thinking and writing about economic history, where our comparative advantage lies ever more emphatically.

Six of the essays included here are classed under 'History of Economics'. I watched three of the developments discussed in them as they occurred and was a minor participant in one. The other three took place long before even my ancient times.

Wassily Leontief's major contribution was input–output analysis, developed in the 1930s and brought to fruition in the 1950s. It still provides the basic framework for most analyses of relationships among sectors of the economy, a position that appears unlikely to be challenged in the visible future. I wrote this essay (Chapter 26) at the behest of the Royal Swedish Academy of Sciences and, sure enough, he received the award.

Gerard Debreu's selection as a Nobel Laureate culminated efforts beginning with those of Léon Walras, more than 100 years ago, and continued by Abraham Wald, Kenneth Arrow and Debreu himself, to formulate mathematically the structure of economic equilibrium. I include my brief essay (Chapter 27) in honour of Debreu's award because it is intended to clear up some misunderstandings (not shared by Debreu) about the nature of his accomplishment. Debreu did *not* confirm Adam Smith's insight that a competitive economy would perform perfectly efficiently without any government intervention. He, along with Kenneth Arrow, *did* establish certain conditions, 'sufficient conditions', under which a competitive economy would be perfectly efficient. But those conditions are so restrictive that no real economy comes close to satisfying them or could conceivably do so. The practical value of Debreu's theorems is that they greatly clarify the conditions in which a real economy can be expected to perform well, even if not perfectly, and the nature of policies that can improve the performance of real economies. The Arrow–Debreu conditions have been somewhat refined and relaxed in the 40-odd years since they were discovered, but basically remain unchallenged.

The story of linear programming (Chapter 28) illustrates how scientific progress stumbles forward. Robert Remak formulated the conditions for economic equilibrium as a system of linear inequalities as early as 1929, but no one had the faintest idea of how to solve them. In 1939, L.V. Kantorovich proposed a method for solving very small (three or four) variable systems. His method rapidly became burdensome for larger systems and, absent the electronic computers still a dozen years in the future, utterly impracticable. Tjalling Koopmans solved a very important special case during World War II. But the first really general and truly implementable solution was Dantzig's 'simplex method', discovered in 1947. Dantzig had the enormous advantage over his predecessors that he did his work when the electronic computer was already in sight (but not yet operational) and he knew in broad outline what it could do.

Almost immediately after the simplex method was announced, linear programming was accepted enthusiastically as the primary method for optimizing complex programmes in both private industry and governmental economic planning. Its use spread quickly all over the world. Some refinements were discovered and adopted, and several alternative methods have been discovered, but none have supplanted it after 50 years of use. Studying and applying linear programming have become a large sub-profession. Linear programming now is not quite as important as it was ten or 20 years ago because fantastic decreases in the cost of computing have made optimization of nonlinear programming problems feasible, and preferable in applications where nonlinearity is too marked to be ignored.

In addition to its usefulness in government and industrial planning, linear programming has led to important advances in economic theory, largely in the form of Tjalling Koopman's generalization called 'activity analysis'. This aspect is based on the duality theorems developed largely by John von Neumann, A.W. Tucker and Dantzig himself. These theorems show more vividly than can be seen without them that finding the prices that induce an economy or firm to function efficiently and finding the quantities of commodities that an economy or firm can produce when functioning efficiently are essentially the same problem; neither can be solved without solving the other, at least implicitly. One important implication, for example, is that charging interest for the use of capital is not an artifact of capitalistic methods of production, but is necessary in all production, no matter what the institutional arrangements, if resources are not to be wasted. The old Soviet economy, where charging interest was heretical, was a sad demonstration of the cost of ignoring these theorems.

Professor I. Bernard Cohen of the Harvard Department of the History of Science was responsible for urging me to write out the story of the birth of linear programming, and offered many valuable suggestions while it was in progress.

Of all the papers in this collection, 'Thünen at two hundred' (Chapter 29) is the one I most enjoyed writing. It is a comment on a paper with the same title by Paul Samuelson. Samuelson, following the precedent of Joseph Schumpeter and several other redoubtable economists, charged Thünen with a mistake in the calculations he used to derive his famous formula for the 'natural wage'. My paper points out that it was the critics who made the mistake. Their mistake was to take it for granted that Thünen's formula was intended to maximize the concept that they would have maximized if they had been in Thünen's shoes. But Thünen, writing at the very beginning of the development of the theory of production, had a very different image of entrepreneurial goals, and maximized his own concept correctly rather than the one that later generations would prefer. Samuelson conceded. Moral: When reading a work in economics written 100 or more years ago, beware the pitfall of imputing to the author the same implicit images of the economy and of economic actors and motivations that you have. Many of the concepts and ideas familiar to first-year students now had not been invented then.

Robert Malthus and David Ricardo (Chapter 30) were the oddest couple in the history of economics. One was a member of the country gentry and the inner circles of the English Establishment, but didn't have much money. The other was an outsider, a member of the London Jewish financial community, and very wealthy. Despite these different backgrounds, they were dear friends and worked intimately together while they argued vehemently with each other in private and in print. Ricardo once said of Malthus, 'I could not love you more if you agreed in opinion with me'. In short, they exhibited a degree of fair-mindedness, civility and tolerance that few people can attain. I wrote this essay because I felt that more economists should be aware that so much decency, humaneness and open-mindedness could exist among members of our profession.

Böhm-Bawerk and Fisher are another interesting contrasting pair. They were not friends; in fact, I'm not sure they ever met, though it seems probable. They are associated because they independently, and not quite simultaneously, undertook the same problem and reached conclusions that are the same in essence though different in most details. The interesting aspect of their relationship is how the characteristics of their separate milieus are reflected in their solutions to their common problem.

The question that seized them both was the legitimacy of charging and paying interest for the use of capital. Each of them found in his own way that interest payments are legitimate and, indeed, inevitable in all but the most primitive modes of production. In fact, they both arrived at the same principles for determining the rate of interest.

But their arguments were quite different. Böhm-Bawerk conceived of an economy that consisted of two classes of people: those who owned property and those who owned only their bare hands, just as in the late 19th-century central European society with which he was familiar. It was perfectly fair for property-owners who placed their property at the disposal of workers to claim a share of the output, equivalent to the increased product that using the property (or capital) made possible. Please look at the essay on the 'Graphical exposition of Böhm-Bawerk's theory', Chapter 8 in this collection, for additional details about Böhm-Bawerk's position.

Fisher, however, observing the one-class society of 19th-century Connecticut and imbibing its scale of values, argued that interest would arise when people who could use profitably more capital than they owned borrowed it from people who had more than they could, or would, use profitably. All that was needed for interest to arise was for capital to be scarce and for people's opportunities to use it to vary. The result was much the same as Böhm-Bawerk's in spite of the radical difference in social images and causations.

The differences between these theories may have some bearing on today's controversies over 'relativism', the doctrine, I gather, that 'truth' is not universal but is related to the culture and circumstances in which it is believed. The contrast between Böhm-Bawerk's and Fisher's theories is somewhat more subtle. The conclusions of the two theories are essentially the same in the two cultures from which they arose, and may very well be the same in any other culture in which the same question could be posed. But the justifications for the conclusions are saturated with the differences between the two. Relativism may relate less to substantive assertions than to their interpretations in differing cultural contexts.

References

Barankin, E.W. and R. Dorfman (1958), 'On quadratic programming', *University of California Publications in Statistics*, **2**, pp. 285–318.

Bentley, Arthur F. (1908), *The Process of Government: A Study of Social Pressures*, Chicago: University of Chicago Press.

Dorfman, Robert, et al. (eds) (1972), *Models for Managing Regional Water Quality*, Cambridge: Harvard University Press.

Keynes, John Maynard (1936), *The General Theory of Employment, Interest, and Money*, New York: Harcourt, Brace and Co.

Maass, Arthur et. al. (1962), *Design of Water-Resource Systems*, Cambridge: Harvard University Press.

MacIntyre, Alasdair (1981), *After Virtue*, Notre Dame, Ind.: U. of Notre Dame Press.

Revelle, Roger (1974), 'Will the earth's land and water resources be sufficient for future populations?' in *The Population Debate: Dimensions and Perspectives*, Papers of the World Population Conference,

Bucharest, 1974, **II**, pp. 3–14. New York: United Nations, 1975.

Rogers, Peter, et. al. (1996), 'Measuring Sustainable Development in Asia: Environmental Quality Indices', Division of Engineering and Applied Science, Harvard University, Cambridge, MA.

Sen, Amartya K. (1987), *On Ethics and Economics*, Oxford, UK: B. Blackwell.

Smith, Adam (1759), *Theory of Moral Sentiments*, Indianapolis: Liberty Classics, 1976. Orig: London: Longman, 1759.

Wilson, Edward O. (1975), *Sociobiology: The New Synthesis*, Cambridge: Harvard University Press.

Wolfe, Philip (1959), 'The simplex method for quadratic programming', *Econometrica*, **57**, pp. 382–98.

PART ONE

STATISTICS

[1]

Made in United States of America

Reprinted from THE ANNALS OF MATHEMATICAL STATISTICS
Vol. XIV, No. 4, December, 1943

THE DETECTION OF DEFECTIVE MEMBERS OF LARGE POPULATIONS

BY ROBERT DORFMAN

Washington, D. C.

The inspection of the individual members of a large population is an expensive and tedious process. Often in testing the results of manufacture the work can be reduced greatly by examining only a sample of the population and rejecting the whole if the proportion of defectives in the sample is unduly large. In many inspections, however, the objective is to eliminate all the defective members of the population. This situation arises in manufacturing processes where the defect being tested for can result in disastrous failures. It also arises in certain inspections of human populations. Where the objective is to weed out individual defective units, a sample inspection will clearly not suffice. It will be shown in this paper that a different statistical approach can, under certain conditions, yield significant savings in effort and expense when a complete elimination of defective units is desired.

It should be noted at the outset that when large populations are being inspected the objective of eliminating all units with a particular defect can never be fully attained. Mechanical and chemical failures and, especially, man-failures make it inevitable that mistakes will occur when many units are being examined. Although the procedure described in this paper does not directly attack the problem of technical and psychological fallibility, it may contribute to its partial solution by reducing the tediousness of the work and by making more elaborate and more sensitive inspections economically feasible. In the following discussion no attention will be paid to the possibility of technical failure or operators' error.

The method will be described by showing its application to a large-scale project on which the United States Public Health Service and the Selective Service System are now engaged. The object of the program is to weed out all syphilitic men called up for induction. Under this program each prospective inductee is subjected to a "Wasserman-type" blood test. The test may be divided conveniently into two parts:

1. A sample of blood is drawn from the man,
2. The blood sample is subjected to a laboratory analysis which reveals the presence or absence of "syphilitic antigen." The presence of syphilitic antigen is a good indication of infection.

When this procedure is used, N chemical analyses are required in order to detect all infected members of a population of size N.

The germ of the proposed technique is revealed by the following possibility. Suppose that after the individual blood sera are drawn they are pooled in groups

436

of, say, five and that the groups rather than the individual sera are subjected to chemical analysis. If none of the five sera contributing to the pool contains syphilitic antigen, the pool will not contain it either and will test negative. If, however, one or more of the sera contain syphilitic antigen, the pool will contain it also and the group test will reveal its presence.[1] The individuals making up the pool must then be retested to determine which of the members are infected. It is not necessary to draw a new blood sample for this purpose since sufficient blood for both the test and the retest can be taken at once. The chemical analyses require only small quantities of blood.

Two questions arise immediately:

1. Will the group technique require fewer chemical analyses than the individual technique and, if so, what is the extent of the saving; and

2. What is the most efficient size for the groups?

Both questions are answered by a study of the probability of obtaining an infected group. Let

p = the prevalence rate per hundred, that is the probability that a random selection will yield an infected individual. Then

$1 - p$ = the probability of selecting at random an individual free from infection. And

$(1 - p)^n$ = the probability of obtaining by random selection a group of n individuals all of whom are free from infection. Then

$p' = 1 - (1 - p)^n$ = the probability of obtaining by random selection a group of n with at least one infected member.

Further

N/n = the number of groups of size n in a population of size N, so

$p'N/n$ = the expected number of infected groups of n in a population of N with a prevalence rate of p.

The expected number of chemical analyses required by the grouping procedure would be

$$E(T) = N/n + n(N/n)p'$$

or the number of groups plus the number of individuals in groups which require retesting.[2] The ratio of the number of tests required by the group technique to the number required by the individual technique is a measure of its expected relative cost. It is given by:

$$C = T/N = 1/n + p'$$

$$= \frac{n + 1}{n} - (1 - p)^n.$$

---

[1] Diagnostic tests for syphilis are extremely sensitive and will show positive results for even great dilutions of antigen.

[2] The variance of T is $\sigma_T^2 = nNp'(1 - p') = nN[(1 - p)^n - (1 - p)^{2n}]$. The coefficient of variation of T becomes small rapidly as N increases.

ROBERT DORFMAN

The extent of the savings attainable by use of the group method depends on the group size and the prevalence rate. Figure 1 shows the shape of the relative cost curve for five prevalence rates ranging from .01 to .15.[3] For a prevalence rate of .01 it is clear from the chart that only 20% as many tests would be required by group tests with groups of 11 than by individual testing. The attainable savings decrease as the prevalence rate increases, and for a prevalence rate of .15, 72% as many tests are required by the most efficient grouping as by individual testing. The optimum group size for a population with a known prevalence rate is the integral value of n which has the lowest corresponding value on the relative cost curve for that prevalence rate.

TABLE I

Optimum Group Sizes and Relative Testing Costs for Selected Prevalence Rates

Prevalence Rate (per cent)	Optimum Group Size	Relative Testing Cost	Percent Saving Attainable
1	11	20	80
2	8	27	73
3	6	33	67
4	6	38	62
5	5	43	57
6	5	47	53
7	5	50	50
8	4	53	47
9	4	56	44
10	4	59	41
12	4	65	35
13	3	67	33
15	3	72	28
20	3	82	18
25	3	91	9
30	3	99	1

Optimum group sizes and their costs relative to the cost of individual testing are given in Table I for selected prevalence rates.

This table, together with the description of the group testing technique as it might be applied to blood tests for syphilis, reveals the two conditions for the economical application of the technique:

1. That the prevalence rate be sufficiently small to make worth while economies possible; and

---

[3] The prevalence rate of syphilis among the first million selectees and volunteers was .0185 for whites and .2477 for other races. Geographically, the prevalence rate for whites ranged from .0505 in Arizona to .0051 in Wisconsin. See Parran, Thomas and Vonderlehr, R. A., *Plain Words about Venereal Disease*, Reynal and Hitchcock, New York.

2. That it be easier or more economical to obtain an observation on a group
   than on the individuals of the group separately.

Where these conditions exist, it will be more economical to locate defective members of a population by means of group testing than by means of individual
testing.

The principle of group testing may be applied to situations where the interest
centers in the degree to which an imperfection is present rather than merely in
its presence or absence.   For example, it could be applied to lots of chemicals
where it is desired to reject all batches with more than a certain degree of impurity.   If n samples of a chemical are pooled and subjected to a single analysis,
the degree of impurity in the pool will be the average of the impurities in the

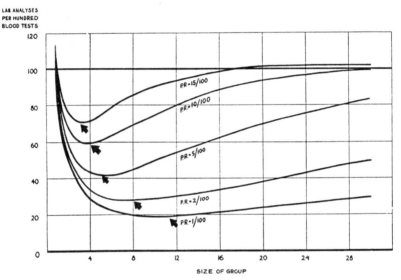

Fig. 1. Economies resulting from blood testing by groups
P.R. denotes prevalence rate

separate samples.   If the criterion were adopted that the members of a pool
would be examined individually whenever the proportion of impurity in the pool
is greater than $1/n$-th the maximum acceptable degree of impurity, clearly no
excessively impure batches would get by.   The extent of the saving accomplished
by this means can be computed by letting p' equal the probability that the pool
will be impure enough to warrant retesting its constituent batches and using the
formulas given above.   The probability, p', can be calculated easily from the
probability distribution of impurities in the separate batches.

It is evident that this approach will produce worthwhile savings only if the
limit of acceptability is liberally above the per cent of impurity encountered in
the bulk of the batches.   It is also evident that under this scheme many of the

ROBERT DORFMAN

retests will indicate that all the batches in the pool are acceptable and that the retesting was not really needed. The criterion for retesting can be raised above $1/n$-th the limit of acceptability at the cost of a relatively small risk of accepting overly impure batches. The probability of failing to detect a defective batch when the retest criterion is raised in this manner will depend upon the form and parameters of the distribution of imperfection in single batches, as well as upon the number of batches in the pool. No simple general solution for this problem has been found.

PART TWO

MATHEMATICAL METHODS

[2]

MATHEMATICAL, OR "LINEAR," PROGRAMMING: A NONMATHEMATICAL EXPOSITION

By Robert Dorfman*

This paper is intended to set forth the leading ideas of mathematical programming[1] purged of the algebraic apparatus which has impeded their general acceptance and appreciation. This will be done by concentrating on the graphical representation of the method. While it is not possible, in general, to portray mathematical programming problems in two-dimensional graphs, the conclusions which we shall draw from the graphs will be of general validity and, of course, the graphic representation of multidimensional problems has a time-honored place in economics.

The central formal problem of economics is the problem of allocating scarce resources so as to maximize the attainment of some predetermined objective. The standard formulation of this problem—the so-called marginal analysis—has led to conclusions of great importance for the understanding of many questions of social and economic policy. But it is a fact of common knowledge that this mode of analysis has not recommended itself to men of affairs for the practical solution of their economic and business problems. Mathematical programming is based on a restatement of this same formal problem in a form which is designed to be useful in making practical decisions in business and economic affairs. That mathematical programming is nothing but a reformulation of the standard economic problem and its solution is the main thesis of this exposition.

The motivating idea of mathematical programming is the idea of a

---

* The author is associate professor of economics at the University of California, Berkeley.

[1] The terminology of the techniques which we are discussing is in an unsatisfactory state. Most frequently they are called "linear programming" although the relationships involved are not always linear. Sometimes they are called "activities analysis," but this is not a very suggestive name. The distinguishing feature of the techniques is that they are concerned with programming rather than with analysis, and, at any rate, "activities analysis" has not caught on. We now try out "mathematical programming"; perhaps it will suit.

Reprinted from AMERICAN ECONOMIC REVIEW, Vol. XLIII, No. 5, Part I, December, 1953

Copyright, 1953, American Economic Association   •   All rights reserved "process" or "activity." A process is a specific method for performing an economic task. For example, the manufacture of soap by a specified formula is a process. So also is the weaving of a specific quality of cotton gray goods on a specific type of loom. The conventional production function can be thought of as the formula relating the inputs and outputs of all the processes by which a given task can be accomplished.

For some tasks, *e.g.*, soap production, there are an infinite number of processes available. For others, *e.g.*, weaving, only a finite number of processes exist. In some cases, a plant or industry may have only a single process available.

In terms of processes, choices in the productive sphere are simply decisions as to which processes are to be used and the extent to which each is to be employed. Economists are accustomed to thinking in terms of decisions as to the quantities of various productive factors to be employed. But an industry or firm cannot substitute Factor A for Factor B unless it does some of its work in a different way, that is, unless it substitutes a process which uses A in relatively high proportions for one which uses B. Inputs, therefore, cannot be changed without a change in the way of doing things, and often a fundamental change. Mathematical programming focusses on this aspect of economic choice.

The objective of mathematical programming is to determine the optimal levels of productive processes in given circumstances. This requires a restatement of productive relationships in terms of processes and a reconsideration of the effect of factor scarcities on production choices. As a prelude to this theoretical discussion, however, it will be helpful to consider a simplified production problem from a common-sense point of view.

I. *An Example of Mathematical Programming*

Let us consider an hypothetical automobile company equipped for the production of both automobiles and trucks. This company, then, can perform two economic tasks, and we assume that it has a single process for accomplishing each. These two tasks, the manufacture of automobiles and that of trucks, compete for the use of the firm's facilities. Let us assume that the company's plant is organized into four departments: (1) sheet metal stamping, (2) engine assembly, (3) automobile final assembly, and (4) truck final assembly—raw materials, labor, and all other components being available in virtually unlimited amounts at constant prices in the open market.

The capacity of each department of the plant is, of course, limited. We assume that the metal stamping department can turn out sufficient stampings for 25,000 automobiles or 35,000 trucks per month. We can then calculate the combinations of automobile and truck stampings which this department can produce. Since the department can accommodate 25,000 automobiles per month, each automobile requires 1/25,000 or 0.004 per cent of monthly capacity. Similarly each truck requires 0.00286 per cent of monthly capacity. If, for example, 15,000 automobiles were manufactured they would require 60 per cent of metal stamping capacity and the remaining 40 per cent would be sufficient to produce stampings for 14,000 trucks. Then 15,000 automobiles and 14,000 trucks could be produced by this department at full operation. This is, of course, not the only combination of automobiles and trucks which could be produced by the stamping department at full operation. In Figure 1, the line labeled "Metal Stamping" represents all such combinations.

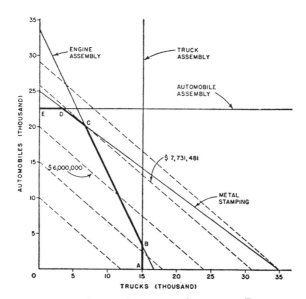

FIGURE 1. CHOICES OPEN TO AN AUTOMOBILE FIRM

Similarly we assume that the engine assembly department has monthly capacity for 33,333 automobile engines or 16,667 truck engines or, again, some combination of fewer automobile and truck engines. The combinations which would absorb the full capacity of the engine assembly department are shown by the "Engine Assembly" line in Figure 1. We assume also that the automobile assembly department can accommodate 22,500 automobiles per month and the truck assembly department 15,000 trucks. These limitations are also represented in Figure 1.

We regard this set of assumptions as defining two processes: the production of automobiles and the production of trucks. The process of producing an automobile yields, as an output, one automobile and absorbs, as inputs, 0.004 per cent of metal stamping capacity, 0.003 per cent of engine assembly capacity, and 0.00444 per cent of automobile assembly capacity. Similarly the process of producing a truck yields, as an output, one truck and absorbs, as inputs, 0.00286 per cent of metal stamping capacity, 0.006 per cent of engine assembly capacity, and 0.00667 per cent of truck assembly capacity.

The economic choice facing this firm is the selection of the numbers of automobiles and trucks to be produced each month, subject to the restriction that no more than 100 per cent of the capacity of any department can be used. Or, in more technical phraseology, the choice consists in deciding at what level to employ each of the two available processes. Clearly, if automobiles alone are produced, at most 22,500 units per month can be made, automobile assembly being the effective limitation. If only trucks are produced, a maximum of 15,000 units per month can be made because of the limitation on truck assembly. Which of these alternatives should be adopted, or whether some combination of trucks and automobiles should be produced depends on the relative profitability of manufacturing trucks and automobiles. Let us assume, to be concrete, that the sales value of an automobile is $300 greater than the total cost of purchased materials, labor, and other direct costs attributable to its manufacture. And, similarly, that the sale value of a truck is $250 more than the direct cost of manufacturing it. Then the net revenue of the plant for any month is 300 times the number of automobiles produced plus 250 times the number of trucks. For example, 15,000 automobiles and 6,000 trucks would yield a net revenue of $6,000,000. There are many combinations of automobiles and trucks which would yield this same net revenue; 10,000 automobiles and 12,000 trucks is another one. In terms of Figure 1, all combinations with a net revenue of $6,000,000 lie on a straight line, to be specific, the line labelled $6,000,000 in the figure.

A line analogous to the one which we have just described corresponds to each possible net revenue. All these lines are parallel, since their slope depends only on the relative profitability of the two activities. The greater the net revenue, of course, the higher the line. A few of the net revenue lines are shown in the figure by the dashed parallel lines.

Each conceivable number of automobiles and trucks produced corresponds to a point on the diagram, and through each point there passes one member of the family of net revenue lines. Net revenue is maximized when the point corresponding to the number of automobiles and trucks produced lies on the highest possible net revenue line. Now the effect of the capacity restrictions is to limit the range of choice to outputs which correspond to points lying inside the area bounded by the axes and by the broken line ABCDE. Since net revenue increases as points move out from the origin, only points which lie on the broken line need be considered. Beginning then with Point A and moving along the broken line we see that the boundary of the accessible region intersects higher and higher net revenue lines until point C is reached. From there on, the boundary slides down the scale of net revenue lines. Point C therefore corresponds to the highest attainable net revenue. At point C the output is 20,370 automobiles and 6,481 trucks, yielding a net revenue of $7,731,481 per month.

The reader has very likely noticed that this diagram is by no means novel. The broken line, ABCDE, tells the maximum number of automobiles which can be produced in conjunction with any given number of trucks. It is therefore, apart from its angularity, a production opportunity curve or transformation curve of the sort made familiar by Irving Fisher, and the slope of the curve at any point where it has a slope is the ratio of substitution in production between automobiles and trucks. The novel feature is that the production opportunity curve shown here has no defined slope at five points and that one of these five is the critical point. The dashed lines in the diagram are equivalent to conventional price lines.

The standard theory of production teaches that profits are maximized at a point where a price line is tangent to the production opportunity curve. But, as we have just noted, there are five points where our production opportunity curve has no tangent. The tangency criterion therefore fails. Instead we find that profits are maximized at a corner where the slope of the price line is neither less than the slope of the opportunity curve to the left of the corner nor greater than the slope of the opportunity curve to the right.

Diagrammatically, then, mathematical programming uses angles where standard economics uses curves. In economic terms, where does the novelty lie? In standard economic analysis we visualize production relationships in which, if there are two products, one may be substituted for the other with gradually increasing difficulty. In mathematical programming we visualize a regime of production in which, for any output, certain factors will be effectively limiting but other factors will be in ample supply. Thus, in Figure 1, the factors which effectively limit production at each point can be identified by noticing on which limitation lines the point lies. The rate of substitution between products is determined by the limiting factors alone and changes only when the designation of the limiting factors changes. In the diagram a change in the designation of the limiting factors is represented by turning a corner on the production opportunity curve.

We shall come back to this example later, for we have not exhausted its significance. But now we are in a position to develop with more generality some of the concepts used in mathematical programming.

II. *The Model of Production in Mathematical Programming*

A classical problem in economics is the optimal utilization of two factors of production, conveniently called capital and labor. In the usual analysis, the problem is formulated by conceiving of the two factors as cooperating with each other in accordance with a production function which states the maximum quantity of a product which can be obtained by the use of stated quantities of the two factors. One convenient means of representing such a production function is an "isoquant diagram," as in Figure 2. In this familiar figure, quantities of labor are plotted along the horizontal axis and quantities of capital

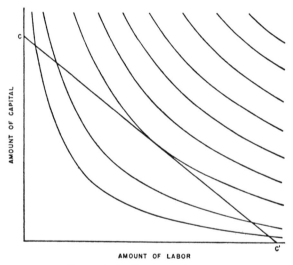

AMOUNT OF LABOR

FIGURE 2. AN ISOQUANT DIAGRAM

along the vertical. Each of the arcs in the body of the diagram corresponds to a definite quantity of output, higher arcs corresponding to greater quantities.

If the prices per unit of capital and labor are known, the combinations of labor and capital which can be purchased for a fixed total expenditure can be shown by a sloping straight line like CC′ in the figure, the slope depending only on the relative prices. Two interpretations follow immediately. First, the minimum unit cost of producing the output represented by any isoquant can be achieved by using the combination of labor and capital which corresponds to the point where that isoquant is tangent to a price line. Second, the greatest output attainable with any given expenditure is represented by the isoquant which is tangent to the price line corresponding to that expenditure.

This diagram and its analysis rest upon the assumption that the two factors are continuously substitutable for each other in such wise that if the amount of labor employed be reduced by a small amount it will be possible to maintain the quantity of output by a *small* increase in the amount of capital employed. Moreover, this analysis assumes that each successive unit decrement in the amount of labor will require a slightly larger increment in the amount of capital if output is to remain constant. Otherwise the isoquants will not have the necessary shape.

All this is familiar. We call it to mind only because we are about to develop an analogous diagram which is fundamental to mathematical programming. First, however, let us see why a new diagram and a new approach are felt to be necessary.

The model of production which we have just briefly sketched very likely is valid for some kinds of production. But for most manufacturing industries, and indeed all production where elaborate machinery is used, it is open to serious objection. It is characteristic of most modern machinery that each kind of machine operates efficiently only over a narrow range of speeds and that the quantities of labor, power, materials and other factors which cooperate with the machine are dictated rather inflexibly by the machine's built-in characteristics. Furthermore, at any time there is available only a small number of different kinds of machinery for accomplishing a given task. A few examples may make these considerations more concrete. Earth may be moved by hand shovels, by steam or diesel shovels, or by bulldozers. Power shovels and bulldozers are built in only a small variety of models, each with inherent characteristics as to fuel consumption per hour, number of operators and assistants required, cubic feet of earth moved per hour, etc. Printing type may be set by using hand-fonts, linotype machines or monotype machines. Again, each machine is available in only a few models and each has its own pace of operation, power and space requirements, and other essentially unalterable characteristics. A moment's reflection will bring to mind dozens of other illustrations: printing presses, power looms, railroad and highway haulage, statistical and accounting calculation, metallic ore reduction, metal fabrication, etc. For many economic tasks the number of processes available is finite, and each process can be regarded as inflexible with regard to the ratios among factor inputs and process outputs. Factors cannot be substituted for each other except by changing the levels at which entire technical processes are used, because each process uses factors in fixed characteristic ratios. In mathematical programming, accordingly, process substitution plays a rôle analogous to that of factor substitution in conventional analysis.

We now develop an apparatus for the analysis of process substitution. For convenience we shall limit our discussion to processes which consume two factors, to be called capital and labor, and produce a single output. Figure 3 represents such a process. As in Figure 2, the horizontal axis is scaled in units of labor and the vertical axis in units of capital. The process is represented by the ray, OA, which is scaled in units of output. To each output there corresponds a labor requirement found by locating the appropriate mark on the process ray and reading straight down. The capital requirement is found in the same manner by reading straight across from the mark on the process line. Similarly, to each amount of labor there corresponds a quantity of out-

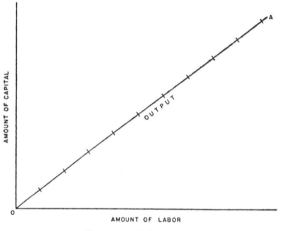

FIGURE 3. A PROCESS

put, found by reading straight up, and a quantity of capital, found by reading straight across from the output mark.

It should be noted that the quantity of capital in this diagram is the quantity used in a process rather than the quantity owned by an economic unit; it is capital-service rather than capital itself. Thus, though more or less labor may be combined with a given machine—by using it more or fewer hours—the ratio of capital to labor inputs, that is, the ratio of machine-hours to labor hours—is regarded as technologically fixed.

Figure 3 incorporates two important assumptions. The fact that the line OA is straight implies that the ratio between the capital input and the labor input is the same for all levels of output and is given, indeed, by the slope of the line. The fact that the marks on the output line are

evenly spaced indicates that there are neither economies nor diseconomies of scale in the use of the process, *i.e.*, that there will be strict proportionality between the quantity of output and the quality of either
input. These assumptions are justified rather simply on the basis of the
notion of a process. If a process can be used once, it can be used twice
or as many times as the supplies of factors permit. Two linotype
machines with equally skilled operators can turn out just twice as much
type per hour as one. Two identical mills can turn out just twice as
many yards of cotton per month as one. So long as factors are available, a process can be duplicated. Whether it will be economical to do so
is, of course, another matter.

   If there is only one process available for a given task there is not
much scope for economic choice. Frequently, however, there will be

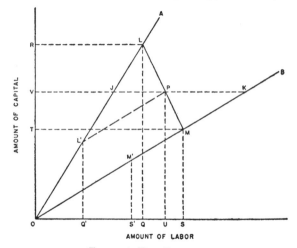

FIGURE 4. TWO PROCESSES

several processes. Figure 4 represents a situation in which two procedures are available, Process A indicated by the line OA and Process B
indicated by OB. We have already seen how to interpret points on the
lines OA and OB. The scales by which output is measured on the two
rays are not necessarily the same. The scale on each ray reflects the
productivity of the factors when used in the process represented by
that ray and has no connection with the output scale on any other
process ray. Now suppose that points L and M represent production of
the same output by the two processes. Then LM, the straight line between them, will represent an isoquant and each point on this line will
correspond to a combination of Processes A and B which produces the
same output as OL units of Process A or OM units of Process B.

   To see this, consider any point P on the line LM and draw a line through P parallel to OB. Let L' be the point where this line intersects OA. Finally mark the point M' on OB such that OM' = L'P. Now consider the production plan which consists of using Process A at level OL' and Process B at level OM'.[2] It is easy to show that this production plan uses OU units of labor, where U is the labor coordinate of point P, and OV units of capital, where V is the capital coordinate of point P.[3]

Since the coordinates of point P correspond to the quantities of factors consumed by OL' units of Process A and OM' units of Process B, we interpret P as representing the combined production plan made up of the specified levels of the two processes. This interpretation implies an important economic assumption, namely, that if the two processes are used simultaneously they will neither interfere with nor enhance each other so that the inputs and outputs resulting from simultaneous use of two processes at any levels can be found by adding the inputs and outputs of the individual processes.

In order to show that P lies on the isoquant through points L and M it remains only to show that the sum of the outputs corresponding to points L' and M' is the same as the output corresponding to point L or point M. This follows at once from the facts that the output corresponding to any point on a process ray is directly proportional to the length of the ray up to that point and that the triangles LL'P and LOM in Figure 4 are similar.[4] Thus if we have two process lines like OA and OB and find points L and M on them which represent producing the same output by means of the two processes then the line segment connecting the two equal-output points will be an isoquant.

We can now draw the mathematical programming analog of the familiar isoquant diagram. Figure 5 is such a diagram with four process lines shown. Point M represents a particular output by use of Process A and points L, K, J represent that same output by means of Processes B, C, D, respectively. The succession of line segments connecting these

[2] An alternative construction would be to draw a line through point P parallel to OA. It would intersect OB at M'. Then we could lay off OL' equal to M'P on OA. This would lead to exactly the same results as the construction used in the text. The situation is analogous to the "parallelogram of forces" in physics.

[3] Proof: Process A at level OL' uses OQ' units of labor, Process B at level OM' uses OS' units of labor, together they use OQ' + OS' units of labor. But, by construction, L'P is equal and parallel to OM'. So Q'U = OS'. Therefore, OQ' + OS' = OQ' + Q'U = OU units of labor. The argument with respect to capital is similar.

[4] Proof: Let Output (X) denote the output corresponding to any point, X, on the diagram. Then Output (M')/Output (M) = OM'/OM and Output (L')/Output (L) = OL'/OL. By assumption: Output (L) = Output (M). So Output (M')/Output (L) = OM'/OM. Adding, we have:

$$\frac{\text{Output (M')} + \text{Output (L')}}{\text{Output (L)}} = \frac{OM'}{OM} + \frac{OL'}{OL} = \frac{L'P}{OM} + \frac{OL'}{OL} = \frac{L'L}{OL} + \frac{OL'}{OL} = 1.$$

four points is the isoquant for that same output. It is easy to see that any other succession of line segments respectively parallel to those of MLKJ is also an isoquant. Three such are shown in the figure. It is instructive to compare Figure 5 with Figure 2 and note the strong resemblance in appearance as well as in interpretation.

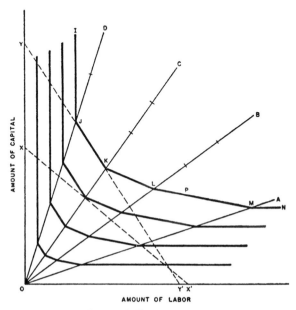

FIGURE 5. FOUR PROCESSES

We may draw price lines on Figure 5, just as on the conventional kind of isoquant diagram. The dashed lines XX' and YY' represent two possible price lines. Consider XX' first. As that line is drawn, the maximum output for a given expenditure can be obtained by use of Process C alone, and, conversely, the minimum cost for a given output is also obtained by using Process C alone. Thus, for the relative price regime represented by XX', Process C is optimal. The price line YY' is drawn parallel to the isoquant segment JK. In this case Process C is still optimal, but Process D is also optimal and so is any combination of the two.

It is evident from considering these two price lines, and as many others as the reader wishes to visualize, that an optimal production program can always be achieved by means of a single process, which process depending, of course, on the slope of the price line. It should be noted, however, that the conventional tangency criterion is no longer applicable.

We found in Figure 5 that an optimal economic plan need never use more than a single process for each of its outputs.[5] That conclusion is valid for the situation depicted, which assumed that the services of the two factors could be procured in any amounts desired at constant relative prices. This assumption is not applicable to many economic problems, nor is it used much in mathematical programming. We must now, therefore, take factor supply conditions into account.

III. *Factor Supplies and Costs*

In mathematical programming it is usual to divide all factors of production into two classes: unlimited factors, which are available in any amount desired at constant unit cost, and limited or scarce factors, which are obtainable at constant unit cost up to a fixed maximum quantity and thereafter not at all. The automobile example illustrates this classification. There the four types of capacity were treated as fixed factors available at zero variable cost; all other factors were grouped under direct costs which were considered as constant per unit of output.

The automobile example showed that this classification of factors is adequate for expressing the maximization problem of a firm dealing in competitive markets. In the last section we saw that when all factors are unlimited, this formulation can be used to find a minimum average cost point.

Both of these applications invoked restrictive assumptions and, furthermore, assumptions which conflict with those conventionally made in studying resource allocation. In conventional analysis we conceive that as the level of production of a firm, industry or economy rises, average unit costs rise also after some point. The increase in average costs is attributable in part to the working of the law of variable proportions,[6] which operates when the inputs of some but not all factors of production are increased. As far as the consequences of increasing some but not all inputs are concerned, the contrast between mathematical programming and the marginal analysis is more verbal than substantive. A reference to Figure 4 will show how such changes are handled in mathematical programming. Point J in Figure 4 represents the production of a certain output by the use of Process A alone. If it is desired to increase output without increasing the use of capital, this can be done by moving to the right along the dotted line JK, since this line cuts successively higher isoquants. Such a movement would correspond to using increasingly more of Process B and increasingly

---

[5] Recall, however, that we have not taken joint production into account nor have we considered the effects of considerations from the demand side.

[6] *Cf.* J. M. Cassels, "On the Law of Variable Proportions," in W. Fellner and B. F. Haley, eds., *Readings in the Theory of Income Distribution* (Philadelphia, 1946), pp. 103–18.

less of Process A and thus, indirectly, to substituting labor for capital. If, further, we assume that unit cost of production is lower for Process A than for Process B this movement would also correspond to increasing average cost of production. Thus both marginal analysis and mathematical programming lead to the same conclusion when factor proportions are changed: if the change starts from a minimum cost point the substitution will lead to gradually increasing unit costs.

But changing input proportions is only one part of the story according to the conventional type of analysis. If output is to be increased, any of three things may happen. First, it may be possible to increase the consumption of all inputs without incurring a change in their unit prices. In this case both mathematical programming and marginal analysis agree that output will be expanded without changing the ratios among the input quantities and average cost of production will not increase.[7] Second, it may not be possible to increase the use of some of the inputs. This is the case we have just analyzed. According to both modes of analysis the input ratios will change in this case and average unit costs will increase. The only difference between the two approaches is that if average cost is to be plotted against output, the marginal analyst will show a picture with a smoothly rising curve while the mathematical programmer will show a broken line made up of increasingly steep line segments. Third, it may be possible to increase the quantities of all inputs but only at the penalty of increasing unit prices or some kind of diseconomies of scale. This third case occurs in the marginal analysis, indeed it is the case which gives long-run cost curves their familiar shape, but mathematical programming has no counterpart for it.

The essential substantive difference we have arrived at is that the marginal analysis conceives of pecuniary and technical diseconomies associated with changes in scale while mathematical programming does not.[8] There are many important economic problems in which factor prices and productivities do not change in response to changes in scale or in which such variations can be disregarded. Most investigations of industrial capacity, for example, are of this nature. In such studies we seek the maximum output of an industry, regarding its inventory of physical equipment as given and assuming that the auxiliary factors needed to cooperate with the equipment can be obtained in the quanti-

[7] *Cf.* F. H. Knight, *Risk, Uncertainty and Profit* (Boston, 1921), p. 98.

[8] Even within the framework of the marginal analysis the concept of diseconomies of scale has been challenged on both theoretical and empirical grounds. For examples of empirical criticism see Committee on Price Determination, Conference on Price Research, *Cost Behavior and Price Policy* (New York, 1943). The most searching theoretical criticism is in Piero Sraffa, "The Laws of Returns under Competitive Conditions," *Econ. Jour.*, Dec. 1926, XXXVI, 535-50.

ties dictated by the characteristics of the equipment. Manpower requirement studies are of the same nature. In such studies we take both output and equipment as given and calculate the manpower needed to operate the equipment at the level which will yield the desired output. Studies of full employment output fall into the same format. In such studies we determine in advance the quantity of each factor which is to be regarded as full employment of that factor. Then we calculate the optimum output obtainable by the use of the factors in those quantities.

These illustrations should suffice to show that the assumptions made in mathematical programming can comprehend a wide variety of important economic problems. The most useful applications of mathematical programming are probably to problems of the types just described, that is, to problems concerned with finding optimum production plans using specified quantities of some or all of the resources involved.

IV. *Analysis of Production with Limited Factors*

The diagrams which we have developed are readily adaptable to the analysis of the consequences of limits on the factor supplies. Such limits are, of course, the heart of Figure 1 where the four principal lines represent limitations on the process levels which result from limits on the four factor quantities considered. But Figure 1 cannot be used when more than two processes have to be considered. For such problems diagrams like Figures 3, 4, and 5 have to be used.

Figure 6 reproduces the situation portrayed in Figure 5 with some

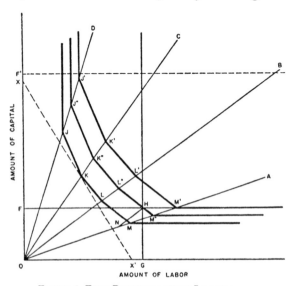

FIGURE 6. FOUR PROCESSES, WITH LIMITATIONS

additional data to be explained below. Let OF represent the maximum amount of capital which can be used and thus show a factor limitation. The horizontal line through F divides the diagram into two sections: all points above the line correspond to programs which require more capital than is available; points on and below the line represent programs which do not have excessive capital requirements. This horizontal line will be called the capital limitation line. Points on or below it are called "feasible," points above it are called "infeasible."

The economic unit portrayed in Figure 6 has the choice of operating at any feasible point. If maximum output is its objective, it will choose a point which lies on the highest possible isoquant, *i.e.*, the highest isoquant which touches the capital limitation line. This is the one labelled J'K'L'M', and the highest possible output is attained by using Process A.

Of course, maximum output may not be the objective. The objective may be, for example, to maximize the excess of the value of output over labor costs. We shall refer to such an excess as a "net value." The same kind of diagram can be used to solve for a net value provided that the value of each unit of output is independent of the number of units produced[9] and that the cost of each unit of labor is similarly constant. If these provisos are met, each point on a process ray will correspond to a certain physical output but also to a certain value of output, cost of labor, and net value of output. Further, along any process ray the net value of output will equal the physical output times the net value per unit and will therefore be proportional to the physical output. We may thus use a diagram similar to Figure 6 except that we think of net value instead of physical output as measured along the process rays and we show isovalue line instead of isoquants. This has been done on Figure 7, in which the maximum net value attainable is the one which corresponds to the isovalue contour through point P, and is attained by using Process C.

It should be noted in both Figures 6 and 7 that the optimal program consisted of a single process, that shifts in the quantity of capital available would not affect the designation of the optimal process though they would change its level, and that the price lines, which were crucial in Figure 5, played no rôle.

The next complication, and the last one we shall be able to consider, is to assume that both factors are in limited supply. This situation is portrayed in Figure 6 by adding the vertical line through point G to represent a labor limitation. The available quantity of labor is shown, of course, by the length OG. Then the points inside the rectangle

---

[9] This is a particularly uncomfortable assumption. We use it here to explain the method in its least complicated form.

OFHG represent programs which can be implemented in the sense that they do not require more than the available supplies of either factor. This is the rectangle of feasible programs. The greatest achievable output is the one which corresponds to the highest isoquant which touches the rectangle of feasible programs. This is the isoquant J"K"L"M", and furthermore, since the maximum isoquant touches the rectangle at H, H represents the program by which the maximum output can be produced.

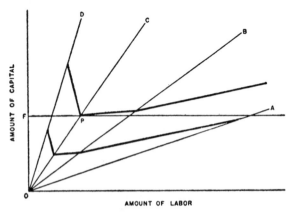

FIGURE 7. FOUR PROCESSES WITH ISOVALUE LINES

This solution differs from the previous ones in that the solution-point does not lie on any process ray but between the rays for Processes A and B. We have already seen that a point like H represents using Process A at level ON and Process B at level NH.

Two remarks are relevant to this solution. First: with the factor limitation lines as drawn, the maximum output requires two processes. If the factor limitation lines had been drawn so that they intersected exactly on one of the process rays, only one process would have been required. If the factor limitation lines had crossed to the left of Process D or to the right of Process A, the maximizing production plan would require only one process. But, no matter how the limitation lines be drawn, at most two processes are required to maximize output. We are led to an important generalization: maximum output may always be obtained by using a number of processes which does not exceed the number of factors in limited supply, if this number is greater than zero. The conclusions we drew from Figures 6 and 7 both conform to this rule, and it is one of the basic theorems of mathematical programming.

Second: although at most two processes are required to obtain the maximum output, which two depends on the location of the factor limits. As shown, the processes used for maximum output were Proces-

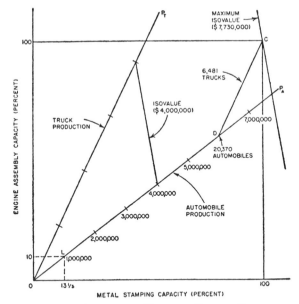

FIGURE 8. AUTOMOBILE EXAMPLE, OPTIMAL PLAN

ses A and B. If somewhat more capital, represented by the amount OF′, were available, the maximizing processes would have been Processes C and D. If two factors are limited, it is the ratio between their supplies rather than the absolute supplies of either which determines the processes in the optimum program. This contrasts with the case in which only one factor is limited. Just as the considerations which determine the optimum set of processes are more complicated when two factors are limited than when only one is, so with three or more limited factors the optimum conditions become more complicated still and soon pass the reach of intuition. This, indeed, is the *raison d'être* of the formidable apparatus of mathematical programming.

We can make these considerations more concrete by applying them to the automobile example. Referring to Figure 1, (p. 799), we note that the optimum production point, C, lay on the limitation lines for engine assembly and metal stamping, but well below the limits for automobile and truck assembly. The limitations on automobile and truck assembly capacity are, therefore, ineffective and can be disregarded. The situation in terms of the two effectively limiting types of capacity is shown in Figure 8.

In Figure 8 the ray P_A represents the process of producing automobiles and P_T the process of producing trucks. These two processes can be operated at any combination of levels which does not require the use of more than 100 per cent of either metal stamping or engine assembly capacity. Thus the rectangle in the diagram is the region of feasible production programs. The optimal production program is the one in the feasible region which corresponds to the highest possible net revenue.[10] Thus it will be helpful to construct isorevenue lines, as we did in Figure 7. To do this, consider automobile production first. Each point on P_A corresponds to the production of a certain number of automobiles per month. Suppose, for example, that the scale is such that point L represents the production of 3,333 automobiles per month. It will be recalled that each automobile yields a net revenue of $300. Therefore, 3,333 automobiles yield a revenue of $1,000,000. Point L, then, corresponds to a net revenue of $1,000,000 as well as to an output of 3,333 automobiles per month. Since (see page 799), 3,333 automobiles require $13\frac{1}{3}$ per cent of metal stamping capacity and 10 per cent of engine assembly capacity, the coordinates of the $1,000,000 net revenue point on P_A are established at once. By a similar argument, the point whose co-ordinates are $26\frac{2}{3}$ per cent of metal stamping capacity and 20 per cent of engine capacity is the $2,000,000 net revenue point on P_A. In the same manner, the whole ray can be drawn and scaled off in terms of net revenue, and so can P_T, the process ray for truck production. The diagram is completed by connecting the $4,000,000 points on the two process lines in order to show the direction of the isorevenue lines.

The optimum program is at point C, where the two capacity limits intersect, because C lies on the highest isorevenue line which touches the feasible region. Through point C we have drawn a line parallel to the truck production line and meeting the automobile production line at D. By our previous argument, the length OD represents the net revenue from automobile production in the optimal program and the length DC represents the net revenue from trucks. If these lengths be scaled off, the result, of course, will be the same as the solution found previously.

V. *Imputation of Factor Values*

We have just noted that the major field of application of mathematical programming is to problems where the supply of one or more factors of production is absolutely limited. Such scarcities are the genesis of value in ordinary analysis, and they generate values in mathematical programming too. In fact, in ordinary analysis the determination of outputs and the determination of prices are but two aspects of the same problem, the optimal allocation of scarce resources. The same is true in mathematical programming.

---

[10] Since the objective of the firm is, by assumption, to maximize revenue rather than physical output, we may consider automobile and truck production as two alternative processes for producing revenue instead of as two processes with disparate outputs.

Heretofore we have encountered prices only as data for determining the direct costs of processes and the net value of output. But of course the limiting factors of production also have value although we have not assigned prices to them up to now. In this section we shall see that the solution of a mathematical programming problem implicitly assigns values to the limiting factors of production. Furthermore, the implicit pricing problem can be solved directly and, when so solved, constitutes a solution to the optimal allocation problem.

Consider the automobile example and ask: how much is a unit (1 per cent) of each of the types of capacity worth to the firm? The approach to this question is similar in spirit to the familiar marginal analysis. With respect to each type of capacity we calculate how much the maximum revenue would increase if one more unit were added, or how much revenue would decrease if one unit were taken away. Since there is a surplus of automobile assembly capacity, neither the addition nor the subtraction of one unit of this type would affect the optimum program or the maximum net revenue. Hence the value of this type of capacity is nil. The analysis and result for truck assembly are the same.

We find, then, that these two types of capacity are free goods. This does not imply that an automobile assembly line is not worth having, any more than, to take a classic example, the fact that air is a free good means that it can be dispensed with. It means that it would not be worth while to increase this type of capacity at any positive price and that some units of these types could be disposed of without loss.

The valuation of the other types of capacity is not so trivial. In Figure 9 possible values per per cent of engine assembly capacity are scaled along the horizontal axis and values per per cent of metal stamping capacity are scaled along the vertical axis. Now consider any possible pair of values, say engine assembly capacity worth $20,000 per unit and metal stamping worth $40,000. This is represented by point A on the figure. Applying these values to the data on pages 798-99, the values of capacity required for producing an automobile is found to be: $(0.004 \times \$40,000) + (0.003 \times \$20,000) = \$220$ which is well under the value of producing an automobile, or $300.[11] In the same way, if engine assembly capacity is worth $60,000 per per cent of capacity and metal stamping capacity is valued at $30,000 per unit (point B), the cost of scarce resources required to produce an automobile will be exactly equal to the value of the product. This is clearly not the only combination of resource values which will precisely absorb the value of output when the resources are used to produce automobiles. The automobile production line in the figure, which passes through point B, is

[11] These unit values are also marginal values since costs of production are constant.

the locus of all such value combinations. A similar line has been drawn for truck production to represent those combinations of resource values for which the total value of resources used in producing trucks is equal to the value of output. The intersection of these two lines is obviously the only pair of resource values for which the marginal resource cost of producing an additional automobile is equal to the net value of an automobile and the same is true with respect to trucks. The pair can be found by plotting or, with more precision, by algebra. It is found that 1 per cent of engine assembly capacity is worth $9,259 and 1 per cent of metal stamping capacity is worth $68,056.

To each pair of values for the two types of capacity, there corresponds a value for the entire plant. Thus to the pair of values represented by point A there corresponds the plant value of (100 × $20,000) + (100 × $40,000) = $6,000,000. This is not the only pair of resource values which give an aggregate plant value of $6,000,000. Indeed, any pair of resource values on the dotted line through A corresponds to the same aggregate plant value. (By this stage, Figure 9 should become strongly reminiscent of Figure 1, page 799.) We have drawn a number of dotted lines parallel to the one just described, each corresponding to a specific aggregate plant value. The dotted line which passes through the intersection of the two production lines is of particular interest. By measurement or otherwise this line can be found to correspond to a plant value of $7,731,500 which, we recall, was found to be the maximum attainable net revenue.

Let us consider the implications of assigning values to the two limiting factors from a slightly different angle. We have seen that as soon as unit values have been assigned to the factors an aggregate value is assigned to the plant. We can make the aggregate plant value as low as we please, simply by assigning sufficiently low values to the various factors. But if the values assigned are too low, we have the unsatisfactory consequence that some of the processes will give rise to unimputed surpluses. We may, therefore, seek the lowest aggregate plant value which can be assigned and still have no process yield an unimputed surplus. In the automobile case, that value is $7,731,500. In the course of finding the lowest acceptable plant value we find specific unit values to be assigned to each of the resources.

In this example there are two processes and four limited resources. It turns out that only two of the resources were effectivly limiting, the others being in relatively ample supply. In general, the characteristics of the solution to a programming problem depend on the relationship between the number of limited resources and the number of processes taken into consideration. If, as in the present instance, the number of limited resources exceeds the number of processes it will usually turn out that some of the resources will have imputed values of zero and that the number of resources with positive imputed values will be equal to the number of processes.[12] If the number of limited resources equals the number of processes all resources will have positive imputed values. If, finally, the number of processes exceeds the number of limited resources, some of the processes will not be used in the optimal program. This situation, which is the usual one, was illustrated in Figure 6. In this case the total imputed value of resources absorbed will equal net revenue for some processes and will exceed it for others. The number of

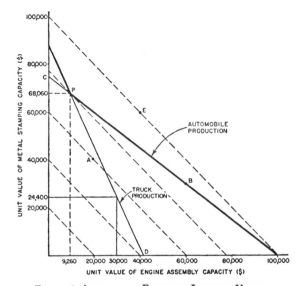

FIGURE 9. AUTOMOBILE EXAMPLE, IMPLICIT VALUES

processes for which the imputed value of resources absorbed equals the net revenue will be just equal to the number of limited resources and the processes for which the equality holds are the ones which will appear at positive levels in the optimal program. In brief, the determination of the minimum acceptable plant value amounts to the same thing as the determination of the optimal production program. The programming problem and the valuation problem are not only closely related, they are basically the same.

This can be seen graphically by comparing Figures 1 and 9. Each figure contains two axes and two diagonal boundary lines. But the boundary lines in Figure 9 refer to the same processes as the axes in Figure 1, and the axes in Figure 9 refer to the same resources as the

[12] We say "usually" in this sentence because in some special circumstances the number of resources with positive imputed values may exceed the number of processes.

diagonal boundary lines in Figure 1. Furthermore, in using Figure 1 we sought the net revenue corresponding to the highest dashed line touched by the boundary; in using Figure 9 we sought the aggregate value corresponding to the lowest dashed line which has any points on or outside the boundary; and the two results turned out to be the same. Formally stated, these two figures and the problems they represent are *duals* of each other.

The dualism feature is a very useful property in the solution of mathematical programming problems. The simplest way to see this is to note that when confronting a mathematical programming problem we have the choice of solving the problem or its dual, whichever is easier. Either way we can get the same results. We can use this feature now to generalize our discussion somewhat. Up to now when dealing with more than two processes we have had to use relatively complicated

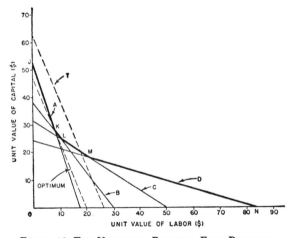

FIGURE 10. THE VALUATION PROBLEM, FOUR PROCESSES

diagrams like Figure 6 because straightforward diagrams like Figure 1 did not contain enough axes to represent the levels of the processes. Now we can use diagrams modeled on Figure 9 to depict problems with any number of processes so long as they do not involve more than two scarce factors. Figure 10 illustrates a diagram for four processes and is, indeed, derived from Figure 6. In Figure 10 line A represents all pairs of factor values such that Process A would yield neither a profit nor a loss. Lines B, C, and D are similarly interpreted. The dashed line T is a locus along which the aggregate value of the labor and capital available to the firm (or industry) is constant. Its position is not relevant to the analysis; its slope, which is simply the ratio of the quantity of available labor to that of capital, is all that is significant. The broken line JKLMN divides the graph into two regions. All points on or above it represent pairs of resource values such that no process gives rise to an unimputed surplus. Let us call this the acceptable region. For each point below that broken line there is at least one process which does have an unimputed surplus. This is the unacceptable region. We then seek for that point in the acceptable region which corresponds to the lowest aggregate plant value. This point will, of course, give the set of resource values which makes the accounting profit of the firm as great as possible without giving rise to any unimputed income. The point which meets these requirements is K, and a dotted line parallel to T has been drawn through it to indicate the minimum acceptable aggregate plant value.

At point K Processes A and B yield zero profits, and Processes C and D yield losses. Hence Processes A and B are the ones which should be used, exactly as we found in Figure 6. To be sure, this diagram does not tell the levels at which A and B should be used, any more than Figure 6 tells the valuations to be placed on the two resources. But finding the levels after the processes have been selected is a comparatively trivial matter. All that is necessary is to find the levels which will fully utilize the resources which are not free goods. This may be done algebraically or by means of a diagram like Figure 8.

VI. *Applications*

In the first section we asserted that the principal motivation of mathematical programming was the need for a method of analysis which lent itself to the practical solution of the day-to-day problems of business and the economy in general. Immediately after making that claim we introduced a highly artificial problem followed by a rather extended discussion of abstract and formal relationships. The time has now come to indicate the basis for saying that mathematical programming is a practical method of analysis.

The essential simplification achieved in mathematical programming is the replacement of the notion of the production function by the notion of the process. The process is a highly observable unit of activity and the empirical constants which characterize it can be estimated without elaborate analysis. Furthermore in many industries the structure of production corresponds to operating a succession of processes, as we have conceived them. Many industrial decisions, like shutting down a bank of machines or operating an extra shift, correspond naturally to our concept of choosing the level of operation of a process. In brief, mathematical programming is modelled after the actual structure of production in the hope that thereby it will involve only observable constants and directly controllable variables.

Has this hope been justified? The literature already contains a report of a successful application to petroleum refining.[13] I have made a similar application which, perhaps, will bear description. The application was to a moderate-sized refinery which produces premium and regular grades of automotive gasoline. The essential operation studied was blending. In blending, ten chemically distinct kinds of semirefined oil, called blending stocks, are mixed together. The result is a saleable gasoline whose characteristics are approximately the weighted average of the characteristics of the blending stocks. For example, if 500 gallons of a stock with octane rating of 80 are blended with 1,000 gallons of a stock with octane rating of 86 the result will be 500 + 1,000 = 1,500 gallons of product with octane rating of $(\frac{1}{3} \times 80) + (\frac{2}{3} \times 86) = 84$.

The significant aspect of gasoline blending for our present purposes is that the major characteristics of the blend—its knock rating, its vapor pressure, its sulphur content, etc.—can be expressed as linear functions of the quantities of the various blending stocks used. So also can the cost of the blend if each of the blending stocks has a definite price per gallon. Thus the problem of finding the minimum cost blend which will meet given quality specifications is a problem in mathematical programming.

Furthermore, in this refinery the quantities of some of the blending stocks are definitely limited by contracts and by refining capacity. The problem then arises: what are the most profitable quantities of output of regular and premium gasoline, and how much of each blending stock should be used for each final product. This problem is analogous to the artificial automobile example, with the added complication of the quality specifications. The problem is too complicated for graphic analysis but was solved easily by arithmetical procedures. As far as is known, mathematical programming provides the only way for solving such problems. Charnes and Cooper have recently published the solution to a similar problem which arose in the operations of a metalworking firm.[14]

An entirely different kind of problem, also amenable to mathematical programming, arises in newsprint production. Freight is a major element in the cost of newsprint. One large newsprint company has six mills, widely scattered in Canada, and some two hundred customers, widely scattered in the United States. Its problem is to decide how much

[13] A. Charnes, W. W. Cooper and B. Mellon, "Blending Aviation Gasolines," *Econometrica* Apr. 1952, XX, 135-59.

[14] A. Charnes, W. W. Cooper, and Donald Farr and Staff, "Linear Programming and Profit Preference Scheduling for a Manufacturing Firm," *Jour. Operations Research Society of America*, May 1953, I, 114-29.

newsprint to ship from each mill to each customer so as, first, to meet the contract requirements of each customer, second, to stay within the capacity limits of each mill, and third, to keep the aggregate freight bill as small as possible. This problem involves 1,200 variables (6 mills $\times$ 200 customers), in contrast to the two or four variable problems we have been discussing. In the final solution most of these variables will turn out to be zero—the question is which ones. This problem is solved by mathematical programming and, though formidable, is not really as formidable as the count of variables might indicate.

These few illustrations should suffice to indicate that mathematical programming is a practical tool for business planning. They show, also, that it is a flexible tool because both examples deviated from the format of the example used in our exposition. The petroleum application had the added feature of quality specification. In the newsprint application there were limits on the quantity of output as well as on the quantities of the inputs. Nevertheless mathematical programming handled them both easily.

On the other hand, it should be noted that both of these were small-scale applications, dealing with a single phase of the operation of a single firm. I believe that this has been true of all successful applications to date. Mathematical programmers are still a long way from solving the broad planning problem of entire industries or an entire economy. But many such broad problems are only enlarged versions of problems which have been met and solved in the context of the single firm. It is no longer premature to say that mathematical programming has proved its worth as a practical tool for finding optimal economic programs.

VII. *Conclusion*

Our objective has been only to introduce the basic notions of mathematical programming and to invest them with plausibility and meaning. The reader who would learn to solve a programming problem—even the simplest—will have to look elsewhere,[15] though this paper may serve as a useful background.

Although methods of solution have been omitted from this exposition, we must emphasize that these methods are fundamental to the whole concept of mathematical programming. Some eighty years ago Walras conceived of production in very much the same manner as mathematical

[15] The standard reference is T. C. Koopmans, ed., *Activity Analysis of Production and Allocation* (New York, 1951). Less advanced treatments may be found in A. Charnes, W. W. Cooper, and A. Henderson, *An Introduction to Linear Programming* (New York, 1953); and my own *Application of Linear Programming to the Theory of the Firm* (Berkeley, 1951).

programmers, and more recently A. Wald and J. von Neumann used this view of production and methods closely allied to those of mathematical programming to analyze the conditions of general economic equilibrium.[16] These developments, however, must be regarded merely as precursors of mathematical programming. Programming had no independent existence as a mode of economic analysis until 1947 when G. B. Dantzig announced the "simplex method" of solution which made practical application feasible.[17] The existence of a method whereby economic optima could be explicitly calculated stimulated research into the economic interpretation of mathematical programming and led also to the development of alternative methods of solution. The fact that economic and business problems when formulated in terms of mathematical programming can be solved numerically is the basis of the importance of the method. The omission of methods of solution from this discussion should not, therefore, be taken to indicate that they are of secondary interest.

We have considered only a few of the concepts used in mathematical programming and have dealt with only a single type of programming problem. The few notions we have considered, however, are the basic ones; all the rest of mathematical programming is elaboration and extension of them. It seems advisable to mention two directions of elaboration, for they remove or weaken two of the most restrictive assumptions which have here been imposed.

The first of these extensions is the introduction of time into the analysis. The present treatment has dealt with a single production period in isolation. But in many cases, successive production periods are interrelated. This is so, for example, in the case of a vertically integrated firm where the operation of some processes in one period is limited by the levels of operation in the preceding period of the processes which supply their raw materials. Efficient methods for analyzing such "dynamic" problems are being investigated, particularly by George Dantzig.[18] Although the present discussion has been static, the method of analysis can be applied to problems with a time dimension.

---

[16] Walras' formulation is in *Éléments d'économie politique pure ou théorie de la richesse sociale*, 2d ed. (Lausanne, 1889), 20° Leçon. The contributions of A. Wald and J. von Neumann appeared originally in *Ergebnisse eines mathematischen Kolloquiums*, Nos. 6, 7, 8. Wald's least technical paper appeared in *Zeitschrift für Nationalökonomie*, VII (1936) and has been translated as "On some Systems of Equations of Mathematical Economics," *Econometrica*, Oct. 1951, XIX, 368-403. Von Neumann's basic paper appeared in translation as "A Model of General Economic Equilibrium," *Rev. Econ. Stud.*, 1945-46, XIII, 1-9.

[17] G. B. Dantzig, "Maximization of a Linear Function of Variables Subject to Linear Inequalities," T. C. Koopmans, ed., *op. cit.*, pp. 339-47.

[18] "A Note on a Dynamic Leontief Model with Substitution" (abstract), *Econometrica*, Jan. 1953, XXI, 179.

The second of these extensions is the allowance for changes in the prices of factors and final products. In our discussion we regarded all prices as unalterable and independent of the actions of the economic unit under consideration. Constant prices are, undeniably, a great convenience to the analyst, but the method can transcend this assumption when necessary. The general mathematical theory of dealing with variable prices has been investigated[19] and practical methods of solution have been developed for problems where the demand and supply curves are linear.[20] The assumption of constant prices, perhaps the most restrictive assumption we have made, is adopted for convenience rather than from necessity.

Mathematical programming has been developed as a tool for economic and business planning and not primarily for the descriptive, and therefore predictive, purposes which gave rise to the marginal analysis. Nevertheless it does have predictive implications. In so far as firms operate under the conditions assumed in mathematical programming it would be unreasonable to assume that they acted as if they operated under the conditions assumed by the marginal analysis. Consider, for example, the automobile firm portrayed in Figure 1. How would it respond if the price of automobiles were to fall, say by $50 a unit? In that case the net revenue per automobile would be $250, the same as the net revenue per truck. Diagrammatically, the result would be to rotate the lines of equal revenue until their slope was 45 degrees. After this rotation, point C would still be optimum and this change in prices would cause no change in optimum output. Mathematical programming gives rise, thus, to a kinked supply curve.

On the other hand, suppose that the price of automobiles were to rise by $50. Diagrammatically this price change would decrease the steepness of the equal revenue lines until they were just parallel to the metal stamping line. The firm would then be in a position like that illustrated by the YY' line in Figure 5. The production plans corresponding to points on the line segment DC in Figure 1 would all yield the same net revenue and all would be optimal. If the prices of automobiles were to rise by more than $50 or if a $50 increase in the price of automobiles were accompanied by any decrease in the price of trucks, the point of optimal production would jump abruptly from point C to point D.

Thus mathematical programming indicates that firms whose choices

[19] See H. W. Kuhn and A. W. Tucker, "Non-Linear Programming," in J. Neyman, ed., *Proceedings of the Second Berkeley Symposium on Mathematical Statistics and Probability* (Berkeley, 1951), pp. 481-92.

[20] I reported one solution of this problem to a seminar at the Massachusetts Institute of Technology in September 1952. Other solutions may be known.

are limited to distinct processes will respond discontinuously to price variations: they will be insensitive to price changes over a certain range and will change their levels of output sharply as soon as that range is passed. This theoretical deduction surely has real counterparts.

The relationship between mathematical programming and welfare economics is especially close. Welfare economics studies the optimal organization of economic effort; so does mathematical programming. This relationship has been investigated especially by Koopmans and Samuelson.[21] The finding, generally stated, is that the equilibrium position of a perfectly competitive economy is the same as the optimal solution to the mathematical programming problem embodying the same data.

Mathematical programming is closely allied mathematically to the methods of input-output analysis or interindustry analysis developed largely by W. W. Leontief.[22] The two methods were developed independently, however, and it is important to distinguish them conceptually. Input-output analysis finds its application almost exclusively in the study of general economic equilibrium. It conceives of an economy as divided into a number of industrial sectors each of which is analogous to a process as the term is used in mathematical programming. It then takes either of two forms. In "open models" an input-output analysis starts with some specified final demand for the products of each of the sectors and calculates the level at which each of the sector-processes must operate in order to meet this schedule of final demands. In "closed models" final demand does not appear but attention is concentrated on the fact that the inputs required by each sector-process must be supplied as outputs by some other sector-processes. Input-output analysis then calculates a mutually compatible set of output levels for the various sectors. By contrast with mathematical programming the conditions imposed in input-output analysis are sufficient to determine the levels of the processes and there is no scope for finding an optimal solution or a set of "best" levels. To be sure, input-output analysis can be regarded as a special case of mathematical programming in which the number of products is equal to the number of processes. On the other hand, the limitations on the supplies of resources which play so important a rôle in mathematical programming are not dealt with explicitly in input-output analysis. On the whole it seems

    [21] T. C. Koopmans, "Analysis of Production as an Efficient Combination of Activities," in T. C. Koopmans, ed., *op. cit.*, pp. 33-97; P. A. Samuelson, "Market Mechanisms and Maximization" (a paper prepared for the Rand Corp., 1949).

    [22] W. W. Leontief, *The Structure of American Economy 1919-1939*, 2nd. ed. (New York, 1951).

best to regard these two techniques as allied but distinct methods of analysis addressed to different problems.

Mathematical programming, then, is of significance for economic thinking and theory as well as for business and economic planning. We have been able only to allude to this significance. Indeed, apart from the exploration of welfare implications, very little thought has been given to the consequences for economics of mathematical programming because most effort has been devoted to solving the numerous practical problems to which it gives rise. The outlook is for fruitful researches into both the implications and applications of mathematical programming.

[3]

VII. A CATECHISM: MATHEMATICS IN SOCIAL SCIENCE
Robert Dorfman

The best way I can comment on Novick's paper is to subject myself to a brief catechism and to compare my responses with those implicit or explicit in Novick's treatment.

What is mathematics? It is presumptuous for an economist to answer this question, but to get on with the argument I propose that mathematics is the technique of expressing relationships, usually symbolically, in such a way as to bring out their formal structure and then of taking advantage of accumulated knowledge about the properties of such formal structures to reveal further relationships which are not immediately evident. The advantage of this procedure is its enormous economy. Consider, for example, the distinction between marginal productivity and net marginal productivity,

[1] I have considered and rejected an alternative answer to the above questions, namely that there is a Gresham's Law according to which bad (mathematical) economics drives out good (literary) economics. Gresham's Law depends on the fact that people are motivated to hoard the undervalued currency. There is no evidence that untold fascinating literary-economic ideas are piling up in the profession's mattresses.

which worried J. B. Clark and J. Robinson among others. It is possible to prove *ab initio* that these two concepts are identical (J. Robinson did so); it saves a lot of brain-wracking to notice that the problem concerns the relationships among certain total and partial derivatives, relationships which were worked out generations ago.

The best clue to Novick's answer is contained in the sentence, "It is high time therefore that we recognize the difference between mathematics as a language form and mathematics as a quantitative method. . . ." Novick seems to feel that there are two kinds of mathematics, one purely linguistic and the other perhaps corresponding to the concept I have proposed. The old aphorism that "mathematics is a language" underlies much of his discussion. This maxim is at best half true, the true half being that mathematics *has* a language and that the first step in "doing mathematics" is to translate non-mathematical concepts into that language. Even as a linguistic device mathematics has a service to perform. Every bilinguist knows that there are things which can be said in French but not in English, and *vice versa*. Every economist knows that there are things which can be said in literary economics but which elude mathematical formulation. But many economists forget the converse: there are some things which can be said in mathematics but which cannot be paraphrased with tolerable accuracy in ordinary English. Consider, for example, that old stumbling block: is marginal cost the cost of the last unit produced or the first one not produced.

Mathematics, I am contending, is neither a language form nor a quantitative method but a branch of logic. I don't know exactly how to distinguish it from the rest of logic, and my definition, apart from the remark about symbols, would apply about as well to logic as to mathematics. The distinguishing mark of mathematics probably lies in the volume of knowledge which has been amassed about certain types of formal relationships; when we make use of these time- and thought-savers we are engaged in mathematics.

Are scientific theories proved by mathematics or statistics or neither? The first question encroached on the mathematician's field of expertness, now we are trespassing in the philosopher's domain. We must proceed, but with diffidence. The situation seems to be that scientific theories are not proved ever, but that both mathematics and statistics (which in this context means merely observation) provide criteria for the provisional acceptance of theories for the purposes and at the times that they are accepted. The mathematical criteria are that if two theories are logically contradictory they cannot both be accepted or, what is the same thing, if any theory is accepted so must be all its logical implications. The statistical criterion is that in choosing among several internally consistent theories that one is to be accepted which would most successfully predict observed phenomena. Both criteria are complicated and they work together in complicated ways.

Two of Novick's passages bear on this question. "The richness of social science today arises chiefly from the stimulus to thinking which follows the fact that little or nothing in the theorems now used is susceptible to

absolute proof and therefore cannot be accepted without challenge." This source of wealth, alas, is open to all sciences; none is paralyzed by the misfortune of absolute proof.

The second relevant passage is, "Mathematics is now used in the social sciences chiefly as it has been used in theoretic physics or chemistry and not as the mathematical results of theory proved by statistics in physics or chemistry are applied in everyday engineering or mechanics." This makes Novick's stand clear. Theories can be proved and, moreover, by statistics. I can barely hint at the reasons for rejecting these positions. In the first place the agreement between observation and theory is never perfect. The possibility always remains, therefore, that a new theory will be discovered which entails fewer discrepancies than any accepted theory. In the second place, agreement with statistics is not the only criterion a theory must meet, and internal consistency and consistency with other accepted theories cannot be verified by statistics. A theory may be supplanted by an alternative whose predictive power is no greater but whose logical implications comprehend a wider realm of phenomena. In the third place, observations do not uniquely determine theory. For example, both underconsumption and overconsumption theories of the business cycle are consistent with the same data. In evaluating a theory statistics and mathematics complement each other, the one testing its logical acceptability and comprehensiveness, the other its empirical relevance. Proof we cannot hope for.

Is the role of mathematics different in social science, physical science, and engineering? It is not. In every case mathematics is used to bring to light relationships implicit in the postulates which are used as a point of departure. Judging from the last passage which I have quoted Novick would hold that the role of mathematics in engineering is different from its role in physical science, that its role in economics is similar to its role in physical science, but that its role in economics should be similar to its role in engineering. I am unable to see the distinction, especially since engineers use precisely the same mathematics and formulas as physicists and chemists.

Is mathematics necessary in social science?

I suppose not. It is quite conceivable that all problems could be solved by verbal means, just as it is quite possible to find that the square root of CLXXXXVI is XIV. Such methods, though, would be not only painful but fearfully inefficient. They would mean, in effect, rediscovering or reproving mathematical theorems every time they arose in a new substantive context. They would eliminate from fruitful research many men who are competent to learn and use some mathematics but not competent to reinvent it when and where needed. I am saying, in effect, that mathematics *is* a practical necessity for the solution of many economic problems. Consider, for example, the elaborate apparatus which was eventually needed to solve the "identification problem" originally raised by E. J. Working in the 1920's. Another example is the theory of general equilibrium and its recent highly technical development. As a matter of history, no one has succeeded in exploring the existence theorems and welfare implications of general equilibrium without a liberal application of fancy mathematics. Superficial treatments of this problem have led to fallacy, and fallacy, I feel, should be extirpated even at the cost of having to learn some mathematics.

Physicists have had to learn tensor analysis willy-nilly, or to come closer to home, statisticians have become involved in the higher reaches of measure theory. This has been hard on those physicists and statisticians who lacked the tools which their developing sciences demanded, but no one seriously contends that this made the tools inappropriate. We economists are in the same fix. If mathematics solves otherwise intractable problems, and it does, there is little point in attacking these solutions because the bulk of the profession cannot understand them.

Mathematics is an aid to reasoning. If we could dispense with it, I'm sure everyone would be glad to and thereby widen his audience and economize on printing bills. But some important problems — I have already mentioned a few — are too hard to solve any other way. This being so, we economists will just have to learn some mathematics.

Novick could hardly deny this, and yet he wrote, "It is not impossible that some day mathematical methods can be applied to economic and social activity. However, that day seems remote. . . ." I should agree that the day is remote and should hazard, just as a guess, 1838 (Cournot).

Are mathematical results often unintelligible and subject to misunderstanding? Alas, they are. This, of course, is Novick's chief charge against mathematical economics, and it is a remarkable charge. I have many times had to argue that the church cannot be attacked because of the sins of the clergy, but this is one of the few times that I have seen the church roundly condemned for the shortcomings of the laity.

The specific misunderstanding which concerns Novick most relates to the significance of mathematical results. All that mathematics purports to establish is statements of the form, "If A is true then B is." What mathematics does is enable use to see more clearly and more deeply into the consequences of assertions which may or may not be true. Novick feels that some economists regard a mathematical theorem as a statement which has been established absolutely, independently of assumptions. Such economists, if such there be, should take warning from his paper and regard it as an important step in their mathematical education.

Should mathematical economists restate their theories in literary form? Novick urges them to do so and Marshall gives the same advice. I must dissent. Practitioners of mathematical economics already have their hands full coping with some of the toughest problems which the science offers and it is unfair to impose on them the special problems of literary lucidity. Mathematical and literary talents do not always dwell in the same man. An amelioration of the communications difficulty lies with translators or popularizers who undertake the ungrateful task of trying to grasp the meaning of the mathematics and restate it with tolerable accuracy in English. The ultimate answer lies with the professional reader, who must equip himself to read what he wishes to understand.

My very strong feeling is that any discussion, like this one, of the legitimacy of mathematical methods in economics is doomed to be fruitless. Time and tide will not be rolled back. The profession will not relinquish power-ful instruments of reasoning. The only real question is a question of fact: do mathematical methods have any power. That they do has been demonstrated repeatedly by the problems they have solved and by the muddled impasses which literary reasoning has not been able to break through.

The Review *of* Economics *and* Statistics

VOLUME XXXVI   MAY 1954   NUMBER 2

THE NATURE AND SIGNIFICANCE OF INPUT-OUTPUT

Robert Dorfman

THERE can hardly be an economist who has not watched with amazement that nova of economics, input-output. Into a science characterized by individual research, piddling grants, and hand-me-down data it brought large, well-financed research teams and fresh resources of statistical material. It prodded a government which has practically never encouraged any but descriptive research to sponsor the development of a radical departure in economic analysis. It reversed a trend from aggregative to disaggregative analysis, leavened the thinking of the profession as the Keynesian hypothesis did two decades ago, and taught us all that "matrix" does not necessarily mean "social milieu." It has been discussed in the general press (for example, *Fortune* and *Dun's Review*) and, latterly, like the Keynesian doctrine, its social implications have become a subject of political controversy.

Two authoritative works on input-output have recently appeared: *The Structure of American Economy 1919–1939* by W. W. Leontief (Ref. 16) [1] and *Studies in the Structure of the American Economy* by Leontief and members of the staff of the Harvard Economic Research Project (Ref. 17). They provide a good opportunity for surveying the accomplishments of input-output and the direction which its development is taking.

The Structure of American Economy 1919–1939 is an enlarged edition of the monograph of 1941 in which Leontief first presented his system in detail. It consists of two main sections. The first is a reprint of the material of the original edition. The second consists of four essays which reflect the development and application of the method since 1941.

Studies in the Structure is, essentially, a

[1] Citations to numbered references will be found in the appendix.

progress report on the work of the Harvard Economic Research Project. It consists of twelve papers, four by Leontief and the rest by other members of the staff. These essays cover the main directions in which research is now progressing: the development of dynamic models, investigation of models for interregional analysis, empirical study of the capital requirements of production and of the determinants of investment in real capital, the detailed study of engineering production functions, continued study of the determinants of household consumption. Thus *Structure of American Economy* presents the basic conceptual and empirical framework of input-output analysis, while *Studies in the Structure* deals largely with supplementary material reexamining the technological assumptions of the theory and paving the way for its extension and amplification.

Input-output belongs in the hard-headed, as distinct from the high-flown, category of economic theories. Leontief's objective, announced at the very outset of *Structure of American Economy*, was "an empirical study of interrelations among the different parts of a national economy" (Ref. 16, p. 3). He wished to avoid both abstract theoretical schemes supported by casual observation and statistical studies based on rudimentary, unexpressed theoretical underpinnings. He attempted to overcome "the persistent cleavage between a preponderantly deductive type of analysis, on the one side, and radical empiricism, on the other." (Ref. 17, p. 5). His method was to erect a sturdy theoretical scaffolding which called for obtainable statistical data, and then to obtain the data.

More specifically, Leontief's procedure was to simplify Walras' general equilibrium schema radically to the point where the equations involved in it could be estimated statistically. There were two essential steps in this simplification. First he aggregated the countless individual commodities which entered Walras' schema into a comparatively few outputs, one for each industrial sector of the economy. Second he dropped the supply equations for unproduced raw materials (chiefly various kinds of labor) and the demand equations for final consumption, and adopted the production equations in their simplest, linear form.

The result is a general equilibrium system of impressive simplicity. To set forth the bare bones, conceive of an economy as being divided into some number of sectors, say n. Suppose that the level of output of each sector depends on the levels of some or all of the other sectors, and on nothing else. Then the formulas relating the output of each sector to the outputs of the other sectors will form a set of n equations in n variables. If, further, these formulas are linear the equations can be solved by straightforward algebra. The result will be a set of sector outputs which are mutually compatible in the sense that each sector produces the quantity called for by the functional relationships assumed at the outset. What we have just sketched is simply a mathematical formalism; Leontief's task was to develop a set of economic concepts which would lead to this kind of mathematical structure and would invest it with meaning. This is just what input-output achieves. An input-output table or matrix is a set of linear formulas connecting the levels of activity in the various segments of an economy. Input-output analysis is the economic justification and interpretation of these formulas and their consequences.

We have already noted that the erection of a well-articulated theory was not Leontief's objective but, rather, only a starting point. Other investigators, for example Walras, might be satisfied with a theory expressed by general functional relationships and connecting constants indicated by letters. Leontief is not satisfied until the functions have been specified and the letters replaced by reliable numerical estimates. The fundamentals of the theory were established some seventeen years ago (See Ref. 15), but the investigations of Leontief and a growing number of followers continue unabated. The major efforts in recent years have taken three main directions. First are applications of

the theory to a variety of economic problems with the objectives both of illuminating the problems and appraising the usefulness of the theory. Second are attempts to estimate the empirical data required by the theory. Third are theoretical investigations designed to overcome and explain short-comings revealed by the first two lines of study and to extend the theory's field of application.

The study and development of input-output is now proceeding vigorously. The extent of the effort can be suggested by a simple listing of the organizations which have undertaken major projects: the Bureau of the Budget, the Bureau of Labor Statistics, the Bureau of Mines, the Department of the Air Force, the Department of Commerce, the Cowles Commission, the Harvard Economic Project, Carnegie Institute of Technology, and perhaps others.

It may be well to summarize the general impression given by the revised *Structure* volume and the *Studies* before going into details. It appears that, after seventeen years, the going is still very rough. That same ingenious and severe simplification which made input-output possible contained the seeds of serious difficulties. Economic relationships are not simple and have stubbornly refused to conform to the model. The reams of careful empirical work have revealed the extent of the approximateness of the model, and attempts to refine the model lead to discouraging complexity. These are the facts; Leontief himself is in the forefront of those bringing them out. Whether, in view of these facts, input-output is a brave failure is a question that we must consider carefully.

The basic model

A number of excellent concise summaries of Leontief's basic framework have already been published.[2] To restate it very briefly, the model depends on the technological interrelationships of the productive sectors of the economy, these connections being regarded as the most stable and reliable structural characteristics of the economy. The economy is divided into a number of sectors on the basis of the nature of the product produced. In different versions the number of sectors has varied from about a dozen

[2] See Ref. 16, pp. 139–46 and Ref. 5, pp. 99–102.

THE NATURE AND SIGNIFICANCE OF INPUT-OUTPUT

to about four hundred. Whatever the number of sectors, each sector is considered to buy its inputs from other sectors and to sell its output to other sectors and, perhaps, to an "autonomous sector" which has no output. The autonomous sector, if there is one, represents final demand and is unexplained within the model.

The model depends on two kinds of relationship: First, the bookkeeping identity that the aggregate sales of any sector must equal the total purchases from the sector by the other sectors, including the autonomous one. Second, the technological relationship that the purchases of any sector (except the autonomous one) from any other sector depend, via a production function, on the level of output of the purchasing sector.

Combining these two relationships we find that the sales of each sector equal autonomous consumption of its output plus a sum each term of which depends only on the output (or sales) of some other sector. For example, the total sales of the coal-mining sector is the sum of its sales to the automobile-producing sector, to the iron and steel products sector, . . . , and finally to final consumption. Now the coal consumption of the automobile industry depends on the number of automobiles produced, and similarly for all other sectors. Thus total production (or sales) of coal equals a sum one term of which depends on automobile production, one term on steel production, . . . , plus, finally, autonomous demand for coal. The upshot of this analysis is a system of equations connecting the outputs of all the sectors and the autonomous demand for the products of each sector. Furthermore there is one equation for each sector. Then, the number of equations is just equal to the number of sector output levels, or sales levels, and, if the autonomous demands be regarded as given, this system of equations may determine the level of output of each sector.

This is the heart of the argument, and, before pushing on, let us consider the significance of the assumptions and conclusions thus far. The bookkeeping relationship is unobjectionable, but it should be kept in mind that the bookkeeping balance relates to sales and purchases and not directly to quantities of production and productive consumption. The difference between the sales of any sector and its output is the change in its inventories of finished goods, and the difference between the purchases of any sector and its productive consumption is the change in its inventories of raw materials. Sales can be identified with output and purchases with input only if inventories do not change. We have come to the first of several reasons for emphasizing that the equations connecting industry outputs are not purely technological and are valid only in static equilibrium.

Several objections can be and have been raised to the technological postulate of the model. First, there is the problem of time. The technological relationships express the common sense fact that the quantities of raw materials used by an industry depend on its level of activity. Since the raw materials are the outputs of supplying industries there is, at first glance, a direct connection between the level of activity in any industry and the levels in its supplying industries. At second glance, though, the connection is not quite so direct (even apart from the inventory problem) for, purely as a matter of technology, inputs (except for services) must be produced before they can be used. Consequently the technological relationships (except for service inputs) connect the current level of each industry with previous levels of its supply industries and subsequent levels of its customer industries. Since the usual input-output model abstracts from the time sequence of production and exchange it applies only to a stationary equilibrium, where time is of no consequence.

Second, there is an aggregation problem. This would not arise if each industry consisted of a number of identical single-product firms. But it does arise as soon as we permit an industry to include firms whose technical methods are not identical or to produce products whose technical requirements are not identical. In an industry which includes some variety of products and technical conditions we can assert that output determines inputs uniquely only if we assume that when the output of one of its products changes, the outputs of all its other products change in the same proportion (in the jargon, we assume that "product-mix" is constant) and also that all technically different segments of the industry (e.g., firms using modern techniques and those using older techniques) expand and contract in the same proportion.[3] The advantage of using a large number of sectors lies, of course, precisely here. The larger the number of sectors in a model, the less need be the diversity within the sectors and the less important is the error incurred by assuming away that diversity. Even with four hundred sectors, however, a considerable amount of variety remains within many sectors.

Third, there is a substitution problem. The model, it will be recalled, assumes that the conditions of production are such that once the level of output of each sector is given the quantity of each of its inputs is uniquely determined. Ordinary production theory, on the contrary, teaches that the amount of each input used in producing a given output will respond to changes in relative input prices. Leontief argues that such responses, that is, factor substitutions, are unimportant, at least in the short run. Samuelson and others[4] have argued that in an economy where labor is the only factor of production not produced within the system, the price structure will lead to the efficient utilization of labor and, since all productive factors will consist in either direct or embodied labor, there will be no scope for changes in relative factor prices, or, therefore, for factor substitutions. Neither of these justifications really disposes of the problem. Leontief's justification applies to time-horizons which are short enough so that the response to changes in final demand does not include changes in technique or in the supply of capital equipment. Such short-run adjustments are inherently transitory and contradict the full static equilibrium assumptions of the model. Samuelson's justification, which assumes that the supplies of all factors except labor can be increased at will, is clearly inapplicable except in the very long run and perhaps there also.

Klein also (Ref. 12) has endeavored to get factor substitutions back into the Leontief model. He assumed a production function of the Cobb-Douglas type which, therefore, permitted factor substitution. Then he showed, just as Cobb and Douglas had done before him, that if producers adopt that combination of factors which minimizes average costs the result will be that in each sector the ratio between the value of purchases from each other sector and the value of the output of the purchasing sector will be the same whatever may be the structure of relative factor prices. On this basis Klein concluded that a Leontief model need not deny the possibility of factor substitution, for the constancy of input-output coefficients is consistent with at least one form of production function which permits substitution. Unfortunately the input-output coefficients whose constancy Klein established are not the ones which appear in a Leontief model. In a Leontief model the coefficients in question are ratios of physical quantities, and Klein's demonstration that ratios of values will not change when prices do is also a demonstration that ratios of physical quantities will change.[5]

The neglect of substitution is the most striking divergence of the Leontief model from conventional economic assumptions. The issue, Leontief maintains, is basically factual, and he suggests that the importance of substitution be decided by empirical studies. We shall consider some statistical results presently, but let us note now that there are not likely to be many empirical data bearing on equilibrium conditions.

Fourth, there is an investment problem. All purchases made by a productive sector may be classified into purchases for purposes of current production and purchases for purposes of investment, that is, increase and replacement of capital plant and equipment. It may be difficult to apply this classification in practice (advertising and maintenance expenditures present problems), but we can consider it in principle. The assumption of a unique relationship between the output of an industry and its purchases from other industries is plausible only with respect to purchases on current account. There are several ways for dealing with capital expenditures. In the first place there is no net

---

[3] These assumptions could be weakened by assuming that the proportions were determinate rather than all the same. But the stricter assumption seems as plausible as the weaker and paves the way for later developments.

[4] See Samuelson, Ref. 19, Georgescu-Roegen, Ref. 6, and Chipman, Ref. 3.

[5] The conclusion which Klein came to in his paper was somewhat different from the conclusion imputed to him above, but the bearing on the question of factor substitutions is the same.

investment and therefore no problem in stationary equilibrium, the state in which the model applies best from other points of view, also.[6] Second, capital expenditures may be separated out from other transactions and treated as part of final demand. To the extent that this expedient is used, of course, the model loses explanatory value. On the other hand this expedient is a recognition of the fact that the model is best adapted to describing the level of current production induced by a given level of final demand, an important problem even though not all inclusive. Third, induced capital expenditures may be considered separately as a component of induced activity. This is the approach used in Leontief's dynamic model, discussed below. Finally, and most crudely, the assumption can be made that net investment in any industry is uniquely related to the level of output of that industry. In any event, investment presents a complication which is not handled very conveniently within the basic framework.

Fifth, there is a limitation inherent in the very notion of a production function. Technologically grounded production functions apply very well to a large part of the economy including manufacturing, mining, and utilities. But there are other areas, such as agriculture (with its large stochastic element), trade, foreign trade, government, finance, and services where the concept is not so compelling. Yet these sectors, too, must be included in the model in order to account for the full output of the sectors with stable production functions. This difficulty can be appreciated best by considering an example taken from the 1939 Inter-Industry Transactions Table (Ref. 16, p. 167). According to this table the construction industry made purchases valued at $636 million from the trade sector in the course of producing an output valued at $10,089 million. This $636 million is not the value of the materials purchased by the construction sector in that year, but only the aggregate of the trade margins on those materials. Can trade margins be regarded as stable technological inputs? An affirmative answer seems to imply an argument along the

lines of full-cost pricing, which, whether or not acceptable, is not a technological argument.

These considerations add up to the conclusion that the Leontief model does not follow directly from such simple and necessary productive relationships as the argument for it implies. (Cf. Leontief, Ref. 16, pp. 143–45.) They indicate that it is not easy to determine the parameters of the model or to verify its adequacy simply by gathering statistical data on intersector transactions. They limit the model to a specification of equilibrium conditions, which qualifies its significance as a predictive tool and compounds the difficulties of empirical verification. And they indicate the necessity for complicating refinements which endanger the practical manageability of the model.

Production assumptions

Our description of the model thus far stands as follows. The essential variables are the outputs of the sectors into which the economy is divided. The output of any sector is determined by finding the amount of its product which each other sector consumes, and adding. The amount of each product which each sector (except the autonomous one, if there is one) consumes depends only on the output of the consuming sector. The economy is in equilibrium when the output of each sector equals the total of purchases from that sector, this total being determined by the outputs of the other sectors. It should be noted that in this model considerations of profit maximization, consumer utility maximization, optimal utilization of resources, and motivation occur in the background if at all. The foreground is occupied entirely by the dictates of productive necessity: each output requires its inputs and that is all there is to it.

In order to implement the model practically it is necessary to specify the production functions involved. This Leontief has done by following the assumption of invariance of technique to its logical conclusion, arriving at the function which Walras originally used. According to this assumption, the quantity of each input consumed by a sector is directly proportional to the quantity of output produced by that sector. The factors of proportionality are Walras' "productive coefficients" and Leontief's "input coefficients."

[6] Even in stationary equilibrium there would be replacement purchases of durable producers' goods, and these would not necessarily be proportional to output. This complication can be allowed for fairly easily, however.

No one recognizes better than Leontief that constant factors of proportionality are only a crude approximation to actual productive relationships. Where new equipment is involved geometry herself rebels against the assumption. The capacity of a pipe, for example, increases rather faster than the square of the diameter, but the amount of material required increases only about in proportion to the diameter. Hence, piping in large plants requires a smaller weight of material per unit of output than piping in small ones. Similar dimensional laws apply to warehouses, ships, boilers, electric wires, and almost every other kind of equipment. When old equipment is involved, maintenance and many other direct expenses do not increase in proportion to output. Warehouses and toll roads are extreme examples of the preponderance of inputs which do not respond to output, but the case is similar with railroads and public utilities generally and with much manufacturing.

The most searching critique of the assumption of input coefficients which are the same over a wide range of outputs comes from Leontief's Harvard Economic Research Project and is reported in *Studies in the Structure* (Ref. 17) in chapters by Chenery, Holzman, Grosse, and Ferguson. In these chapters engineering data were used to study the technical production relationships in natural gas transmission (H. B. Chenery), metal machining (M. Holzman), cotton textile manufacture (A. P. Grosse), and air transport (A. R. Ferguson). Only in the case of cotton textile manufacture was proportionality found to exist between inputs and outputs, and there only by assuming an unchanging product-mix and neglecting maintenance and other indirect inputs.

A theoretical defense of the assumption is, of course, conceivable. It would run along the lines of abstract economic theory and allege that an industry in equilibrium is composed of a number of identical economic units, each of optimum size, and that expansion and contraction of output are attained by changing the number of economic units. Leontief declines to retreat to this level of idealization which, in any event, runs counter to his concept of aggregating firms into broad economic classes. His defense is frankly that only this simple assumption will lead to a manageable theory of general equilibrium. Leontief writes, ". . . the question is not whether these ratios are constant or not — they certainly cannot be expected to be constant in the strict sense of the word. The real questions are: How does the actual range of their variations affect the empirical validity of the analytical computations based on the assumption of fixed coefficients . . .?" (Ref. 16, p. 214).

In practical applications the Leontief system has been freed partially from the assumption of constant input coefficients by using a simple device. To illustrate this device, assume that some industry requires 1 unit of labor per unit of product up to an output of 50 units and that thereafter $1\frac{1}{2}$ units of labor are required per unit of product. Then if we are sure that at least 50 units of product will be required when the equilibrium levels of output are calculated, we can write the equation:

Labor units required by this industry
$$= 50 + 1\frac{1}{2} \times (\text{Output} - 50)$$
$$= -25 + 1\frac{1}{2} \times \text{Output}.$$

That is, we can arrive at the correct result by using the higher, or marginal, input ratio as if it were a constant coefficient and balancing the resulting overstatement by deducting 25 units from the final demand for labor. Rising marginal inputs can thus be incorporated in the model, perhaps to a considerable extent, as Evans and Hoffenberg (Ref. 5, p. 100) have pointed out.

It is possible that future Leontief models will make extensive use of this and similar devices. The studies of engineering production functions, which permit the calculation of marginal input requirements at different levels of output (Ref. 17, chs. 8–11), look in this direction. At the same time those studies indicate that there are serious difficulties involved in developing engineering production functions for broad industrial sectors rather than for well-specified products, and the statistical problems of compiling such functions for all the sectors in the economy are impressive. The assumption of constant input coefficients is therefore of practical importance, even though not theoretically mandatory, and we shall consider it below in the light of empirical testing.

Models: closed, open, and ajar

We have alluded from time to time to the autonomous sector which is present in some versions of the model and absent in others. This sector is of key importance in the interpretation of a Leontief model. The mathematics is always essentially the same, but the economic interpretation changes in response to the treatment of the autonomous sector and final demand.

In the original version, presented in the first edition of *Structure of American Economy* (Ref. 16), there was no autonomous sector. Consumers were regarded as a "household industry" which consumed the outputs of the other sectors in direct proportion to its output, which consisted chiefly of labor services. The government and foreign trade were treated similarly. Thus there was no final demand. All consumption was consumption for further production and was explained within the model in the course of determining the levels of output of the household, government, and other sectors which form part of a mutually consistent pattern of sector output levels. This kind of model, since it attempts to account for all consumption, is called "closed." It is the most ambitious version, since it attempts to explain more than any other, but also it requires the most unpalatable assumptions and is the most restrictive since it provides no room for autonomous investment, exogenous changes in government demand, or the like. For these reasons the general tendency has been away from closed models toward "open" models which include a final demand for products of the various sectors which is unexplained within the model. In order to account for this final demand in the input-output framework an autonomous sector is introduced which consumes but does not produce. There is clearly a wide choice regarding which sources of demand are to be included in the autonomous sector and which are to be explained within the model. The choice depends particularly on the disposition to be made of government demand, household consumption, net exports, and investment.

The most important models for governmental purposes are those in which the autonomous sector comprises final consumption by households, government demand, and net exports. Household consumption cannot be determined within a Leontief model unless the dubious concept of a household production function is invoked. On the other hand, since household consumption does not depend on the details of the outputs of the various sectors, it is frequently placed in the autonomous sector and estimated independently from a general estimate of the level of national income, via some sort of consumption function. Net exports also can best be estimated independently of the internal model by taking account, nowadays, of the government's foreign aid program. Finally, government demand, both civil and military, is almost entirely unrelated to the levels of activity in the private productive sectors. After autonomous demand has been determined by adding these three components, the Leontief equations can be used to estimate private sector outputs consistent with that demand.

No mention has been made thus far of investment in either plant and equipment or inventories, and we have already seen that such investment cannot be derived from the basic Leontief equations. If we regard the model as describing the equilibrium levels of the various sectors in response to a continuing given level of final demand there would be no need for accumulation of inventories or changes in the stock of capital equipment. The open model, then, does not yield the levels of economic activity consequent upon any government program or assumptions about final demand but, rather, only equilibrium levels in the sense that each sector produces just enough to meet its demands without either drawing down or adding to inventories or capital equipment. In order to have a more complete explanation of the levels of economic activity, investment would have to be allowed for. This may be done by estimating investment independently and including it in the autonomous sector, by the crude assumption that investment is proportional to output, or by making the model dynamic. We shall discuss this last alternative later.

Placing household consumption in the autonomous category is, of course, a serious limitation, all the more so since the modern theory of the consumption function is tending to explain consumption endogenously in terms of the level of economic activity. Leontief early abandoned his first crude approximation in which the consumption of each final product was regarded as proportional to the level of employment. But he has not abandoned the hope of reintroducing the level of consumption as one of the variables explained within the system, using a more realistic consumption function.

Ordinary consumption functions, with household expenditure as a dependent variable and disposable income and the like as independent variables, do not quite fill the needs of Leontief models, because what is required is a formula for predicting the consumption of major categories of goods item by item rather than total consumption expenditure. But individual item consumption predictors should involve prices along with measures of over-all income and activity, and the treatment of prices is one of the weak points of the input-output model. Besides, even with respect to aggregate consumption, attempts at prediction have not been notably successful to date.

Duesenberry and Kistin have been studying this range of problems (Ref. 17, ch. 12). Their standpoint is that economic variables like income and prices influence consumption of various goods within a framework set by quasi-economic variables like established consumption habits and the distribution of population among socio-economic strata. Thus the effects of economic variables have to be studied under circumstances where changes in quasi-economic variables can be avoided or allowed for. This leads Duesenberry and Kistin to use area budget studies, which show the consumption patterns of individual socio-economic groups, in preference to nationwide time-series data. Their method for making over-all consumption estimates, however, does not allow for the effects of changes in the sizes of socio-economic strata, with the consequence that their estimates are no more successful than the results of cruder and more convenient methods of calculation. Their procedure, though, has the very considerable virtue of identifying some of the hitherto anonymous "autonomous variables" which influence consumption, and of paving the way for incorporating those variables in economic analysis. Nevertheless, we are still a long way from being able to estimate consumption with tolerable accuracy within the framework of an input-output model.

The upshot seems to be that the open models omit the two driving forces of economic activity: consumption and investment. What open models amount to then is a device for calculating the level and pattern of gross economic activity (gross in the sense that intermediate goods are counted along with final ones whenever they pass from one sector to another) consistent with any specification of net final output. In normal circumstances this may be a very limited objective for such a formidable apparatus. But in time of war or economic mobilization, when consumption and investment cease being the prime movers of economic activity, this objective is extremely important. Much of the interest in open models stems from their application to problems of mobilization.

Dynamic models

The basic Leontief model is concerned with the conditions of a static equilibrium. We have already discussed some of the limitations thereby imposed. The model loses significance as an empirical predictor, it cannot be used to trace the time-paths of readjustment to changed conditions, time-lags in technological relationships have to be neglected, investment cannot be explained within the model. At least three dynamic extensions of the basic model have been proposed to overcome these limitations.

Hawkins (Ref. 9) and Leontief (Ref. 17, ch. 3) have developed models based on a generalization of the accelerator principle. The essential idea is that net investment in any sector is proportional to the rate of change of output of that sector. Leontief's accelerator model is, moreover, irreversible, that is, it assumes that the factor of proportionality takes different values according to whether or not there is excess capacity in the sector. The formal mathematics of this model is a natural extension of the basic scheme, the major difference being that total demand for the product of each sector is now the sum of three terms: (1) the quantity used as inputs by other sectors, which is proportional to the outputs of those sectors; (2) the quantity required for net investment, which is proportional to the rate of change of output of other sectors; and (3) the quantity required for final demand exclusive of net investment. Unfortunately, the irreversibility feature, which seems logically unavoidable in an accelerator model, leads to mathematical complications, because use of the excess-capacity proportionality factor for a sector may imply a level of output inconsistent with excess capacity while the use of the full-capacity-utilization factor for the same sector implies a level of output inconsistent with full-capacity utilization. This paradox requires further research but need not detain us.

Aside from this ambiguity, the theory of the acceleration Leontief model is neat, and extensive work has been undertaken by the Harvard Economic Research Project to implement it. Two reports on this work are contained in *Studies in the Structure of the American Economy*, chapter 6, by R. N. Grosse, on the estimation of capital input coefficients, and chapter 7, by P. G. Clark, on a test of the acceleration theory of investment in the telephone industry.

The estimation of capital input coefficients, that is, the number of units of output of each sector required per unit of new capacity of each sector, presents difficulties over and above those encountered in estimating the ordinary input coefficients. For one thing, the statistical data are less adequate. For another, statistical averaging is less appropriate, since the characteristics of new equipment are not, in general, reflected in the older installed equipment accessible to statistical compilation. Thirdly, the assumption that the value of new investment is directly proportional to the volume of output it will support is particularly questionable. With respect to the inventory investment, Whitin [7] has shown that the optimal level of inventories increases significantly less than in proportion to the level of output. With respect to plant and equipment the usual theories of long-run economies of scale and the scale-laws of geometry and physics to which we have already alluded indicate that capacity is likely to increase faster than the physical volume of equipment inputs.

Leontief, A. P. Grosse, and collaborators are well aware of all these *a priori* difficulties, and others as well, but are not deterred by them.

Their policy is to produce estimates on the most practicable assumptions they can find and then submit the results to empirical test. When, however, the same coefficient was computed by two different plausible methods the results were frequently at variance. It is impossible to say as yet whether the discrepancies are due to the theoretical problems mentioned or to the inadequacy of statistical records. Whatever may be the cause of the difficulties, this type of dynamic model must be regarded as still in the process of construction.

The underlying assumption of the accelerator model is, of course, the acceleration principle. A case study of the reasonableness of this assumption was made by P. G. Clark (Ref. 17, ch. 7), who investigated the determinants of investment in the telephone industry. Clark's work, along with that of Chenery, A. P. Grosse, and Duesenberry,[8] seems to be moving toward a new theory of investment which may turn out to be one of the major contributions of the Harvard Economic Research Project. In Clark's hands the acceleration theory is modified almost beyond recognition into a "capital-requirements theory" composed of three hypotheses: "(1) The firm's demand estimates depend via a fixed expectations coefficient upon the recent trend of its output. (2) The firm's net investment depends via a fixed capital coefficient and a fixed spare-capacity coefficient upon these demand estimates. (3) The firm's retirement [plan] depends via a fixed retirement coefficient upon its present stock of capital equipment." (Ref. 17, p. 249.) Clark has tested each of these hypotheses against data taken from the telephone industry but, I think, tended to be overgenerous in finding conformity between theory and fact. For example, the first hypothesis implies that a firm would expect its demand to grow exponentially, but data given on page 270 indicate that the telephone company expected the volume of messages to grow linearly or a little less. The "confirmations" found for the other hypotheses consist in success in finding *ad hoc* explanations for discrepancies between hypothesis and

---

[7] See T. M. Whitin, *The Theory of Inventory Management* (Princeton, 1953), p. 147 ff.

[8] See Hollis B. Chenery, "Overcapacity and the Acceleration Principle," *Econometrica*, xx (January 1952), 1–28; A. P. Grosse, "Innovation and Diffusion" (mimeographed); A. P. Grosse and J. S. Duesenberry, "Technological Change and Dynamic Models" (mimeographed).

fact rather than in finding gratifying degrees of conformity. Nonetheless, this is not a crucial test of the capital-requirements theory of investment and the theory itself is both plausible and empirically usable. If it works out it will free economic models from the mechanistic confines of the acceleration principle.

A second type of model is based on an extension of the multiplier principle. Such models have been developed by Solow (Ref. 20) and, as by-products to other work, by Goodwin (Ref. 9) and Chipman (Ref. 2). The underlying idea is that of lead-times; the output of a sector in any period is related to the output of other sectors in previous periods. Various justifications of such relationships are possible. Goodwin and Chipman use expenditure considerations; increases in the output of any sectors generate income flows which show up as increases in the demand for other sectors in later periods. Solow relies on an equilibrium argument: because most commodities must be outputs before they are inputs, supplies will not equal demands unless the various sectors expand and contract in an equilibrium sequence. This point of view, also, is appropriate to mobilization planning. It does not, of course, explain investment but, in compensation, it does not require capital coefficients. Theoretical equilibrium conditions have been derived from these models (see esp. Ref. 9), but little or no empirical work has been done and so they stand aside from the main stream of input-output analysis, which is, above all, empirical.

The third major type of dynamic model rests on the two assumptions that installed capacity must at all times be at least equal to productive requirements and that no capacity should be installed before its product is required (i.e., neither capacity nor product should be stored against future requirements). This type of model was worked out by an Air Force group headed by J. Holley (Ref. 11) and is the only type whose full operation has been tested. The test consisted in applying flow and capital input coefficients derived for the year 1944 to final consumption data for the years of rapid expansion, 1940–44, and comparing the levels of sector outputs and capital formation resulting from the model with *post hoc* estimates. The only reason for being interested in this

model is that it has been tested, because the economic assumption that capacity should be adequate to meet peak loads without drawing on inventories cannot be defended either as a descriptive or as a normative postulate. One would hope that an economic model based on this assumption would lead to substantial overestimates of capital formation and of total output, and that is just what occurred. To this extent the model "makes sense." Its positive contributions are two: (1) it is an ultra-conversative procedure for testing whether a proposed program of outputs can be produced, (2) it established by actual example that a fairly elaborate dynamic model can be worked out numerically.

The present status of dynamic models is one of work still in process. The work bids fair to advance our understanding of the determinants of investment and to produce techniques which will contribute to the planning of economic mobilization. It may lead to formulations useful for more general normative or descriptive economic analyses. As to that, it is a little too early to say.

Empirical validation

As Leontief sees it, the crucial test of his system, constant input coefficients and all, is the accuracy of the predictions it yields. In this spirit he has applied three separate tests to his static model. First, he has used technical data based on the 1939 Census of Manufactures to calculate a set of sector levels corresponding to the final demand existing in 1929, and compared those levels with the ones actually experienced (Ref. 16, pp. 152-58). Second, he has used 1939 technical data to estimate sector outputs corresponding to the final demand patterns of 1919 and 1929 and compared the errors resulting from this method of estimation with the errors found in two simple regression procedures (Ref. 16, pp. 216-18). Third, and most elaborate, he has made a study of the pattern of variation in input coefficients over the two decades 1919–39 and made a number of calculations of the effects of the observed changes on the output levels corresponding to observed levels of final demand (Ref. 17, ch. 2).

The results of these tests are inconclusive at best. The data available for the testing are known to be subject to appreciable statistical error. The tests are all based on a model in which the economy was divided into about a dozen sectors, involving therefore a violent amount of aggregation. And, in a sense, they are tangential to the main point since they test secular stability over fairly long periods rather than constancy in respect to changes in the scale of output. Because of these considerations, the results of the tests cannot be given decisive weight, and this is just as well because the results are not very encouraging. In the first test, four out of the nine sectors tested showed errors greater than 10 per cent. The third test had many aspects. The most significant findings were that over the two decades studied the input coefficients fell at an average rate of about 1 per cent per annum (with considerable dispersion, of course), the labor input coefficients fell at better than 3 per cent per annum during 1919–29 and at about 1½ per cent per annum during 1929–39, and, as a result, if the manpower requirements of the 1939 final demand had been estimated by using 1929 technical data an error of about 23 per cent would have been made. Leontief's second test hardly shows more than that two estimating methods can be found which are inferior to input-output, but another investigator has proposed another method which in one test proved superior to input-output.[9]

In sum, the direct statistical testing performed thus far leaves the crucial issue in doubt. There is still another way, though, to test the model. After all, the model is not designed primarily to assist in predictions over a period of a decade or so. Its purpose is to permit the estimation of the impact on an economy of various changes in surrounding circumstances. How successful has the model been in performing this task?

Leontief has given his system a number of trial applications. The most interesting are:

1. Calculation of multipliers which show the effects on the sales of the various sectors and on total employment of a million dollar change in the final demand for products of the various sectors (Ref. 16, pp. 139–62);

2. Estimation of the effects on industrial levels and on employment of changes in the level of exports (Ref. 16, pp. 163–86);

3. Estimation of effects on the price structure of changes in wage and profit rates (Ref. 16, pp. 188–202);

4. Calculation of effects on economic activity in separate geographic regions of changes in the level and pattern of national demand (Ref. 17, ch. 5).

The fruitfulness of each of these applications depends on the appropriateness of the assumptions of the basic model to the problem in hand and on the plausibility of the additional assumptions required by the specific problem. The first application flows directly from the basic model without requiring additional assumptions. The most serious restriction on the meaning of the results is the fact that they refer to a static equilibrium. The Leontief model tells how much the equilibrium levels of sector outputs and employment will shift in response to exogenous changes in final demand, and only in this restricted sense does it predict the effects of changes in demand. The second application runs afoul of a difficulty we have noted previously, the ubiquitous application of technical input coefficients. Exports are treated as an industrial sector which purchases from the other sectors in technically fixed proportions and the calculations rest on this convention (it can hardly even be called an assumption). The third application depends on the accounting identity that the total value of output of any sector equals the value of purchases from other sectors plus value added. This plus a little algebra permits the calculation of the effect on the price structure of a change in wage rates in any sector if two additional assumptions be made: (1) that profits, depreciation charges, and taxes per unit of output do not change; and (2) that the change in the price structure does not induce substitutions. These assumptions imply that increases in cost are passed along in full. It seems difficult to grant the additional assumptions. The reverberations which are assumed away are, to be sure, secondary effects, but the whole input-output method depends on the calculation of

[9] H. J. Barnett, "Specific Industry Output Projections," a paper prepared for the Rand Corporation, 1951. Barnett's test involves a number of statistical complications which prevent it from being conclusive either.

indirect demand which is also a secondary effect, and who is to say that the secondary effects which are neglected by assumption are not more important than those which are included by calculation? Students of taxation have long ago reached a degree of sophistication about the shifting, incidence, and absorption of cost changes which should not be forgotten when applying the methods of interindustry analysis.

The application to problems of regional economics also requires difficult special assumptions. In effect it requires us to regard each industry in each economic region as a separate economic sector and to regard as constant not only the technological linkages among industries but also the regional distribution of purchases and sales of each industry.

This review of applications of the model is necessarily cursory. It indicates, though, that assumptions and complexities accumulate as soon as the model is pushed beyond the most straightforward technological applications.

Conclusion

It is not surprising that in this appraisal we have found more deficiencies than triumphs. Economic life is just not simple enough to be comprehended within a system of linear equations, and when we impose this format on it we must be content with a pretty liberal degree of approximation. We must be content also to note that the approximate model may be accurate enough for some purposes and still be inapplicable where the changes to be studied are no larger than the errors inherent in the model.

The situation in which these limitations are not crippling or even serious is clear. This is the case of economic mobilization, where large programs are envisaged, technical requirements are the predominant consideration, and consumption and investment are not allowed to interfere with the plan. Leontief's model comprehends the important relationships involved in such a problem, and the errors in the model can be tolerated. The model works better as an instrument of planning than as a tool for analyzing the operation of a free economy.

In using an input-output model for mobilization planning the major components of final demand — household consumption, government requirements, and net exports — are all regarded as part of the plan and therefore subject to government control. It is true that the government can place an upper limit on these components of demand and, in the circumstances envisaged, it is reasonable to assume that actual final demand will achieve this upper limit. Thus the most difficult problems of economic forecasting are tractable to a mobilization planner.

The input-output model then determines the level of activity of each sector and the total requirement for each original factor as implied by the assumed levels of final demand, on the assumption that the observed input-output ratios will be maintained. If the required quantities of original factors do not exceed the quantities available, the plan can be carried out and this, after all, is the primary question involved in such work. On the other hand, if the factor requirements of the plan exceed the available supplies then either the plan is infeasible or the input-output ratios must be altered by the use of *ersatz* materials or other expedients. In either event the use of the model will lead to a set of final demands and activity levels which are internally consistent though not necessarily optimal.

In focusing our attention on the objectives of input-output and the extent to which they have been achieved we have done scant justice to one of its most valuable products, the vast amount of organized empirical knowledge concerning the interrelations of industrial sectors which has been obtained. A storehouse of data now exists telling us where the products of various industries go and where their raw materials come from. We are beginning to learn more about the capital requirements of production and even about that well-tilled field, empirical production functions, than was ever before available. In short, input-output analysis provides a much-needed framework for gathering and understanding data about our industrial economy. Much of this information is contained in *Studies in the Structure of the American Economy* (Ref. 17), much more will be forthcoming as the work progresses.

It appears now that input-output is not likely to supplant traditional methods for studying industrial or price problems, or even to replace the Walrasian conceptual framework for thinking in terms of general equilibrium. Even so, we are not yet in a position to say what input-output analysis cannot do. The shift from the original closed models to the open models now in use increases the applicability of the technique many fold, though at the cost of theoretical completeness and explanatory content. The study of dynamic and regional models is only beginning at present; they may be susceptible of similar improvement. The Leontief group, and especially Duesenberry and Kistin, are laboring to close the model again in a more sophisticated manner.[10] Not a small part of Leontief's achievement was to open up a vast and hopeful field for exploration, and the work is not yet far advanced.

Whatever is to come of all this work, the improved models will rest on Leontief's original insight. Even in its present unperfected form interindustry analysis is a promising approach to analysis of our complicated industrial structure, and the most feasible technique yet developed for over-all industrial planning.

[10] See Reference 17, ch. 12.

APPENDIX
Selected References on Input-Output

1. Kenneth J. Arrow, "Alternative Proof of the Substitution Theorem for Leontief Models in the General Case," in Reference 13, 155–64.
2. John S. Chipman, "The Multi-Sector Multiplier," *Econometrica*, XVIII (October 1950), 355–74.
3. ———, "Linear Programming," this REVIEW, XXXV (May 1953), 101–17.
4. J. Cornfield, W. D. Evans, and M. Hoffenberg, "Full Employment Patterns, 1950," *Monthly Labor Review*, LXIV (February and March 1947), 163–90 and 420–32.
5. W. D. Evans and M. Hoffenberg, "The Interindustry Relations Study for 1947," this REVIEW, XXXIV (May 1952), 97–142.
6. Nicholas Georgescu-Roegen, "Leontief's System in the Light of Recent Results," this REVIEW, XXXII (August 1950), 214–22.
7. ———, "Some Properties of a Generalized Leontief Model," in Reference 13, 165–73.
8. R. M. Goodwin, "The Multiplier as Matrix," *Economic Journal*, LIX (December 1949), 537–55.
9. David Hawkins, "Some Conditions of Macroeconomic Stability," *Econometrica*, XVI (October 1948), 309–22.
10. David Hawkins and H. Simon, "Some Conditions of Macroeconomic Stability," *Econometrica*, XVII (July–October 1949), 245–48.
11. Julian L. Holley, "A Dynamic Model," Part I, *Econometrica*, XX (October 1942), 616–42; Part II, *Econometrica*, XXI (April 1953), 298–324.
12. L. R. Klein, "On the Interpretation of Professor Leontief's System," *Review of Economic Studies*, XX (No. 2, 1952–53), 131–36.
13. T. C. Koopmans, ed., *Activity Analysis of Production and Allocation* (New York, 1951).
14. ———, "Alternative Proof of the Substitution Theorem for Leontief Models in the Case of Three Industries," in Reference 13, 147–54.
15. Wassily W. Leontief, "Quantitative Input and Output Relations in the Economic System of the United States," this REVIEW, XVIII (August 1936), 105–25.
16. ———, *The Structure of American Economy 1919–1939*, first edition (Cambridge, Mass., 1941); second edition, enlarged (New York, 1951).
17. ——— and collaborators, *Studies in the Structure of the American Economy* (New York, 1953).
18. J. von Neumann, "A Model of General Economic Equilibrium," *Review of Economic Studies*, XIII (No. 1, 1945–46), 1–9.
19. P. A. Samuelson, "Abstract of a Theorem Concerning Substitutability in Open Leontief Models," in Reference 13, 142–46.
20. Robert Solow, "On the Structure of Linear Models," *Econometrica*, XX (January 1952), 29–46.
21. Abraham Wald, "On Some Systems of Equations of Mathematical Economics," *Econometrica*, XIX (October 1951), 368–403.
22. Leon Walras, *Éléments d'économie politique pure ou théorie de la richesse sociale*, second edition (Lausanne, 1889).

[5]

OPERATIONS RESEARCH

By ROBERT DORFMAN*

Once upon a time, within the memories of men who think they are still young, there was no such thing as operations research, or at least no such phrase. Today the Operations Research Society of America has more than 2,300 members, the Institute of Management Science has more than 2,600 members (there is considerable overlap, of course) and at a recent international conference on operations research no less than sixteen countries from four continents were represented. It is a flourishing movement.

The proper way to begin an inquiry into this movement would be to define it. But this is difficult; for operations research is not a subject-matter field but an approach or method. And, even after a study of hundreds of examples of work classified as operations research, it is by no means clear just what the method is other than that it is scientific (like all respectable methods), because operations analysts are typically resourceful and ingenious men who tackle their problems with no holds barred. I propose, nevertheless, to advance a definition; but it will help to prepare the way for that hazardous attempt if I try to convey the flavor of operations research by sketching a pair of contrasting caricatures, one of a conventional business consultant and one of an operations analyst.

Suppose that a soap company seeks advice as to whether its advertising budget next year should be larger than, the same as, or smaller than this year. They might engage a business consultant who, in this case, would be a specialist in either advertising or marketing. He would have had substantial experience with advertising the same or similar products and would have at his finger tips a good many relevant data and, besides, would be familiar with all the standard sources of such data. In addition he would be aware of the maxim that it takes five cents worth of advertising to sell a dollar's worth of soap, though he would not necessarily take it very seriously. With this background at his disposal he would marshal the pertinent facts. He would examine the experience of his client and would correlate sales with advertising

* The author is professor of economics, Harvard University. [This is the second in a series of survey articles for which the Rockefeller Foundation has provided support. The first of the series appeared in the June 1959 issue.—*Editor.*]

expenditures for past years, doing it by eye if his research budget were stringent or by least-squares if he anticipated a fee that justified a more imposing report. He might well consider data by states or marketing areas, for both his client and competing firms, and might also analyze sales and advertising exposure broken down by city size. If the project were at all large he would almost certainly have a field survey made, finding out from a random sample of housewives what soaps they bought and what advertisements they were aware of. Finally, with this information all carefully organized, he would determine the level of advertising expenditure appropriate to the budgeted level of sales. In all likelihood this figure would turn out to be fairly close to 5 per cent of anticipated gross sales, partly because you can't go far wrong by sticking close to an established norm, and partly because nearly all his data will be in this range with the exception of a few observations relating to attempts to launch brands that, for one reason or another, did not catch on, or relating to advertising campaigns that had been successful beyond reasonable hope of duplication. In short, he would arrive at a recommendation based on a reasoned scrutiny of past experience.

But now suppose that the soap company turned to an operations analyst for advice. Typically, this man or firm would have no particular experience with either soap or advertising, and would feel the need of none. More likely than not, the analyst would be a graduate physicist or mathematician. With this background at his disposal he would formulate the problem. The first words he would say to himself might be: "Let p_{xt} be the probability that the xth household will buy my client's soap during the tth week.[1] Then p_{xt} is the product of two factors: p'_{xt}, the probability that they will buy any soap during the week, and a_{xt}, the probability that if they buy any soap it will be my client's brand. Assume that p'_{xt} cannot be influenced by my client's advertising but that a_{xt} can be. In fact, suppose that the Weber-Fechner law applies so that the rate of increase of a_{xt} with respect to advertising expenditure is inversely proportional to the level of advertising expenditure already attained, i.e.,

$$\frac{da_{xt}}{dE} = \frac{c}{E}$$

where E is the level of advertising expenditure and c is a constant of proportionality. Then, integrating this differential equation, $a_{xt} = \log kE^c$ where k is a constant of integration to be determined from the data. Then $p_{xt} = p'_{xt} \log kE^c$ and total expected sales can be estimated by integrating this expression over the entire population (i.e.,

---

[1] In this and most later examples the mathematical details are not essential to the general discussion and may be skimmed.

all values of x). Thus, assuming p'_{xt} and k to be given data, total sales can be estimated as:

$$s_t = \log kE^c \int p'_{xt}dx$$

and

$$\frac{ds_t}{dE} = \frac{c}{E} \int p'_{xt}dx.$$

Thus the optimal level of advertising can be found by finding the value of E at which the profit per dollar's worth of sales multiplied by this derivative equals 1, the cost of an additional dollar's worth of advertising."[2] In short, he would arrive at a recommendation based on logical deduction from simple first premises which are a plausible approximation to the laws underlying the phenomenon being studied.

Each of these approaches is "scientific" according to its own canons, but they are quite different. We can characterize this difference by saying that the operations analyst, in contrast with the conventional business analyst has a strong predilection for formulating his problems by means of formal mathematical models. By a model I mean a symbolic description of a phenomenon in which its observable characteristics are deduced from simple explanatory first principles (i.e., assumptions) by manipulating symbols in accordance with the laws of some formal logic (usually ordinary mathematics).

Argument *ad hominem* is generally regarded as unscholarly, but in trying to characterize operations research it seems important to note who the operations analysts are. According to a survey conducted by the American Management Association [2], more than 40 per cent of operations analysts are engineers by training, another 45 per cent are mathematicians, statisticians, or natural scientists. It is only natural that the point of view in which these men are schooled should permeate operations research. The essence of this point of view is that a phenomenon is understood when and only when it has been expressed as a formal, really mechanistic, quantitative model, and that, furthermore, all phenomena within the purview of science (which is probably all the phenomena there are) can be so expressed with sufficient persistence and ingenuity. A second characteristic of men of science, amounting to a corollary of the first, is their preference for symbolic, as opposed to verbal, modes of expression and reasoning. These characteristics I take to be the style of operations research, and I define operations research to be all research in this spirit intended to help solve practical,

---

[2] In constructing this fable I have followed the spirit of the only operations research study of advertising with which I am acquainted, but have carefully diverged from that study in all details.

immediate problems in the fields of business, governmental or military administration or the like.

There is an important corollary to the tendency of operations analysts to cast their thinking in terms of formal mathematical models. Operations research is not a descriptive science but a prescriptive one. Therefore the deduction of adequate descriptive models is only part of the task of the operations analyst. In the end he must come up with a recommendation for action and this requires that he know what the operation in question is intended to accomplish. We rather side-stepped this issue, in the fable at the beginning of this essay, by assuming that the objective of the advertising was to attain the maximum possible excess of gross sales over the sum of production costs and advertising expenditure. But the conscientious operations analyst does not so glibly assume the objective of the operation he studies; and the extensive literature devoted to studying the objectives of business enterprise shows that he is wise to be circumspect about this point. In the soap example, it may well be highly important to maintain total sales at a level that makes it worth while for retailers to stock the brand in question, even if the marginal net return is negative. The long run may have to be considered, if the brand has to establish or maintain a market position in the face of vigorous competition. In short the objectives of an operation are likely to be complicated, obscure, and composed of several incommensurable aspects. A major part of the task of the operations analyst is to construct a "measure of merit" for the operation he studies to accompany his formal description of it. The logical precision of the model enforces corresponding precision in expressing the objectives that the operation is intended to attain. The orthodox business consultant, on the other hand, is under no such pressure to formulate precisely the goals of the enterprise he studies.

When the operations analyst has formulated the model of his undertaking and the goals it serves he is still nearer the beginning of his analysis than the end. He must still particularize his model by estimating the values of the various "given" parameters that enter into it. For this purpose he employs, usually, more or less advanced statistical methods. Then he must solve the model, that is, find explicit relationships between the parameters under the control of his client, on the one hand, and the measure of merit on the other. When this has been done he is in a position to determine the optimal values of the decision parameters, to make his recommendations, and to try to persuade the management to adopt them.

In the next two sections we shall discuss a number of aspects of the problem of model formulation. Then we shall examine some of the problems and pitfalls of determining measures of merit or objective functions. The concluding section is devoted to the conditions for successful operations research and to some general conclusions and remarks.

I. *Some Standard Models*

There are three aspects to model building, closely related to each other but requiring different skills. The first is straightforward description; expressing the situation under study in terms of the symbolism adopted. This involves inventing symbols for the various components of the system and writing down the relationships connecting them. Usually the symbolism adopted is algebraic and the basic relationships take the form of equations and inequalities. Frequently, though, block diagrams are used. Then the components are represented by labeled boxes and the relationships by lines connecting the boxes. Less frequently, a logical symbolism is employed, with the elements of the problem conceived of as classes or members of classes and the relationships being those of class inclusion, overlapping, and the like. In any event, the process is one of translating the real world situation into a set of abstract and simplified symbols. The result is an essentially tautological and sterile description of the problem, for it yields almost nothing more than definitions and identities.

The second stage we can call creative hypothesizing. This is the stage at which the motivational, behavioral, and technological assumptions are introduced. It entered the soap example in two ways. First in the selection of relevant variables, as when we decided that the price of the soap, competitors' advertising expenditures, the level of national income, the season of the year, and many other conceivable variables could all be omitted. Our fictitious operations analyst made the same kind of conjectural judgment when he decided that the probability that a household's total purchases of soap of all brands was uninfluenced by his client's advertising. But the most vigorous exercise of creative hypothesizing occurred when he conjectured the form of the relationship between advertising and the conditional probability that any soap purchased would be his client's brand. The first aspect of model formulation is a craft but the second is an art and introduces the crucial assumptions of the model.

The final aspect of model formulation is quantification: the assignment of numerical values to the parameters of the model. In the soap example these parameters are c and p'_{zi}, the latter being a different number, presumably, for each class of household. This last aspect is clearly a more or less involved problem in statistical estimation.

It is clear that the operations analyst works, basically, as an applied mathematician with some statistics and numerical analysis thrown in.

His principal tools, aside from his own judgment and imagination, are algebra, the calculus, differential equations, probability theory and statistics. In addition he has some special-purpose tools of his own.

In principle, each time a problem is referred to an operations analyst he could construct a tailor-made model to fit the case, and in practice he does so a large proportion of the time. But fortunately problems of essentially similar form arise repeatedly in widely differing contexts. Consider, for example, the problems of providing facilities for checking customers out of a supermarket, accommodating aircraft arriving at an airport, servicing locomotives at a repair depot, and meeting the needs of telephone subscribers. In each case the problem is to provide tolerably prompt service to a demand whose timing cannot be predicted exactly, by means of expensive facilities. This problem, in all its variants, is the problem of queuing theory. Similarly, the problem of allocating limited resources among a number of uses pervades businesses and administrative organizations of all kinds. This family of problems is the concern of programming, linear and otherwise. And in like manner, game theory, inventory theory, servo-mechanism theory all study types of problems that are likely to occur throughout a wide variety of business and administrative circumstances. The operations analyst has at his disposal a large and growing kit of such tools and is thus provided with an efficient apparatus whenever he recognizes that a particular problem fits into one of these tidy categories. Naturally these ready made models are the most communicable, teachable, and talked about aspects of the craft and tend to receive a disproportionate emphasis both in the public image of operations research and in professional instruction. They will also receive disproportionate emphasis here.

1. *The Linear Programming Model*[3]

Essentially linear programming is a mode of expressing the problem of allocating scarce resources that has the peculiar virtue of lending itself to statistical estimation and numerical solution. It applies when the activities of an enterprise are limited by a number of resources in limited supply and when these resources are to be allocated to a number of activities each of which absorbs them in proportion to its level of utilization. Each of the activities also contributes to the attainment of the objectives of the enterprise in proportion to its utilization. The problem is to discover a set of activity levels attainable within the resource limitations which leads to the maximum possible attainment of the objectives.

[3] For a more complete discussion of linear programming from an economist's point of view see Baumol [6] or Dorfman [14].

One of the most frequent and successful practical applications of linear programming is to the scheduling of oil refinery operations.[4] We can convey the flavor of the method by laying out a highly simplified example of this application. Suppose a refinery has 1000 units of blending capacity which it uses to produce regular and premium motor fuel (to be denoted by subscripts 3 and 4 respectively) from two grades of blending stocks (to be indicated by subscripts 1 and 2). Introduce four decision variables x_{13}, x_{14}, x_{23}, x_{24} where x_{ij} denotes the number of barrels of blending stock i devoted to the production of motor fuel j. Now consider the consequences of decisions regarding these four variables. The total input of blending stock 1 is $x_{13} + x_{14}$ and that of blending stock 2 is $x_{23} + x_{24}$. If the two stocks cost \$1.26 and \$1.68 per barrel respectively, the total cost of fuel inputs is:

$$1.26(x_{13} + x_{14}) + 1.68(x_{23} + x_{24}).$$

The total output of regular-grade gasoline is $x_{13} + x_{23}$, that of premium-grade is $x_{14} + x_{24}$. If the regular grade is worth \$4.20 per barrel at the refinery and premium grade is worth \$5.04 per barrel, the value of product is:

$$4.20(x_{13} + x_{23}) + 5.04(x_{14} + x_{24}).$$

By subtraction we find the excess of the value of outputs over the value of inputs to be:

$$2.94x_{13} + 3.78x_{14} + 2.52x_{23} + 3.36x_{24}.$$

We suppose that the objective of the plan is to make this number as large as possible.

Now turn to restrictions on choice. Suppose that the only quality specification to be considered is octane rating. The octane rating of any blend is a weighted average of the ratings of its components. Thus suppose that the octane rating of blending stock 1 is 75 and that of blending stock 2 is 93. Since regular-grade motor fuel is a blend of x_{13} barrels of stock 1 with x_{23} barrels of stock 2, its octane rating is:

$$\frac{75x_{13} + 93x_{23}}{x_{13} + x_{23}}.$$

Similarly the octane rating of the premium fuel is:

$$\frac{75x_{14} + 93x_{24}}{x_{14} + x_{24}}.$$

Now suppose that regular fuel must have an octane rating of at least 82 and premium fuel a rating of at least 88. Then we have the constraints on the decision variables:

---

[4] See Charnes, Cooper, and Mellon [12] and Manne [28] for more realistic examples.

$$\frac{75x_{13} + 93x_{23}}{x_{13} + x_{23}} \geq 82,$$

$$\frac{75x_{14} + 93x_{24}}{x_{14} + x_{24}} \geq 88,$$

which are equivalent to:

$$-7x_{13} + 11x_{23} \geq 0,$$

$$-13x_{14} + 5x_{24} \geq 0$$

respectively.

Finally suppose that each barrel of regular fuel produced requires 1 unit of blending capacity, and each barrel of premium fuel requires 1.2 units. Then, since 1000 units are available in all, we have the capacity constraint:

$$(x_{13} + x_{23}) + 1.2(x_{14} + x_{24}) \leq 1,000$$

Gathering all these formulas we have the purely formal problem: Find $x_{13}, x_{23}, x_{14}, x_{24}$ so as to make:

$$2.94x_{13} + 3.78x_{14} + 2.52x_{23} + 3.36x_{24}$$

as large as possible, subject to the restrictions:

$$7x_{13} - 11x_{23} \leq 0$$

$$13x_{14} - 5x_{24} \leq 0$$

$$(x_{13} + x_{23}) + 1.2(x_{14} + x_{24}) \leq 1,000.$$

The rest is arithmetic calculation.

Besides being of substantial practical importance, this example has a number of pedagogical virtues. In the first place it illustrates the flexibility of linear programming. Note that the numbers we had to choose, $x_{13}, x_{14}, x_{23}, x_{24}$ were "activities" in only a very strained sense. In this context, what we would ordinarily think of as an activity would be blending one of the grades of motor fuel by a specified chemical formula (e.g., blending a barrel of regular fuel by using .6 barrels of blending stock 1 and .4 barrels of blending stock 2). Linear programming cannot take account of more than a finite and fairly small number of activities (say 200) when defined in the ordinary way, but with our particular choice of variables we have admitted to consideration an infinite number of activities, viz., all physically possible blends. The resource scarcities, also, represent resource scarcities in only a very extended sense. The "1000" is the quantity of a genuine limiting resource, but the two zeros of the right-hand side of the restricting inequalities are artifacts resulting from the manipulation of the quality specifications. This flexibility—the fact that the words "activity" and "resource limitation" do not have to be taken at all literally in setting up a linear programming problem—is largely responsible for the widespread applicability of the method. Any problem that can be expressed by means of linear equations and inequalities is amenable to linear programming, whatever the physical interpretation of the variables and relationships. Indeed there are methods for incorporating nonlinear relationships, at the cost of substantially increased difficulty in computation.

One important limitation of linear programming has always been that the variables whose values are to be determined must be continuously variable, but recently methods have been developed for solving problems where the decision variables must be integers (e.g., the number of aircraft flights per day between two points).[5] Another important limitation, on which less progress has been made, is that linear programming formulations do not allow for uncertainty.

Let us return to the blending example for another remark. A key theorem of linear programming states that there always exists an optimal solution in which the number of decision variables with positive values does not exceed the number of constraints, in this case three. Now suppose, for example, that the positive variables turn out to be x_{13}, x_{23}, x_{24}. This indicates that the premium fuel would be 100 per cent pure blending stock 2. But this cannot be optimal since the quality specification for premium fuel would be overfulfilled and money could be saved by adding in some of the cheaper blending stock. Clearly, no admissible combination of three positive values can be optimal in this problem, so there must be a solution with only two of the decision variables at positive value. This means that only one of the two products is made, i.e., the refinery produces either regular or premium fuel but not both. Which product should be made can be ascertained readily by computing which of the two yields a greater gross revenue per unit of blending capacity absorbed. Thus the arithmetic turns out to be even more trivial than it promised to be at first glance.

An even more common application of linear programming than the refinery blending problem is the so-called transportation problem, which arises whenever a standardized commodity is to be shipped from a variety of sources to a variety of destinations.[6] Newsprint companies use it to decide which of their customers should be supplied from each of their mills, oil companies use it in assigning bulk distribution plants to refineries, the National Coal Board in England uses it to allocate markets among mines, Henderson applied it to an appraisal of the economic efficiency of the coal industry in this country [20]. There has accumulated a large literature which deals with such complications as

---

[5] See Gomory and Baumol [19] and Markowitz and Manne [30].

[6] For a typical small-scale example see Vazsonyi [39, p. 26 ff].

differences in production costs at different supply points, limitations on the capacity of shipping routes, fixed charges for opening or constructing shipping routes, and a cascading of problems such as where distribution involves a chain of factory to warehouse (of limited capacity) to retail store.

All the problems in this wide family are surprisingly easy to solve (though I wouldn't recommend that you try a large one with pencil and paper) for a number of technical reasons, among them the fact that all the restraints take the form of simple sums like: for any factory the sum of shipments to all its customers cannot exceed its capacity. As a result transportation problems involving literally thousands of origins and destinations can be solved readily. It seems that even more efficient methods of solution result when the linear programming point of view is abandoned and the problem is conceived of as routing a flow through a network, so that shipments of commodities are analyzed as if they were currents in electric circuits or flows of liquids through systems of pipes.[7] To use electrical terminology, transportation costs are analogous to resistances, and differences in the value of the commodity at different points are the voltages.

2. *Information Theory*

Information theory rests on the discovery of a quantitative measure of information, originally by R. V. L. Hartley and put into its current form by C. E. Shannon [36]. The unit of information is the "bit," which is the amount of information in a message that tells which of two equally likely possibilities is the case. Thus the telegram "It's a boy" conveys (approximately) one bit of information to a receiver who knew previously that a birth had occurred. Or consider a kind of message that is more common in industry: a requisition sent by a production department to a store-room. It contains at least three kinds of information: (1) which item is desired. This selects one of a large number of not-equally-likely possibilities, but its information content is measurable in bits by a formula that we do not have space to explain. (2) The quantity desired—again a selection from a large number of not-equally-likely possibilities. (3) Which department desires the items—again quantifiable in the same way. The formulas for information quantity are constructed in such a way that the information content of the message is the sum of these three components (and any others, such as the date desired, that may be present). Of course, there are many messages whose information content cannot be measured. For example, I do not

---

[7] The network approach to transportation problems is due mostly to Ford and Fulkerson. See [17] [18].

suppose that the information-content of this essay can be quantified.[8] But equally obviously, the smooth running of any organization depends on the flow of messages that are sufficiently standardized so that their information content can be estimated numerically.

The metric for information content is accompanied by measures of the information-carrying capacity of channels and the information-processing capacity of centers. A center is any person or group who originates messages or receives and acts on them. A channel is any group of devices or persons that transmits messages between centers. E.g., a channel might be typist-messenger boy-receptionist-secretary; or microphone-transmitter-radio waves-receiver-loud-speaker).

The capacity of a center depends on the kinds of messages it processes, the kind of action or decision required, and the technical characteristics of the center. The capacity of a channel depends on the amount of interference present in it (i.e., irrelevant signals, technically called "noise"), the forms of the messages it handles, the rate at which it can transmit the elementary symbols of which messages are composed, its susceptibility to error, etc. The capacities of the physical components of a channel (e.g., electronic amplifiers) can often be estimated from engineering considerations, the capacities of the human components have to be derived from statistical studies.

The relevance of the form of message to the capacity of a channel is particularly significant. It is contained in the notion of "redundancy," i.e., the ratio of the actual information content of the message to the maximum amount that could be packed into a message of the same length (subtracted from unity, of course). Thus the information content of the vital statistic telegram mentioned above is entirely contained in the zero-redundancy message "B" or the somewhat more redundant "Boy." Redundancy of form is expensive, but it is also useful, up to a point. Thus if a channel is subject to error (as all are) redundancy often saves the day. The message "F" conveys no information, but "Foy" is practically as good as the correct message. Mail order companies recognize the virtue of redundancy when they require that an order include the name of the item desired along with the catalogue number. The optimal amount of redundancy in a system, i.e., the optimal form of message, is an important field of application of information theory. For example, the ordinary method of transmitting television signals is more than 99 per cent redundant (because it is practically certain that the spot following a bright spot will also be bright; the only information needed after a few bright spots is when the first dark spot

---

[8] But an upper limit can be placed on it by using the estimate that text written in English contains about 1.5 bits per letter.

occurs). One of the more important advances that made color television feasible, since color TV requires much more information per second, was a less redundant scheme for encoding the signals for transmission.

The relevance of information theory to communications engineering is evident but would not qualify it as a model for operations research. Its contribution to operations research derives from its bearing on the structures of organizations. Here the essential principle is that an organization will not function smoothly if the amount of information to be sent on any channel or processed at any center exceeds the capacity of that channel or center. Thus the information structure of an organization can be depicted by representing it as a kind of network with the centers shown by capacitated nodes and the channels by capacitated links. Then the required flow of information between any pair of centers can be compared with the maximal attainable flow.[9] Bottlenecks as well as underutilized channels can then be detected and corrective actions indicated. Possible ameliorative measures are: (a) increasing physical channel capacity (e.g., increasing the number of trunk lines), (b) reducing the redundancy of messages (which is always unduly high in organizations that have not given conscious attention to this problem), (c) routing messages indirectly via underutilized channels. (d) increasing the capacities of centers (e.g., installing more counters in the storeroom), and (e) reassigning functions away from overloaded centers.

[9] From this point of view Paul Revere's communication system (two lanterns, one if by land, two if by sea) was just adequate. There was one bit of information to be transmitted and his channel had a capacity of one bit per night. It was insufficiently redundant, however, and if there had been much noise (mist, gusty winds) the course of the Battle of Lexington might have been other than it was.

3. *Simulation and Gaming*

This extended example may suggest the extreme mathematical, statistical, and technical difficulties that confront the operations analyst. They occur whether special-purpose or general-purpose models are employed. I have already mentioned that in the area of general systems analysis the equations describing the performance of an organization defy solution more often than not. The same is true of inventory problems and queuing problems. Even linear programming, whose salient virtue is the ease with which it lends itself to solution, is constantly pressing against the limitations of the most modern and powerful computing machines.

As a result, the operations analyst, like every other research worker, lives nearly always near the end of his tether. He simplifies his problems as much as he dares (sometimes more than he should dare), applies the most powerful analytic tools at his command and, with luck, just squeaks through. But what if all established methods fail, either because the problem cannot be forced into one of the standard types or because, after all acceptable simplifications, it is still so large or complicated that the equations describing it cannot be solved? When he finds himself in this fix, the operations analyst falls back on "simulation" or "gaming."

Simulation is to the operations analyst what a pilot model or experiment is to a natural scientist. If you can't predict how a machine will behave the only thing to do is to try it out and see. The operations analyst cannot usually try out an enterprise of the characteristics he is considering, but he can frequently duplicate it, at least approximately, on paper. To see how this works, pretend that we had failed to solve the machine-shop inventory problem of the last section. Then we should have to analyze it by simulation.

The most popular methods of simulation use high-speed computing machines. To simulate our inventory problem we should select a starting inventory at random, read the data of the problem into the machine and instruct the machine to follow some specific inventory policy. The machine would then look at the given starting inventory and decide in accordance with the assigned inventory policy whether to place an order for replenishment and if so how large. Then it would draw a random number from the range 0 to 9 inclusive. If the number were in the range 0-4 it would interpret this to mean that no parts were demanded in the first month, if it were in the range 5-7 it would assume that one part was demanded, an 8 would mean that two parts were demanded, and a 9 would represent a demand for three parts. Whatever the result, the machine would satisfy the demand as far as possible, subtract those sales from the initial inventory, increase the inventory by the replenishment stocks received in response to orders placed, if any, print out the results of interest, and go on to perform the same calculations for the second month.

All this would take about a thousandth of a second.[18] In this way the machine would generate a thousand months of synthetic experience with the assigned policy, equivalent to nearly a century, in a second.

[18] So much celerity is, unfortunately, extremely rare. Half a minute to a minute of machine time (costing $5 to $10) per cycle would be more typical.

When a sufficient amount of experience with a given inventory policy had been accumulated the machine would calculate the average inventory, average number of sales per month, average number of refusals, average reorder and inventory carrying cost, etc. Then it would turn to a new inventory policy and perform the same calculations.

In this way very large samples of synthetic experience can be obtained quickly and estimates can be obtained of all desired characteristics of probability distributions that are too complicated to be calculated mathematically. Analyses by simulation can do even more than that. The machine can be programmed so that after it has tried a few inventory policies assigned by the analyst it will then review the results and decide which would be the most promising inventory policy to try next. Then it could try the policy it has selected, again review the results, concoct a new promising policy, try it, and continue this process of trial and revision until it could not find any avenue that promised improvement within the range of inventory policies that it was permitted to explore. All this a calculating machine can do quickly, accurately, and without human intervention. What more could be desired?

Well, unfortunately, a great deal more. The result of a simulation is always the answer to a specific numerical problem without any insight into why that is the answer or how the answer would be influenced by a change in any of the data. In our inventory example, a change in the probability distribution of demand, in the length of the delivery lag, in the reorder cost or in net profit per sale would presumably change the solution, but a simulation with given data gives no hint of size or direction of changes in inventory policy resulting from such changes in data. Thus each variant of a problem analyzed by simulation has to be solved by a separate computation; and computation is expensive. In practical affairs, of course, it is usually more important to know how to respond to changes in conditions than how to behave optimally in any single set of circumstances. This is so because, first, circumstances do change, and second, because we never do know precisely what circumstances are but have to base decisions on estimates and, therefore, have to know how consequential errors in these estimates are.

There is a second serious limitation, also. Above I said that a computing machine could be programmed to search iteratively through a family of possible inventory policies and, through a guided process of trial and error, pick out the best. This is an oversimplification if the problem is at all complicated, say complicated enough to warrant simulation. Most decision problems tackled by operations research involve a number of interrelated variables. In the inventory example the variables are the numbers of parts to be ordered when the inventory is at each of its possible levels. In transportation problems the variables are the quantities to be delivered by each supply point to each consumer. A review of the other models we have discussed will show that typically they are multidimensional and that much of their difficulty stems from the wide variety of possible solutions to be contemplated. When explicit methods of solution cannot be found, therefore, we find ourselves in an area known as "analysis of response surfaces," about which a few words have to be said.

Suppose that we are interested in maximizing profit or minimizing cost, or something else of the sort, where the profit or cost in question depends on a number of variables under our control but where the manner of dependence is so complicated that we cannot actually write it down in the form of an equation. Then we can select any set of values of the variables under our control and, say, by simulation, estimate the value of the profit corresponding to that selection. This profit, together with the values of the variables that gave rise to it is "a point on the response surface," and, subject only to limitations of patience and expense, we can calculate any number of such points that we please. What we now need is some procedure for finding the set of values of the decidable variables that gives rise to the highest possible profit, by means of a practicable number of simulations or similar computations. All that simulation provides is a method for finding single points on the response surface and the best that can be said about finding optimal points is that research on this problem is being prosecuted vigorously [9] [10]. As things stand at present no fully satisfactory general-purpose method is known.

Be that as it may, simulation comes nearer to solving the unsolvable than any other device known, a fact that justifies fully its importance as a tool of operations research. Except in problems as trivial as our inventory example it is, however, a difficult tool to use well. It entails two main kinds of technical difficulties, those relating to the exploration of the response surface, which we have already discussed, and statistical problems such as deciding how large a sample to take of each set of circumstances and policies. E.g., in our inventory example the statistical problem is how many months of synthetic experience should be accumulated with each inventory policy examined. With a given research appropriation, more policies can be examined if each examination employs a smaller sample, but the disadvantages of using unduly small samples is evident. These are formidable problems in technical mathematical analysis and statistics and have an important bearing on the cost and precision of the analysis, but do not have much influence on the result, or, at least, should not.

A device quite similar to simulation in form but entirely different in objective is "gaming" or "operational gaming." Formally, gaming is simulation with human intervention. To "game" our inventory example we should omit the inventory policy from the machine program and replace it by the following routine. Each time that a new initial inventory is computed, the machine would print out the results of the previous period's operations, including the terminal inventory, and wait. Then the subject, which might be either an individual or a team, would decide on the basis of his best judgment how many parts to order. This would be read into the machine which would then compute the results of the period's operations, print them out, and wait for the next decision. In working through an operational game of this sort, the subject might or might not be informed of the basic data, for example the probability distribution of demand. If he is not informed of some of the relevant data he would be expected to deduce them as experience accumulates.

This device will not, of course, disclose the optimal policy to be followed, but it can serve any of several other purposes. It can be used to investigate how close an experienced subject can come to the mathematical optimum in given circumstances and how long it takes him to do so. It can be used to test how changes in the circumstances and in the data available change the performance of subjects, and in this way to throw light on the practical value of additional information in the real life situation being simulated. Thus, in the inventory example, if the probability distribution of demand is not known such an experiment could reveal how much should be spent on market research or other methods for ascertaining it.

Gaming can also be used as a psychological-experimental device for studying executive behavior. Thus, in one set of such experiments it was found that executives started by basing their decisions on rough rules of thumb and revised them, in the light of experience, much too slowly in the sense that when they changed their policies they usually moved them only a small fraction of the distance between the current policy and the optimum, and only very rarely overcorrected. Further it was found that this conservative bias tended to be more marked in proportion to the importance of random and unpredictable elements in the game.

Gaming can also be used to study the optimum of some decisions when other decisions are too complicated or are based on considerations too vague to be formalized. In this application, various policies for making the decisions to be optimized are programmed into the machines while the unmanageable decisions are made by a team as required. Finally, gaming can be used as a pedagogical device.

Gaming is fun but, if a skilled team is required, very expensive. The expense frequently precludes sufficient replication to generate reliable probability distributions of consequences; and even where expense is not prohibitive, the memories, learning processes, and tendencies to habit formation on the part of the teams make much replication impracticable. Even if the replication problem can be surmounted there is a more fundamental difficulty in using gaming as a research tool. In any series of repetitions of a game, the teams will either base their decisions on some well-defined policy or, more usually, will "play it by ear," using their best judgment as experience accumulates. In the former instance the results of the experiment will be an assessment of the consequences of the policy used but, as we have seen above, any well-defined policy can be assessed more cheaply and conveniently by programming a computing machine to follow that policy and conducting a simulation experiment. In the latter instance it is hard to say what the results mean since no expressable or reproducible policy was followed. The results will reflect an amalgam of the potentialities of the situation, the approximations used in constructing the game, the abilities of the teams under somewhat unnatural conditions, and the vagaries of chance. If a large number of teams is used, the gaming may produce an evaluation of how well an "average" team will perform under the conditions of the game, but still another dimension of sampling variability crops up in this application [38].

As a result of these problems, the literature does not indicate that gaming has played a significant role in solving operations research problems. It seems to hold more promise as a device for executive training, for investigating the psychology of decision making, and for stimulating effective planning by confronting managers vividly with various contingencies they should be prepared to meet. Even in these last applications, however, it does not seem feasible to impose rewards and penalties cruel enough to approximate the pressures of real-life decision problems.

IV. *The Role of Operations Research*

Such is the nature of operations research. I hope that I have made an adequate case for the assertion that its essence lies in a strong tendency to tackle administrative problems via formal models constructed in the spirit of the natural sciences. We turn now, and finally, to the role of operations research in business and economic administration.

If an experienced operations analyst were asked to describe the problem he would most like to meet, I suspect that he would mention four characteristics: first, the objective of the operation should be clearly defined, second, the operation should be describable by a reasonably manageable model, third, the data required for estimating the parameters of the model should be readily obtainable, and fourth, current operating practice should leave plenty of room for improvement. These are the characteristics of the ideal problem, from the analyst's point of view, and sometimes he encounters it, but more often he must be content with projects that fall short of perfection in one respect or another. Each of these characteristics deserves a little discussion.

For an operation to have a clearly defined objective it is not necessary, of course, that the businessman or other client be able to write down its objective function at a moment's notice. It does require that the analyst be able to obtain a consensus on the purpose of the operation, specific enough so that he can judge how conflicts in goals are to be resolved. With a little care to assure that the objective function does not conflict with higher-level goals and that the measure of cost is appropriate, the definition of objectives should present little difficulty at the operating levels. More trouble is likely to occur at the executive levels, where decisions are likely to have widespread and incommensurable ramifications. Glen Camp, in fact, warns against undertaking such problems: ". . . best results will be obtained if the scientist meticulously avoids the evaluation of intangibles" [11, p. 630]. The narrower and more specific the problem, then, the more likely it is to possess this characteristic.

The second characteristic of a promising project was that it be possible to formulate a manageable model to describe the impact of various possible decisions on the objective function. Again we may cite Glen Camp: "The function of the operations research team is to assist the responsible authority of an organization by clarifying those uncertainties in the factors on which action is based, and *only* those, which can be clarified by scientific study" [11, p. 629]. Now, how is one to tell, in a preliminary survey of a problem, whether its essence can be caught in a manageable model or whether, in Camp's words, it can be clarified by scientific study?

Model building is the analyst's primary skill and contribution, and he cannot expect when he approaches a problem to find that his work has already been done for him. Thus the question is not whether a model exists ready-to-hand, but whether one can be built in reasonable time. The answer depends basically on whether or not the problem involves kinds of relationships that have not been established by previous scientific study or, as I shall say, whether or not it involves gaps in fundamental scientific knowledge. Consider, for example, the advertising fable that we used to characterize the operations analytic approach. In that fable the analyst boldly extemporized a model of the relationship of advertising expenditure to sales. It was, of course, a shot in the dark. No one really knows what the relationship in question is. The problem involved a gap in scientific knowledge.

When he encounters such a gap, the operations analyst has a choice of three options: he can proceed on the basis of a bold conjecture, he can undertake the substantive research necessary to fill the gap, or he can abandon the problem as unsolvable at the current state of knowledge. Much of the analyst's skill lies in determining which option to choose in given circumstances. A bold conjecture is refreshing, but an insubstantial foundation for an important decision. Abandoning the project is manifestly distasteful. Undertaking fundamental research entails the usual hazard that it may not be successful, plus an unwelcome delay in arriving at a useful recommendation.

In practice, this third option is frequently chosen and frequently well advised. Much of the work of the practicing analyst is the work of filling gaps in substantive knowledge, just as much of the value of the model-building approach resides in disclosing and defining those gaps. There is much testimony to indicate that the most valuable results of operations research are by-products. Again and again businessmen have stated gratefully that they learned more about their business by answering an analyst's questions, supplying data for his model, and checking over the model with him than they did from his final report. (Is the analogy with psychoanalysis a coincidence?) Similarly the substantive research undertaken as part of an operations research project is often of great value, quite apart from the value of the final recommendations.[20] Thus the attempt to construct a model may be worthwhile even in unpromising circumstances.

But not always. Frequently the gaps in knowledge that prevent constructing a reliable model are already perfectly well known to the client, and not of a kind to be filled by short-term research. The advertising fable is, very likely, a case in point. Such gaps in knowledge are frequently what induce the client to call in the operations analyst. If he could fill them, he could solve the problem himself, and his hope is that the magic of operations research will help him to reach a well-founded decision in spite of certain areas of ignorance. Such hopes are doomed to disappointment. Operations research is not a substitute for substantive knowledge, but a way of employing it, nor can the operations analyst be expected to complete scientific knowledge to order as required by his clients.

If gaps in substantive knowledge prevent the formulation of a complete model, clearly the analyst cannot hope to ascertain the optimal decision. He may then address himself to a more modest, but still useful goal, as pointed out by P. M. S. Blackett in one of the earliest and most important papers on operations research methodology [8]. He can seek to discover a policy that is better than the current one, though not necessarily best. This approach is one that economists are schooled in. Blackett recommended that instead of attempting to ascertain the objective function as a function of the various decision variables, the analyst undertake the much easier task of estimating its partial derivatives with respect to each decision variable (essentially the net marginal productivities of the decision variables) in the neighborhood of the currently used values of those variables. If any of those partial derivatives is substantially different from zero (i.e., if any marginal productivity is substantially different from the corresponding marginal cost) then a direction in which current policies can be improved is apparent.

Just as the operations research approach is not peculiarly adapted to solving fresh scientific questions, so it is not well adapted to discovering fresh lines of action or technological innovations (with an exception to be noted below). A range of possible actions or decisions is

---

[20] For a famous and fascinating illustration see Thornthwaite, "Operations Research in Agriculture" [27, pp. 368-80].

built into the model from the outset; the solution of the model yields the best solution within that range. For example, linear programming yields the optimal combination of the activities listed in the matrix; it will not disclose the existence of some still better activity not foreseen in advance. In short, the technique of operations research is designed to uncover better ways of organizing the use of given resources by means of given techniques; it does not extend the range of technical possibilities.

This is not to say that operations analysts have not been instrumental in technical innovations. They are typically imaginative and resourceful men, unfettered by traditions of which they are frequently unaware, and often do suggest courses of action that would never occur to men schooled in the habits of an enterprise or branch of technology. But the methods of operations research are of little help in the field of substantive invention though the practitioners often do have patents to their credit.

There is, however, one field of operations research that does bear directly on the process of technical invention, namely "requirements studies." In a requirements study an operation is surveyed in order to determine the characteristics of desirable technical innovations. Models are built which incorporate as yet nonexistent hardware and the performance characteristics of the hardware are varied (on paper) in order to ascertain their influence on the over-all operation. Thus a set of specifications for new equipment can be established and the gain flowing from meeting those specifications can be estimated. This type of analysis has been most prevalent in establishing military requirements—the RAND Corporation was studying the usefulness of artificial satellites as early as 1946—and has also been used by commercial airlines in planning for new equipment. Thus studies are now in progress on the usefulness of supersonic passenger aircraft.

The third characteristic of a promising operations research project was that an adequate fund of experience be available to permit statistical estimation of the parameters required by the model. This requirement will be satisfied most adequately by repetitious, even routine, types of operation. Morse and Kimball, for example, state, "Patrol or search is an operation which is peculiarly amenable to operations research. The action is simple, and repeated often enough under conditions sufficiently similar to enable satisfactory data to be accumulated" [32, p. 38]. Nearly all our examples, indeed, have been of this sort. They concerned scheduling a refinery, which is done at least once a month, reordering inventories, similiarly periodic, and so on. In all such repetitive decisions, the necessary statistics are accumulated over time as an administrative by-product if not as part of a formal reporting system. If the requisite statistics are not available, the situation is analogous to that which occurs when there is a gap in scientific knowledge, discussed above, except that gathering statistics is less of a gamble than undertaking to establish a new scientific relationship.

If the problem being studied is nonrepetitive, even the statistical outlook is more doubtful since, after all, statistics require a population from which a sample can be drawn. The statistical characteristic also, therefore, is more likely to be fulfilled at the operating levels of an enterprise than at the highest executive levels, since operating decisions are much less likely than broad policy and strategy decisions to be *sui generis*.

The final characteristic of a promising operations research study was that current operations admit of substantial improvement by means of the kinds of decisions discoverable by studying the operation of a model. This last characteristic, unfortunately, works somewhat in opposition to the first three. If an operation is repetitive, well recorded, intended to serve a well-defined goal, and of a kind in which the influences of decisions on the attainment of the goal do not transcend available technical knowledge, then it is not likely that current practice will fall far short of the most efficient practice attainable. And, indeed, the usual upshot of a linear programming analysis or a transportation problem study is to find a plan that will reduce costs by 2 or 3 or 5 per cent. To be sure, in a large operation, 5 per cent is not contemptible. But neither is it dramatic; and in view of the approximations used in reaching such solutions and the possible errors in the statistical estimates it cannot even be certain that such small savings are genuine rather than paper results. This finding stands in unhappy contrast to the state of affairs during the second world war, on the basis of which Morse and Kimball wrote, ". . . successful application of operations research usually results in improvements by factors of 3 or 10 or more" [32, p. 38]. This is as if a successful operations research project can be expected to treble the capacity of a factory or divide its unit costs by three.

The contrast between the peacetime and wartime yields of operations research is explained by the fact that the second world war was largely a race of technological improvements. Efficient submarines led to the development of airborne search-radar; airborne search-radar induced the invention of snorkel-equipped submarines. Technological innovations followed each other so quickly that a new device was in the field before trial-and-error methods could discover efficient means for employing its predecessor. Operations research proved to be a very effective means for accelerating the discovery of effective ways of using novel equipment. In more stable circumstances, however, the situation is otherwise. Blackett, also relying on wartime experience, wrote ". . . in the course of repeated operations by many different participants, most of the possible variations of tactics will be effectively explored, so that any large derivatives will eventually be discovered, and given intelligent control, improved tactics will become generally adopted" [8, p. 33]. On the other hand, considerable room for improvement may remain even under fairly stable technological conditions, as the dragline example showed. The explanation in that instance probably lay in the numerousness and the complexity of the decision variables, which precluded efficient exploration of possibilities by unsystematic means.

These considerations suggest that in just those kinds of business operation in which the first three requirements for productive operations research are likely to be met, the requirements for the discovery of efficient methods by more traditional means are also likely to be met, and there may not be very much improvement left for the operations analyst to discover. The major exception to this conclusion is problems of adapting to new circumstances or of employing novel techniques or instruments. In those cases, operations research can often speed up the process of adaptation. An optimal situation for operations research is one in which conditions are changing too rapidly for experience to be assimilated by informal, unsystematic methods, but slowly enough to permit the formulation of a model applicable to both the recent past and relevant future, and to permit the accumulation of the data needed for estimating the parameters of the model.

All in all, conditions auspicious for operations research are more likely to be met at the middling and lower levels of an organization than at the topmost ones: the clarity of objectives, the simplicity of relationships, and the availability of technical knowledge and statistical data all point in this direction. Thus the device of "suboptimization" recommends itself. Suboptimization is defined by Hitch and McKean, its principal expositors, as the ". . . process of choosing among a relatively small number of alternatives by an administrative level other than the highest" [21, p. 172]. More explicitly it is the organizational policy in which the higher echelons of an organization assign tasks to the lower echelons and establish performance criteria for them, and then leave the lower echelons free to perform the tasks in the best way they can as judged by the criteria established. That, after all, is how a market economy works. Suboptimization is a new word for decentralization, and its advantages are the familiar advantages of decentralization. From the point of view of operations research its major advantage is that it enables the relatively manageable problems of detailed operation to be solved separately from each other and from the more intractable problems that arise on the higher executive levels.

The foregoing summarizes the circumstances in which operations research is likely to be successful in the sense of disclosing significantly improved policies and practices. But operations research can be successful in other senses also. We have already noted the educative value of collaborating with an analyst and looking at problems from his viewpoint. We have seen that operations research often suggests and sometimes accomplishes valuable substantive research. In many instances the contribution of operations research is to improve the planning process itself, without improving the quality of the plans.

Consider planning petroleum refinery operations, which now is quite prevalently accomplished with the use of programming models. Before programming was introduced, monthly refinery schedules were developed by a planning section in the refinery engineer's department and required about two weeks of computation by highly trained engineering personnel. After a programming system is introduced, the same plans are developed in three or four hours by clerical personnel and computing machine operators under the general supervision of an engineer. The new planning system has at least three advantages over the old one, even though the resultant plans are not appreciably superior to those developed by tedious hand calculations using the same data. First, it is vastly cheaper in terms of both monetary cost and drain on scarce, highly trained manpower. Second, because of its speed, more timely data can be employed. Before the mechanized planning made possible by operations research, the forecasts for, say, the March plan had to be based on data available on February 14; after mechanization the closing date for forecast data becomes February 26. Thus, even where programming does not produce superior plans given the same data, the speed with which it can be performed permits the use of improved data. Third, the probabilities of errors in both arithmetic and judgment are greatly reduced when formalized, mechanized planning supersedes informal, skilled-judgment methods. The programming procedure includes a built-in guarantee that the resulting plan is optimal, avoiding the hankering worry that a misjudgment was made somewhere in a protracted computation.

In more general terms, where plans or decisions are based on large masses of data and complicated interrelationships—where, for example, a large number of operations have to be coordinated—the model developed by an operations research study provides a framework within which the data can be assembled, analyzed, and digested in a swift, mechanical, error-free, and inexpensive way. Such a model makes the planning process itself more efficient and reliable.

Finally, consider the really tough and important problems where there is no objective basis for making a usefully precise evaluation of the consequences of possible actions or policies. Contending with such imponderables is the primary responsibility of the high executive, a responsibility that cannot be delegated, not even to an operations analyst. Nevertheless, an operations research study of such a problem can help the executive by organizing the data, focussing the issues, bringing out the implications of possible assumptions and hunches, delimiting the range of the inevitable uncertainty. Any detached, analytic, skeptical viewpoint can help clarify such problems, and the analyst has such a viewpoint to contribute.

There is much room for folly, though, when an operations analyst participates in conjecturing answers to unanswerable questions. The executive is under a strong temptation to pass the buck to the analyst, and the analyst is tempted just as strongly to accept it. When there is no "right" decision, there is a tendency to adopt one that can be justified—for who can be blamed for following a recommendation supported by an imposing dossier? And what dossier is more imposing, these days, than an operations research report? Thus the analyst may find that his simplifying assumptions, perhaps made for exploratory purposes, have become the basis for weighty decisions, even decisions important to the safety of the nation.

It is all very well to inveigh against the executive who permits his judgment to be overborne by elaborate calculations that he does not understand. Though the executive must retain the responsibility, he must also accept much on faith, and when his analyst assures him that the recommendations are well-founded, what is he to do? The businessman cannot audit the technical reasoning. Though the analyst can remain detached and impartial as regards the affairs of his client, he is as liable as any man to fall under the spell of his own handiwork. I see no satisfying way to resolve this difficulty. Glen Camp, as we saw, advised analysts to abstain from such dangerous enterprises but also, as we remarked, the analyst can serve usefully in smoothing the way for a decision. The accumulation of experience in the use of operations research will probably help some, particularly by reducing the pressure on the analyst to produce clear-cut recommendations

It appears, in summary, that operations research is best adapted to dealing with routine, semitechnical, quantifiable problems, and that it can also contribute in a larger realm by showing businessmen how to view their problems from a sophisticated scientific standpoint. It has developed powerful methods for solving the day-to-day problems of middle management and, I think, can fairly claim to be an indispensable tool at that level. Operations analysts aspire higher, of course.[21] But when they will attain a special competence in dealing with larger, more conjectural problems is itself a very conjectural question.

[21] See for example Ellis A. Johnson [22] and Russell Ackoff [1].

We noted at the outset that operations research is dominated by, and takes its style from, men trained in the natural sciences. There is, however, a large handful of practising operations analysts who were trained as economists and, permitting myself a parochial evaluation, these men have contributed to the development of the science far out of proportion to their numbers. The economist comes to operations research with a number of important ideas already instilled, among them an appreciation of the importance of substitution, a sophistication about the objectives of enterprises, an awareness of the importance of marginal trade-offs, and most important, a realization that physical quantities are subsidiary to "values" in a decision process. He also inherits from his training a number of disabilities, including ignorance of the technical side of business and industry and a belief in the existence of production functions. On balance it appears that the older science has more to contribute to the younger than the other way round, as is right and proper. But still we can learn from our juniors, and we fail to do so at our own risk.

The most important lesson operations research has to teach is how much we are asking of businessmen when we ask them to behave "rationally." Even when businessmen would dearly like to do so, it turns out that the most powerful tools of mathematics cannot, for example, help them discover a "rational" inventory policy; and that is only one small part of the businessman's problem. Since the profit-maximizing or risk-minimizing course of action is undiscoverable, he must perforce rely on hunches and rules of thumb. It is by no means clear what rational behavior consists of in such circumstances. On the other hand it turns out that business performance is frequently quite close to the rational optimum for problems of the sort that operations research is able to solve.

Thus the lesson of operations research appears to be a heavy score against the belief that firms maximize anything, either in the short run or the long. Instead we must conceive of actual firms as operating according to certain rules of thumb that would be rational if life were much simpler than it is and that are not disastrous under actual circumstances. It makes one tolerant of such practices as pricing by conventional mark-ups, costing with conventional overhead burdens, and investing in accordance with tried and proven pay-off periods. These practices are what businessmen must follow until operations research provides them with better standards. The success of operations research testifies to the willingness of businessmen to abandon operation by rule-of-thumb when a better alternative becomes available. The best we can say is that businessmen would like to behave "rationally" and are eager to be taught how.

For many purposes of economic analysis the current crude image of the firm, as a responsive extension of the personality of a fully informed, aggressive entrepreneur, is probably adequate. But for some other purposes—the understanding of inventory and investment behavior, for example—we must recognize the firm for what operations research has disclosed it to be: often fumbling, sluggish, timid, uncertain, and perplexed by unsolvable problems. Since its discriminating power is low it responds only to gross stimuli; since its decision processes are uncertain the timing and vigor of its responses are unpredictable. It reacts in familiar ways to the familiar and avoids the novel as long as it dares. We need economic theories that incorporate these ingredients. They will remain valid until operations research has made much more progress against businessmen's problems.

References

1. R. L. Ackoff, "Operations Research and National Planning," *Op. Res.*, Aug. 1957, *5*, 457-68.
2. American Management Association, "Progress in Industrial Operations Research, Results of a Survey," *Management News*, Dec. 1957.
3. K. J. Arrow, "Alternative Approaches to the Theory of Choice in Risk-Taking Situations," *Econometrica*, Oct. 1951, *19*, 404-37.
4. K. J. Arrow, S. Karlin and H. Scarf, *Studies in the Mathematical Theory of Inventory and Production*. Stanford 1958.
5. W. J. Baumol, "On the Theory of Oligopoly," *Economica*, Aug. 1958, *N. S. 25*, 187-98.
6. ———, "Activity Analysis in One Lesson," *Am. Econ. Rev.*, Dec. 1958, *48*, 837-73.
7. R. Bellman, *Dynamic Programming*. Princeton 1957.
8. P. M. S. Blackett, "Operational Research," *Advancement of Sci.*, Apr. 1948, *5*, 26-38.
9. G. E. P. Box, "The Exploration and Exploitation of Response Surfaces," *Biometrics*, Mar. 1954, *10*, 16-60.
10. S. H. Brooks, "A Comparison of Maximum-Seeking Methods," *Op. Res.*, July-Aug. 1959, *7*, 430-57.
11. G. D. Camp, "Operations Research: The Science of Generalized Strategies and Tactics," *Textile Res. Jour.*, July 1955, *25*, 629-34.
12. A. Charnes, W. W. Cooper and B. Mellon, "Blending Aviation Gasolines—A Study in Programming Interdependent Activities in an Integrated Oil Company," *Econometrica*, Apr. 1952, *20*, 135-59.
13. C. W. Churchman, R. L. Ackoff and E. L. Arnoff, *Introduction to Operations Research*. New York 1957.
14. R. Dorfman, "Mathematical or Linear Programming: A Non-Mathematical Exposition," *Am. Econ. Rev.*, Dec. 1953, *43*, 797-825.
15. J. W. Dunlap and H. H. Jacobs, "Strip Mining Phosphate Rock with Large Walking Draglines" [26, Ch. 9].

16. A. DVORETZKY, J. KIEFER AND J. WOLFOWITZ, "On the Optimal Character of the (s,S) Policy in Inventory Theory," *Econometrica*, Oct. 1953, *21*, 586-96.

17. L. R. FORD, JR. AND D. R. FULKERSON, "Solving the Transportation Problem," *Mgt. Sci.*, Oct. 1956, *3*, 24-32.

18. ———, "A Primal Dual Algorithm for the Capacitated Hitchcock Problem," *Nav. Res. Log. Quart.*, Mar. 1957, *4*, 47-54.

19. R. E. GOMORY AND W. J. BAUMOL, "Integer Programming and Pricing." *Econometrica*, forthcoming.

20. J. M. HENDERSON, *The Efficiency of the Coal Industry*. Cambridge, Mass. 1958.

21. C. HITCH AND R. C. MCKEAN, "Suboptimization in Operations Problems" [27, 168-86].

22. E. A. JOHNSON, "The Long-Range Future of Operations Research," *Op. Res.*, Jan.-Feb. 1960, *8*, 1-23.

23. B. O. KOOPMAN, "Fallacies in Operations Research," *Op. Res.*, Aug. 1956, *4*, 422-26.

24. R. F. LANZILLOTTI, "Pricing Objectives in Large Companies," *Am. Econ. Rev.*, Dec. 1958, *48*, 921-40.

25. R. D. LUCE AND H. RAIFFA, *Games and Decisions*. New York 1957.

26. J. F. MCCLOSKEY AND J. M. COPPINGER, ed., *Operations Research for Management*, Vol. II. Baltimore 1956.

27. J. F. MCCLOSKEY AND F. N. TREFETHEN, ed., *Operations Research for Management*, Vol. I. Baltimore 1954.

28. A. S. MANNE, *Scheduling of Petroleum Refinery Operations*. Cambridge, Mass. 1956.

29. H. M. MARKOWITZ, *Portfolio Selection*. New York 1959.

30. H. M. MARKOWITZ AND A. S. MANNE, "On the Solution of Discrete Programming Problems," *Econometrica*, Jan. 1957, *25*, 84-110.

31. P. M. MORSE, *Queues, Inventories and Maintenance*. New York 1958.

32. P. M. MORSE AND G. E. KIMBALL, *Methods of Operations Research*. New York 1951.

33. E. S. OLCOTT, "The Influence of Vehicular Speed and Spacing on Tunnel Capacity" [26, Ch. 3].

34. R. SCHLAIFER, *Probability and Statistics for Business Decisions*. New York 1959.

35. G. L. S. SHACKLE, *Expectation in Economics*. Cambridge 1949.

36. C. E. SHANNON AND W. WEAVER, *The Mathematical Theory of Communication*. Urbana 1949.

37. H. A. SIMON, "Theories of Decision-Making in Economics," *Am. Econ. Rev.*, June 1959, *49*, 253-83.

38. C. J. THOMAS AND W. L. DEEMER, JR., "The Role of Operational Gaming in Operations Research," *Op. Res.*, Feb. 1957, *5*, 1-27.

39. A. VAZSONYI, *Scientific Programming in Business and Industry*. New York 1958.

40. T. M. WHITIN, *The Theory of Inventory Management*. Princeton 1953.

[6]

An Economic Interpretation of Optimal Control Theory

Capital theory is the economics of time. Its task is to explain if, and why, a lasting instrument of production can be expected to contribute more to the value of output during its lifetime than it costs to produce or acquire. From the explanation, it deduces both normative and descriptive conclusions about the time-path of the accumulation of capital by economic units and entire economies.

Traditionally, capital theory, like all other branches of economics, was studied in the context of stationary equilibrium. For example, the stationary state of the classical economists, and the equilibrium of Böhm-Bawerk's theory of the period of production, both describe the state of affairs in which further capital accumulation is not worthwhile. A mode of analysis that is confined to a distant, ultimate position is poorly suited to the understanding of accumulation and growth,[1] but no other technique seemed available for most of the history of capital theory.

For the past fifty years it has been perceived, more or less vaguely, that capital theory is formally a problem in the calculus of variations.[2] But the calculus of variations is regarded as a rather arcane subject by most economists and, besides, in its conventional formulations appears too rigid to be applied to many economic problems. The application of this conceptual tool to capital theory remained peripheral and sporadic until very recently, and capital theory remained bound by the very confining limitations of the ultimate equilibrium.

All this has changed abruptly in the past decade as a result of a revival, or rather reorientation, of the calculus of variations prompted largely by the requirements of space technology.[3] In its modern version, the calculus of variations is called optimal control theory. It has become, deservedly, the central tool of capital theory and has given the latter a new lease on life. As a result, capital theory has become so profoundly transformed that it has been rechristened growth theory, and has come to grips with numerous important practical and theoretical issues that previously could not even be formulated.

The main thesis of this paper is that optimal control theory is formally identical with capital theory, and that its main insights can be attained by strictly economic reasoning. This thesis will be supported by deriving the principal theorem of optimal control theory, called the maximum principle, by means of economic analysis.

I. The Basic Equations

In order to have a concrete vocabulary, consider the decision problem of a firm that wishes to maximize its total profits over some period of time. At any date t, this firm will have inherited a certain stock of capital and other conditions from its

---

[*] The author is professor of economics at Harvard University.
[1] A point made most forceably by Joan Robinson in [9] and elsewhere.
[2] Notable examples are Hotelling [6] and Ramsey [8].

[3] The twin sources of the new calculus of variations are R. Bellman [4] and L. S. Pontryagin, et al. [7]. Bellman emphasized from the first the implications of his work for economics.

817

past behavior. Denote these by $k(t)$. With this stock of capital and other facilities k and at that particular date t, the firm is in a position to take some decisions which might concern rate of output, price of output, product design, or whatnot. Denote the decisions taken at any date by $x(t)$. From the inherited stock of capital at the specified date together with the specified current decisions the firm derives a certain rate of benefits or net profits per unit of time. Denote this by $u(k(t), x(t), t)$.[4] This function u determines the rate at which profits are being earned at time t as a result of having k and taking decisions x.

Now look at the situation as it appears at the initial date $t = 0$. The total profits that will be earned from then to some terminal date T is given by:

$$W(k_0, \vec{x}) = \int_0^T u(k, x, t)dt$$

which is simply the sum of the rate at which profit is being earned at every instant discounted to the initial date (if desired) and added up for all instants.[5] In this notation $\vec{x}$ does not denote an ordinary number but the entire time path of the decision variable x from the initial date to T. This notation asserts that if the firm starts out with an initial amount of capital k_0 and then follows the decision policy denoted by $\vec{x}$, it will obtain a total result, W, which is the integral of the results obtained at each instant; these results in turn depending upon the date of the pertinent instant, the capital stock then and the decision applicable to that moment. The firm is at liberty, within limits, to choose the time path of the decision variable $\vec{x}$ but it cannot choose independently the amount of capital at each in-

stant; that is a consequence of the capital at the initial date and the time path chosen for decision variable. This constraint is expressed by saying that the rate of change of the capital stock at any instant is a function of its present standing, the date, and the decisions taken. Symbolically:[6]

$$(1) \qquad \dot{k} = \frac{dk}{dt} = f(k, x, t).$$

Thus the decisions taken at any time have two effects. They influence the rate at which profits are earned at that time and they also influence the rate at which the capital stock is changing and thereby the capital stock that will be available at subsequent instants of time.

These two formulas express the essence of the problem of making decisions in a dynamic context. The problem is to select the time path symbolized by $\vec{x}$ so as to make the total value of the result, W, as great as possible taking into account the effect of the choice of x on both the instantaneous rate of profit and the capital stock to be carried into the future. This is truly a difficult problem, and not only for beginners. The essential difficulty is that an entire time path of some variable has to be chosen. The elementary calculus teaches how to choose the best possible number to assign to a single variable or the best numbers for a few variables by differentiating some function and setting partial derivatives equal to zero. But finding a best possible time path is an entirely different matter and leads into some very advanced mathematics. The strategy of the solution is to reduce the problem which, as it stands, requires us to find an entire time path, to a problem which demands us to determine only a single number (or a few numbers), which is something we know how to do from the ordinary cal-

---

[4] In the sequel we shall often omit the time-arguments in the interest of simplicity, and thus write simply $u(k, x, t)$.

[5] The argument t allows the introduction of any discounting formula that may be appropriate.

[6] The dot will be used frequently to denote a rate of change with respect to time.

culus. This transformation of the problem can be performed in a number of ways. One way, which dates back to the eighteenth century, leads to the classical calculus of variations. Another way, which will be followed here, leads to the maximum principle of optimal control theory. This method depends very heavily on introducing the proper notation. First, introduce a formula for the value that can be obtained by the firm starting at an arbitrary date t with some amount of capital k and then following an arbitrary decision policy $\vec{x}$ until the terminal date. It is

$$W(k_t, \vec{x}, t) = \int_t^T u[k, x, \tau]d\tau$$

which, of course, is just a generalization of the W formula introduced previously.

Now break W up into two parts. Think of a short time interval of length Δ beginning at time t. Δ is to be thought of as being so short that the firm would not change x in the course of it even if it could. Then we can write

$$\begin{aligned}W(k, \vec{x}, t) &= u(k, x_t, t)\Delta \\ &+ \int_{t+\Delta}^T u[k(t), x, \tau]d\tau.\end{aligned}$$

(2)

This formula says that if the amount of capital available at time t is k and if the policy denoted by $\vec{x}$ is followed from then on, then the value contributed to the total sum from date t on consists of two parts. The first part is the contribution of a short interval that begins at date t. It is the rate at which profits are earned during the interval times the length of the interval. It depends on the current capital stock, the date, and the current value of the decision variable, here denoted by x_t. The second part is an integral of precisely the same form as before but beginning at date $t+\Delta$. It should be noticed that the starting capital stock for this last integral is not $k(t)$ but $k(t+\Delta)$. This fact, that the capital

stock will change during the interval in a manner influenced by x_t, will play a very significant role. We can take advantage of the fact that the same form of integral has returned by writing

$$W(k_t, \vec{x}, t) = u(k, x_t, t)\Delta + W(k_{t+\Delta}, \vec{x}, t + \Delta)$$

where the changes in the subscripts are carefully noted.

Now some more notation. If the firm knew the best choice of $\vec{x}$ from date t on, it could just follow it and thereby obtain a certain value. We denote this value, which results from the optimal choice of $\vec{x}$ by V^*, as follows

$$V^*(k_t, t) = \max W(k_t, \vec{x}, t).$$

Notice that V^* does not involve $\vec{x}$ as an argument. This is because $\vec{x}$ has been maximized out. The maximum value that can be obtained beginning at date t with capital k does not depend on $\vec{x}$ but is the value that can be obtained in those conditions from the best possible choice of $\vec{x}$. Now suppose that the policy designated by x_t is followed in the short time interval from t to $t+\Delta$ and that thereafter the best possible policy is followed. By formula (2) the consequence of this peculiar policy can be written as

$$V(k_t, x_t, t) = u(k_t, x_t, t)\Delta + V^*(k_{t+\Delta}, t + \Delta).$$

In words, the results of following such a policy are the benefits that accrue during the initial period using the decision x_t plus the maximum possible profits that can be realized starting from date $t+\Delta$ with capital $k(t+\Delta)$ which results from the decision taken in the initial period.

Now we have arrived at the ordinary calculus problem of finding the best possible value for x_t. If the firm adopts this value, then V of the last formula will be equal to V^*. The calculus teaches us that one frequently effective way to discover a value of a variable that maximizes a given function is to differentiate the function with respect to the variable and equate the partial derivative to zero. This is the method that we shall use. But first we should be warned that this method is not sure-fire. It is quite possible for the partial derivatives to vanish when the function is not maximized (for example, they may vanish when it is minimized), and cases are not rare in which the partial derivatives differ from zero at the maximum. We shall return to these intricacies later. For the present we assume that the partial derivative vanishes at the maximum, differentiate $V(k_t, x_t, t)$ with respect to x_t, and obtain

$$(3) \quad \Delta \frac{\partial}{\partial x_t} u(k, x_t, t) + \frac{\partial}{\partial x_t} V^*(k(t + \Delta), t + \Delta) = 0.$$

The trouble with that formula, aside from the fact that the function V^* is still unknown, is that we are told to differentiate V^* with respect to x_t, whereas it does not involve x_t explicitly. To get around this, notice

$$\frac{\partial V^*}{\partial x_t} = \frac{\partial V^*}{\partial k(t + \Delta)} \frac{\partial k(t + \Delta)}{\partial x_t}.$$

Both of these expressions merit some analysis and we shall start with the second. Since we are dealing with short time periods we can use the approximation

$$k(t + \Delta) = k(t) + \dot{k}\Delta.$$

That is, the amount of capital at $t+\Delta$ is equal to the amount of capital at t plus the rate of change of capital during the interval times the length of the interval. Remembering formula (1), $\dot{k}$ depends on x_t:

$$\dot{k} = f(k, x_t, t).$$

Thus we can write

$$\frac{\partial k(t + \Delta)}{\partial x_t} = \Delta \frac{\partial f}{\partial x_t}.$$

Turn, now, to the first factor, $\partial V^*/\partial k$. This derivative is the rate at which the maximum possible profit flow from time $t+\Delta$ on changes with respect to the amount of capital available at $t+\Delta$. It is, therefore, the marginal value of capital at time $t+\Delta$, or the amount by which a unit increment in capital occurring at that time would increase the maximum possible value of W. We denote the marginal value of capital at time t by $\lambda(t)$, defined by

$$\lambda(t) = \frac{\partial}{\partial k} V^*(k, t).$$

Inserting these results in formula (3), we obtain

$$(4) \quad \Delta \frac{\partial u}{\partial x_t} + \lambda(t + \Delta)\Delta \frac{\partial f}{\partial x_t} = 0$$

and furthermore, the constant Δ can be cancelled out. We have one more simplification to make before arriving at our first important conclusion. The marginal value of capital changes gradually over time and so, to a sufficiently good approximation,

$$\lambda(t + \Delta) = \lambda(t) + \dot{\lambda}(t)\Delta.$$

That is, the marginal value of capital at $t+\Delta$ is the marginal value at t plus the rate at which it is changing during the interval multiplied by the length of the interval. Insert this expression in equation (4), after cancelling the common factor Δ in the equation as written, to obtain

$$\frac{\partial u}{\partial x_t} + \lambda(t) \frac{\partial f}{\partial x_t} + \dot{\lambda}(t)\Delta \frac{\partial f}{\partial x_t} = 0.$$

Now allow Δ to approach zero. The third term becomes negligibly small in comparison with the other two. Neglecting it, there results:

$$(5) \quad \frac{\partial u}{\partial x_t} + \lambda \frac{\partial f}{\partial x_t} = 0.$$

This is our first major result and constitutes about half of the maximum principle. It makes perfectly good sense to an economist. It says that along the optimal path of the decision variable at any time the marginal short-run effect of a change in decision must just counter-balance the effect of that decision on the total value of the capital stock an instant later. We see that because the second term in the equation is the marginal effect of the current decision on the rate of growth of capital with capital valued at its marginal worth, λ. The firm should choose x at every moment so that the marginal immediate gain just equals the marginal long-run cost, which is measured by the value of capital multiplied by the effect of the decision on the accumulation of capital.

Now suppose that x_t is determined so as to satisfy equation (5). On the assumption that this procedure discovers the optimal value of x_t, $V(k_t, x_t, t)$ will then be equal to its maximum possible value or $V^*(k, t)$. Thus

$$V^*(k, t) = u(k, x_t, t)\Delta + V^*(k(t+\Delta), t+\Delta).$$

Now differentiate this expression with respect to k. The derivative of the left-hand side is by definition $\lambda(t)$. The differentiation of the right-hand side is very similar to the work that we have already done and goes as follows:

$$\lambda(t) = \Delta\frac{\partial u}{\partial k} + \frac{\partial}{\partial k}V^*(k(t+\Delta), t+\Delta)$$

$$= \Delta\frac{\partial u}{\partial k} + \frac{\partial k(t+\Delta)}{\partial k}\lambda(t+\Delta)$$

$$= \Delta\frac{\partial u}{\partial k} + \left(1 + \Delta\frac{\partial f}{\partial k}\right)(\lambda + \lambda\Delta)$$

$$= \Delta\frac{\partial u}{\partial k} + \lambda + \Delta\lambda\frac{\partial f}{\partial k} + \Delta\lambda + \lambda\frac{\partial f}{\partial k}\Delta^2.$$

We can ignore the term in Δ^2 and make the obvious cancellations to obtain

$$(6) \qquad -\lambda = \frac{\partial u}{\partial k} + \lambda\frac{\partial f}{\partial k}.$$

This is the second major formula of the maximum principle and possesses an illuminating economic interpretation.

To a mathematician, λ is the rate at which the value of a unit of capital is changing. To an economist, it is the rate at which the capital is appreciating. $-\lambda(t)$ is therefore the rate at which a unit of capital depreciates at time t. Accordingly the formula asserts that when the optimal time path of capital accumulation is followed, the decrease in value of a unit of capital in a short interval of time is the sum of its contribution to the profits realized during the interval and its contribution to enhancing the value of the capital stock at the end of the interval. In other words, a unit of capital loses value or depreciates as time passes at the rate at which its potential contribution to profits becomes its past contribution.

This finding is reminiscent of the figure of speech employed by the nineteenth century capital theorists. They said that a capital good embodied a certain amount of value which it imparted gradually to the commodities that were made with its assistance. That is just what is going on here. Each unit of the capital good is gradually decreasing in value at precisely the same rate at which it is giving rise to valuable outputs, either currently saleable or stored for the future in accumulated capital. We can also interpret $-\lambda$ as the loss that would be incurred if the acquisition of a unit of capital were postponed for a short time.

II. *The Maximum Principle*

In effect we have been led to construct the auxiliary or Hamiltonian function

$$H = u(k, x, t) + \lambda(t)f(k, x, t),$$

to compute its partial derivative with respect to x, and to set that partial derivative equal to zero. This construction has substantial economic significance. If we imagine H to be multiplied by Δ, we can see that it is the sum of the total profits earned in the interval Δ plus the accrual of capital during the interval valued at its marginal value. $H\Delta$ is thus the total contribution of the activities that go on during the interval Δ, including both its direct contribution to the integral W, and the value of the capital accumulated during the interval. Naturally, then, the decision variable x during the current interval should be chosen so as to make H as great as possible. It is for this reason that the procedure we are describing is called the maximum principle. A simple and frequently effective way to do this is to choose a value of the control variable for which the partial derivative vanishes, as we have done.

We have also, in effect, computed the partial derivative of H with respect to k and equated that partial derivative to $-\lambda$. The common sense of this operation can be seen best from a modified Hamiltonian,

$$H^* = u(k, x, t) + \frac{d}{dt}\lambda k$$

$$= u(k, x, t) + \lambda \dot{k} + \dot{\lambda}k.$$

$H^*\Delta$ is the sum of the profits realized during an interval of length Δ and the increase in the value of the capital stock during the interval, or in a sense, the value of the total contribution of activities during the interval to current and future profits.[7] If we maximize H^* formally with respect to x and k we obtain:

$$\frac{\partial u}{\partial x} + \lambda \frac{\partial f}{\partial x} = 0,$$

$$\frac{\partial u}{\partial k} + \lambda \frac{\partial f}{\partial k} + \dot{\lambda} = 0,$$

---

[7] H^* differs from H by including capital gains.

which are equations (5) and (6).

Of course, the firm cannot maximize H^* with respect to k since k is not a variable subject to choice. But we now see that equations (5) and (6) advise the firm to choose the time-paths of x and λ so that the resultant values of k are the ones it would choose, if it could do so, to make the sum of profits and increment in capital value as great as possible in every short time interval.

As a technical note, in differentiating H, the marginal value λ is not regarded as a function of x and k, but as a separate time path which is to be determined optimally.

Now we have before us the basic ideas of the maximum principle. There is naturally much more to the method than these two formulas. A good deal of mathematical elaboration is required before the two formulas can be implemented, and we shall indicate later some of the complications that can arise. But there is one additional feature that has to be mentioned before we have finished dealing with fundamentals. This concerns the boundary conditions; for example, the amount of capital available at the beginning of the planning period and the amount required to be on hand on the terminal date.

To see how these boundary data affect the solution to the problem, consider how the three basic formulas operate. They are:

(I) $\dot{k} = f(k, x, t)$

(II) $\dfrac{\partial u}{\partial x} + \lambda \dfrac{\partial f}{\partial x} = 0$

(III) $\dfrac{\partial u}{\partial k} + \lambda \dfrac{\partial f}{\partial k} = -\dot{\lambda}.$

The first of these is part of the data of the problem. It specifies how capital grows at any instant as a result of its current standing and the choices made. The other two formulas are the main results of the maximization principle. Formula II says that the choice variable at every instant should be selected so that the marginal immediate gains are in balance with the value of the marginal contribution to the accumulation of capital. Formula III says that capital depreciates at the same rate that it contributes to useful output.

The three formulas are conveniently written and remembered in terms of the Hamiltonian. In this form they are:

$$\text{(I')} \qquad \frac{\partial H}{\partial \lambda} = \dot{k}$$

$$\text{(II')} \qquad \frac{\partial H}{\partial x} = 0$$

$$\text{(III')} \qquad \frac{\partial H}{\partial k} = -\lambda.$$

Notice the reciprocal roles played by k and λ in these equations. The partial derivative of H with respect to either is simply related to the time-derivative of the other.

These three formulas jointly determine completely the time paths of the choice variable, the capital stock, and the value of capital. We shall start at time zero with a certain capital stock and a certain initial value for capital. Now look at formula II written out a bit more explicitly:

$$\text{(II)} \quad \frac{\partial}{\partial x} u(k, x, t) + \lambda(t) \frac{\partial}{\partial x} f(k, x, t) = 0.$$

With k and λ known, this formula determines the value of x, the choice variable.[8] Putting this value in formula I we obtain $\dot{k}$, the rate at which the capital stock is changing. Putting it in formula III we similarly obtain λ the rate at which the value of a unit of capital is changing. Thus we know the capital stock and the value of a unit of capital a short time later. Using these new values, we can repeat our sub-

stitutions in the three formulas and so find, in order, a new value of the choice variable, a new rate for the change in the capital stock and a new rate for the change in the value of capital. Repeating this cycle over and over again, we can trace through the evolution of all the variables from time zero to time T.

In short, these three formulas working together determine the optimal paths of all the variables starting out from any given initial position. In another sense, then, the problem of the choice of an optimal path has been reduced to a much simpler problem, the problem of choosing an optimal initial value for the value of a unit of capital. This is not by any means an easy problem, but it is obviously a great deal easier than finding an entire optimal path without the aid of these formulas.

III. *The Boundary Conditions*

We can now mention the role of boundary conditions. They are of two sorts. Initial conditions describe the state of the firm or economy at the initial date, t = 0. In particular, they set forth the initial stock of capital. Terminal conditions prescribe the values of some, or all, of the variables at the terminal date, t = T. For example, the problem may require that the firm have at least some specified stock of capital, say $\overline{K}$ on hand at the terminal date, which can be imposed by including $k(T) \geq \overline{K}$ in the conditions of the problem. Or, again, if the problem is strictly one of maximizing profits during a finite interval, 0 to T, it is clear that capital on hand at date T cannot contribute to that objective; it exists too late to be of service before date T. Such a problem gives rise to the terminal condition $\lambda(T) = 0$.

Now we have seen that the three equations (I), (II), (III) jointly determine the entire evolution of x, k, and λ once the starting values have been prescribed. In particular they determine the terminal

---

[8] Some mathematical complications arise here. We assume that with k, λ, and t given, formula (II) is satisfied by a unique value of x.

values. We have only[9] to determine a set of starting values that leads to acceptable terminal values to find an entire time path that satifies the necessary conditions for being optimal. In our example, since the initial capital stock is given, the critical initial value to be determined is $\lambda(0)$, the marginal value of capital at the initial date. The three basic formulas, abstract though they may appear, in fact constitute a constructive solution to the problem of choosing an optimal time path. They are a solution, in principle, of the problem of optimal capital accumulation.

We have now found that the old-fashioned technique of equating margins, used with a little ingenuity, leads to the maximum principle, which is the fundamental theorem of optimal control theory.

IV. *An Example*

About the simplest known example of the application of these principles to an economic problem is the derivation of the socially optimal path of capital accumulation for a one-sector economy with an exponentially growing population and production under constant returns to scale.[10]

Let us set forth some notation and data. $N(t)$ is population at date t. Since population grows exponentially, at rate n, say,

$$N(t) = N(0)e^{nt}.$$

It will save clutter if we assume $N(0) = 1$ (measured in hundreds of millions of people). Denote per capita consumption by c and the utility enjoyed by a person consuming at rate c by $u(c)$. The total utility enjoyed by all the persons alive at time t with per capita consumption at rate c is

$$e^{nt}u(c).$$

Let ρ be the social rate of time preference.

Then the importance at time 0 of the consumption achieved at time t is

$$(7) \qquad e^{-\rho t}e^{nt}u(c) = e^{(n-\rho)t}u(c).$$

A defensible social objective for a society with time horizon T (conceivably infinite) is to maximize

$$(8) \qquad W = \int_0^T e^{(n-\rho)t}u(c)\,dt,$$

or the sum of the utilities enjoyed between 0 and T.[11]

Consumption is limited by output and output by capital stock. Let $K(t)$ denote the capital stock at date t and let $k(t) = K(t)/N(t)$ denote capital per capita. By virtue of constant returns to scale, we can write the production function of the economy as

$$Y(t) = N(t)f(k(t))$$

or, omitting the confusing time-arguments,

$$Y = Nf(k) = e^{nt}f(k).$$

Gross investment equals output minus consumption, or $Y-Nc$. Net investment equals gross investment minus physical depreciation. Suppose that physical capital deteriorates at the rate δ per unit per annum so that the total rate of decay of the physical stock, when it is K, is δK. Then net capital accumulation is

$$\dot{K} = Y - Nc - \delta K = N(f(k) - c) - \delta K$$
$$= N(f(k) - c) - \delta Nk$$
$$= N(f(k) - c - \delta k).$$

Finally, eliminate $\dot{K}$ by noticing:

$$\dot{k} = \frac{d}{dt}\frac{K}{N} = \frac{K}{N}\left(\frac{\dot{K}}{K} - \frac{\dot{N}}{N}\right)$$

$$(9) \qquad = k\left(\frac{\dot{K}}{Nk} - n\right)$$

$$= f(k) - c - \delta k - nk$$

$$= f(k) - c - (n + \delta)k.$$

---

[9] Only! Reputations have been made by solving this problem in important instances.

[10] A more extended discussion of a very similar model can be found in Arrow [1].

[11] It is best to assume $\rho > n$ or else the integral will be infinite for $T = \infty$.

Equations (8) and (9) constitute our simple example. Equation (9) is an example of equation (I). To derive equation (II), differentiate equations (7) and (9) with respect to the choice variable, c:

$$\frac{\partial}{\partial c} e^{(n-\rho)t}u(c) = e^{(n-\rho)t}u'(c),$$

$$\frac{\partial}{\partial c} [f(k) - c - (n + \delta)k] = -1.$$

Hence equation (II) is:

(10) $e^{(n-\rho)t}u'(c) - \lambda = 0,$

or the value of a unit of capital at time t is the marginal utility of consumption at that time, adjusted for population growth and the social rate of time preference.

Equation (III) is obtained similarly by differentiating equations (7) and (9) with respect to k. There results:

$$-\dot\lambda = 0 + \lambda[f'(k) - (n + \delta)],$$

or

(11) $f'(k) = n + \delta - \dfrac{\dot\lambda}{\lambda}.$

Equation (10) can be used to eliminate the unfamiliar λ. Differentiating it with respect to time:

$$\frac{\dot\lambda}{\lambda} = n - \rho + \frac{u''(c)}{u'(c)} \frac{dc}{dt}.$$

Thus equation (11) becomes

$$f'(k) = \rho + \delta - \frac{u''(c)}{u'(c)} \frac{dc}{dt}.$$

This is our final equation for the optimal path of capital accumulation. It asserts that along such a path the rate of consumption at each moment must be chosen so that the marginal productivity of capital is the sum of three components:

(1) ρ, the social rate of time preference,
(2) δ, the rate of physical deterioration of capital, and

(3) the rather formidable looking third term which, however, is simply the percentage rate at which the psychic cost of saving diminishes through time. This can be seen by noting that the psychic cost of saving at any time is $u'(c)$, its time rate of change is $u''(c)dc/dt$, and its percentage time rate of change is the negative of the third term in the sum.

In other words, along the optimum path of accumulation the marginal contribution of a unit of capital to output during any short interval of time must be just sufficient to cover the three components of the social cost of possessing that unit of capital, namely, the social rate of time-preference, the rate of physical deterioration of capital, and the additional psychic cost of saving a unit at the beginning of the interval rather than at the end. All of these are expressed as percents per unit of time, which is also the dimension of the marginal productivity of capital.

The evolution of this economy along its optimal path of development can be visualized most readily by drawing a phase diagram as shown in Figure 1. We have found that the rates of change of k and c can be written:

(9) $\dot k = f(k) - (n + \delta)k - c,$

$$\dot c = \frac{u'(c)}{u''(c)} [\rho + \delta - f'(k)].$$

Thus $\dot k = 0$ whenever c and k satisfy the equation

$$c = f(k) - (n + \delta)k.$$

In Figure 1, k is plotted horizontally and c vertically. The curve labelled $\dot k = 0$ shows the combinations of c and k that satisfy this equation. It has the shape drawn because of the conventional assumptions that the marginal productivity of capital is positive but diminishing (i.e., $f'(k) > 0$,

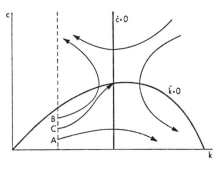

FIGURE 1

$f''(k) < 0)$, and the very plausible assumption that for very low levels of capital per worker, $f'(k) > n + \delta$. We also assume that no output is possible without some capital, i.e., $f(0) = 0$. If consumption per capita is less than the rate on the locus just described, capital per capita increases $(\dot{k} > 0)$. Above the locus $\dot{k} < 0$.

Similarly, consumption per capita is unchanging $(\dot{c} = 0)$ if

$$f'(k) = \rho + \delta.$$

The vertical line in Figure 1, labelled $\dot{c} = 0$, is drawn at this level of k. If we accept the usual assumptions of positive but diminishing marginal utility $u'(c) > 0$, $u''(c) < 0$. Then $\dot{c} > 0$, i.e., per capita consumption grows, to the left of this line. The reason is that with low levels of capital per capita the amount of depreciation is small and the amount of capital needed to equip the increment in population with the current level of capital per capita is also small.

These considerations enable us to depict qualitatively the laws of motion of the system. Imagine an initial low level of capital per capita, represented by the dashed vertical in the diagram. The entire evolution of the system is determined by the choice of the initial level of per capita consumption. If a low initial level is chosen, such as at point A in the figure, both consumption and capital per capita

will increase for some time, following the curved arrow that emanates from point A. But when the level of capital per capita reaches the critical level, consumption per capita will start to fall though capital per capita will continue to increase. This is a policy of initial generosity in consumption followed by increasing abstemiousness intended, presumably, to attain some desired ultimate level of capital per capita.

Similarly, the path emanating from point B represents a policy of continually increasing consumption per capita, with capital initially being accumulated and eventually being consumed. The other paths drawn have similar interpretations.

The path originating at point C is of particular interest. It leads to the intersection of the two critical loci, the steady state of the system in which neither per capita consumption nor per capita income changes. Once at this point all the absolute values grow exponentially at the common rate n.

It is now seen that if the initial capital per capita is given, the entire course of the economy is determined by the choice of the initial level of per capita consumption. This choice determines, among other things, the amount of capital per capita at any specified date.[12] If the conditions of the problem prescribe a particular amount of capital at some date, the initial c must be the one with a path that leads to the specified point. If there is no such prescription for capital accumulation, the initial c will be the one that causes the capital stock to be exhausted at the terminal date under consideration. And if there is no terminal date (i.e., $T = \infty$) the problem becomes much trickier mathematically and, indeed, the theory of optimization with an infinite time horizon is not yet completely established. But, in this simple case, we can see that the only

[12] The position of the economy at particular dates cannot be read off the phase diagram.

possible solution is the path that originates at point C and terminates at the point where $\dot{c} = \dot{k} = 0$. For, the figure shows that all other paths that satisfy the optimizing conditions lead eventually to situations in which either c or k is negative. Since such paths cannot be realized, the only feasible optimizing path is the one that approaches $\dot{c} = \dot{k} = 0$.

This result is quite characteristic of infinite horizon problems: the optimal growth paths, under many conditions, approach the situation in which consumption and the capital stock grow exponentially at a rate determined by the rate of population growth and the rate of technical progress (here assumed zero), just as in this case.

For finite horizon problems, it can be shown that the more remote the terminal date considered, the closer the path will come to the steady state position $(\dot{c} = \dot{k} = 0)$ before veering away to either high consumption or high capital accumulation as the case may be. This is a version of the turnpike theorem.

V. *Derivation via Finite Maximizing*

Those who distrust clever, intuitive arguments, as I do, may find some comfort in seeing the same results deduced from the more familiar method of maximizing subject to a finite number of constraints. Let us suppose that the entire period of T months is divided into n subperiods of m months each. $u(x_t, k_t, t)$ then denotes the rate at which profits are being earned or other benefits derived during the t-th subperiod, with x_t being the value of the decision variable during that subperiod, and k_t the value of the state variable at its beginning. Since the subperiod is m months long, the total profit earned is $u(x_t, k_t, t)\, m$.

The rate of change of the state variable during the t-th subperiod is $f(x_t, k_t, t)$. Then the values of the state variable at the beginnings of successive subperiods are

connected by the equation

$$(12) \qquad k_{t+1} = k_t + f(x_t, k_t, t)m.$$

Finally, the finite version of our problem is to choose $2n$ values, x_t, k_t so as to maximize the total profit over the entire period,

$$\sum_{t=1}^{n} u(x_t, k_t, t)m$$

subject to the n constraints (12), and to any boundary conditions that may apply. To be specific, suppose that initial and terminal values for the state variable are preassigned. These give rise to the side conditions

$$k_1 = K_0$$
$$k_{n+1} = K_T.$$

This problem is solved by setting up the Lagrangean function

$$L = \sum_{t=1}^{n} u(x_t, k_t, t)m$$
$$+ \sum_{1}^{n} \lambda_t[k_t + f(x_t, k_t, t)m - k_{t+1}]$$
$$+ \lambda_0[K_0 - k_1] + \mu[k_{n+1} - K_T]$$

and setting each of its partial derivatives equal to zero. The Greek symbols in this formula are the Lagrange multipliers, one for each constraint. We shall interpret them after we have completed our calculations.

The same Hamiltonian expression that we encountered before is beginning to emerge, so it is convenient to write

$$H(x_t, k_t, t) = u(x_t, k_t, t) + \lambda_t f(x_t, k_t, t)$$

and

$$L = m \sum_{1}^{n} H(x_t, k_t, t) + \sum_{1}^{n} \lambda_t(k_t - k_{t+1})$$
$$+ \lambda_0(K_0 - k_1) + \mu(k_{n+1} - K_T).$$

Now differentiate and equate derivatives to zero:

$$\frac{\partial L}{\partial x_t} = m \frac{\partial}{\partial x_t} H(x_t, k_t, t)$$

(13)
$$= [u_1(x_t, k_t, t) + \lambda_t f_1(x_t, k_t, t)]m = 0$$

$$\text{for } t = 1, \ldots, n,$$

which is analogous to equation (5). And

$$\frac{\partial L}{\partial k_t} = m \frac{\partial}{\partial k_t} H(x_t, k_t, t) + \lambda_t - \lambda_{t-1} = 0$$

or

(14)
$$-\frac{\lambda_t - \lambda_{t-1}}{m} = u_2(x_t, k_t, t)$$

$$+ \lambda_t f_2(x_t, k_t, t), \text{ for } t = 1, \ldots, n,$$

which is the discrete analog of equation (6).

Finally

$$\frac{\partial L}{\partial k_{n+1}} = -\lambda_n + \mu = 0.$$

Thus $\mu = \lambda_n$ and can be forgotten.

These equations are applicable to problems in which time is regarded as a discrete variable. The Lagrange multipliers have their usual interpretation. In particular, λ_t is the amount by which the maximum attainable value of $\sum u(x_t, k_t, t)m$ would be increased if an additional unit of capital were to become available by magic at the end of the t-th period. In other words, λ_t is the marginal value of capital on hand at date mt.

The maximizing conditions found previously should be the limit of these equations as m approaches zero and n approaches infinity, and they are. To show this, we have to revise our notation slightly. The subscripted variables now denote the values that the variables have in the t-th period. When m changes, the dates included in the t-th period change also. So we need symbols for the values of the variables at fixed dates. To this end, let τ denote any date and $x(\tau)$, for example, the

value of x at that date. The connection between x_t and $x(\tau)$ is easy. Any date τ is in the subperiod numbered t where t is given by

$$t = 1 + [\tau/m].$$

In this formula, [ ] is an old-fashioned notation meaning "integral part of." For example: $[3.14159] = 3$. Then $x(\tau)$ is defined by

$$x(\tau) = x_{1+[\tau/m]},$$

and similarly for the other variables. Equations (13) and (14) can now be written in terms of τ:

(15)
$$u_1[x(\tau), k(\tau), \tau]$$
$$+ \lambda(\tau)f_1[x(\tau), k(\tau), \tau] = 0,$$

(16)
$$-\frac{\lambda(\tau) - \lambda(\tau-m)}{m} = u_2[x(\tau), k(\tau), \tau]$$
$$+ \lambda(\tau)f_2[x(\tau), k(\tau), \tau].$$

Notice in equation (16) that λ_{t-1} has been replaced by $\lambda(\tau-m)$, reflecting that the beginnings of the intervals are m months apart.

Equation (15) is identical with equation (II). As m approaches zero, the left-hand side of equation (16) approaches $-\lambda(\tau)$, taking for granted that it approaches a limit and applying the definition of the derivative. The whole equation, therefore, approaches equation (III). Equation (I) is similarly and obviously the limiting form of equation (12).

Thus the basic equations of the maximum principle are seen to be the limiting forms of the ordinary first-order necessary conditions for a maximum applied to the same problem, and the auxiliary variables of the maximum principle are the limiting values of the Lagrange multipliers.

VI. *Qualifications and Extensions*

This entire development has been exceedingly informal, to put it kindly. The calculus of variations is a difficult and delicate subject, so that a choice always has to be made between stating a proposition correctly, with all the qualifications that it deserves, and stating it forceably and clearly so that the essential idea can be grasped at a glance. The more intelligible alternative has been chosen throughout this paper since all the theorems have been stated and proved rigorously elsewhere in the literature.[13] This choice, as it happens, has especial drawbacks in the present context because much of the virtue of the maximum principle lies precisely in the qualifications that have been suppressed: it is valid under more general conditions than the classical methods that yield almost the same theorems.

As an example of the alternative mode of exposition, our main conclusions can be stated more formally and correctly as follows:[14]

THEOREM 1. Let it be desired to find a time-path of a control variable $x(t)$ so as to maximize the integral

$$\int_0^T u[k(t), x(t), t]dt$$

where

$$\frac{dk}{dt} = f[k(t), x(t), t],$$

where $k(0)$ is preassigned, and where it is required that $k(T) \geq \overline{K}$. It is assumed that the functions $u(k, x, t)$ and $f(k, x, t)$ are twice continuously differentiable with respect to k, differentiable with respect to x, and continuous with respect to t. Then if $x^*(t)$ is a solution to this problem, there exists an auxiliary variable $\lambda(t)$ such that:

(a) For each t, $x^*(t)$ maximizes $H[k(t), x(t), \lambda(t), t]$ where $H(k, x, \lambda, t) = u(k, x, t) + \lambda f(k, x, t)$;

[13] For example, in Arrow and Kurz [3] and Halkin [5].
[14] The given theorem is adapted from Arrow [2], Propositions 1 and 2. More elaborate theorems can be found in that source.

(b) $\lambda(t)$ satisfies

$$\frac{d\lambda}{dt} = -\frac{\partial H}{\partial x}$$

evaluated at $k = k(t)$, $x = x^*(t)$, $\lambda = \lambda(t)$; and

(c) $k(T) \geq \overline{K}$, $\lambda(T) \geq 0$, $\lambda(t)[k(T) - \overline{K}] = 0$.

This theorem applies to the type of problem that we have been considering, with the useful elaboration that a lower limit has been imposed on the terminal value of the state variable, k. Part (c) of the conclusion, called the transversality condition, arises from this added requirement. It asserts that the terminal value of the auxiliary variable cannot be negative and that it will be zero if, at the end of the optimal path, $k(T)$ exceeds the required value.

The principle difference between this formal statement and our previous conclusions lies in conclusion (a) of the Theorem. The assertion that the Hamiltonian function, H, is maximized at each instant of time is not the same as the assertion that its partial derivatives vanish, made in our equations (II) and (II'). Equating partial derivatives to zero is neither necessary nor sufficient for maximization, though it is especially illuminating to economists, when it is appropriate, because conditions on partial derivatives translate readily into marginal equalities. There are three complications that can make the vanishing of partial derivatives an inadequate indication of the location of a maximum.

First, there are the so-called higher order conditions. First partial derivatives can vanish at a minimum or at a saddle-point as well as at a maximum. To guard against this possibility, second partial derivatives, and even higher ones, have to be taken into account.

Second, the vanishing of partial derivatives, even when higher order conditions are satisfied, establishes only a local maximum. It does not preclude that there may be some other value of the variables, a finite distance away, for which the function to be maximized has a still higher value. For reassurance on this point, one must inspect global rather than merely differential or local properties of the functions involved.

Finally, where the range of variation of the functions involved is limited in some manner, the maximum may be attained at a point where the partial derivatives do not vanish. This is a frequent occurence in economic applications, made familiar by linear programming. For example, it may be optimal for a firm with great growth possibilities to reduce its dividends to zero, though negative dividends are not permissible. In terms of our formulas this would be indicated by finding

$$\partial H/\partial x_t < 0 \quad \text{for all } x_t \geq 0,$$

where x_t denotes dividend payments per year at time t. H would be maximized by choosing $x_t = 0$, its smallest permissible value, although the partial derivative does not vanish there.[15] This maximum could not be found by the ordinary methods of the calculus. Other methods are available, of course, for example those of mathematical programming. It is in just these circumstances that the maximum principle yields more elegant and manageable theorems than the older calculus of variations, which is more closely akin to the differential calculus.

For all these reasons, the fundamental condition for an optimal growth path is the maximization of $H(k, x, \lambda, t)$ at all moments of time, and the vanishing of $\partial H/\partial x$ is only an imperfectly reliable device for locating this maximum. It is, however, a very illuminating device and contains the conceptual essence of the matter, which is why we have concentrated on it.

[15] Technically this is called a "corner solution."

Throughout the discussion we have tried to be ambiguous about the exact nature of the time paths, $x(t)$ and $k(t)$. We have treated x and k as if they were one-dimensional variables, such as the quantity of capital or the rate of consumption. In many economic problems, however, there are several state variables and several choice variables. In such problems, it is profitable to think of $x(t)$, $k(t)$, their derivatives, and so on, as vectors. Then $\lambda(t)$ should also be regarded as a vector, with one component for each component of $k(t)$. When this viewpoint is taken, all our conclusions and the theorem still apply with scarcely a change in notation. That is why we were so ambiguous: it is easiest to think about ordinary numbers, but our conclusions and even most of our arguments are applicable when the variables are vectors.

The last remark raises some important new possibilities. Many economic problems concern the time paths of interconnected variables. For example, a problem may deal with the growth paths of consumption (c), investment (i), government expenditure (g), and income (y) in an economy. These four variables can be regarded as four components of a decision vector, x, connected by an income accounting identity $c(t) + i(t) + g(t) = y(t)$. Then the optimizing growth-path problem requires finding optimal growth paths for these four variables (and perhaps others) that satisfy the income accounting identity.

The new feature that we have encountered is the introduction of constraints or side conditions on the values of the decision variables. The same line of reasoning that we have been using applies, with the sole modification that when the function $V(k, x_t, t)$ is maximized, the vector x_t has to be chosen so as to satisfy all the side constraints. The algebra becomes somewhat more complicated but leads to conclusions like those discussed above and with the same economic import. In 1968, Kenneth Arrow derived a lucid version of the formal statement of the theorem applicable to problems in which the decision variables are constrained. See [2, Proposition 3, p. 90]. Of course, this argument, too, presumes that circumstances are such that the proper partial derivatives vanish at the maximum.

REFERENCES

[1] K. J. ARROW, "Discounting and Public Investment Criteria," in A. V. Kneese and S. C. Smith, eds., *Water Research*, Washington 1966, pp. 13–32.

[2] ———, "Applications of Control Theory to Economic Growth," American Mathematical Society, *Mathematics of the Decision Sciences, Part 2.* Providence 1968, pp. 85–119.

[3] ———, AND M. KURZ, *Public Investment, the Rate of Return, and Optimal Fiscal Policy.* Stanford University Institute for Mathematical Studies in the Social Sciences, 1968.

[4] R. BELLMAN, *Dynamic Programming.* Princeton 1957.

[5] H. HALKIN, "On the Necessary Condition for Optimal Control of Nonlinear Systems," *Journal D'Analyse Mathématique*, 1964, *12*, 1–82.

[6] H. HOTELLING, "A General Mathematical Theory of Depreciation," *J. Amer. Statist. Ass.*, Sept. 1925, *20*, 340–53.

[7] L. S. PONTRYAGIN, V. G. BOLTYANSKII, R. V. GAMKRELIDZE, AND E. F. MISHCHENKO, *The Mathematical Theory of Optimal Processes*, (tr. by K. N. Trirogoff). New York 1962.

[8] F. P. RAMSEY, "A Mathematical Theory of Saving," *Econ. J.* Dec. 1942, *38*, 543–59.

[8] J. ROBINSON, *The Accumulation of Capital.* Homewood, 1956.

PART THREE

ECONOMIC THEORY

[7]

OPTIMAL ADVERTISING AND OPTIMAL QUALITY

By Robert Dorfman and Peter O. Steiner*

Lawrence Abbott discussed some of the principles of quality competition in a recent issue of this *Review*.[1] Most of the conclusions obtained by Abbott and a number of other results of some interest can be derived more easily by approaching the problem of differentiated competition from a broader point of view than Abbott's, using rather simple analytic tools. We demonstrate the technique which we have in mind, along with some results of intrinsic interest, by applying the technique to a few problems including Abbott's.

1. *Joint Optimization of Advertising Budget and Price*

Theorem: A firm which can influence the demand for its product by advertising will, in order to maximize its profits, choose the advertising budget and price such that the increase in gross revenue resulting from a one dollar increase in advertising expenditure is equal to the ordinary elasticity of demand for the firm's product. The proof of this statement will be given immediately. As a clarifying preliminary we state that we mean by advertising any expenditure which influences the shape or position of a firm's demand curve and which enters the firm's cost function as a fixed cost, *i.e.*, a cost which does not vary with the quantity of output. This concept corresponds generally, but not exactly, to the usual concept of advertising. It includes expenditures on billboards, newspaper space, radio time, interior decoration of a place of business, air conditioning of sales space, etc. And now, the proof.

We consider a firm which makes two kinds of choice: the price of its product and the amount of its advertising budget. Assuming this to be so, the relationship between the quantity the firm can sell per unit of time, q, its price, p, and its advertising budget, s, can be denoted by the formula

$$q = f(p, s). \tag{1}$$

We assume that $f(p, s)$ is continuous and differentiable.

In order to determine the optimal price-quantity-advertising con-

---

* The authors are associate professor and assistant professor of economics, respectively, at the University of California, Berkeley.

[1] Lawrence Abbott, "Vertical Equilibrium under Pure Quality Competition," *Am. Econ. Rev.*, Dec. 1953, XLIII, 826–45.

Reprinted from THE AMERICAN ECONOMIC REVIEW, Vol. XLIV, No. 5, December, 1954
Copyright, 1954, American Economic Association · All rights reserved

stellation it is convenient for expository reasons to analyze the situation in two steps. In the first step we regard the quantity of output as fixed and specify the optimal price-advertising constellation for selling that predetermined quantity. Then we let quantity vary and seek its optimum. The advantage of this procedure is that cost considerations, other than the cost of advertising, do not enter the first step.[2]

Suppose, then, that price be changed by a small amount, dp, and advertising expenditure by a small amount, ds. The change in the level of sales will be the total differential of equation (1) or:

$$dq = \frac{\partial f}{\partial p}\,dp + \frac{\partial f}{\partial s}\,ds.$$

In order for quantity not to change as a result of these variations, dp and ds must be chosen in such a way that they have equal and opposite effects on quantity; so that $dq=0$. That is,

$$dp = -\frac{\dfrac{\partial f}{\partial s}}{\dfrac{\partial f}{\partial p}}\,ds,\ \text{assuming}\ \frac{\partial s}{\partial p} \neq 0. \tag{2}$$

The result of these variations is to change gross revenue by the amount qdp, change advertising expenditure by ds, and leave the volume of sales and aggregate production cost unchanged. The net effect on profit is, therefore:

$$qdp - ds = -\left(q\,\frac{\dfrac{\partial f}{\partial s}}{\dfrac{\partial f}{\partial p}} + 1\right)ds. \tag{3}$$

Now we must consider two cases: first, where the original level of advertising from which the variations were measured was positive, and second, where the original level of advertising was zero. We now show that a positive level of advertising cannot be optimal unless the quantity in parentheses in equation (3) is zero. For, if that quantity were positive we could choose a negative value for ds (signifying a decrease in advertising) which would have the effect of making the whole expression positive. It would therefore indicate that a decrease in advertising and a compensating decrease in price (as specified in equa-

---

[2] This two-stage mode of analysis has, of course, no effect on the result. It is unnecessary from a purely mathematical point of view, since we could handle this as a problem in the maximization of a function of several independent variables. The procedure adopted makes the problem amenable to more elementary methods.

tion [2]) would increase profit. Hence, the original level of advertising was too large to be optimal. Similarly if the parenthesis were negative, slight increases in both advertising expense and prices would serve to increase profits.

Analogous reasoning for the case where the original level of advertising was zero shows that profits could not be maximized if the quantity in parentheses were negative. Thus we have a *necessary* condition for profit maximization at any level of output (and therefore at all levels). It is:

$$q \, \dfrac{\dfrac{\partial f}{\partial s}}{\dfrac{\partial f}{\partial p}} + 1 \begin{cases} = 0 \text{ if } s > 0, \\ \geq 0 \text{ if } s = 0. \end{cases} \tag{4}$$

Let us now define the ordinary elasticity of demand, denoted by η, by

$$\eta = - \frac{p}{q} \frac{\partial f}{\partial p}$$

and the marginal value product of advertising, denoted by μ, by

$$\mu = p \frac{\partial f}{\partial s} .$$

This last concept is simply the rate of increase of gross receipts as advertising expenditure increases, price remaining constant. Substituting these concepts for the partial derivatives in equation (4) we find:

$$- q \, \frac{\dfrac{\mu}{p}}{\dfrac{q}{p} \eta} + 1 \begin{cases} = 0 \text{ if } s > 0, \\ \geq 0 \text{ if } s = 0. \end{cases}$$

or, cancelling the p's and q's, multiplying through by η, and transposing:

$$\begin{cases} \mu = \eta & \text{if } s > 0, \\ \mu \leq \eta & \text{if } s = 0. \end{cases} \tag{5}$$

This equation proves the theorem.

Furthermore, inequality of η and μ indicates the direction of change in price or advertising that will increase profits. If $\mu > \eta$, it will pay to increase advertising expenditure and price, as we saw in the discussion following equation (3). Inequality in the other direction leads to the reverse course of action in order to maximize profits.

Although the volume of sales, q, was assumed constant throughout this argument, the generality of the result is not restricted by this assumption. If a firm's position can be improved without changing its sales volume then, *a fortiori*, it can be improved if the possibility of changing sales volume is open to it. Therefore a condition which must be met if profit is to be maximized while holding volume constant must also be met if volume is permitted to change.

Figure 1 may help bring out the significance of this result. The figure consists of three parts, each representing a different conceivable situation. In each part the advertising budget, s, is measured horizontally. To each value of s there corresponds a certain price which maximizes

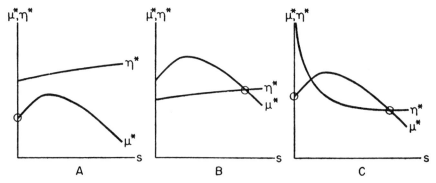

FIG. 1. OPTIMAL LEVELS OF ADVERTISING: ILLUSTRATIVE CASES.

profit regarding that advertising expenditure as given. To each such pair of advertising budget and optimal price there corresponds a certain elasticity of demand, which we denote by η^*, and a certain marginal value product of advertising, which we denote by μ^*. The three parts of Figure 1 show three possible ways in which η^* and μ^* may vary in response to changes in the advertising budget.

Our theorem shows that a nonzero level of advertising can maximize profits only if it corresponds to a crossing point of the η^* and μ^* curves. But not every crossing point, if there is more than one, is a profit maximizing point. Indeed, only points where μ^* crosses η^* from above correspond to profit maximization.[3] The circled points in the diagram indicate points of possible profit maximization.

What can be said about the shapes of the elasticity and revenue productivity functions portrayed? It seems plausible to assume that the effectiveness of advertising, indicated by the height of μ^*, increases initially but eventually shows decreasing returns. The effect of increased advertising expenditures on the elasticity of demand may work in either

---

[3] The proof is lengthy and, since it is fairly straightforward, it is omitted. It depends upon forming $\mu^* - \eta^*$ and finding its derivative in the neighborhood of crossing points.

direction,[4] and we offer no conjectures about it. In so far as the *existence* of an optimal level of advertising is concerned, the shape of the elasticity function is not critical. For if μ^* is ever greater than η^* (the necessary condition for advertising to pay at all), it must eventually cross it from above. This is because eventually μ^* will become less than unity, but η^* never will—by the classical arguments. In our illustrative figures we have arbitrarily drawn the elasticity curves as rising slightly in response to increases in advertising expenditures. It should be noted that changes in advertising budgets correspond to movements along these curves rather than to shifts of them.

A few market predictions follow at once from these considerations. In a perfectly competitive market the elasticity of demand for each firm's output is infinite. If we were to draw a diagram like Figure 1A for such a market, the η^* curve would be well above the top of the page. In this case the marginal value product of advertising is always less than the elasticity of demand and there will be no advertising.

At the other extreme are markets in which products are differentiated and in which product differences are important to consumers but are difficult for them to measure. Typically such markets offer a structure of prices for different brands. Either or both of two reasons conduce to relatively low elasticities of demand for the individual brands. First, there is a strong likelihood that the market structure will lead to retaliatory pricing if important changes in the structure of prices are attempted unilaterally. For this reason the relevant elasticity of demand may be approximated along a *mutatis mutandis* demand curve. Second, the price-brand preferences will reflect an uncertainty on the part of consumers which will make them reluctant to respond to changes in price differentials. To see this most clearly, imagine that consumers did know exactly what the differences between brands were worth to them. Then if any brand reduced its price it would immediately attract the "marginal" customers of other brands. Indeed we should have the case where the different brands were essentially competing commodities. But consumers' uncertainty blurs the sharp edge of preferences and replaces a cardinal ranking by something more like an ordinal one. The result is reduction in the effectiveness of changes in the price gaps between brands.

At the same time consumers' uncertainty has the effect of increasing the marginal effectiveness of advertising because consumers will not hold firmly to their appraisals of the relative merits of competing products. These circumstances are conducive to heavy advertising expenditure. Figure 1B would be typical of such a market.

----

[4] *Cf.* Neil H. Borden, *The Economic Effects of Advertising* (Chicago, 1947), esp. pp. 438, 850–51, 879.

A third important type of market occurs when product differentiation would not be important economically in the absence of advertising but when appropriate advertising can induce consumers to attach importance to the distinguishing characteristics of competing brands. Our previous conjecture concerning the effects of advertising on elasticity would not apply to this kind of market. Instead the elasticity of demand faced by any such firm would be infinite in the absence of advertising and would be decreased to finite levels by advertising. Figure 1C portrays the behavior of the curves in such a market. The perfectly competitive situation corresponding to zero or merely nominal levels of advertising would be transformed into the imperfectly competitive market corresponding to the circled intersection of the curves if aggregate profit were greater under the latter condition than under the former. Which of the two possible equilibrium situations is the more profitable will depend on the shape of the firm's cost curves and cannot be judged from this diagram alone.

In a monopolized industry as compared with an imperfectly competitive one both the effectiveness of advertising and the elasticity of the firm's demand curve are likely to be low. The appropriate level of advertising will depend very heavily on the special characteristics of the product, *e.g.*, necessity or luxury, major expenditure item or minor, closeness of substitutes, etc.

2. *Joint Optimization of Quality and Price*

In this section we find the optimal price-quality position for a firm which can influence its sales by modifying either the quality of its product or its price.

By quality we mean any aspect of a product, including the services included in the contract of sales, which influences the demand curve. The essential difference from advertising is that changes in quality enter into variable costs. Each conceivable quality will have a definite average cost curve, but there may be several different qualities with the same average cost curve. In this case we may assume that only that quality which has the most favorable demand curve will be given serious consideration. Thus we may assume that quality can be improved only at the expense of operating on a higher average cost curve. By quality improvement we mean any alteration in quality which shifts the demand curve to the right over the relevant range *and* raises the curve of average variable costs.

Now we can find the profit-maximizing conditions. Since the technique is parallel to that used in the preceding section we shall abbreviate the exposition. Consider a firm which produces a differentiated product whose quality can be measured (*e.g.*, in terms of horsepower, tensile strength, denier, etc.) and whose rate of sales per unit of time, q, is a continuous and differentiable function of price, p, and a quality index, x. We write as its demand function:

$$q = f(p, x)$$

The average cost of production, c, is a function of q and x:

$$c = c(q, x).$$

Just as in Section 1 we consider the effect on profit of arbitrary small changes in price and quality which have precisely offsetting effects on sales. This effect is expressed by the following equation, which is analogous to equation (3):

$$q dp - q dc = -q \left(\frac{\frac{\partial f}{\partial x}}{\frac{\partial f}{\partial p}} + \frac{\partial c}{\partial x} \right) dx.$$

By an argument similar to that following equation (3), the condition for profit maximizing equilibrium is found to be that the quantity in parentheses is zero, or:

$$-\frac{\partial f}{\partial p} = \frac{\frac{\partial f}{\partial x}}{\frac{\partial c}{\partial x}}.$$

This is the condition sought.

The left-hand side of this equation is the slope of the ordinary demand curve. The right-hand side measures essentially the rate at which sales increase in response to increases in average cost incurred in order to increase quality.[5] If the expression on the right-hand side of equation (6) is greater than that on the left, the indication is that an increase in quality will increase demand more than enough to compensate for the loss of sales that would result from an increase in price just sufficient to cover the increase in cost. Under such a circumstance quality should be increased.

Thus the general level of quality in any market depends on the relative magnitudes of two market characteristics and one technical characteristic of the product. Quality tends to be higher the greater the

---

[5] For example, if sales would increase by 100 units if the quality index were increased by one unit, and if this would raise average cost by $20, the right-hand side would be 5 units per dollar.

DORFMAN AND STEINER: OPTIMAL ADVERTISING AND QUALITY   833

sensitivity of consumers to quality variation (measured by $\partial f/\partial x$), the lower the sensitivity of consumers to price variation (measured by $\partial f/\partial p$), and the lower the effect on average costs of quality changes (measured by $\partial c/\partial x$). These are the three co-ordinate determinants of the general level of quality.

This analysis also suggests the conditions which conduce to quality variety in a market on the one hand and standardization on the other. If a market consists of a number of groups of consumers having identical demand curves but differing in their responsiveness to quality changes it will pay to provide different qualities at different prices. Similarly, if the groups are uniformly sensitive to quality changes but different in price consciousness (*i.e.*, if $\partial f/\partial x$ is the same for all groups, but $\partial f/\partial p$ differs among groups), there will be a range of qualities offered in order to exploit the differences in the demand curves. The analogy to discriminating monopoly is apparent. *A fortiori*, if, as frequently happens, those members of a market who have relatively high sensitivity to price changes have low sensitivity to quality and vice versa, then a spectrum of qualities will be offered. In all other cases, the commodity will tend to be standardized.

The optimizing condition of the quality variation case can be made more comparable to that for the price variation case by introducing the elasticity of demand with respect to quality variation, defined by the formula:

$$\eta_c = \frac{c}{q} \; \frac{\dfrac{\partial f}{\partial x}}{\dfrac{\partial c}{\partial x}}.$$

This formula gives simply the ratio of the percentage change in demand to the percentage change in average cost, both induced by a small change in quality. If we multiply both sides of equation (6) by p/q and then multiply the right-hand side by c/c, we obtain

$$-\frac{p}{q}\frac{\partial f}{\partial p} = \frac{p}{c}\frac{c}{q}\frac{\dfrac{\partial f}{\partial x}}{\dfrac{\partial c}{\partial x}}$$

which, recalling the definition of the ordinary elasticity of demand, is equivalent to:

$$\eta = \frac{p}{c}\,\eta_c. \tag{7}$$

3. *Joint Optimization of Advertising, Quality, and Price*

In Section 1 we discussed the equilibrium conditions for a firm which makes decisions with respect to both price and advertising expenditure; in Section 2 we dealt with a firm which makes decisions with respect to price and quality. The combined case, that of a firm which makes decisions of all three types, is probably of greater practical interest than either of these separated cases. This combined case presents no difficulties. We note that since advertising expenditure and quality can be varied independently a firm will not be in equilibrium unless it is in equilibrium with respect to each of these variables separately. Thus all of the preceding analyses apply and a firm will not be maximizing profits in the combined case unless its price, quality, and advertising expenditure are such that:

$$\mu = \eta = \frac{p}{c}\, \eta_c.$$

We here assume, of course, that advertising is at a positive level.

4. *Optimal Advertising with Fixed Prices*

Theorem: If the price which a firm can charge is predetermined by conventional, oligopolistic, legal or other considerations, and if the firm can influence its demand curve by advertising, it will, in order to maximize its profits, choose that advertising budget and the resulting rate of sales such that

$$\text{Marginal Cost} = p\left(1 - \frac{1}{\mu}\right).$$

The reader will notice that this formula is formally identical to the familiar relationship connecting price, marginal revenue, and elasticity where price is a variable of choice.

This is a simplified variant of the problem of Section 1. In order for an optimum to obtain, the advertising expenditure needed to increase sales by one unit must equal the profit on the marginal unit, *i.e.*, the excess of the given price over marginal production cost, MC. The equilibrium condition is then,

$$\frac{\partial s}{\partial q} = p - MC. \tag{8}$$

Since the marginal revenue product of advertising is

$$\mu = p\frac{\partial q}{\partial s},$$

equation (8) can be written

$$\frac{p}{\mu} = p - MC$$

which, after transposing and factoring out p proves our theorem.

By solving this formula for μ it can be seen that when advertising expenditure is optimized, the marginal revenue product of advertising equals the reciprocal of the mark-up on the marginal unit produced.

5. Optimal Quality with Fixed Prices

Theorem: If the price which a firm can charge is predetermined and if the firm can influence its demand curve by altering its product, it will, in order to maximize its profits, choose the quality such that the ratio of price to average cost multiplied by the elasticity of demand with respect to quality expenditure equals the reciprocal of the mark-up on the marginal unit. In symbols, the maximizing condition is

$$\frac{p}{c} \eta_c = \frac{p}{p - MC}.$$

This is Abbott's[6] problem and is a simplified variant of the problem discussed in Section 2. To solve it we notice that for profits to be maximized the marginal cost of production plus the total increase in quality cost necessary to sell one more unit at the given price must be equal to the given price. Furthermore, the average increase in quality cost necessary to sell one more unit at the going price is the increase in quality cost per unit increase in the quality index, divided by the increase in sales at the going price per unit increase in the quality index.[7] From these two considerations we have, at the optimal quality for the given price:

$$p = MC + q \frac{\dfrac{\partial c}{\partial x}}{\dfrac{\partial f}{\partial x}}. \tag{9}$$

Recalling the definition of elasticity with respect to expenditure on quality and inserting it, we obtain

$$p = MC + \frac{c}{\eta_c}$$

[6] Abbott, *op. cit.*

[7] To see this more clearly suppose that average cost will increase by $2 if the quality index is increased by one unit and that sales will increase by 10 units if the quality index is increased by one unit. Then a one unit increase in sales will result if quality is increased by 1/10 unit and this will raise average cost by $2/10=$.20.

from which our theorem follows by elementary algebra. It may be noted that equation (9) appears to be the result given by Abbott.[8] It clearly conforms to common sense. What it says is that if a small increase, say Δc, in average cost suffices to improve quality enough to increase sales by one unit at the going price, then the total increase in production costs will be $q\Delta c$ (to increase quality of all units) plus the marginal cost (to produce one more unit) and this must be just equal to marginal revenue (price, in this case) in profit-maximizing equilibrium.

In a zero-profit group equilibrium without advertising $p=c$ and equation (9) shows that for each firm average cost exceeds marginal cost. Thus the firms are operating in the decreasing range of their cost curves, a result also noted by Abbott.[9]

6. *Conclusion*

There are good grounds for doubting the economic significance of the whole business of writing down profit functions (or drawing curves) and finding points of zero partial derivatives (or graphical points of tangency). Such devices are merely aids to thinking about practical problems and it may be an uneconomical expenditure of effort to devote too much ingenuity to developing them. Yet such devices are aids to clear thought and, if sufficiently simple and flexible, they help us find implications, interrelationships, and sometimes contradictions which might escape notice without them. Such aids are particularly needed in the field of nonprice competition. We hope that the techniques suggested here will be of assistance in developing this field and bringing out its connections with the theory of price competition. The examples we have solved above are not only of importance in themselves but, we hope, demonstrate the flexibility and convenience of the technique which we suggest.

[8] Abbott, *op. cit.*, pp. 837–38.
[9] *Ibid.*, p. 844.

[8]

A Graphical Exposition of Böhm-Bawerk's Interest Theory[1]

This note will expound the mechanics of Böhm-Bawerk's theory of interest.[2] It is well-known that this theory depends on the idea of " the period of production." There is an extensive literature that suggests that this concept cannot be defined with any satisfactory degree of precision.[3] Nevertheless we can conceive of it intuitively as the average time that elapses between the instant when labor is expended and the instant when its fruits are available for consumption. This will serve for the purposes of this discussion. This period, measured in years, will be denoted by p.

A second fundamental notion in Böhm-Bawerk's scheme is that of capital itself. The formal definition is " produced means of production " but it is not very suggestive, in this approach, to think of capital as a stock of completed buildings, machinery, etc. Instead, capital is best conceived of as a stock of incomplete consumables, what accountants call " goods in process." Thus an electric generator is to be regarded as a stock of partly finished kilowatts. By taking this point of view we see that the stock of capital at the beginning of a year permits an economy to have a flow of consumables during the year that exceeds the yield of the labor devoted to producing goods that can be consumed during the year, simply because a portion of the work has already been done. In short, capital is a fund of congealed labor and also a fund from which the community can draw subsistence while devoting its labor to activities whose output will not be available for consumption for some time in the future.

Clearly, the size of the capital stock, regarded as a subsistence fund, limits the delay that the community can afford between the present and the time when the results of its current labor will be ready for consumption. This delay is the period of production. The heart of Böhm-Bawerk's analysis is the discovery of relationships among the stock of capital, the wage rate, the labor force, and the length of the period of production.

Consider, now, a stationary economy in which, on the average, C years elapse between the date when work is started on a product and the date when it reaches a consumer's hands. Let N denote the labor force and w the annual wage rate. Then goods incorporating labor valued at Nw are produced each year, and goods incorporating labor valued at NwC are produced in each production cycle. We can calculate at once the value of the labor which must be invested in the capital stock of the economy in order to achieve these levels of output, wages, and employment. In each time interval dt (small or large), production is completed on goods that incorporate labor valued at $Nw\,dt$. For simplicity, assume now that labor is expended on each good at a steady rate[4] so that goods started up t years ago have invested in them the fraction t/C of their ultimate labor cost. Then goods started up in the time interval t years ago to $t + dt$ years ago incorporate at present labor valued at $Nw(t/C)dt$. And, since the goods now in

153

process are those that were started up C years ago and at every instant since, the total value of the labor tied up in the capital stock is:

$$\int_0^C Nw \frac{t}{C} \, dt = \frac{NwC}{2}.$$

Thus, with the simplifying assumption, the amount of labor invested in the capital stock at any time is just half the value invested in the total amount produced in a production cycle. We may then write for the value of the capital stock:

$$K = \frac{NwC}{2}.$$

Böhm-Bawerk's famous 'period of production' is the length of time that elapses on the average between the time that a unit of labor is devoted to a product and the time that the product reaches the hands of the consumer. Under the simplifying assumption that labor is expended on the product at a constant rate, the period of production, to be denoted by p, is just half the length of the production cycle, i.e., $p = C/2$.

Then the value of the capital stock is

$$K = Nwp. \tag{1}$$

Considered as a physical stock, the capital is the accumulated result of $\frac{1}{2}NC = Np$ work-years, since one-half of the work performed since work was initiated on the oldest goods still in process was devoted to goods that have passed out of inventory. If the wage rate (which is the same as the rate of consumption per worker per year) rises, the flow of consumables provided by this stock will be drawn down at a greater rate and the period for which the stock will suffice (the period of production) will fall. Thus with a given capital stock and labor force there is an inverse relationship between the wage rate and the period of production. This is one of the two main relationships determining the levels of the interest rate and of wages in Böhm-Bawerk's system.

The quantity of capital invested per laborer employed is simply :

$$\frac{K}{N} = wp$$

Now let us turn to the technical conditions of production. The basic technical relationship that explains the emergence of interest is the fact that the output per worker per period expands more than in proportion to the length of the period of production. Expressed alternatively : the output per worker per year is an increasing function of the period of production. Let $f(p)$ denote output per worker per year. Then Böhm-Bawerk assumes that $f(p)$ has the shape shown in Figure 1. Note that even if $p = 0, f(p)$ is positive; $p = 0$ is the happy situation of the South Sea Islander who picks his breadfruit just before breakfast and his bananas just before lunch. As productive activities become less direct and more time consuming, $f(p)$ increases, but increases constantly at a decreasing rate.

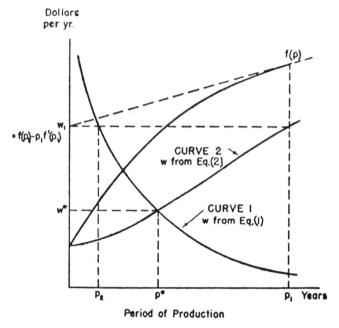

Figure I.

If the wage rate is given, the length of the production period is determinate and can be determined in two instructive ways which, naturally, give the same answer. First suppose that the production period is determined by entrepreneurs so as to maximize the annual rate of profit. The annual rate of profit per worker is :

$$\pi = \frac{f(p) - w}{wp}.$$

Maximizing this with respect to p we find :

$$\frac{d\pi}{dp} = \frac{wpf'(p) - w(f(p) - w)}{w^2 p^2} = 0$$

which simplifies to :

$$f(p) - pf'(p) = w. \tag{2}$$

Each entrepreneur can maximize his annual income by investing his capital in productive processes whose length is the value of p given by this formula. This is the second of Böhm-Bawerk's two main relationships.

Equation (2) may seem more natural if we note its kinship to the residual theory of value imputation. Imagine that there are two factors of production, labor and " time," and that $f(p)$ is the output of one man-year of labor combined with p years of " time ".

Then $f'(p)$ is the marginal productivity of " time," $pf'(p)$ is the total imputed value of the " time " used in conjunction with a man-year of labor, and the left-hand side of equation (2) is the excess of the value of output over the total imputed value of " time ". The equation asserts that in equilibrium this excess is equal to the wage.

Before bringing equations (1) and (2) together it will be instructive to deduce the second in a different way. Let us compute the marginal productivity of labor. Total annual output is :

$$Y = Nf(p).$$

Marginal productivity of labor is obtained by differentiating this definition with respect to N to obtain :

$$\frac{dY}{dN} = f(p) + Nf'(p) \frac{dp}{dN} .$$

But, by equation (1) :

$$\frac{dp}{dN} = \frac{d}{dN} \frac{K}{wN} = -\frac{K}{wN^2} = -\frac{p}{N} .$$

Substituting in the previous equation we find :

$$\frac{dY}{dN} = f(p) - pf'(p).$$

Thus, if we require that the period of production be such that the marginal productivity of labor is equal to its wage we obtain equation (2) again.

These relationships are shown on Figure 1, where the equilibrium period of production and wage are determined. We have already described the curve labelled $f(p)$. Curve 1 represents equation (1). We have already noted that if the capital stock and the level of employment are given, equation (1) prescribes that the period of production must be inversely proportional to the wage rate. Curve 1, which is a rectangular hyperbola, shows this inverse relationship with the level of wages, measured vertically, plotted against the length of the production period, measured horizontally, for which the given capital stock will provide full employment.

Curve 2 shows the marginal productivity of labor corresponding to each value of p, and is derived from $f(p)$ in the following manner. Choose a value of p arbitrarily ,say p_1, and go up vertically to the corresponding value of $f(p)$. Then go back along the tangent of $f(p)$ to the vertical axis. The point at which the tangent hits the vertical axis will be $f(p_1) - p_1 f'(p_1)$, or the desired marginal productivity. Finally go back horizontally until the ordinate through p_1 is reached ; the result is a point on Curve 2, and Curve 2 can be traced out by finding all such points.

Consider an arbitrary wage level, say w_1, that lies above the intersection of Curves 1 and 2. In response to this wage employers will adopt productive processes of length p_1, as shown on Curve 2. But at that wage Curve 1 shows that the available capital will provide full employment only if the period of production is p_2, which is shorter than p_1. Thus there will be insufficient demand for labor and the wage will fall. A similar argument shows that wages will be bid up if we start from any wage below the crossing point. And, therefore, the intersection of Curves 1 and 2 determines the equilibrium level of wages and of the production period. Clearly the equilibrium wage will be greater the greater is the quantity of capital per laborer, $f(p)$ being given.

The rate of interest or profits (the words are synonymous in this context) is also determined by this construction.   We can find the profit rate directly from the ratio of annual profits per worker to investment per worker, or :

$$\frac{f(p) - w}{wp} = \frac{p f'(p)}{wp} = \frac{f'(p)}{w} .$$

Substituting in the equilibrium values of w and p, the equilibrium interest rate follows. Alternatively we can calculate the marginal productivity of capital.   Differentiating $Y = N f(p)$ we obtain :

$$\frac{dY}{dK} = N f'(p) \frac{dp}{dK} = N f'(p) \frac{d}{dK} \frac{K}{Nw} = \frac{f'(p)}{w}$$

The results, of course, agree.

Böhm-Bawerk's quaesitae have all been found, but a few remarks seem in order.   In the first place, the last equation shows that so long as extension of the period of production is productive, in the sense of increasing annual output per worker, the rate of interest will not be zero.   Böhm-Bawerk apparently felt this never would happen.   In the second place, inspection of the diagram shows, and easy algebra will verify, the wage will always be greater if p is greater than zero than if p is zero.   From this it follows that the workers benefit from co-operating with capital and from the accumulation of capital.

Finally, there is one loose end to be tied up.   Throughout the argument we, like Böhm-Bawerk, have valued capital at the value of the labor embodied in it.   This procedure is inconsistent with modern valuation theory, with capital theory itself, and even with sound business practice.   Capital tied up in goods-in-process commands interest, and we must allow for it.

Consider the batch of goods started up in the time interval of width dt, t years before any definite valuation date. On completion (i.e., C years after initiation) these goods will incorporate labor worth $Nw\, dt$. Thus, assuming that labor is expended on these goods at an even rate throughout the time production takes, that rate must be $\dfrac{Nw}{C}\, dt$. Then the current valuation of the batch of goods started up t years ago, allowing for interest at rate r, continuously compounded, is:

$$dt \int_0^t \frac{Nw}{C} e^{r\tau} d\tau = \frac{Nw}{C} \frac{e^{rt} - 1}{r} dt.$$

Adding up for all goods begun in the p years preceding the valuation date gives:

$$K = \int_0^C \frac{Nw}{C} \frac{e^{rt} - 1}{r} dt = \frac{Nw}{C} \frac{e^{rC} - 1 - rC}{r^2} \qquad (3)$$

To obtain a practical approximation, expand the exponential as a power series:

$$K = \frac{Nw}{C} \frac{\tfrac{1}{2}(rC)^2 + \tfrac{1}{6}(rC)^3 + \ldots}{r^2}$$

$$= Nwp\,(1 + \tfrac{2}{3}\,rp + \ldots)$$

Thus Böhm-Bawerk's formula for the value of the capital stock is an acceptable approximation if rp is not too large.

The value of r may be calculated by equating the value of the labor expended on a batch of goods, accumulated at interest, to the final value of that batch. This comparison gives:

$$\frac{Nw}{2p} \frac{e_2^{rp} - 1}{r}\, dt = N f(p)\, dt.$$

In order to see what the solution for r looks like, we expand the exponential, disregard terms involving $(rp)^2$ and higher orders of r, and, after elementary cancellations and re-arrangements obtain :

$$r \approx \frac{f'(p)}{w} \tag{4}$$

confirming previous calculations. The value of capital per worker, allowing for the accrual of interest, is found from equation (3) by inserting the values for r and for $(e^{rp} - 1)/r$ that we have just found. It is :

$$\frac{K}{N} = \frac{f(p) - w.}{r}$$

Thus, the capital stock per worker is appraised at the capitalized value of a perpetuity equal to the annual net profit per worker. Finally, using equations (2) and (4),

$$\frac{K}{N} = \frac{p f'(p)}{r} \approx wp\,,$$

for the third time. Thus the pieces all fit together when values in terms of embodied labor are replaced by values that incorporate accrued interest in accordance with the dictates of modern capital theory.

Cambridge, Mass.   R. DORFMAN.

Notes

¹ This paper was written during the tenure of a Ford Foundation Faculty Research Fellowship, and I wish to express my gratitude. It incorporates the beneficial results of some heated discussions with Professor William Baumol, and for those, too, I am grateful.

² In the attempt to make Böhm-Bawerk clear we have been preceeded by Böhm-Bawerk himself and by Wicksell on at least two occasions. But Böhm-Bawerk's brilliance in concept is matched only by his obscurity in exposition, and, as to Wicksell, the treatment in *Value, Capital and Rent* is nearly as tortuous as Böhm-Bawerk's while his discussion in *Lectures on Political Economy, Volume* 1 departs significantly from Böhm-Bawerk's point of view.

³ This concept was the center of a fine controversy involving Böhm-Bawerk, Clark, Taussig and a number of other difficult writers some two generations ago. As an example of the criticism to which it is open, see Wicksell, *Value, Capital and Rent*, pp. 115-119. More favorable views, though, have been expressed by C. H. P. Gifford (*Economical Journal*, December 1933) and J. Marschak (*Economic Journal*, March 1934).

⁴ This assumption does not affect the conclusions that will be reached, but it makes the argument much simpler and more transparent than is possible in the general case.

This article has been corrected by the author and thus differs to that originally published in the Review of Economic Studies.

[9]

General Equilibrium with Public Goods [1]

R. Dorfman

1 INTRODUCTORY

It is becoming fashionable nowadays for economists to dabble in political theory. Partly, we are forced into it; the principal application of economics is to political decisions. Partly we are enticed into it, when we perceive that the tools we have fashioned for our own purposes can be applied with profit to the problems of politics. I am responding here to both motivations.

The current wave of interest began with the writings of Kenneth Arrow [1] and Duncan Black [5], who applied a set-theoretic approach to some problems of political decision-making. It was continued by Anthony Downs [8], who took a very economic point of view. He reasoned that a rational decision in any field is a 'best' decision, which can always be regarded as a decision that maximises something. In the case of politics that something is political support. Once that is recognised, the usual economics of maximising decisions applies. More currently, Charles Lindblom [15] is reacting against the ultra-rationalistic approach and is reminding us that politics is the art of compromise among the conflicting interests of incommensurable groups. Though none of these deal specifically with the problems of public goods, their insights are pertinent and I have borrowed from all of them. In the same strain, I have made use of the point of view expounded by Chester Barnard [2] in the context of maintaining the effectiveness and integrity of an organisation, the approach that emphasises the importance of maintaining a favourable balance of the inducements extended to participants in an organisation over the contributions exacted from them, even when no monetised values are at issue.

The welfare economics of public goods has been set forth, probably definitively, by Paul Samuelson in three influential papers [16, 17, 18] on which I lean heavily. Samuelson's argument was amplified by Strotz [19], with special emphasis on the distributional implications of the provision of public goods. But these contributions had to do with welfare

[1] This research was undertaken during tenure of the Ford Faculty Rotating Research Professorship at the University of California, Berkeley.

optima and paid no attention to the peculiarities of decision-making about public goods.

The best bridge between the ideals established in the framework of welfare economics and the pulls and pushes recognised by the institutional-political approaches is provided by a paper by Howard Bowen [6], which proposes a voting procedure intended to perform the same functions in the political sphere that competitive markets perform in the economic one. I shall discuss Bowen's proposal more extensively below.

All of these streams of writing, and some others that I haven't noted, bear on the problem that I wish to confront: how to formalise the considerations that enter into decisions about public goods. I shall take the time to discuss the concept of public goods in the very next section, but the upshot will be simply that public goods are ordinary economic goods except that their use cannot be rationed nor can their benefits be allocated. In the nature of the case, therefore, decisions about public goods transcend the competence of markets and decentralised decision making. Those decisions stand squarely on the boundary between economics and politics, and we shall so regard them.

How these decisions are made in practice depends on the structure of the government that makes them, and governments are very varied. In a federalised government, such as that of the United States, these decisions are arrived at very differently from the way they are in a centralised government, such as that of France. My formalisation is intended to be non-committal enough to cover all such variations, but in thinking about the problem I have usually had in mind the procedures prevalent in America. According to these procedures, decisions about public goods are part-and-parcel of the regularly recurrent budget-making process. It is then that the levels of expenditure on police and fire protection, public health, national defence, highway maintenance, education and all the rest are proposed, debated and settled. It is the considerations that are debated in this budgeting process that we have to formalise.

In the next section I shall, mostly for the record, discuss the concept of public goods. Section 3 will set forth an abstract, descriptive model of public goods decisions, in the spirit of stationary general equilibrium analysis. In the final section some of the concepts invoked in this model will be mulled over and evaluated.

2 THE CONCEPT OF PUBLIC GOODS

There are certain goods that have the peculiarity that once they are available no one can be precluded from enjoying them whether he contributed to their provision or no. These are the public goods. Law and order is an example, and there are many others too familiar to make further exemplification worth while. Their essential characteristic is that they are enjoyed but not consumed, or that benefit can be derived from them without any act of appropriation. In fact the enjoyment of public goods is often unconscious and even involuntary. For example, if a community fluoridates its water supply even those who object most strenuously to tampering with the natural purity of water will find that their children have fewer cavities. There is then, often in the case of a public good, no definable act of consumption and therefore no way of measuring or defining the amount of it consumed or the marginal cost of providing a small amount of it to a single beneficiary or an individual's private demand curve for its services to him. All this very useful apparatus of economics is irrelevant to public goods.

It was Baumol [3] who, to my knowledge, most clearly enunciated this attitude toward the nature of public goods. Since none can be precluded from enjoying them it is in the interests of each to avoid contributing to them if he can. Therefore the coercive power of the state must be enlisted to compel contributions. And when this is done, wisely, all benefit, for then goods desired by all (or virtually all) can be provided which would otherwise be unavailable to any. Goods of this nature, then, can be provided only by the state, by philanthropists, and as by-products of certain private goods.

The extreme or pure category of public goods are those to which I have already called attention: where the usufruct cannot be denied and where the receipt of benefit is not associated with any deliberate choice or act. There are many such goods but they are a bit hard to list because, like the air, they tend to be invisible. But there are other categories, too. One goes under the heading of 'externalities'. There are some public goods that are produced as joint products with private goods. Leading instances occur in the fields of education and public health.[1] I, myself, have never bothered to be innoculated against infantile paralysis. Nevertheless, I am immune because there are virtually no carriers left in my community. The private good of those who submitted to innoculation has become my public good.

There is a similar side to education. It is brought out in an inverse sort of way by the fact that in the good old days of the American South it was

[1] Recognition of the importance of mixed public–private goods goes back to Adolph Wagner at least. See the passage from *Finanzwissenschaft* cited by Wicksell [21, p. 98]. More recently, Leif Johansen appealed to these very same examples [13, p. 180].

illegal to teach a slave to read or write. I submit that the reason for government interest in education, public health, postal services and airways control, to mention only a few instances, is that in each of these cases the use of private service carries as a joint product a widely diffused communal benefit. The State therefore takes steps to assure that the private good is consumed in amounts deemed adequate. But the gains to the direct, private beneficiaries are distinct from the public benefits derived.

Still another kind of public good exists when the derivation of benefit is associated with an explicit act of consumption but where it is unduly inconvenient or expensive to exact a user charge. In such cases, particularly if there is a joint product side to the matter, the commodity may be treated as if it were a pure public good. Typical examples are roads and outdoor recreational facilities. Often no charge is made for their use, though in principle there could be user charges. Curbside parking is an interesting example. It is treated as an unappropriable public good until the supply becomes nearly exhausted, then it is found convenient to levy a user charge.

Finally, we have to consider whether appropriable commodities produced under conditions of low or negligible marginal cost ought to be considered public goods. Often they are so considered, and sometimes negligible marginal cost has been used as the definiendum of public goods, but I shall exclude them. Urban transit and sewage disposal may be public goods (under the joint product interpretation) but they are not so by virtue of the strongly decreasing costs of producing their services. That characteristic makes them 'public utilities' and, though the public at large has a legitimate interest in having them provided in adequate amounts, the principles that determine what is adequate provision are different from the questions that I am confronting.

In short, public goods are those that are consumed jointly rather than severally. They are goods that place us all in the same boat willy-nilly. They have no marginal cost that can be assessed, even conceptually, against an individual occasion of use. Therefore they cannot have declining marginal costs.

There is a fine distinction to be made, which I am afraid I shall not always respect. It concerns the notion of the quantity of a public good. Consider a park as a public good. Is the amount of it the number of acres of parkland, or the number of 'visitor-days' of use, or what? All that the government can decide is the number of acres of parkland and the facilities provided in them, and I am forced to use these magnitudes to measure the amount of the public good provided. A public good so defined and measured is an intermediate product, analogous to a productive facility. The benefits, both public and private, yielded by such a good depend on the use that is made of it and this is often a matter for private decision, as in the case of parks.

For public goods, as I have said, there can be no individual choice of quantity and no individual expression of preference in the market-place. All decisions have to be made socially, which is to say politically. Our central task is the formalisation of these political decisions.

3 A DESCRIPTIVE MODEL

I am about to propose a descriptive model of decision making concerning public goods. I do so with a great deal of diffidence. These decisions are political as well as economic, and my acquaintance with the literature of political science is very spotty. So I am a 'primitive' in this field, a man who has to rediscover the first principles for himself and who is likely to drop into the pitfalls that the professionals have avoided for generations. On top of that an economist suffers from a special disability when dealing with political problems: his deeply ingrained habits of mind practically compel him to view everything as an economic problem in which each of the participants is striving to maximise something and the social institutions co-ordinate their efforts toward the maximisation of something else. There is no guarantee that the political world is like that. My amateurishness and my mental set will be amply reflected in what follows.

My approach will be to conceive of a standard stationary general equilibrium model to which a government sector has been added, and to determine some properties of the general equilibrium of this government plus private sector model. For the private sector I borrow heavily from Debreu [7], including even his notation. For the government sector I find it necessary to proceed on my own.

Since my concern is with public goods I shall conceive of a government that does nothing except provide public goods and levy the taxes necessary to finance them. It does not, in particular, make transfer payments or concern itself with economic policy.

I assume that this government is sensitive to the needs and wishes of its body politic. It may have a will of is own, but its first concern is to find some resolution of the conflicting desires and utilities of its citizenry so as to enlist and maintain their loyal support. The citizenry, of course, consists of individuals, but it seems important to me that they form themselves into interest groups, formed largely along socio-economic lines.

These interest groups are, in fact, very complicated phenomena: they overlap (there must be some people who are members of both the Junior Chamber of Commerce and the N.A.A.C.P.), their edges are blurred, from time to time they split, consolidate, and reform. But I shall abstract from all that and assume that there are given interest groups the members of each of which share a common set of preferences as regards public goods. The government, whose officials are themselves members of some of these interest groups, must consult the preferences of each of these groups in arriving at its decisions. How this is done constitutes the heart of my model of the government sector.

As a further simplification I shall assume that decisions concerning tax policy can be separated from decisions concerning public goods. This is not unrealistic. Decisions about public goods are normally made annually as part of the routine of preparing the government's budget. The total burden of taxes must be consistent with these decisions. But the distribution of taxes, or tax policy, is reconsidered much more infrequently and with primary attention to distributive and aggregative considerations. For the purpose of studying public goods decisions we shall take the tax policy as given.

Now I can present my model. The structure of the private sector will be discussed only cursorily so that proper emphasis can be placed on the government and its decisions. A fuller statement of the overall model will be found in the appendix.[1]

The economy cum body-politic, then, consists of a finite number of consumer-voters, a finite number of firms and a government. The government, as we shall see more fully below, provides a vector of public goods, g. In the presence of these public goods, the typical consumer, Mr α, selects a vector of private good consumptions, x^α (negative components signifying contributions), from a closed, convex set X^α, g available to him in the circumstances. The public goods vector, g, is itself a member of a closed, compact set, G, available to the government. The consumer's choice is made in the light of a preference ordering over the elements of X^α, G which has the usual convenient convexity and continuity properties. This choice is constrained by a budget limitation: given any set of prices of private goods, Mr α's net value of consumption cannot exceed the value of his initial resources (if any) plus the value of his shares in the profits of firms less his tax liability. Mr α is assumed to own a share $\theta_{\alpha j}$ of firm j

---

[1] A mathematical appendix is to be prepared and will be available from the author. Reference to it is unnecessary, however, because the principal theorems have been derived independently by Duncan K. Foley [9].

(usually zero) and to be liable for a share $\theta_{\alpha 0}$ (rarely zero) of the expenses of the government.

The typical firm, firm j, produces a vector y^j of private goods (negative components denote net inputs). Its range of choice is restricted to a closed, convex production set Y^j, G, but it does not select the g elements of its choice vector. Instead, taking them as given and taking the prices of private goods as given, it chooses y^j so as to maximise its profit. Its profit is then distributed, with proportion $\theta_{\alpha j}$ going to Mr α.

The government, which will be denoted by subscript 0, is formally very like a firm except that it and it alone can choose the vector of public goods, g, which enters into the available sets of all participants in the economy. The role of the government in this model at least, is to provide public goods. It does this by selecting a vector y^0, g from the closed, convex set Y^0, G available to it. When it makes this choice, it provides the vector g of public goods to the community and a vector y^0 of private goods, most of whose components will presumably be negative. Given a price vector p for private goods, the government also levies a tax of $-\theta_{\alpha 0} p . y^0$ on consumer α.

The coefficients $\theta_{\alpha 0}$ express the tax policy of the government. We shall regard them as given data not subject to decision. The institutional assumption here is that whereas the actual level of taxation is part and parcel of decisions concerning public goods the general tax policy is not, and is not very frequently revised. We shall see below that the separation of tax policy from public goods decisions entails some social inefficiency. But, in fact, these decisions tend to be separated in practice, in the interest of reducing the complexity of the alternatives confronted by government officials and legislators.

Superficially, our assumption seems to specify a very simple tax policy: it is a simple head tax; there are no excises, income taxes, taxes on firms, or tariffs. But it can be interpreted more generously. It can be taken to mean that Mr α knows that in the end, after all the shiftings and complications, he will be assessed about the proportion $\theta_{\alpha 0}$ of the expenses of the government. This formulation does ignore, however, the distortions introduced into the price structure by indirect taxes and, to a lesser extent, by direct taxes.

This describes our economy-polity except for its most crucial feature for our purposes: the principles on which y^0, g is to be selected from the government's available set. It is at this stage that we must break our own ground. Up to this point our concepts and assumptions have had the authority of generations of close thought and scrutiny behind them. Now we are entering a territory in which I have not been able to discover any compelling concensus. We must therefore construct our own principles out of the bits and pieces of doctrine that I have been able to find. What I am about to say, now, has no particular authority behind it.

Decisions about the provision of public goods are conveyed in the government's annual budget. They are reached through a political process in which it is useful to distinguish three groups of participants: government officials, other political leaders and ordinary citizens. The proposals for the budget originate with the government officials, for only they have the staff and information needed to prepare them in the required detail. These proposals, however, cannot be implemented without widespread public understanding and support. Formally, this public assent is conveyed by legislative enactment of the budget, and for this reason I include legislators among the 'other political leaders'. But in fact, and in this model, the process of gaining public acceptance includes much more than pushing a budget bill through the legislature. It involves convincing the great bulk of the members of the public, minorities along with majorities, that their needs and interests have been dealt with fairly.

This process of gaining widespread public acceptance is the most elaborate and noisy step of the whole procedure. The trial balloons, the political breakfasts, legislative hearings and debates, speeches, leaks, editorials, press conferences are all part of it. The key actors are the 'other political leaders': the congeries of politicians, in and out of office, prominent citizens, political commentators, interest-group leaders and others who devote a major portion of their time and efforts to political affairs. The political leaders are the main channel of communication between the government officials and the general public, largely because the general public, being uninformed about political matters, and knowing that it is, relies heavily on *ad hominem* arguments.[1] A member of the public will tend to approve the government's proposals if they come with the endorsement of leaders in whom he has confidence. The leaders therefore play a double role; they are the targets of the government's persuasive efforts and almost simultaneously the conveyors of the government's programme to their followings.

A political leader's authority and influence stems from his constituency: the ordinary people who have confidence in him and who regard his endorsement of a proposal as a powerful argument in its favour. A

[1] The rational state of ignorance of the general public is one of the main themes of Anthony Downs's *An Economic Theory of Democracy*.

leader's following consists of people who have come to believe, on the basis of past experience and pronouncements, that the conclusions he comes to on political matters are close to the ones that they would reach if they took the trouble to become informed and to think things through. Expressed somewhat differently, each political leader has a following that consists of people who believe that he thinks and acts on the basis of their broad preconceptions about right, justice and the objectives of political policy. Such a following is likely to be drawn from a fairly homogeneous socio-economic group of citizens, and we shall consider each political leader to be a representative of some definable socio-economic group. In my opinion, it is unrealistic to assume that the ordinary citizen has clearly defined preferences about political decisions and policies, but he accepts the appraisals of political leaders who do have such preferences. Thus, in my economic-political model I conceive that individual consumers have preference maps over bundles of private goods, but that only socio-economic groups (via the leaders in whom they have confidence) have preference maps for public goods.

I have described thus far one direction of the flow of information in the political process, the flow from government officials to political leaders to ordinary citizens. There is also a significant reverse flow. It is obvious that a political leader cannot choose his positions entirely in accordance with his personal whims and preferences. His influence depends upon his followers' confidence in him, and this is constantly being reassessed in the light of his current stands and accumulating evidence. The leader can therefore endorse only proposals that he can 'sell', and that he believes will turn out to enhance, rather than impair, the confidence on which his position depends. He is constantly appraising the fairly vague opinions of his constituents to determine what he can sell, and is simultaneously conveying the results of these appraisals to the government officials to persuade them to frame proposals that he can endorse.

Out of this two-way flow of information emerges a government programme, or budget, that virtually every significant political leader finds acceptable. Some of the leaders may not like it very well, but at the very least they will be able to present it to their constituents as the best compromise attainable in the circumstances. For politics is not a game of 'winner take all'. I am not at all sure why this is, but quite obviously a great deal of effort is expended on providing to each leader and the group he represents at least a fair minimum recognition of their demands. Wicksell [21] recognised this characteristic of public decisions long ago, and asserted it as a moral demand: that taxes should not be levied

against any citizen unless he felt that he was receiving adequate government services and benefits in return. I do not wish to rest my case on
moral grounds, but merely on the empirical recognition that stable
governments. appear to act this way. New revolutionary regimes, of
course, do not; they run roughshod over the interests of the recently
ousted group. But a stable government does not discredit any political
leaders or alienate any significant minority. Perhaps my empirical
observation is not much more than a definition of a responsible, legitimate government. If so, there are such governments, and my theory
is restricted to them.

In summary, then, we imagine a body politic to be made up of a number
of socio-economic groups.[1] A typical member of one of these groups has
only very general ideas about what he would like his government to do,
but each group is represented in the political decision process by one or
more spokesmen who have quite definite preferences and quite definite
ideas about costs and benefits and trade-offs, and whose ideas are consistent with the vague notions of their constituents. The government
officials strive to formulate a programme of government activities that will
be at least acceptable to all these leaders. That is the first, and most
demanding, task of the government officials. It may be that there are
several programmes that are acceptable all around. If so the government
has some latitude for choosing among them, and we must now conjecture
how this latitude is exercised.

In terms of our formal model, when the government has found a vector
y^0, g that satisfies all the groups that comprise its body politic, i.e. all
their spokesmen, it has done most of its work. But there may be numerous
vectors that meet this requirement, and some basis is needed for selecting
among them.

Should we be content with the doctrine of 'satisficing', saying only
that the government will select some element from the set of universally
acceptable vectors? Should we adopt some version of search and scanning
theory, saying that the government will choose the acceptable vector that
is closest, in some sense, to the vector accepted last year or in some average
of past years? Both of those, I think, are acceptable approaches, the
second not far from Lindblom's [15], but they seem to me to imply an
excessively bloodless government without any purposes of its own or
interest in leadership. It is trite that 'power corrupts', and I am not sure

---

[1] These socio-economic groups should not be confused with the interest groups that
play a central role in the thinking of David Truman [20] and his school. Their model
of political decisions is substantially different from this one.

that I believe it, but at least power does evoke an interest in getting things done. An aspirant government seeks political power in order to accomplish some objectives, and it attains the power by mobilising public support for those objectives and disarming resistance to them. So I say, but without undue conviction, that we ought to conceive of the government of our model economy-polity as having definite goals that it wishes to attain to the maximum extent possible within the limitations of the political and economic constraints already described.

Furthermore, these goals do not come out of the air. They are the goals of one or more of the socio-economic groups that constitute the body politic. The leaders of the government are themselves members of these groups, and are interested in the welfare of their own and other groups, they have acceded to power by enlisting the support of a sufficient preponderance of those groups, and they can remain in power only by meriting the loyalty of many of the groups while not incurring the excessive hostility of the others. So we shall not impose a separate set of goals for the government, though that would be a defensible, and even interesting, alternative to the formulation being presented. Instead, we shall assume that the goals of the government are the goals of the socio-economic groups that comprise its body-politic with, however, varying degrees of attention to the interests of the different groups. From this point of view, different political parties would be distinguished not by differences in their objectives or programmes but by differences in their degrees of attentiveness to the interests of the various socio-economic groups. What a government so motivated seeks to maximise is some function of the welfares of these socio-economic groups, as perceived by themselves.

I am being subtle here, even to the point of deviousness. De Viti de Marco insists, and rightly, that there is some room for altruism in individual consumers' decisions and substantially more in political decisions. There is room for altruism in this formulation. The discussion of public goods in Section 2 made it clear that the external effects of consumption are public goods. It often happens that the members of group A feel that the members of group B ought to have something for which the latter have no felt need. Bath-tubs for slum-dwellers are often advanced as a notorious example (usually by members of group C, who don't see the point of it). In that case, bath-tubs in rehabilitated slums will enter group A's welfare function, but not group B's (and may enter group C's deleteriously). The individual groups' welfare functions as here conceived do not measure the benefits directly received by the members of that group, but rather benefits to the whole community as perceived by that group. That is how altruism enters the government's objective function, though it is based exclusively on the welfare functions of the constituent groups. Presumably, benefits received directly by members of a group will bulk especially large in the welfare function of that group, but there is room for other considerations.

The government's objectives, then, are an amalgam of the objectives of the groups it governs. The government's leadership is leadership in the direction of the goals of the groups that have predominant influence in it. But, we should reiterate, this leadership is tempered by the need to conciliate all the groups.

In order to express these ideas with adequate precision we must somehow quantify the benefits of public goods as seen by members of citizen group α, and moreover must do so in monetary terms so that the benefits from the provision of public goods can be compared with those of private consumption. The idea of monetary equivalent of a benefit in kind is inherently artificial. Furthermore, the procedure for constructing one is necessarily somewhat arbitrary, as the number of variorum 'compensating variations' attests. The particular method that will be followed is recommended by its conventionality and its convenience.

Our approach is in the willingness-to-pay tradition. Suppose that the government proposes to provide levels of public goods g and to do so by utilizing private goods in quantities y^0. At prices p, which will be regarded as being preassigned until further notice, this will impose on a member of group α a tax burden amounting to $-\theta_{\alpha 0} p y^0$ (remember that $p y^0$ is normally negative). A member of group α will be at least acquiescent if this tax burden does not exceed the most that he is willing to pay for the proposed provision of public goods. But how much is that? To answer this question we conceive of some minimum, basal level of public goods, $\bar{g}$, to which corresponds a low tax burden $-\theta_{\alpha 0} p \bar{y}^0$. There also corresponds a consumption good vector $\bar{x}^\alpha$ which is the best that the consumer can afford at the low level of taxation. (In considering alternative government programmes, the citizen-taxpayer is assumed to ignore the aggregative effects of the government budget, and so shall we.) This combination $\bar{x}^\alpha$, $\bar{g}$ places the consumer-citizen on some one of his indifference curves or, stated more elaborately, on the boundary of one of his preferred consumption sets. We may now associate with the proposed government output g (as I shall sometimes, rather inaccurately, call the provision of public goods) a private consumption vector x^α chosen as the cheapest consumption vector at the assigned prices such that x^α, g is indifferent to

$\bar{x}^\alpha$, $\bar{g}$. The value of the proposed programme as seen by this citizen may then be taken to be

$$F^\alpha(g, p) = p(\bar{x}^\alpha - x^\alpha),$$

since this is the maximum tax he could afford to pay over and above the inevitable tax $-\theta_{\alpha 0} p \bar{y}^0$ without being forced below the level of welfare corresponding to $\bar{x}^\alpha$, $\bar{g}$. (We do not preclude that this expression may be negative, for an ill-chosen programme.) This is the citizen's gross benefit from the programme. His net benefit, or citizen's surplus, is the excess of his gross benefit over the increase in taxation necessitated by the government's consuming $-y^0$ instead of $-\bar{y}^0$, or

$$\phi^\alpha(y^0, g, p) = F^\alpha(g, p) + \theta_{\alpha 0} p(y^0 - \bar{y}^0).$$

In effect $\phi^\alpha(y^0, g, p)$ compares the tax that a member of group α would be willing to pay to have government output g instead of $\bar{g}$ with the tax that he would actually have to pay. It is necessarily a concave function of y^0, g. For consider any two government programmes $(y^{0\prime}, g')$ and $(y^{0\prime\prime}, g'')$, and their corresponding levels of private consumption x'^α and x''^α chosen so that

$$(x'^\alpha, g') \sim (x''^\alpha, g'') \sim (\bar{x}^\alpha, \bar{g}),$$

where $\sim$ symbolises indifference to a member of group α. Consider also any linearly intermediate government programme

$$(y^{0\lambda}, g^\lambda) = \lambda(y^{0\prime}, g') + (1 - \lambda)(y^{0\prime\prime}, g''), \qquad 0 < \lambda < 1.$$

Because of the assumed convexity of consumer's preferences:

$$(\lambda x'^\alpha + (1 - \lambda)x''^\alpha, g^\lambda) > (x'^\alpha, g') \sim (x''^\alpha, g'')$$

where $>$ denotes strict preference. Hence, surely

$$p x^{\alpha\lambda} \leq \lambda p x'^\alpha + (1 - \lambda) p x''^\alpha,$$

where
$$(x^{\alpha\lambda}, g^\lambda) \sim (x'^\alpha, g'). \quad \text{Now}$$
$$\phi^\alpha(y^{0\lambda}, g^\lambda, p) = p(\bar{x}^\alpha - x^{\alpha\lambda}) + \theta_{\alpha 0} p(y^{0\lambda} - \bar{y}^0).$$

Subtracting these two expressions and applying the definitions of $\phi^\alpha(y^{0\prime}, g', p)$ and $\phi^\alpha(y^{0\prime\prime}, g'', p)$ we obtain

$$\phi^\alpha(y^{0\lambda}, g^\lambda, p) \geq \lambda \phi^\alpha(y^{0\prime}, g', p) + (1 - \lambda)\phi^\alpha(y^{0\prime\prime}, g'', p)$$

or concaveness.

We can now pose the problem of choosing the government's programme in the following form: For a given set of prices of private goods, p, find an element in the government's production set Y^0, G so as to maximise

$$\sum_\alpha w_\alpha \{F^\alpha(g, p) + \theta_{\alpha 0} p(y^0 - \bar{y}^0)\}$$

subject to

$$F^\alpha(g, p) + \theta_{\alpha 0} p(y^0 - \bar{y}^0) \geq 0, \text{ all } \alpha.$$

The maximand merits a word or two. The weights w_α in it measure the government's relative concern for the different socio-economic groups indexed by α. They are a compound of the political influence of these groups and of attention paid to their welfares for more disinterested motives. Altogether it is the kind of social welfare function employed by Samuelson, in [16] and elsewhere, and by Strotz [19] in their studies of the ideal output of public goods.

Thus stated, the problem is seen to be almost a standard concave programming problem, the only unconventional feature being that the optimal point must be selected in a specified closed, convex set, in addition to satisfying the usual concave inequalities. It is close enough to concave programming so that the following theorem applies:

Lemma. Suppose that $f^0(z)$ is a concave function, $f(z)$ is a concave vector-valued function, both defined for $z \in Z$, and that S is a closed, convex subset of Z with an interior. Suppose also that for every non-trivial vector $u \geq 0$ there exists a $z \in S$ such that $uf(z) > 0$. (Inner products will be written in the same way as products of scalars.)

Then, if $f^0(z^*)$ is a maximum of $f^0(z)$ for $z \in S$ satisfying $f(z) \geq 0$, there exist vectors u, v satisfying:

(a) $u \geq 0$, $uf(z^*) = 0$,
(b) $v(z - z^*) \geq 0$ for all $z \in S$, and
(c) $f^0(z) + uf(z) + vz \leq f^0(z^*) + vz^*$ for all $z \in Z$.

The proof, which will not be presented, is a straightforward application of the method used by Karlin [14, p. 200 ff.] to demonstrate the Kuhn–Tucker Theorem.

In applying this theorem to the choice of a government programme, the couple y^0, g plays the role of z and a valuation couple, r, q has to be introduced to play the role of v. Whereupon, if y^{0*}, g^* is an optimal government programme, there exist vectors u, r, q satisfying:

$$u \geq 0, \quad \sum_\alpha u_\alpha \{F^\alpha(g^*, p) + \theta_{\alpha 0} p(y^{0*} - \bar{y}^0)\} = 0,$$

$$r(y^0 - y^{0*}) + q(g - g^*) \geq 0 \text{ for all } y^0, g \in Y^0, G$$

and

$$\sum_\alpha (w_\alpha + u_\alpha)\{F^\alpha(g, p) + \theta_{\alpha 0} p(y^0 - \bar{y}^0)\} + ry^0 + qg$$

$$\leq \sum_\alpha w_\alpha \{F^\alpha(g^*, p) + \theta_{\alpha 0} p(y^{0*} - \bar{y}^0)\} + ry^{0*} + qg^*$$

for all y^0, g for which the functions are defined.

To interpret this, first let $g = g^*$ and $y^0 = y^{0*} + \Delta y^0$. Most of the terms then cancel, leaving:

$$\sum_\alpha u_\alpha \{F^\alpha(g^*, p) + \theta_{\alpha 0} p(y^{0*} + \Delta y^0 - \bar{y}^0)\} + \sum_\alpha w_\alpha \, \theta_{\alpha 0} p \Delta y^0 + r \Delta y^0 \leq 0.$$

Most of the first summation drops out because of the second condition on the vector u, so that

$$\{\sum_\alpha (u_\alpha + w_\alpha)\theta_{\alpha 0} p + r\}\Delta y^0 \leq 0$$

for all Δy^0 for which $y^{0*} + \Delta y^0$ lies in the domain of definition of the functions. Consider the ith component of y^0. If y_i^{0*} is in the interior of its domain, Δy_i^0 can be either positive or negative and the last inequality requires

$$r_i = -p_i \sum_\alpha (u_\alpha + w_\alpha)\theta_{\alpha 0}.$$

It is convenient to write $u_0 = \sum_\alpha (u_\alpha + w_\alpha)\theta_{\alpha 0}$, so that if Δy_i^0 can vary freely

$r_i = -u_0 p_i$. If Δy_i^0 cannot vary freely we have to be content with an inequality, but this will happen only in rare and uninteresting cases, essentially only when y_i^0 is restricted to be non-positive and $y_i^{0*} = 0$. I have tried to think of a significant commodity for which a government's net input is likely to be zero, and have come to the conclusion that governments use practically everything, even lipsticks. So, for all intents and purposes we may take $r = -u_0 p$.

Next, to interpret the auxiliary vector q it helps to suppose that the citizens' surplus functions $F^\alpha(g, p)$ are differentiable at g^* at least. Then we can choose $y^0 = y^{0*}$, $g = g^* + \Delta g$ and obtain

$$\sum_\alpha (u_\alpha + w_\alpha)\{F^{\alpha*} + \Delta g \nabla F^{\alpha*} + \theta_{\alpha 0} p(y^{0*} - \bar{y}^0)\} - u_0 p y^{0*} + q(g^* + \Delta g)$$

$$\leq \sum_\alpha w_\alpha \{F^{\alpha*} + \theta_{\alpha 0} p(y^{0*} - \bar{y}^0)\} - u_0 p y^{0*} + qg^*$$

for all $g^* + \Delta g$ in the domain of definition, apart from an approximation error of order higher than that of Δg, which can be ignored, using the notation

$$F^{\alpha *} = F^\alpha(g^*, p), \text{ and}$$
$$\nabla F^{\alpha *} = \text{gradient of } F^\alpha(g, p) \text{ at } (g^*, p).$$

By the same operations as before this reduces to

$$\Delta g\{\sum_\alpha (u_\alpha + w_\alpha)\nabla F^{\alpha *} + q\} \leq 0.$$

For single-component variation, then

$$\Delta g_k\{\sum_\alpha (u_\alpha + w_\alpha)F_k^{\alpha *} + q_k\} \leq 0,$$

the subscript denoting partial differentiation. It seems sensible to restrict g, the output of government goods, to be non-negative. Then if g_k^* is positive Δg_k can vary freely and the inequality requires

$$q_k = -\sum_\alpha (u_\alpha + w_\alpha)F_k^{\alpha *}.$$

That is, the component q_k of q is the negative of a politically weighted sum of the marginal valuations placed by the members of the different socio-economic groups on g_k. If that particular public good is not provided, the variation cannot be negative and the inequality demands only that q_k does not exceed the negative of this weighted sum.

Furthermore, $(-u_0 p, q)$ are the coefficients of the support plane of Y^0, G at y^{0*}, g^* so that

$$q\Delta g - u_0 p\Delta y \geq 0$$

for all $y^{0*} + \Delta y$, $g^* + \Delta g$ belonging to Y^0, G. Then if only one component of g changes from g^* and that change is positive

$$q_k \geq u_0 \frac{p\Delta y}{\Delta g_k}.$$

The fraction on the right is easily interpreted. For any $\Delta g_k \neq 0$ the product $p\Delta y$ has a maximum in the government's production set. The negative of the ratio of this maximum value to Δg_k is the incremental cost per unit of Δg_k, i.e.

$$IC(\Delta g_k) = -\max_{\Delta y} \frac{p\Delta y}{\Delta g_k}$$
$$\text{for } y^{0*} + \Delta y, g^* + \Delta g \in Y^0, G.$$

If the boundary of the production set is differentiable, $IC(\Delta g_k)$ will approach a well-defined limit as $\Delta g_k \to 0$. This limit is the marginal cost of g_k, to be denoted by $MC(g_k)$. Then we have found

$$q_k \geq -u_0 MC(g_k)$$

if $g_k > g_k^*$ is technically possible. For negative values of Δg_k the sense of the inequality is reversed. If Δg_k can vary freely the inequality becomes an equality.

Now we can combine our two results on q_k. If g_k can be varied upward from g_k^* we have found

$$-\sum_{\alpha}(u_\alpha + w_\alpha)F_k^{\alpha*} \geq q_k \geq -u_0 MC(g_k)$$

or

$$\sum_{\alpha}(u_\alpha + w_\alpha)F_k^{\alpha*} \leq MC(g_k)\sum_{\alpha}(u_\alpha + w_\alpha)\theta_{\alpha 0}.$$

In words, the weighted sum of the marginal valuations placed upon the kth public good by the socio-economic groups cannot exceed the marginal cost of that good multiplied by a factor of proportionality. If g_k can be varied downward from g_k^* the inequalities are reversed. An equality results if free variation is possible. That is, in the case of free variation

$$\sum_{\alpha}(u_\alpha + w_\alpha)F_k^{\alpha*} = MC(g_k)\sum_{\alpha}(u_\alpha + w_\alpha)\theta_{\alpha 0},$$

or the politically weighted sums of the marginal valuations placed upon the public goods by the different groups are proportional to their marginal costs.

Finally, the u_α are the shadow prices associated with the constraints that no group shall have a negative citizens' surplus. If any group has a positive citizens' surplus the corresponding u_α will be zero. The u_α may be positive for groups with zero citizens' surplus at y^{0*}, g^*. In fact, this vector may be taken as measuring the social cost, as viewed by the government, of meeting the minimum demands of the several socio-economic groups. This can be seen most easily by looking back at the statement of the lemma on concave programming. From conclusions (b) and (c) of that lemma it follows that

$$f^0(z) - f^0(z^*) + uf(z) \leq 0 \text{ for all } z \in Z.$$

If, then, we consider a value of z for which $f^i(z) = f^i(z^*) - 1$ and $f^j(z) = f^j(z^*)$ for all $j \neq i$, then, using conclusion (a),

$$f^0(z) - f^0(z^*) \leq u_i.$$

The coefficient u_i is therefore an upper limit to the amount that the objective function could be increased by permitting a unit violation of the ith constraint. If the functions are sufficiently smooth at z^* this limit is approached by infinitesimal variations.

This throws a little light on one of the ground-rules of our formulation. If some u_α should be very large the indication would be that society could benefit substantially, from the government's viewpoint, from a small infraction of the constraint with respect to that group. The government might therefore be tempted to override the protests of that group in the larger interest. This suggests that we might wish to contemplate negative lower limits to the citizens' surpluses accorded the different groups within the society, and it seems probably that governments do sometimes impose negative citizens' surpluses on politically weak or morally undeserving groups. But we shall not follow this lead.

This is all very fine as a matter of conceptualisation, but in fact the government has to solve its problem by the exercise of judgement, by appeal to previous and analogous experience, and by trial-and-error, just as does the businessman in his attempt to maximise profit. Indeed, regarded as a descriptive formulation, which is what I wish, this apparatus is methodologically identical with the familiar doctrine of business decision making. It proposes an impracticable calculation which, if it could be carried out, would approximate the results obtained by practical decision makers using other means. Some question must surely arise as to the descriptive significance of this model. Such considerations as the stern test of the market and economic Darwinism can be enlisted in support of the descriptive relevance of the received theory of production, but what forces can I summon to enforce the optimal solution of the public goods problem? As far as the constraints go there is the stern test of the voting booth or, in other contexts, of the need to hold a supporting coalition together. For the rest I feel, as I have said before, on even weaker ground. My justification is simply the conventional one: in government affairs as in business if there is an evident opportunity for cutting costs or improving output it will be taken eventually.

In government as in business affairs one of the advantages of decentralisation is that there are many units that can try experiments and that successful innovations can be emulated. This makes the behaviour of local governmental bodies somewhat more analogous to that of independent businessmen. The central government may, perhaps, be slower in exploring its production set but even there there is strong pressure for economical operation.

But I do not wish to claim too much, only to make it plausible that the solution to this programming problem approximates the behaviour of a government in the presence of given pressures, preferences and prices. Let us take it to be so. Then the government decides on an output g of public goods and a net consumption $-y^0$ of private goods. These are connected to what goes on in the private sphere by the fact that the government places the same relative valuations on private goods (our $-u^0p$) that the private sector does. Now the private sector takes over. In the presence of the public goods g and the net drain of $-y^0$ exerted by the government on the private sector, it possesses a general equilibrium position in which $\Sigma y - \Sigma x = -y^0$, where the first summation is taken over all firms and the second over all consumers. This equilibrium will of course be a technically efficient and Pareto-optimal configuration of the private sector. This is discussed in more detail below. This equilibrium includes an equilibrium set of prices for private goods, which will not necessarily be the same as the p on which the government decision was predicated. If the output-p resulting from the general equilibrium differs from the input-p used as a basis for the government's decisions, the government-plus-private economy will not be in full equilibrium and the government would reassess its programme in the light of these market prices. But, it is argued below on the usual fixed-point grounds, there does exist a price vector which if used by the government in formulating its programme will induce a general equilibrium configuration of the economy in which that same set of prices will reappear as the equilibrating price vector.

The set of levels of public goods predicated on this fixed-point price vector has some claim to be considered the equilibrium levels of public goods outputs, with all the efficiency properties appertaining thereto. In particular, it will be technically efficient. The marginal cost of each public good produced will be proportional to a politically weighted sum of the incremental tax burdens that the populace would be willing to assume to obtain a small increment in the level of that good. Some potential public goods may not be provided. If so, the politically weighted sum of the tax burdens that the populace is willing to assume to obtain them will not exceed their marginal costs at zero output multiplied by the same factor of proportionality. It will be impossible to improve the level of the government's objective function either by transfers of resources between the government and private sectors or by reallocation of resources within the government sector.

If the citizens' surplus should be positive for every group at the solution point, then $u=0$ and the output level of good k would satisfy

$$\sum_\alpha w_\alpha F_k^{\alpha^*} = MC(g_k) \sum_\alpha w_\alpha \theta_{\alpha 0}.$$

That is, the sum of the marginal desirabilities of the good to all the groups, weighted in accordance with the government's concern for them, would equal the sum of the tax burdens required for a small increase in output, weighted in the same way. If, for example, the government weights the groups in proportion to the numbers of people in them, say n_α, and if the tax burden is equally shared so $\theta_{\alpha 0} = 1/\Sigma n_\alpha$, then $\Sigma w_\alpha \theta_{\alpha 0} = 1$ and the condition becomes $\Sigma n_\alpha F_k^{\alpha^*} = MC(g_k)$, a formula for which there are precedents. But if some of the citizens' surpluses are zero the u will not vanish and this appealing formula will not apply. No more can be claimed for our solution than that. Income transfer could still improve the lot of some socio-economic groups at the expense of others and could increase the value of the government's objective function. Relaxation of the political constraints could also increase the value of the objective function. If a different government should come to power with a different political influence vector w a different equilibrium would emerge, with all the same justifications.

The conclusions reached by this analysis should be compared with the results of previous studies of the public goods problem. I know of three comparable studies, those of Bowen [6], Samuelson [16] and Strotz [19]. All three, in contrast to the present one, take a normative point of view; they seek to specify the ideal output of public goods, in some sense. Samuelson and Strotz lay great emphasis on the importance of tax policy and income transfers as part of the problem of attaining ideal output; Bowen and I exclude those expedients. Bowen works within a partial equilibrium framework, the rest of us are general equilibrators. Still there remains enough similarity to make comparisons worth while.

Bowen, as I said, considers the ideal output of a single public good in a partial equilibrium framework. He does not divide the body politic into socio-economic classes with divergent interests but does admit that individuals will have different preferences with respect to the level of provision of the public good. Each individual's preferences are expressed by his marginal rate of substitution between disposable income and the public good, regarded as a function of the level of output of the public good. In other words, the basic psychological datum is the amount that each individual would be willing to be taxed per unit increase in the output of the public good, for a small increase in its level. The sum of these marginal rates of substitution is the amount that the community in the aggregate would be willing to pay per unit for a small increase in the level of the good. At the ideal level of provision this total willing marginal contribution should be just equal to the marginal cost of the good.

For comparison with this ideal, our model political-economic system would produce the level g_1 for which

$$\sum_\alpha (u_\alpha + w_\alpha)F_1^\alpha = u_0 MC(g_1)$$

where the summation is taken over all individuals and $u_0 = \sum_\alpha (u_\alpha + w_\alpha)\theta_{\alpha 0}$. Our F_1^α is the same concept as Bowen's marginal rate of substitution. Bowen assumes that all individuals are given equal weight in political decisions, so that $w_\alpha = \frac{1}{n}$ for all α. $\Sigma \theta_{\alpha 0} = 1$. With these simplifications our formula becomes

$$\sum_\alpha u_\alpha F_1^\alpha + \frac{1}{n}\sum_\alpha F_1^\alpha = MC(g_1)\left(\sum_\alpha u_\alpha \theta_{\alpha 0} + \frac{1}{n}\right).$$

This shows that if $u_\alpha = 0$ for all α, or if the political constraints are disregarded, our optimum is the same as Bowen's. But this is not a likely result. Recall the political constraints:

$$F^\alpha(g, p) + \theta_{\alpha 0}p(y^0 - \bar{y}^0) \geq 0$$

for all groups α or, taken literally in Bowen's case, for all individuals α. For any single public good, there are likely to be groups that have a very low desire for it from the very outset. These constraints require that the output of the good stop expanding when the citizen's surplus of the least enthusiastic group falls to zero, which is likely to be well below Bowen's ideal level. Fluoridation of water supplies and education in family planning are two extreme examples. With respect to them there are politically effective groups such that $F^\alpha(g, p) \leq 0$ for all $g \geq 0$. And in point of fact, there are many jurisdictions in which these public goods are not provided. There are, of course, many less extreme instances. So it appears that the political constraints operate in the direction of under-provision of public goods.

This downward bias results from the rigidity of tax policy and the exclusion of income transfers from our model, but these are not unrealistic exclusions. Its effect is exaggerated when the model is applied to a single good. An important part of the art of politics is skill in holding a coalition together by offering a package of public goods that is satisfactory to each of the groups in the coalition, taken all in all, though some groups may regard some components in the package as being irrelevant or even noxious to their interests.   A blatant example is the National Seashore Act in the United States, which mobilised widespread support by proposing the preservation of four widely separated areas, one on each of the seacoasts.   Thus, packaging public goods together moderates the bias toward underprovision by depriving individual groups of item-by-item vetoes, but it probably does not obliterate it.   Galbraith [10], for one, has complained about this tendency.   On the other hand, it is not possible for our model to yield more than ideal output, in the single good case.   For if $u_\alpha = 0$ at the ideal level of output Bowen's criterion and our optimality condition are identical.

The studies by Samuelson and Strotz are so closely related that they can be discussed together.   Both are set in general equilibrium frameworks, and both seek the vector of public goods levels that maximises the value of a social welfare function.   Samuelson's social welfare indicator is an increasing function of individuals' utilities; Strotz' is linear in individual utilities.   Both assume that the output of public and private goods together is constrained by some aggregate social transformation function. As regards the ideal output of public goods they arrive at the same criterion, which Samuelson expresses thus:

$$\sum_\alpha \frac{u_{n+j}^\alpha}{u_r^\alpha} = \frac{F_{n+j}}{F_r}$$

where u_{n+j}^α is the marginal utility of public good j to consumer α,
   u_r^α is the marginal utility of private good r to him, and
   F_{n+j}/F_r is the marginal rate of transformation of private good r into public good j according to the social transformation function.

These concepts do not appear explicitly in our model, and so must be translated.   In our notation the marginal utility of public good j to consumer α is proportional to F_j^*, that of private good r is proportional to its price, so Samuelson's left-hand side becomes

$$\sum_\alpha \frac{u_{n+j}^\alpha}{u_r^\alpha} = \sum_\alpha \frac{F_{n+j}^{\alpha*}}{p_r}.$$

The aggregate social transformation function does not come up explicitly in our model but our assumptions on the firms' and the government's production sets are sufficient to assure that there is a social production set and that it has proper convexity. Furthermore, at the private plus government general equilibrium point the supporting plane of the social production set has coefficients proportional to $(p, -q/u_0) = (p, MC(g)_1, \ldots, MC(g_m))$, i.e. the same as the supporting plane of the government's production set. The marginal rates of transformation being simply the ratios of coefficients of the supporting plane, we have $F_{n+j}/F_r = MC(g_j)/p_r$. Accordingly, Samuelson's criterion reduces to

$$\sum_{\alpha} F_{n+j}^{\alpha*} = MC(g_j),$$

that is, each public good should be produced at the level at which its marginal cost equals the sum of the marginal willingnesses to pay for it on the part of all the citizen-consumers. This is the same as Bowen's criterion, as Samuelson remarked. Both Samuelson and, particularly, Strotz laid great emphasis on the importance of income redistribution, i.e flexible tax policy, in the attainment of this optimum. Since income redistribution is precluded in our model and since there are political constraints besides, such a government as we are imagining could not attain this ideal. All the remarks we made in comparing our model with Bowen's apply with equal force to the comparison with Samuelson's (Strotz concurring).

4 SOME IMPLICATIONS

It will be recalled that when Dupuit wrote his famous paper on the utility of public works he introduced the notion of consumer's surplus but despaired that the demand curves on which it depended could ever be measured. He argued that his concept was useful in spite of the fact that quantification appeared to be impossible. We now know that his pessimism was not altogether justified, although demand curves have remained very difficult to estimate to this very day.

I find myself in a very similar situation, seeing little or no reason to hope that the citizen's surpluses that I have described can be ascertained numerically. Dupuit was wrong; so may I be, but I regard the outlook as bleak.

I know of only one really serious effort to grapple with this problem, and it merits discussion here. In 1943, Howard Bowen proposed a voting procedure for determining the socially ideal level of output of a public good [6].

Bowen's proposal is to put the level of expenditure on a public good to a referendum. Before the referendum the voters are to be made as well informed as possible about the consequences of different levels of expenditure and, in particular, that the cost is to be shared equally among them. At the referendum each voter indicates the level of expenditure that he prefers. The mode of these voters' preferences is then adopted.

It is assumed explicitly that each voter will indicate the level that he, individually, prefers. This level is, of course, the one at which the marginal contribution of a dollar spent on the public good to that voter's welfare, as he sees it, is equal to the marginal worth to him of his tax contribution or of one-*nth* of a dollar. Then, assuming that the individual voters' marginal utilities for the public good are symmetrically distributed, Bowen argues that the mode of the voters' preferences 'may be presumed to indicate the point of intersection between the curve of marginal cost per person and the modal or average curve of marginal substitution [between the public good and disposable income]' [6, p. 37]. This level, moreover, is shown to be the ideal level of the public good in most cases.

Now there are some technical difficulties with this proposal, which are not very instructive to pursue, but, more pertinent to our interest, there is a nasty, game-theoretic side to it, which Bowen would not have passed over as lightly as he did if he had been writing a few years later. For, to keep things simple suppose that two voters, Mr A and Mr B are the whole electorate and that Mr A would like a higher level of the public good than Mr B. This is the sort of information that would be known, at least vaguely, to both of them. If Mr A and Mr B both vote for the levels that they desire, Mr A would get less of the public good than he wants (taking, crudely, the mode of two votes to be the midpoint between them). Mr A can remedy this situation easily by voting for somewhat more than he actually wants. He would be foolish not to do so, just as Mr B would be foolish not to vote for somewhat less than he really wants. This is an especially easy game. The Nash equilibrium point is for Mr A to vote for twice the level that he really wants, and for Mr B to vote for zero. Mr A wins. The assymetry results from the fact that Mr A can vote for as large a scale as he chooses, but Mr B cannot vote for less than zero.

This is a defect to worry about but not necessarily decisive. To add a little realism, suppose there are a number of Mr A's and a number of Mr B's, e.g. some families and some elderly couples all of whom want schools, but do not feel their urgency with equal keenness. The difficulty of co-ordinating even the slight amount of duplicity required to win the game would make Bowen's voting procedure work somewhat better than in the case where all group consultations could be conducted within a single head.

When there are several social groups with divergent interests, then, as Bowen recognised, another difficulty in principle arises. An unweighted mean, median, or mode can be used to average the preferences of symmetrically distributed individuals, but how are the votes of contending interest groups to be averaged? A small cabal from the A group could distort either the arithmetic average or the mode; a small cabal from the B group could capture the mode; even without any connivance the numerically larger group would control the median. Bowen's suggestion is to use a sequence of referenda administered to the groups separately and to adjust the allocation of cost between the groups after each referendum until both groups vote for the same level. But then the proposal looses its intriguing simplicity.

I conclude, then, that Bowen's procedure could not work and, at any rate, is not descriptive of any extant political procedure. In the light of these and other difficulties, which he recognised, Bowen urged strongly the use of public opinion polls for ascertaining citizens' preferences [6, p. 43]. Hotelling has made the same suggestion in a similar connection [12]. More recently Holt recommended the use of questionnaire methods for assistance in determining welfare objectives [11]. My own opinion is that no matter how informative public opinion polls may be for many purposes, they cannot be relied on to disclose the willingness-to-be-taxed functions $F^\alpha(g, p)$.

A great deal is known about the structure and determinants of voters' preferences but I cannot pretend to knowledge of this subject. These preferences appear to be a complex mixture of firmly held convictions and lightly held opinions. The man in the street is swayed easily by arguments about matters remote from his daily concerns and fundamental beliefs. Should the United States be spending $50 billion on national defence? The average citizen is willing to hope that someone in Washington has figured it out about right, or else to accept the authority of his party's spokesmen. What else can he or I do? So it seems that these $F^\alpha(g, p)$ reflect the preferences of group leaders, professional and volunteer, more nearly than they do the preferences of the great rank-and-file. The leaders, who have occasion to become informed and to think things through, know better than the followers where all will stand when the chips are down.

Thus the $F^\alpha(g, p)$ are quite different from demand curves, to which they have a formal resemblance. Demand curves pertain to individuals. Citizens' preferences pertain to groups: they are formed, articulated, and changed by group leaders (with due respect for deep-seated preconceptions beyond their reach) and are accepted, as long as current, by all the members of the group. The citizens' surplus functions, and the preference maps from which they are derived, reflect the limit to the exercise of sovereignty by individual citizens. The $F^\alpha(g, p)$ on the basis of which a citizen's spokesman makes his decisions is only one of a great number of such functions consistent with the citizen's desires, as sharply as he cares to formulate them. A political leader can, under the pressure of expediency or changed convictions, change his preference map substantially and carry most of his constituency with him. Herein lies the 'leadership' of political leaders and their scope for constructive initiative. They do more than reflect the wishes of their constituents; they define, articulate and apply them to practical problems.

I am not saying that voters have no preferences worth considering with respect to public goods. I am saying that we voters don't know our preferences; that we have to be told what they are by people who accept our prejudices and premises and who also understand the consequences and implications of particular political decisions. In consequence, surveying voters' preferences is like surveying castles in the sand. Firm bedrock is somewhere else.

For an essay that began with an attempt to insert a government sector into a quantitative model of economic equilibrium, we have come to a strange result. We have been led to base our approach on a concept – citizen's surplus – whose quantifiability is very doubtful. But we should not be under any illusions about how quantitative the theory of general equilibrium is. It contains no numbers, and its significant theorems are all qualitative in nature. So we do no violence to the spirit of the theory by adding still another concept that defies empirical measurement. In so far as the formulation just proposed has merit, it permits the apparatus of general equilibrium theory to be used to provide guidance for decisions about public goods. It indicates the social losses that arise from not integrating decisions about public goods with tax and income policy. It helps explain that the discrepancies that have been noted between the marginal social benefits of public expenditures on different programmes may be due, not to inattention or maladministration, but to the built-in protections that the political process provides to minorities in a world where the delicateent adjustm of tax policy and income distribution is not always feasible. Above all, it provides a conceptual framework that may help bridge the gap between professional economists and practising politicians.

If the economist could free himself of his lofty disdain for the considerations foremost in the mind of the practising government official, he might enhance the sympathetic understanding between himself and officials. With the best will in the world, there is only one way for him to do that. He must accept that a government can no more violate its political constraints than it can transgress its production possibility set, and he must build these constraints into the core of his thinking, as we have done, instead of grudgingly admitting that in the end his recommendations have to be warped in the interests of political feasibility.

It is conventional, and almost obligatory, at the end of a theoretical essay to remind the reader that it is only a crude, first, tentative approximation and that a great deal more work remains to be done. I follow this convention with special enthusiasm in the present instance because the shortcomings of the political model I have proposed are so numerous and significant. Yet I do not believe that they entirely smother the germ of truth that it contains.

In the first place, the 'government' in this model is so simplified that it is practically emasculated. It does nothing but levy taxes and produce public goods. The social waste that we detected stems largely from the failure of this government to co-ordinate its tax policy with its public goods decisions and from its inability to make compensating income transfers. The reader should recall that we excluded these ameliorative fiscal devices by assumption. This assumption seems justified, however: governments in fact do not co-ordinate their tax policies very finely with their expenditure programmes, and it probably would be impractical for them to try to do so. Income transfers would certainly mitigate some of the social waste, but it should be recognised that they introduce distortions of their own and can provide only a limited offset to the costs of meeting what I have called 'political constraints'. Still, a more adequate treatment of the taxation side of governmental decisions would be highly desirable, particularly one that took account of the price structure distortions that taxes inevitably cause.

No attention has been paid to public goods provided by entities other than the government, or to externalities of any kind. Yet these are closely akin to the phenomena we have studied and should be included in any complete treatment.

I am not well satisfied with my characterisation of socio-economic groups or with my treatment of their relationship to their leaders.

Particularly I am aware that the preference maps of government officials, other political leaders, and the general public all are altered in the course of the give-and-take of the political process. I see no objection to conceiving of them as being concrete and definite at any one time (apart from the vagueness of the preferences felt by ordinary citizens), but I am sorry to have to treat them as immutable, which they surely are not. The laws of change of preference maps are a subject for a separate investigation that I could not undertake. In regard to these matters of political theory, I feel that I have gone about as far as my competence and duty as an economist can justify.

I am aware also of some technical defects in the formulation. The most bothersome is that the definition of citizens' surplus, on which so much depends, is ambiguous. The surplus functions of the different socio-economic groups will be affected by the basal level of government activity with which proposed programmes are compared. There is no reason why all groups should compare a proposed programme to the same base. The concept of citizens' surplus seems fundamentally sound, but the formulation permits improvement. I do not know how to improve it.

I have reservations also about the requirement that *no* group receive a negative citizens' surplus. It is a great mathematical convenience and it has Wicksell's blessing, but still I wish I had been able to construct my argument without it.

Finally, this model is subject to all the strong limitations of general equilibrium analysis. It is thoroughly static. It ignores the risks and the uncertainties that are so important an aspect of political as well as economic affairs. It excludes the possibilities of increasing returns in production and of non-convexity of consumers' and citizens' preferences.

The model is, in short, only a beginning which I hope is on the right track.

REFERENCES

[1] Kenneth J. Arrow, *Social Choice and Individual Values* (New York, 1951).
[2] Chester I. Barnard, *The Functions of the Executive* (Cambridge, Mass., 1954).
[3] William J. Baumol, *Welfare Economics and the Theory of the State* (Cambridge, Mass., 1952).
[4] Abram Bergson, 'A reformulation of certain aspects of welfare economics', *Quarterly Journal of Economics*, LII (Feb 1938) 310–34.
[5] Duncan Black, 'On the rationale of group decision-making', *Journal of Political Economy*, LVI (Feb 1948) 23–34.

General Equilibrium with Public Goods   275

[6] Howard R. Bowen, 'The interpretation of voting in the allocation of economic resources', *Quarterly Journal of Economics*, LVIII (Nov 1943) 27–48.
[7] Gerard Debreu, *Theory of Value* (New York, 1959).
[8] Anthony Downs, *An Economic Theory of Democracy* (New York, 1957).
[9] Duncan K. Foley, 'Resource allocation and the public sector', *Yale Economic Essays*, forthcoming.
[10] J. Kenneth Galbraith, *The Affluent Society* (Boston, 1958).
[11] Charles C. Holt, 'Quantitative decision analysis and national policy', in Bert G. Hickman (ed.), *Quantitative Planning of Economic Policy* (Washington, 1965) 252–66.
[12] Harold Hotelling, 'The general welfare in relation to problems of taxation and of railway and utility rates', *Econometrica*, VI (Jul 1938) 242–69.
[13] Leif Johansen, *Public Economics* (Amsterdam and Chicago, 1965).
[14] Samuel Karlin, *Mathematical Methods and Theory in Games, Programming, and Economics*, vol. I (Reading, Mass., 1959).
[15] Charles E. Lindblom, *The Intelligence of Democracy* (New York, 1965).
[16] Paul A. Samuelson, 'The pure theory of public expenditure', *Review of Economics and Statistics*, XXXVI (Nov 1954) 387–9.
[17] Paul A. Samuelson, 'Diagrammatic exposition of a theory of public expenditure', *Review of Economics and Statistics*, XXXVII (Nov 1955) 350–6.
[18] Paul A. Samuelson, 'Aspects of public expenditure theories', *Review of Economics and Statistics*, XL (Nov 1958) 332–8.
[19] Robert H. Strotz, 'Two propositions related to public goods', *Review of Economics and Statistics*, XL (Nov 1958) 329–31.
[20] David B. Truman, *The Governmental Process: political interests and Public opinion* (New York, 1960).
[21] Knut Wicksell, 'A new principle of just taxation', in R. A. Musgrave and A. T. Peacock (eds.), *Classics in the Theory of Public Finance* (London and New York, 1964) pp. 72–118.

[10]

Reprinted from THE REVIEW OF ECONOMICS AND STATISTICS
Published for Harvard University. Copyright, 1979, by North-Holland Publishing Company
Vol. LXI, No. 1, February, 1979

A FORMULA FOR THE GINI COEFFICIENT

Robert Dorfman*

The Gini Coefficient is well established as a conventional, ad hoc measure of income inequality. Recently there has been a flurry of interest in it, stirred up by a debate about its significance as a measure of economic welfare (Atkinson, 1970; Dasgupta et al., 1973; Newbery, 1970; Rothschild and Stiglitz, 1973; Sen, 1973; Sheshinski, 1972) in the course of which a confusing variety of formulas for the coefficient have been published, some of them quite complicated (Atkinson, 1970; Fei, 1978; Sen, 1973; Theil, 1967, for example). This note will propose a simple formula for the Gini Coefficient that will apply to both discrete and continuous distributions of income and will be well-defined and valid whether or not there is a finite upper limit to the income that can be received by anyone, provided the mean of the distribution is finite.

Received for publication February 28, 1978. Revision accepted for publication November 1, 1978.
* Harvard University.

Gastwirth (1972) has published a similar formula without proof, attributing it to Kendall and Stuart (1977), where the proof also is omitted.

The formula to be proposed is

$$G = 1 - \frac{1}{\mu} \int_0^{y^*} (1 - F(y))^2 dy, \tag{1}$$

where

$F(y)$ is the cumulative probability distribution of income,

μ is its mean, assumed finite, and

y^* is its upper limit, which may be infinite.

The Gini Coefficient can be approached from either of two directions. First, it can be regarded as the salient summary statistic of the Lorenz Curve of the income distribution. The Lorenz Curve, to be denoted $L(u)$, is the proportion of the total income of the economy that is received by the lowest $100u\%$ of income receivers. (A more formal definition will be given below.) From this point of view, the Gini Coefficient is the area between a given Lorenz Curve and the Lorenz Curve for an economy in which everyone receives the same income, expressed as a proportion of the area under the curve for the equal distribution of income. This definition leads to the formula

$$G = 1 - 2 \int_0^1 L(u)du, \tag{2}$$

as will be demonstrated below. A formula for the area under a Lorenz Curve will be derived en route. It is

$$\int_0^1 L(u)du = \frac{1}{2\mu} \int_0^{y^*} (1 - F(y))^2 dy. \tag{3}$$

Equation (1) follows immediately from equations (2) and (3).

Second, Gini himself proposed the coefficient that now bears his name as a measure of the variability of any statistical distribution or probability distribution. (See Gini (1912), for example.) Specifically, he based his coefficient on the average of the absolute differences between pairs of observations, and defined it to be the ratio of half of that average to the mean of the distribution. We shall see that that definition also leads to equation (1).

Derivation from the Lorenz Curve

In this section we derive the formula for the Gini Coefficient from its definition in terms of the Lorenz Curve. But first we must formulate the Lorenz Curve in more detail.

Let $F(y)$ denote the proportion of the population that receives incomes no greater than y. $F(y)$ need not be continuous but since it is monotonic it can have no more than a countable infinity of points of discon-

tinuity. Furthermore, it is everywhere one-sided continuous both to the left and to the right, and by virtue of its definition $F(y+) = F(y)$. We assume throughout that the points of discontinuity, if any, are isolated, that $F(y)$ is differentiable between those points, and that the income distribution has a finite mean, μ.

The Lorenz Curve, $L(u)$, is the function of u, for $0 \leq u \leq 1$, that specifies the proportion of aggregate income that goes to the members of the population in the lowest $100u\%$ of the income distribution. To relate $L(u)$ to the distribution of income, regard y as the function of u, say $y(u)$, that specifies the largest income such that the proportion of the population whose incomes do not exceed any lower income does not exceed u. Then $y(u)$ is defined by $F(y(u) -) \leq u \leq F(y(u))$.

We shall write

$$I(y) = \int_0^y xdF(x),$$

a Stieltjes integral, for the total income accruing to members of the population whose incomes do not exceed y divided by the total number of members of the population. We shall also use the convention

$$\int_a^{z^-} f(x)dg(x) = \lim_{\epsilon \to 0} \int_a^{z-\epsilon} f(x)dg(x).$$

In this notation the total income accruing to the lowest $100u\%$ of the population is

$$I(y(u) -) + y(u)[u - F(y(u) -)]$$

multiplied by the size of the population. Since the aggregate income of the population is μ times the size of the population, the proportion of income received by the lowest $100u\%$ is

$$L(u) = \frac{1}{\mu} [I(y(u) -) + y(u)(u - F(y(u) -))].$$

The definition of the Gini Coefficient depends on the area, A, under the Lorenz curve, or

$$A = \int_0^1 L(u)du.$$

To evaluate this integral divide the range of u into segments at the values of u corresponding to the (isolated) discontinuities of $F(y)$. Suppose these discontinuities occur at $y_0 = 0, y_1, y_2, \ldots, y_k$ (k may be infinite). $y(u) = y_i$ when $F(y_i -) \leq u \leq F(y_i)$, which we shall abbreviate by $F_i^- \leq u \leq F_i$. Then

$$A = \sum_{i=1}^k \int_{F_{i-1}}^{F_i} L(u)du + \int_{F_k}^1 L(u)du \tag{4}$$

where k (possibly infinite) is the index of the largest discontinuity of $F(y)$.

The contribution of the ith segment is

$$\frac{1}{\mu} \int_{F_{i-1}}^{F_i} [I(y(u) -) + y(u)(u - F(y(u) -))]du.$$

For $F_{i-1} \le u \le F_i^-$, the second term is zero and $F(y(u)) = u$. For $F_i^- \le u \le F_i$, the first term is constant ($= I(y_i^-)$) and $y(u) = y_i$. Thus

$$\int_{F_{i-1}}^{F_i} L(u)du = \frac{1}{\mu}\left[\int_{y_{i-1}}^{y_i^-} I(y)dF(y)\right.$$
$$\left. + (F_i - F_i^-)I(y_i -) + \tfrac{1}{2}(F_i - F^-)^2 y_i\right].$$

To simplify, notice

$$I(y_i -) = I(y_i) - y_i(F_i - F_i^-)$$

and

$$\int_{y_{i-1}}^{y_i} I(y)dF(y) = -\int_{y_{i-1}}^{y_i^-} I(y)d(1 - F(y))$$
$$= -(1 - F_i^-)I(y_i -) + (1 - F_{i-1})I(y_{i-1})$$
$$-\int_{y_{i-1}}^{y_i^-} (1 - F(y))y\, d(1 - F(y)).$$

Further, the last integral equals

$$\tfrac{1}{2}\int_{y_{i-1}}^{y_i^-} yd(1 - F(y))^2 = \tfrac{1}{2}\int_{y_{i-1}}^{y_i} yd(1 - F(y))^2$$
$$- \tfrac{1}{2} y_i((1 - F_i)^2 - (1 - F_i^-)^2).$$

Putting these all together, the terms involving y_i cancel out and there remains

$$\int_{F_{i-1}}^{F_i} L(u)du$$
$$= \frac{1}{\mu}\left[-(1 - F_i)I(y_i) + (1 - F_{i-1})I(y_{i-1})\right.$$
$$\left. - \tfrac{1}{2}\int_{y_{i-1}}^{y_i} yd(1 - F(y))^2\right].$$

By similar manipulations,

$$\int_{F_k}^1 L(u)du = \frac{1}{\mu}\left[(1 - F_k)I(y_k) - (1 - F(y^*))I(y^*)\right.$$
$$\left. - \tfrac{1}{2}\int_{y_k}^{y^*} yd(1 - F(y))^2\right],$$

and, adding up,

$$A = \frac{1}{\mu}\left[-(1 - F(y^*))I(y^*) - \tfrac{1}{2}\int_0^{y^*} yd(1 - F(y))^2\right].$$

Finally, integrating by parts,

$$A = \frac{1}{\mu}\left[-(1 - F(y^*))I(y^*) - \tfrac{1}{2}(1 - F(y^*))^2 y^* \right.$$
$$\left. + \tfrac{1}{2}\int_0^{y^*} (1 - F(y))^2 dy\right] \tag{5}$$

where y^*, which may be infinite, denotes the upper limit of the income distribution.

If y^* is finite, $F(y^*) = 1$ and the integral is all that remains.[1] Otherwise we must assure ourselves that the

[1] Professor Andrew Gleason assisted greatly with the following argument.

expression on the right converges as $y^* \to \infty$. By straightforward algebra, for any finite y^*:

$$\int_0^{y^*} (1 - F(y))^2 dy - (1 - F(y^*))^2 y^*$$
$$= \int_0^{y^*} (F(y^*) - F(y))^2 dy$$
$$+ 2(1 - F(y^*))\int_0^{y^*} (F(y^*) - F(y))dy. \tag{6}$$

Similarly, we can see that

$$\int_0^{y^*} (F(y^*) - F(y))dy = I(y^*).$$

Thus the right hand side of equation (5) reduces to

$$\frac{1}{2\mu}\int_0^{y^*} (F(y^*) - F(y))^2 dy \le \frac{1}{2\mu}$$
$$\int_0^{y^*} (F(y^*) - F(y))dy \le I(y^*)/2\mu \le 1/2$$

since $I(y^*) \le \mu$. Convergence is therefore assured. If there is no upper bound to the distribution of income,

$$A = \lim_{y^* \to \infty} \frac{1}{2\mu}\int_0^{y^*} (F(y^*) - F(y))^2 dy$$
$$= \frac{1}{2\mu}\int_0^\infty (1 - F(y))^2 dy, \tag{7}$$

which is valid in any case.

In the important special case in which $F(y)$ is a step-function with jumps at $y_0 = 0, y_1, y_2, \ldots;$ $F(y) = F_{i-1}$ for $y_{i-1} \le y < y_i$. Then equation (7) reduces to

$$\int_0^1 L(u)du = A = \frac{1}{2\mu}\sum_{i=0}^\infty (1 - F_i)^2(y_{i+1} - y_i). \tag{8}$$

We can now derive the Gini Coefficient itself. It is defined as the difference between A and the area under the Lorenz Curve for a population in which everyone receives the same income (namely μ), to be denoted A_e, expressed as a proportion of A_e. That is,

$$G = \frac{A_e - A}{A_e}.$$

For the curve of equal distribution, $F(y) = 0$ for $y < \mu$ and $F(y) = 1$ for $y \ge \mu$. By either equation (7) or (8),

$$A_e = \frac{1}{2\mu}\mu = \frac{1}{2}$$

and

$$G = 1 - \frac{1}{\mu}\int_0^\infty (1 - F(y))^2 dy,$$

which is equation (1).

Example 1

For the Pareto Distribution, $F(y) = 0$, $y \le 1$; $F(y) = 1 - y^{-\alpha}$, $y \ge 1$; $\mu = \alpha/(\alpha - 1)$; $\alpha > 1$. Formula (1) yields

$$G = 1 - \frac{\alpha - 1}{\alpha} \left[\int_0^1 dy + \int_1^\infty y^{-2\alpha} dy \right]$$

$$= 1 - \frac{\alpha - 1}{\alpha} \left[1 + \frac{1}{2\alpha - 1} \right] = \frac{1}{2\alpha - 1}.$$

Example 2

Consider a geometric distribution with $i = 0, 1, 2, \ldots$; $k = \infty$, $y_i = i$; and where the proportion of the population that receives i is $f_0 = 0$, $f_i = (1 - a)/a)a^i$, $i = 1, 2, \ldots$; $0 < a < 1$. Then $\mu = 1/(1 - a)$, $F_i = 1 - a^i$. Equation (8) gives

$$\int_0^1 L(u)du = \frac{1 - a}{2} \sum_0^\infty a^{2i}$$

$$= \frac{1 - a}{2} \frac{1}{1 - a^2} = \frac{1}{2(1 + a)}.$$

Then, by equation (2),

$$G = 1 - \frac{1}{1 + a} = \frac{a}{1 + a}.$$

Derivation from the Income Distribution[2]

The second definition of the Gini Coefficient, Gini's own, is based directly on the distribution of income, $F(y)$. In words, it is half the ratio of the average absolute difference between pairs of observations to the mean, μ. In symbols, let $\Delta = E|x - y|$. Then $G = \Delta/2\mu$. Now

$$|x - y| = 2\left(\left(\frac{x + y}{2} \right) - \min(x,y) \right)$$

so

$$\Delta = 2(\mu - \text{E min }(x,y)).$$

[2] The theorem in this section and its proof were contributed by the referee, Joseph L. Gastwirth.

Further,

$$\text{Prob}(\min(x,y) \le z) = 1 - \text{Prob}(x > z)\, \text{Prob}(y > z)$$
$$= 1 - (1 - F(z))^2,$$

which is the cumulative distribution function of $\min(x,y)$. So

$$\Delta = 2\mu - 2 \int_0^\infty z d(1 - (1 - F(z)))^2$$

$$= 2\mu + 2 \int_0^\infty z d(1 - F(z))^2.$$

We have already evaluated this integral in the course of deriving equation (5). Thus

$$G = \Delta/2\mu = 1 - \frac{1}{\mu} \int_0^{y^*} (1 - F(y))^2 dy,$$

as before, since the term $y^*(1 - F(y^*))^2$ vanishes whether y^* is finite or not.

REFERENCES

Atkinson, Anthony B., "On the Measurement of Inequality," *Journal of Economic Theory* 2 (1970), 244–263.

Dasgupta, Partha, Amartya Sen, and David Starrett, "Notes on the Measurement of Inequality," *Journal of Economic Theory* 6 (1973), 180–187.

Fei, John C. H., Gustav Ranis, and Shirley W. Y. Kuo, "Growth and the Family Distribution of Income by Factor Components," *Quarterly Journal of Economics* 92 (1978), 17–53.

Gastwirth, Joseph L., "The Estimation of the Lorenz Curve and Gini Index," this REVIEW 54 (1972), 306–316.

Gini, Corrado, *Variabilità e Mutabilità* (Bologna: Tipografia di Paolo Cuppini, 1912).

Kendall, Sir Maurice, and Alan Stuart, *The Advanced Theory of Statistics*, 1 (4th ed.) (London: Charles Griffin, 1977), 48–51, 54.

Newbery, D. M. G., "A Theorem on the Measurement of Inequality," *Journal of Economic Theory* 2 (1970), 264–266.

Rothschild, Michael, and Joseph E. Stiglitz, "Some Further Results on the Measurement of Inequality," *Journal of Economic Theory* 6 (1973), 188–204.

Sen, Amartya, *On Economic Inequality* (Delhi: Oxford University Press, 1973).

———, "Poverty: An Ordinal Approach to Measurement," *Econometrica* 44 (1976), 219–231.

Sheshinski, Eytan, "Relation between a Social Welfare Function and the Gini Index of Inequality," *Journal of Economic Theory* 4 (1972), 98–100.

Theil, Henri, *Economics and Information Theory* (Chicago: Rand McNally, 1967).

[11]

THE JOURNAL OF FINANCE • VOL. XXXVI, NO. 5 • DECEMBER 1981

The Meaning of Internal Rates of Return

ROBERT DORFMAN

ABSTRACT

Nearly one hundred years after Irving Fisher's persuasive argument that net present value is the fundamental criterion for appraising investment projects, businessmen and bankers continue to consider the internal rate of return. Business practice is justified in some circumstances. It has long been recognized that a firm will grow asymptotically at a rate equal to the largest real positive root of an individual project's rate of return equation if the net cash flows are continually reinvested in projects of the same type. That same root also controls the firm's asymptotic growth rate if any fixed proportion of the cash flows is reinvested. The other roots of the equation are important also, since the stability of the firm's growth path depends on them.

FOR A VERY LONG time, two families of criteria for capital investment decisions have coexisted: net present value criteria, most forcefully advanced by Irving Fisher [9], and internal rate of return criteria. Throughout most of this time the Fisherian criteria have received the endorsement of orthodox economic theory, but the rate of return criteria have survived in business and banking practice, as attested by the fact that the most popular financial hand calculator contains a built-in program for computing rates of return. The purpose of this paper is to explore the element of validity in the rate of return criteria and, secondarily, to clarify the meaning of the internal rates of return—there are almost always several.

The debate between net present value criteria and internal rate of return criteria goes back to the inception of modern interest theory. A definitive statement of the case for net present value criteria appears in Irving Fisher's *The Rate of Interest* [8]; that argument remains the foundation of the dominant school of capital investment appraisal to this day. The internal rate of return criterion is implicit in Boehm-Bawerk's *Positive Theorie des Kapitales* [3]. There, Boehm-Bawerk took it for granted that businessmen would (and should) invest so as to obtain the greatest annual net cash flow in perpetuity per dollar invested—a simple version of the internal rate of return principle. This approach has remained popular ever since (though not so popular among theorists, with some exceptions including Keynes [15]). The list of intervening contributors, expositors, and commentators is too long to be worth recounting. A few have to be mentioned, however.

Alchian [1] clarified the conceptual relationships among the internal rate of return, the net present value criterion, and a subsidiary concept, Fisher's "rate of return over cost". Hirschleifer's influential paper [13] explored the implications of imperfections in the capital markets for the net present value criterion. Marglin, in a pair of elegant articles [16, 17], showed how to incorporate the possibility of reinvesting proceeds in the present value criterion. Wright [19], Fleming and

Wright [10], and, independently Arrow and Levhari [2] threw light on the most confusing technical aspect of the internal rate of return criterion by showing that if the duration of an investment project is subject to choice and if it is chosen to maximize the internal rate of return, then the equation for the rate of return can have only one real root.

The strongest influence on the present paper is the work of John S. Chipman. In a series of papers [5, 6] he developed the insights that when the net proceeds resulting from investments in an economy are wholly or partially reinvested, the growth of the economy can be described by a renewal equation, and, under some appropriate assumptions, the formula for the roots of that equation is identical with the rate of return equation for the typical investment in that economy.

The net present value criterion is supported by a powerful argument. The argument has its limitations, however, three of which are relevant in the present context. First, in its original and fundamental form, the present value is computed from the cash flows generated by an initial act of investment, without allowance for the results of possible reinvestment of those cash flows or even full maintenance and replacement of the physical capital originally procured. Beside ignoring some important consequences of an investment, this convention makes it difficult to compare undertakings with different economic lives. To take the starkest example, two alternative investment opportunities cost $1,000 each; the first yields $1,100 in one year, the second yields $1,166 in two years, the market rate of interest is 5%. Straightforwardly, the net present value of the first is $48, that of the second is $58; the second is preferable. But which leaves the investor better off at the end of two years? On the Fisherian assumption, he will have to reinvest his $1,100 at the market rate and end with $1,155, which is certainly inferior to the second alternative's result. Alternatively, the investor might be able to repeat his investment after the first year, and obtain $1,210 at the end of the second. Which assumption to make is obscure, and with that obscurity the decisiveness of the net present value argument fades. (See Hildreth [12]).

Later work (Galenson and Leibenstein [11], Eckstein [7], Marglin [16] and [17]) has corrected this deficiency. One has only to impose a reinvestment and replacement policy and then to include in the calculation the cash flows attributable to the daughter investments, and their daughters, and so on forever. Of course, the assumptions about the original investment's progeny have to be pretty tenuous. But, as the example shows, to ignore them is to assume that after the initial investment no opportunities more promising than the market rate of interest will become available, which is not a very appealing assumption.

The second limitation is that the Fisherian argument presumes perfect financial markets. The "separation theorem" rests on this assumption. Because of it, the precise pattern of cash flows is irrelevant; any pattern can be exchanged in the financial markets for any other of the same present value. Hirschleifer [13] has made clear the consequences of dropping it; the pattern of cash flows can then matter a great deal, and the net present value is an incomplete criterion for investment appraisal.

Those two limitations weaken the case for the net present value criterion; the third limitation cuts deepest. Fisher's whole structure is an elaboration of the tension between opportunities to invest and impatience to consume. It assumes that the purpose of investing is to be able to afford the greatest possible amount of consumption. (In the presence of the perfect financial market assumption, the greatest amount of consumption is well-defined as the consumption pattern with greatest possible present value). If the purpose of investment is anything other than enhancing the ability to consume, then some other criterion may well be appropriate. The literatures of both corporate behavior and economic development suggest that quite frequently promoting consumption is not the dominant goal. A number of plausible goals have been hypothesized and supported with more or less evidence, so that one tends to conclude that the purpose to be served by investment is not the same in all instances, and that the appropriate investment criterion varies correspondingly. One particularly appealing alternative objective is growth: growth of the enterprise or growth of the economy as the case may be. In the sequel, we shall develop the implications of the maximum growth objective, and shall see that in conjunction with some assumptions about reinvestment opportunities, it entails an internal rate of return criterion for selecting investments. We shall first develop this thesis in the context of a firm that desires to grow as rapidly as possible by using internally generated funds.

I. Investment Appraisal for Internally Financed Projects

We now develop a rule for project selection for a firm that desires to grow as rapidly as possible. In this section we assume that this growth is to be financed entirely by retained earnings and depreciation charges. But not all retained earnings are available for reinvestment. A certain proportion of them is claimed by income taxes and another proportion has to be paid out as dividends. The residue, say proportion θ of retained earnings after depreciation, will be reinvested along with the entire amount charged to depreciation. These assumptions enable us to formualte the growth path that will result from a policy of investing in undertakings of any specified type.

A particular type of investment project can be characterized adequately for our purposes by specifying the net cash flow that it generates, per dollar of initial investment, in each year of its economic life. The net cash flow in the τth year will be denoted by $f(\tau)$. For example, if a type of investment costs 1,000 initially and generates successively cash flows of 3,250, − 6,500, 5,000 in its three-year life it would be characterized by the table

τ	$f(\tau)$
1	3.25
2	−6.50
3	5.00

In each year also, the investment depreciates. Depreciation in year τ will be denoted by $\delta(\tau)$. Then, following the rule of reinvesting each year the depreciation charge plus the proportion of θ of cash flow after depreciation, the reinvestment generated in the τth year of the project's life per dollar of initial investment will be

$$y(\tau) = \delta(\tau) + \theta(f(\tau) - \delta(\tau))$$
$$= \theta f(\tau) + (1 - \theta)\delta(\tau) \qquad (1)$$

We assume that the daughter projects have the same cash flows as the parent, and denote by $Y(t)$ the total amount of gross investment in calendar year t. This will be the total amount of investment that will result from projects initiated 1, 2, ..., T years previously, where T is the length of the individual project's life. Symbolically,

$$Y(t) = \sum_{\tau=1}^{T} Y(t - \tau)y(\tau) \tag{2}$$

The $y(\tau)$ are simply constants, determined by Equation (1). Then Equation (2) is a Tth order difference equation in $Y(t)$, with constant coefficients. The solution of such an equation has the form

$$Y(t) = \sum_{i=1}^{T} c_i(1 + u_i)^t \tag{3}$$

on the assumption (which avoids a good deal of algebraic complexity) that all the roots $(1 + u_i)$ are distinct. The roots $(1 + u_i)$ are the solution to the polynomial equation

$$\sum_{\tau=1}^{T} \frac{y(\tau)}{(1 + u_i)^\tau} = 1 \tag{4}$$

Notice the similarity of this equation to the internal rate of return equation for the individual projects. The only difference is that $y(\tau)$ appears in the numerator instead of $f(\tau)$. The c_i are constants which are determined by any T values of $Y(t)$ along the growth path, usually the first T.

Our remaining task is to determine the roots $(1 + u_i)$, which depend on the relations among $y(\tau)$, $f(\tau)$, and $\delta(\tau)$. To this end, the depreciation formula must be specified. It appears that only one depreciation formula leads to a tractable solution. This is the formula for "economic depreciation" introduced by Hotelling [14].

It goes as follows. Let $V(\tau)$ denote the value of the assets per dollar of initial investment at the end of the τth year of the project's life. By convention, the initial value is denoted $V(0)$ and, by definition, $V(0) = 1$. The value $V(\tau)$, at the end of any year is the present value of future cash flows discounted at an appropriate rate of interest, r, or

$$V(\tau) = \sum_{s=\tau+1}^{T} \frac{f(s)}{(1 + r)^{s-\tau}} \tag{5}$$

At once $V(T) = 0$. Applying this formula to $\tau = 0$:

$$V(0) = \sum_{1}^{T} \frac{f(s)}{(1 + r)^s} = 1 \tag{6}$$

Thus, r can be any root of the internal rate of return equation. We leave in abeyance for the moment which root should be chosen.

The depreciation formula follows at once. Depreciation in the τth year of a project is the decrease in the value of the assets during that year, or

$$\delta(\tau) = V(\tau - 1) - V(\tau)$$

By comparing Equation (5) for $V(\tau)$ and $V(\tau - 1)$, we obtain the recursion relation

$$V(\tau) = (1 + r)V(\tau - 1) - f(\tau)$$

and thence

$$\delta(\tau) = f(\tau) - rV(\tau - 1) \tag{7}$$

The economic commonsense of these formulas is apparent.

Inserting the formula for $\delta(\tau)$ and Equation (5) in Equation (1) we obtain

$$y(\tau) = f(\tau) - (1 - \theta)rV(\tau - 1)$$

$$= f(\tau) - (1 - \theta)r \sum_{s=\tau}^{T} \frac{f(s)}{(1 + r)^{s-\tau+1}}$$

We are now in a position to determine the roots of Equation (4). Insert the equation for $y(\tau)$ in that equation to obtain

$$\sum_{\tau=1}^{T} \frac{f(\tau)}{(1 + u_i)^{\tau}} - (1 - \theta) \frac{r}{1 + r} \sum_{\tau=1}^{T} \frac{1}{(1 + u_i)^{\tau}} \sum_{s=\tau}^{T} \frac{f(s)}{(1 + r)^{s-\tau}} = 1 \tag{8}$$

The double sum is

$$\sum_{\tau=1}^{T} \left(\frac{1 + r}{1 + u_i}\right)^{\tau} \sum_{s=\tau}^{T} \frac{f(s)}{(1 + r)^{s}} = \sum_{s=1}^{T} \frac{f(s)}{(1 + r)^{s}} \sum_{\tau=1}^{s} \left(\frac{1 + r}{1 + u_i}\right)^{\tau}$$

$$= \sum_{s=1}^{T} \frac{f(s)}{(1 + r)^{s}} (1 + r) \frac{1 - \left(\dfrac{1 + r}{1 + u_i}\right)^{s}}{u_i - r}$$

$$= (1 + r) \sum_{s=1}^{T} f(s) \frac{(1 + r)^{-s} - (1 + u_i)^{-s}}{u_i - r}, \quad u_i \neq r$$

Using this fact, the equation becomes

$$\sum_{1}^{T} \frac{f(\tau)}{(1 + u_i)^{\tau}} - \frac{(1 - \theta)r}{u_i - r} \sum_{1}^{T} f(\tau)[(1 + r)^{-\tau} - (1 + u_i)^{-\tau}] = 1, \quad u_i \neq r$$

or

$$\frac{u_i - \theta r}{u_i - r} \sum_{1}^{T} \frac{f(\tau)}{(1 + u_i)^{\tau}} - \frac{(1 - \theta)r}{u_i - r} \sum_{1}^{T} \frac{f(\tau)}{(1 + r)^{\tau}} = 1$$

We can solve this equation by inspection. Denote the roots of Equation (6) by $r_1, r_2, \cdots, r_T$ with $r_1 = $ the smallest real positive root. Choose $r = r_1$. Then the second summation above becomes unity and the whole equation becomes

$$\frac{u_i - \theta r_1}{u_i - r_1} \sum_{1}^{T} \frac{f(\tau)}{(1 + u_i)^{\tau}} = \frac{u_i - \theta r_1}{u_i - r_1}$$

This equation is obviously satisfied by $u_1 = \theta r_1$ and also by $u_i = r_i$, $i = 2, 3, \cdots$, T, for then the summation equals unity.

We now have the solution to Equation (3). It is

$$Y(t) = c_1(1 + \theta r_1)^t + \sum_{i=2}^{T} c_i(1 + r_i)^t \tag{9}$$

In words: the growth path of investment, and thereby of total cash flows, dividends, and capital assets, is a sum of exponentials, one of which grows at the rate θr_1, and the others at the rates given by the other roots of the internal rate of return equation.

To see clearly what this formula is telling us, we perform the calculation for the three-period illustration given at the outset, which was constructed to be both transparent and ill-behaved. The internal rates of return are readily found to be

$$r_1 = \tfrac{1}{4}, r_2 = i\sqrt{3}, r_3 = -i\sqrt{3} \ (i = \sqrt{-1})$$

Then the growth path resulting from investing in this type of undertaking and reinvesting in the same type is

$$Y(t) = c_1(1 + \tfrac{1}{4}\theta)^t + c_2(1 + i\sqrt{3})^t + c_3(1 - i\sqrt{3})^t$$

It is convenient to write

$$1 + i\sqrt{3} = 2 \ (\cos 60 + i \sin 60)$$

and similarly for $1 - i\sqrt{3}$. Then, for instance,

$$(1 + i\sqrt{3})^t = 2^t(\cos 60t + i \sin 60t)$$

Furthermore, for the growth path to consist of real numbers, c_2 and c_3 must be complex complements, say $a(\cos \omega + i \sin \omega)$ and $a(\cos \omega - i \sin \omega)$. Then, doing a little algebra,

$$c_2 2^t \ (\cos 60t + i \sin 60t) = a2^t \ (\cos(60t + \omega) + i \sin(60t + \omega))$$

and

$$c_3 2^t \ (\cos 60t - i \sin 60t) = a2^t \ (\cos(60t + \omega) - i \sin(60t + \omega))$$

and finally

$$Y(t) = c_1(1 + \tfrac{1}{4}\theta)^t + 2^{t+1} a \cos(60t + \omega)$$

The growth path consists of an exponential term with growth rate $\theta/4$ and a cosine wave of exponentially growing amplitude. The disposable constants c_2 and c_3 have been replaced by a and ω, which specify the amplitude and phase of the trigonometric term.

Although the principal root displays a substantial rate of growth, this growth path as a whole can clearly be disastrous because of the exponentially increasing oscillations. One can draw either or both inferences. Either this type of undertaking is not a healthy steady diet for a growing firm, or else the firm must choose the initiating three levels of investment, $Y(1)$, $Y(2)$, $Y(3)$, so as to start along a growth path on which $a = 0$. The initial investments $Y(1) > 0$, $Y(2) = (1 + \theta/4) Y(1)$, $Y(3) = (1 + \theta/4) Y(2)$ will serve nicely. Thereafter, with such an unstable growth path, the firm must be watchful for random disturbances, and take prompt action to return to the exponential path if any occur.

It should be emphasized that the example was chosen to be badly behaved, so as to make clear the sort of thing that can happen in principle. Notice that each \$1,000 invested obligates the firm to invest a further \$6,500 two years later. More normal cash flow patterns do not generate such instability. They may have no complex roots at all, or all the complex roots may have amplitudes smaller than $1 + r^*$, where $r^* = $ largest real positive root. In those more normal cases, whatever the initial investments, the firm will tend to grow asymptotically at the rate r^* if there are several real positive roots, or θr^* if there is only one.

We thus have justified the following internal rate of return criterion:

> *For a firm to achieve the greatest possible rate of growth by investing in a succession of similar projects, with a fixed proportion of the net cash flow of each generation used to finance the net investment in the next generation, it should choose a type of project in which the greatest positive real root of the internal rate of return equation (i.e., Equation (6)) is as great as possible.*

Furthermore, in choosing a type of investment project, all the roots of the internal rate of return equation should be taken into account because all of them influence the potential growth path. If there is any negative or complex root with an absolute value as great as $1 + r^*$, the growth path will be intolerably unstable; such investments should be avoided no matter how great the principal root. On the other hand, if $1 + r^*$ is greater than the absolute value of any of the other roots, the enterprise will approach asymptotically an exponential growth path with the greatest growth rate achievable.

Two technicalities remain to be cleared up. First, can we be sure that there will be a positive real root? It is easy to see that a sufficient condition is $\sum f(\tau) > 1$. For then, if $r = 0$, the middle member of Equation (6) is greater than unity, whereas that middle member can always be made less than unity by choosing r sufficiently large. By continuity there must be an intermediate value of r that satisfies the equation.

The other dangling technicality is the case $\theta = 1$, i.e., the case where the entire net cash flow is available for reinvestment. The Xerox Corporation during its first decade was as good an approximation of this case as is likely to be found in the real world. The demonstration given above does not apply to this case (because the restriction $u_i \neq r$ is violated). Nevertheless, Equation (9), with $\theta = 1$, remains valid. Simply notice that if $\theta = 1$ in Equation (1), $y(\tau) = f(\tau)$. Thereupon, Equation (4) becomes identical to the internal rate of return equation and has the same roots.

II. Investment Appraisal Admitting Debt-finance

The analysis can now be extended to admit debt-finance. As before, a financial and investment policy has to be specified, and only a special, though economically sound, policy leads to an intelligible analysis.

All the assumptions of the previous section will be retained except those relating to internal financing of net investment. Instead we shall assume that the firm maintains a prescribed degree of leverage by borrowing a proportion b of net investment. (Then its leverage will be $b/(1 - b)$, $0 \leq b < 1$.) To maintain the prescribed leverage, we specify also that the firm retires its debt *pari passu* with the depreciation of the underlying assets. This can be achieved, for example, by issuing serial bonds to finance the net investment. We now show that this more general case is formally the same as the previous one.

With these assumptions, the net profit earned by an investment of \$1, or an equity investment of $(1 − b), in the τth year of its life will be

$$f(\tau) - \delta(\tau) - r^0 b V(\tau - 1)$$

where r^0 is the rate of interest on the borrowed funds. Then, if the proportion (1 − θ) of net profit is paid to stockholders and for taxes, $r^0 b V(\tau - 1)$ is paid for interest, and $b\delta(\tau)$ is used to retire debt, the contribution of a unit investment to the internal funds available for reinvestment will be

$$f(\tau) - (1 - \theta)(f(\tau) - \delta(\tau) - r^0 b V(\tau - 1)) - r^0 b V(\tau - 1) - b\delta(\tau)$$

$$= \theta(f(\tau) - \delta(\tau) - r^0 b V(\tau - 1)) + (1 - b)\delta(\tau)$$

in the τth year of its life. Allowing for the fact that the proportion b of new gross investment is to be financed by borrowing, these internal funds will support an investment of

$$y(\tau) = \theta'(f(\tau) - \delta(\tau) - r^0 b V(\tau - 1)) + \delta(\tau)$$

where $\theta' = \theta/(1 - b)$. Now substitute for $\delta(\tau)$ by Equation (7) to obtain

$$y(\tau) = f(\tau) + \theta'(r V(\tau - 1) - r^0 b V(\tau - 1)) - r V(\tau - 1)$$

$$= f(\tau) - ((1 - \theta')r + \theta' r^0 b) V(\tau - 1)$$

The law of growth of the sequence of investments is again given by Equation (2), and its solution has the form of Equation (3). The equation for the roots of Equation (3) then becomes

$$\sum_1^T \frac{y(\tau)}{(1 + u_i)^\tau} = \sum_1^T \frac{f(\tau)}{(1 + u_i)^\tau} - ((1 - \theta')r + \theta' r^0 b) \sum_1^T \frac{V(\tau - 1)}{(1 + u_i)^\tau} = 1$$

Remembering that

$$\sum_1^T \frac{V(\tau - 1)}{(1 + u_i)^\tau} = \sum_1^T f(\tau) \frac{(1 + r)^{-\tau} - (1 + u_i)^{-\tau}}{u_i - r}$$

and that r is a root of the internal rate of return equation, this simplifies to

$$\sum_1^T \frac{f(\tau)}{(1 + u_i)^\tau} - \frac{(1 - \theta')r + \theta' b r^0}{u_i - r} \left(1 - \sum_1^T \frac{f(\tau)}{(1 + u_i)^\tau}\right) = 1$$

or

$$\frac{u_i - \theta'(r - b r^0)}{u_i - r} \sum_1^T \frac{f(\tau)}{(1 + u_i)^\tau} = \frac{u_i - \theta'(r - b r^0)}{u_i - r}, \qquad u_i \neq r \qquad (10)$$

Now select one of the real positive roots of the internal rate of return equation to be used in the formula for depreciation, Equation (5). Call the selected root r_1. Then Equation (10) is satisfied when $u_i = r_i$, $i = 2, \cdots, T$, and also when

$$u_1 = \theta'(r_1 - b r^0)$$

$$= \theta \frac{r_1 - b r^0}{1 - b} \qquad (11)$$

$$= \theta(r_1 + \frac{b}{1 - b}(r_1 - r^0))$$

Notice that the solution obtained in the preceding section is the special case of this solution in which $b = 0$.

Notice also that for any value of b, u_1 is an increasing function of r_1 if $r_1 > r^0$. It is therefore advantageous to choose the largest positive real root, r^*, for r_1 unless $r^* \leq r^0$. In the latter case, debt finance should not be used at all.

Assuming $r_1 = r^* > r^0$, when borrowing is permitted the firm can grow more rapidly than if confined to internally generated funds in direct proportion to (a) the leverage, and (b) the excess of the largest real positive root of the internal rate of return equation over the interest rate on borrowed funds.

The foregoing discussion has presumed that b is somehow prescribed to the firm. More normally, the leverage is a matter of financial policy. If b can be chosen with no restrictions other than $0 \leq b < 1$, and if r^0 is not affected by the choice of b, both of which are unlikely, then Equation (11) shows that the firm can be made to grow as rapidly as desired, simply by choosing a large enough leverage. The analysis of the choice of the leverage in more plausible circumstances is straightforward, and is left to the reader.

III. Conclusion

We have argued that an enterprise may have any of a number of objectives in mind when it selects investment projects. If its objective is to maximize the value of its distributions, then some version of the net present value criterion is likely to be appropriate. Otherwise, the investment criterion should be designed to reflect the objective that is in view.

We paid particular attention to situations in which the objective was to maximize the enterprise's rate of growth, and found that in certain circumstances this objective was best achieved by adopting an internal rate of return criterion. The reason was that when growth is the objective, the critical consideration in choosing among opportunities is the extent to which they generate funds available for reinvestment, and the best opportunity from this point of view is not necessarily the one with the highest net present value of cash flows.

The circumstances we assumed in order to prove those assertions were implausible. We envisaged a firm like McDonald's or Fotomat that used the investable funds from each generation of investments to build more McDonald's or Fotomats with cash flows precisely the same as their predecessors, *ad infinitum.*

Referring to earlier arguments along the same lines (Boulding [4, pp. 680-81, and earlier editions], Chipman [5]), Samuelson [18] derided this argument as "far-fetched", and, indeed, it is. Farfetchedness is a characteristic of all economic theories which are simple enough to yield intelligible insights, which is why none of them ought to be taken literally. The question that continually confronts the applied theorist is which simplified "stylized model" most adequately (or least inadequately) incorporates the essential features of the real-life phenomena he is trying to understand. In the choice between the internal rate of return and the net present value criteria, the question is whether the firm or firms under consideration are more like firms which are interested primarily in growing and are in a position, for some considerable period of time, to invest in a succession of similar investment projects with similar time-paths of returns per dollar, or whether they are more like firms interested primarily in net payouts to their proprietors who have access to perfect capital markets. Both models are far-fetched enough to generate legitimate qualms, and each catches the essence of some situations. Businessmen do pay attention to the internal rate of return of prospective investment projects, and often justify doing so by emphasizing the importance of reinvestment and affirming their confidence that opportunities similar to those now available will continue to open up in the future.

Two implications of our formulation and analysis ought to be made explicit. The first is constructive. If a type of investment project has several real positive internal rates of return, the one that is relevant for decision is the greatest of· them, for that rate of return corresponds to the growth rate that will dominate eventually and may dominate all along the line.

The second implication is limiting. Suppose that an enterprise has several types of investment opportunity with different rates of return and, for some reason, follows the policy of reinvesting a fixed (non-zero) proportion of its investable cash flow in each of them. Then it is easy to show that the enterprise's dominant rate of growth will not be any simple average of the dominant growth rates of the individual types of investment but, rather, will depend on all the rates of return (positive, negative, and complex) of all the types of investment. It follows that the analysis cannot be extended to enterprises which diversify their undertakings. In essence, such an enterprise sacrifices its opportunity to grow at a maximal rate in the interest of diversification, and the extent of the sacrifice depends in a very complicated way on all the terms of the growth paths of the individual types of investment.

Many significant questions remain unanswered. The most pressing, perhaps, concern the implications for the choice of investment projects by a developing economy that is determined to grow as rapidly as possible. There are also intriguing theoretical questions concerning the nature of general equilibrium in an economy in which all firms select their investments in order to maximize their rates of growth. Preliminary explorations indicate that all such questions are too complicated to be dealt with in the confines of this paper.

REFERENCES

1. A. A. Alchian. "The Rate of Interest, Fisher's Rate of Return Over Costs and Keynes' Internal Rate of Return." *American Economic Review* 45 (December 1955).
2. K. J. Arrow and D. Levhari. "Uniqueness of the Internal Rate of Return with Variable Life of Investment." *Economic Journal* 79 (September 1969).
3. E. V. Boehm-Bawerk. *Positive Theorie des Kapitales*. Jena: Fischer, 1889.
4. K. E. Boulding. *Economic Analysis, Vol. I, Microeconomics*. New York: Harper & Row, 1966.
5. J. S. Chipman. "A Renewal Model of Economic Growth: The Discrete Case." In *Mathematical Topics in Economic Theory and Computation*, R. H. Day and S. M. Robinson, eds. Philadelphia: SIAM Publications, 1972.
6. ———. "A Renewal Model of Economic Growth: The Continuous Case." *Econometrica* 45 (March 1977).
7. O. Eckstein. "Investment Criteria for Economic Development and the Theory of Intertemporal Welfare Economics." *Quarterly Journal of Economics* 71 (February 1957).
8. I. Fisher. *The Rate of Interest*. New York: Macmillan, 1907.
9. ———. *The Theory of Interest*. New York: Macmillan, 1930.
10. J. S. Fleming and J. F. Wright. "Uniqueness of the Internal Rate of Return: A Generalization." *Economic Journal* 81 (June 1971).

11. W. Galenson and H. Leibenstein. "Investment Criteria, Productivity, and Economic Development." *Quarterly Journal of Economics* 69 (August 1955).
12. C. Hildreth. "A Note on Maximization Criteria." *Quarterly Journal of Economics* 61 (November 1946).
13. J. Hirshleifer. "On the Theory of Optimal Investment Decision." *Journal of Political Economy* 66 (August 1958).
14. Harold Hotelling. "A General Mathematical Theory of Depreciation." *Journal of the American Statistical Association* 20 (September 1925).
15. J. M. Keynes. *The General Theory of Employment, Interest, and Money.* New York: Harcourt, Brace, 1936.
16. S. A. Marglin. "The Social Rate of Discount and the Optimal Rate of Investment." *Quarterly Journal of Economics* 77 (February 1963).
17. ———. "The Opportunity Costs of Public Investment." *Quarterly Journal of Economics* 77 (May 1963).
18. P. A. Samuelson. "Economics of Forestry in an Evolving Society." *Economic Inquiry* 14 (December 1976).
19. J. F. Wright. "The Marginal Efficiency of Capital." *Economic Journal* 69 (December 1959).

[12]

TRANSITION COSTS OF CHANGING REGULATIONS

Robert Dorfman

Transition costs are the costs of adapting to a change in circumstances. Before the change, the industry affected or the economy may have been more or less in equilibrium. After the change and after sufficient time has elapsed, the industry or economy will have found its way to a new equilibrium consistent with new circumstances. The intervening time is the transition. During the transition some costs will be incurred that would not have been incurred if circumstances had not changed, and that will not recur once the transition is completed. These are the transition costs. They are the costs of change and should be distinguished, though the distinction is often hard to maintain in practice, from the change in costs resulting from the change in circumstances. This is the difference between the costs of production in the preexisting equilibrium and those that will be incurred in the equilibrium that results from the change.

Transition costs are of several kinds, not all of which arise in response to every change in circumstances. The kinds of

Robert Dorfman is professor of political economy at Harvard University. Participants in his workshop on the dynamics of regulatory change were Robert Friedland, rapporteur, Joseph Cordes, Robert Frank, Richard Klem, Jack Pearce, Tanya Roberts, and Fred Thompson.

40   ATTACKING REGULATORY PROBLEMS

costs that are relevant depend on the nature of the change in circumstances and the corresponding change in the equilibrium position. I am concerned primarily with transitions induced by changes in governmental regulations, and therefore I discuss only that kind of exogenous change.

Government regulations, even in our free-market economy, are numerous and varied. For our purposes they can be classified into the following types:

1. Price controls, which can take the form of minimum prices (perhaps enforced by a support program), maximum prices, or requirements that all price changes by approved by some governmental body.
2. Restrictions on entrance into an industry, which may take the form of licensing requirements or requirements for permission to enter the industry, for example, "certificates of necessity and convenience."
3. Quality requirements, including regulations on service standards for public utilities, safety and other performance specifications for consumer products, disclosure requirements for credit and banking services, and so on.
4. Employee protections, including work-safety requirements, other limitations on working conditions, regulations affecting hiring practices, and the like.
5. Environmental regulations and some others, including zoning restrictions and constraints on technologies and processes used and on effluents and emissions.

Furthermore, the change in any regulation may take several forms: an introduction of that type of regulation for the first time, a recision of all or some of the regulations of that sort, or an alteration in one or more regulations. The kinds of transition costs that will be incurred and their magnitude, of course, depend to a great extent on the kind of regulation that is involved and whether the change is an introduction, a recision, or an alteration.

The costs of transition depend also on the relationship between the preexisting equilibrium and the new equilibrium that eventually will be established. In particular, if the new equilibrium rate of output will be smaller than the old one, then some of the fixed capital equipment in the industry and some of that labor employed will become redundant. Both the owners of that capital equipment and the workers who are displaced sustain losses, the extent depending on how successful they are in finding alternative employments. Whether these private losses are also social losses is a somewhat different matter, which will be discussed with some care below.

Many regulatory changes affect the cost curves in the industries concerned. If a regulation increases costs, then, in the new equilibrium, prices are likely to be higher and output lower than before, with the consequences just discussed. If a regulatory change reduces costs in an industry, it may give rise to similar displacements in competing industries. Regulatory changes often alter the equilibrium structure of the affected industry. The relaxation of the Civil Aeronautics Board (CAB) controls over airline fares is a recent instance. Then the costs of groping toward the newly appropriate structure will have to be sustained.

TRANSITION COSTS ASSOCIATED WITH FIXED CAPITAL

Consider an industry on which more stringent environmental constraints have been imposed, increasing costs of production at all levels of output. The economic consequences can be visualized as an upward shift in the supply curve, which will now intersect the unmoved demand curve at a higher price and lower quantity than before. The sum of consumers' and producers' surpluses will be reduced, and this reduction is generally taken to be a crude but adequate measure of the social cost of the new requirements. All this is entirely conventional, but is it really all there is to it?

To answer this question we must look more closely at the reasoning on which the conventional analysis is based. Figure 3–1 shows a conventional Marshallian cross with one demand curve and two supply curves. Before the change, the market was in equilibrium at E_1 and the sum of consumers' and producers' surpluses was the area A_1E_1D. This total social surplus is the area under the demand curve up to the

42   ATTACKING REGULATORY PROBLEMS

Figure 3–1   Static equilibrium analysis of cost of regulation

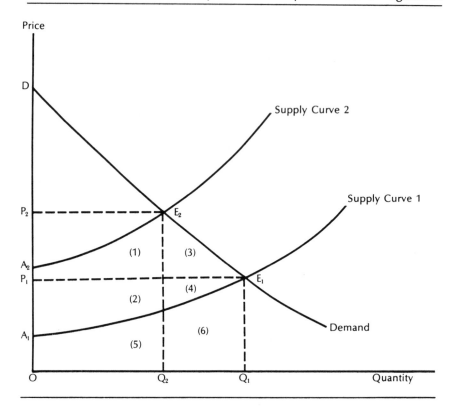

quantity produced Q_1 minus the resource costs of producing
that output, represented by the trapezoid $A_1E_1Q_1O$. That
trapezoid is excluded from the social surplus because the resources whose cost it represents are not available to other
sectors of the economy in which they could make equivalent
contributions to the value of economic output. In the presence
of the stricter regulations, supply curve 2 comes into operation. The equilibrium moves to E_2, and the social surplus is
reduced by the sum of the areas (1), (2), (3), and (4). Areas (1)
and (2) indicate the additional resource costs of producing the
new equilibrium output in the presence of the stricter regulations. Areas (3) and (4) represent the deadweight loss in so-

cial surplus that results from the shrinkage in output. The critical area for present purposes is area (6). It represents the value of the resources no longer required by the industry. Their value was not included in the social surplus before the change on the grounds that they could make as great a contribution to social output if employed elsewhere. Given enough time for the new equilibrium to be established, this is a reasonable presumption as to what will happen. But in the interim, during the transition, it is not reasonable, at least not without further inspection.

Many of these resources, both capital equipment and skilled labor, are specialized to their current employments. The capital equipment is worth only its salvage value to other industries. The productivity elsewhere of the displaced employees depends on how transferable their skills are. They may be employable only after expensive retraining, or they may be employable only at lower levels of skill, or they may not be employable at all. Thus during a substantial transition period the resources released by the industry are not likely to contribute as much to the national output as they did before the regulatory change.

The issue still remains whether this loss in productivity is a social or only a private loss. Notice that it has now been revealed to be an illusion to count area (6) as part of the social cost of producing the larger output Q_1. In fact the social cost of producing the increment $Q_1 - Q_2$ was smaller than area (6), the discrepancy being absorbed by the factors that received rents, or payments, in excess of what they could earn in alternative employments. These rents have now evaporated, which is a purely private loss. But also the rents should have been included in the social surplus arising from the preexisting equilibrium, so that the sum of the areas (1) to (4) is actually less than the total loss in social surplus inflicted by the change in regulations. This is not a case in which a rent is redistributed among members of the population; the rents have been simply annihilated. Hence a social loss has been incurred that is measured by the extent of those rents, or by the reductions in productivity of the displaced factors.

Capital equipment, of course, is often not as adaptable as workers. It cannot be retrained, but often it can be remodeled, and sometimes it is readily transferable, as are rolling stock, standard furniture and fixtures, and unspecialized storage space. During the transition period the resources that would have been used to maintain and replace the redundant specialized capital equipment are released to other sectors of the economy at undiminished productivity. Eventually, by the end of the normal economic lives of the redundant equipment, all the released resources will be of this sort, and the conventional diagram will be an adequate portrayal of the reduction in social surplus. But during the transition there will be a gradually diminishing transitional loss resulting from the forgone contribution to the value of output that the capital would have made in its employment before the change.

Measuring the extent of this loss is straightforward in principle. For each unit of capital equipment, it is the difference between the present value of its net product during the remainder of its normal economic life and its salvage value, which is the market's estimate of its value in alternative employments. There is a readily available estimate of the value of the equipment's contribution during the remainder of its normal economic life, namely, its depreciated book value. An asset's depreciated book value depends on its original acquisition cost and the accounting conventions used in calculating depreciation, which are strongly influenced by provisions of the internal revenue code that often have little relation to economic worth. It is therefore an open question whether reported book values are adequate representations of the transitional costs that arise from premature retirements caused by regulatory changes.

In estimating the transitional capital losses that are likely to result from a proposed regulatory change, the question arises of which components of the fixed capital employed by an industry are likely to be retired or transferred to other industries. One would expect that they would be the marginal components, those close to retirement in any event because of either age or obsolescence. To the extent that this is true, the transitional capital losses will be small or even negligible. This, however, is merely conjectural, and some study of actual experiences is required to ascertain how far one can rely on this conjecture.

In some cases capital goods that are not close to retirement can be remodeled in order to continue operating under changed regulatory rules. This possibility can be allowed for by applying a somewhat more general definition of the transitional capital cost: the present value of the net product that the plant and equipment would have yielded under the preexisting regulations minus the present value of its net product under the changed conditions and plus any costs of modification. For plant and equipment that are retired prematurely because of the change, the present value of the net product under the new conditions is just the salvage value (if any), and the cost of modification is zero. For capital assets that are remodeled, this formulation allows for the possibility that operating costs are likely to be higher for remodeled equipment than for assets that were designed originally for the changed conditions of operation.

The strategy of estimating transitional capital costs appears to be completely unexplored. It would clearly be impractical to make an inventory of all the fixed plant and equipment in an industry in an attempt to foresee the fate of every capital asset. Many recent economic impact analyses do classify the plants in an affected industry by size, vintage, and other pertinent characteristics and, for each category, estimate production costs with and without the regulatory change. It is a natural presumption that the retirements would occur chiefly in the high-cost categories of plant, and the modifications primarily in the low-cost ones. Here, again, empirical studies of actual instances are needed.

For policy purposes, perhaps the most significant characteristic of transition costs is that they depend heavily on the transitional provisions incorporated in the regulatory change. At one extreme, the regulation may include a grandfather clause that exempts existing plants from the new requirements; no transitional capital losses are imposed by such a regulation. (They may even gain in value, as did second-hand cars that could continue to use leaded fuel.) Sometimes particular categories of existing plants are exempted, for example, plants below a specified size. An important decision is the promptness with which the new requirements come into force. The most important instance of this decision was probably the Energy Policy and Conservation Act of 1975, which required automobile manufacturers to improve the average fuel efficiencies of the cars they produced gradually according to a prescribed timetable that extended over ten years. The legislated timetable was based, clearly, on anticipations about the relative costliness of attaining the desired ultimate fuel efficiency by different possible deadlines. Similarly, nearly all the recent changes in fuel price regulations include provisions designed to moderate the abruptness of transition. All such provisions attest to a concern over transition costs, and to a belief that they can be reduced by moving slowly. Unfortunately, there is very little solid knowledge, either theoretical or empirical, on which to base a belief about the effects of the speed of transition on the transition costs. Studies at many levels will be required before we are in a position to make well-founded decisions about desirable speeds of transition. It is virtually certain that transitional capital costs can be reduced by slowing down the rates at which compliance with new regulations is required. Quantitative estimates, however, or even techniques for making them, are nonexistent.

The entire field of transitional capital costs remains unexplored territory. It is, furthermore, important territory. In some cases these costs may be large enough to affect judgments of the advisability of proposed regulations. More frequently, probably, they will be critical to decisions about the transitional provisions of regulatory changes. In our present state of knowledge, we can anticipate that substantial economic waste, and even hardship, will result from ignoring or misjudging these costs.

TRANSITION COSTS ASSOCIATED WITH DISPLACED WORKERS

In principle, the transition costs associated with displaced workers are no different from those associated with prematurely retired capital equipment. Applying this principle we can say that the cost attributable to each worker displaced is the present value of the net product that the worker would have produced without the regulatory change minus the present value of the net product in new employment (if any) and plus the cost of retraining and relocating. Nevertheless, workers are essentially different from capital equipment. Whereas the terms of the corresponding formula for capital equipment were relatively easy to estimate, the prospective net products for workers are extraordinarily difficult.

The task divides into two components. The first is to estimate how many workers will be displaced and some of the salient characteristics (such as age, skill, and location) of the displaced workers. The second is to estimate the transition costs per displaced worker, which will differ according to personal characteristics. Each of these components divides, in turn, into a number of subcomponents.

Estimating the number and characteristics of workers whom a regulatory change is likely to displace is by now a familiar task since it forms a significant part of the standard economic impact analysis. Though it is a familiar task, each effort appears to be largely ad hoc. There is little or no literature on the theoretical underpinnings of economic impact analyses. One consequence is that these studies cannot be compared with one another; they use different sets of assumptions and different conceptual frameworks that frustrate attempts to relate the findings of the individual studies. At present, therefore, it is very difficult to compare the economic impacts of different regulatory changes that have been studied separately. This is serious enough, but also in doubt is the significance of analyses that have been undertaken without the benefit of a well-established theory. For example, it is commonly assumed in economic impact analyses that all the workers in a plant that closes in consequence of a regulatory change will be displaced. In fact, because of normal labor turnover, many of them would have left that plant even without any regulatory change. This example illustrates only one of the considerations that tend to be ignored for lack of an established framework for analysis.

Plants close and workers are displaced for many reasons other than regulatory change, for example, technological changes and increasing competition from imports. Many such episodes have been studied, and those studies are relevant both methodologically and empirically. Yet the displacement effects of regulatory changes are very likely different from those of other disturbances. Therefore, while studies of worker displacement made in conjunction with the Trade Adjustment Assistance Program and similar programs are suggestive, they are probably not applicable to the consequences of regulatory changes. In particular, it seems unlikely that workers displaced by regulatory changes will have the same personal and reemployability characteristics as those displaced by other types of disturbance.

The second component of the analysis of the transitional costs of worker displacement is the estimation of the social cost attributable to displaced workers of different types. This, too, has been studied many times in the context of job losses from other kinds of disturbances. Studies of income losses and unemployment experience are probably more pertinent to regulatory disturbances than are the analyses of the numbers of workers affected. All the literature, theoretical and empirical, on job search behavior is pertinent and helpful. Nevertheless hardly anyone would deny that both the theory and practice of estimating the duration of unemployment, the costs of relocation, and the changes in the lifetime earnings profile that ensue when a worker is displaced are still in their infancy. Perhaps the most promising approach is the one pioneered by Louis S. Jacobsen (1976), which uses data from the Social Security System's longitudinal employee-employer data file to estimate both durations of unemployment and subsequent losses in earnings. Another promising method is the one used by Glenn Jenkins and Claude Montmarquette (1979), which is based heavily on job search theory. All the available studies are experimental and are based on rather scanty empirical data. A great deal remains to be done before we can make reliable estimates of workers' losses in earnings from regulatory changes. These early studies have identified some of the factors that influence the displaced workers' experience, but it is clear that much more research is needed.

The speed of transition and other transitional provisions of the regulatory change have at least as much influence on costs attributable to job displacement as on losses associated with fixed capital. At an extreme, if a very slow rate of transition is permitted, normal labor turnover may take care of all or nearly all required reduction in the labor force. Hence studies of the effects of different rates of transition, of retraining and relocation assistance programs, and of other transitional provisions will be extremely helpful.

MANAGING THE TRANSITION

The adjustment to a regulatory change does not take place overnight. Frequently, indeed, it begins long before the change goes into effect—during the hearings that precede a new law or at the inception of the administrative rulemaking procedures that precede a new regulation. The adjustments to a regulatory change continue long after, throughout the period required for the capital stock and work force of the affected industry to adjust to the new regulatory regime.

During the transition, many things happen that are difficult to foresee. The transitional effects, moreover, are strongly influenced by many details of the regulation and by whatever provisions may be included to ease and guide the adjustments. I have already mentioned the importance of the speed with which the new regulations become operative and some of the implications of such provisions as grandfather clauses. Many other ostensibly secondary details are critical also. For example, if a toxic chemical is to be banned, it matters greatly whether further manufacture of the chemical is prohibited, or whether sale of the chemical is made illegal, or whether the prohibition applies to its use. In the long run all three of these forms of prohibition may produce the same results, but during the transition, while inventories are being run down, the consequences can differ dramatically.

It seems obvious that the quicker the regulatory change goes into effect, the sooner the anticipated benefits will accrue. But there are offsetting drawbacks. One motivation, surely, for the prevalence of introducing regulations or dismantling them by graduated steps is uncertainty about the consequences of the regulatory change. It is felt to be desirable to be able to watch the adjustments as they evolve and to be able to make midcourse corrections as they are needed. CAB's gradual relax-

50   ATTACKING REGULATORY PROBLEMS

ation of its controls over airline fares is a typical instance. In retrospect it appears that the gradualism was unnecessary, since there were no significant adverse developments, but no one could have been confident of that in advance.

A second consideration relates to the ability of the markets affected to respond efficiently to the disturbance created by the regulatory change. In every market there is an accustomed range of disturbances to which the participants can react with confidence; beyond that range no one is sure of the appropriate response, and miscalculations are likely. The airline fare deregulation, gradual though it was intended to be, illustrates this problem. The airlines responded to their newly conferred freedom to engage in competitive pricing by cutting fares substantially. The public response, which disclosed a price elasticity of demand some three or four times as great as had been estimated, was a surprise to everyone. A severe shortage of aircraft resulted, which lasted for at least a year.

A third reason for being reluctant to impose abrupt regulatory changes relates to their distributional consequences. Thus far this chapter has not emphasized the private gains and losses caused by regulatory changes, though clearly they are of first importance both socially and politically. I have already noted that the severity of both capital losses and employee displacement can be reduced by moving gradually. Since these losses often give rise to demands for compensatory or ameliorative programs, the entire task of managing the transition is eased when the adjustments required can be made slowly. These considerations ought to be weighed against the advantages of an early termination of the inefficiencies, hazards, or externalities that the regulatory change is designed to accomplish.

At present only highly subjective and impressionistic comparisons can be made between the advantages and the disadvantages of speed. We cannot tell in any specific instance whether the disadvantages are present at all, let alone estimate their magnitude. The root of the problem lies deeper than just our lack of theory and empirical analysis of responses to regulatory changes. For a variety of good reasons the economic analysis of equilibriums and therefore of comparative statics is much more highly developed than the analysis of the transitional behavior that leads from one equilibrium to another when any market condition changes. Yet the behavior of the market and the participants in it while they are groping their way from the preexisting equilibrium to the equilibrium that corresponds to the changed circumstances is just what generates the transitional costs and transitional problems. Reliable assessments, then, of the transitional tradeoffs and of the transitional costs of alternative modes for introducing a regulatory change must await further development of the theory of markets in disequilibrium.

The distribution of the costs of the transition is particularly important. Suppose that New York City, or any other city, were to decide to relax its control over taxicabs by issuing medallions to all applicants who satisfied reasonable insurance and safety requirements. If this were done abruptly, current taxicab owners would suffer severe capital losses, of the order of $40,000 per taxicab. If it were done gradually by limiting the number of new medallions issued per year to 5 percent, say, of the current fleet, the desired result would be attained eventually while the capital losses and other disturbances would be greatly moderated.

There are other methods for ameliorating the private losses and hardships that inevitably accompany many regulatory changes. Certainly, special attention has to be paid to methods for easing the transition on the part of employees and owners of small enterprises. There is much empirical evidence on the effectiveness of ameliorative measures arising from experiences with competitive imports and technological changes. These experiences need to be studied further with a view to application to regulatory changes.

One especially important ameliorative measure is to compensate losers in whole or in part, in cash or in kind. To plan any compensatory program requires, in the first instance, estimates of the extent of the losses suffered by different classes of individuals or firms. In the deregulation of airline fares, compensation was extended to communities that might suffer reductions in airline service, in the form of special subsidies for continuing to serve them. The effectiveness of different forms of compensation in improving the distribution of transitional costs deserves special study. So also do the motivational consequences of different forms of compensation, some of which may give rise to distortions comparable to those that the regulatory change is intended to correct.

One apparently minor detail that has a substantial bearing on the costs of regulatory changes is the method used to convey information about them to the industry concerned, to state agencies, and to the general public. When a change is impending or is recent it is normal for the administering agency, and some irrelevant agencies as well, to be besieged by inquiries from a variety of people wishing to know whether the change applies to them, what they are expected to do about it, or what they can expect from employers or sellers to whom they believe the new regulations apply. There are numerous complaints and misunderstandings. All of these are costly, often beyond the scale of petty annoyance.

The standard procedure for publicizing changes is to publish announcements in the *Federal Register* and to prepare press releases in the hope that the news media and trade publications will disseminate the necessary information. There is reason to doubt that this is the most effective means of communication between the government and the general public. Serious studies of the channels by which information about regulatory changes is now disseminated and those by which it is acquired by affected industries and the general public, which may be quite different from those intended, would be worthwhile. These studies should include appraisals of the accuracy and completeness of the information transmitted through different channels. Experiments with alternative channels would also be informative.

In general, the costs of a transition and the distribution of its burdens depend on many fine details of the regulatory change and of its transitional provisions. They are too numerous and sometimes too subtle to be treated in a general overview such as this one. But they are important. An adequate program of research in this area would have to begin with a survey of the expedients that have been tried and with an analytic framework for assessing and comparing their effects. The results of such studies would enable us to ease the problems both of introducing and of dismantling regulations.

CONCLUSION

In an area where so little work has been done, an inventory of research needs is doomed to be incomplete and, worse than that, unduly general. One of the first valuable products of research efforts is the discovery of well-defined studies that need to be undertaken; we do not really know what we do not know until we make a serious effort to formulate and extend what we believe we know. In advance of this effort it is premature to attempt to delineate a research program.

I have attempted, nevertheless, to sketch some of the more important problems that are now visible. For the most part these have been fairly conventional problems—issues relating to capital redundancy, to the displacement of skilled and unskilled workers, to the distribution of the transitional gains and losses, and to the effects of varying speeds of adjustment and other provisions intended to moderate the disturbances created by the change. Some issues have been implied rather than made explicit, for example, the differing impacts of a change on declining and expanding industries and in static and growing regions.

Furthermore, the emphasis has been spotty. A great deal of attention was paid to adjustments that reduce employment in an industry or region; none to changes that lead to increased economic activity, though they too entail transitional costs. The most serious omission, perhaps, is the slight attention paid to problems of information and uncertainty. One of the major consequences of either increased or decreased regulation of an economic sector is the change in the nature of the uncertainties that participants in that sector have to confront. Increasing regulation may reduce some kinds of uncertainty—for example, price fluctuations—but it always increases another kind, namely, uncertainty about what the government will do next. Every regulatory change, except complete withdrawal from a sector, enhances this kind of uncertainty by reinforcing the recognition that regulations change and that the present regime cannot be expected to endure. This increased uncertainty is one of the costs of the regulatory change, and one that is exceedingly difficult to measure. Can anything be done to moderate it? Can a government undertake a commitment to make no more changes of a certain type or to render them more predictable? With a little ingenuity I think that it can go a long way in that direction, but I am not sure that it would be worthwhile to do so.

This aspect of regulatory change has one characteristic that should be noted. In addition to affecting the transitional responses, it changes the ultimate equilibrium since it inhibits capital commitments predicated on the current state of the regulations. This characteristic, though striking here, is not altogether peculiar. It is very likely true that many specific regulatory changes affect the ultimate equilibrium in ways that cannot be detected by conventional comparative equilibrium analyses because of the transitional behavior that they generate.

These and many other issues remain unexplored in this survey. They will be disclosed in useful detail only as the work progresses. What has been sketched is not really an agenda for research, but suggestions for the next steps.

REFERENCES

Jacobson, Louis S. 1976. "Earnings Losses of Workers Displaced from Manufacturing Industries." Arlington, Virginia: Public Research Institute, Professional Paper 169. (November).

Jenkins, Glenn P. and Claude Montmarquette. 1979. "Estimating the Private and Social Opportunity Cost of Displaced Workers." *Review of Economics and Statistics* 61 (August): 342–353.

[13]

JOURNAL OF ENVIRONMENTAL ECONOMICS AND MANAGEMENT 11, 91–106 (1984)

On Optimal Congestion[1]

ROBERT DORFMAN

Department of Economics, Harvard University, Cambridge, Massachusetts 02138

Received August 14, 1980; revised September 1981

A number of classic papers conclude that if a congestible facility is the property of a profit maximizing entrepreneur, he will impose a charge for use that induces the socially optimal level of use and congestion. All these papers happen to deal with a special case in which that conclusion holds, but it is not true in general. In general, the socially optimal level of use of a congestible facility is the level at which the marginal cost of providing the service is equal to the sum of the decreases in the users' willingnesses to pay for a unit of service when the level of congestion is optimal, and need not coincide with the level resulting from a profit-maximizing charge. This sum is derived from the integral under a fictitious demand curve constructed by imagining that the level of congestion is the same (and optimal) at all levels of the use-charge.

Congestion is a type of externality. It occurs when some resource or facility is used in common by a number of people who affect each other's use or enjoyment of it more or less symmetrically. The facility in question may be a common property resource, such as a park, beach, or public library, or it may be private property, such as a ski slope, cinema, supermarket, or university library. The reciprocal effects may be to enhance each user's enjoyment or benefit from the use of the resource, or it may be to diminish it. The adverse effect is probably more prevalent. In either case, the benefit that each user derives from his use of the resource can be regarded as a function of the number of other users at the time that he uses it.

The analytic problem presented by congestion is to derive criteria that characterize the socially optimal level of use of a congestible resource or facility and to appraise the efficiency of various social arrangements for managing the resource in the light of these criteria. The two most common social arrangements are free access, which is widely recognized to be inefficient, and the imposition of use-charges of one sort or another. When use-charges are imposed the problem becomes, more narrowly, the determination of the optimal level of those charges and the appraisal of different methods for setting them. In particular, the most prominent proposal for determining the charges is that they should be set so as to generate the greatest possible net revenue to the owners or managers of the facility. This paper will be concerned particularly with clarifying the conditions under which revenue maximizing use-charges will induce the socially optimal use of a congestible resource or facility.

A discussion of the socially optimal level of use of a congestible facility can be conducted at either (or both) of two levels of discourse. The more profound is the level of general equilibrium welfare. Analyses at this level take as their point of departure individual utility functions or indicators and a Bergson-type social welfare function. The utility indicators employed generally take as their arguments the extent of the individual's use of each congestible facility considered, level of

---

[1] This paper grew out of fruitful discussions with Professor David Zilberman.

0095-0696/84 $3.00
Copyright © 1984 by Academic Press, Inc.
All rights of reproduction in any form reserved

congestion of those facilities, and an index of the individual's consumption of noncongestible goods and services. The optimality conditions derived from these data are then elaborations of the fact that at the social optimum the partial derivative of the social welfare function with respect to the level of congestion of each congestible facility must be zero.

Oakland [12] and Diamond [3] are excellent examples of this level of analysis. Its strength lies in its generality. It can and does incorporate a wide class of consumer utility indicators, and need not assume that the benefit that a consumer derives from using any facility is additively separable from his benefits from other facilities or from the consumption of noncongestible commodities. It also does not require strongly limiting assumptions about the structure of the social welfare indicator, and in particular does not presume that social welfare is a simple sum of the welfares of the individuals in the society. Furthermore, it allows for extensive repercussions throughout the economy of changes in the use and conditions of use of each congestible facility. But this level suffers from the defects that go with its advantages. Precisely because it is so noncommittal about the structures of social and individual welfare, its conclusions are confined to the same abstract level, and require elaboration with the aid of specializing assumptions in order to be applied to any concrete problem.

The other level of discourse, which will be adopted here, is much cruder. It is conducted at the level of partial equilibrium. Its primary data are consumers' demand curves for the use of a particular congestible facility, which take as their arguments only the use-charge for that facility and its level of congestion. The effects of changes in this use-charge and level of congestion on the use of other congestible facilities, on prices in general, and on the distribution of income are all regarded as negligible. The benefit that the consumer derives from using the facility is the unpaid-for area under his demand curve, the Dupuit measure of consumer's surplus. The corresponding contribution of the facility to social welfare at any level of use is simply the sum of these individual consumer surpluses plus the net revenue or producer's surplus accruing to the operator of the facility if there is one.

All these are strong and limiting simplifications, but where they are acceptable the partial equilibrium level gains in intelligibility and implementability what it loses in generality. Its decisive advantage is that is uses the same conceptual framework as benefit-cost analysis, which is the principle tool for appraising social decisions concerning the use of resources. Knight [8] and Gordon [6] illustrate this level of discourse. Knight's paper, undoubtedly the most influential in this whole area, will be discussed below.

Taking the partial equilibrium point of view, the social surplus resulting from a level of use, X, of a congestible facility can be written as

$$SS(X) = CS(X) + PS(X)$$

that is, as the sum of the aggregate consumers' surplus from the use of the facility and producer's surplus or net revenue. Immediately, at the optimal level of use,

$$CS'(X) = -PS'(X).$$

At the level of use that maximizes the net revenue generated by a facility

$$PS'(X) = 0$$

and therefore if that is also the socially optimal level

$$CS'(X) = 0.$$

Most of our results will be consequences of this simple criterion.

For example, these equations assert that if net revenue maximization is to induce a socially optimal level of use, then the derivative of aggregate consumers' surplus must vanish at the price-use level pair that maximizes producer's surplus. One way, not the only one, in which this can happen is for aggregate consumers' surplus to be the same at all levels of use. As we shall see, this is the case in Knight's famous toll road example, which is why he found that the toll that maximized the profits of the owner of a congestible toll road would also induce the socially optimal level of traffic.

The two central sections of the paper present two models of the use and social benefits generated by a congestible facility or resource. In the first model it is assumed that the extent to which any consumer uses the resource is a continuous variable, and depends continuously on the use-charge and the level of congestion. The second model, in the following section, treats the case in which each user decides simply whether or not to use the resource on a particular occasion. In this case the individual demand functions are inherently discontinuous; the consumer either uses the resource or he does not at a particular configuration of price and congestion. The two cases are fundamentally the same and will lead us to identical conclusions, but the techniques of analysis are so different that it pays to treat them separately. The paper concludes with a recapitulation and a few concluding remarks.

THE MAIN CONGESTION PROBLEM

Consider some congestible facility used by a number of people and, perhaps, firms. The users differ in a number of characteristics such as age, income, tastes, family size, etc., that affect the amount of use they make of the facility. We shall assume that they can be divided into a finite number of types of identical users, with n_i denoting the number of users of the ith type.[2] The typical user of type i decides on the amount that he will use the facility per unit of time in the light of the price per use, p (which may be zero), and the degree of congestion. The degree of congestion is an increasing function of the amount the facility is used by users of all types. Letting x_i denote the amount of use by a type i user, and X the total amount of use, $X = \Sigma n_i x_i$. Then, at use-price p and congestion level X, a user of type i will use the facility to the extent

$$x_i = f^i(p, X).$$

We shall assume that these demand curves are continuous and differentiable, and that $\partial f^i / \partial p < 0$ if $x_i > 0$ and $\partial f^i / \partial X < 0$. This last assumption is not innocuous. Situations are frequent in which consumers prefer more congestion to less. Many consumers prefer to use city parks and subways when they are well frequented. As an extreme instance, there is no point in going to Times Square on New Year's Eve

---

[2] The analysis is similar if some of the relevant characteristics, such as income, are regarded as continuous variables, but the notation is more cumbersome.

unless it is expected to be very congested. Nevertheless, for reasons that will soon emerge, this assumption must be imposed.

With those data, the total amount of use demanded at a given price and congestion level will be

$$X^d = \sum n_i f^i(p, X) = F(p, X).$$

Anderson and Bonsor [2] have aptly called $F(p, X)$ for a given value of X a "constant crowding demand curve" (ccdd, for short). These ccdd curves are the key conceptual device that distinguishes the analysis of behavior with respect to congestible facilities from ordinary demand behavior. They will be used extensively below.

Users will be in equilibrium, however, only when the amount of congestion experienced is the same as the amount anticipated, that is, when $X^d = X$. Thus the equilibrium level of use when the use-charge is p satisfies the equation

$$X = F(p, X).$$

This equation is the market demand curve in implicit form. It is here that the strong assumption $\partial f^i/\partial X < 0$ becomes necessary. Without it the market demand equation need not have a unique solution, in which case the market demand curve will not be well defined. For example, suppose there are 1000 potential users, all of the same type, and that the individual demand curves are

$$x_i = f^i(p, X) = 5 - \frac{1}{250,000}(X - 3000)^2 - \frac{p}{2}.$$

Then the total amount of use demanded at any p, X combination will be

$$X^d = 5000 - \frac{1}{250}(X - 3000)^2 - 500p.$$

If $p = 1$, then $X^d = X$ when $X = 2250$ or when $X = 3500$, and if $p = 4$, $X^d = X$ is satisfied if $X = 2750$ or 3000 and so on. The mathematical consequence is that the market demand curve is not well defined. The practical consequence is that the facility manager or monopolistic owner cannot control the level of use merely by setting the price of admission. The unpleasant assumption that we have made precludes such behavior and assures that the market demand curve is well defined, continuous, differentiable, and downward-sloping.

To each p, X combination on the market demand curve there corresponds a value of consumers' surplus. The surplus accruing to a consumer of type i is the area to the left of his demand curve and above the ordinate for the price charged, taking the level of congestion as given. Note that the relevant demand curve is the consumer's ccdd curve, for this curve expresses the consumer's judgment of the value to him of his use of the facility at the given level of congestion. Thus we write

$$CS^i(X) = \int_p^\infty f^i(w, X) \, dw$$

provided that the integral is convergent. Total consumers' surplus is the sum of these integrals taken over all individuals, or

$$CS(X) = \sum_i n_i \int_p^\infty f^i(w, X) \, dw$$
$$= \int_p^\infty F(w, X) \, dw.$$

Alternatively, it is generally convenient to express the consumers' surplus in terms of the inverse ccdd curve, which under our assumptions exists and is well defined. This curve can be written $p = \Phi(X^d, X)$ so that Φ denotes the price at which X^d units of service will be demanded when the level of congestion is X. As usual consumers' surplus is then the area below $\Phi(X^d, X)$ and above the ordinate for the price, or

$$CS(X) = \int_0^X \left[\Phi(X^d, X) - p \right] dX^d.$$

For later use we compute the derivatives of these expressions obtaining[3]:

$$CS'(X) = \int_p^\infty F_2(w, X) \, dw - F(p, X) \frac{dp}{dX}$$
$$= \int_0^X \left[\Phi_2(X^d, X) - \frac{dp}{dX} \right] dX^d.$$

In computing the second variant of $CS'(X)$ we have used the fact that $\Phi(X, X) = p$ when p, X is on the market demand curve. The derivative of p is also taken along the market demand curve. What the formula says is simply that the rate of change of consumers' surplus is the sum, taken over all units of service used, of the rate of reduction of the value of the service to the user when congestion increases less the corresponding reduction in the price charged.

It is now easy to calculate the socially optimal charge and level of use, taking advantage of the fact, already noted, that at the optimum $CS'(X) = -PS'(X)$. The producers' surplus or net revenue is

$$PS(X) = pX - TC(X)$$

and its derivative is

$$PS'(X) = p + X\frac{dp}{dX} - MC(X).$$

Comparing this result with the formulas for $CS'(X)$ we obtain immediately a pair of equivalent necessary conditions for a price and level of use to be socially optimal:

$$p = MC(X) - \int_p^\infty F_2(w, X) \, dw \tag{1}$$

$$p = MC(X) - \int_0^X \Phi_2(X^d, X) \, dX^d. \tag{2}$$

---

[3]Subscripts to functions will be used to denote partial derivatives.

In deriving formula (1) use was made of the fact that $F(p, X) = X$ along the market demand curve.

The interpretations of both of these conditions are evident. For instance, formula (2) asserts that the socially optimal price must cover the marginal cost of serving a user plus the sum of the rates of decrease (with respect to congestion) of the value to the user of each use made of the facility at the level of use induced by that price. Note again the interplay of the market demand curve, which relates p and X, and the ccdd curve which is used to calculate the change in consumers' surplus.

The conditions in which net revenue maximization leads to a socially optimal outcome are also immediate. Let p^*, X^* denote the socially optimal point on the market demand curve. If producer's surplus is maximized at that point, $PS'(X^*) = -CS'(X^*) = 0$, or

$$\int_0^{X^*} \left[\Phi_2(X^d, X^*) - \Phi_2(X^*, X^*) \right] dX^d = 0,$$

where we have used the fact that $p^* = \Phi(X^*, X^*)$. Clearly, this condition will be satisfied only in special circumstances. One circumstance in which it will hold—not the only one, but the most likely— is for $p = \Phi(X^d, X)$ to be constant with respect to X^d, that is, for the ccdd curve to be infinitely elastic. In that case consumers' surplus itself will be zero at the optimal level of congestion (at least). Note that this condition of infinite elasticity of demand is also the condition under which an ordinary monopolist of a product free from congestion effects will choose the socially optimal level of output.[4]

Criteria essentially the same as Eqs. (1) and (2) have been presented previously, though derived rather differently. The most similar argument, though without allowance for individual diversity (which does not affect the conclusions in any important way), is that of Anderson and Bonsor [2].

The import of our conclusions can be illuminated by applying them to an example derived from Garrett Hardin's famous parable of the commons [7]. This fable concerns a village with N households, each of which is entitled to graze its sheep freely on the village commons. The amount of mutton yielded by a sheep is a decreasing function of the total number of sheep grazed. Denote this function by $m(X)$ with $m'(X) < 0$. Mutton sells for v per pound and the cost of tending the sheep is c. From these data, a villager will be in equilibrium when he has x sheep in his herd and x satisfies $vxm(X) - cx = 0$ with $X = Nx$. If we regard the villagers as consumers of the services of the commons, their consumer's surpluses will be zero whatever the level of X. This is inefficient. The villagers, by ignoring the effect that each has on the average yield of the sheep, have equated average revenue per sheep with the cost of tending. But the marginal revenue per sheep, $v[m(X) + xm'(X)]$, is less than the average revenue and therefore less than the cost.

Now suppose that a rapacious baron seizes the commons and exacts a tax of p on each sheep grazed, choosing the tax to maximize his revenue, pX. In the presence of this tax, the equilibrium size of the average flock is x such that $vm(X) = c + p$, $X = Nx$, so that the revenue that the baron maximizes can be written as $X[vm(X)$

---
[4] I thank professor Richard Zeckhauser for calling my attention to this resemblance between the socially optimal level of congestion and the conditions in which ordinary monopoly will lead to a socially optimal level of output of the monopolized product.

$- c$]. This is simply the social surplus that ought to be maximized. The congestion externality has been internalized. The baron profits and the villagers are no worse off assuming that c is a true measure of the opportunity cost of tending a sheep.[5]

The data of this example can be translated easily into the notation of the general model. But the crucial point is that $CS(X)$ equal 0 for all values of X, so that the condition for revenue maximization to be socially optimal is satisfied. The same is true in Gordon's example of the demersal fishery [6] and in many other instances. But not always.

CONGESTION WITH DISCONTINUOUS DEMAND CURVES

Dichotomous choices are a part of everyday life. We either go to the museum this afternoon or we do not, we buy either one videotape recorder this year or none. In a market characterized by such choices, each consumer's demand curve is discontinuous, and if we make the standard simplifying assumption that the market is comprised of identical consumers, the market demand curve is discontinuous too. The standard market analyses then do not apply. The discontinuity problem is especially important in the markets for congestible facilities, where each consumer's decision depends on his beliefs about how other consumers are likely to decide. A close inspection of the Pigou–Knight toll road example [13, 8] will make the difficulty vivid. In that example, there are two routes from A to B: a toll road that is fast at low traffic densities but has limited capacity, and a slower free road of unlimited capacity. Say that the time advantage of the toll road is $t(X)$, where X is the number of drivers who choose it. It is assumed that time is the only consideration, that drivers value their time at v_0 per minute, the same for all drivers, and that all drivers have the same information. Then any of three things can happen. If the drivers expect X to choose the toll road and the toll is less than $v_0 t(X)$, they will all choose it. If the toll exceeds $v_0 t(X)$ none will choose the toll road. Clearly, neither of these is a viable situation. Knight, being a sensible man, took it for granted that at any given toll, p, X will settle down to the value that satisfies the third possibility, $p = v_0 t(X)$. He then moved on to discuss the implications of that implicit demand curve. But, in fact, when that equation is satisfied, every driver is indifferent between using the toll road and the free road; there is nothing in the model to determine the number who choose the toll road. Some additional mechanism would have to be adduced to render the model determinate. We shall return to this example below.

Thus, in this type of problem the "simplifying" assumption instead generates complications. There are several conceivable ways to avoid them. We choose to meet the real problem head-on by conceding that we consumers are infinitely diverse. To this end, we formulate as follows the market for a congestible facility where consumers make simple use–don't use choices. For any level of congestion, X, there is a highest price at which any particular consumer will choose to use the facility. For consumer i we write this price as $w = \phi_i(X)$. For the present, we shall regard X as fixed, and shall discuss the properties of $\phi_i(X)$ later. Now consider any willingness-to-pay value, w, and all the consumers who share it for the given level of congestion. They need not be identical in any respect except just this one, but there

[5] Weitzman [15] showed that the villagers could not benefit from the intrusion of the baron and would be harmed if either (1) the increase in the output of mutton led to a fall in its price, or (2) the reduction in the average size of the flocks induced the villagers to accept a lower net return per sheep.

will be a certain number of them, and we shall imagine that the market is large enough so that the number of consumers who are just willing to pay w or very close to it is a continuous variable with respect to w. More formally, we shall take the frequency density of consumers for whom $\phi_i(X) = w$, to be written $h(w, X)$, to be a continuous function of w for any X. This frequency density function will be the basic datum of the analysis.

We impose a few mild requirements on it, in addition to continuity in w. First, there should be no gaps in it. That is, if $h(w, X) > 0$ for any $w \geq 0$, then also $h(w', X) > 0$ for $0 \leq w' \leq w$. Second, for any X there should be a maximum value that anyone is willing to pay. Formally, for any X there is a number $\bar{w}(X)$ such that $h(w, X) > 0$ for $0 \leq w < \bar{w}(X)$ and $h(w, X) = 0$ for $w > \bar{w}(X)$. Together with the continuity assumption, this implies $h(\bar{w}(X), X) = 0$. We shall let W denote the highest price that anyone is willing to pay, no matter what the value of X. Then $\bar{w}(X) \leq W$ for all values of X. With some additional restrictions to assure that certain integrals converge, W can be permitted to be infinite, but we shall not go into them.

The ccdd curve follows immediately. For any price, the level of use demanded is the number of consumers who are willing to pay at least that price, or

$$X^d = F(p, X) = \int_p^W h(w, X)\, dw.$$

By our construction, $F(p, X)$ is continuous and differentiable with respect to p, and

$$F_1(p, X) = -h(p, X) < 0. \tag{3}$$

This $F(p, X)$ possesses an inverse, $p = \Phi(X^d, X)$, which is continuous with respect to X^d.

For any value of X and the corresponding market price, $p = \Phi(X, X)$, the consumers' surplus is the sum over all users of the excesses of their willingnesses to pay over that price, or

$$CS(X) = \int_p^W h(w, X)(w - p)\, dw.$$

Integrate this expression by parts, using Eq. (3), to find:

$$CS(X) = \int_{p = \Phi(X, X)}^W F(w, X)\, dw, \tag{4}$$

which is the usual integral under the ccdd curve. To express the consumers' surplus in terms of the inverse ccdd curve, change the variable of integration to $X^d = F(w, X)$. Then $dw = d\Phi(X^d, X)$ with respect to variations in X^d. If $\Phi(X^d, X)$ is differentiable at that point, which we have not established, $d\Phi(X^d, X) = \Phi_1(X^d, X)\, dX^d$. Otherwise, the resultant integral will be a Lebesgue-Stieltjes integral. We must then assume that $h(w, X)$ is smooth enough so that $\Phi(X^d, X)$ can be differentiated except at isolated points. With this mild assumption we can write

$$CS(X) = \int_X^0 X^d d\Phi(X^d, X)$$
$$= -pX + \int_0^X \Phi(X^d, X)\, dX^d = \int_0^X \left(\Phi(X^d, X) - p\right) dX^d \tag{5}$$

after integrating by parts. Thus, all the usual formulas apply to these ccdd curves.

Now we can turn to the market demand curve, characterized implicitly by p, X satisfying $X = F(p, X)$. Immediately we confront the same difficulty that arose in the continuous case: If some of the consumers prefer more congestion to less that function may not be well defined, in which case neither the public planner seeking to induce the optimal level of use nor the monopolist seeking to maximize net revenue could do so simply by choosing p and allowing consumers to respond according to their preferences.[6] To rule out this possibility, we introduce the assumption that all consumers always prefer less congestion to more, i.e., that $\phi_i(X)$ is always a strictly decreasing function of X. We shall also assume, more reasonably, that for all consumers $\phi_i(X)$ is continuous and differentiable.

We can now consider how $F(p, X)$ behaves when X changes. To be concrete, suppose that X increases by a small amount, δX. (The analysis for decreases in X is exactly the same.) By our assumptions about preferences, this change will not induce any nonusers to use the facility, but it will induce some users to drop out. Consider user i for whom $w = \phi_i(X \geq p$. He will drop if and only if $w + \phi_i'(X)\delta X + o(\delta X) < p$.[7] For this to occur, $\phi_i'(X)$ must be small enough so that $\phi_i'(X) < (p - w)/\delta X$. Now recall that the consumers who happen to share the common value $\phi_i(X) = w$ may have very different tastes in other respects, and in particular that the derivative $\phi_i'(X)$ may differ among them. It will, however, have some average value, say $\bar{\phi}'(w, X)$.

This is sufficient information to establish the behavior of $X^d = F(p, X)$. By integrating the responses of consumers for whom $\phi_i(X) = w$ for all values of w, $w \geq p$, it can be shown, albeit tediously, that the increase in congestion by δX will decrease X^d by $-\bar{\phi}'(p, X)h(p, X)\delta X + o(\delta X)$. (In interpreting this formula, remember that necessarily $\bar{\phi}'(p, X) < 0$.) Allowing δX to approach zero establishes the continuity of $F(p, X)$. Dividing by δX and taking the limit as $\delta X \to 0$ yields $F_2(p, X) = \bar{\phi}'(p, X)h(p, X)$, which shows that $F(p, X)$ is differentiable with respect to X and, indeed, is the formula for the derivative. Furthermore, $F_2(p, X) < 0$, of course, so the inverse $p = \Phi(X^d, X)$ exists and is continuous and differentiable with respect to X.

We can now determine the socially optimal level of use and the corresponding price. We have already seen (Eq. (5)) that consumers' surplus at any level of use is

$$CS(X) = \int_0^X \left[\Phi(X^d, X) - p \right] dX^d.$$

For later use its derivative is

$$\frac{dCS}{dX} = \int_0^X \left[\Phi_2(X^d, X) - \frac{dp}{dX} \right] dX^d. \tag{6}$$

The socially optimal level of use maximizes the sum of consumers' and producer's surpluses, which is

$$SS(X) = CS(X) + pX - TC(X)$$
$$= CS(X) + X\Phi(X, X) - TC(X).$$

---

[6] Example: Suppose $F(p, X) = 6 + 0.125X + 0.03X^2 - 0.00025X^3 - 4p$. Then, taking $p = 1$, $F(1, X) = X$ is satisfied for $X = 2.5$, 43.1, and 74.4. Besides, regarding X as the independent variable, there is no solution with nonnegative p to $F(p, X) = X$ if X is in the range $10 < X < 30$.

[7] $o(\delta X)$ denotes an unspecified remainder term with the property that $o(\delta X)/\delta X \to 0$ as $\delta X \to 0$.

Differentiate, set the derivative equal to zero, and make some obvious cancellations to obtain the result that at the social optimum

$$p^* = MC(X^*) - \int_0^{X^*} \Phi_2(X^d, X^*)\, dX^d. \tag{7}$$

This is the same as Eq. (2), and has exactly the same interpretation. Specifically, the socially optimal price equals the marginal cost of serving the level of use that it induces plus the integral over all those uses of the rate of decrease in the user's willingness to pay for the use, with respect to increases in the level of congestion. Freeman and Haveman [5] obtained a virtually identical criterion.

Just as in the continuous case, if net revenue maximization is to lead to the social optimum, it is necessary to have $PS'(X) = 0$, and therefore $CS'(X) = 0$, at the socially optimal level of use. This, in turn, requires

$$\int_0^{X^*} \left[\Phi_2(X^d, X^*) - \frac{dp}{dX^*} \right] dX^d = 0$$

(see Eq. (6)). We cannot expect this condition to be satisfied in general, but it will be in special circumstances. In particular, if $\Phi(X^d, X^*)$ is constant with respect to X^d, i.e., if the ccdd curve is infinitely elastic, it will be satisfied. As in the continuous case, the divergence between the social optimum and the net revenue maximizing level of use arises from a slope in the ccdd curve, which creates the opportunity for a kind of monopolistic exploitation.

The Pigou–Knight toll road example provides an application. We shall assume, as Pigou and Knight did not, that the value of time is not the same for all drivers. Let v_i be the value of time for a particular driver and, as before, let $t(X)$ be the time saved by using the toll road when X drivers use it. Of course, $t'(X) < 0$. Then that driver's willingness to pay function is $\phi_i(X) = v_i t(X)$. To describe the diversity of valuations of time let N be the total number of potential users and $g(v)$ be the frequency density function that specifies the proportion of drivers with valuations in the neighborhood of v. In terms of the general notation, $h(w, X)$ denoted the frequency density of drivers for whom $vt(X) = w$, regarded as a function of both w and X. Therefore $h(w, x) = Ng(w/t(X))/t(X)$. The general notation is not convenient in this application, however, and we shall not use it.

The demand function follows at once. At any toll p and congestion level X, the number of drivers who will use the toll road is the number for whom the value of time saved is at least as great as the toll or $vt(X) \geq p$. Thus

$$X^d = F(p, X) = N \int_{p/t(X)}^{\bar{v}/t(X)} g(v)\, dv, \tag{8}$$

where $\bar{v}$ (perhaps infinite) denotes the highest value of time of any driver. All the functions we need are derived from this basic datum.

To apply the social optimality condition, Eq. (7), we require $\Phi_2(X^d, X)$, the derivative with respect to X of the price at which X^d drivers will use the road. To this end differentiate Eq. (8) with respect to X, holding X^d constant:

$$0 = -Ng\left(\frac{p}{t(X)} \right) \frac{d}{dX} \frac{p}{t(X)}.$$

Then, if $g(p/t(X)) \neq 0$, the other factor must be zero, or

$$t(X)\frac{dp}{dX} - pt'(X) = 0.$$

Yielding

$$\frac{dp}{dX} = \Phi_2(X^d, X) = \frac{p}{t(X)}t'(X).$$

Inserting this in Eq. (7) produces

$$p^* = -\int_0^{X^*} \frac{p}{t(X^*)}t'(X^*)\,dX^d$$

$$= -\int_0^{X^*} vt'(X^*)\,dX^d, \tag{9}$$

taking $MC(X^*) = 0$ and letting v denote price per minute saved that will induce a usage of X^d. The integral is, naturally, the aggregate decrease in the value of using the road that results from a marginal increase in congestion.

The optimality criterion takes a more familiar form if we change the variable of integration from X^d to p. Their relationship can be found by differentiating equation (8) with respect to p:

$$\frac{dX^d}{dp} = -N\frac{1}{t(X)}g\left(\frac{p}{t(X)}\right).$$

Inserting this in Eq. (10), and adjusting the limits correspondingly yields

$$p^* = -N\int_{p^*}^{\bar{v}t(X^*)} \frac{p}{t(X^*)}t'(X^*)g\left(\frac{p}{t(X^*)}\right)\frac{dp}{t(X)}$$

$$= -N\int_{p^*/t(X^*)}^{\bar{v}} vt'(X^*)g(v)\,dv.$$

This is essentially the formula derived by Layard [9] by a more informal method. In this version the optimal price is the sum over all valuations of time at which the toll road will be chosen of the density of users with that valuation multiplied by the value of the time lost by those users when there is a marginal increase in congestion.

Inserting the formula for $\Phi_2(X^d, X)$ in Eq. (6), the derivative of consumers' surplus at the optimum is found to be

$$CS'(X^*) = \int_0^{X^*}\left[\frac{p}{t(X^*)}t'(X^*) - \frac{dp}{dX^*}\right]dX^d$$

$$= -p^* - X^*\frac{dp}{dX^*}.$$

Note that a necessary condition for revenue to be maximized is that the third member of this equation vanish. Hence $CS'(X^*) = 0$ is a necessary condition for the socially optimal level of traffic to maximize net revenue, as we expected.

But the Pigou–Knight discussion reached the conclusion that a revenue maximizing toll would always induce the socially optimal level of traffic. Consideration of the consumers' surplus formula will show why. That formula can be written

$$CS(X) = \int_0^X \left(p(X^d) - p(X) \right) dX^d$$

where $p(X^d) = \Phi(X^d, X) =$ the valuation of $t(X)$ minutes by the marginal user when the price induces a demand for X^d uses, and $p(X)$ is the same function evaluated for $X^d = X$. If the valuations are uniform, as Pigou and Knight assumed, $p(X^d) = p(X)$ for all values of X^d. Then $CS(X) = 0$ for all X and the condition for coincidence is satisfied. As we saw at the outset, however, if the valuations are uniform the function described by Eq. (8) is not well defined; there is no p such that $X^d = F(p, X)$ for $0 < X^d < N$. Then, strictly speaking, this argument fails. It can be salvaged to some extent by showing, with the aid of Tchebycheff's inequality and some patient algebra, that as the variance of $g(v)$ approaches zero so does $CS(X)$, for any X. Basically, though, the simplification led into error. Apart from the rare case of uniform valuations of time, a Lerner-type mandate to maximize revenue or a Knight-type inducement to maximize profit cannot be relied on to lead to the socially optimal level of traffic. Edelson [4], using a very different model, reached the same conclusion.

Markets formally similar to the toll road example, in which identical consumers make dichotomous choices, have probably received more attention in the literature of congestion than any other type. Examples subsequent to Pigou–Knight are Gordon [6] and Walters [14]. In all such cases the demand curves that reflect consumers' motivations are infinitely elastic and do not possess inverses. Any analysis that invokes inverses, as these papers generally do rather surreptitiously, is therefore unfounded. (Gordon's application narrowly escapes this stricture because there is an obvious dynamic mechanism for bringing about his equilibrium.) Fortunately, this type of market is rarely encountered in practice.

CONCLUDING REMARKS

We have studied the necessary conditions for the socially optimal level of use of a congestible facility, with particular emphasis on the comforting thought that tendencies toward nonoptimal use arise from the absence of a market for the facility's services, and can be corrected by entrusting the facilities to private ownership or to management that acted as private owners would. We considered two models at length: in one the individual users had continuous demand functions for the services of the facility, in the other they did not. Not surprisingly, the two models led to identical conclusions.

Our major conclusions can best be expressed in terms of the "inverse constant crowding demand curves," which played a central role in the analysis. The general inverse demand curve for the use of a congestible facility can be written $p = \Phi(X^d, X)$, where p is the price at which X^d units of service of a congestible facility will be demanded when the level of congestion or total usage is X. This becomes an inverse ccdd curve when X is regarded as constant. The importance of these curves derives from the fact that they are the relevant curves for calculating consumers' surplus. In fact, the consumers' surplus that is conferred by any level of use X and the price p that induces that level of use is

$$CS(X) = \int_0^X \left[\Phi(X^d, X) - p \right] dX^d,$$

which is the integral under the inverse ccdd curve and above the ordinate for the price. In these terms, a necessary condition for a price–use level pair, p^*, X^*, to be socially optimal was found to be

$$p^* = MC(X^*) - \int_0^{X^*} \Phi_2(X^d, X^*) \, dX^d.$$

This is the basic optimality criterion found here and also by several previous writers using a variety of methods. It asserts, reasonably enough, that the socially optimal price should cover the marginal costs of service plus the sum of the reductions in the value of each unit of service to the consumer thereof that would result from a marginal increase in the level of congestion. This criterion can also be written

$$p^* = MC(X^*) - X^* \frac{dp^*}{dX} - CS'(X^*),$$

where dp^*/dX denotes the derivative of price with respect to the level of congestion taken along the ordinary demand curve and computed at the optimal level of congestion. Since the net revenues yielded by the use of the facility are maximized when $p + Xdp/dX = MC(X)$, it is seen readily that for net revenue maximization to lead to a socially optimal price—usage configuration, it is necessary that $CS'(X^*) = 0$. This was our second main conclusion.

One cannot expect the condition for net revenue maximization to lead to socially optimal results to be satisfied in general, though it is satisfied in many of the simplified models that figure large in the literature. In the real world, however, the essential simplifying conditions are likely to be violated, particularly the assumption that all users of a facility have identical demand curves for its use. Perhaps the only important circumstance in which this assumption applies is that in which the users are themselves firms in a competitive industry. Then the zero profit condition for competitive equilibrium implies that consumers' surplus will be zero at all levels of congestion and therefore that the socially optimal use-charge will also generate the maximum net revenue to the operator of the facility. Knight's toll road example and Gordon's model of a fishery illustrate this class of cases.

A number of assumptions that underlie this entire treatment should be made clear. In the first place, attention has been confined to a single facility, holding everything else in ceteris paribus. This precludes consideration of situations in which a number of highly substitutable facilities compete for the user's patronage, for example, recreational beaches or ski slopes. The problem and its analysis change radically when there is a group of highly substitutable facilities.[8] Then the central issue becomes the optimal distribution of users among the facilities rather than the optimal level of congestion on any single one. In the context of a dichotomous choice type of market, this is an assignment problem as the term is used in

---

[8] The following discussion is consciously cursory, intended to only suggest the outlines of the problem.

mathematical programming. Taking that point of view, it is straightforward to find that the socially optimal use-charge, p_α, and level of use, X_α, for a typical facility, the αth, are connected by

$$p_\alpha = MC_\alpha(X_\alpha) - \sum_i x_{i\alpha}\phi_i'(X_\alpha)$$

where $x_{i\alpha} = 1$ if user i uses facility α and zero otherwise. This is just what one would expect. Furthermore, if the optimal use-charges are imposed and the users choose the facilities at which their individual consumer's surpluses are greatest, they will distribute themselves optimally.

An immediate consequence of this relationship is that even if a number of facilities have the same cost curves and would be perfect substitutes apart from the effects of differing levels of congestion, it need not be socially optimal to impose the same use-charge for all of them. Anderson and Bonsor [1974a] noted the same phenomenon in their treatment of the multiple facilities case.

Thus, necessary conditions for a socially optimal distribution of consumers among the facilities are found easily. The conditions attained by a market equilibrating process in which the operators of individual facilities are free to choose their own use-charges are another matter. The market structure is no longer monopolistic, but is of the nature of monopolistic competition (or worse). The simplest applicable concept of equilibrium is a Nash equilibrium in which each facility imposes a use-charge that maximizes its producer's surplus taking the use-charges of the competing facilities as given. To characterize such an equilibrium, one needs demand curves for use of the various facilities, for each one regarding the prices and congestion levels of the others as given data. These demand curves, however, require far more information than is necessary for the analysis of a single facility. In the notation of the preceding section, the demand for use of the αth facility in a group of perfect substitutes is the number of users, i, for whom

$$\phi_i(X_\alpha) - p_\alpha \geq \max\left[0, \max_\beta\left(\phi_i(X_\beta) - p_\beta\right)\right].$$

This formula clearly generates extremely awkward and complicated demand curves, and I do not know the conditions under which a monopolistic competitive equilibrium will agree with the social optimum but suspect that they are restrictive. Anderson and Bonsor [1] conclude otherwise, but their treatment is so terse that the underlying assumptions are hard to discern. McConnell [11] attempted to estimate demand curves for a group of substitutable recreational beaches, but he assumed, in effect, that a single demand curve could be applied to all the beaches, which is clearly inappropriate.

A particularly important instance of the distribution of users among substitutable congestible facilities occurs when the "substitutes" are, in fact, the same physical facility at different times. The degree of congestion on a toll road at 8 AM is influenced by the toll charged and the degree of congestion at 8:30 AM and even 9:30 AM. Thus, the congestion problem converges on the familiar peak-load pricing problem. Even without invoking the device of allocating users by user-charges, the socially optimal level of congestion of a facility at any time will depend on the levels of congestion at other times.

But the multiple facilities case and the multiple time-of-use case move the analysis toward the general equilibrium framework which we consciously eschewed at the outset. It does not appear that basically new insights can be attained by adapting that framework, but in practical applications it is likely to be misleading to consider individual facilities or times of use in isolation when there are close substitutes.

Second, our treatment has been short-run in the sense that the physical characteristics of the facility considered were assumed to be fixed and unalterable. This is frequently a valid assumption, but many significant social decisions escape it, as when decisions have to be made about the width, grades, and other specifications of a proposed toll road, or the area and public facilities to be provided at a park. Oakland [12] included such a decision in his study, but as we noted above, that study was conducted at a highly abstract level. It does not appear that the inclusion of long-run decisions would entail any fundamental complications in the approach or analysis, and Oakland's results suggest that the conclusions would not be altered in essence.

Finally, we should note the ambiguous role played by congestion in the foregoing analysis. For the purpose of establishing the demand curves, expected or anticipated congestion was the relevant concept, but for appraising the results in terms of the social and consumers' surpluses the actual level of congestion experienced was appropriate. The same term and symbol was used for both of these concepts. There was therefore an implicit assumption that the two magnitudes were the same when the market equilibrium was achieved, but no mechanism for bringing this about was mentioned. It is excusable and even judicious in a theoretical paper to avoid becoming entangled in the dynamic mechanisms by which an equilibrium is attained, but it is dangerous to apply the theoretical conclusions without considering whether an effective equilibrating process is likely to be operative.

Congestion per se is an important problem but it is not quite sui generis. The theory of congestion applies to all markets in which the purchasers' satisfaction depends to a significant extent on the total amount of the good or service purchased in the market. Leibenstein's [10] bandwagon and snob effects are a case in point. The economics of agglomeration is closely related if not identical. And there are doubtless many other phenomena to which the theory can fruitfully be applied.

REFERENCES

1. F. J. Anderson and N. C. Bonsor, Allocation, congestion, and valuation of recreational resources, *Land Econ.* **50**, 51–57 (1974).
2. F. J. Anderson and N. C. Bonsor, Pricing and valuation of transport facilities in the presence of congestion, *Economica* **41**, 424–431 (1974).
3. P. A. Diamond, Consumption externalities and imperfect corrective pricing, *Bell J. Econ.* **4**, 526–538 (1973).
4. N. M. Edelson, Congestion tolls under monopoly, *Amer. Econ. Rev.* **61**, 873–890 (1971).
5. A. M. Freeman, III and R. H. Haveman, Congestion, quality deterioration, and heterogeneous tastes, *J. Public Econ.* **8**, 225–232 (1977).
6. H. S. Gordon, The economic theory of a common-property resource: The fishery, *J. Pol. Econ.* **62**, 124–142 (1954).
7. G. Hardin, The tragedy of the commons, *Science* **162**, 1243–1248 (1968).
8. F. H. Knight, Some fallacies in the interpretation of social cost, *Quart. J. Econ.* **38**, 582–606 (1924).
9. R. Layard, The distributional effects of congestion taxes, *Economica* **44**, 297–304 (1977).
10. H. Leibenstein, Bandwagon, snob, and Veblen effects in the theory of consumers' demand, *Quart. J. Econ.* **64**, 183–207 (1950).

11. K. E. McConnell, Congestion and willingness to pay: A study of beach use, *Land Econ.* **53**, 185–195 (1977).
12. W. H. Oakland, Congestion, public goods and welfare, *J. Public Econ.* **1**, 334–356 (1972).
13. A. C. Pigou, "The Economics of Welfare," Macmillan & Co., London (1920).
14. A. A. Walters, The theory and measurement of private and social cost of highway congestion, *Econometrica* **29**, 676–699 (1961).
15. M. L. Weitzman, Free access vs. private ownership as alternative systems for managing common property, *J. Econ. Theory* **8**, 225–234 (1974).

PART FOUR

NATURAL RESOURCE AND ENVIRONMENTAL ECONOMICS

[14]

An Economist's View of Natural Resource and Environmental Problems

ROBERT DORFMAN

The task of economists with respect to natural resource and environmental policy is to provide a framework within which the data provided by experts in other fields can be viewed and the social implications drawn. Economists can only repeat, without quite understanding, what geologists, ecologists, public health experts, and others say about physical and physiological facts. Their craft is to perceive how economies and people in general will respond to those facts.

It must be emphasized that the analysis of these responses, though predicated on secondhand knowledge, is critically important. What is happening and what is going to happen to our natural resource base and our environment depend not only on the facts of nature but also on human responses to them. The efficacy of any policy that may be adopted depends as much on how it affects human behavior as on how it is intended to influence natural phenomena. Judgments about the desirability of different policies are based on judgments about how they affect people's welfare. All these are matters that economists study and that they have come to treat with some sophistication.

The following discussion relates facts only insofar as necessary —others can speak to these facts with much more authority. Rather it bears down heavily on social interpretation. It is hoped that it can contribute some necessary unifying threads to the discussion of natural resource and environmental problems. Inevitably, such discussion dismembers unified problems into manageable segments to the neglect of both their basic unity and the fact that the same principles of human response apply to all of them.

One unifying thread has been mentioned already; that is, how people react to problems related to natural resources or the environment. This depends on what they know about the problem, what options are open to them, and what their motivations are. These things deserve attention whether we are dealing with deforestation, acid rain, or whatever.

One widespread and important factor is how much things cost. Often the most effective way to get people to exercise their ingenuity in economizing on the use of a resource is simply to make it expensive. Sometimes the best way to persuade people to stop desecrating their environment is to widen the alternatives open to them. These and other expedients appear in different guises in different contexts.

Therefore, the discussion is divided roughly in accordance with the kinds of information and incentives that are appropriate. The major division is between natural resource problems and environmental quality problems. The natural resource section is subdivided according to renewable or nonrenewable resources. In the environmental section, problems of planning and evaluation are discussed first, then problems of implementation, which are subdivided further according to whether the environmental problem occurs in an industrial nation, a less developed nation, or transcends national boundaries.

The first distinction, between natural resources and the environment, is not an easy one. For example, is a forest a natural resource, or a part of the environment, or both? It is both, as most people use the terms; these categories are not mutually exclusive. If we were legislators, we might have to define these words more precisely, but for our present purpose hairsplitting is not in order. Whether a particular item is to be regarded as a natural resource or an environmental feature, or a human artifact for that matter, depends on the problem under consideration and on the point of view being taken. A graded and drained field is a human artifact to the farmer who invested in it, a natural resource to the economic geographer, and part of the environment to the ecologist. For working purposes we can be satisfied with the crude distinction that a natural resource is something that can be reduced in quantity when used, whereas an environmental feature can be altered in quality but not diminished in quantity. We shall consider natural resources first.

NATURAL RESOURCE PROBLEMS

The first distinction to be made in discussing natural resource problems is that between exhaustible and self-renewing resources. Exhaustible resources are typically of geologic origin, and any amounts consumed will be replaced on a geologic time scale, if at all. Any amount used is gone forever for all practical purposes. Self-renewing resources are typically biological, and the amounts harvested will be replaced by natural forces rather quickly, within limits. But there are borderline cases. Groundwater is one example—left to itself, a depressed water table will rise in a few years or decades. Another is a climax forest—the biological processes that generated it may take millennia and, indeed, may never be repeated. Again, fine distinctions are unnecessary.

There is a paradox. Exhaustible resources are never totally exhausted. The general rule is that as a deposit is worked, the successive units of the resource become increasingly expensive to extract, until finally the deposit is abandoned with much of the resource still in place. Typically, an oil well is capped with 50-60 percent of the original oil still in the reservoir. It is said that there is still gold in Vermont, but the ore is of such poor grade that it is not worth extracting even at current high prices.

On the other hand, self-renewing resources can be annihilated. Simple mention of the passenger pigeon and the American buffalo establishes that. Thus, exhaustible and self-renewing resources present quite different problems of resource management.

Exhaustible Resources

Economists have an elegant theory for the use of exhaustible resources. It is frequently attributed to Harold Hotelling, but the main lines were presented by Lewis Gray about a generation earlier. The basic theory has several variants. The one discussed here is not quite the simplest, but it is the simplest that has empirical relevance.

The theory concentrates on the behavior of a mine-owner, who may be an entire nation. At any time, the owner has to decide how much to extract, taking into account the fact that the more extracted right away, the greater will be the cost of each unit extracted in the future. The reasoning is a bit subtle but is essentially as follows. Suppose that in any month the owner should extract one unit less than he is now planning and make it up the next month. Then in the current month he would sacrifice the net profit on one unit at this month's price. In the second month two things would happen. First, he would gain the net profit on one unit at the second month's price. Second, the net profit on every unit extracted in the second month would be increased because the reserves in place at the time that unit was extracted would be one unit greater, thereby reducing extraction cost.

It would be advantageous to cut back the first month's output if the sum of these two effects on the second month's profits were greater than the first month's sacrifice accumulated at interest for a month. Similar reasoning applies to the option of increasing production in the first month. And the current plan is just right if the price is increasing just quickly enough that no shift in either direction is advantageous.

To continue, if the price were not increasing, or were increasing only slowly, all producers would be induced to increase their current output to obtain their profits now rather than later. But the increase in current output would reduce the going price, while its effect on future prices would be, if anything, to increase them, because the reserves available for the future would be reduced. Hence, the market behavior would be to accelerate the increase in the price, and the process would continue until prices were growing quickly enough that producers were content with their current rates of production.

This theory thus leads to the conclusion that, left to itself, the market for any exhaustible resource will generate a path of gradually increasing prices. Further, if the prices at any two dates are compared, the price at the later date, the net of extraction costs discounted to the earlier date, will equal the price at the earlier date, also net of extraction costs. Moreover, to the extent that the price of a unit of a resource, net of extraction costs, measures the social benefit of extracting that unit, this price path reflects the fact that the resource is being extracted at just the rate that a wise, beneficent planner would recommend.

Of course, the gradual increase in price will be an inconvenience to future generations. It will induce them to use the resource more sparingly, to extract and process it more carefully, to reclaim and recycle it more extensively, and to substitute other, somewhat less suitable resources for it if they are cheaper. That is as it should be. The inconveniences in the future are offset by the advantages in the present of using the resource at the rate induced by the price path, if the discount rate that generates the market behavior reflects the relative social evaluation of present and future net benefits.

There is some empirical confirmation for this theory, but not much. When the oil-exporting nations abruptly increased their prices, inducing a reduction in worldwide consumption, all the other producers increased their outputs as much as possible, just as the theory predicts. But the main prediction of the theory, that the prices of exhaustible resources would rise faster than prices in general, was not supported in this case. It is easy to think of reasons for this. The basic one probably is the great continuing advances in the technologies of finding, extracting, and processing exhaustible resources, accompanied by the development of substitutes for expensive minerals. Another important reason is the notorious instability in the price of raw materials, which fluctuates so much that producers are reluctant to forego current profits for uncertain gains in the future.

So the theory, though perhaps correct in principle, merely points to one consideration, the effects of which may be swamped in practice by other considerations. For predictive purposes the theory has a poor record. Prescriptive purposes—telling us how fast exhaustible resources ought to be extracted—are another matter, although they depend on similar reasoning. The essence is to recognize that every unit of an exhaustible resource that is extracted confers an immediate social benefit, the extent of which is measured by the price that people are willing to pay for the unit less the cost of the resources used to extract it. It also imposes costs on the future, their extent being measured by the increase in the cost of extracting future units because of the reduced amount of the resource in place. The proper balance between present and future is struck when the immediate benefits are just balanced by the deferred costs.

The problem lies in the estimation of the deferred costs. They have to be assessed from the point of view of the present, since our future selves and our descendants cannot express their views. This assessment is a difficult task for several reasons. One has already been mentioned: the impossiblity of foreseeing technological improvements in the production and use of a resource or the development of substitutes for it. A second is the problem of "discounting." Today's needs always seem more urgent than the future's. To some extent this habit of discounting the future is justifiable, since the future will be more technically adept than the present. It will also be richer, in the sense of having larger stocks of productive capital to work with and therefore more ample flows of most consumable goods. Justifiable or not, we always do it, so the question arises as to how much we should discount future consequences of current actions. This question is important and has generated an enormous literature, but it is far from being resolved. In this circumstance, the best way to contend with a practical problem of exhaustible resources is to estimate the consequences of applying a wide range of discount rates. It may turn out that the rate of extraction will be influenced strongly by the rate of discount that is applied. Then the decision is thrown into the realm of judgment. But the analysis that leads to such an indecisive result is not futile. One man's good judgment is another man's folly. Where there are differing judgments about social decisions, it is important to clarify the source of the difference. If different opinions about proper extraction policy arise from differing opinions about the proper rate of discount, then that is the issue on which public debate should be focused. If agreement is unobtainable, as is generally the case, it is nonetheless helpful to know what people are disagreeing about and where they stand.

A third problem is associated with the concept of reserves. Reserves are, in fact, a kind of bugbear. Geologists make estimates of the amounts of various minerals in the earth's crust. For example, there are about 2×10^{18} metric tons (mt) of aluminum. But nearly all of this enormous quantity is in such low concentrations or otherwise unavailable that for practical purposes it might as well not be there. So the significant quantity is the amount in usable deposits. Although usable deposits is not a geological concept, we rely on geologists to estimate it. The US Geological Survey makes estimates for a number of conceptual quantities such as "proved reserves," "inferred reserves," or "recoverable resources," which are distinguished by the degree of confidence that geologists have in the actual existence of the deposits and by their judgment of the economic practicality of extracting the minerals. Those estimates are interesting but of little value in formulating extraction policies. As we have noted, deposits are invariably abandoned before they are exhausted, because the cost of further extraction has risen. For policy purposes, there is a need for estimates of the cost of further extraction from the best deposits remaining after various quantities have been mined. Such estimates require a knowledge of both geology and mining economics, and just plain future vision. They are extraordinarily difficult to make and can rarely be made with much confidence.

The final problem that deserves mention is this. To ascertain the desirable current rate of extraction of an exhaustible resource, we need to know the costs that any choice will impose at future dates. But future costs will depend on the rate of extraction at the time. We seem to be caught in a bind of circular reasoning: to know the proper rate at one date, we need the answer to the same question for all future dates. Happily, the problem is not so much circular as simultaneous. The proper current rate of extraction cannot be estimated without forecasting the whole course of extraction until an inevitable day when costs have risen so much that further exploitation of the resources costs more than it is worth. Then the resource is exhausted from an economic point of view, though geologically a great deal remains in place. Charting this proper course of extraction, where every year along the way present benefits are balanced against future costs, is a difficult technical problem, but solvable within the limits imposed by the problems of prediction and discounting mentioned before.

Things now stand as follows. To establish the proper rates of use of any exhaustible resource, we must make necessarily tenuous projections of future uses and future extraction and processing costs and agree on an appropriate discount rate. With those data we can calculate the proper rate of extraction currently and in the future. Simultaneously, we can calculate the future course of prices for the resource, since the price at any time must equate the amount demanded with the proper rate of extraction. The prices that obtain at present and that will obtain in the future are, in fact, the key to the problem. If the price of a resource could be made to follow its proper course, the amounts of the resource extracted and used would automatically allocate its use over a time in the best way possible. This theory maintains that for any exhaustible resource, there is a course of prices that will induce producers, all trying to exploit their deposits as profitably as possible, to extract the resource at the socially optimal rate. Further, though this course of prices is difficult to estimate, by making use of the available pertinent knowledge, we can make estimates that will be the best attainable guides to policies for use and conservation. But now there is another difficulty to be faced: If we knew the socially optimal price path, how could we implement it?

Most of the critical exhaustible resources are traded in world markets. They are extracted, typically, in both industrial and developing countries. The industrial countries are generally net importers and depend on imported raw materials for their industries. They have a great stake in rational allocation of resource use over time. The developing countries also depend on the resource as a way of paying for current imports and storing wealth with which to finance their own development. Optimal allocation over time is a secondary concern to them;

high prices in the immediate future are more important. Management of resources is particularly complicated in developing countries, where both the nation itself and multinational mining companies participate according to elaborate contractual arrangements. There is little basis for expecting the international markets thus created to generate socially optimal prices. Institutional arrangements for coordinating the policies of the mining companies and the nations with the deposits are lacking, but there is no lack of conflicts of interest.

In these circumstances, the outlook for implementing any farsighted plan for extracting nonrenewable resources in a way that will service the interests of all the countries concerned is dim indeed. The only expedient appears to be to alter the structure of the markets so that they induce more satisfactory performance. I will suggest one way in which this might be done.

One notorious problem in the markets for exhaustible minerals is that the prices fluctuate erratically, quite unlike the smooth evolution required to induce optimal rates of extraction. These fluctuations are harmful in many ways: high prices contribute to inflationary pressures in the importing countries, whereas low prices exacerbate foreign exchange problems and generate unemployment in developing countries. Whether prices are high or low, their variability interferes with the process described above; decisions about the rate of extraction become dominated by short-run speculative considerations instead of a long-run concern for how best to allocate use over time.

One expedient for moderating these fluctuations and some of their consequences is rarely used. It is a type of loan that an international lender, either an international agency or an institution like the National Westminster Bank, might make to a developing country when the price of a mineral export is depressed. The loan would be secured by a mortgage on a stated amount of the still unmined deposit. The amount of the loan per unit would be a fraction, say one-half, of the long-run value of the resource-in-place calculated by means of the theory discussed above. The loan would be retired in, say, quarterly instalments, each payment being the amount secured by the ore extracted in the previous quarter plus accumulated interest. Such loans would ease the pressure on a developing country to maintain production when the price of its resource was depressed and would also reduce the amount extracted at times when the social value, as indicated by the price, was lower than the long-run socially optimal value. To the extent that it succeeded in reducing the volume produced during troughs in demand, it would also moderate the violence of the price fluctuations.

Surely many other devices are available for improving the performance of the international markets in exhaustible commodities. We shall have to continue to rely on the markets, however, to control the rate of extraction of exhaustible resources, and this is not altogether a bad thing. Properly performing markets reflect the assembled knowledge and judgment of the people who are in the best position to assess the present and future values of the resource, who have a canniness that central planners cannot be expected to equal. The important thing is that the markets should not be dominated by speculative or narrowly acquisitive motivations.

Of course, we do not know at present which markets are performing well and which are inducing excessive rates of mineral extraction. The only way to find out is to gather the pertinent data, apply the normative theory, and compare the actual course of prices and extractions with the socially optimal one. This is no mean task, but the stakes are so high that studies of this kind would be worthwhile for at least some of the more important minerals such as copper, nickel, and tin.

Self-renewing Resources

The problems presented by self-renewing resources are different from those presented by exhaustible resources. For one thing, there is a real possibility that the world's stock of a self-renewing resource will be depleted permanently and irretrievably. Nevertheless, there is a close kinship in the conflict, present in both cases, between the enticements of immediate harvesting and the awareness that large current harvests increase the costliness of future harvests.

This awareness has given rise to the doctrine of "maximum sustainable yields," which is a good starting point for discussing the complications introduced by self-renewal. The doctrine is based on the "logistic law of population growth," which holds that any environment or habitat has a maximum carrying capacity for each species that inhabits it. When the population of any species is small in relation to the carrying capacity for it, the population grows rapidly in terms of percentage but slowly in terms of absolute mass, simply because the number of individuals growing and reproducing is small. As the population increases, the percentage growth rate declines (in part because food becomes harder to find and predators become more numerous), but the growth rate in absolute numbers and weight increases—up to a point. After that point, the decrease in the percentage growth rate overcompensates the increase in numbers to which that percentage is applied, and the growth rate in terms of absolute population becomes smaller and smaller as the carrying capacity is approached.

The maximum sustainable yield is the absolute growth rate at that critical point at which the population is growing most rapidly. For if the harvest taken each year is equal to the natural annual amount of growth, the population will remain stationary, and that size of harvest can be sustained indefinitely. Without appraising this ecological theory, it can be stated empirically that it appears to apply to some species and not to others. However, it is often maintained that the population of any economically significant species should be allowed to grow to the level at which the natural rate of growth is fastest and then be held at that level by an annual take equal to the maximum sustainable yield.

The doctrine may be ideal from the point of view of the species in question, but from a social or economic point of view, there are at least three things wrong with it. First, it takes no account of the cost of harvesting. Whatever the species may be—fur-bearing animals or fish or teak or truffles—it is generally cheaper to find and capture any given number the more numerous they are in the particular area. It follows, then, that if the population were held at a level somewhat greater than the one that affords the maximum sustainable yield, the saving in the average cost of harvesting would be greater than the value of the (slight) decrease in the sustainable yield.

The second defect in the maximum sustainable yield theory is complementary to the first. The doctrine ignores the fact that the social value of units of any commodity falls when the supply increases. Thus, if the population of a commercial species were held somewhat above the level of the maximum sustainable yield, the annual harvest would be reduced but the value of the units forgone would be lower than the value of those harvested and the average cost of harvesting would be reduced, for the reason just explained. It can be shown, in fact, that there is always a sustainable yield somewhat smaller than the maximum that gives rise to a perpetuity of social benefits that is preferable to the one corresponding to the maximum sustainable yield.

The third defect is somewhat less obvious. It is that this doctrine and almost any policy based on maintaining a constant harvest in perpetuity ignores the cost of attaining the population at which that harvest can be sustained. Consider the "socially optimal sustainable yield," the yield that takes into account the effect of harvest size on the average harvesting cost and the social value of each unit harvested. Suppose that the current population is smaller than the one at which the socially optimal yield can be sustained. Then, for the population to grow to the optimal level, the current harvest must be reduced below the sustainable take, thus reducing current social benefits. That reduction is the cost.

On the other hand, if the current population is at least equal to the one at which the socially optimal yield can be sustained, the current harvest and social benefits can be increased, although it will not be possible to harvest the optimal sustainable yield thereafter. It turns out, nevertheless, that the temporary increase would be worthwhile, since the current gains would outweigh the future costs. In a nutshell, it is not best to maintain the socially optimal sustainable yield even if you are in a position to do so. Economists will recognize the analogy between this finding and the distinction between "the golden rule of economic growth" and the "modified golden rule."

We conclude that all policies based on constant annual harvests are socially wasteful. The socially optimal policy has to be deduced from an analysis similar to the one that applies to exhaustible resources, but amended to allow for the natural replenishment of the population. The result of such analysis is almost inevitably a recommendation against harvests that remain the same year after year.

So much for the economic theory of self-replenishing resources. It has been discussed here largely to discredit the maximum sustainable yield doctrine, but now its limitations must be emphasized. All the principles of economically optimal harvesting are derived from some variant of the logistic growth assumption that the growth of a natural population depends primarily on its own numbers. But this is rarely, if ever, the case. The growth of a population is likely to be influenced at least as strongly by the abundance of its food, its competitors, and its predators, of which human beings are usually only one. Often the dominant influence on the growth of a population is a subtle change in its environment such as a slight change in water temperature or acidity, or a variation in the amount or timing of rainfall. Thus few natural populations grow in accordance with logistical laws, and harvesting policy, within wide limits, is an ineffective way to control population growth. On the whole, the best way to sustain a population is to control the factor that influences its growth most strongly. This is frequently the extent and condition of the population's habitat. Even if no one had ever hunted the American buffalo, there would not be millions of them roaming the western plains today. Acid rain has eliminated the trout from many lakes despite determined efforts to limit the annual catch. And so on.

Although limits on harvesting cannot be relied on to maintain a population at a desired level or constrain its growth to a desired path, uncontrolled harvesting can reduce a population to the critical level below which reproduction fails to compensate for natural mortality. There is a strong tendency for just that to happen to commercially valuable species. Animals and plants in the wild are common property—that is, no one's property—so fishers, hunters, and gatherers do not feel that they have much influence over the size or costs or even the existence of future harvests. Sensibly, they take what they can now, instead of leaving it for someone else to reap. Occasionally, common-pool problems afflict exhaustible resources also, but they are much more prevalent with regard to renewable resources.

Probably the most ominous instance of the common-pool problem today is the overuse of forests and rangelands in the developing countries. Free access to forests and ranges has been part of the way of life in those countries, at least since the invention of slash-and-burn agriculture. With the growth of human populations, the practice has become more destructive than the resources can bear. Garrett Hardin's "tragedy of the commons" is being enacted on Java, in the Sahel, in the Amazon Basin, and in many other parts of the world.

Coping with this deeply ingrained practice is difficult. Direct control is futile; the intruders are too numerous and the control apparatus too feeble. Besides, to the extent that controls are effective, they impose cruel hardships. The only effective approach seems to be to make available satisfactory and competitive substitutes for the goods and services now provided by the open lands: fuel and building materials to protect forests, alternative forage or crops to protect grazing lands, and so on. The roles of central governments and international agencies would then be twofold: first, to provide the substitute commodities needed to make life tolerable without incursions into fragile areas of the environment; and second, to provide strong incentives to local authorities—village elders, panchayats, and the like—to protect and reclaim the forests, grazing lands, and other natural resources in their districts. Such efforts, if widespread, would make greater demands on the budgets and administrative apparatus of the developing countries than they could meet. Programs would therefore have to be concentrated on the most severely threatened localities and, even then, given adequate support by international agencies.

ENVIRONMENTAL PROBLEMS

Natural resource problems shade imperceptibly into environmental problems, as the discussion of common pools may have suggested. After all, the environment consists of resources, some, such as the air we breathe, of supreme importance. The rough distinction adopted here is that natural resource problems relate to the quantity and environmental problems to the quality of the resources that constitute the environment.

Environmental problems, then, concern the quality of our shared surroundings—terrestrial, aquatic, and atmostpheric. In some interpretations, they concern both man-made and natural components of the environment. But this is another difficult distinction. The natural features will be emphasized here, although without paying much attention to the boundary between them and human artifacts.

It has been conventional to divide environmental problems according to whether they related to the condition of the air, land, or water. Fortunately, that division seems to be falling into disuse. The same principles apply to all three, since they are all common pools, and the conditions of the three are intimately linked. The classic example is sulfuric emissions into the atmosphere, most measures to reduce which generate nasty sludges that must be disposed of either on land or in water. The land-air-water distinction will therefore not be used much here. Instead, the discussion will be organized around two aspects of environmental protection programs: planning or appraisal, and implementation.

As used here, *planning* means deciding on the goals to be achieved in specific situations, whereas *implementation* means deciding on the means to be used to attain those goals. The two are not really separable. Planning requires knowledge of the means available, since they affect the costliness and even the practicability of attaining various goals. Implementation, of course, requires knowing what is to be achieved. But it is best to talk about one thing at a time, and planning is discussed first.

Planning Problems

Planning, then, is the selection of goals—for example, the level of dissolved oxygen to be attained in a waterway or the rate of emission of sulfur oxides to be permitted in a region. It is always a compromise among evils and, in practice, amounts to a form of benefit-cost analysis.

Although benefit-cost analysis is a banner to some people and a red flag to others, it is unavoidable. To choose among courses of action, one must compare the advantages and drawbacks of the permissible alternatives. Since this must be done, it is best done consciously and systematically.

Nevertheless, the use of benefit-cost analyses is a subject of controversy, and the results are regarded with skepticism. This low esteem is well-merited, for few analyses can command respect or confidence. As a result, most have come to be paper exercises, undertaken for the record, while actual decisions are made without the guidance accorded by careful analysis of their consequences.

There are numerous reasons for this costly and unsatisfactory state of affairs. A half-dozen of the leading problems that can be corrected will be discussed below.

ABSENCE OF STANDARDS. It is not too much to say that every benefit-cost analysis is ad hoc, an exercise in the analyst's judgment and ingenuity. Every analyst goes about this work in a distinctive way and, in general, carries out each task differently. This state of affairs has numerous disastrous consequences. The analogy that comes to mind is auditing, in many ways a similar enterprise. How much confidence would financial reports deserve if every auditor had wide latitude to define the various classes of assets and liabilities and to devise valuation assumptions? That is essentially the situation with benefit-cost analysis.

The burden placed on readers of these analyses is excessive. They must search through the footnotes in the appendixes to the annexes to find out what the innocent sounding words really mean. More often than not they discover that the definitions are inappropriate and the assumptions implausible. But that is not all. Environmental plans have long histories during which diverse alternatives are supposedly evaluated. Each time one of the alternatives is studied, it is done differently, using different assumptions and definitions. To make use of these reports, frequently thousands of pages in total, the details of what was done have to be rooted out, and rough-and-ready adjustments have to be made to render them at all comparable. It is a task to be approached not without dread. Policymakers might do better relying on "trained intuition," or "expert judgment," or "wise experience."

Clearly, planning will not be effective while these conditions persist. There have been attempts to deal with the problem. Both the Organization for Economic Cooperation and Development (OECD) and the United Nations Industrial Development Organization (UNIDO) have sponsored handbooks on the conduct of benefit-cost analysis, and numerous government agencies have issued manuals and guidelines (for example, the Water Resources Council of the United States). The extent of their effectiveness is indicated by the fact that more than ten years after the OECD and UNIDO reports were issued, nothing has changed, and for good reason. Both were scholarly, subtle, general, abstract, demanding of data, difficult to apply, and, above all, unenforced. In fact, both contain disclaimers assuring the reader that they have no official status. As it happens, neither deals explicitly with environmental problems.

There is need for some influential agency or group of agencies concerned with environmental problems to set forth specifications for benefit-cost evaluations and to require that studies submitted to, or generated by, the agency conform to them. That is not easy in the present state of the art. To be useful, the specifications would have to be explicit and detailed. Undoubtedly, several formats would have to be permitted, to allow for differences in the scale of the appropriate analytic effort, in the availability of data, and in the nature of the problem. Preparing such a document will require difficult negotiations and some experimentation. The effort would certainly not be worthwhile if the need were not so urgent. But considering the amount of effort now devoted to preparing benefit-cost analyses of doubtful usefulness and questionable validity, it would be a sure winner.

The promulgation of acceptable standards is only first step, though a major one. The standards would have to be brought up to date from time to time as experience and knowledge accumulated. Most important, any benefit-cost analysis invokes numerous assumptions—about population growth, trends in price levels and interest rates, and other matters. For comparability of studies, therefore, standard sets of assumptions would need to be prescribed. They need not pretend to precision and in fact should not. The important thing is that they impose uniformity and be reasonably plausible.

For these purposes, some continuing organization or institution must be established. It is hoped that such an institution and its standards would in time acquire the authority of the Institute of Certified Public Accountants and similar organizations. No other single development could do as much to advance the practice and usefulness of benefit-cost analysis.

NEGLECT OF DISTRIBUTIONAL EFFECTS. At least nine out of ten benefit-cost studies adopt the time-honored procedure of adding up benefits and costs "to whomsoever they may accrue." This alone is enough to disqualify them as guides for making practical decisions. Decisions about environmental policies are—and ought to be—political decisions. Their effectiveness depends ultimately on public acceptance. Under any form of government, the officials who make the decisions must be alert to the reactions of the constituencies to which they owe their positions and influence. Analyses that omit the effects of policies on relevant population groups—farmers in the affected region, workers in the affected industries, richer and poorer nations, the poor wherever they may be—thereby leave out the very information that is or should be most significant to the people who make the decisions. A major concern of political decision-makers is to get that information. If it is left out of benefit-cost analyses, they will get it from other sources, ignoring the analyses in the process.

Practical politicians and administrators often point out that it is indiscreet to be explicit about who benefits and who pays for environmental measures, that it can lead to nothing but dissension. It can be countered that it is impossible to hide the fact of distributional consequences and that it is far better to admit them openly than to leave a vacuum to be filled by tendentious claims.

UNPERSUASIVE TREATMENT OF NONMONETARY EFFECTS. Environmental problems are undoubtedly the most difficult field of application of benefit-cost analysis. This is because the major benefits and many of the costs have no natural monetary values: examples are protection of public health, preservation of natural areas and wildlife, improvement in air quality, reduction in urban noise levels. There have been endless efforts to put dollar values on these things and equally endless debates about those efforts. The very propriety of trying to place dollar values on such ultimate goods has been challenged. The problem is built in and it is also inescapable. It has been pointed out many times that every decision involving an environmental problem entails an implicit or explicit judgment about how much we ought to be spending on the goals that it is designed to achieve.

Since there is no generally accepted way of assigning monetary value to many of the benefits that motivate environmental programs, benefit-cost analyses will not be persuasive if their conclusions depend on monetary values selected by the analyst. Instead, estimates of the physical results (for example, number of untimely deaths averted, number of hectares preserved, increase in the level of dissolved oxygen) should stand at the heart of the analyses, so that the reader can judge whether the results are worth the cost according to his or her own scale or values.

The reader will often be helped if the physical results are translated, after they are presented, into monetary equivalents by applying a plausible range of values to those results. Occasionally this translation will show the cost to be so small or so great as to force a decision but the analyst has no right to presume this.

NEGLECT OF UNCERTAINTY. The future is always uncertain, but never more so than when attempting to foresee the benefits and costs of environmental interventions. We know painfully little about the effects of human actions on environmental or ecological conditions, or about the way in which people respond to programs intended to alter their behavior with respect to the environment. Thus, the effects of environmental programs cannot be predicted with any accuracy, and it is pretense to behave otherwise. Yet that is the almost invariable practice. It is standard for benefit-cost analyses to present point estimates of decreases in death rates, increases in net social benefits, and the like, with no indication of how uncertain those estimates are.

No reader, of course, takes those estimates literally, but neither does he have a basis for judging how skeptical he should be about them. It is the responsibility of the analyst to provide such a basis, by indicating the ranges within which there is good reason to believe the true values lie. Lip service is often paid to this dictum in qualifying phrases and footnotes, but that doesn't help the reader much or instill much confidence. The analyst should recognize that these ranges define the limits of his knowledge and should base his reasoning and his interpretation on them rather than on fictitiously precise point estimates. Most important, the tables that summarize the results of an analysis should emphasize the ranges that are believed to include the true values rather than follow the current, misleading practice.

This aspect of benefit-cost analyses has an important link with the implementation problems to be discussed below. The choice of implementation strategy often depends on where the uncertainties lie. For example, one of the critical choices may be whether to rely on economic incentives or to impose direct regulations. Poor information about the private costs of abating emissions will produce less confidence in estimates of the effects of economic incentives than in those of the effects of regulations. On the other hand, if the major uncertainties relate to the beneficial effects of abatement, then the economic and administrative advantages of economic incentives will loom large. Information about the reliability of the various estimates in a benefit-cost analysis is therefore critically important to the design of an implementation plan.

INADEQUATE ATTENTION TO ALTERNATIVES. There are always a number of potential responses to an unsatisfactory environmental condition—in fact, often more than one can conceive of, much less analyze. The possible alternatives differ in the amount of protection they afford and in their cost, side effects, and methods of implementation. Sound planning requires, first, identifying a variety of plausible responses to a problem, though a complete listing is out of the question. Second, it requires that the identified alternatives be assigned a price tag and compared incrementally—that is, that each alternative be compared with the one whose costs are just below its own so that readers can see what improvements are bought with the additional expense.

SUPERFICIAL TREATMENT OF COSTS. So much effort is generally expended in estimating the benefits of environmental protection measures that cost is relatively neglected. But this neglect can be costly. For example, when the use of a dangerous pesticide is banned or restricted, farmers are likely to resort to some other pesticide that may also be dangerous. The dangers imposed by the second pesticide are one of the costs of restricting the first, and they should be taken into account. Again, when tall stacks were recommended as a means of dispersing the sulfur dioxide generated in congested areas, the effects of long-distance transport were not taken into account. We are now worrying about them, a bit late. Many other examples could be cited of adverse but foreseeable side effects that might well have influenced environmental decisions. It is a mistake to assume that the visible expenses of implementation are the only costs of environmental policies.

ALLOWANCE FOR DEGREE OF EFFECTIVENESS. Finally, benefit-cost studies invariably take it for granted that the policies studied will be executed with 100-percent faithfulness by all concerned. Alas, life isn't like that. Emissions, for example, are never abated by quite as much as a plan calls for; endangered species continue to be trapped and gathered despite determined efforts to protect them; and so on. Benefit estimates should not presume 100-percent efficiency in execution; the actuality may be far lower.

Thus far the discussion has concentrated on some technical aspects of planning, which is where the most pervasive and serious shortcomings lie at present. There are naturally, substantive issues as well, at least one of which should be mentioned.

No planner leaves costs, in the narrow dollars-and-cents sense—entirely out of account in environmental planning, although sometimes the United States pretends to do so. However, one implication of these costs is rarely taken into account, perhaps because it is so unpleasant. It is that some countries and communities can afford more protection than others. Many countries adopt American or German environmental standards to avoid the onerous task of establishing their own. The World Health Organization has recommended some uniform environmental standards as guides to individual nations. All such blanket proposals are misguided. In environmental matters, as in education, nutrition, health care, and so on, sound planning requires that aspiration levels be adapted to available resources. In any country, the stricter the environmental standards the greater the resources that will required to attain them, and the less the resources that will be available for other urgent needs such as health care and developmental investments.

The poorer countries of the world confront tragic choices. They cannot afford drinking water standards as high as those to which the industrial countries are accustomed. They cannot afford to close their pristine areas to polluting industries that would introduce technical know-how and productive capital and thereby earn urgently needed foreign exchange. They cannot afford to bar mining companies from unexploited regions. Nor can they afford to impose on those companies antipollution requirements that are as strict and expensive as those in richer industrialized countries. They should always realize that environmental protection measures are financed out of the stomachs of their own people, since the multinationals cannot be made to pay for them. It follows that every country, and particularly the poorer ones, has to choose its own environmental standards, adapted to its needs and resources.

These remarks apply to global pollutants, particularly carbon dioxides, as well as to local and regional pollutants. The richer countries are beginning to cut back on globally polluting emissions. The poorer countries can say, justly, "You fellows have increased the carbon dioxide concentration in the atmosphere by at least 12 percent. Now it's our turn." Is there any really satisfactory response to that? The world can neither stand by complacently while India, China, and the others pour carbon dioxide into the atmosphere, nor can it expect them to desist. A partial response would be for a consortium of the richer countries to subsidize the more expensive fuels and processes that would permit poorer countries to expand their production of energy with small emissions of carbon dioxide than they could otherwise afford.

Implementation Problems

Implementation is concerned with the means for attaining goals. The central difficulty of implementation is that governments cannot abate injuries to the environment directly; they must induce other people to do so. Thus, implementation amounts to the choice and administration of instruments that will induce people to cut back on polluting behavior. It is no less than an application of the art of government to a particular field.

One would not, therefore, expect implementation to be a simple matter, and it is not, though surprisingly little systematic thought has been given to it. The choice of instruments to be used in attaining any given environmental goal depends on many things, including three that will receive special attention here: the nature of the activities that cause the damage, the people who engage in polluting activities, and the array of instruments available to the government. All these variables are different in developing countries than modernized countries, and pollutants that traverse national boundaries cannot be controlled by the ordinary instruments of government at all. These three cases therefore are dealt with separately, beginning with environmental impairments specific to industrialized countries.

INDUSTRIALIZED COUNTRIES. It is easy to take for granted the progress that has been made by the industrialized countries. Drinking water and urban waste ceased being transmitters of infectious diseases three or four generations ago. More recently, the atmospheric concentrations of particles and sulfur oxides have been diminishing in most industrialized countries. But other problems have come to the fore. New harmful substances that conventional treatments do not eliminate are being released into the atmosphere and public waters, and new hazards presented by some conventional pollutants are being recognized. In addition, the hazards of land disposal of urban and industrial wastes are becoming evident, as are the dangers of open-sea disposal.

The implementation problems presented by release of pollutants into the air and public waters are entirely conventional. The new pollutants, like the old ones, are unwanted by-products of industrial activities, with major contributions from automobiles and space heating. Such activities cannot be conducted without generating undesirable waste products. From the generator's point of view, the most efficient way to dispose of the waste is to release it and allow the air or water, as the case may be, to carry it away. This time-honored method of disposal is also efficient from the social point of view to the extent that waste products are harmless when sufficiently diluted. However, since frequently they are not harmless, questions arise: Are the producers acting efficiently from their own point of view, generating too much waste? Are they releasing too much? The benefit-cost analyses already discussed are designed precisely to answer those questions.

If the answer to either of those questions is yes, then the implementation question is how to induce the generator to act in a socially acceptable manner. The answer in any instance depends on circumstances—for example, on who the generator is. We will consider industrial and commercial polluters first.

The instruments applicable to industrial and commercial polluters are classed under the two broad headings of regulations and economic incentives. If regulations are used, firms can be expected to respond grudgingly and to comply in the most economical way possible from their own point of view. This is frequently not the most economical way from the social point of view, because regulations are inherently blunt instruments. They must be designed so that violations can be detected easily and unambiguously, and they cannot make fine distinctions. As a result, regulations typically either require or prohibit some easily observable behavior, which is not likely to be the behavior that abates the pollution most efficiently from anybody's point of view. This is why so many regulations require the installation of equipment for end-of-pipe treatment of waste flows, though it is well known that simply having the equipment on hand does not guarantee that it is used or used effectively, and that end-of-pipe treatment is frequently not the efficient way to abate polluting discharges. The presence of equipment for waste treatment can be checked easily, but its effective use is harder to observe, and the desired result, the reduction of polluting discharges, much harder still. Designing pollution control regulations therefore requires considerable ingenuity and technical expertise to attain an efficient compromise between effectiveness when the regulations are complied with and ease of enforcement. The problems are aggravated by the politics of the regulatory process. The industry that will be subject to the regulation is sure to press for regulations that are economical from its point of view and, if possible, difficult to enforce.

Further, circumstances differ, so that a regulation that is reasonable and effective for some firms in an industry is ineffective or unduly onerous for others. Therefore, a practice called segmenting has developed, in the United States at least. The firms in an industry are divided into classes by size or some other criterion, and different regulations are imposed on each class. Segmenting somewhat reduces the bluntness of the regulatory instrument but still without making it very sharp, and it introduces a new complication, that of defining the classes. There is no need to recount the litigation that ensues when a firm with 102 employees in one month demands to be classified according to the 98 workers it claims it "normally" employs. Even with segmenting, no regulation can be attuned to each firm's circumstances. In addition, segmenting greatly reduces the effectiveness of regulations. The firms that qualify for the most lenient treatment are likely to be the smaller ones, located in the most congested places, where their discharges are most harmful.

Indeed, a pervasive inefficiency of most such regulations is that they are designed to reduce discharges rather than the harm that the discharges inflict. A plant in an isolated location with ample diluting water is required to go to the same expense as one in a densely populated place with only a thin stream to carry its waste away. Several studies, relating to both atmospheric and aquatic discharges, have shown that abatement costs could be reduced by 25 percent or more without reducing the amount of protection afforded by taking such considerations into account, but it is difficult to do so.

The other major class of instruments is economic incentives, which may take the form of subsidies for abatement or fees for discharging or variants on those themes. Let us right away dismiss the subsidy approach. Aside from the administrative problem of establishing the base level of discharge to be used in computing the subsidy, subsidies have the perverse effect of transferring some of the social cost of pollution from the industry that generates it to the general public, thereby encouraging production of the very pollutants they are intended to abate.

We are left then with fees for discharging and with variant schemes such as expensive discharge permits. As compared with regulations, discharge fees are exquisitely sensitive to the special technology of each polluting firm and lead it to reduce its discharges to the optimal extent and to do so in the most efficient possible way. For this reason, economists typically advocate the use of fees and zealously cite studies that show the great savings that could be attained by relying on fees instead of regulations to secure a given level of abatement. Polluting industries generally object to the use of fees, despite the greater discretion they afford, pointing out that fees cost them more than regulations that would achieve the same amount of abatement, because they must bear both the cost of abatement and the cost of the fees on the discharges that remain. This contention is entirely correct. By the same token, fees, more than regulations, tend to discourage firms from entering the industry, thereby making it more concentrated than is socially desirable. The trouble is that, for the reasons already recited, there are no regulations that will do the same job.

The advocacy of fees has been seriously marred by the fact that it is generally based on an unfair comparison. Fees levied on discharges are compared with regulations designed to be monitored easily. If the regulations were imposed directly on discharges, leaving the firms free to use their own discretion in deciding how to abate them, they would attain virtually the same level of economic efficiency as fees. It is overlooked that control by fees presents the same monitoring problem as control by regulation. A fee levied on operating without a prescribed end-of-pipe treatment plant is little more efficient than a regulation requiring such a plant. The ostensible difference in effciency arises from a difference in the point at which the control is presumed to operate.

Practical experience with fees is limited, but such experience as there is shows them to be powerfully effective. Much of that experience relates to liquid discharges. Some of it is inadvertent, as when treatment charges are levied on waste delivered to public treatment facilities. Invariably it is surprising to see the alacrity with which industries reduce the amounts of pollutants they discharge once a fee is levied that makes abatement worth their while.

What has been said here far from exhausts the points that have been raised in the continuing debate over economic inducements versus regulatory controls. But enough has been said to indicate that the difference does not appear to be as vast or as vital as the contending parties often maintain. On balance, there is some advantage in the use of fees, largely because they are easier to administer and because direct monitoring of discharges seems to be almost always feasible, whichever approach is taken, by using carefully designed sampling methods.

Discharge fees are not able to control discharges by individuals operating automobiles or home heating plants or garbage disposers, all of them significant sources of pollution. There are too many individuals, all too long accustomed to unrestricted discharge of their wastes. The only feasible control here lies in the equipment used. This is the strategy used in controlling automobile exhausts, and it is sound. It can be implemented either by direct regulation or by imposing license fees on equipment that does not meet specified discharge standards. The only basis for choice appears to be administrative convenience.

The really difficult problems relate to some quite different forms of pollution that were, surprisingly, overlooked in the early days of concern for environmental protection. They are the disposal of solid wastes and of toxic and otherwise hazardous wastes. Solid wastes traditionally were deposited in municipal or industrial dumps, which were unsightly but thought to be otherwise innocuous. Dangerous substances used to be generated in relatively small volumes and were dealt with ad hoc, often simply by making the disposer liable for any damages that might result. Altogether, the hazards imposed by these forms of waste were largely unrecognized until recently.

The industrial nations now realize that things are already pretty far out of hand. Many substances deposited in sanitary landfills have been leached into groundwater. In addition, in congested areas, many of the established landfills are reaching capacity, and there are few if any available sites for new ones. Chemicals too toxic to be discharged into waterways were formerly also deposited in dumps or, illegally, along roadsides. That is now recognized as an extremely hazardous practice, but it continues.

These problems relate to the law of the conservation of matter, hazardous or not; the waste has to go somewhere, and there does not seem to be any place to put it. Toxic chemicals present an additional problem. They frequently are generated in a dilute, but insufficiently dilute, mixture along with harmless substances. Removing them from the mixture so that they can be handled with the care they require turns out to be technically difficult as well as expensive. Generators would naturally much prefer just to throw the whole mixture away.

I regard the disposal of solid wastes and toxic substances as the most urgent environmental problem now confronting the industrial nations, but I have no tidy solutions. A good deal can be accomplished by not throwing so much away: by making things more durable, using less elaborate packaging, and recycling waste materials. Some incentive could be provided by increasing the charges for disposal and making them proportional to the volume of waste, but unfortunately this also provides an incentive for illegal disposal. Any tight system for controlling waste disposal would require elaborate record keeping. This is not practical for household and commercial waste and is difficult for the toxic by-products of industry because of the problem of estimating the amount that was generated. So I have to conclude lamely that a solution, or a battery of solutions, will have to be sought. There is opportunity for a number of worthy research projects.

DEVELOPING COUNTRIES. It is an illusion to think that environmental problems afflict only rich countries. On the contrary, they are more severe and more ominous in poor countries. Water is no longer a carrier of infectious disease in the industrial countries, but that is hardly true of many of the poor ones. The air in Cairo and Mexico City is dirtier than any rich country would tolerate. And the poor countries suffer from many environmental threats that are peculiar to themselves. To be sure, it would be inappropriate for poor countries to aspire to the environmental standards of richer countries—poverty means doing without. But hardly any country is so poor that it has to endure waterborne epidemics, pandemic intestinal worms, or massive soil erosion.

An important aspect of both planning and implementation in developing countries is that the instruments available for implementing plans are much weaker than those in industrialized nations. The civil service is not of the same quality, statistical and other records are scanty and unreliable, and communication is slow and difficult. In many developing countries, the arm of the central government does not extend effectively much beyond the limits of the major cities, and civil unrest is not far away. Major capital investments have to be financed from external sources, meaning that policies and plans are not entirely under the government's control.

These limitations dictate a good deal of modesty. Plans must be simple to understand and administer. Programs for implementation must be designed so that misunderstanding and negligence are easily detected. And, whatever precautions are taken, only partial effectiveness can be expected. Most important, however many the urgent needs, the administrative apparatus must not be stretched too thin. Only a few of the urgent problems in a few localities can be handled at any one time. The rest will have to wait, and it is small comfort to remark that the people are used to waiting.

The typical developing country contains both a modern and a traditional sector. The issues presented by the modern sector are much like those encountered in the industrial countries, though, as just noted, the instruments available are far less adequate. The issues presented by the traditional sector are entirely different, since this sector consists largely of farmers plus some artisans and small merchants, none far from subsistence level. These people are very hard on their environment; they have no choice. They have to cultivate every accessible bit of land, gather every available twig of wood, poach all the game they can, dispose of wastes in any way they can. Neither regulations nor taxes can reach them, since folkways are stronger than "lawways," and need is stronger than either. These problems have already been referred to in the context of natural resource management, and the same remarks apply here.

The key to controlling environmentally harmful activities in the traditional sector is to provide effective alternatives and simultaneously to provide economic incentives to the community, rather than to the individual, to protect and restore the environment. Only then will governmentally imposed penalties, either charges or legal sanctions, have any chance of being effective. It is important to enlist the cooperation of community leaders because only they, and not the formal government apparatus, are in a position to influence and monitor the behavior of the community's members.

I do not minimize this task or the financial and administrative resources required to perform it. That is why I said earlier that the central government's plans have to be very selective, to the neglect of many urgent problems. It is better to succeed at a few enterprises than to make passing attempts at many.

INTERNATIONAL AND GLOBAL PROBLEMS. We are ascending the ladder of difficulty. Pollution that crosses national boundaries is the most difficult of all to control. There are no instruments available and there would be no one to wield them if there were. The matter was discussed, naturally, at the lengthy Law of the Sea Conference, and Part XII of the draft convention is devoted to it. According to this, the signatory states accept the obligation to protect and preserve the marine environment; undertake to pass laws and enter treaties designed to minimize the release of harmful pollutants into international waters by their nationals; agree to cooperate in monitoring the marine environment, to promote research on marine phenomena, to publish findings of the research, and so on. No agreement seems to have been reached on any specific problem, and no organ was established to keep track of performance with respect to these provisions. This upshot is symptomatic. International pollution is controlled only by the consciences of the individual nations and the pressures that nations can exert on their neighbors.

Neighborly pressures are effective up to a point. The United States has agreed to limit the amount of salt introduced into the Rio Grande and is negotiating with Canada over the transport of sulfates and sulfur oxides from the Midwest to eastern Canada. In Europe, West Germany has accepted responsibility for controlling the quality of the Rhine where it enters the Netherlands. There are many other examples. These bilateral agreements fail, however, where the responsibilities and the damages are more difficult.

The two most ominous current problems of this sort are the increasing concentration of atmospheric carbon dioxide and the depletion of the ozone layer. There appears to be no way to deal with either of these problems in the absence of a competent international organization or authority. The experience with the Law of the Sea Conference and at the Stockholm Conference on Environmental Problems underscores the difficulty of establishing any such institution, given deep-seated conflicts of interest. Nothing can be done until the urgency of the problem is appreciated by all or nearly all the nations that contribute to it. Moreover, these global environmental problems appear to result from insidious, slow-acting, and irreversible processes. To be effective, correctives have to be initiated before severe damage is visible to the naked eye.

The first step, then, toward averting irremediable damage to the global environment is to obtain persuasive indications of impending impairments before they occur. Such indications can come only from a system for monitoring the state of the world environment, operated by an authoritative and widely respected organization. There is no such system at present, not even on the part of the United Nations Environment Programme, the obvious agency for the undertaking. In 1986 the World Resources Institute, in cooperation with the International Institute for Environment and Development, is planning to initiate annual reports on the state of the environment. This will be an important beginning, but whether those organizations will have the resources needed to maintain surveillance over the world's environment remains uncertain.

Assuming that a global monitoring system detects a serious hazard, the second step is to do something about it. Corrective measures will undoubtedly require sacrifices and self-denials on the part of many nations, which will not be forthcoming until they, individually, see themselves threatened. Under such circumstances, nations are capable of great sacrifices for a common goal, as countless military alliances have demonstrated.

Under such pressure, then, I can see the possibility of an alliance for global protection. To operate, such an alliance would first have to ascertain the highest level of global emissions or other insults that the environment can tolerate without crippling damage. Then it would have to determine the total national emissions implied by reasonable plans for economic growth. To reconcile these two figures would undoubtedly require reducing the growth aspirations of selected nations, allowing for higher growth rates in developing countries than in the developed nations.

Thus, national quotas for harmful emissions could be established. Compliance could be monitored as part of the continuing surveillance of the global environment, and infractions punished by imposing discouragingly heavy fines on nations that exceed their quotas. The fines could be enforced, if need be, by liens on the violators' property within the territories of other members of the alliance. The alliance might also make grants-in-aid to selected developing countries to help them achieve their growth rates within the constraints imposed by the quotas. Flexibility could be introduced by permitting nations to sell or donate portions of their quotas to one another. All this, I am persuaded, can be achieved if the peoples of the world are really convinced that they face a common danger and that the required sacrifices are being shared equitably. But not otherwise.

[15]

Resources and World Development,
eds. D.J. McLaren and B.J. Skinner, pp. 767–785
John Wiley & Sons Limited
© S. Bernhard, Dahlem Konferenzen, 1987

Food for a Developing World

R. Dorfman* and W.P. Falcon**

Dept. of Economics, Harvard University
Cambridge, MA 02138
**Food Research Institute, Stanford University*
Stanford, CA 94305, USA

Abstract. The problems of food and agriculture in both less developed countries (LDCs) and developed market economies (DMEs) have poverty as their common cause. Hunger in low-income countries typically does not arise from inadequate food supplies or resource bases but rather from the lack of purchasing power among poor people. Development of the agricultural sector represents the best medium-run alternative for redressing this problem. Moreover, the experience of the 1970s shows that those LDCs that had the most successful agricultural development programs also increased their imports from DMEs. Reducing poverty in both sets of nations can thus be complementary rather than competitive activities.

INTRODUCTION

When we undertook to write this paper the front pages of the American newspapers were dominated by two seemingly contradictory sets of headlines. One set narrated day by day the unfolding horrors of famines, particularly in the Sahel region of Africa. The other set related the financial distresses of farmers, particularly in the American Midwest, who confronted glutted markets where the prices for their crops were lower than the costs of raising them. Many farmers were going bankrupt, others were on the verge. Altogether the headlines portrayed a world in which farmers were growing more food than their customers could buy at prices that covered costs, while millions of these customers were undernourished and even starving.

Further analysis of the data shows that the appearance of paradox is illusory. In fact, we shall endeavor to demonstrate that the troubles of the farmers who produce the food and the suffering of the consumers who need it are two aspects of a single, very obvious problem. Most of the one billion people who are undernourished are simply too poor to buy nutritious diets at prices that cover the cost of production. The main cause of this undernourishment is poverty. The problem of the struggling farmers is also poverty — the poverty of the people who might be their customers. These two poverty dilemmas are compounded by the fact that many rural people themselves are among those who are too poor to buy farm products.

The assertions we have just made about the close links among the problems of poverty, undernutrition, and even famines are part of a growing convention-al wisdom among specialists on rural development. We emphasize them here because they do not seem to be well understood outside that small circle. Yet if progress is to be made against this triplet of urgent problems, it must be based on correct diagnosis.

This realization presents us with three tasks: first, to establish our contention that the problem of hunger is inseparable from that of poverty in general; second, to consider the nature and causes of the widespread "farm problem"; and third, to discuss the policies and programs that these diagnoses suggest. We undertake the first of those tasks in the next section. The third section deals with the contrasting farm problems of the LDCs and the DMEs. The final section is devoted to the implications of the food-farm problem for continued economic development, especially for the LDCs, and to some of the policy measures that seem indicated.

POVERTY AND UNDERNUTRITION

It is important to keep in mind that the two-sided, food-farm problem is pervasive. Undernutrition is not restricted to the Sahel; it is found virtually everywhere. The Food and Agriculture Organization publishes annual reports (1) that show the number of calories per day available per capita in some 140 cooperating countries*. Figure 1 is based on the reports from the 112 cooperat-ing countries that had populations of at least one million in 1979. It shows the percentage of the total population of those countries (amounting to 3.9 billion in 1979) that lived in countries where daily per capita supply of calories was no greater than the amounts shown along the abscissa. Thus, 4 percent of the population of those countries lived in nations where the average number of calories per day available for human consumption was less than 1,900, about 65 percent lived in countries where the average number of calories was less than 2,500, and virtually no one lived in a nation with more than 3,700 calories per capita per day.

These are abstract numbers. To assess their meaning: in the United States, where caloric availability is regarded as substantially greater than minimal, the average daily per capita supply was about 3,650 calories in 1979; in West Germany it was 3,540 calories; and in Bangladesh, where undernutrition is prevalent, it was 1,880 calories per capita per day. As a broad average,

---

* For discussion of the interpretation and limitations of these data, please see Appendix.

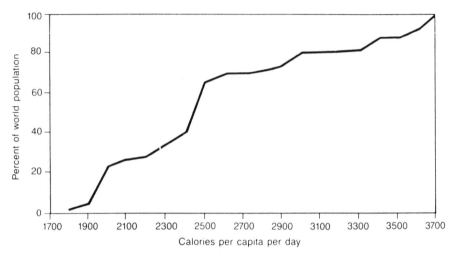

FIG. 1 — Cumulative distribution of world population by average calories per capita per day available in countries in which they live.

2,400–2,500 calories per day is a generally accepted level of adequacy. Of course, since caloric intake is not equally distributed throughout a population, if the average in any country is barely 2,500 calories per capita per day, a large proportion of the population is receiving less than that, i.e., is undernourished.

In 59 of the 112 countries in the 1980 sample the average daily caloric supply was less than 2,500. These deficient countries included the two largest, China and India, although China's very rapid agricultural growth since 1979 has moved that country above the 2,500 caloric level. It should not be inferred, however, that undernutrition occurs only in these 59 countries; it is a problem among the lower-income groups in all the countries of the world, although the FAO data do not disclose this point directly.

We have asserted that the widespread inadequate levels of nutrition can be attributed chiefly to widespread inadequate levels of income. Figures 2A and 2B are presented in support of this claim. They show the relationship between the FAO data (1) on average caloric availability in different countries in 1978–80 and World Bank data (6) on per capita gross national product (GNP) in 1980. Figure 2A displays the relationship for 49 low-income countries, those with per capita GNP of less than $1,000 in 1980, and Fig. 2B shows the same data for 31 middle-income LDCs with per capita GNP greater than $1,000 but less than $4,500.

The relation between caloric availability and per capita GNP is not very tight in either case, but its presence is indubitable. The visual impression is confirmed in both cases by computing the rank correlation coefficients. For the poor LDCs the (Spearman) correlation coefficient is 0.48, for the middle-income countries it is 0.57. For all 80 countries with per capita GNPs of $4,500

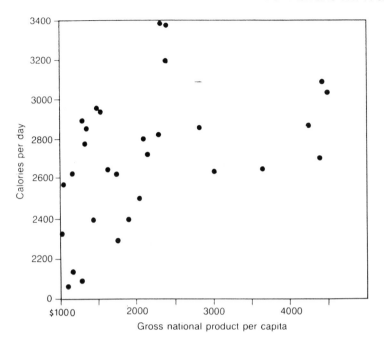

FIG. 2A — Relation between average calories per capita per day and GNP per capita in countries with GNP per capita less than $1,000 (1980).

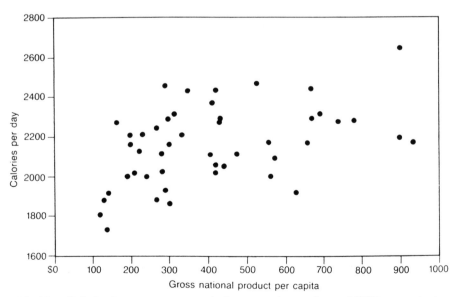

FIG. 2B — Relation between average calories per capita per day and GNP per capita in countries with GNP per capita between $1,000 and $4,500 (1980).

or less in 1980, the rank correlation coefficient between per capita GNP and available calories per capita per day is 0.77. The probability that chance variation would lead to such high correlations in the absence of a genuine relationship is less than one in ten thousand.

We are always careful to tell students that a correlation does not establish causality. We should (but usually do not) accompany that warning with the counter-warning that correlations are often highly suggestive indications of some causal connection, and therefore should not be dismissed lightly. In the present instance it seems highly probable that there is causality that runs in both directions. Low income has a strong tendency to reduce caloric intake, and low-caloric intake has a mild positive feedback by reducing energy and productivity.

At any rate, it appears from these data that inadequate diets and poverty (as indicated by low per capita GNP) go together in the LDCs. The relationship between caloric availability and per cpaita GNP does not extend to countries with per capita GNPs above $4,500, however. In all 22 such countries in the FAO sample, per capita calorie availability is comfortably above 2,500 per day, and the data do not indicate any relationship between calorie availability and average per capita income in those DMEs. Part of the low correlation is due to the nature of the calories consumed. FAO "consumption" data do not include the indirect calorie "costs" of using grain to produce meat. Thus, high-cost diets containing large amounts of grain-fed meat seriously underestimate total (direct plus indirect) calorie consumption. There can be undernutrition associated with poverty even in these countries, but it is associated with poverty of the individual household or population segment rather than with a measure of the average poverty or income in the nation.

It may appear that throughout this discussion we have been evading the obvious explanation of undernourishment: the Malthusian explanation that the growth of population has outrun the capacity of the world to provide nourishment. That certainly would account for food shortages and for general poverty in the nations where they are most severe. But it would not be consistent with the coincident economic distress of the agricultural sectors in most countries or with some of the other characteristics of the current situation.

The analysis of a situation in which the population is too great for the food-producing sector to support traces to the work of Malthus and Ricardo early in the nineteenth century. According to this analysis, as population grows in relation to the available amount of farmland, less and less productive land is brought under the plow. More labor and other resources are then required to grow and market a unit of food or food energy on the average or, more importantly, at the margin. An increasing proportion of the economy's resources must then be devoted to growing food, leaving less for all other purposes and resulting in a general decline in living standards and an increase in the price of food relative to the prices of other commodities.

TABLE 1 Percent of labor force in agriculture and index of food output per capita, selected regions and country groups, 1970 and 1980 (from (1), 1980, Tables 3 and 6; for production indices, 1969–71 = 100).

Country group	Percent of labor force in agriculture		Index of food output per capita	
	1970	1980	1970	1980
World	51.3	45.3	100	105
Africa	71.5	65.4	100	91
North and Central America	13.8	11.6	98	107
South America	38.1	31.7	102	112
Asia	64.9	57.8	101	108
Europe	20.8	15.2	100	116
Oceania	23.7	21.6	99	105
DMEs	12.9	8.5	99	111
LDCs	66.4	59.2	101	108

Consider Table 1 in the light of this analysis. In the decade of the 1970s the proportion of the labor force in agriculture declined on all continents and in both DMEs and LDCs, while food output per capita increased on all continents except Africa, which was beset by droughts and persistent civil disruptions. Moreover, food prices did not increase during the decade, although world population grew by 20 percent. On the contrary, the agricultural nations and sectors complained of the adverse trend in their terms of trade. All these facts conflict with the Malthusian explanation.

A further indication that the world population is not pressing on the biological capacity of the Earth to provide food is contained in the data already discussed on the availability of calories in 1980. The worldwide average of the available number of calories per capita per day is more than sufficient. Or it would be so if the calories were equally distributed throughout the world and the income strata and if there were no losses or waste between the farms and the tables. These "ifs" are far from the case. On the other hand, the actual production of food fell far short of potential. Many of the most important food-producing countries, including the USA, restricted output or destroyed crops in order to prevent price declines. About a third of cereal production was fed to livestock, used industrially, or otherwise diverted from direct human consumption. Inefficient farming practices were still used in many of the LDCs, though yields per hectare increased steadily during the decade. For these and other reasons it is evident that if there had been effective demand the world's production of food would have been substantially greater.

Counterfactuals, of course, are hard to establish. One other indication of the world's food production potential can be seen by considering the physical dimensions of its agricultural resources. There are about 1.4 billion arable hectares in the world, although what constitutes arable land depends in part on the price of food. The number of calories produced on each hectare in the course of a year depends on the crop that is planted, the number of crops planted during the year, and many other factors. The worldwide average productivities to land planted to a few important sources of food energy were*:

	Kg/Ha	Calories/Ha
Wheat	1,870	6.6 million
Rice	2,750	9.6 million
Maize	3,000	10.5 million
Potatoes	12,520	9.6 million
All cereals	2,110	7.4 million

As a conservative average, suppose that the 1.4 billion arable hectares can produce seven million calories each per year. In total, they would produce ten quadrillion calories, without allowing for double or triple planting. The average annual caloric requirement per capita is 2,500*365*1.1 = 1 million, introducing a 10 percent allowance for waste (which is probably low). Thus, the calories produced on arable land could support a population of ten billion, about twice the current population, without allowance for multiple cropping or for food energy supplied by fish, livestock, or orchard crops.

The number of calories produced would have been more than adequate to meet the food-energy needs of the population if it had been distributed equally. However, actual cereal production by region, including that used for feed or nonfood uses, showed enormous variation:

Cereal production: Calories/Capita–Day by Region
(from (1), 1984)

World	2965
Developed Market	5488
West Europe	4286
North America	9207
Oceania	16043
Other	961
Less developed Market	1728
Africa	968
Latin America	2287
Near East	2258
Far East	1708
Centrally Planned	3547

---

* Kilogram yields are taken from ((1), 1980). Conversion to energy: 3,500 calories per kg for cereal crops, 770 calories per kg for potatoes.

Although global food-production systems may have been operating at less than 50 percent capacity, the real problem was not aggregate production. The problem was instead a need for greater capacity in some countries as well as economic and political arrangements that promote trade and more efficient distribution of produce among those and other regions.

Looking toward the future introduces new elements of uncertainty. Some considerations indicate that food-production capacity will grow during the next two, or three, or five decades; others indicate that it will decline. Which forces will predominate is a matter for conjecture without the benefit of much factual support.

The annual losses of arable hectares to waterlogging, groundwater depletion, erosion, salinization, desertification, and urban sprawl are immediate and visible. On the favorable side is the spread of effective methods of cultivation, pest control, and fertilization along with the steady development of high-yielding crop varieties adapted to local conditions. Promised, but still at the horizon, are improved methods for developing high-yielding tropical corn varieties, crops for semiarid areas, and genetic engineering efforts that may serve a variety of ecological zones.

Thus far the favorable tendencies have been winning. The number of cultivated hectares has been growing, very slightly, and yields per hectare have been increasing steadily. The balance could be reversed in the future, but we see no reason to expect that.

We conclude on these grounds that the global farm sector is well able to feed the world's population now and believe that it will remain so for the visible future. At the same time, the world's population is not being fed adequately at present. Urgent attention is needed to develop and implement economic policies that will stimulate the farm-food sector to a level of output that makes fuller use of its capacity and distribute the resultant output more equitably and efficiently.

THE FARM PROBLEM

Hunger occurs wherever there are poor people, but it is a prevalent problem only in poor countries. Agricultural distress and depression, in contrast, strike the rich countries and the poor ones alike. It is not surprising, however, that the causes and nature of the farm problem differ substantially between the LDCs and the DMEs. It is not much of an exaggeration to say that in LDCs farmers are not productive enough, whereas in the DMEs they are entirely too productive for their financial health.

The low-income countries tend to have a large proportion of their population engaged in farming. Figures 3A and 3B show this connection. In them, the percentage of the labor force engaged in agriculture is compared with per capita GNP. Both sets of data relate to 1980 and are taken from the *World*

Development Reports published annually by the World Bank (6).

The relationship for the poorer countries, those with per capita GNP less than $1,000, is shown in Fig. 3A. The connection is evident visually and is confirmed by a Spearman rank correlation of −0.54. The connection is even more striking for countries with per capita GNP of at least $1,000 in 1980, shown in Fig. 3B. As GNP per capita increases over this wider range the percent of the labor force in agriculture falls rapidly, practically to the vanishing point. These figures suggest that agriculture is a relatively unproductive economic sector, where productivity is measured by value of output per worker engaged.

This suggestion is confirmed by a more direct comparison. The *World Development Reports* (6) also include data on the percent of GDP originating in agriculture, which are comparable with the estimates of the percent of the labor force engaged in agriculture that we have used before*. In a country where the percent of GDP arising in agriculture is the same as the percent of the labor force engaged in that sector, the value produced per worker in agriculture would be the same as the value produced per worker, on the average, in the nonagricultural sectors. A percent of GDP arising in agriculture that is smaller than the percent of the labor force engaged there would indicate lower productivity for agricultural workers than for other workers. Specifically, the ratio between the value contributed per worker outside agriculture to that contributed per agricultural worker is easily seen to be

$$LF/(1\text{-}LF)*(1\text{-}PR)/PR, \tag{1}$$

where LF denotes the proportion of the labor force engaged in agriculture and PR denotes the proportion of GDP originating in agriculture†. This productivity ratio is shown in Fig. 4A for 83 LDCs and in Fig. 4B for 17 DMEs for which comparable data for 1980 are available. Notice that the ratio of productivity outside agriculture to that in agriculture was greater than unity in 98 percent of the LDCs and was more than ten in one eighth of them. Predominantly, among the LDCs, work outside agriculture produced between three and four times as much economic value as work in agriculture.

The contrast between productivity in and out of agriculture was much less sharp among the DMEs for which the data were available. In about two thirds of them productivity outside agriculture was between one and two times as great as in agriculture, but in two of them (New Zealand and the USA) value

---

* Since many farmers or members of their households hold nonfarm jobs on a part-time basis, the concept of "a labour force engaged in agriculture" presents many problems. Those difficulties are ignored in the broad discussion that follows.

† The preceding statements presume that the unemployment rate is about the same in the agricultural labor force as in the nonagricultural. This presumption is unlikely to be valid, but there is no feasible way to verify it because of the difficulty of measuring or even defining agricultural unemployment.

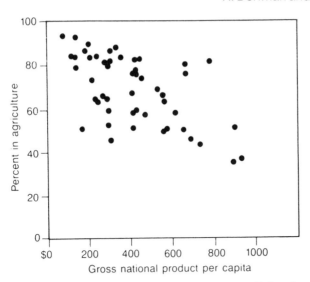

FIG. 3A — Relation between GNP per capita and percent of labor force in agriculture for countries with GNP per capita less than $1000 (1980).

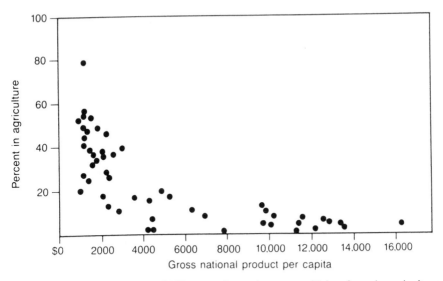

FIG. 3B — Relation between GNP per capita and percent of labor force in agriculture for countries with GNP per capita greater than $1,000 (1980).

produced per worker was greater in agriculture than in the rest of the economy. The comparatively low value of product per worker in the agricultural sector in most countries entails low incomes to factors employed in that sector, since value produced is what pays incomes.

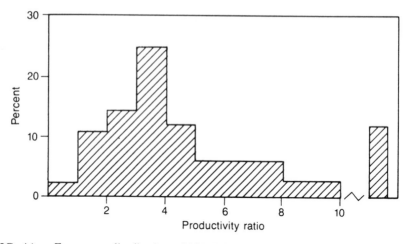

FIG. 4A — Frequency distribution of 83 LDCs by nonagriculture/agriculture productivity ratios (1980).

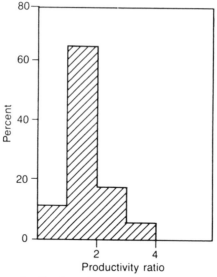

FIG. 4B — Frequency distribution of 17 DMEs by nonagriculture/agriculture productivity ratios (1980).

The LDCs tend to be short of arable land. The FAO data show that in Bangladesh and China the average member of the farm labor force cultivates about one third of a hectare. In Egypt there is less than half a hectare per farmer or farmworker. In about half of the 49 low-income LDCs for which reasonably adequate data were available, the average farm worker or farmer worked less than a hectare. These included the most populous countries such as China, India, Bangladesh, and Indonesia.

R. Dorfman and W.P. Falcon

The productivity of the land, as measured by value added in agriculture per hectare cultivated, was less in the LDCs than in most developed countries, but not dramatically less. To calibrate, GDP per hectare in the USA was $416 in 1980, but land is not cultivated intensively on American farms. In Western Europe GDP per hectare was in the $1,500–$2,000 range, in Japan it was more than $9,000. By comparison, the lowest GDP per hectare reported was $90 for the Saharan country of Chad. The highest of the LDCs were around $1,000, reported for Liberia and El Salvador. Clearly differences in the productivity of the land cannot account for the vast differences between the incomes of farmers in the LDCs and those in the DMEs.

The differences in the amount of land available per agricultural worker is clearly much more important. In the United States the average worker cultivated about 90 hectares, in Western Europe 8 to 9 hectares, whereas, as we have seen, in most of the LDCs the average worker cultivated a hectare or less. In consequence, the average GDP per farm worker in Western Europe is $13,000 or more (as of 1980); the highest comparable figure reported for an LDC was only a tenth as great (Nicaragua, $1,400), and for only seven of the LDCs was GDP per agricultural worker as great as $1,000.

In short, the density of farm workers per arable acre is so great in the low-income LDCs that the workers do not produce enough to live on despite obtaining respectable crop yields per hectare, often in very adverse conditions. Although yields can be increased in most countries, any permanent improvement must depend on reducing the agricultural work force. This reduction can occur slowly through population policy but most effectively by absorbing many of the agricultural workers into employment in other sectors. Failing this basic solution, most of the LDCs resort to palliatives. We revert to the policy problems thus created in the final section.

In the DMEs the farm problem is also severe, but the cause is quite different. In those countries farming is among the most progressive industries technologically, thanks to constantly improving seeds, more effective methods of cultivation, fertilization, and pest control and to highly effective managerial practices and marketing organization. At the same time, as Houthakker (2) pointed out some years ago, the farmers in an advancing developed economy cannot expect to share in generally expanding markets and increasing levels of real income to the same extent as other sectors. The reason is one of the best-established empirical generalizations of economics, called Engel's Law. According to this law, as a family's income grows, its expenditures on food and farm products do not increase proportionately; therefore, as a country's income grows, its domestic market for food and farm products does not expand as rapidly as its overall economic activity. Neither generally do its export markets (if it exports farm products), for the demand by its customers also lags because Engel's Law applies to them as well.

We have already noted the sharp decline in the proportion of the labor force devoted to agriculture that is experienced as a nation's per capita income rises: a decline from more than 80 percent in the poorest countries to 5 percent or less in most Western European countries, Canada, the USA, and so on. Even so, not enough farmers leave the land. Those that remain, aided by the impressive advances in agricultural technology and increases in agricultural capital equipment, continue to increase their output of farm products faster than the domestic markets will increase their consumption without reductions in the prices of farm products. Since the DMEs are experiencing difficulties, they do not provide commercial export markets for each other. The consequence is a general tendency of farm prices to fall in real terms. This decline, in conjunction with heavy fixed costs and declining land prices, creates severe distress and hardship among farm operators in developed economies.

A tragic paradox is thus generated in which the DMEs produce more food than they can dispose of at market prices while the LDCs can neither produce enough to feed themselves nor afford to buy from the DMEs. The only enduring cure from the viewpoint of the DMEs is to reduce their agricultural labor force still further and so abate the unsalable flood of agricultural products. But that is not easy. The farmer has invested his human, physical, and financial capital in his farm, and they cannot readily be removed. In fact, the extent to which farm populations have fallen already should be considered remarkable. Thus, the DMEs also resort to palliatives to relieve farm distress. They support farm prices artificially, subsidize farm exports and the consumption of farm products, and encourage the restriction and even destruction of farm outputs. These are costly, wasteful, and inefficient policies, compelled by the hardships otherwise imposed on a politically potent segment of the population.

IMPLICATIONS FOR POLICY

Long-run structural change, in which agriculture's share of GDP declines, is the ultimate hope of all developing countries. Unfortunately, this long-run vision has too often generated an inappropriate short-run policy response. While it would seem to follow that rapid industrialization was the proper strategy in LDCs, efforts to industrialize have often been inefficient and capital-intensive. It is a paradox of history, therefore, that the best chance for reducing agriculture's role in the long run is by stressing it in the short run! Even more ironically, improving LDC agricultures also offers the best hope for DMEs' agricultural exports. Explaining the logic of these two propositions and describing a few of the needed policy changes are the tasks of this final section.

Our previous arguments have emphasized the link between poverty and hunger. For the world as a whole, and even for most regions, food supply is not the issue, nor is resource-carrying capacity for the population of the foreseeable future. Undernourishment is instead primarily due to inadequate purchasing power. This is an extremely important observation because it changes the policy argument on hunger alleviation away from food production and toward policies that generate income, create productive employment at low investment costs, and provide poor people with access to resources.

Global prescriptions to achieve the foregoing objectives are almost impossible to develop. There is simply too much variation in the physical, social, and economic settings within and between continents to paint policy suggestions with anything but the broadest of brushes. The comments that follow, therefore, focus relatively more on Africa (even though there are more undernourished individuals in Asia) and are derived from a growing specialized literature on rural development. From this literature we draw three broad lessons from the post-World War II experience of LDCs: first, there is an important distinction between famine and nonfamine causes of undernutrition; second, development strategies must focus critically on the profitability of the farming sector; and third, in analyzing development strategies a distinction should be made between projects and programs for the food sector.

Famine is one of the most used and abused words to describe LDC food situations. By famine we mean a severe interruption in food production or food supply, caused typically by weather or wars. The causes, cures, and consequences of famine thus defined are vastly different from undernutrition caused from general poverty and a lack of purchasing power*. Failing to distinguish between the two types of undernutrition is a central problem in understanding and solving global food problems.

Fortunately for the world, there now exists adequate logistical capability and sufficient political and moral commitment to solve most famine problems. What is often missing, however, is a willingness on the part of host governments in afflicted countries to seek assistance. At times food has been used as an instrument of war, and at other times governments have simply been too embarrassed to admit the existence of famine conditions. There is also plenty of room for famine-relief improvements in the form of greater food-aid commitments, fewer political constraints on aid by both donors and recipients, better early-warning systems in famine-prone countries, and more adept efforts by nongovernmental organizations that have generally played the critical role in the actual food-distribution process. We would contend, however, that the world is much further ahead in coping with famine problems — when host governments will permit help — than it is in dealing with the problems of undernutrition created by chronic and widespread poverty.

The policies required to attack chronic undernutrition in poor countries require a fundamental attack on poverty†. Without being at all sanguine about

---

* Sen (5) would argue that many famines (even by our definition) are caused by a failure to provide entitlements to poor people rather than by an absolute shortage of food.

† We believe that there are few *international* food policies, and that most policy initiatives must be undertaken at the country level. For a slightly more internationalist view, see McCalla and Josling (4).

the difficulties that will be encountered, we believe that creation of a rapidly growing rural sector is the best short-run hope for providing poor people the purchasing power necessary to buy food. Investments per productive job are likely to be lower in agriculture than in industry, and the development of a growing and broad-based rural sector will assist concurrent and later industrialization efforts. In short, feeding the hungry in LDCs is likely to be achieved best by assuring a profitable farming sector in these countries.

Our review of the LDC agricultural successes and failures of the past 25 years suggests that profitability at the farm level depends on four integrated components — improved technology, realistic prices, adequate infrastructure, and well-balanced macro policy. Unfortunately, especially for Africa, the presence of only one or two of these components is unlikely to be sufficient for getting agriculture moving.

The great technological advances in wheat and rice during the 1970s were major factors in Asia's improved agricultural performance. This technology lowered costs, raised yields, and helped a number of poor nations to become self-sufficient in grains. So great were these advances that they may have lulled the rest of the world into believing that "the" technology problem had been resolved for all the LDCs. Such a conclusion is unwarranted. Almost no wheat varieties now (or perhaps ever) will exist for the humid tropics; corn yields in LDCs are still only about 20 percent of those in DMEs, and progress in semiarid regions can be described as slow at best. The need for African nations and the rest of the world to invest in relevant agricultural technology is an obvious policy implication. This obvious solution will entail a major effort to increase the very limited number of trained specialists, particularly those from Africa.

The urban bias in food pricing, whereby food prices have been kept low to placate vocal urban dwellers, has been a second factor affecting rural dynamism. Throughout most of the 1970s there was a strong correlation between agricultural stagnation and low food prices. In the short run these low prices were not all bad because the poor in both rural and urban areas are net purchasers of food. But the long run consequences of the discouragement to agricultural development from these hidden taxes on agriculture have been disastrous. Low food prices, rural stagnation, and the creation of few jobs has been the dismal result in a great many countries.

Since 1980 agricultural pricing policies have become far more complex in LDCs. In part, countries have learned the low domestic prices and stagnation lesson; in part also, world grain prices have reached historic lows (in real terms), thereby raising questions about what constitutes prices that are too low*. In spite of these caveats, it is still the general rule that price policy in

---

* Timmer (this volume) raises an interesting new set of dilemmas for LDCs caused by low world prices for grain.

LDCs is anti-agriculture, with consequent adverse effects on rural development.

Inadequate rural infrastructure has been a third factor that inhibited rural development, particularly in Africa. By contrast, investment in irrigation in Punjab and roads in Java have clearly been key elements in the agricultural successes of India and Indonesia. The much greater distance from an all-year road for the average farmer in Africa versus Asia explains part of the cost disadvantage of African farmers. It also underscores some of the sheer physical problems of marketing rural output in Africa.

A fourth component of profitability, macroeconomic policy, may be less obvious but even more important than the previous elements. Budget, foreign-exchange, and credit policy, typically developed in the Ministry of Finance and the Central Bank, affect farmers' lives in LDCs much more often than do decisions made in the Agricultural Ministry. The following sequence is all too familiar: overambitious development plans, a resort to deficit financing to pay for projects, consequent inflation, and an increasingly overvalued exchange rate that impedes agricultural exports. This distortion, together with tariffs to protect inefficient domestic industry, provides a powerful mechanism that, intentionally or not, impoverishes agriculture and drives capital to other sectors.

It is no wonder, therefore, that successful rural development is so difficult in LDCs. Technology, sectoral policy on investments and prices, and macro policy must all be in harmony. Too often they are not and the result is discordant nondevelopment. We see no alternative to a concerted focus on this set of simultaneous policies for the rural sector in LDCs. Certainly one broad alternative — a focus on development *projects* rather than on policies or programs — has *not* worked in the 1970s and 1980s. "Bad" policy has destroyed "good" projects; moreover, many projects, because of their foreign-resource intensity, have not been replicable in sustainable programs. Finally, key government personnel simply do not have time to manage centrally all the projects that foreign donors or domestic ministries can put forward. This problem is especially severe in countries where product and factor markets are so distorted as to require a maze of special regulations to make projects financially feasible.

"Projectitis" in Africa is especially revealing, Kenya, a country of less than 20 million people, has over 1,200 agricultural projects, 47 of which deal with agricultural research alone. Fortunately, Kenya is improving its pricing policy, in part because the government has realized that it must establish more realistic incentives for agriculture. These market rules are needed so that rural development can take place on a more decentralized basis and so that donor interests in specific projects can be curtailed and coordinated.

The DMEs have a very strong vested interest in the rural development of poor countries. Indeed, it is that vested interest which provides the final link to our global poverty argument.

We have already shown that global food supply is not the fundamental cause of undernutrition, much conventional wisdom notwithstanding. We also wish to take issue with those who argue that increased food output in LDCs means reduced food exports from DMEs. Although this conclusion might seem to follow, empirical experience from the 1970s shows that it did not. Kellogg (3), in one of the most interesting assessments to date, shows that the poor countries whose domestic agriculture grew most rapidly imported from DMEs twice as much corn per capita and four times as much soybean per capita as did poor countries whose domestic agriculture was stagnant. In short, in those countries with growing and dynamic rural sectors, the demand for food is likely to increase even faster than supplies. This demand for grain is likely to be important especially in support of the livestock sector that typically assumes much greater importance as economies grow.

Whether trading patterns established in the 1970s and early 1980s will continue into the 1990s is a critical question. It involves issues of debt, protectionism, and the general economic health of the global economy. At least the 1970s have shown, however, that curing poverty-related hunger in LDCs via a focus on rural development is consistent with helping to solve the market-related poverty of farmers in the DMEs. Maintaining this complementarity over the rest of the twentieth century is critical in buying the necessary time for both sets of countries to move human and other resources out of agriculture.

APPENDIX

Nutritional Data

One informative source on the adequacy of nutrition in the countries of the world is the *FAO Production Yearbook* (1). A key table for our purposes is "Food Supply (excluding fish): Calories per Caput per Day." Since we make considerable use of this table, a few explanatory comments are in order.

First, in spite of this title, the data are more closely related to human ingestion of calories than they are to the usual concepts of supply or production. This is so because they are computed by adding to each country's production of foods that provide calories, the imports of such foods, and then subtracting the country's exports of calories in foods, the increases in the caloric content of its food stocks, and the amounts of calories fed to livestock, used for seed, or used as industrial inputs, and finally making other, less important adjustments. The result of these computations is the number of calories available for human consumption at the end of the chain of distribution and, apart from a minor allowance for changes in inventories at the end of the chain, is an estimate of the amounts actually procured by the population of the country.

Though we refer to these data as estimates of "caloric availability per capita per day," we treat them as approximations to actual caloric intake, differing from it by losses in food preparation and household storage (perhaps of the order of 10 percent of the amount procured), changes in household inventories (a minor allowance), and statistical errors.

The "statistical errors" just mentioned are not necessarily small, particularly in the LDCs. Note should be taken of the numerous statistical adjustments that are applied to derive the estimates; each makes its contribution to inaccuracy. As is normal for international agencies, FAO obtains its data from the statistical bureaus of the cooperating nations. Definitions and standards are therefore not strictly uniform among countries. Besides, the quality of statistical reporting varies widely among countries — highly professional statistical organizations are luxuries typically found only in rich countries. Poor countries are often content with fairly crude estimates of even such fundamental and comparatively simple data as the sizes of their populations. All these considerations reduce the reliability of the FAO estimates of caloric availability per capita-day. Nevertheless, they provide a broad picture of agricultural activity and nutritional status throughout the world.

Finally, we should call attention to our decision to use per capita caloric availability as our indicator of nutritional adequacy. Analysis is much simpler with a single, scalar measure, and for several reasons we believe that caloric intake is a reliable enough indicator of nutritional conditions for general analytic purposes. One reason is that the cereals which are the main sources of calories in most countries (rice, wheat, and the coarse grains) contain substantial amounts of proteins, fats, and the other essential ingredients. For example, a person who obtained 2,500 calories a day entirely from wheat would ingest more than the recommended daily allowance of protein as a by-product; enough rice to provide 2,500 calories contains about two thirds of the daily protein intake recommended for men. A second reason is that people who obtain sufficient calories almost invariably do so from a sufficient variety of foods to supply their needs of the other nutrients. We do not ignore that nutritional diseases are common in some countries; we allege merely that they are common only among people who do not consume sufficient calories in the first place.

Gross National Product and Income Data

The data on gross national product, gross domestic product, etc., are taken from the *World Development Reports* (6) published annually by the World Bank. The estimates are made by the countries in question and vary greatly in quality just as in the case of the nutritional data.

There is an additional problem. All the economic values used in this paper are stated in terms of U.S. dollars, which requires that accounts compiled in terms of local currency be converted to U.S. dollars. For this purpose the

World Bank uses official exchange rates, with considerable reluctance, and we follow. Official exchange rates are recognized to be poor approximations to the relative purchasing powers or other measures of the values of different currencies. They are used because no other measures of the values of currencies are compiled regularly for most of the countries of the world.

As a result the economic values that we use herein are known to be subject to error, sometimes seriously so. This imparts a downward bias to correlations involving these values and strengthens our confidence when statistical tests indicate that the correlations are "significant."

REFERENCES

(1) Food and Agriculture Organization. Annual. Production Yearbook. Rome: FAO.
(2) Houthakker, H.S. 1967. Economic Policy for the Farm Sector. Washington, DC: American Enterprise Institute.
(3) Kellogg, E.D. 1985. University involvement in international development alternatives: important issues for public education. In Proceedings. Athens, GA: Association of U.S. University Directors of International Agricultural Programs.
(4) McCalla, A.F., and Josling, T.E. 1985. Agricultural Policies and World Markets. New York: MacMillan.
(5) Sen, A.K. 1981. Poverty and Famines. London: Oxford University Press.
(6) World Bank. Annual. World Development Report. Washington, DC: Oxford University Press.

[16]

World Development, Vol. 19, No. 1, pp. 103–110, 1991.
Printed in Great Britain.

0305–750X/91 $3.00 + 0.00
Pergamon Press plc

Protecting the Global Environment:
An Immodest Proposal

ROBERT DORFMAN
Harvard University, Cambridge, Massachusetts

Summary. — As the other essays in this symposium note, the threats to the global environment are an aggravated instance of the Prisoners' Dilemma game. On the assumption that one nation's environmental behavior does not affect the behaviors of other nations, each nation serves its interests best by continuing to abuse the environment, no matter what other nations do. As a result, the benign global environment is doomed unless the nations of the world, or most of them, learn how to restrain each other's environmentally destructive activities. The experience of the thinning of the ozone layer and the signing of the Montreal Protocol in response shows that the countries can cooperate when the conditions are right, and indicates the conditions that are required.

The impact of human activities on our environment is insistently on our minds these days. Whether those activities pose a serious threat to the environment, and whether it is imperative that we mend our ways are no longer live questions. The live questions are in what ways our behavior should be changed, and how those necessary changes can be brought about. That last question is the subject of this paper.

The problem that I shall deal with is as follows: no country, not even the United States, can cope single-handedly with the threats to the integrity of the worldwide environment such as the "greenhouse problem," acid precipitation, the threatened annihilation of the great whales, etc. Although the nations of the world have been making substantial progress in protecting themselves against practices within their own borders that pollute or otherwise damage their own environments, they have not made comparable progress in dealing with environmental threats that cross national frontiers. The frustrating history of the struggles of the International Whaling Commission is an all too typical example of the formidable obstacles to international cooperation on behalf of the environment. On the other hand, the Montreal Protocol limiting the production and use of substances that deplete the ozone layer is an all too rare instance of what can be achieved when the gravity of an environmental threat is widely appreciated. I shall review the history of the Montreal Protocol below because it illuminates so clearly the

conditions required for effective international cooperation in defense of the environment. But first, we should examine in general terms the problem that has to be solved.

The conditions that make it difficult to restrain nations from abusing the global environment are an exaggerated version of the same ones that nations confront in protecting the environments within their borders. A nation that permits its citizens to abuse the global environment does so because the benefit that it gains thereby appears greater than the harms that it expects to accrue to its own citizens; harm to other nations and their citizens is considered at a deep discount, if at all. By the same token, a nation that restrains its citizens from behavior that harms the environment beyond its borders is likely to find that its sacrifices are entirely frustrated unless other nations do the same.

In consequence, environmental damages and threats that cross national boundaries can be combatted only by arrangements by which nations reciprocally agree to restrain their citizens from environmentally harmful behavior. Such agreements may be advantageous to all participants, although each cooperating nation would lose by imposing those restraints unless the others reciprocated. In this respect, the situation is an instance of the famous "prisoners' dilemma."

International cooperation for protecting the environment depends on widespread recognition of the advantages, indeed the necessity, of such agreements. How much is involved in securing such recognition is exemplified by the fact that 15 years of pressure and difficult negotiations were required to attain an effective treaty regulating the use and release of the chlorofluorocarbons (CFCs) that erode the protective ozone layer.

Meanwhile, the environment is not waiting patiently. There is good reason to believe that acid precipitation is killing forests on several continents. The concentration of carbon dioxide (CO_2) in the atmosphere is increasing measurably year by year, with consequences that we do not understand. There is no indication that the nations are about to agree to slow down the accumulation of atmospheric CO_2, although there is an encouraging amount of talk to that effect. Migratory species in the oceans and in the air are being exterminated because no one nation is in a position to protect them from citizens of other nations.

The recently ratified protocol limiting releases of CFCs is the one significant exception to this ominous state of affairs. It is appropriate, therefore, to review the strategy followed in that instance since it reveals the most promising approach for gaining international cooperation in solving a human-made environmental problem.

I shall discuss the lessons I derive from the CFC experience in three stages. First, I shall discuss the principles that will have to be followed to succeed in any effort to control mankind's environmentally destructive behavior. Second, I shall describe the institutions that these principles show to be necessary. And finally, I shall indicate the steps that I think will be required in order to create these institutions. In short, I shall start from the final destination and trace the route back to where we stand at present.

I turn first to the principles on which any program for worldwide environmental preservation will have to be based. Most obviously, such a program will have to elicit widespread cooperation among the countries of the world, be they members of the so-called First World, or Second World, or Third World. The program must therefore not affront the principles of any of these "worlds." At the same time, it must not endorse the principles or political objectives of any group of nations. It must, indeed, be so far removed from the rivalries of nations and blocs that it does not create a forum for airing international quarrels. There already is such a forum in the General Assembly of the UN, and experience indicates clearly that an institution where nations debate their competing aspirations and views of the world is not well suited to mobilizing the united efforts that environmental problems demand.

The first of these principles is that *an institution that is designed to deal with global, or even regional, environmental problems must be sharply and narrowly focused on those problems.* Such an institution cannot be a world government, nor even be a step toward a world government. It must not even deal with so broad a realm as "the environment," but only with very specific problems, such as ozone depletion.

In specifying this sharp focus, I have in mind the difficulties faced by the United Nations Environmental Program from its inception. Right away, at the Stockholm Conference that gave birth to the United Nations Environmental Program (UNEP), the Third-World participants drove home the reasonable point that economic development and environmental protection are inseparable. Much abuse of the environment is a direct consequence of desperate poverty, and, at any rate, no country can be expected to divert resources to preserving the environment while its population still lacks food, medical facilities, and other requisites of bare existence. Granted that an economy cannot develop soundly if it destroys its environmental base, still an impoverished nation's first concern must be the nutrition, health, and education of its population. Besides, many Third World nations contend, most of the poverty and most of the environmental abuse in the world are the heritage of heedless exploitation by the formerly imperial countries of the First World.

The conference nearly foundered on this kind of embittered acrimony, and only strenuous exercise of tact and forbearance kept it going. The Third World countries had their way, up to a point. The industrial countries made no hard commitments for combatting world poverty, but they did agree to having economic development included in the agenda of the UNEP. UNEP's solicitude for the aspirations of the less-developed countries (LDC) was symbolized, perhaps, by the choice of its headquarters: Nairobi. Nairobi is neither a convenient nor an economical location for an institution charged with protecting the world's environment, but it is the capital of a less-developed nation.

For the ensuing 10 or more years UNEP devoted at least as much effort to articulating the views of the LDCs as to defending the integrity of the environment. It thereby impaired its standing as a politically neutral agency devoted to environmental protection. It has only recently emerged from the distrust engendered by that period.

History consists of samples of size one, which is too small to prove anything. Still, this experience, and some similar ones, strongly suggest that if an environmental program is to be successful it must not be admixed with other causes, no matter how worthy or how passionately felt. It must not allow its attention to be diverted to other desirable goals, for every widening of scope is also a widening of the things about which the cooperating nations can disagree.

I dwell on the need for negotiations and treaties concerning environmental protection to be focused narrowly on a specific, urgent problem because that recommendation is at variance with a standard doctrine of political science. The standard doctrine holds that broad terms of reference facilitate negotiations by permitting concessions in different areas to be traded. The peculiarity of international environmental negotiations that makes this doctrine inapplicable is the critical need to solicit and retain widespread participation. To meet this need, it is wise to have an agenda that offers as few subjects for disagreement as possible. Provision for facilitating trades and compromises is indeed important; some examples are discussed below.

A second basic principle relates to the insistent and legitimate need for economic growth. Although an institution concerned with preserving with global environment cannot simultaneously be devoted to fostering economic growth, neither can it ignore the need for it. Therefore, *environmental protection cannot be predicated on a zero-growth policy*. The LDCs in particular cannot be expected to acquiesce in any policies that condemn them indefinitely to their current levels of poverty.

It is very likely that a world in which the per capita consumption of fossil fuel in India and China was the same as it is in Western Europe today would be an ecological disaster. It is also surely true that a world in which India and China continue to consume energy at their current severely limited levels is a human impossibility. No matter what the expected environmental cost, a viable environmental policy must take that requirement into account. Less dramatically, but equally undeniably, the nations that are currently called "developed" have their pockets of poverty and their growth aspirations that will have to be accommodated to some extent if they are to cooperate.

In short, all the nations have reasonable aspirations, sometimes appearing to be imperious necessities, which, when added up, impose more stress on the environment than it can be expected to bear. Some must be disappointed, or, more plausibly, all must be partly disappointed.

A program for global environmental protection must therefore persuade its participants to accept painful reductions in some of their hopes and goals. Two things are necessary for meeting this requirement. First, the overall cut-back must be seen to be unavoidable, and second, the allocation of the cut-back among nations must be seen to be fair. The requirement of fairness is particularly hard to meet in a world where there are such disparities in the sizes and wealths of nations, and such diversity in concepts of fairness as there are in our world.

Finally, on a more workaday level, *a plan for environmental protection must provide for executing the practical tasks of implementation*. These include monitoring the state of the environment and the performances of the participating nations, maintaining communication with the participants, promoting research and disseminating the results, and, when necessary, enforcing compliance with whatever international conventions or treaties exist.

The four requirements that have been mentioned here are difficult ones to meet, but they can be met. I hope to establish that claim by exhibiting one scheme that meets them all. I am sure that it is not the only scheme that does so, nor even the best one conceivable, but it will serve the purpose of showing that international organizations that can protect the environment are not hopelessly visionary, even in a world as polarized as ours.

Recall that the first requirement that I laid down for an instrument by which the nations of the world could cooperate to protect their joint environment was that it be so sharply focused on an environmental problem that nations could leave their rivalries and enmities behind when they came to participate. There already are many such international undertakings, for instance, the International Union for Conservation of Nature and Natural Resources, the International Postal Union, the International Whaling Commission, the International Bureau of Weights and Measures. They vary greatly in effectiveness, but they survive and function.

The effort to protect atmospheric ozone exemplifies sound strategy from this point of view. The sequence of events that led to the Montreal Protocol indicates clearly the scale of the obstacles that have to be overcome to secure international acceptance of measures that conflict with individual economic goals. In evaluating this ozone experience, one should keep in mind the fact that the CFCs that have to be controlled, while very useful, are not among the critically important chemicals in any economy.

Mario Molina and F. S. Rowland (1974) were the first to recognize the threat to the ozone layer and the human contribution to ozone depletion. It took some time before even the scientific community was convinced that the suspected danger was real, but over the next few years a number of countries took individual actions to reduce the use of CFCs in aerosol sprays, a major contributor to the problem. The rapid growth in the production and use of CFCs was halted, even reversed in some countries. Proposals for an international agreement, however, made no progress.

In 1981, after seven years, the United Nations Environmental Program established an "Ad Hoc Working Group of Legal and Technical Experts to Elaborate a Global Framework Convention for the Protection of the Ozone Layer." That group and its subcommittees conferred numerous times during the following four years, finally achieving the framework convention that was signed by representatives of 20 countries in 1985. That convention set general goals and provided for further negotiations, but did not specify the responsibilities of the individual signatories. Two more years of negotiations elapsed before representatives of 31 nations (meeting in Geneva) signed a draft of a protocol that spelled out most of those responsibilities, 13 years after the problem was recognized and seven years after serious international negotiations were begun. In September 1987, a final protocol laying out specific responsibilities was endorsed in Montreal by representatives of 45 nations. During 1988 this protocol was ratified by enough nations to go into effect.

But that does not quite end the story. In the course of 1988, the growth of the "ozone holes" near the North and South Poles, as well as additional indications of thinning of the ozone layer in the temperate zones, persuaded most countries that the Montreal Protocol was not stringent enough to arrest the deterioration of the ozone layer. Accordingly, the UNEP has summoned the expert working group to meet again in 1990.

In the course of the seven years of effort that finally resulted in the Montreal Protocol, initial high ambitions had to be compromised substantially to keep the costs acceptable to an adequate number of nations. The final limits on the production and use of CFCs are about half as severe as the ones the scientists initially recommended. A provision for the working group to reconvene after five years to consider the adequacy of the limits was deleted, and replaced by the weaker provision that the Executive Director of UNEP might call such a meeting under certain conditions. The delicate issues of monitoring emissions of CFCs, the state of the ozone layer,

and the performances of the signatory nations were deferred until later meetings. So was the even more delicate issue of enforcing the production and consumption limits, but it was understood that each nation would be responsible for securing the compliance of its own nationals. On the other hand, the "free-rider" problem was recognized by an agreement not to trade with nonsigners in CFCs or in products made with them.

In short, the Montreal Protocol, with all its weaknesses and strengths, is the hard-wrought result of years of patient and adroit negotiation. Compromises were patiently worked out. East-West and North-South conflicts of interest and ideology were sedulously avoided. The fact that controlling CFCs was the only subject on the agenda was essential to achieving the agreement. Nothing more far-reaching or ambitious could have been attained.

I shall combine the discussions of the second and third principles that I proposed, for they are related. These principles must allow for economic growth and must be equitable to nations at all stages of economic development. We can combine these into a provision for equitable economic growth with fair sharing of sacrifice.

Here is the point at which the greatest difficulties inevitably arise. What seems equitable to the rich frequently seems most unjust to the poor, what seems fair to the young is likely to appear egregiously partial to the old. The only way to prevent deadlock when dearly held national goals conflict with environmental imperatives is to avoid direct confrontation. This can be done by substituting general principles for explicit mandates, prohibitions, or requirements.

To be specific, I feel that the principle of economic growth must be accepted, and also the principle that the LDCs must be expected to grow faster than the relatively more developed ones. How much growth must be accepted, and how much faster the poorer countries must be expected to grow are difficult matters, but still much easier than decisions about growth targets for this, that, or the other named countries. The discussion should be confined to the general, anonymous level of principle if agreements are to be possible at all.

My suggestion for conducting such discussions is to divide the concept of economic growth into two components: growth of population and growth of per capita income. The first component is easy. Most nations now accept, at least in principle, that their population growth must be slowed down, perhaps even halted. Many nations have already attained this objective, some apparently inadvertently. A growth rate of 1% per year, or preferably a bit less, with no distinction among nations, would very likely be acceptable to virtually all national governments. Note that this is not set forth as a prescription for a desirable scenario: even growing at 1% per year, the population of the world would double in about 70 years. The principle of a 1% annual growth rate is based, rather, on an observation of growth rates that the industrial nations have found acceptable. It would be hoped that the figure, as a standard, could realistically be revised downward over time.

The growth rate in per capita income is a more delicate matter, and the differential of growth rates between rich and poor countries is most delicate of all. Judgments about fairness are not factual matters, but facts are often very helpful in reaching them. The relevant facts in the current instance are the implications of different rates of growth and different environmental policies for the integrity of the environment.

The critical data needed are the answers to three sorts of factual questions. The first sort of question is essentially technical. It deals with the relationship between a country's per capita income and its impositions on the environment, i.e., its discharges of fluorocarbons, CO_2, sulfur oxides, heavy metals, and so on. We already have much information about these questions thanks to the work of Professor Leontief and his colleagues who studied the relationship between economic activity and polluting emissions in different regions of the world under the auspices of the United Nations several years ago. (See Leontief *et al.*, 1977).

The second type of question is physical. It deals with the relation between the world's discharges of harmful substances and the consequent state of environmental media, particularly the atmosphere and the oceans. These questions, of course, have been widely studied and, though many uncertainties remain, much is known about the answers. Finally, the third type of question is predominantly biological. It deals with the relationship between the state of environmental media and the health of human beings and other species of fauna and flora.

The answers to these three types of question put together provide estimates of the implications of alternative rates of national income growth for the health and survival of human beings and other living creatures. That is as far as facts can take the decision process. From there it is a matter of judgment to decide how much impairment of ecological health can be accepted in the interest of faster growth of per capita income and, reciprocally, how much sacrifice of income growth can be accepted in the interest of a healthier environment.

To be sure, these are usually not easy decisions to be made in the context of an international conference, though sometimes they are. The ozone case appears to have been a relatively easy one. No country judged that much impairment of public or environmental health would be justified for the convenience of more than the current use of CFCs. The only significant impediment to regulation was concern for easing the transition costs for countries that had made large investments in the use or production of these chemicals. We cannot expect decisions about environmental control to be that easy always, or even usually, but at least they can be discussed at the level of broadly applicable criteria and principles rather than at the acrimonious level of specific instances.

The decision about the allocation of growth rate limitations among countries can be approached, within the framework of the overall global growth rate, in a similarly anonymous manner. It would be hopeless to strive for agreements about the relative growth rates of Bangladesh, Argentina, and Switzerland in any international forum. But the relative growth rates of the low-income developing countries, the middle-income developing countries, and the more developed countries can be discussed profitably, with reasonable grounds to hope that agreement can be reached on rates of catching up.

Finally, within the framework of the targets for economic and population growth for countries in broad income groups, permissible discharges of harmful substances per capita can be calculated from the relationships developed in the Leontief and other studies.

The targets for population and per capita income growth rates should be regarded as computational devices rather than as quotas to which the countries are expected to adhere. Every country should be free to follow whatever population and economic growth policies it regards as suitable. What is not free is the amount of pollutant discharges or other intrusions on the environment to which the country is entitled. Quotas for these would be calculated for each country from its calculated growth rates and would not be altered if actual growth diverged from the calculated path.

For example, suppose it has been accepted that the poorest LDCs should be permitted to increase per capita GNP at a rate of 3.5% a year, and suppose that one of them in fact succeeds in growing for several years at 5% All observers would applaud this performance, but nevertheless the amount of atmospheric pollutants that the country is permitted to discharge would be calculated to increase over time only on the basis of the 3.5% growth rate.

In many instances (CFC emissions for one) continuing economic growth will have to be reconciled with actual reductions in environmentally harmful releases. In these cases, the emissions quotas cannot be calculated by simple continuation of established relationships between economic activity and polluting discharges. Instead, the discharge quotas have to be computed on the assumption of feasible changes in consumption patterns and production methods that will make it possible to attain the growth targets without violating the quotas.

These considerations lead me to find some fault with the ozone protocol. It does not provide for growth, and it does not distinguish adequately among nations at different stages of economic development. Very likely, those flaws in principle are not serious in the instance of the CFCs, whose use is only loosely related to economic development or per capita income. But we should not expect to avoid the difficulties I have been considering when the nations confront the need to limit the use of pesticides, or heavy metals, or fossil fuels. Those substances are closely connected to economic income, and the implications for economic growth of limiting their use cannot be ignored.

As argued above, it will be most practical to take up the various threats to the environment one at a time, to negotiate agreements about them separately, and to have separate secretariats to administer each of the agreements. For instance, in addition to the institution handling ozone depletion and its relation to CFCs, one would look for an organization charged with designing standards for human interaction with rain forests, and ways of sharing the unequal burden of meeting those standards. One organization would monitor, and, where necessary, interfere with, disposal of nuclear wastes; other bodies would confront other specific waste disposal issues; and so on. Such arrangements will help insulate environmental protection from *Weltpolitik*.

But some cooperation among the various environmental secretariats would be efficient and helpful. In particular, it would be inefficient and confusing for emission targets for different substances to be predicated on different projections of overall rates of economic growth. Much of the work of economic estimation and projection, some of the work on health effects, and some of the administrative work still to be described could be performed cooperatively, either by joint committees or through contracts with other international organizations such as the UNEP,

the World Health Organization, the International Union for the Preservation of Nature, or the International Council of Scientific Unions.

So far I have described the kind of decision-making apparatus that seems feasible and attractive. Implementation mechanisms are also required. It seems inevitable that they will continue to rely on each participating government to regulate or otherwise control the behavior of its nationals. There is too much diversity of national custom and law to think of doing otherwise. Besides, to attempt to regulate the behavior of citizens directly would intrude unacceptably on national sovereignties. Each participating government would then assume responsibilty for the compliance of its nationals with the international agreement. The steps taken by each signer to assure its citizens' compliance would depend upon its own customs, legal system, and economic policies. Many nations, undoubtedly, would discourage environmentally harmful acts by taxing them or by introducing similar economic incentives.

The secretariat that administers each agreement would have three principal continuing responsibilities. First, it should have a continuing program for monitoring the environmental conditions under its jurisdiction. For many conditions, the monitoring might well be performed by the UNEP's Global Environmental Monitoring System (GEMS) or an affiliated agency.

Second, it should monitor the performance, and particularly the emissions, of the participating nations. This could generally be done by meteorological or oceanographic observations, by satellite observations, or by sampling inspections on the ground. Some such assurance to the participating countries that the others are complying with their agreement will doubtless be necessary.

Third, each secretariat should have some power to enforce compliance when violations are detected. How this is to be done will depend for each problem on the kind of performance that has been agreed to. The experience of the International Whaling Commission is instructive. In that case, the United States assumed much of the responsibility for obtaining compliance by reducing the amount of fishing in US waters that ships from countries not in compliance with international whaling agreements were permitted to do. This turned out to be a reasonably effective enforcement measure.

In general, enforcement measures should be tailored to the peculiar requirements and properties of the environmental abuse or infraction involved. One quite generally useful type of sanction is for an environmental protection convention to provide that signers will not trade with a violator in commodities related to the infraction. A variant of this device was used in the Montreal Protocol to penalize nations that declined to sign, i.e., "free riders."

A more severe enforcement method would be to impose fines on participants whose nationals violated the environmental agreements. The fines should be calibrated to the economic advantage gained by the violation, and should be large enough to make continued violation not worthwhile. The fines might be set, for example, to be approximately equal to twice the increase in the violator's GNP that was gained by the violation. Such a penalizing procedure would require a monitoring system that was sensitive enough to establish the severity of the violation and the amount of economic gain that it provided. A procedure that relies on fines should be effective against all but the most desperately impoverished nations.

One principle, however, should be inviolate: an environmental protection treaty should be binding upon nations rather than upon individual nationals who might commit violations.[1] As mentioned earlier, for an international authority to be empowered to proceed against individuals would be a questionable invasion of national sovereignty.

A special difficulty arises in gaining the cooperation of the poorer nations. The United States can forgo the use of DDT without great sacrifice; India, which depends on DDT for controlling malaria as well as for other purposes, cannot. Therefore, India with considerable justification could decline to subscribe to any convention that denied it the use of this practically miraculous (but ecologically dangerous) pesticide.

Economists have a device for coping with reluctance to cooperate in a socially beneficial change when, as in instances such as this one, the reluctance is justified. It is called "the compensation principle," and is based on the idea that if a social change is in the general interest there must be some members of the society who would be made better off, and sufficiently better off, so that they could afford to compensate the members who would be harmed, if there are any, liberally enough so that they, too, would be better off after they are compensated. For example, the richer countries who feel that they can forgo using DDT could gain India's assent by agreeing to bear the additional cost of controlling malaria by more expensive methods that are ecologically safer.

In general, the compensation principle can help solve many problems in which the interests

of different nations diverge. One of the most common types is upstream-downstream conflicts. For example, West German forests are suffering severe damage from precipitation containing sulfates produced by emissions from East German power plants. An agreement could be reached whereby West Germany compensated East Germany for part or all of the cost of flue gas desulfurization in those plants.

Another vexatious type of problem occurs when environmental degradation within a country affects the welfare of other countries. A leading example is destruction of the rain forests in several tropical countries, which releases large amounts of carbon dioxide and has other harmful ecological effects outside the boundaries of the countries that contain the forests. The more affluent countries could assume the costs of preserving the forests, including the cost of maintaining the forest guards and fire-fighters, and even the opportunity cost of maintaining the forests in their pristine state.

There is another way also in which the richer nations could help the poorer ones to meet the costs of protecting the environment. During the next few decades, many of the LDCs will not use the full emission quotas that would be allocated to them by the economic growth formulas that I have described. At the same time, some of the richer nations will want to use more than their allotments. Then the LDCs should be permitted to sell some of their emission allotments to the more developed countries, thereby earning welcome foreign exchange.

It is interesting, but not yet very profitable, to speculate about further administrative details. Before that will be worth while, however, the countries of the world must become receptive to the idea of making significant economic sacrifices in order to avoid environmental damage. The final topic to be considered is how (and if) that receptivity can be created.

Fortunately, recent events spare me from the charge of being impossibly visionary. I have mentioned repeatedly major progress toward restraining use and releases of CFCs. In May 1989, one of the world's greatest whaling fleets agreed, under some pressure, to submit to the moratorium on whaling declared by the International Whaling Commission. To be sure, these are relatively easy cases. Neither CFCs nor whale oil are fundamental to any nation's economy. This confirms UNEP's wisdom in beginning with those threats. For the more painful and difficult cases, more elaborate preparations will be needed to persuade the nations of the world to submit to mutual discipline.

I think there is general agreement that the

most ominous dangers at the moment are the warming of the biosphere by the increasing concentration of CO_2 and other heat-reflecting gases, and the destruction of forests, with their enormous genetic reservoirs, by acidic precipitation. Both of these dangers are byproducts of fossil fuel combustion, and fossil fuels are the stuff of which modern, high-tech life-styles are made. Nations are not likely to forbid or severely restrict their use until they are completely convinced of imminent and painful dangers. There must, therefore, be an utterly reliable and impartial monitoring system that will keep track of the state of the environment and will report its findings without bias, giving good news as much emphasis as bad. GEMS was designed for such a purpose, although it is woefully underfinanced.

At the moment, GEMS' reports on the state of the environment are not influential. But the monitoring system has not been in operation very long or on an adequate scale, and reputations for reliability are not created overnight. I should like to see UNEP assign very first priority to strengthening GEMS and increasing the repute and influence of its reports worldwide. To be more pointed, currently UNEP, like most environmental organizations, has a reputation for special pleading that has to be lived down before its credibility can be re-established.

GEMS seems to me to be the best hope we have for mobilizing world opinion in support of the inevitably painful restraints that will be needed to ward off the impending doom of the temperate-zone forests from acidic precipitation, and the unpredictable consequences of increasing the concentration of heat-retaining gases in the atmosphere. Nothing is likely to be done until we are thoroughly frightened, but once we are there is a good chance that world opinion can insist that governments deal with the threats.

NOTE

1. There are entities that are not answerable to any national government: in particular, some multinational corporations. It would appear to be necessary for the administration of any environmental convention to have means of dealing more directly with such entities. Formal recognition, perhaps in the UN, of the growing role in the modern world of transnational groups of various kinds may be a necessary first step to bringing them into the sphere of responsibility proposed, in this paper, for nations and their nationals.

REFERENCES

Leontief, Wassily, *et al.*, *The Future of the World Economy, A United Nations Study* (New York: Oxford University Press, 1977).

Molina, Mario, and F. S. Rowland, "Stratospheric sink for chlorofluoromethane: Chlorine atom catalyzed destruction of ozone," *Nature*, No. 249 (1974), pp. 810–812.

PART FIVE

SOCIAL DECISIONS

The Functions of the City

Robert Dorfman

Harvard University

I take it for granted that something is wrong with the American city. Though we are in the midst of a war, the newspapers and magazines are devoting unaccustomed space to urban problems: safety in the streets, education, traffic congestion, air pollution, water supply, slums, and even the technical complications of urban finance. As is only natural, we are attempting to grapple with each of these problems on its own merits. Such an approach is appropriate because the means for dealing with, for example, air pollution and the inadequacies of the schools are disconnected, at least on a superficial level. But it is also inappropriate because the problems are clearly interconnected at a deeper level and because a piecemeal series of attacks is not a strategy and does not provide an intelligent order of priorities. It is in order, therefore, to search for the unifying elements in all these problems.

There is obviously one urban problem that dominates all the others in urgency and in importance: the predicament of the colored minority. This is clearly the source of the troubles in the streets, the decay of the central cities, the deterioration of the schools, and much else. Thus, any significant discussion of our cities must be focused on our race problem. But the race problem is not a peculiar property of the Negroes. The Puerto Ricans in Harlem and the Mexicans in California display many of the same social pathologies. It follows that we should look for the source of the problem not in the characteristics of the Negro but in those of the city, which is what I intend to do.

To this end we need a nonevaluative description of an American city, which will take the form of a highly simplified model to highlight the sources of the stresses we are experiencing.[1] These stresses result from the fact that a city performs a number of functions in our society whose demands are discordant with each other. Thus, we begin by inspecting the functions of a city.

A city can be regarded from four points of view. First, it is *a very elaborate physical, technological, and spatial layout.* From this aspect a city is a complex of buildings, wires, pipes, wireless communications, ventilation facilities, surface and subsurface means of access, and so on. It is a large and complicated machine for housing, maintaining, and transporting its population and for storing and transporting the materials they use and disposing of their wastes. In contrast with most other machines, a city comes into being by growth rather than by design and construction. As a result the parts are not well designed to fit each other; they are in varied states of disrepair and obsolescence, and they are replaced and modernized seriatim. Blighted areas and slums are a normal characteristic of a city just as obsolete components are a normal part of a large factory. In short, the physical aspect of a city is that of a great machine in a perpetual state of construction and chronic inadequacy; but, as Parkinson observed long before me, physical inadequacy is a sign of growth and vitality.

From a second point of view a city can be regarded as *a governmental or political entity.* From this point of view an American city is a fantastically complicated and unwieldy institution, a circumstance from which many of its difficulties flow. A survey of Cook County disclosed that there are more than 1,300 governmental jurisdictions, legally independent of each other, each of which discharges some governmental functions within the county. This situation is typical: our overlay of state, federal, municipal, county, sewage district, school district, and other jurisdictions guarantees it. Coordination among all these units is, of course, impossible. In fact, coordi-

[1] By "city" I shall always mean a standard metropolitan statistical area (SMSA) as used by the Census Bureau.

The Functions of the City

33

nation within any one of them, say the municipal government itself, is difficult because many of the officials are independently elected and have independent constituencies and authorities that render them only partially subject to the control of the mayor or other titular head. In short, governmentally, as well as physically, a city is a jumble of poorly integrated parts.

The foregoing two aspects of the city are, however, subsidiary and instrumental. The city as physical facilities and as governmental organization exists to serve the city's other two aspects: the city as *an economic unit* and the city as *a social unit*. It is to these two aspects, and particularly the second, that we have to pay the most attention. I shall argue that much of the complexity of city life results from the conflicting demands made upon the city by its economic and social functions.

The primary economic function of the city is to house one or more markets. A city is not a good place for a farm or a mine or even a factory. But for those economic activities that depend upon numerous contacts and flows of information, location in the right city is practically indispensable. In spite of all the marvels of electronics, it remains true that the everyday conduct of business requires quick, cheap, informal, and intimate communication between a business firm and its suppliers, customers, and even rivals. This kind of communication is going on all the time in the city, in its employment offices, its businessmen's restaurants, its display rooms, its stores, its streets, its conference rooms. Telephones and jet travel are all very well; but frequently in large affairs, and almost always in the multitude of small ones, it pays to be on the spot. Economists refer to the advantages of close contact as "economies of agglomeration." If you want to cast a TV serial, you had better be in Hollywood, where the actors are; and if you are an actor, you had better be there also because that is where the producers expect to find you. If you want buyers to see your dresses, you had better have a New York showroom. And so on.

Economically speaking, each city is a center or market of one sort or another, and the particular industries it serves define its primary economic functions. Or, in slightly different words, each city specializes in providing quick, cheap, day-to-day communication facilities for the firms in one or a few of the nation's economic sectors.

*Municipal
Objectives
and
Organization*

34

The economic function of the city is, therefore, to serve as the communication center, or market, for some industries. The size and character of the city are dictated to a large extent by the size and physical requirements of the markets it houses. Not only must it provide working space and communications for its industries, but it must provide living space, public utilities, protective services, and logistic support of every sort for the industries and for the people who staff them.

From the economic point of view the city is a marketplace and its population is the staff of the market and of the firms that participate in it. The inhabitants of the city are, therefore, in close day-to-day contact with each other in the course of performing their economic functions, and these contacts disregard, very largely, the social likes and dislikes of the people involved. These social likes and dislikes are, however, the essence of the fourth aspect of the city, its aspect when regarded as a social entity.

The most superficial glance at an American city will disclose that it includes a wide variety of people who sort themselves out into neighborhoods largely on the basis of ethnic affinity and socioeconomic similarity. These neighborhoods have neither economic nor administrative nor legal significance. They are social entities purely, and they discharge most of the social functions of the city insofar as they are discharged at all.

This clustering on grounds of ethnic and income similarity is the contemporary expression of one of mankind's most deep-seated urges: the need to be a loyal member of a well-defined and somewhat exclusive social group. I mention below some of the specific psychological satisfactions derived from such membership, but the central fact, which probably requires no further analysis, is that a man needs to attach himself emotionally to some tribe, clan, or community, and feels lost, isolated, and meaningless when he cannot do so. Once upon a time, I suppose, this trait had important survival value, for the ability of the clan to prey upon its competitors and resist their depredations depended upon the loyalty of its members. Nowadays the antagonistic aspect of group identification is disfunctional, though it persists and accounts for many of the characteristics of the American city. The constructive, communal-minded aspect remains essential.

The need for identification with a group accounts for the subdivision of the city into homogeneous neighborhoods. A group is a group of allies. It cannot be all-inclusive, for the vitality and solidarity of the alliance depend on the existence of potential enemies. As James Stephens once said, there cannot be an inside without an outside. Moreover, this same need explains why the neighborhoods must stand in very complicated relationships to one another. Overt and unmitigated enmity cannot be tolerated, but some amount of distrust, hostility, and xenophobia is part of the cement that solidifies the group.

The group or neighborhood provides other satisfactions to its members in addition to the general feeling of belonging to something and of purpose in life (namely, promoting the general welfare of the group). One of these is the comfort and security that comes from being among people who share rather than challenge our presuppositions, tastes, and values. This particular satisfaction dictates the formation of neighborhoods on the basis of similarity of ethnic and cultural backgrounds and also explains why virtually all of an individual's social life may be lived within the confines of his ethnic community.

In the second place, the group provides the anonymous individual with vicarious feelings of significance and accomplishment through his identification with talented or influential members of his group. And we should not overlook that the ethnic group provides a safe and socially accepted channel for expressing aggression. We all experience more frustrations and more occasions for rage than we can respond to under the conditions of modern urban life. Frustration cannot be bottled up indefinitely, but it can be displaced. When, for example, we should like to beat our wife or insult our boss, we can gain considerable relief from our necessarily suppressed rage by calumniating the members of some other social group. Under extreme provocation, we can even join a riot.

In short, there are real and important psychological needs —for identification, for approval and support, for discharge of hostility—that can be met by belonging to an appropriate social group. In a small and homogeneous town, the whole community may coalesce into such a group. In a large and diverse city, the populace divides itself into ethnically oriented neighborhoods (primarily) in its attempt to satisfy these needs. These neighborhoods are generally too amorphous and unstable, I should think, to provide much sense of communal effort or purpose. They do provide the security of being among

*Municipal
Objectives
and
Organization*

36

people of similar beliefs and tastes, and they do provide outlets for deflected aggression, which are all the more important because of the feebleness of the positive, constructive satisfactions.

The functions mentioned so far all follow from perceiving a neighborhood or social group as one of a number of associated and competitive groups that occupy the same living space. There is another vital social function that any community must discharge, irrespective of the presence of competing groups: it must socialize its members, particularly its young. This is done by inculcating the traditions and culture of the community (including, importantly, loyalty to it) and by providing a sufficient variety of models of desirable behavior and of social roles so that an individual can find adequate scope for self-expression and personal development within the confines of his community. In our cities part of the task of social indoctrination is carried on by the city as a whole (for example, through its formal educational system) and part, less formally, by the ethnic neighborhoods which otherwise would atrophy. Models of personal development, however, have to be provided almost entirely by the ethnic communities because young people do not have sufficient contact with outsiders, nor can they, simply because they are outsiders, identify with them. It should be remarked at once that Negro communities are particularly deficient in models of social behavior and development.

From these considerations there emerges a simplified model of an American city. It consists of a cluster of ethnically distinguished neighborhoods whose members collaborate in staffing the firms, markets, and other economic and political organizations of the city. Economic cooperation brings the members of the diverse ethnic communities into intimate and daily contact with each other. Social predilections separate them at the end of the day. There emerges a delicate balancing of economic and social forces. On the one hand, the demands of economic life render the diverse groups dependent upon each other and enforce cooperation among them. On the other hand, competition for economic opportunity creates an arena for the virulent expression of social antagonism. The economic life of the city depends upon moderating the diverse tendencies, while social vitality reinforces them.

The tensions just described are mitigated, to an extent, by

The Functions of the City

37

carrying over into economic life the ethnic divisions of social life. Certain occupations and industries become segregated, just as neighborhoods are. It would be surprising if it were otherwise. People wish to work, as to live, among people with whom they feel most at ease. Some aspects of economic performance are transmitted in the cultures of the groups, as emphasis on scholarliness and bookishness among Jews. Wherever markets are imperfect, the tendency of members of any group to favor their fellows draws them together, just as the suspiciousness, prejudice, and competitiveness of members of each group against outsiders drives them apart. And, finally, just because personal contacts are much richer within groups than between them, the flows of information, which are an important part of markets and of city life, facilitate economic relationships within groups more than among them.

The consequence is that the diverse ethnic groups within the city come to dominate different industries and occupations. Though this fact has its regrettable side from the viewpoint of individualistic and egalitarian standards, it contributes to the viability of the city and to the stability and health of the social groups. It diminishes the tensions of the economic life of the city by reducing the frequency and intimacy of contacts between members of alien groups, that is, it extends to economic life some of the coziness of social life. But I attach more importance to its impact on the vitality of the ethnic groups which provide most of the social satisfactions of the city. The esteem and status of the group is derived in substantial part from its contribution to the economic life of its city, and in particular from the industries in which it plays a dominant role. Thus, the specialization of ethnic groups to industries is an important support to their self-regard and to their feelings of security and belongingness in the city as a whole. Furthermore, through this means the structure of economic status in the city as a whole is duplicated within its ethnic communities. The models of personal conduct and development that were mentioned above as one of the requisities for a healthy community are a by-product of this industrial specialization. They could be created without the specialization to be sure, and sometimes are; but their vividness and effectiveness are reinforced by the circumstance that the career pattern is part of the group culture and tradition, is contained largely within it, and includes some elements of exploitation of alien groups.

Municipal Objectives and Organization

38

The economic and social functions of the city thus impinge very forcefully upon each other. The economic functions provide the city's unity and define the opportunities for the ethnic groups that comprise it. The social functions create the city's diversity and strongly influence all aspects of behavior, including economic.

This vision, or image, of the nature of the American city has implications for our understanding of what is wrong with it today and what can be done about it. In the first place it maintains that many of the important social functions of the city depend upon the vitality of the ethnic communities and neighborhoods within it. Integration, in the sense of cultural homogenization of the population, is not in the field of possibility in the visible future and may not even be desirable if, as this analysis suggests, a man needs to be a member of a psychologically manageable subgroup less diverse and overwhelming than an entire city.[2] It suggests, indeed, that the neighborhoods and subgroups in American cities are less vital and coherent than they should be if they are to provide their members with meaningful social satisfactions.[3] It suggests, furthermore, that since subgroups will persist so will tensions among them. If the social development of the cities can be influenced at all by conscious planning, which is doubtful, emphasis should be placed on strengthening the positive, constructive satisfactions of life within the ethnic neighborhoods so as to reduce the emotional importance of the hostility relations among them.

More specifically, it should be noted that the quality of housing has not come up in this discussion. Improvement of housing may well be desirable on various grounds, but this analysis implies that it is not one of the critical elements in our urban problem. Perhaps this is the reason public housing schemes have not had the beneficent social effects expected from them. Improvement of housing is an attractive social expedient because we know how to accomplish it simply by spending money; but it should not, for that reason, be made

---

[2] This conclusion is supported by the findings of Oscar Handlin, "The Goals of Integration," *Daedalus*, vol. 95 (winter, 1966), pp. 261–286, and Talcott Parsons, "True Citizenship for the Negro American? A Sociological Problem," *Daedalus*, vol. 94 (fall, 1965), pp. 1009–1054, in the *Daedalus* symposium on the Negro American.

[3] This finding is strictly in the tradition of Emile Durkheim.

the centerpiece of our attack on the problem of the cities if the problem actually lies elsewhere.

Formal education, also, has played only a small role in this analysis, which perhaps is fortunate because it is so terribly difficult to improve. The Coleman Report indicates that the success of formal education depends more on the cultural environment of the students than the other way round, which is a conclusion that this analysis tends to also. This, again, implies that the strategic focus of our attack should not be on the formal educational system.

Jobs are important as everyone knows, but this analysis indicates that not any old jobs will contribute to a lasting solution of our urban problems. Specifically, developing employment opportunities in the lowest occupational levels of scattered industries may contribute more to perpetuating exploitative and hostile relationships among ethnic groups than to enhancing the integrity of the disadvantaged ones.

The positive implication of this discussion is that the social health of the ethnic groups that comprise a city is strongly influenced by their roles in the economic life of the city. In particular, the social health of a group seems to require that there be some significant markets in which its members occupy influential, if not dominant, positions. Surely the Negroes are distinguished from the other ethnic groups in precisely this regard: that they have no such economic bases of power, status, and social mobility.[4] If this be so, effort should be concentrated on creating such economic foundations for social health for the Negro communities. I am well aware of the difficulties of this enterprise, and I am struck also that none of the major programs with which I am acquainted are pointed in this direction, which may be the essential one.

[4] See St. Clair Drake, "The Social and Economic Status of the Negro in the United States," *Daedalus,* vol. 94 (fall, 1965), pp. 791–814, and Eugene P. Foley, "The Negro Businessman: In Search of a Tradition," *Daedalus,* vol. 95 (winter, 1966), pp. 107–144, both in the *Daedalus* symposium on the Negro American.

*Municipal
Objectives
and
Organization*

40

[18]

Social Decisions without Social Preferences

Robert Dorfman

HARVARD UNIVERSITY, U.S.A.

One of the most sacred foundations of economic reasoning is that decisions are a reflection and implementation of preferences. Consumers' decisions reveal 'revealed preference'. Business decisions are intended to maximise profits because businessmen prefer higher profits to lower. All decisions are intended to obtain the more preferred in lieu of the less preferred.

Naturally, then, we carry this presupposition over to social decisions; they would be incomprehensible and unanalysable without it. And we do so a full twenty years after Arrow [1] showed that there cannot exist any social welfare or preference function that meets minimal requirements of rationality, consistency and responsiveness to the preferences of individual members of the society.

Not only that, but over the years a substantial body of practical experience has accumulated, in which sincere and intelligent efforts to formulate social preference functions have invariably failed. This experience has stemmed from attempts to formulate benefit–cost criteria for the selection and design of governmental projects. The benefit–cost concept does imply the existence of a social preference function and is, I think, the leading practical illustration of an attempt to implement one. The numerator measures the extent to which the project would improve society's position as measured by the social preferences, the denominator measures the extent to which the project detracts, and the whole ratio compares the project's potential contribution to its costs. In the beginning it was taken for granted, rather naïvely as it turned out, that the effect of an economic development project on national income was a good indicator of social preferences with respect to the project. In application this meant that if the market value of the products that would be produced as a result of the project exceeded the costs of the project, then the project would contribute positively to national welfare. Beginning in about 1936, benefit–cost ratios in this spirit have been estimated routinely for certain classes of government investment projects in the United States, and the technique of making the estimates has become increasingly refined.

But I think it is fair to say that the belief that government investment decisions were guided by rationally estimated benefit–cost ratios was an act of self-deception from the very outset. The policy of requiring the estimates was very valuable, and remains so. It compels the comparison of the strictly economic contributions and costs of proposed projects, and that comparison is an important consideration in deciding about them. But the early history of benefit–cost appraisal indicates that another consideration, entirely omitted from the official benefit–cost criteria, was the crucial one: namely the location of projects. At that time it was a national policy to develop the natural resources of the arid, uninhabited West, and that is where virtually all important projects were built. The benefit–cost ratios of the projects actually built varied substantially, but the section of the country in which they were located was uniform. It seems clear that the social criterion actually employed was different from the one that was alleged.

Since that time more difficulties have accumulated than have been overcome. Concern with intangible consequences, with externalities, with effects on quality of life, with effects on the distribution of income and other benefits has forced proponents of benefit–cost analysis to advance their claims in more and more modest terms. Obviously, measurable economic effects are not an adequate indicator of social desirability, and all the considerable effort that has been devoted to enhancing the significance of benefit–cost estimates has been unavailing. No way has been found to make them reflect the social consequences of public projects well enough so that they can be used as a basis for decisions. Arrow's theorem suggests that no way will be found.

So there are both theoretical and empirical grounds for believing that social, or at least governmental, decisions are not derived from any comprehensive scale or measure of social preferences. It is hard to accept that, because an economist feels lost without his compass if he doesn't have something to maximise. But I want to accept it – it appears to be the case – and I hope to show that we can formulate a coherent theory of social choice without the presumption that there is something to be maximised.

We must therefore take a different tack and consider how social choices are made. By social choices I shall mean decisions that affect large numbers of members of a community – decisions that are, in effect, public goods (or bads, as the case may be). Every society has an institution for making and implementing such decisions: its government. Thus we are concerned with governmental decision-making. There is a long and impressive tradition of political philosophy that deals with the moral principles of governmental behaviour and the grounds of governmental legitimacy, but that literature is irrelevant to our present task. I know of but two major attempts to formulate the principles of governmental behaviour descriptively, and both of them are fairly recent. Both, also, arise from the American political context. One, espoused particularly by Charles Lindblom [3] and Aaron Wildavsky [7], is summarised by the rubric of 'disjointed incrementalism'. It holds that governments, like business firms, do not make bold leaps to precomputed optima, but feel their way timidly, each year adjusting last year's policies slightly to correct old deficiencies and to meet new problems. That is probably true, but it is not very informative. Methodologically it is much like predicting that next year's G.N.P. will be within a few percentage points of this year's. So I shall follow the other approach.

The alternative approach, which stems from the work of Arthur Bentley [2] and David Truman [6], depends on the notion that a community can be divided conceptually into a number of interest groups, and that governmental decisions depend on the relations between the government and these groups. In order to pursue this approach I have to state more precisely what I mean by 'government' and by 'interest group' and have to specify how these entities interact.

The word 'government' is used in English discourse in two senses, one of which I have already employed. In that sense it means the institution in a society that is empowered to make a wide range of decisions about matters that affect a large number of members of the society and that are binding on all members of the society. A government can use force, if need be, to compel action in accordance with its decisions, but that is not its distinguishing characteristic – the Mafia uses force also. The critical characteristic that defines a government is that compliance with its decisions is accepted as a moral obligation by the vast majority of the members of its society, i.e. that it is 'legitimate'. This mysterious attribute of legitimate authority is the central concern of political philosophy, and I shall not pursue it further. It is quite possible for a society, during transitional periods, not to have any government, if there is no institution whose dictates are accorded moral force by the requisite vast preponderance. But the need for widely accepted decisions is so imperious that a society without a government is seriously crippled, and such episodes are short-lived. Briefly, then, a government in this sense is an institution by which a society makes decisions that are morally binding on all its members.

Even to write that definition I have had to use words in a metaphorical and unpragmatic way. I wrote that a 'society makes decisions'. But a society can't really make any decisions; only individual men can. The second meaning of the word 'government' corrects this defect in part. It recognises that at any time the powers of the government (in the first sense) are vested in particular men. The decisions made by those men in accordance with prescribed rules (the written or unwritten constitution) are the decisions of the government (in the first sense) and thereby of the society. The men in whom the governmental powers are vested are the government in the second sense. It should be noted that it is only when the word is used in this second sense that a government can be said to have any objectives, and even then I find some difficulty in imputing objectives to a group of men rather than to individuals. From here on I shall use the word freely in both senses, and I do not think that that will give rise to any confusion.

It is fruitful to regard the society or the body politic as being divided into a number of interest groups. My concept of an interest group is entirely conventional and I shall not elaborate upon it here. (It is discussed at some length in [4].) Very briefly, an interest group is a set of individuals of similar tastes and similar circumstances who can be expected to be in agreement about social decisions. This agreement doesn't just happen; it is brought about by particular individuals, whom I shall call politicos or political leaders, who devote themselves to formulating and articulating the desires of the various interest groups. The unanimity that I have ascribed to interest groups consists essentially in unanimity in accepting the formulations and recommendations of particular politicos. The authority and influence of any politico depends on the confidence that the interest groups he appeals to have in him; it is never entirely secure. The members of the government are politicos. Other politicos aspire to governmental positions. Still others are merely prominent citizens of various sorts in whom other citizens repose confidence.

In these terms, the government at any instant consists of a coalition of interest groups whose members are sufficiently numerous and weighty to enable them to select (in accordance with the constitution) the men who occupy the governmental positions. To be more exact, I should have said that the government consists of a coalition of politicos whose followings are sufficiently weighty. The remark that the government is a coalition alerts us to the applicability of the theory of n-person games, whose central concern is the principles of coalition formation and behaviour. The first thing to notice about n-person games is that coalitions do not have any objectives; only their individual members do. So we must formulate this political game more explicitly, with particular attention to the objectives of the individual participants. I shall refer to the participants as 'interest groups', though it is important to remember that the objectives of interest groups are filtered through, and to a large extent formulated by, the politicos. But the politicos are so constrained by their need to maintain the confidence of their followers that the substitution is innocuous. That is to say, a politico can and must sharpen and define the deep-seated predilections of his followers, but he cannot depart substantially from them without losing his claim to influence. With these understandings we can talk about the interests and objectives of individual interest groups.

Each interest group, to be typified by α, is affected by governmental decisions in two ways: it derives benefits from them (perhaps negative benefits) and it bears its share of any economic costs. Since the group is homogeneous with respect to tastes and circumstances, it is meaningful to assume that there is a preference ordering by which the group (i.e. its politicos) can rank the various potential decisions of the government. More than that, each decision imposes an economic or monetary cost (or saving) on the group. So in arriving at its evaluation of any potential decision the group implicitly expresses how much more (or less) it is willing to pay to have decision X^1, say, instead of decision X^2. The preferences of the group are thereby brought into contact with the measuring-rod of money, just as the preferences of a consumer are. We can therefore assume more than an ordinal preference scale defined over governmental decisions; we can assume a numerical utility indicator, to be denoted by $U^\alpha(X)$, which measures the economic burden that the group is just willing to bear in order to have decision X executed. There are serious problems of measurement involved in this concept, which I have discussed elsewhere [5] and which merit further exploration, but I shall not go into them here.

From any decision X, then, group α will receive a benefit, or gross benefit $U^\alpha(X)$, which is the amount that it is willing to pay to enjoy the consequences of that decision. It will also have to meet some economic costs. If the decision entails a cost of $C(X)$ *in toto* and the group has to bear a proportion θ_α of the total, the economic cost to group α will be $\theta_\alpha C(X)$. The net benefit or citizens' surplus accruing to α will then be $U^\alpha(X) - \theta_\alpha C(X)$. The group's attitude towards the decision depends entirely on this magnitude. For short, I shall designate it $CS^\alpha(X)$. Group α, therefore, would like the decision X that makes $CS^\alpha(X)$ as large as possible. But the group cannot choose X unilaterally. Its only means for making its wishes felt is to combine with other groups – with different citizens' surplus functions – into a winning coalition, that is, a coalition that under the rules of the society can either designate the government or, by threatening to do so, compel the current government to adopt a desired decision.

We make a few simple assumptions about the rules that determine which coalitions are winners and which losers:

1. No interest group can control the government unaided. That is, the coalition consisting of group α alone is a losing coalition.
2. There is at least one winning coalition.
3. If S is a winning coalition and R is any collection of interest groups, then $S \cup R$ is a winning coalition. From this and the previous assumption it follows that the coalition of all groups, to be denoted by S^u, is a winning coalition.
4. If S is a winning coalition and the intersection $S \cap R$ is empty, then R is not a winning coalition. In particular, if S is a winning coalition and $-S$ denotes its complement, then $-S$ is not a winning coalition.

So we come to the principles of coalition formation. There are two cases to be considered, one in which utility is transferable and the other in which it is not. The first of these will turn out to be almost trivial and the second very nearly intractable, but they are both worth discussing nevertheless.

Transferable utility means that there is some external unit in terms of which the citizens' surpluses received by all coalitions can be measured, and in terms of which we can talk meaningfully of the aggregate citizens' surplus received by all members of a coalition. Willingness to pay, as we have conceived it, is not necessarily such a unit. It may make a very great difference to the members of a coalition how the total amount that they are willing to pay for a particular decision is distributed among the members (in general, it will) and they may be quite restricted in their ability to arrange compensations, side-payments or bribes that will make a particular decision more agreeable to disgruntled members. Transferable utility presumes that there are no such restrictions on side-payments, in which case all that matters to a coalition is the aggregate citizens' surplus available for distribution among its members. This is so because, as between any two decisions X^1 and X^2, if X^1 affords the coalition the greater aggregate citizens' surplus, then each individual member of a coalition can be made better off if X^1 is adopted than if X^2 is. Whether or not utility is transferable in governmental affairs depends upon the particulars of the case. We shall first consider the cases where it is.

The key to the analysis is, in game-theoretic terms, the characteristic function. This is the aggregate citizen's surplus that would accrue to any coalition of interest groups if it should be formed. This aggregate will be denoted by $v(S)$, where S designates any coalition. The simplest coalition is one that consists of a single interest group operating on its own. The coalition that consists of group α operating by itself is denoted by $\{\alpha\}$, and the corresponding value of the characteristic function by $v(\{\alpha\})$. We make two assumptions about $v(\{\alpha\})$. First, no interest group is influential enough to control the government single-handedly. Second, constitutional and other considerations (such as the 'due process of law' clauses of the United States constitution) protect every group and set a floor below which the citizens' surplus accruing to any group cannot be pushed by act of government. The floor for group α is some number, m_α, presumably negative. By this assumption $v(\{\alpha\}) \geq m_\alpha$, which asserts that group α can assure itself of at least m_α without the co-operation of any other group. By the first assumption, however, group α on its own cannot control the government, cannot protect itself against the most adverse possible decision, and therefore cannot assure itself of $v(\{\alpha\}) > m_\alpha$. It follows that $v(\{\alpha\}) = m_\alpha$.

Larger coalitions are of two sorts: losing coalitions and winning coalitions. Losing coalitions are those that, under the prevailing political rules and practices, cannot control the government. They therefore cannot protect their members from adverse decisions. If S is a losing coalition its members cannot be assured of more than their constitutional minima. Therefore $v(S) = \Sigma m_\alpha$, where the sum is taken over all members of S.

Finally, if S is a winning coalition it can control the government. Accordingly it will have the government choose the decision X which makes the aggregate citizens' surplus accruing to its members as great as possible. Then for a winning coalition

$$v(S) = \max_X \Sigma CS^\alpha(X),$$

where the sum is taken over all groups in S.

We have now defined completely the characteristic function of the political game. In principle, and perhaps in practice, it is computable. The values of $v(S)$ for losing coalitions, including those that consist of single interest groups, follow at once from the maximum degrees to which individual groups can be exploited under the rules of the game. The computations for winning coalitions are more interesting and informative. Part of the data of a real decision problem consists of physical, financial and legal restrictions to which any governmental decision must conform. These restrictions specify an admissible set, say A, from which X must be selected, no matter which coalition forms. Often this set can be described by a system of inequalities, linear or otherwise, constraining the detailed specification of decision X. Then the computation required to determine $v(S)$ is the more-or-less standard programming problem:

Choose X so as to maximise

$$v(S) = \Sigma CS^\alpha(X),$$

the sum taken over all $\alpha \in S$, subject to the conditions:

$$X \in A$$
$$CS^\alpha(X) \geq m_\alpha, \text{ for all } \alpha.$$

This computation has to be made only for winning coalitions.

I now want to establish that in such a situation the government will arrive at a decision that makes the sum of the citizens' surpluses of all the groups in the community as great as possible; i.e. joint welfare maximisation is inevitable. To do this we need a few more notions from game theory. An imputation is a detailed specification of the gains accruing to all the participants in a game. If we allow for side-payments, s_α, which may be negative, an imputation is a vector u with one component,

$$u_\alpha = CS^\alpha(X) - s_\alpha,$$

for each interest group. We presume that when side-payments are made they are made only by members of a coalition to one another, so that $\Sigma s_\alpha = 0$ when the sum is taken over the members of any coalition. No side-payments are made within any losing coalition, but they may be within a winning coalition.

We say that an imputation u can be blocked if there exists any coalition S such that $\Sigma u_\alpha < v(S)$, where the sum is taken over all members of S. This is sensible because if such an imputation were proposed, the coalition S would form and distribute its aggregate citizens' surplus to its members in such a way that every one of them would receive more than u_α. Notice that any imputation in which $u_\alpha < m_\alpha$ for any group α can be blocked, since each group, acting independently, can assure itself of at least m_α.

The core of a game consists of all imputations that cannot be blocked. One of the more distressing findings of game theory is that the core of a game may be empty. That is, every possible imputation may be blocked by one coalition or another. This is as true of political games as it is of games in general, and examples are easy to construct. But if the core is not empty the outcome of the game will be one of the imputations in the core.

Now in our political game an imputation will not be in the core unless it corresponds (in a sense to be defined immediately) to a decision that maximises aggregate citizens' surplus. To define this idea, suppose that decision X maximises $\Sigma CS^\alpha(X)$ for some winning coalition S. Then an imputation u corresponds to X only if $\Sigma u_\alpha = v(S)$, taking the sum over groups that comprise S, and $u_\alpha = m_\alpha$ for all other groups.

Now suppose that the greatest attainable aggregate citizens' surplus is W^u. Consider any decision X and a winning coalition S that would select X if it formed. The groups in S together receive $v(S)$; the excluded groups receive a total of $v(-S)$, say. If X does not maximise aggregate citizens' surplus, then $v(S) + v(-S) < W^u$. But no imputation consistent with those coalitions can be in the core. For one possible coalition is the all-inclusive coalition, say S^u, and $v(S^u) = W^u > v(S) + v(-S) = \Sigma u_\alpha$. Any imputation arising from the coalitions S versus. $-S$ could therefore be blocked. It follows that if the core is not empty it will include only imputations that correspond to joint-welfare-maximising decisions. As a by-product it is worth recording that all imputations in the core must be Pareto-optimal. The converse is not true; the requirements for being in the core are more stringent than those of Pareto-optimality.

But the core might be empty. In that case no coalitions would be stable, but some might be particularly vulnerable. These, which I shall call non-viable coalitions, are those in which every member could benefit from a merger with some outside groups to form a larger coalition. Explicitly: a coalition S would be non-viable if, by itself, it would select a decision that did not maximise the aggregate citizens' surplus of the community as a whole. For if this were the case the members of S could be included in a larger coalition, say $S \cup R$, such that $v(S \cup R) > v(S) + v(R)$. All the members of S could join $S \cup R$ without abrogating any previous commitments or promises, and all would benefit. Non-viable coalitions would be merged into viable ones until a coalition was formed that selected a decision that maximised aggregate community-wide citizens' surplus.

Whether the core is empty or not, then, the coalition that finally forms will be one that chooses an X such that $\Sigma CS^{\alpha}(X) = W^{u}$, its greatest possible value.

The conclusion that we have reached by this elaborate argument is really very transparent. If, as it assumes, utility is transferable, then we can talk meaningfully about the total amount of utility in the community and about its maximisation. That provides us forthwith with a scale of social preferences and a social welfare function, more utility being better than less. The apparatus of benefit–cost analysis applies validly to a special case of this case, viz. that in which utility is measured adequately by the market value of goods produced, perhaps discounted and otherwise adjusted. In those special instances, and there undoubtedly are some, where life is that simple, there is an unambiguous way to measure the desirability of the results of different governmental decisions, and political decisions simply don't arise. That is the upshot of the trivial case.

We now turn to the more significant case in which utility is not transferable. In that case, if decision X is taken, the only possible imputation is $u_{\alpha} = CS^{\alpha}(X)$. This case does not require institutionally that it be absolutely impossible to make side-payments or compensations. There must, however, be substantial restrictions on those side-payments. We can regard the specifications of the decision as incorporating any side-payments that are permissible and agreed upon. Formally, then, no side-payments at all are allowed.

Since side-payments are not permitted, it is no longer meaningful to regard the reward to any coalition as the sum of the rewards to its members. Each member receives his own reward, the distribution cannot be rectified, and it matters greatly what it is. We lose, therefore, the concept of the characteristic function and its analytic advantages. (Generalisations of that concept can be constructed for games with non-transferable utilities, but the construction is too complicated to be justified in the present context.)

It is still helpful, however, to retain the notion of the core to designate all achievable imputations that are not clearly ruled out by the interests of the participants. To be in the core an imputation u must, in the first instance, be achievable. That is, there must be some decisions X such that $CS^{\alpha}(X) = u_{\alpha}$ and $u_{\alpha} \geq m_{\alpha}$ for all α. Second, there must be some winning coalition S for which u is undominated. That is, there must be some winning S for which there is no achievable imputation v such that $v_\alpha \geq u_\alpha$ for all α in S, with at least one strict exceedence. And, third, u must not be blocked by any winning coalition.

The requirements for blocking are more delicate now than in the transferable utility case. Indeed, the major difficulty in this case is to define blocking in a way that is both analytically fruitful and institutionally reasonable. In our context it appears that an imputation will be blocked in either of two circumstances: (*a*) if there exists a winning coalition S and an achievable imputation v for which $v_\alpha > u_\alpha$ for all $\alpha \in S$. In such a case the imputation u will surely be supplanted by v or some other, since it is in the interests of all potential members of S to combine against u and they can overturn it.

Alternatively, (*b*) u will not be in the core if there exists an achievable imputation v for which $v \geq u$ and $v_\alpha > u_\alpha$ for some α in a winning coalition S. It is immediate by this second condition that all imputations in the core are Pareto-optimal, simply by noting that the universal coalition is a winning coalition. The force behind this condition is that if a decision can be improved upon from the point of view of any interest group without harming any other, then that interest group will be motivated and able to organise a coalition against that decision.

The tendency of political manœuvring to achieve Pareto-optimal decisions depends heavily on the second sort of blocking, which requires that interest groups that are indifferent with regard to a number of decisions be willing to go along with any interest group that cares. This is far from completely compelling. Yet I suspect that our difficulties in accepting it arise chiefly from the artificial clarity of the definitions. There probably are few instances in which an interest group is totally indifferent among decisions, though they often do not care very much. There are probably few instances in which side-payments are completely prohibited, though they may be small and nebulous (e.g. sense of obligation). Our intuition is not a safe guide to the realm where, in the interests of theoretical precision, the rough edges of reality are honed to razor-sharpness. The second form of blocking amounts to assuming that when a choice between imputations is of small concern to an interest group, then a small inducement will suffice to elicit its co-operation.

That seems sensible for simple situations. To be sure, specific decisions are often embedded in a larger context, and then malevolence, beneficence, prior obligations and considerations of high strategy affect the behaviour of the interest groups. The analysis must presume that the decision under study is self-contained and inclusive enough to be insulated from such influences. Otherwise important, and unascertainable, data have been omitted from the interest groups' utility functions.

The analysis in terms of game-theoretic concepts provides little information about which coalitions will form or which decisions will be taken, other than that they will tend to be Pareto-optimal or nearly so. But we can go further, with this analysis as background, by noticing that one coalition is of particular interest: the coalition that happens to control the government at the moment. That coalition's decisions are, at least temporarily, the government's decisions, and we must inspect the grounds on which they will be taken.

The first consideration is surely maintenance of control. This requires that decisions taken afford sufficient citizen's surplus to a sufficient number of the interest groups in the coalition to maintain their loyalty. The sort of considerations involved in maintaining loyalty are suggested by the preceding analysis. A decision that can be blocked in the first way threatens the integrity of the coalition; one that can be blocked in the second way forgoes an opportunity to solidify the coalition. The second kind of blocking can be avoided simply by choosing a Pareto-optimal decision, but the first kind is a good deal more intricate.

The government must compare any proposed decision with all alternatives, ascertain which interest groups prefer the alternative, and determine whether those interest groups constitute a winning coalition. If they do, the proposed decision is blocked. This scanning process can be formalised in terms of two-person game theory: the government *versus* all potential coalitions. The government is the minorant player. Whichever decision it makes, it must anticipate the alternative proposal that costs it the most support. It must therefore choose a proposal, if it can, against which the most adverse possible coalition does not win. If there is no such proposal it must minimise the amount of opposition it arouses. Governments clearly do this all the time, by offering budget programmes that are sufficiently attractive to a sufficient variety of interest groups to continue them in power. The former calculations, however, appear to be very difficult. It pays to set them forth schematically to see what is involved.

For this purpose we have to state explicitly what constitutes a winning coalition. Let us assign a measure of political importance, q_α, to each of the interest groups. It will depend on the number of members in the group, their wealth, and perhaps other things. The political power of a coalition is the sum Σq_α taken over all groups in the coalition. If it is sufficiently great, at least as great as some number R, say, then that is a winning coalition.

To ascertain whether any decision will induce the formation of a winning opposing coalition, we notice that the significant characteristic of the decision is the imputation $u = CS^\alpha(X)$ that corresponds to it. The test of any proposed imputation u is whether there exists any alternative that could defeat it. This test amounts to the following mixed-integer programming problem. Introduce a vector of (0, 1) variables k_α where $k\alpha = 1$ signifies that group α would oppose the government. Then, given a proposed imputation u, search for a decision X and a k-vector which maximise $\Sigma q_\alpha k_\alpha$ subject to the requirements that

$$X \in A$$
$$CS^\alpha(X) \geq m_\alpha \text{ for all } \alpha$$
$$CS^\alpha(X) \geq u_\alpha - M(1 - k_\alpha) \text{ for all } \alpha$$
$$\text{and for some large number } M.$$

If the maximum so found is greater than R, then the proposed imputation can be blocked. This is an integer programming problem but may be a fairly simple one if the number of interest groups that have to be distinguished is not very large.

The problem faced by the government, the minorant player, does not necessarily have a solution. Whether it has a solution or not depends on the extent to which the interests of the interest groups conflict, and has a great deal to do with the stability of the government.

If unblocked decisions exist, that is, decisions that will satisfy enough interest groups to maintain the government in power, the government will have some room for choice among them. It uses any such freedom to enhance the citizens' surpluses of its members. That is, it chooses a decision X for which there is no alternative Y such that $CS^\alpha(Y) \geq CS^\alpha(X)$ for all α in the governing coalition, with some strict exceedance. This also can be expressed readily as a programming problem, but I shall not go into the details here.

In this paper I have discussed in a programmatic way how a theory of governmental decisions can be constructed without appeal to an inclusive social preference function. It applies only to comparatively simple decisions that are not too deeply enmeshed in a complicated context. Such decisions do occur, particularly at the more technical levels of government.

I have not deduced any theorems, other than weak and obvious ones about Pareto-optimality. My intent has been to exhibit the structure of the problem. But I am sure that with a bit more specificity theorems can be found that will throw some light on the conditions that influence the welfares of the different interest groups and on the nature of the governing coalitions that are likely to form.

REFERENCES

[1] K. J. Arrow, *Social Choice and Individual Values* (New York, 1951).
[2] A. F. Bentley, *The Process of Government* (New York, 1907).
[3] R. A. Dahl and C. E. Lindblom, *Politics, Economics and Welfare* (New York, 1953).
[4] R. Dorfman, 'General Equilibrium with Public Goods', in J. Margolis and H. Guitton (eds), *Public Economics* (London and New York, 1969).
[5] —— and H. D. Jacoby, 'A Model of Public Decisions Illustrated by a Water

Pollution Policy Problem', in R. H. Haveman and J. Margolis (eds), *Public Expenditures and Policy Analysis* (Chicago, 1970).

[6] D. B. Truman, *The Governmental Process: Political Interests and Public Opinion* (New York, 1951).

[7] A. Wildavsky, *The Politics of the Budgetary Process* (Boston, 1964).

[19]

ROBERT DORFMAN

The technical basis for
decision making

MY TASK is a very important and difficult one. It is no less than to set forth a fruitful conceptual framework for the discussions to follow. It is also a very great privilege, because it gives me the opportunity, before anyone else can present their view, to advocate my own penchants and to derogate other people's, which I fully intend to do.

First of all, I have to address myself to the concept of common property resources. Each of us knows what they are, generally speaking, but as I read the literature I am sure that we are not all in exact agreement. By that I mean that there are many questionable cases in which I should say, "This is a common property resource," and you would say, "It is not." As a homely example, consider ski slopes. Some are privately owned but nevertheless can, and do, give rise to serious congestion problems on occasion. They are not common property resources as commonly understood. But the slope on the next mountain may be in a public park. Is that a common property resource, or is it also a private resource that happens to be owned by the state? I am not going to insist on an answer, since we could waste a great deal of time if we attempted to find a rational basis for resolving all such quibbles. The exact definition is unimportant; what is important is its relation to other economic concepts that have similarly fuzzy edges.

The key concept is *externalities*. An externality occurs whenever an action taken by some economic unit has a *direct* impact on the welfare or productivity of some other economic unit. Usage of this term is not exactly uniform in the literature in a couple of respects, and some confusion has resulted. In the interest of uniformity where it matters, let me call attention to two nebulous aspects. First is the question of reimbursement. My definition did not mention reimbursement, but some

The author is David A. Wells Professor of Political Economy, Harvard University.

5

THE TECHNICAL BASIS FOR DECISION MAKING

definitions require that it be absent.[1] Consider the famous Pigouvian example of the railway whose engines emit sparks that sometimes ignite farmers' fields. There is an externality there by my definition. Furthermore the externality would still be present if the farmer owned the right-of-way and were able to charge the railroad for the privilege of sending an engine past his field. That is where definitions diverge. It seems most useful to say, in this latter case, that there is still an externality but that the price can be set so that the proper (in some sense) amount of it will be generated. In general, I should say, externalities are technological relationships and not matters of law or institutional arrangements. Institutional arrangements are significant because they affect the amount of the externality that is produced, but the externality will be there, paid for or not, unless the offending activity is suspended entirely or the offended people move out of range. Unless we define externalities in this way we are in danger of confusing two fields of discourse—technological and institutional—when we discuss externalities.

The other ambiguity about which I wish to take a position is the distinction between technological and pecuniary externalities. The operative phrase in the definition I proposed as a ground rule is *direct impact*. That definition does not admit effects transmitted via the price mechanism as externalities at all. Though I presume that that position is generally accepted nowadays, pecuniary externalities do survive in the literature. The phrase appears to go back to Viner's authoritative paper on cost curves (9), and in that connection it is interesting to recall what he had to say about the kinds of externalities that concern us: "External technological diseconomies, or increasing technical coefficients of production as output of the industry as a whole is increased, can be theoretically conceived, but it is hard to find convincing illustrations." The world has changed a great deal since 1931.

Those comments should make the concept of externalities sufficiently precise. Any economic unit's behavior can affect the welfare or productivity of others in a vast number of different ways, through altruism, envy, congestion, pollution, and a myriad of other kinds of connection.

---

[1] For example, Mishan: "External effects may be said to arise when relevant effects on production or welfare go wholly or partially unpriced" (7, p. 6). Mishan is explicit about what he means by this; in particular he means to include all cases in which a firm pays a factor of production less than its social value in alternative occupations. This definition includes the draft, hard bargaining, and a host of other market imperfections as sources of externalities, which I find confusing.

6

ROBERT DORFMAN

Sometimes the connection is physical. That is to say, sometimes there is an identifiable physical medium through which the effects of one agent's activities are transmitted to other agents. Such a medium is what I shall mean by a common property resource.

This point of view has some immediate consequences for our discourse. It means that all problems attributable to the misuse or abuse of common property resources are instances of externalities, and the entire theory of externalities applies to them. But the converse is not true. There are externalities that do not involve common property resources, for example, those attributable to altruism and envy, the advantages of living among better-educated people with habits and tastes agreeable to us, and the benefits conferred by the extension of knowledge and the creation of art. All of those are real externalities, but common property resources are not involved, according to my concept, and we shall only imperil a useful, delimited concept if we try to stretch it to cover too wide a range of externalities.

Second, notice that this concept makes no reference to property rights. The private ski slope and the public park confront exactly the same technological problems, and the admission fee or usage-discipline that is right for one is right for the other. They are classified identically according to this concept, as seems sensible. In Garrett Hardin's now-classic parable (5), the commons is a common property resource, but would remain so if the lord of the manor appropriated it and charged a grazing fee per head. The distinguishing feature of a common property resource is that it transmits influences directly from one economic agent to another. It may, legally, be private property.

At this juncture I must digress briefly onto the topic of property, which has become part of this literature under the well-merited influence of Ronald Coase. It seems to me that much of the literature is confusing, and even wrong, when it discusses the relationship between property rights and the use of common property resources. It is often said that the difficulties arise either because there are no property rights or because they are ill defined. Typically, nothing could be further from the truth. In Garrett Hardin's case, every properly certified member of the village had a perfectly clear entitlement to graze his livestock on the common, and it was enforceable at law. In the famous Pigou-Coase railway example, also, the rights of the participants are clearly defined although, as Coase is at pains to point out, they are not exactly what Pigou assumed them to be (2, sec. VIII). The same is true of fisheries, aquifers, and oil pools, all of which have been used to illustrate gaps

7

THE TECHNICAL BASIS FOR DECISION MAKING

in the definition of rights. But there are no gaps in these instances; on the contrary, there are overlaps. Several people have clearly established rights that, when exercised, turn out to be incompatible. I believe that lawyers call this kind of situation a "conflict of rights," and it is far from rare. When it comes to the surface, the courts must decide which right is to prevail. Once the precedent is set, it has the effect of redefining the rights so that they are no longer in conflict. But the point is that clear rights existed before the precedent, and the conflict arose, not from any deficiency of rights or definition, but rather from a superfluity of them. And so it is with common property resources: there are too many rights to them, and when exercised, the rights impair each other.

We come out of this terminological excursion with the conclusion that a common property resource is a kind of public good with the peculiarities that it cannot be augmented, but it can be saturated. It is not easy to say precisely what that means because it is not easy to say precisely what is meant by *using a public good* and because the ways in which users of a public good affect each other are so varied. Let me mention a few examples to remind you of the possibilities.

First there is the oil-pool kind of problem. Each person with access to the pool is under an incentive to withdraw all the oil he can as quickly as he can, before his neighbor does the same. He knows that by drilling and operating superfluous wells he is expending resources without increasing the ultimate yield of the pool; indeed he is likely to diminish it, but he does so all the same. In this case the users do not affect each other at all in the short run, and even if they did not affect the total yield in the long run, the problem would remain.

The fisheries kind of problem is somewhat different. The yield on any day displays diminishing returns to the total amount of fishing effort, so each trawler reduces the productivity of all the others present on the same fishing grounds. In addition, the catch on any day increases the cost of the catch on subsequent days, and the catch in any season impairs the productivity of the grounds in future seasons. There are both short-run and long-run interferences.

In both these examples the mode of damage to the common property resource is the removal of something of value from it, in one case something that regenerates, in the other something that does not. But that is far from the only mode of mutual interference. On the overcrowded beach or congested highway the individual user does not remove anything from the common property resource or change it

8

ROBERT DORFMAN

physically in any way. The mere fact that he is using it is enough to impair its serviceability to others.

Air pollution is quite different again. Here the mode of impairment is the addition of something deleterious to the common property resource. There are short-run effects, and there may be long-run or even permanent effects also.

In all these instances the interferences are reciprocal; each user affects all the others in much the same way. But that need not be the case; the externalities generated by use may be unidirectional. This is so, for example, when birdwatchers and hunters use the same wilderness area or when tanneries and swimmers use the same river.

Now it does not seem possible for a single theoretical formulation to encompass all these modes of interaction: the abstraction of exhaustible components or self-replenishing ones, the insertion of noxious ingredients, mere congestion, and variants of all these. *Common property resources* seems to be a catchall concept for a variety of essentially different circumstances that require different definitions and formulations. The one common element seems to be the presence of numerous users, or of decentralized decision making subject to a shared constraint.

In this circumstance, instead of striving for a general formulation or an exhaustive taxonomy, it seems best to bring out the issues that arise and the possibilities for analysis by examining a series of special cases, and that is what I plan to do.

In all these cases I shall emphasize the distinction between socially optimal or socially efficient behavior, on the one hand, and equilibrium behavior on the other. This is always an important distinction in economic analysis. Where there are no externalities or market imperfections, these two sorts of behavior turn out to be the same, thanks to the skill of the invisible hand. When externalities are present, the equilibrium and the social optimum tend to diverge unless some corrective action is taken, as is well known and as we shall see exemplified repeatedly in what follows. One type of corrective social action, often practically useful and always conceptually illuminating, is to assess some appropriate charges on externality-creating behavior so as to restore the efficacy of the invisible hand. These brief analyses will pay special attention to the existence and characteristics of such corrective charges.

My first case is Garrett Hardin's famous and moving parable of the commons (5). The story is too simple and familiar to need retelling. In essence, there are some herdsmen who share a commons. Each one

9

THE TECHNICAL BASIS FOR DECISION MAKING

gains in proportion to the size of his own herd and ignores the collective effects of overgrazing. As a result, Hardin tells us,

> the rational herdsman concludes that the only sensible course for him to pursue is to add another animal to his herd. And another; and another. . . . But this is the conclusion reached by each and every rational herdsman sharing a commons. Therein is the tragedy. Each man is locked into a system that compels him to increase his herd without limit—in a world that is limited. Ruin is the destination toward which all men rush, each pursuing his own best interest in a society that believes in the freedom of the commons. (5, p. 1244)

That is very plausible, and surely there is some truth it it. But wherein is the tragedy? Hardin has rushed on toward his grim conclusion too swiftly to make that clear; I want to take it a good deal more slowly.

One possible interpretation is the following. Let $p(X)$ be the probability that an animal will survive to be marketed when the total herd sharing the commons is X. Then the socially optimal size of herd is the one that maximizes $Xp(X)$. We are tempted to rush right in, compute the derivative, and show that the independent herdsmen will try to graze ruinously many cattle. But things are not necessarily that bad. It might be, for example, that

$$p(X) = \frac{a+1}{a+X}, a \geq 0,$$

so that the probability of survival is a certainty if a lone animal is grazed, and falls harmonically toward zero for larger herds. If that be the case,

$$\frac{d}{dX} Xp(X) = \frac{a(a+1)}{(a+X)^2} > 0.$$

There is no "tragedy."[2] The size of the marketable herd is an always-increasing function of the number of cattle grazed, and the invisible hand of self-interest leads the herdsmen in the optimal direction. Things are more complicated than Hardin told us. To produce a real tragedy, or even a serious misallocation of resources, from decentralized use of a common property resource, we must introduce additional considerations.

[2] Not in the usual sense, that is. Hardin uses the word in a different sense, to mean "the solemnity of the remorseless working of things" (5, p. 1244). In this sense there is a tragedy, but it is a beneficent one.

10

ROBERT DORFMAN

It will not even suffice to assume that the carrying capacity of the commons is finite (as Hardin probably does.)[3] Substantially stronger assumptions are needed. One that will suffice is that after some point the marginal productivity of cattle is negative, i.e., that the addition of animals to the herd will actually reduce the number that survives to be marketed. Another line of argument that would buttress Hardin's point is to assume that there is some other scarce resource that is wasted when too many cattle are grazed on the limited commons. For example, the cattle may need tending, or water may be in short supply. Then grazing too many cattle will waste this cooperating resource, even though the carrying capacity of the commons is not reached. In short, the model can be saved by taking other economic considerations into account, but as it stands it is too simple to establish its main conclusion.

My second case follows the route of introducing a second factor, namely labor. Let the commons be a berry patch in which the number of bushels picked on any day shows diminishing returns to the number of person-hours devoted to picking. If $F(X)$ is the number of bushels picked in X person-hours, then the social optimum is attained when $pF(X) - wX$ is maximized. (The definitions of the symbols are conventional.) But none of the individual pickers is concerned about the social optimum. Each is concerned with his own net gain, which we write for the ith picker:

$$pf(x_i, X) - wx_i.$$

In this notation x_i is the number of person-hours spent by the ith picker, and his individual production function, the same for all pickers, shows that his harvest depends both on his own effort (positively) and on the total effort, $X = \Sigma x_i$ (negatively). Furthermore, the individual production functions are related to the aggregate production function by

$$\sum_i f(x_i, X) = F(X).$$

It can be shown that the only function that satisfies this relation and the side-condition $f(0, X) = 0$ (no hours, no berries) is the linear one

$$f(x_i, X) = \frac{x_i}{X} F(X).$$

---

[3] If the carrying capacity of the commons is finite, the marginal productivity of cattle must approach zero rapidly after some point. In more concrete terms, the addition of one more animal to the herd must, after some point, increase the expected number of premature deaths by virtually unity.

THE TECHNICAL BASIS FOR DECISION MAKING

This entails that if $pF(X)/X > w$, the individual pickers will spend more time, and additional pickers will be attracted to the field. If the inequality is reversed, usage will shrink. Equilibrium requires exact equality. The equilibrium condition $pF(X)/X = w$ is sufficient to determine X (at a level that is greater than the social optimum), but the x_i remain indeterminate, just as in ordinary competitive models with constant returns to scale.[1]

An immediate moral to be drawn from this simple case is that the frequent and natural assumption—that the aggregate yield from a common property resource depends only on the aggregate use made of it—is very stringent. In particular, it entails that each user's production function has strictly constant returns to scale.

It is well known that the users of the common property resource can be induced to use it to an optimal extent by imposing either a user charge on their labor or a royalty on their harvests. The appropriate user charge in this case is

price x [average product − marginal product]

per person-hour, both products computed from $F(X)$. The corresponding royalty is

price x [1 − elasticity of $F(X)$]

per bushel. The two instruments lead to identical results because of the postulated rigidity of the individual production functions. Whichever device is used, the level of the unit impost that maximizes the net social product also maximizes the aggregate of fees collected. In fact, the two are the same: the optimal charge simply imputes the total net product as rent on the common property resource.

If institutional arrangements permit fairly frequent revision of the royalty rate or user charge, the socially optimal rates can be found by trial and error even if the production function, $F(X)$, is not known.

There are, I think, some real situations—not only berry picking—to which this formulation applies. To be sure, there are few or no produc-

---

[1] I believe that this formulation is the same as Cheung's fishery model (1), but he purports to determine the x_i. The divergence arises from the fact that in Cheung's version each user regards all alien x_i as fixed when choosing his own value (a Chamberlinian assumption), while in mine, each user simply disregards the effect of his choice on the aggregate. Cheung's assumption is more appropriate for small-group problems, mine for large.

tion processes in which a common property resource is combined with only a single private resource, but some consumption processes, particularly recreational ones, are like that. Besides, this model does not really depend on the singleness of the private resource but, rather, on the absence of possibilities for substitution among private resources. Therefore, any sufficiently rigid production situation can be analyzed by this model—in particular, any situation with fixed coefficients of production.

We must now consider the new features that appear when there are possibilities for substitution among private resources that affect the productivity of the common property resource. It will be sufficient to consider the case where there are just two privately provided resources.

Things are sophisticated enough now that instead of telling a story, I shall just set forth a formal model. Suppose, then, that there are n firms (or other users) that share a common property resource. They all produce the same product and have the same production function that uses as inputs two private resources and the common property resource. To be specific, the rate of output (or satisfaction) of the ith user is

$$f(x_{1i}, x_{2i}, X_1, X_2, Y, A).$$

In this notation, x_{1i} and x_{2i} are the amounts of the two cooperating resources employed by the ith user, X_1 and X_2 are the total amounts of those resources applied by all users, Y is the total output, and A is the amount of the common property resource. We assume that $f(\quad)$ has positive partial derivatives with respect to x_{1i}, x_{2i}, and A, and zero or negative partials with respect to the other three variables. Furthermore, we assume that $f(\quad)$ is homogeneous of first order with respect to x_{1i} and x_{2i}, so that each user operates under constant returns to scale as far as its private decisions are concerned, and is homogeneous of zeroth order with respect to X_1, X_2, Y, and A. This last assumption means that the output of the individual firm would not be affected if total usage and availability of the common property resource were increased in the same proportion. This is only a virtual condition on the functional form, of course, since by hypothesis the availability of the common property resource cannot be changed. This formulation seems to catch the essence of the fisheries type of situation (apart from long-run considerations) and many others, but it is far from general. It does represent a considerable loosening-up from the previous case, since total output is now

$$Y = \sum_i f(x_{1i}, x_{2i}, X_1, X_2, Y, A)$$

13

THE TECHNICAL BASIS FOR DECISION MAKING

and depends on the distribution of inputs among firms as well as on their total.

The common property resource is most efficiently utilized when $pY - w_1X_1 - w_2X_2$ is as great as possible. The uninstructed, independent decisions of the users will not attain this result since each user, quite sensibly, ignores the effect of his decisions on the aggregate arguments. But, as is well known, properly chosen royalties and use charges (r, c_1, c_2, say) can guide the individual users to the social optimum. By straightforward algebra, one such schedule is found to be

$$r = p \frac{\sum_i \frac{\partial f^i}{\partial Y}}{\sum_i \frac{\partial f^i}{\partial Y} - 1}$$

$$c_1 = -(p - r) \sum_i \frac{\partial f^i}{\partial X_1}$$

$$c_2 = -(p - r) \sum_i \frac{\partial f^i}{\partial X_2}$$

where the symbol f^i indicates that the partial derivative is to be evaluated with the variables for the ith user at their optimal values.

There are actually more instrument variables in this solution than are needed. The royalty can be set at any desired level less than p (including zero), and the input charges can be adjusted according to a rather messy formula to take up the slack. The formula given is the simplest one mathematically, though not necessarily administratively. Though the use of a royalty is optional and the rate somewhat arbitrary, the charges for the use of complementary inputs are not. They must be set in proportion to the relative marginal damage inflicted on the common property resource, damage being measured in terms of its ability to support production.

Whichever optimal schedule of royalties and user charges is used, it turns out that the total collections just absorb the total net value produced, as a consequence of the homogeneity assumptions. Therefore, maximizing collections or rents is equivalent to maximizing net social product. In contrast to the previous, simpler case, there are now so many variables that it does not seem conceivable that the social optimum can be found by trial and error. Pretty fair estimates of the production technology and of the effects of the externality variables are needed for setting the appropriate charges.

14

ROBERT DORFMAN

Institutionally, this setup corresponds to some real situations but ignores some important possibilities. In terms of our catalog of possible modes of interaction, the cases of pure congestion and of removal of valuable ingredients from the common property resource are covered, with Y as the predominant or sole carrier of the interactions.[5] The case of the insertion of noxious ingredients is also covered to the extent that the quantities introduced are fully determined by the quantities of cooperating factors used. This rules out the possibility of end-of-pipe treatment, which is an important possibility in practice. The range of applicability of this formulation is pretty much the same as that of the various process weight formulas used for environmental regulation.

It should be noted that the production function on which this formulation is based,

$$f(x_{1i}, x_{2i}, X_1, X_2, Y, A),$$

contains three classes of variables: privately determined variables (x_{1i} and x_{2i}), externality-carriers (X_1, X_2, Y), and the quantity of the common property resource or public good (A). The privately determined variables are chosen so as to maximize the attainment of private objectives. The externality-carriers are by-products or functions of the privately determined variables and are not independently determined. The amount of the common property resource is determined exogenously to the system.

This classification is characteristic of a much wider range of externality or public goods problems and displays the way in which the generation of externalities interacts with the available quantities of shared resources.

The approach just illustrated can be generalized, on a formal level, to incorporate the possibility of end-of-pipe treatment. One need only write the basic production function as

$$f(x_{1i}, x_{2i}, u_i, U, Y, A),$$

[5] Here I should make explicit some terminological distinctions that help to keep thinking straight. Some goods have the property that their production or use creates externalities. I call these *externality-conveyors* or *externality-carriers*, and distinguish them from *externalities* per se. Thus gasoline is an externality-carrier; the associated externalities are the increase in average travel time and the smarting eyes, bronchial complaints, and so on caused by the widespread use of gasoline. An externality-conveyor is also distinguished from the medium or common property resource through which it conveys, just as a ship is distinguished from an ocean.

15

THE TECHNICAL BASIS FOR DECISION MAKING

where u_i (perhaps a vector) measures the impact of the ith user on the common property resource and U is the sum or some other symmetric function of the u_i. The previous formulation is a special case of this one. Straightforward mathematics will disclose the optimal levels of all variables as well as the scheme of royalties and charges that will induce the users to select those optimal levels. There are no surprises or new insights to be found by so doing, and I shall not go through the formalities. Besides, when waste treatment comes into the picture, the assumption of constant returns to scale becomes especially unpalatable since increasing returns are a notorious feature of treatment plants of nearly all types. In short, we are now reaching the level of abstraction at which it seems best to turn back to ad hoc, special-purpose models that take advantage of the special features of special situations.

Let me call attention to the fact that all the models I have analyzed are stationary equilibrium models. They do not apply at all to the oil-pool kind of problem or any problem in which resource exhaustion is a significant feature. They apply to fisheries-type problems only to the extent that depletion of the breeding stock can be ignored. To contend with problems of those classes, it is necessary to introduce considerations derived from capital theory.

The most elegant treatments that I know of the economics of depletable resources are those of Hotelling (6) and Weinstein and Zeckhauser (10). Neither, unfortunately, deals with the common-pool aspect of the problem. In the following, I use a simplification of the Weinstein-Zeckhauser analysis as a point of departure.

Consider an oil pool with multiple users. At any moment there are S barrels of oil in the pool. The total cost of extracting oil at the rate of y barrels per year is $C(y, S)$, and, for given y, increases as the underground stock is drawn down. In fact, I want it to increase so rapidly that it climbs toward infinity while there is still some oil left. This device is not only realistic; it frees us from having to worry about terminal constraints on the total amount to be withdrawn over time.

On the demand side, we assume that the demand curve for oil from this pool is constant over time. The area under the demand curve to the left of the current rate of withdrawal is $D(y)$, and this represents the gross social value of that rate of withdrawal. The current price at any moment is then $p = D'(y)$.

At any moment the rate of net social benefit from the operation of the pool is $D(y) - C(y, S)$. Therefore, using a discount rate of r, the optimal time-path of withdrawals is the one that maximizes

16

ROBERT DORFMAN

$$\int_0^\infty e^{-rt}\,[D(y) - C(y, S)]\,dt,$$

taking account of the fact that each moment's withdrawal reduces the stock in the pool—$dS/dt = -y$—and therefore increases the cost of extraction forever in the future. This is a standard control theory problem. The necessary condition for an optimal time-path is that there exist a shadow-price variable, $u(t)$, such that at every moment when $y > 0$

$$p - C_1(y, S) - u(t) = 0$$

and

$$\frac{du}{dt} - ru = C_2(y, S).$$

These laws of motion determine the time-paths of y, S, p, and u when oil is extracted at the socially optimal rate. The first of them identifies the shadow-price with the marginal net profit per barrel. The second shows how the marginal net profit changes over time as the stock of oil is drawn down. In fact, integrating the second law, it can be seen that

$$u(t) = -\int_t^\infty e^{-r(z-t)} C_2(y, S)\,dz,$$

which is the present value at time t of the marginal increases in extraction costs over all time entailed by a marginal increase in the rate of output at time t.

So far we have not even mentioned the common-pool aspect of the problem which is our main concern, but we can do so now. The individual oil well operator is motivated by the value of $u(t)$ at present and in the future. If $u(t)$ is increasing faster than the rate of interest, he can maximize his wealth by not extracting oil now, but waiting until the future when it will be more profitable to do so. Contrariwise, if the rate of interest is greater than the rate of growth of $u(t)$, he is best advised to withdraw all he can right now and invest the net proceeds at the current rate of interest (the individual owner ignores the future increase in costs that he imposes on everyone by drawing down S). He will be induced to extract a positive finite quantity only when the marginal profitability of withdrawals grows at a rate just equal to the current rate of interest. The proper inducement can be provided by imposing a unit withdrawal tax or royalty equal to $u(t)$. Then the after-tax net marginal

17

profits will grow at the rate r, and the operators will be content to withdraw oil at the socially optimal rate.

Thus the oil-pool problem leads to the same kind of conclusion that we reached in the static cases. The charges that induce efficient individual behavior are those that absorb the total net rent attainable from using the common property resource, and are maximized when those net rents are maximized. Similar conclusions apply to the somewhat more complicated problems of partially depletable resources, as in the fisheries case.

All the preceding models were symmetric: all the participants were similarly placed and suffered reciprocally from each other's use of the common property resource. We turn now to asymmetric problems—those in which some users impose external costs on others while receiving none (or very different ones) in return. The asymmetry introduces a range of new, intriguing, and very difficult problems, namely those relating to equity and distributional considerations.

Distributional considerations are not entirely absent from the symmetric-use problems, of course. In the foregoing cases we simply took it for granted that the proceeds of the charges, royalties, or whatnot were redistributed to the users of the common property resource in such a way that all benefited, which is not difficult to achieve since those charges enhance the productivity of the resource. The formula for redistribution can give rise to lively disagreement, the more vociferous in proportion as the situation departs from exact symmetry. For symmetry is a powerful solvent of disagreements; people tend to sympathize with the claims and problems of others in proportion as they are in the same situation. Now we must confront the kind of problem that arises when this close bond of human sympathy is stretched.

There is another marked difference between the symmetric and asymmetric cases. In the symmetric cases, all users of the common property resource suffer from uninstructed individualistic use. In fact, individualistic use is not even technologically efficient. For in those cases the common property resource is used to produce some relatively homogeneous product (which may be a particular kind of consumer satisfaction), whose total amount is actually diminished if externalities are ignored. An unambiguous improvement is achieved by imposing or inducing moderation, insofar as more is better.

The situation is otherwise in asymmetric cases. There, more downstream output can be attained only at the expense of less, or less economical, upstream output. Uninstructed use can be on the produc-

18

ROBERT DORFMAN

tion possibility frontier, and the social waste, if any, is to that extent more subtle and more difficult to measure.

The philosopher's stone for all such problems is the social welfare function, but the philosopher's stone has yet to be found. Failing that helpful aid, the fall-back position is Pareto-optimality, admittedly a modest aspiration level just because it evades questions of equity and distributional wisdom. But even Pareto-optimality is not a clearly defined test, especially in the context of common property resources. We say that a situation is Pareto-optimal if it cannot be altered without harming at least one person, but we do not say what constraints have to be honored in considering various possibilities for alteration. Suppose, for example, that if an upstream user spent $1,000 more on effluent treatment, downstream productivity would be increased by many times that amount, but that there is no socially sanctioned method by which he can be reimbursed. Is the current situation Pareto-optimal? I know of no authoritative answer to that question. The current situation does fail the compensation tests. Nevertheless, I should say that it is Pareto-optimal, because I regard social constraints as being just as genuine and immutable as physical constraints. Both kinds can change over time, and on the whole, physical constraints have proved to be more flexible than social and institutional ones. So I shall regard a situation as Pareto-optimal, even if it fails the compensation tests, if there is no socially acceptable way to compensate losers for a change that benefits others.

This brings us back to our earlier discussion of "conflict of rights." If we impose some restraint on an upstream user, we impair his recognized rights. If we compensate him by imposing a charge on downstream beneficiaries, then we are taxing them for the mere exercise of their legitimate rights. Whether we compensate or not we affront someone who is likely to be justifiably adamant about the inviolability of his rights. What should be done in such a pickle?

I have already said, in part. In individual cases the parties go to court, and the court decides, on the legalistic grounds that courts employ, whose right is genuine and whose is spurious. Economists have a role to play in such legal determinations. As Coase (2) documents, the courts often take economic costs and benefits into account in resolving conflicts of rights. Economists can therefore contribute by estimating those quantities. Fortunately for us, we do not have to make the final determination of whose benefits should preponderate over whose costs.

Once the court has decided, it may be possible to arrange compensation without infringing anyone's rights; if so, the compensation test

19

THE TECHNICAL BASIS FOR DECISION MAKING

applies. The result of this test is to maximize to all users the aggregate value of using the common property resource.

But that is not the usual or most important way to resolve conflicts of rights to the use of a common property resource. The most important way is to redefine those rights by legislative enactment. Here, for example, lie the roots of one of the arguments against the concept of effluent fees. It is said that they are "licenses to pollute," and thus confer a right that the opponents regard as altogether dubious. I desist from entering that debate, which I have mentioned only by way of illustration.

Now, an economist is well advised to avoid making pronouncements about who has the right to do what, and to whom, but he cannot evade the responsibility for offering whatever illumination economics can shed on the consequences of various allocations of rights. For example, the Federal Water Pollution Control Amendments of 1972 gave primacy to the rights of those who like unpolluted water over the rights of those who use public waters for the discharge of wastes.[6] Economic analysis has some light to shed on the wisdom of this assignment of rights.

On the other hand, this determination having been made, it is bootless to reexamine the question in the context of particular watersheds. From now on, until further notice, the right to clean water has to be regarded as an operative constraint in estimating Pareto-optimal possibilities for utilizing public waters. This means that any plan of use that impairs the quality of the water has to include adequate compensation to downstream riparians.

On these grounds, I conclude that the economist working on problems relating to common property resources need not confront the unsolvable problems of distributional equity. He can accept the inherited assignment of rights as establishing the comparative levels of welfare to which the various users of the resource are entitled and can devote himself to

---

[6] Federal Water Pollution Control Amendments is a very complicated document, and my interpretation is open to some question. The interpretation in the text is derived from the statements of congressional intent to the effect that ultimately public waters shall be returned to their unpolluted state and that, pending that happy day, no public waters shall have their qualities degraded below their current levels. The operative sections of the law, however, are much less ambitious. They require only that in the near future effluents be subjected to "best practical" treatment and that in the intermediate future "best available" treatment be applied. The phrases in quotation marks are subject to administrative definition, and nowhere does the act reconcile them with the high aspiration level of the statement of intent. It seems to be assumed that "best available" will eventually be defined in a way that is consistent with the stated goals of the act.

20

ascertaining the most efficient way to utilize the resource while respecting this constraint.

I have taken the position that the practicing economist is not equipped or obligated to adjudicate rights and equities. On the other hand, he is virtually forced to make judgments about political feasibility. The reason is that political expediency is a dominant—and proper, in my opinion—consideration in decisions concerning the use and development of common property resources. Economic analyses that lead to recommendations that flout political expediency are simply wasted, and the more skillful the analysis, the more lamentable the waste. To avoid squandering our efforts on such enterprises, we must design our analyses to recognize political constraints along with all the others. In some circumstances, at least, a decision has to be accepted as Pareto-optimal if all the possibilities that seem superior on strictly economic grounds are politically impracticable.

I have a modest proposal for incorporating political considerations. This proposal takes off from a variant of "multiobjective programming." The variation consists in considering as the outputs obtained from a common property resource, not qualitatively different commodities or services, but the contribution to the welfares of different, relatively homogeneous groups of citizens. Taking this point of view, suppose that there are a finite number of alternatives for managing some common property resource. Then we can construct a table, or matrix, with a column for each alternative and a row for each class of citizens to be considered. The entries consist in the changes in the welfares of the row citizens that would result from adopting the column alternatives. Since the various alternatives generally cost money (or real resources) and there are options as to how the financial burden is to be distributed, an additional row is needed for the joint or initially unallocated costs of the alternatives.

Such a table may disclose at once that certain alternatives are inadmissible, using the word in the usual sense that an alternative is inadmissible if there is some other one that costs no more on the joint cost row, that enhances the welfare of every group at least as much, and that enhances the welfare of some group more. This is a weak test, however, and most sensible alternatives will survive it.

To obtain a more powerful principle of discrimination, we revert to the joint cost row and recognize that these costs must be assessed against the benefiting groups in some manner, reducing their welfares thereby. Now I can state a theorem that is virtually obvious intuitively:

21

THE TECHNICAL BASIS FOR DECISION MAKING

Consider two alternatives and suppose that the sum of the group net benefit entries for Alternative No. 1 minus its joint cost is greater than the same quantity computed for Alternative No. 2. Then no matter how the joint costs of Alternative No. 2 are assessed among the beneficiaries, there will be some way of assessing the costs of Alternative No. 1 so that every group is better off with Alternative No. 1 (so assessed) than with Alternative No. 2 (so assessed).

This theorem extends immediately to any finite number of alternatives. If the sum of group net benefits minus joint costs is greater for Alternative No. 1 than for any other alternative, then no matter which other alternative is chosen and how its joint costs are allocated, there is a way to allocate the costs of Alternative No. 1 that makes every group better off.

In a sense, then, Alternative No. 1 is dominant in these circumstances. Notice that this is a restricted version of the usual compensation test, since reallocating joint costs is a restricted and somewhat devious form of compensation. Notice, more particularly, that the various allocations of welfare attainable by adopting Alternative No. 1 and allocating its costs in some manner satisfy the von Neumann-Morgenstern definition of a solution to an N-person game. So we can invoke the entire literature of N-person game theory to both justify and criticize the claim that an alternative like Alternative No. 1 of the theorems has a special plausibility and interest. I can summarize that literature by saying that von Neumann-Morgenstern solutions do have a strong intuitive attraction, but that on moderately close inspection they are not very compelling. They are, however, the most nearly satisfying solutions for such situations that anyone has proposed thus far.

Let me recall some of the characteristics of von Neumann-Morgenstern solutions that lead to this qualified advocacy. On the favorable side, we have seen that they are efficient economically in the narrow sense that the excess of total benefits over costs, to whomsoever they may accrue, is greater for outcomes in the solution than for any others. For this reason, the economist who recommends the alternative that generates the solution set is in a strong position. Whatever other alternative may be proposed, he can suggest a cost allocation based on his proposal that will confer greater net benefits on everybody. He even has something to say about how the costs of the favored alternative should be allocated—namely, so as to placate potential opponents by giving them about as much net welfare gain as they could hope to obtain by

ROBERT DORFMAN

any expedient. So the alternative chosen by this simple (and conventional) test has much to recommend it.

To see the salient weakness of the solution concept, we must recognize that neither in politics nor in game theory is unanimity required for a decision. Now, given any outcome in the solution set (that is, a management alternative together with an allocation of its joint cost), it is quite possible for there to be an outcome outside the set that is preferred by a politically effective plurality. The only rejoinder to such an objection is that there must be some other outcome in the solution set that will be preferable to the outside one from everybody's point of view. But, alas, this third outcome need not be preferred to the first one by any politically effective grouping or coalition. To restate: Any outcome in the solution set may be defeated politically by some outside outcome, but that outside outcome in turn can be defeated by some other outcome inside the set which, in its turn, may be defeated by some other outside outcome. And so on forever. Such are the caprices of lack of transitivity.

Now we have opened the door to the full richness and confusion of *N*-person game theory: coalition formation, characteristic functions, and all the rest. We shall not go through that door, however, after this glance inside. Instead, I have to point out that the application of game theory to the management of common property resources is more complicated than I may have suggested.

The two key theorems that I presented are not really applicable in that simple form to most actual common property resource problems. The reason is that those theorems, and all similar theorems, depend on the ability to make side-payments either explicitly or implicitly. In common property resource problems, under current institutional conditions, the scope for side-payments is limited to the range of choice for allocating the joint costs. If the joint costs are small or nil, there will be very little room for maneuver.[7] Besides, even if the joint costs are large in toto, the ability to allocate them strategically is confined by legal and

[7] Lest I appear to contradict the theorems, I have to mention that the proofs require the possibility of negative cost allocations in some situations, since the net benefits conferred on some group by an outcome outside the solution set may be so much greater than those conferred by the alternative generating the set that, even if that group bore none of the costs, it would still be worse off than under the outside outcome. I recently came across just such a situation. The optimal alternative happened to be disastrous for a decisive group. They had to be assigned a negative share of the costs to make it acceptable to them and, by an artful adaptation of what was legally and politically possible, this was arranged. So negative cost shares are more than a mathematical figment.

23

institutional limitations on the taxes and other instruments that have to be used.

This complication means that conventional game theory needs some modification before being applied to common property resource problems and similar problems of public decisions. The essential modification required is to recognize that, whereas in game theory as usually presented a coalition wins a specified total of resources which it can distribute among its members as it wills, in these applications a coalition wins access to a specified and limited set of distributions of individual gains, from which it can choose. In technical language, the characteristic function—conventionally denoted by $v(S)$—has to be regarded as a set of attainable distributions rather than as a simple scalar sum. This modification has been dealt with to some extent in the literature and leads to a theory similar to the familiar one, but somewhat weaker. But this it not the place to pursue so specialized a topic.

The elaboration of game theory to take account of restrictions on side-payments is intriguing intellectually but, I suspect, not very important practically. At the Environmental Systems Program we are beginning to build a small inventory of documented case studies of political decisions about environmental matters. It is still too fragmentary to permit reliable inferences, but so far we have found only a small minority of instances in which it can be suspected that limitations on side-payments prevented the adoption of an economically efficient plan, and in no instance have we found that those limitations were clearly inhibiting. Moreover, we have found that it is very difficult to ascertain just what the limitations are in any instance. The situation is analogous to that found in applications of linear programming to production problems, where ingenious and highly motivated businessmen have a tendency to discover "activities" that the more disinterested analysts do not foresee when constructing their matrices. Just so, in environmental decision problems, the people actually concerned display extraordinary resourcefulness in discovering expedients that permit the allocation of costs needed to effectuate the decision that they want. I won't go so far as to say that in practice there are no limitations on attainable cost allocations, but will say that those limits are generally so flexible that disregarding them is a fair approximation in practice.

Throughout this extensive review of analytic techniques applicable to decisions about common property resources, I have never gotten to a number of very important technical matters. It is a far cry from any of the models that I have sketched to numerical models that can be applied

24

to real decision problems by simulation or other means. The chasm is not just computational; it contains real conceptual difficulties such as how to allow for uncertainty, how to find relevant rates of discount for time streams of costs and benefits, how to value and compare benefits and costs that cannot be reduced readily to monetary equivalents. All those are respectable obstacles that must be surmounted in crossing the chasm. But I have elected to stay on the theoretical side of the gorge on the grounds that those very important issues are nonetheless one step removed from the main business of this conference, which is what principles should guide decisions about the use of common property resources after all the technical problems of gathering data and analyzing their implications have been surmounted.

REFERENCES

1. Cheung, Steven N. S. "The Structure of a Contract and the Theory of a Nonexclusive Resource," *Journal of Law and Economics*, vol. 13 (April 1970), pp. 49–70.
2. Coase, Ronald. "The Problem of Social Cost," *Journal of Law and Economics*, vol. 3 (October 1960), pp. 1–44.
3. Dales, J. H. *Pollution, Property and Prices*. Toronto: University of Toronto Press, 1968.
4. Freeman, A. Myrick, III, and Haveman, Robert H. "Clean Rhetoric and Dirty Water," *The Public Interest*, vol. 7 (Summer 1972), pp. 51–65.
5. Hardin, Garrett. "The Tragedy of the Commons," *Science*, vol. 162 (December 13, 1968), pp. 1243–48.
6. Hotelling, Harold. "The Economics of Exhaustible Resources," *Journal of Political Economy*, vol. 39 (April 1931), pp. 137–75.
7. Mishan, E. J. "Reflections on Recent Developments in the Concept of External Effects," *Canadian Journal of Economics and Political Science*, vol. 31, no. 1 (February 1965), pp. 1–34.
8. Ruff, Larry E. "The Economic Common Sense of Pollution," *The Public Interest*, vol. 5 (Spring 1970), pp. 69–85.
9. Viner, Jacob. "Cost Curves and Supply Curves," *Zeitschrift für Nationalökonomie*, 1931.
10. Weinstein, Milton C., and Zeckhauser, Richard J. "The Optimal Consumption of Depletable Natural Resources." John F. Kennedy School of Government Discussion Paper No. 13A. Cambridge, Mass.: Harvard University, August 1972. Processed.

25

[20]

Towards a Social Index of Environmental Quality

Robert DORFMAN

Not very long ago when we explained that economics studied the production and distribution of scarce goods, the standard example of an undoubted good that was not scarce was air. I don't know what example we would use today. Neither air, nor water, nor even the ozone layer in the stratosphere seems to qualify. Kittens, maybe.

A whole new range of scarce commodities, called "the environment", has seized public attention and entered the jurisdiction of economics. But they have not entered the marketplace, and their production, preservation, and distribution are not governed by the institutions that apply to the traditionally scarce commodities. There were precursors of the current awareness of the importance of environmental commodities – Pigou made factory smoke an economic topic nearly a century ago, and congestion was the subject of a famous controversy of the 1920's – but appreciation of the scale and pervasiveness of environmental commodities is novel.

Largely because these commodities have only recently become scarce we have not inherited institutions for managing them – for preserving them and allocating their use. We have not even inherited a proper vocabulary for thinking about them, but have to adapt a hodge-podge of concepts developed in other contexts.[1] At the moment societies are busy inventing the requisite institutions, and economists are working on the tools for analyzing the emergent social devices. The current situation is so unsettled that normal decision processes have become awkward to the point of paralysis.

Petroleum refineries are a case in point. They are notorious consumers (in the strict sense of the word) of clean air and clean water. Before those commodities became scarce, refineries were sited according to well-tested business principles: with an eye to cheap land, ample intake water, and access to transportation. Nowadays, though, the community, as custodian of the newly scarce commodities, becomes involved and, failing any established procedure for reconciling the plusses and minuses, the

[1]For example, we sometimes say that everyone consumes the same amount of a public good. But if "consumes" means "uses up", no one really consumes a public good at all.

decision process stalls. Clearly neither the old way of locating refineries nor the new one is tolerable.

I am not about to take on the large task of resolving such perplexities. New social decision processess will have to be evolved painfully. My concern in this paper is with only one ingredient, an important one, namely the factual basis. One reason, surely, that disputes about environmental decisions are so unresolvable is that we are substantially ignorant about the consequences of any alternative. One source of this ignorance is a remarkable deficiency of technical understanding – meteorological, hydrological, epidemiological, geological, ecological, and more – which an economist cannot help to overcome. But there is more to it than that. Even if the hard scientists knew the physical and biological facts there would remain an unsolved problem of social evaluation. These newly scarce commodities are now simply omitted from our economic accounts – for good reasons that have become obsolete. What was the point of including in GNP the services of 414 million acre-feet of fresh water a year at a value of zero per acre-foot? But now the unit value is no longer zero and, failing the traditional method of social evaluation in the marketplace, it is far from clear what the value is. That is the area in which I wish to probe.

There is, then, a well-recognized gap in the GNP accounts that leads to serious distortions. Under the current rules, if a factory increases its emissions of smoke, imposing increased medical and maintenance costs on its neighbors, GNP will rise; there is no off-setting entry for the reduced value of services of the atmosphere. But more important things are involved than tidying up our economic accounts. Protecting and improving the environment are undertakings of deep public concern. The official estimate is that an average of $20 billion a year (1973 dollars) will be spent during the next decade to carry out the federal laws and programs for environmental protection. The costs of local programs and requirements, and the opportunity costs of undertakings precluded for environmental reasons add more billions. In short, we are serious about conserving the newly scarce commodities.

In this circumstance there is clear need to monitor the state of the environment and to assess the results of the heavy expenses sustained on its behalf. The same sorts of data are needed to plan future programs and expenditures, to perform the function normally discharged by market prices. There is a limited budget available for environmental protection, and we do have to allocate it to the specific tasks where it will be most effective socially as well as technically. So we have to measure the social as well as the technical effects of various anti-pollution, anti-depletion, and anti-deterioration measures.

1. Some Recent Attempts

In this country the Council on Environmental Quality (as well as numerous other people and organizations) has long been alert to the importance of keeping tabs on the environment, and the history of their efforts is instructive. In their Third Annual Report (August 1972) the lead chapter was entitled "The Quest for Environmental Indices", and was devoted in large part to presenting a number of indices of national air and water quality that had been constructed under their sponsorship. We do not have to go into the methods used to construct those indices because in the next (Fourth Annual Report September, 1973) they were discontinued. Instead, in the measured prose appropriate to the annual reports of official agencies, there was a perceptive discussion of the conceptual problems that rendered the previous year's indices unsatisfactory, and a reaffirmation of intent to continue wrestling with the problem. The Fifth Annual Report (December 1974) initiates a more modest approach and one more consistent with the current state of competence. It includes a compendium of thirty statistical tables covering various aspects of the environment and the loads imposed on it, and offers a pilot effort toward a statistical abstract of environmental trends and conditions. No social or economic evaluations are attempted.

While the Americans are thus regrouping their forces, the Canadians are persisting with the construction of comprehensive environmental indices. Since the approach being followed in Canada is in the same general family as the American attempts, though with some significant differences, their work can be used to characterize the entire family.[2]

The result striven for is an array of indicators to depict the state of the environment in Canada as a whole and in individual provinces and metropolitan areas. For each geographic area there are separate indices for air quality, water quality, land quality, and miscellaneous aspects (meaning pesticide use and radioactivity), which can be combined into a comprehensive environmental quality index for the region.

Though the details vary, the basic strategy used to construct all these indices is uniform. The elementary unit of analysis is an annual (or monthly) average of physical measurements of some aspect of the environmental quality in some locality, say the annual average concentration of sulfur dioxide in the atmosphere of Ottawa. The ratio of the physical measurements to some objective or standard is then computed to obtain a specific aspect index, which is a dimensionless number. The

---

[2]The following discussion is based on Inhaber (1974). This paper reports on the work of the Federal Department of the Environment, Ottawa.

specific aspect indices are combined into a more inclusive index by computing a weighted root-mean-square, with the weights reflecting judgments of the relative importance of the different components. (Most of the American experiments used the same procedure, including root-mean-square averaging, to obtain indices of specific aspects and to average them.) Two examples will suffice.

One of the components of the air quality index is the "Index of Specific Pollutants", which is

$$I_{sp} = \sqrt{0.2I_{SO_2}^2 + 0.1I_{SPM}^2 + 0.1I_{COH}^2 + 0.2I_{CO}^2 + 0.2I_{NO_x}^2},$$

where the subscripts on the right denote sulfur dioxide, suspended particles, coefficient of haze, carbon monoxide, and nitrogen oxides, respectively. I_{SO_2}, for example, is the ratio of the observed annual average concentration of SO_2 in the atmosphere of, say, Ottawa to the prescribed atmosphetic standard.

The formula for the comprehensive index of environmental quality is

$$I_{EQI} = \sqrt{0.3I_{air}^2 + 0.3I_{water}^2 + 0.3I_{land}^2 + 0.1I_{miscellaneous}^2}.$$

Each component of this formula is constructed by averaging subcomponents, such as I_{sp}, according to the same root-mean-square procedure.

As these formulas indicate, the environmental quality indices are in all cases composites of physical measurements, with social judgments and evaluations entering only through the selection of the weights and the standards used to convert the physical averages to dimensionless numbers. These two judgments affect the index in opposite ways. Broadly speaking, the relative importance of any component is proportional to its weight and inversely proportional to the standard used in computing it. The importance–weights are *very* rough judgments; in the American trials uniform weights were used for lack of clear reason to emphasize any aspect of the environment more than any other. The Canadian weights are equally crude, as can be seen from the formulas. The standards used to convert the physical measurements to dimensionless, and formally comparable, numbers are somewhat less arbitrary. In the American formulas, the secondary standards promulgated by the Environmental Protection Agency were used; the Canadian indices, being more comprehensive, use government standards when available and expert judgment of a satisfactory norm otherwise.

The result is an arithmetic artifact that is very difficult to interpret, and that no one cares to defend very staunchly. It shares the shortcomings of all index numbers. The absolute level is admittedly arbitrary and meaningless, but the trends exhibited by a time-series or comparisons of indices for different regions can be meaningful under proper conditions. If the components all point in pretty much the same direction, then the index constructed from them is meaningful, and the relative weights, the comparison standards, and even the formula used for averaging are all inconsequential details. If the component-by-component comparisons diverge substantially, then the weighting scheme and other technical details determine the comparative standing of the combined indices, but in that circumstance the usefulness of calculating any index at all is questionable. Sudbury has a higher SO_2 index than Ottawa while Ottawa has a higher particulate index than Sudbury; no mathematical formula can determine which city suffers more from air pollution (cet. par.) unless that formula is accepted as the definition of the degree of pollution. To put the matter starkly, an *ad hoc*, pragmatic index is either unnecessary (if all components agree) or meaningless (if they do not).

It does not appear, then, that indices of this type hold much promise for monitoring environmental trends or comparing regional conditions. Nor do such formulas appear any more suitable as guides to environmental policy. To stay with relatively proximate choices the measures that have to be taken to combat SO_2 pollution are entirely different from those that reduce NO_x. How should scarce resources be allocated between them? A mechanical formula is no guide, unless, of course, the social goal is simply to reduce the reading of the official pollution index. Since, in fact, if an index becomes official it is likely to become the measure of achievement employed by government bureaus and chambers of commerce, adopting such an index entails real dangers; the formula may usurp social judgment of the relative importance of the different components.

2. An Alternative Proposal

The upshot of the foregoing review is that a meaningful environmental quality index cannot be fabricated out of physical first-principles and a snippet of social judgment. The task is far more difficult than that. I cannot perform it, but I can suggest where to begin.

Because the environment is too big to be studied as a whole, it must be divided into segments. The approach discussed above divided it into physical components, but it seems more appropriate for purposes of social evaluation to divide it into areas of human concern. Three broad areas seem to provide a fruitful basis for division: commercial and industrial productiveness, healthfulness, and amenities. We may aspire to indices of environmental quality from each of these points of view; it does not seem reasonable to hope to combine them.

The productiveness of the environment can be measured in ordinary economic terms. Its healthfulness can be appraised in terms of its effect on vital statistics, in particular, mortality and morbidity rates. The amenities provided by the environment are a more diverse group of effects for which there does not appear to be any natural common unit. Because there is no common metric for these broad areas of concern, any consolidation into an overall measure of the quality of the environment is inherently arbitrary and none will be proposed here.

Each of these broad areas can be subdivided along physical lines into comparatively homogeneous types of physical conditions and measurement problems. Table 1 indicates the kind of schema that results. It seems feasible to construct environmental quality indices for each of the subheadings. An overall productiveness index can be constructed by combining its components without invoking arbitrary weights, as will be explained below. Overall indices of healthfulness can be constructed similarly. Beyond that it does not seem possible to go.

The categories listed in the table are self-explanatory except for the subdivision of outdoor recreation. This subdivision reflects the repeated social choice between leaving rural areas relatively undisturbed, to be used by hikers, campers, bird-watchers, and the like, or developing them with roads, picnic areas, and other facilities to make them accessible to large numbers of casual users. This is an important family of choices, and many considerations enter.

A table such as Table 1 constitutes an implicit definition of the environment and of our concerns with it, so attention should be drawn to some of its implications. "Environment" is one of the most elastic words in the dictionary. In some usages it includes the work environment, the housing environment, and much more. All such extensions are omitted from Table 1 by design. The table concentrates on the interaction between human activities and the status of non-human, natural forces and conditions. There is no intention to derogate the importance of housing, work places, schools, streets, and the other places inhabited by people. They are simply not part of the "environment" as here construed, and belong elsewhere in our thinking and social accounting.

There is no explicit mention in the table of population trends, which is heavily featured in the tables in the CEQ Fifth Annual Report, or of trends in the discharges of pesticides and other pollutants, which both the CEQ tables and the Canadian indices incorporate. These are important data, too, and are reflected in the table through their effects on environmental productiveness, healthfulness, and the other indices. To do more would be a form of double-counting. For example, if pesticide use were to increase with sufficient control so that there were no effect on healthful-

TABLE 1

MAJOR CATEGORIES OF ENVIRONMENTAL EFFECTS.

Commercial and industrial productiveness

    1.1   Water (fresh, oceanic)
    1.2   Air
    1.3   Land and forests
    1.4   Exhaustible resources

Healthfulness

    2.1   Water (local public waters, global)
    2.2   Troposphere
    2.3   Upper atmosphere

Amenities

    3.1   Urban atmospheric conditions
    3.2   Urban outdoor recreation
    3.3   Non-urban outdoor recreation
        3.3.1   Mass recreation facilities
        3.3.2   Specialized recreation opportunities
    3.4   Integrity of nature
        3.4.1   Endangered species
        3.4.2   Natural spectacles, geological formations, etc.
        3.4.3   Wetlands, wildlife preserves, etc.

ness or the other indices, then the proposed formulation would show no deterioration of environmental quality, and properly. The motivating idea is to measure environmental quality, which is a matter of consequences, rather than causes of change.

In that same spirit, a single physical change can enter the indices in the table in several places. For example, a change in the concentration of atmospheric suspended particles may affect productiveness (item 1.2), healthfulness (item 2.2), and urban environmental amenities (item 3.1). If a change has consequences in several dimensions, each kind of consequence is accounted for separately, though the physical change itself is not recorded explicitly. As remarked above, changes in emissions and discharges of pollutants are not exhibited, though their consequences are.

Each of the categories in the table presents its individual challenges for measurement and evaluation. I shall discuss them enough to indicate the broad outlines of the approach recommended, but shall not weary us by attempting to cover every item. In every instance the aim of the index will be to measure social consequences in appropriate units rather than physical conditions. There will be no attempt to aggregate or average consequences in dissimilar units.

3. Commercial and Industrial Productiveness

The principle to be applied is that the effect of environmental conditions on commercial productiveness is measured by the difference between the net value added by a given bundle of transferrable resources in the observed environmental conditions and the value that would be added by those same resources in entirely "natural", or pristine conditions. Thus, the environmental productiveness index for any region is a comparison of its actual value of output with the value that the same resources would have yielded in a completely undeteriorated environment. This principle, of course, has to be modified in practice.

Consider the fresh water resources of a region. Their productiveness index will be built up by making an inventory of the region's lakes, rivers, and aquifers and estimating the change in the productiveness of each of them or of a representative sample. The heart of the task is to estimate the productiveness change for a single body of water.

It will not do, however, simply to study each lake or river separately and to compare the value added by the enterprises that use it with what they would have added if the water were in pristine condition. The reason is that the change in value added, so measured, depends both on the physical condition of the water and on the kinds and amounts of the resources that employ the water. An index of environmental quality should be influenced by only the first of these factors. For example, if discharges of plant nutrients reduce the dissolved oxygen concentration in a lake, we should want a measure of environmental quality to reflect this fact even though there may be no commercial use of the lake at the moment. In other words, a measure of environmental quality is conceived to measure social value or potential rather than social costs actually sustained.

For this reason, the measure of environmental quality for any body of water (or other component of the environment) has to be made with reference to some standard amount and mode of development, the same for all similar bodies in the region and for all the times to be compared. Then the first step in constructing a regional index of the productiveness of public waters is to establish a standard mode of commercial development for each class of waters (a task for an economic geographer); the second step is to estimate the effect of the water quality change on value added in these standard conditions.

The second step amounts to estimating the partial derivatives with respect to water quality of the production function of the standard mode of development. A couple of examples will indicate what is involved.

One important commercial use of water is to cool in process or exhaust streams of fluids by means of condensers, heat exchangers, and similar devices. The rate at which an industrial process can be operated is often limited by the rate at which undesired heat can be removed. The rate at which a heat exchanger of given design can remove heat (in, say, BTU per hour) is very close to proportional to the difference in temperature between the heat-source and the intake-water. For example, assuming a 400° heat-source, a 60° stream can remove 3% more heat per hour than a 70° stream. Each degree of increase in the temperature of a stream or lake therefore reduces by an easily calculable amount the rate at which industrial processes that use it for cooling can be operated. The reduction in the rate of value added per degree of increase in water temperature can therefore be computed.[1]

Things are not always, or often, that simple. Another important commercial use of public waters is fishing and shellfish culture. The size of the catch to be expected from a given level of fishing effort depends on, among other things, the temperature of the water, dissolved oxygen concentration, acidity, turbidity, salinity, and concentrations of a number of trace chemicals. Furthermore, the relationships are complex and, in spite of a great deal of research, not well enough understood to permit the kind of calculation just sketched for cooling water. Yet that is the kind of calculation that has to be made, not merely to construct environmental quality indices, but more basically to guide our management of water resources. Even at present enough is known about the environmental requirements of water life so that the various specialized research results can be pieced together into a useable estimate of a fisheries production function in which the principal dimensions of water quality enter as arguments.

To generalize: for each significant commercial use of public waters the productiveness of a standard level of cooperating resources has to be estimated as a function of the relevant physical dimensions of water quality. A meaningful index of environmental quality, for either a single body of water or all the public waters in a region, would then be the ratio between the value added under observed water quality conditions and that added under pristine conditions, expressed as a percentage of the pristine yield.

The first two components of the productiveness index relate primarily to pollution, the second two to exhaustion and depletion. Nevertheless, the same general kind of indices can be computed for all. The productive-

[1]This calculation makes no pretense to high precision. Heat-exchanger design and other aspects of operation can be adapted to the temperature of the intake-water, thus moderating the effects of changes in temperature. The basic heat-removal efficiency principles are as stated, however.

ness of agricultural land is reduced by some atmospheric pollutants, particularly sulfates and sulfur dioxide; that environmental cost is part of the air productiveness index. Agricultural productiveness is also reduced by soil erosion and by the depletion of plant nutrients. These effects belong in the productiveness index for land and forests. Forestry yields are also reduced by over-cutting. This effect can be estimated by comparing the annual economic yield of the forest as it now stands with a norm that is an estimate of the economic yield that could have been obtained if the forest had been cropped from the beginning so as to maintain its yield. A similar comparison applies to minerals and other exhaustible resources.

Thus the same general approach applies to appraising the productiveness of all components of the environment. Whether it be for the air, agricultural land, forests, or mineral resources, the relevant measure is a comparison of the annual value added by some standard level of economic effort under observed environmental conditions, with what would have been added under pristine conditions. A comprehensive index of environmental productiveness can be constructed either by summing the reductions resulting from the deterioration of the different components of the environment, or by averaging the separate indices of percentage loss, using the values added under pristine conditions as weights.[4]

4. Healthfulness

In principle, indices of the healthfulness of the environment can be constructed in much the same way, though not in terms of dollars and cents. The health costs of environmental deterioration can be measured by the mortality and morbidity experienced by a standardized population (standardized with respect to age distribution, sex, racial composition, etc.) under observed environmental conditions as compared with the same experience under pristine conditions. Table 1 suggests that separate healthfulness indices be computed for public waters, the lower atmosphere, and the upper atmosphere. Further distinctions might be made, as among urban, suburban, and rural conditions.

Though the principle is simple, the task is formidable and currently appears to be beyond our capability in spite of a vast amount of research on the effect of environmental conditions on human health. The current

---

[4] It seems a reasonable approximation to regard the deterioration or exhaustion of the different components of the environment as acting additively.

lack of indicators of environmental healthfulness does not indicate that they cannot be constructed; the literature that I have found deals with bits and pieces and nowhere attempts to put them together. Perhaps the best single survey of the subject is the National Academy of Sciences report (1974) *Health Effects of Air Pollutants.* This report reviews separately the health effects of carbon monoxide, nitrogen oxides, photochemical oxidants and ozone, airborne particles and sulfur oxides, and concludes with a brief digest (11 pages) of laboratory experiments in which the effects of pairs of pollutants were observed and compared with the effects of the pollutants in isolation. Instances of synergism, antagonism, and simple additivity were all observed. In the end it was concluded that the interactions among pollutants and other variables in real-life atmospheres are too complicated to permit reliable extrapolation from controlled laboratory experiments. The authors of the report did not find, or at least did not cite, any epidemiological studies of the effects of pollutants in combination. There are some well-known synergisms, for example that between sulfur dioxide and suspended particulates. Apart from them, simple additivity of effects appears to be an adequate working approximation. It seems therefore entirely feasible to construct comprehensive indices of environmental healthfulness by assembling the many studies that have been made of the effects of individual pollutants.

I should not, however, pass over the difficulties of estimating the health effects of individual pollutants, the subarea in which most relevant research has been done. Two kinds of effect have to be distinguished: acute effects, which are shown by abrupt increases in daily mortality and morbidity during episodes of exceptionally high pollution (counterbalanced by subnormal mortality and morbidity when the air is exceptionally clean), and chronic effects, which result in regularly higher death and illness rates in populations exposed to relatively high levels of pollution for long periods of time.

Acute effects have been observed frequently and measured occasionally. The type of data available is exemplified by a study by Buechley et al. (1973).[5] They compared the number of deaths in the New York–New Jersey metropolitan area on each day of the period 1962–1966 with the atmospheric concentration of SO_2 on that day and certain other atmospheric data. After allowing for the effects of other pollutants and temperature they found a close relationship between the number of deaths on each day and the logarithm of the atmospheric concentration of $SO_2 (R^2 = 0.92)$. The relationship shows decreasing sensitivity to increases

---

[5]The estimates in the text are derived from a chart taken from Buechley et al. and published in a National Academy of Sciences report (1974, p. 424).

in SO_2 concentration as the concentration increases. At a concentration of 200 micrograms of SO_2 per cubic meter, which is about average for the region, the number of deaths per day increases by one per unit increase (in micrograms per cubic meter) in concentration. At a concentration of 1,200 micrograms per cubic meter, corresponding to a very bad day, the rate of increase is about a quarter that great. At least one other study confirms this general pattern – Glasser and Greenburg (1971).

Such findings of short-run effects are very suggestive but require careful interpretation to allow for peculiarities of age, socioeconomic status, and other factors in the population observed.

The effects of long periods of exposure to atmospheric pollutants are generally harder to detect. One of the frustrating aspects is that people move around a great deal and pollution concentrations vary greatly even within a single city. We therefore cannot tell from climatological data how much pollution the people who die within a given year, or who survive, have been exposed to. There are occasional exceptions. Children have comparatively small radii of operation and so can be expected to be exposed to the pollution concentrations in the neighborhoods of their homes and schools. A much cited study of second-graders in Chattanooga found that the frequency of respiratory illness rose by 0.01 cases per week per 100 children for each increase of 1 microgram per liter in the atmospheric concentration of nitrogen dioxide, up to concentrations of 150 micrograms per liter. No increase in morbidity was detected for higher concentrations.[6]

These examples suggest the kind of data one has to work with. The studies leave no room to doubt that death and illness rates increase with atmospheric pollution, but estimates of how fast they increase are few and far between. Even the examples cited are unreliable, for reasons I cannot go into.

There is probably no area where more work has been done and more remains to be done than the health effects of pollution, particularly atmospheric pollution. This work, focussed more than heretofore on quantitative estimates of the relation between pollution levels and mortality and morbidity rates, has to be accomplished before the construction of meaningful indices of environmental healthfulness.

Once the epidemiological research is in hand, the construction of healthfulness indices is straightforward. Two indices are needed, one for mortality and one for morbidity. A region's index for, say, mortality

[6]Computed from data in Shy et al. (1970). For further details and examples see the aforementioned National Academy of Sciences report (1974) and Lave and Seskin (1970).

would then be the death rate for a standardized population in a pristine atmosphere expressed as a percentage of the death rate for the same population exposed to the observed levels of pollutant concentrations.

No such indices have ever been computed, so one can have only unsubstantiated conjectures about what they would show. The fragmentary hints that I have seen suggest that few or no places in the country would have mortality indices of less than 85. Such data, if we had them, would help us form a more reasonable appreciation than we have at present of the seriousness of the environmental threat.

5. Amenities

The two previous categories were relatively homogeneous, and each gave rise to a natural measure of its aspect of environmental quality. In both cases the conceptual problem of scaling was simplified by being able to appeal to a comparison between actual and reasonably well-defined ideal conditions. None of these facilitating circumstances apply to amenities. Environmental amenities are a potpourri whose ingredients range from the absence of urban noise and haze to the availability of prospects of nature's grandeur. I see no way in which they can be added up and no uniform standard by which they can be assessed, let alone valued.

The amenity aspect of urban atmospheric conditions can perhaps be described by the kind of index described above. For example, we could compare the percentage of clear days under actual conditions with the percentage under pristine conditions in the same locality. That device, though, does not avail for recreational amenities or for the vitality of natural life.

At the moment the route already taken by the Council of Environmental Quality (1974, pp. 335–366) seems to be the only feasible one: compilation of time series to exhibit the trends in the relevant variables. The assortment of series presented, which is only preliminary and tentative, could profitably be expanded and focussed on the categories suggested in Table 1. For example, the current compilation includes only two series dealing with outdoor recreation, and both are devoted to the use of facilities rather than to availability and adequacy while neither shows any geographical detail. There are no data on the wildlife population. There are data on pesticide use, but none on fish- or bird-kills, residue concentrations, or other consequences. But it is captious to criticize the first attempt in a constructive endeavor.

6. Conclusion

The need to measure and monitor the state of the environment is widely recognized. After some forgetting, men have again come to appreciate their dependence on natural forces, and have become alarmed by realizing that now, as never before, they have the power to do irremediable harm.

The recent and current attempts to meet this need have approached the problem from a physical point of view, and have tried to describe the state of the environment in terms of formal averages of physical conditions. This approach is inherently inadequate and can be misleading. The ability of the environment to support economic activity and to contribute to the healthfulness and pleasantness of life bears no simple relation to the weight of pollutants discharged, to the ratio of pollutant concentrations to official standards, or to other physical measurements. Meaningful indicators of environmental conditions must measure directly the degree to which its ability to satisfy social needs has been impaired.

The main outlines of a system of environmental quality indices constructed from this point of view have been described. I discussed at some length the difficulties that stand in the way of constructing such a set of indices, and concluded that they could be overcome, with the possible exception of measurements of amenity values.

My intent in setting forth this proposal is twofold. First, I hope to trigger a debate about the merits of the specific set of concepts recommended, a debate from which a better set will emerge. Second I hope that the establishment of an appropriate set of concepts for describing the state of the environment will serve to focus the current extensive but diffuse research on environmental conditions. Usable indices of environmental quality are still a long way off. Their construction is impeded by the complexity of the effects of environmental conditions and by the difficulty of studying them. But also it is retarded by the lack of an integrating focus and unifying set of concepts and objectives to tie the numerous and diverse detailed researches together. The goal of constructing environmental quality indices could serve this coordinating role.

7. References

Buechley, R. W., W. B. Riggan, V. Hasselblad and J. B. Van Bruggen, 1973, SO_2 levels and perturbations in mortality; A study in the New York–New Jersey metropolis, Archives of Environmental Health 27, pp. 134–137.

Council on Environmental Quality, 1974, Fifth annual report (Government Printing Office, Washington, DC).

Glasser, M. and L. Greenburg, 1971, Air pollution, mortality, and weather; New York City; 1960–1964, Archives of Environmental Health 22, pp. 334–343.

Inhaber, H., 1974, Environmental quality: Outline for a national index for Canada, Science 186, Nov., pp. 798–805.

Lave, L. B. and E. P. Seskin, 1970, Air pollution and human health, Science 169, Aug., pp. 723–733.

National Academy of Sciences, Coordinating Committee on Air Quality Studies, 1974, Air quality and automobile emission control – vol. 2, Health effects of air pollutants, U.S. Senate Committee on Public Works Print Serial no. 93–24 (Government Printing Office, Washington, DC).

Shy, C. M., J. P. Creason, M. E. Pearlman, K. E. McClain, F. B. Benson and M. M. Young, 1970, The Chattanooga school study: Effects of community exposure to nitrogen dioxide – II, Incidence of acute respiratory illness, Journal of the Air Pollution Control Association 20, pp. 582–588.

[21]

Incidence of the Benefits and Costs
of Environmental Programs

By ROBERT DORFMAN*

This paper is concerned with the distribution among segments of the population of the benefits and costs of programs for protecting the environment. The matter is important from several points of view, including political viability and simple equity as expressed, for instance in Knut Wicksell's principle of just taxation. The paper consists of two parts. In the first we present some indications of how the benefits and costs of the current program impinge on different segments of the population classified by income level. In the second part we urge that the distribution of benefits and costs be taken into account in selecting and designing programs, and offer a suggestion for doing this.

Table 1 is a reminder of the magnitudes involved, which are far from negligible. It presents Department of Commerce estimates of the cash flows incurred for pollution control and abatement in 1972, divided according to the

TABLE 1—POLLUTION CONTROL EXPENDITURES
UNITED STATES, 1972
($ billion)

Sector	Current Account	Capital Account	Total
Households[a]	2.0	.9	3.0
Business	4.1	4.0	8.2
Government			
Federal	.9		.9
State and local	2.1		2.1
Government enterprises	1.1	3.5	4.6
Total	10.2	8.4	18.8

Note: The federal pollution abatement program was in only partial operation in 1972.
Source: Council on Environmental Quality, Sixth Annual Report, Dec. 1975, p. 526.
[a]Including increased cost of home operation.

*Harvard University.

broad sector on which the costs fall initially. It should be read with the understanding that several major components of the Federal pollution control program were just getting under way in that year.

The total outlays in 1972 amounted to about $19 billion. Nearly half consisted of costs imposed on business enterprises by various environmental protection regulations, more than two-thirds if government enterprises be included along with private businesses. The remaining third was divided about equally between costs imposed directly on households and expenditures of governments of all levels. It is anticipated that for the next ten years at least the level of expenditure will be maintained at about the level indicated for 1972.

All the costs, whatever their point of initial impact, are defrayed ultimately by households. The governmental expenditures are transmitted by increases in taxes and by reductions in governmental services of other sorts. Business expenditures are shifted to households primarily by increases in prices. Both of these processes for shifting the burden from the initial point of impact to the ultimate payer are very complicated. The requisite analyses have been made by the Public Interest Economics Center working under contract with the Environmental Protection Agency. Our interest now is not in the technique of estimating ultimate incidence, which is intricate and requires a number of questionable simplifying assumptions, but in the results, some of which are shown in Figure 1. This figure shows the cost to households of different income categories imposed by the pollution control programs operative in three years, 1972, the current year, and 1980. The cost is measured as a percentage of family income. A perfectly neutral sharing of the burden

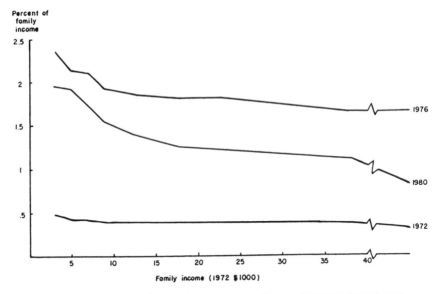

FIGURE 1. COST OF POLLUTION CONTROL PROGRAM, SELECTED YEARS, AS PERCENT OF FAMILY INCOME

Source: Public Interest Economics Center

would be represented on the graph by a straight horizontal line. The sharing in 1972 was essentially neutral. In 1976, however, and especially in 1980 the distribution of the burden is distinctly regressive.

Figure 2 gives some insight into how this comes about. It shows, for 1976, the ultimate incidence of the costs borne initially by governments and industries and also the incidence of the costs of the mobile sources or automobile program, which is the major component of the costs borne by households from the outset. The costs of the mobile sources program are seen to be strongly regressive, and the costs borne initially by industries are almost as regressive. It is unfortunate that the data do not divide the costs attributed to government expenditures according to whether those expenditures are made by the Federal or by state and local governments. The total shown has a progressive impact. If the division were made it would show

even more progressiveness for Federal expenditures and either neutrality or some regressiveness for the expenditures of state and local governments.

The benefits of pollution control programs are even more difficult to estimate either in toto or as distributed among segments of the population. We do not have to review here the diversity of the benefits of those programs, the difficulties of estimating their magnitudes, or the obscurity of their values to different segments of the population. All available estimates are open to serious question. For our purposes the most appropriate and inclusive estimates appear to be ones derivable from some surveys made by the Gallup Organization on behalf of the National Wildlife Federation, which has provided the survey results to us. In 1969 the National Wildlife Federation survey of public opinion about environmental matters included the following question: "Would you be willing to

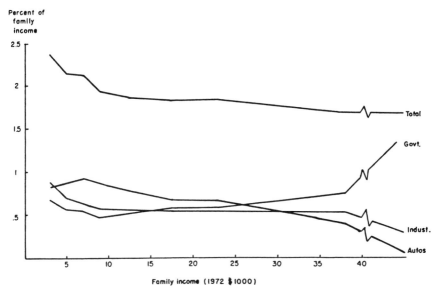

FIGURE 2. COMPONENTS OF COST OF POLLUTION CONTROL PROGRAM, 1976, AS PERCENT OF FAMILY INCOME

Source: Public Interest Economics Center

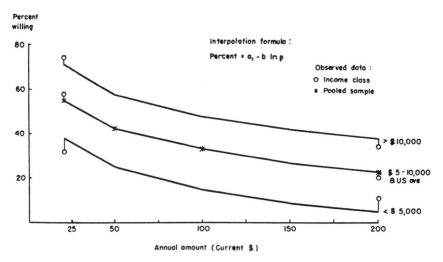

FIGURE 3. ASSERTED WILLINGNESS TO PAY FOR ENVIRONMENTAL CLEANUP, 1969 SURVEY

Source: National Wildlife Federation and interpolated data

accept a $X per year increase in your family's total expenses for the cleanup of the natural environment?'' The question was asked for $X =$ $20, $50, $100, and $200. The tabulations available show the percent willing at all four levels for the survey population as a whole, and the percent willing to pay $20 and $200 for three income ranges.

Figure 3 shows the results. The little circles show the observed percentages for the three income levels, the asterisks show the observed responses for the national sample as a whole. For no reason that we can discern the national data lie precisely on the following curve:

Percent willing $= 98 - 14.3 \ln p$.

This formula is shown as the middle curve in the figure and can be interpreted as a demand curve since it shows the proportion of the population that alleges that it would be willing to purchase a commodity called "clean natural environment" at various prices if it could do so as a matter of individual choice. According to this formula if the clean environment commodity were essentially free 98 percent of the population would buy it, and virtually no one would buy it at a price greater than $900 a year. The demand curves shown for the three income levels were calculated by assuming that they all had the same functional form and slope coefficient but different intercepts. The pooled sample curve lies so close to the curve for the middle income bracket that it is not feasible to show it separately. The main conclusion to be drawn is the unsurprising one that clean environment is a superior good and that at any stated price more people at higher income levels are willing to buy it than at lower incomes.

A similar question was asked in a survey two years later. Then respondents were asked how great a tax increase they would accept willingly to finance improvement in our natural surroundings. The responses are shown in Figure 4. The main impression is the same as that given by the earlier survey, but no simple family of curves could be found to represent the

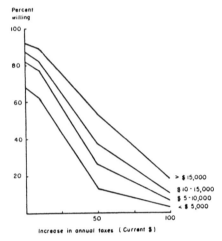

FIGURE 4. ASSERTED WILLINGNESS TO PAY TAXES FOR ENVIRONMENTAL IMPROVEMENT, 1971 SURVEY

Source: National Wildlife Federation

results. For that reason, and because the question asked in the earlier survey was more inclusive, we have used the 1969 data in our analysis.

Thus far we have seen estimates of the costs and the benefits of the national pollution control programs distributed by income classes. Now we wish to bring the two estimates together, but before doing so we should make it clear that we do not regard the computations to come as having any high degree of reliability. They are perhaps suggestive but certainly untrustworthy. Starting with the willingness to pay data for 1969 we can calculate the area under each of the "demand curves" and from that compute the average willingness to pay for families in the corresponding income bracket. The Public Interest Economic Center estimates, with the help of some interpolation, provide directly estimates of the average costs per family in each income bracket. These two sets of estimates are compared in Table 2 for the 1976 level of

TABLE 2—INCIDENCE OF BENEFITS AND COSTS OF
POLLUTION CONTROL PROGRAM, 1976
(Current dollars)

(1) Income Class	(2) Average Willingness to Pay Per Family	(3) Average Cost Share Per Family	(4) Excess Burden Per Family
>$5,710	$ 60	$121	$ 61
$5,710 –$11,410	214	205	−9
<$11,410	608	549	−59

Sources: Col. (2): Computed from demand curves fitted to National Wildlife Federation, 1969 survey. Col. (3): interpolated from estimates of Public Interest Economics Center.

expenditure.[1] According to this table which, we repeat, should be accompanied by the Surgeon General's warning, the cost of the pollution control program to middle bracket families was just about what they would be willing to pay to obtain a clean environment. Lower bracket families, on the average, were required to pay some $60 more per family than they regarded environmental cleanup as worth, while the average burden on the upper income families was about $60 less than they said they would be willing to contribute to obtain a clean environment.

It is hard to resist believing these estimates, though we should not do so. Together with other indications they suggest very strongly that the environmental protection programs entail a redistribution of income, perhaps of substantial magnitude. But redistributing income is not a proper function for the Environmental Protection Agency. Some people object vigorously to redistributing income as an incident to government programs enacted for other purposes. We cite only Wicksell and, currently, Robert Nozick. Furthermore it is bad politics and imperils the acceptability of programs that would be desirable except for their redis-

tributive side effects. Now, the amount and nature of the redistribution incidental to any government program are not unalterable. They can be changed by changing the techniques used to achieve the objectives and by changing the method of financing. For example, federal taxes are much more progressive than state and local taxes; to the extent that the program is implemented by federal activity or by state and local activity financed by federal subventions, the incidence of the costs will be correspondingly progressive. It appears desirable and sensible in planning programs —environmental as well as others—to give thought to ways of minimizing the amount of redistribution that they entail.

But redistributive effects are not symmetrical. There is no particular harm in charging some citizens less for programs than they would be willing to pay. The harm inheres in compelling some citizens to pay more for government programs than they would be willing to but for the coercive powers of the government. There also lies the political peril. So the thing to be minimized is the extent to which the government compels citizens to buy things that they do not want (at least at the price charged) rather than the aggregate amount of funds redistributed. We call this undesirable aspect of implicit redistribution "exaction," meaning by that term the total amount of the burden imposed on citizens in excess of the amount that they would be willing to pay for the program being financed. The amount of exaction entailed by the pollution abatement program cannot be estimated from the data in Table 2, but it must be considerable because the net excess burden on the families in the lowest income stratum is nearly $800 million a year.

A little example will help make this notion concrete and will bring out some of its implications. Suppose, then, that there are four towns who share a lake and contribute to polluting it. The State Pollution Control Board requires that the level of some pollutant in the lake be reduced by ten parts per million *(ppm)*. Any of the towns could achieve this goal individually by

[1]The rather strange income levels result from inflating incomes of $5,000 and $10,000 as of 1969 to 1976 price levels.

TABLE 3—FOUR POLLUTING TOWNS
(Hypothetical data)

Town	Cost Per Thousand Gallons Treated	Abatement Per Thousand Gallons Treated (.1 ppm)	Cost Per .1 ppm Abated	Willingness to Pay Per .1 ppm Abated
1	$3,000	8	$ 375	$ 80
2	4,000	10	400	40
3	3,600	6	600	120
4	4,000	4	1,000	160

treating a sufficient volume of its discharges, but the costs are widely different. The data are shown in Table 3. In Town 4, for example, the costs of treatment are $4,000 per thousand gallons and the abatement achieved is .4 *ppm*. Thus a reduction of 1 *ppm* would cost Town 4 $10,000. The data for Town 1 show that they could achieve a 1 *ppm* reduction in pollution at a cost of only $3,750. The final column shows the value that each town places on a unit of pollution abatement. The dice have been loaded in this example so that the towns that are situated where they can reduce pollution cheaply are also the towns that place least value on that achievement.

Clearly the cheapest way to reduce pollution by 10 *ppm* is to have Town 1 do the whole job. Aggregate costs will then be $37,500. But then an exaction would fall on Town 1 amounting to $29,500 ($37,500–$8,000) and they would take little comfort from the knowledge that the other three towns were receiving unpaid-for benefits of $4,000, $12,000, and $16,000. Indeed, that method of reducing pollution in the lake might seem to them, and to the courts, to be intolerably unfair.

A little arithmetic will show how very unfair that method of pollution abatement is. If Town 1 were permitted to treat five gallons less, the exaction levied on it would decline by $15, provided that some other town made up the deficiency in treatment. Town 2 could make up the deficiency by treating four gallons, at a cost of $16. This would not constitute an exaction from Town 2 but would only reduce their

unpaid-for benefits. Total exactions would thereby be reduced by $15, but at the cost of increasing the aggregate costs of water treatment by $1. In short, it would cost $1 to reduce exactions by $15.

At this point an essential issue arises. Any sensible economist will ask: If exactions are to be reduced by $15, wouldn't it be better simply to have Town 2 pay Town 1 $15 (or $15.50) instead of spending $16 on its own, less efficient, treatment facilities? We are now looking at the Achille's heel of all compensation arguments. That certainly would be better if the compensatory payment could be arranged, and in this little example it is easy to think of suitable institutional arrangements. But in fact, there are often virtually insurmountable obstacles to arranging compensatory payments, particularly if the groups involved are not legal entities, as is frequently the case. If compensation cannot be arranged, then to have Town 1 sustain the entire burden is no more justifiable than any other social change in which the losers are not compensated though they could be. It is Pareto-efficient for Town 1 to sustain the entire burden; it is also Pareto-efficient to have some of the other towns share. Which is desirable socially depends on the relative evaluation placed on expending resources and imposing exactions, or perhaps merely on where you happen to live.

If a $15 reduction in exactions is deemed to be worth $1 or more in resource cost, then it will be advantageous to have Town 2 join in treatment up to the point where its treatment costs are as great as the benefits that it derives from the reduction in abatement, after which Town 2 will also be subject to exactions. At this point Town 3 could join in, reducing exactions further but increasing economic resource costs.

This reasoning is traced through completely in Figure 5, which shows the entire tradeoff diagram between resources costs and exactions. At the left-end all treatment is done by Town 1 at a cost of $37,500 and an exaction of $29,500. At each corner a new town joins in, reducing exactions and increasing economic costs. At the

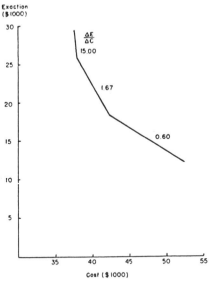

FIGURE 5. FOUR POLLUTING TOWNS,
COST-EXACTION TRADEOFF

found by an adaptation of the linear program-ming algorithm. The procedure is to start with a guess as to which segments of the population will suffer exactions and which will not. Then solve the linear programming problem in which the objective is to minimize total exaction from the designated segments and the constraints are the usual ones plus the requirements that no exactions be imposed on the protected segments and that exactions from the designated segments be non-negative.

The resulting solution gives the minimum possible exaction from the designated segments, and the corresponding cost. But the initial guess might well be in error. This can be detected by inspecting the dual variables for the constraints. If, for example, the dual variable for any of the protected segments is greater than unity, that segment should be added to the exacted-from set. The reasoning is as follows. Suppose some protected segment has a dual variable of, say, 1.5. Then if an exaction of $1 be imposed on that segment, the exaction on the previously designated segments will fall by $1.50 and there will be a net decrease in exactions of $.50. Similar reasoning shows that if the dual variable for any of the segments exposed to exaction is greater than unity, that segment should be added to the protected set.[2]

If, therefore, any of the dual variables is greater than unity the initial guess should be revised by changing the designation of the segment with the largest dual variable, and the resulting linear programming problem should then be solved. It is an easy theorem that eventually a set of exacted-from segments will be found for which none of the dual variables exceeds unity, and that such a division of the population into exacted-from segments and pro-tected segments corresponds to the minimum possible exaction. Once the minimum has been found, the tradeoff frontier can be traced by parametric programming. If the situation is

right-end all four towns treat. Exactions are then as low as possible, namely $12,250, but costs have risen to $52,250. Every point on this frontier is Pareto-efficient. Which should be chosen depends on the relative evaluations placed on economic efficiency and equity in this sense.

This example is so simple that the minimum possible exaction and the entire cost-exaction frontier where institutional circumstances pre-clude compensatory arrangements were dis-covered by commonsense reasoning. In general, this will not be possible. However, if the necessary data or estimates are available it is scarcely more difficult to calculate the minimum possible exaction or the cost-exaction tradeoffs than it is to make the conventional estimates of minimum cost or the benefit-cost ratio. If the situation permits the cost-minimizing plan to be found by linear programming, then the exaction-minimizing plan and the tradeoff frontier can be

[2] An obvious generalization applies if the groups are not of equal weight or importance.

such that linear programming will not suffice for the basic problem, the computations are more difficult but, in principle, the same.

Therefore, no significant conceptual or computational problems are introduced by taking exactions into account in designing and selecting government programs. This is fortunate because the extent of exactions is an important characteristic of any program, already taken into consideration by political leaders and moralists, but heretofore neglected by economists and program analysts, at least in their formal work. Program recommendations that flout this consideration face unnecessary difficulties in being adopted. Recommendations that avoid imposing unacceptable exactions are likely to have much better prognoses as well as being, indeed, more desirable socially.

As applied to the national pollution control program, concern for exactions together with the data previously introduced argue for relying as heavily as feasible on abatement measures whose ultimate incidence is progressive. In particular, this means emphasizing measures executed or financed by the federal government and imposing relatively stringent abatement requirements on polluting commodities and activities that are consumed by households in the upper income brackets. Unfortunately, there appears to be no way to avoid severe restrictions on automotive emissions. Any subsidy on automotive pollution control devices would only introduce a perverse incentive. It seems that we have to reconcile ourselves to highly regressive methods for reducing atmospheric pollution, and to redouble our efforts to compensate for them by using methods with progressive incidences for water pollution control.

[22]

Forty Years of Cost–Benefit Analysis

Robert Dorfman

HARVARD UNIVERSITY

I THE BEGINNINGS

This year is a triple anniversary. With great fanfare the United States is celebrating the 200th anniversary of its Declaration of Independence. With considerable solemnity but less fanfare economists all over the world are celebrating the 200th anniversary of *The Wealth of Nations*. And with almost no fanfare whatsoever benefit-cost analysts are celebrating the 40th anniversary of their craft, which had its official inception in the Flood Control Act of 1936.[1]

My paper is a contribution to this third and smallest celebration. The three events are not unrelated. A great deal has happened to the functions of democratic governments and to the nature of economic analysis in the forty years since the Flood Control Act, and these changes have had a noticeable effect on the chequered history of benefit-cost analysis. This is therefore, an opportune occasion for reappraisal. My main theme will be that all is not well with benefit-cost analysis, and never has been.

Let us go back to the beginning. The words that launched benefit-cost analysis are few and eloquent, and I cite them essentially in full:

> *Section 1*. It is hereby recognized that destructive floods upon the rivers of the United States, upsetting orderly processes and causing loss of life and property, including the erosion of lands, and impairing and obstructing navigation, highways, railroads, and other channels of commerce between the States, constitute a menace to national welfare; that it is the sense of Congress that flood control on navigable waters or their tributaries is a proper activity of the Federal Government in cooperation with the States, their political sub-divisions, and localities thereof; that investigations and improvements of rivers and other waterways, including watersheds thereof, for flood control purposes are in the interest of the general welfare; that the Federal Government should improve or participate in the improvement

---

[1] This also is the fortieth anniversary of *The General Theory*, but no one seems to be commemorating it.

of navigable waters or their tributaries, including watersheds therefore, for
flood control purposes if the benefits to whomsoever they may accrue are
in excess of the estimated costs, and if the lives and social security of
people are otherwise adversely affected. [4, Sec.1]

The operative words are 'if the benefits to whomsoever they may accrue are
in excess of the estimated costs', and that standard soon was generalised to
apply to much more than flood control projects, indeed to a wide variety of
the public investment activities of the government of the United States and
of many other governments.

There is not another word in the act about the benefit-cost standard, and
at this late date it is impossible to discern what the few words that I have
quoted were intended to accomplish. There is some reason to think that they
were intended to placate some mean-minded members of the Congress, who
feared that the flood control legislation would serve as an excuse for
squandering public monies on undertakings that were largely without merit.
If that was the purpose then the clause was successful because the act passed
both houses of Congress without difficulty. On the other hand, the intent
may have been actually to inhibit the construction of projects for which there
was not much real justification. If that was the intent, then the clause was
only partially successful. The remainder of the act dealt with some legal
technicalities and then went on to authorise by name a large number of flood
control projects costing in the aggregate some $300 million, which was a large
sum in those days. It is a portent of things to come that there is good reason
to believe that not all of the projects authorised in the later sections met the
standard so bravely announced in Section 1. It is certainly true that in the
intervening forty years many projects have been undertaken by the United
States government, with the consent of Congress, that fail to meet the
standard.

Nevertheless, it would be wrong to say that Section 1 of the Flood
Control Act of 1936 has been ineffectual. Beside creating a new branch of
economic analysis, it compelled first the Corps of Engineers and later many
other branches of the Federal Government and other governments to make
explicit estimates of the gains and losses to be expected from their proposals,
and to defend the proposals in the light of these estimates. In the nature of
the case no scores were kept, but it is beyond doubt that many thousands of
projects were scrubbed and many more were improved because of the
necessity of showing that the benefits of each project were great enough to
justify the cost, in some sense.

The passage of the Flood Control Act initiated a struggle which still
continues. On one side are the proponents of projects, on the other the

defenders of the public purse and conscience. The foci of the struggle are the words 'benefits' and 'costs', which are nowhere defined in the act — an omission that makes me suspect that the restriction was not meant entirely seriously. But it does not matter whether the restriction was serious or not; it became part of the law and commanded obedience. Project proponents began forthwith to construe 'benefits' as broadly as possible and 'costs' as narrowly as they could. The defenders responded by issuing a long series of documents — which still continues — defining those words in great detail. The most famous of those documents in the United States are the 'Green Book' of 1950 [6], Budget Bureau Circular A-47 of 1952, and Senate Document No. 97 of 1962 [7], all long since superseded. I shall not recount this history in detail. In its early years it is merely a reflection of the ingenuity exercised by project proponents in finding ways of calculating benefits and costs so as to have the benefits predominate, and of the persistence of the watchdogs in plugging loopholes and clarifying ambiguities. The story can be regarded as rather sordid, but that is not my reaction. It was, in fact, beneficial because out of those struggles came a much deepened understanding of those innocent-sounding words. It was, besides, extremely instructive because the history demonstrated and still demonstrates the inadequacy of a simple economic criterion for guiding political and social decisions. That, indeed, is the main moral that I want to derive from this reappraisal. I am not the first to notice this by any means. In fact, the recent history of benefit-cost analysis in the United States — to which I shall return below — discloses an increasing awareness of the inadequacy of the benefit-cost criterion in its original form, along with a protracted effort to improve it.

In the remainder of my paper I shall first discuss the rationale of benefit-cost analysis as originally proposed. This rationale will provide us with criteria for choosing appropriate definitions of benefits and costs and with suitable formulae for comparing them. It will also bring out some of the crucial limitations of the original concept. After that I shall discuss the recent efforts in the United States to overcome these limitations and shall advance some conjectures about developments still to come. In tracing the development of benefit-cost analysis I shall concentrate on the experience of the United States because I know that experience best and also because I believe that most of the difficulties have been encountered first in the United States and that the major evolution is going on there.

II RATIONALE OF BENEFIT-COST ANALYSIS

The most obvious justification of benefit-cost analysis is to regard the formula prescribed by the Flood Control Act as a non-technical way of expressing the Kaldor-Hicks compensation test. This is the interpretation adopted by Mishan [3] in his authoritative text. It implies, incidentally, that Congress legislated the compensation test some three years before Kaldor published his ingenious paper [1]. But I do not think that that interpretation is entirely adequate, because in practice only one-half of the compensation test is used. According to the test if two alternative policies are compared it will be found, Scitovsky's paradox aside, that the people who gain from one of them will be able to afford to overcompensate the people who prefer the other. Then the test recommends that that alternative be adopted. Benefit-cost analysis however, is used in quite a different way. A proposed project that fails to meet the benefit-cost test cannot be undertaken. On the other hand, the number of projects that meet the test at any time is likely to be greater than the number that can be initiated in the current year or other planning period for macro-economic, political, or other reasons. Therefore, projects that meet the test are not automatically adopted (as the compensation criterion would demand) but are subjected to a further screening, for which the benefit-cost analysis is also used. In other words, the selection of projects is controlled by a budget constraint, usually implicit but still effective.

I therefore recommend a different justification. To formalise the actual application of benefit-cost analysis it is necessary to conceive of an economy with at least two sectors, a government sector and a private sector. For institutional reasons economic undertakings are divided between the sectors, some kinds being reserved for the private sector and some for the public. There is not much overlap. The government's investment decisions, with which we are concerned, can then be regarded as consisting of two stages. The first is a decision about the total amount of economic resources to be devoted to public investment. This decision is made largely on macroeconomic grounds and I shall have little to say about it. When the Flood Control Act was written, the United States was in the midst of the Great Depression, and the government accordingly was anxious to invest as much as it could without flagrant waste in order to 'prime the pump'. In those circumstances the criterion in the act made excellent sense, as we shall see. Nowadays the American government, as well as many others, is constrained by concern over adding to inflationary pressures. We shall see some of the implications of this below. In all circumstances the aggregate level of government investment is strongly influenced by considerations of economic policy for which benefit-cost analysis is not well adapted.

The second stage, for which benefit-cost analysis is an appropriate tool, is the allocation of the aggregate investment budget among projects, including particularly the selection of projects to be undertaken. I shall show how benefit-cost criteria emerge under particularly simple circumstances. The same principles apply to more complicated circumstances, to which I shall allude after the basic demonstration.

To this end suppose that there is an inventory of n proposed projects, and suppose also that the investment costs and other consequences of adopting any of the projects are not affected by choices with respect to the other projects. We shall denote the amount to be invested in a typical project, the i'th, by x_i and shall assume that the amount of this investment can be chosen anywhere in the range $0 \leqslant x_i \leqslant \bar{x}_i$. In year t the beneficial results are expected to be worth $y_i(t)$ and the costs are $c_i(t)$, both being functions of x_i. Both y_i and c_i are to be estimated on the basis of a constant price level, to reflect results in terms of a uniform measure of value. Then the net benefits of the i'th project are

$$B_i(x_i) = \sum_{t=0}^{\infty} \frac{y_i(t) - c_i(t)}{(1 + \rho)^t}$$

where ρ denotes the social rate of discount. (I shall have more to say below about the social rate of discount and the estimation of y_i.) We shall assume throughout that the function B is continuous and differentiable, that its first derivative is not negative and its second derivative not positive.

In addition to the n genuine projects it is convenient to introduce a null project, to be identified by subscript 0, which consists of not laying claim to all the resources permissible. The net benefit function for the null project is assumed to be $B_0(x_0) = b_0 x_0$ where b_0 is a positive constant about which more will be said.

The problem of allocating the fixed government investment budget, say C, among the n + 1 projects can now be written as:

$$\text{maximise} \quad \sum_{i=0}^{n} B_i(x_i)$$

$$\text{subject to} \quad \sum_{i=0}^{n} x_i \leqslant C,$$

$$0 \leqslant x_i \leqslant \bar{x}_i, \qquad i = 1, \ldots, n.$$

We have now arrived at a standard convex programming problem. The necessary conditions for a set of x_i to be a solution to this problem are that there exist numbers λ and μ_i, $i = 1, \ldots, n$ such that:

$$B'_i(x_i) - \lambda - \mu_i \leqslant 0, \qquad\qquad i = 0, 1, \ldots, n, \tag{1}$$

$$x_i[B'_i(x_i) - \lambda - \mu_i] = 0 \qquad\qquad i = 0, 1, \ldots, n, \tag{2}$$

$$C - \sum_{i=0}^{n} x_i \geqslant 0, \tag{3}$$

$$\lambda[C - \sum_{i=0}^{n} x_i] = 0,$$

$$\bar{x}_i - x_i \geqslant 0, \qquad\qquad i = 1, \ldots, n,$$

$$\mu_i[\bar{x}i - x_i] = 0, \qquad\qquad i = 1, \ldots, n,$$

$$\lambda, \mu_i, x_i \geqslant 0, \qquad\qquad i = 0, 1, \ldots, n.$$

Clearly λ is the 'shadow price' associated with the aggregate investment constraint, and the μ_i are the shadow prices of the upper limits on investment in the various projects. By convention, μ_0 is defined to be 0.

The relationship between these mathematical conditions and practical benefit-cost analysis depends on the fact that $B'_i(x_i)$ is an incremental benefit-cost ratio — the rate at which benefits increase with increases in the level of investment in the i'th project. This remark has two immediate implications. The first is that benefit-cost ratios properly relate to incremental changes rather than to aggregate levels of investment. This is good advice, often enunciated and nearly as often disregarded. The only time that it is permissible to disregard this advice is when, for practical purposes, the level of investment can take only two values, 0 and $\bar{x}_i$. The second implication is that the costs in the benefit-cost ratio have to be defined as the project's drain on the constraining investment budget. This interpretation of costs is not typically followed in practical benefit-cost analyses but, nevertheless, is the only interpretation that permits such analyses to be used legitimately in selecting the combination of projects that will be most beneficial socially in the presence of a limitation on the amount of resources to be devoted to public investments.

To go further, notice that formula (1) with $i = 0$ becomes

$$B'_0(\dot{x}_0) = b_0 \leqslant \lambda$$

so that λ is surely positive and formula (3) holds with strict equality. Two cases have now to be distinguished. If $x_0 > 0$ then $\lambda = b_0$ and $B'_i(x_i) \leqslant b_0 + \mu_i$. If x_i is positive, so that there is some investment in the i'th project, then because of formula (2), formula (1) holds with strict equality and we have

$$B'_i(x_i) = b_0 + \mu_i \geqslant b_0, x_i > 0.$$

Then b_0 serves as a critical benefit-cost ratio. Only project increments for which the incremental benefit-cost ratio is at least as great as b_0 are permissible in an optimised allocation of public investment. On the other hand, if $x_i = 0$ then $\mu_i = 0$ and the formula becomes $B'_i(0) \leqslant b_0$. In words, the initial incremental benefit-cost ratio for a project that is not undertaken cannot exceed b_0.

The other case, and perhaps the more usual one, occurs when $x_0 = 0$. Then the same kind of analysis shows that λ has to be at least as great as b_0. It follows as before that for any project to be undertaken its marginal benefit-cost ratio, $B'_i(x_i)$, must be at least as great as b_0.

It should be noticed that to apply these principles it is not necessary to solve the convex programming problem formally or to compute the shadow prices explicitly. Because the constraints take such simple forms the optimal allocation can be discovered by fairly obvious trial-and-error procedures that I shall not take time to describe.

The interpretation of benefit-cost analysis just presented depends heavily on the concept of b_0, which also is closely related to one of the most hotly debated issues in the literature of benefit-cost analysis, namely the relevance of the rate of return on private investments to public investment decisions. The coefficient b_0 measures the social value per dollar of resources released by the government for use in the private sector. Its numerical value depends on the use that will be made of the released resources. To the extent that they will become net increments to current consumption it seems reasonable to value them at \$1 per dollar. To the extent that they become net increments to the kinds of investment undertaken in the private sphere it seems most reasonable to assume that they will increase the economy's annual output by an amount equal to the marginal rate of return on private investments, say r. In that event the social value per dollar of the released funds can be approximated by the present value of a perpetuity of r per year calculated at a discount rate of ρ, the social rate of discount. This present value is r/ρ. From these considerations, if we estimate that the released funds will be divided between consumption and private investment with the proportion θ going to investment, b_0 will be

$$b_0 = (1 - \theta) + \theta \frac{r}{\rho}.$$

In most circumstances it seems fair to assume that r will be greater than ρ and that θ will be between 0 and 1, inclusive. (One needn't worry about the multiplier effect of the additional consumption since it merely replaces the similar multiplier of the relinquished government investment.) The division coefficient θ will presumably depend largely on the effects of the level of government investment on the market rate of interest and on credit conditions generally. On this showing b_0 can be expected to be at least one and possibly much greater.

The rate of return on private investment thus enters the benefit-cost criterion by way of the cut-off point for acceptable incremental benefit-cost ratios rather than through the rate of discount used to convert time-streams of returns to present values. To be sure, the weight of authority in the literature tends to the opposite conclusion. The standard reasoning is that if it is possible to obtain a perpetuity of r per year by investing a marginal dollar in the private sector, it is wasteful to invest it in the public sector for a rate of return lower than r. Therefore, the government should accept only projects for which the internal rate of return is at least as great as the rate of return on private investments.

There are two troubles with that line of reasoning. First, a country can neither consume nor invest rates of return. It can consume and invest net benefits, so the objective of investment policy has to be to maximise net benefits rather than average or marginal rates of return. As Fisher emphasised long ago, the two objectives need not coincide. They do happen to coincide in the special case in which each dollar of government investment displaces a dollar of private investment ($\theta = 1$) and in which the government investment also gives rise to a perpetuity. Otherwise, ordinary Fisher-type investment analysis shows that the present value of the net benefits of a government investment project, evaluated at the social rate of discount, can very easily exceed the present value of a perpetuity of r, evaluated at the same rate of discount, even if the internal rate of return on the government project is less than r. This will normally be the case if the Fisherian 'rate of return over cost' (the rate of discount at which the government project will have the same present value as the private perpetuity purchasable for the same amount of investment) is greater than the social rate of discount.

The other difficulty with the conventional line of reasoning is that it presumes that the govenment is in a position to choose whether resources are to be invested in the public or in the private sector, i.e., in effect that $\theta = 1$. This is by no means the case. Resources relinquished by the government need not be invested at all. They can be consumed, as we have noted, and because of the possible difference between the private and social rates of discount this may be an inferior use of the resources from the social point of view. It may even be the case that government investment facilitates or stimulates private investment instead of displacing it, i.e., $\theta < 0$.

For these reasons, benefit-cost criteria in which future results are discounted at the rate of return to private investments should be regarded as dangerous short-cuts to be used only in very special circumstances if any. Despite these strictures, they are, unfortunately, used frequently.

One further implication of these formulas is worth noting. It may turn out when the maximisation problem is solved that $\lambda > b_0$. In that case, if $x_i > 0$, $B'_i(x_i) > b_0$. In words: the marginal benefit-cost ratios of the projects undertaken strictly exceed the marginal social value of the resources left at the disposal of the private sector. If that occurs, the overall government investment budget should be re-examined; it may be too stringent. On the other hand, it may not be. The benefit-cost evaluations of the individual projects of necessity exclude the macroeconomic externalities of government investments, that is, the possible effects of the level of government investment on inflationary pressures, the foreign exchange balance, and other macroeconomic conditions. Be this as it may, the value of λ is a significant datum for appraising the overall level of the government investment budget.

In the last paragraph I talked as if there were a single overall government investment constraint. This is not usually the case. More prevalently there are separate budgets for water resource developments, investments in educational facilities, environmental protection, and so on. Such a separation of budgets is essential if project appraisal is not to become impossibly unwieldy. Then each component of the budget has its own λ, and if the methods of project appraisal in the different components are reasonably comparable, then any major discrepancies among the λ's is a signal that the overall budget may be misallocated.

I have taken a bit of time to indicate the rich implications of interpreting benefit-cost analysis as a practical method for finding an optimal allocation of a government investment budget among more proposed undertakings than can be afforded at any one time. That, I believe, is the sound interpretation. But it is clear that the formula that emerges from it is not precisely the same as any that are currently in use. The main divergences of the formula that we found from conventional ones[2] are:

1. It is incremental rather than total. This conforms to much good practice and standard doctrine, but not to usual practice.
2. It employs a social rate of discount where as much authoritative

[2] There is no single conventional benefit-cost formula. Every agency of the US Government and others goes about its benefit-cost analyses in a somewhat different way from other agencies, and even within agencies the practices and definitions often vary from one analysis to another. The principles and practices employed are chronically controversial and are perpetually being revised. That is why it is so difficult to say exactly what benefit-cost analysis is.

literature recommends a private market rate of discount. United States Government practice, however, leans towards this practice.

3. It defines the cost of a project increment (the denominator of the ratio) to be its drain on the government's limited investment budget, a most unusual definition.
4. It arrives at a cut-off or critical ratio greater than unity, which is an unusual conclusion though not unprecedented in the literature.

These discrepancies appear to be a vestige of the economic conditions that obtained when benefit-cost analysis was formalised. Recall that that occurred in the midst of the Great Depression, at a time when the US Government was anxious to spend as much as it could to relieve economic distress and support the faltering economy. Benefit-cost analysis was introduced to enforce some consideration of economic prudence in this 'spend and spend' effort.

This was just the situation that I passed over too lightly in sketching the rationale of benefit-cost analysis. The aggregate cost constraint was ineffective. The coefficient of the null project, b_0, was actually negative: the rate of return on private investment was virtually zero, and resources released by the government would reduce rather than increase consumption, on Keynesian grounds. Under these conditions λ was zero and equation (1) required that every investment project undertaken be built either up to its physical limit ($x_i = \bar{x}_i$) or to the point where $B'_i(x_i) = 0$, since $\mu_i = 0$ if $x_i < \bar{x}_i$. But $B'_i(x_i) = 0$ requires that the present value of marginal gross benefits equal that of marginal costs or, if you prefer, that the marginal benefit-cost ratio be unity, where 'cost' now means the present value of all the economic costs of the project. This is a completely conventional benefit-cost formula. Thus, when benefit-cost analysis originated, logic did call for the formulae that are still standard. Conditions are very different now, but the formulae remain as a heritage from a former era. They persist, I believe, because the people who use them have had no occasion to re-examine their foundations.

I hasten to add that I am not about to recommend the criterion we have deduced for general application. It suffers from some fundamental limitations that I shall discuss presently. But before I get on to those I want to point out a few more of its consequences and implications.

In the first place, we arrived at a criterion dependent on a benefit-cost ratio only because we took account of a single aggregative resource constraint. If we had taken account of more than a single aggregative limitation, and that is frequently appropriate, we should have arrived at an entirely different form of criterion — a criterion that would have involved the entire panoply of shadow prices and the whole apparatus of maximisation under several constraints. In principle such problems are solvable and in practice they are solvable too, provided that they are well formulated. But they are vastly more difficult, not mathematically so much as organisationally. To solve an allocation problem that requires the optimal utilisation of several resources requires that all the alternative uses of those resources be specified in advance and that a great deal of data about those alternatives be assembled in a consistent, standardised format. This I believe to be an impracticable achievement for any large and dispersed bureaucracy that deals with complicated matters. In contrast, criteria based on benefit-cost ratios require only that a total resource budget and a cut-off ratio be established. With those data only, rough and ready methods can be used to identify the acceptable projects and increments. It is this administrative feasability that recommends the benefit-cost approach so strongly. But it should be kept in mind that that approach requires that only a single resource limitation be regarded as constraining.

The use of benefit-cost ratios also requires that all the benefits and all the kinds of cost considered be measured in units that can be made commensurate with the measurements of the constraining resource that appears in the denominator of the ratio. This is a very restrictive requirement and often cannot be satisfied without a great deal of artificiality and arbitrariness. In fact, the strain induced by this requirement is at the root of much of the current dissatisfaction with benefit-cost analysis, which I share.

Finally, some technical aspects should be mentioned. The less important is that the simple formulation that we analysed above is rarely applicable. It assumed that the benefit and cost streams resulting from each project considered were not affected by decisions about the other projects. This is rarely the case. An extreme, but frequent, form of interdependence arises when two or more of the alternative projects preclude one another. Less severe forms of interdependence are also common. These interdependencies complicate the formal analysis but do not affect the conclusions in any essential way.

The more severe technical complication arises from the presence of uncertainty — that is, from the circumstance that the estimates of the benefits and costs of the several projects are not precise, and ought, in all propriety, to be expressed as probability distributions rather than as numerical values. At a deep level this difficulty is insuperable, since decision-making in the face of uncertainty is no more tractable in benefit-cost analysis than in any other branch of applied economics. It is, in a way, one aspect of the problem of multiple objectives since the consequences of any decision are not properly a single scalar magnitude but, rather, a vector of probabilities. The problem of uncertainties in benefit-cost analysis has accumulated an extensive literature in which we cannot afford to become entangled. For practical purposes, practical expedients (and not very satisfactory ones) have to be employed. From here on I shall neglect this serious but specialised problem which

benefit-cost analysis shares with the rest of economics, and shall devote my
attention to the problems more peculiar to benefit-cost analysis.

III PRESENT AND FUTURE OF BENEFIT-COST ANALYSIS

To this point I have discussed the origin of benefit-cost analysis and its
development as originally conceived. That development consisted mostly in
spreading use of the method, along with gradual refinement of the definitions
of benefits and costs. In the course of my review I emphasised that the basic
formulae employed, though superficially plausible, were not grounded in any
sound theory. But I could not avoid hinting in a few places that there were
even deeper difficulties. Like the hero of a Greek tragedy, benefit-cost analysis
from its very inception and nature contained the seeds of its own destruction,
and these seeds sprouted visibly some fifteen to twenty years ago.

In one sentence: benefit-cost analysis suffered from being an economic
approach to a political problem. Economic analyses have an essential role to
play in political decisions, since economic consequences have to be taken into
account along with other considerations. The fundamental flaw was that as the
Flood Control Act was interpreted and practices developed and became en-
trenched, the results of benefit-cost analyses were presumed to be
determinative. That is, if a project's benefit-cost ratio turned out to be less
than one it was assumed that that project was precluded, no matter how
desirable it might be for reasons not incorporated in the benefit-cost calculation. This was an unfair burden and an unrealistic expectation. Sensible men
do not relinquish a project they desire just because an arithmetic requirement
is not met, when they are perfectly aware that the arithmetic ignores the considerations that are really motivating them.

Let me be a little more specific. In the United States a typical government
investment will give rise to costs diffused over the entire tax-paying population
and to benefits concentrated in the immediate vicinity of the project. That
circumstance is a frequent motivation for water resource developments, highways, and many other federal projects. In the 1930s many projects were
intended to resuscitate agriculture in the Midwest and the far West, which was
then in desperate condition economically. More recently projects have been
designed to stimulate economically backward regions. But the benefit-cost
formulas, because of the words 'to whomsoever they may accrue', do not
permit emphasising purely localised benefits. It thus became necessary, in
order to achieve the desired local stimulation, to find a way to incorporate
these effects surreptitiously. Accordingly the Corps of Engineers discovered
'secondary benefits', that is, benefits consisting of increases in employment
and business activity in the localities directly affected by the project. In

economic terminology, secondary benefits are regional employment and expenditure multipliers. Subsequently, the Federal Interagency River-Basin Committee and the Water Resources Council, which are responsible for defining admissible benefits, gave limited consent to the inclusion of secondary benefits. They approved their inclusion in the benefit-cost calculation to the extent that the economic resources involved would not otherwise have been employed so productively. This permission was qualified by the remark that the admissible secondary benefits would generally be minor. Judging from the internal evidence, the approved definition was a typical bureaucratic compromise between the promoting agencies and the Bureau of the Budget. It had the effect of largely disallowing the secondary benefits, without quite saying so.

By dint of such compromises the benefit-cost procedure remained workable for quite a while despite insistent pressures to include considerations not originally intended. After World War II, however, the nature of the investment projects to which benefit-cost analysis applied changed substantially. Beginning around 1955 the scope and diversity of government activity, including government investments, began a rapid growth. This is indicated by some gross statistics. In 1955, government consumption of goods and services, exclusive of national defence consumption, amounted to about 11½ per cent of GNP. By 1975 this had grown to over 16 per cent, implying that governmental nondefense activities were growing about 1½ times as rapidly as economic activity in general. Moreover, the character of government investments changed. Instead of emphasising assistance to agriculture and other types of economic activity, they were devoted increasingly to directly consumable outputs: recreation facilities, public housing, public health, environmental protection, and the like. Benefit-cost analysis is not nearly as well adapted to appraising the values of these new types of investment as it was to the older type. The intermediate goods and services produced by government projects appraised by benefit-cost analysis during the first twenty years or so could be valued readily and interpreted as contributions to the gross national product — such as water for agricultural irrigation, hydro-electric power, and flood protection for standing crops, livestock, and rural property. In recent years projects have been designed increasingly to provide recreational opportunities, to facilitate transportation, to enhance environmental amenities, and so on. Such project outputs are very difficult to evaluate in monetary terms and most of them are excluded from national income accounts. Nevertheless there are clearly good reasons (as well as bad ones) for undertaking such projects and the ability of benefit-cost analysis, as originally construed, to evaluate undertakings convincingly was increasingly strained. in the academic literature Arthur Maass published an authoritative paper [2] pointing out the stresses created by evaluating projects according to a criterion that did not reflect the objectives that they were intended to attain. The protests and objections from the practitioners and from Congressmen were even more vehement. In 1969 these pressures induced a thorough re-examination of the benefit-cost standard. The result was a new evaluative procedure promulgated by the Water Resources Council in 1973 [8]. This procedure, even after being watered down by compromises, constituted a radical departure.

In fact the new evaluative standards departed from time-honoured traditions in at least three significant ways. First, they formally demoted the benefit-cost calculations from their decisive role. Under the new procedures, in addition to the traditional calculation of benefits and costs, a table has to be constructed showing the beneficial and adverse affects of the proposal on the environment (not necessarily in monetary terms). In selecting projects agencies are permitted to trade off the environmental account against the benefit-cost calculation, so that a project with a benefit-cost ratio less than one can be approved if its net effect on the environment is sufficiently favourable. In addition the new procedures call for a display of the effects of a project on the economy of the region in which it is located, and one of a catch-all category called 'social well-being'. How these latter displays are to affect the project's appraisal is not made clear.

The thought underlying this change is that there is a social welfare function with at least two arguments, economic output and environmental quality. This social welfare function is admittedly unknown. Nevertheless administrators are instructed to consider the values of both arguments and to recommend a project if in their judgement no alternative promises a preferable combination of the two. The administrators are also instructed to report not only their recommendation but the benefit-cost analysis, and the summary of environmental consequences, so that Congress can exercise its own judgement on the appropriate compromise between the two kinds of national goals.

The second radical change is implicit in these instructions. It is the open admission that no single number can measure the social desirability of a project and, indeed, that no formula or formal procedure is adequate for the purpose. The final determination of the suitability of a project has to rest with the judgement — essentially a political judgement — of the administrator and the Congress, balancing the designated pair of considerations. After those admissions, it is a much smaller step to recognise that there may be n rather than only two kinds of consideration to be taken into account. There are already indications that this next step will be taken shortly.

Finally, the third critical innovation occurs in several of the non-operative, explanatory passages. It is a candid avowal that no project is likely to be good for everybody, and a refusal to restrict attention to aggregative effects as called for by the original 'whomsoever' phraseology. The recognition of individual differences is expressed most explicitly in the following passage:

> The priorities and preferences of the various individuals affected will vary and, accordingly, there will likely not be full agreement among all affected on whether certain effects are beneficial or adverse or on the relative trade-offs between objectives. [8, Sec. II-E]

Taken all together, then, the 1973 regulations mark an order of magnitude increase in political sophistication and realism. The arithmetic of benefit-costs remains primary, nominally at least, but is no longer the sole criterion of social or political desirability. The public is recognised to have diverse goals that have to be compromised among one another, and, furthermore, the public is recognised as containing disagreements within itself that also may have to be compromised. The true complexity of public investment decisions is finally reflected in the new regulations.

It is obvious that the new standards, for all their increased sophistication, are rather mushy in comparison with the neat simplicity of the established benefit-cost criterion. Their intent is to place openly on the table consideration that had to be buried surreptitiously in the original benefit-cost procedures. How this new candour and complexity will work out has yet to be seen. About five years from now, if the 1973 regulations last that long, the time will be ripe to survey decisions taken under their guidance and to appraise their effects.

For better or for worse, as I have hinted, the 1973 regulations are not likely to remain in force for very long. Less than six months after those regulations became effective, Congress instructed the President to 'make a full and complete investigation and study of principles and standards for planning and evaluating water and related resources projects' [5]. The motivation, apparently, was the feeling that more attention should have been paid to the subsidiary considerations, namely, regional economic development and social well-being. Congress being what it is, one suspects that regional economic development loomed especially large in its view. Be that as it may, the Water Resources Council went back to work and now the administration is debating a new proposal, which has not yet been made public. Although the new proposals are not yet public knowledge, enough of the preliminary thinking has leaked to indicate that more importance will be accorded to regional economic development. If so, this will be another step toward realism since regional economic benefits already receive great attention, unofficially so to speak.

So stands the current situation with respect to the use of benefit-cost analysis for water resource planning in the United States. I have reviewed it because water resource planning in the United States is where it all began forty years ago, and has since been the bell-wether of the practices for evaluating other sorts of projects and projects in other jurisdictions. New departures in this one area are very likely to spread unless they encounter unexpected difficulties.

For the future it seems inevitable to me that the stranglehold of the benefit-cost ratio will be relaxed. It has proved to be impracticable in such applications as environmental protection, public education, and public investments in health services, all of which are nowadays highly significant aspects of governmental activity. Inevitably there will be a great deal of fumbling and stumbling until we learn how to apply the so-called 'multi-objective' standards just as there was with benefit-cost analysis when it was new. Just as then, we shall learn by experience how to perform the task.

But I do not believe that multi-objective presentations will be the ultimate form of appraisal of government investment projects. At its present stage it is an invitation to *ad hoc* decisions — that is, to adopting trade-offs among objectives that are widely at variance from each other on different occasions. Some guidance for deciding on these trade-offs is surely needed and will surely be supplied when there has been sufficient experience to show what form implementable guidance should take.

Besides, as we have seen, benefit-cost analysis in its original form foundered on a built-in illogicality. The new formulation is illogical too, in a more subtle way. It presupposes a social welfare function, though economists have known for twenty years that there isn't any. I quoted above a foreshadowing of this difficulty, the recognition that the public is made up of individuals with divergent priorities and preferences. It seems very likely to me that the next radical revision will take this recognition to heart instead of merely mentioning it in passing. Analyses will then indicate which sub-groups of the population are most favoured by any proposal and which least so. This is essential information for the ultimate decision makers, sometimes pretty obvious but often obscure. Current research suggests that it will be feasible for project analysts to produce such information. The reason for optimism is that homogeneous sub-groups of a population can possess group welfare functions, simply by reason of their homogeneity, although an entire population made up of diverse groups does not possess a social welfare function.

This further step of displaying how proposed projects would affect the welfares of groups within the population instead of only their effects on different aspects of national welfare is a long way in the future. It is not entirely visionary, however. I am impressed by how faithfully the development of benefit-cost analysis thus far has followed the track of academic

Income Distribution, Welfare and Taxation

study, with a lag of ten to twenty years. Indeed, I can hardly think of any other branch of applied economics in which scholarly research has so regularly flowered into operating practice. The continuing study of the basic principles of government investment decisions is as likely to be fruitful as any other branch of economic analysis that I am acquainted with.

REFERENCES

[1] Kaldor, Nicholas, 'Welfare propositions of economics and interpersonal comparisons of utility', *Economic Journal*, 49, (September 1939) pp. 549–52.
[2] Maass, Arthur, 'Benefit-cost analysis: its relevance to public investment decisions', *Quarterly Journal of Economics*, 80, (May 1966) pp. 208–26.
[3] Mishan, E. J., *Cost-Benefit Analysis* (New York: Praeger Publishers, 1976).
[4] US Congress, Flood Control Act of 1936 (74th Congress, Public Law 738, 22 June, 1936).
[5] US Congress, Water Resources Development Act of 1974 (Public Law 93-251), Section 80 (c).
[6] US Federal Inter-Agency River Basin Committee, *Proposed Practices for Economic Analysis of River Basin Projects*, May 1950.
[7] US Senate, 'Policies, Standards and Procedures in the Formulation, Evaluation, and Review of Plans for Use and Development of Water and Related Land Resources', 87th Congress, 2nd Session, Senate Document 97, 29 May, 1962.
[8] Water Resources Council, 'Establishment of principles and standards for planning water and related land resources', *Federal Register* 38 (10 September, 1973) pp. 24778 ff.

[23]

THE LESSONS OF PESTICIDE REGULATION

Robert Dorfman

I want to make it clear from the outset that I have no particular interest in pesticides and no competence in most of the disciplines that have to be employed in studying them. I am not a farmer, agronomist, or horticulturist, nor do I have training in toxicology, oncology, or the chemistry of harmful substances. My own humble crop of tomatoes is harvested every year by some unknown bug rather than by me, and I have about given up the struggle against the magnificent crabgrass that now occupies most of my lawn.

I became involved with pesticides because I wanted to make a case study of some manageable area of environmental regulation that would reveal in concrete form the issues and problems involved. The Environmental Protection Agency (EPA) nominated pesticides so, under the sponsorship of the National Research Council (NRC), I recruited a team that included highly qualified specialists in most of the relevant disciplines. We conducted a detailed review of the kinds of decisions that had to be made and of how EPA is organized to make those decisions. In some instances, we also audited the quality of the resultant decisions.

This paper is based to a large extent on my experience as chairman of the National Research Council Committee on Pesticide Regulation. See National Academy of Sciences, Environmental Studies Board. 1980. *Regulating Pesticides*. Washington, D.C.

14   REFORM OF ENVIRONMENTAL REGULATION

A case study of pesticide regulation, of course, is a sample of only one, but I believe that it exemplifies most of the issues and problems that arise in environmental regulation of all types. All of us members of the NRC panel on pesticide regulation, whatever our home disciplines, found the experience instructive and left the committee a good deal wiser than we were when we joined it.

The legal basis for regulation is the Federal Insecticide, Fungicide, and Rodenticide Act of 1947 as substantially amended in 1964, 1975, and later, called by its few friends, FIFRA. FIFRA in its present form requires that all pesticides manufactured or imported for use in the United States be registered by the administrator of EPA, and that the registration must specify, among other things, any limitations on their use. The administrator can decline to register a pesticide if, in his judgment, the hazards of its use outweigh its benefits. He may also place restrictions on its use on the same grounds. In addition, he may suspend or cancel registrations that have already been granted if he learns that they permit chemicals or practices that generate greater hazards than can be justified by their beneficial effects. On top of all that, an amendment passed in 1972 requires the administrator to review the registrations of the some 50,000 pesticides then in use. (About 5,000 new pesticides are proposed for registration every year.) The administrator's responsibilities under this act are discharged through the Office of Pesticide Programs (OPP), which is under the jurisdiction of an assistant administrator for toxic substances and pesticide programs.

CURRENT STATE OF AFFAIRS

The task that a plethora of pesticides (1.6 billion pounds used in nearly 50,000 formulations) and current legislation have set before EPA, and OPP in particular, is awesome. Despite great effort, little progress has been made on this monumental assignment. The current status report indicates that final determinations have been reached on the usability and conditions of use of some fifty pesticides. Thousands still remain on the agenda. It is important to understand why so little has been accomplished.

It must be said that numbers like 50,000 pesticides are scare numbers, useful chiefly for calling attention to a problem. In the first place, these pesticides are compounded out of a much smaller number of active ingredients, variously estimated at 800 to 1800—still an impossible number considering the rate of progress. In the second place, there are no grounds to suspect the safety of many, if not most, of the chemicals utilized—a fact that can be verified without elaborate procedures. This fact has not expedited EPA's progress, however, because the agency has chosen (properly) to turn its attention first to the pesticides about which there are substantial grounds for concern. To understand why the review process is virtually at a standstill, one must understand what is involved in reviewing a pesticide about which there are grounds for suspicion.

EPA responded to the 1972 amendments by establishing a formalized procedure for reviewing the registration of a pesticide. The procedure is called the rebuttable presumption against registration procedure, RPAR for short. The RPAR process begins when a pesticide is placed on the review agenda. Ninety days are then permitted for assembling the requisite data on the risks and benefits associated with that pesticide and for digesting the data. But of course delays may be encountered. At the end of this period, if it appears that there is good cause to deny or limit registration, a notice (RPAR) is published in the *Federal Register.* The applicants for registration, other government agencies, and the general public then have forty-five days in which to submit evidence and briefs in rebuttal of the presumption. Next, the agency considers the responses to the RPAR and, six months after the original publication, is required to issue a document responsive to the registrants' and public's comments, either granting their justness or presenting reasons for refusing to accept them. The packet is then forwarded to the administrator or an assistant administrator for decision. When the decision has been reached, a formal notification of a proposal to regulate is published in the *Federal Register,* together with justifications and supporting documents. Thirty days are then permitted for public comment and thirty more for consideration of these comments before the final decision is reached and published.

In all, the process requires somewhat more than a year if all deadlines are met, which is not to be expected. Some proceedings begun in 1976 are still in progress. Of course, the process can be snarled by lawsuits at any time, even after its completion. The number of years and dollars required to process a single pesticide is considerable. Clearly, handling thousands of such processes is out of the question and yet, in every instance, people are involved whose legal rights must be protected.

16   REFORM OF ENVIRONMENTAL REGULATION

It should not be imagined that the lengthy process that I have just sketched is devoted entirely to shuffling legal documents. They are merely the visible tip of the iceberg underneath. A great deal of good, hard, and expensive work is done by the agency, the registrants, and the interested public. For instance, the application for registering a new compound must include reports on field trials of its efficacy, on chemical determinations and analyses of its composition and properties, and on laboratory and biological tests of its riskiness. All take time and money. The bill for the biological assay alone typically runs above $250,000. All of the other data required by the RPAR process must be laboriously assembled. EPA is not expected to perform scientific research into the properties and effects of the pesticides that it registers. But it often does perform such research (either in its own laboratories or by contract) long before the procedure begins in order that the requisite data may be available when required.

This brief sketch of the procedure followed in regulating a pesticide should make it clear that it is elaborate, time consuming, and costly. This appears to be inevitable if the safety of the public and the rights of the people concerned are to be protected. But in fact it is so solicitous of the rights of the people concerned that the public safety is not protected, as indicated by the negligible process that has been made in the past half decade toward actually conducting the review of the pesticides in use. The officials at EPA are concerned about this problem, but have not been able to devise a way to expedite the processing.

OPP has not been idle all these years. It is keenly aware of the need to systematize and simplify the procedure and has proposed an approach called generic review, which takes advantage of the fact that all pesticides are based on 1800 or fewer active ingredients. Generic review is not entirely safe since an apparently minor change in molecular structure can make a great deal of difference in effects. But it is a good deal safer than proceeding at the current negligible rate of progress.

All efforts, however, have been frustrated by two great impediments. One is the "pesticide of the month" problem. Perhaps you remember the Kepone disaster in Virginia or the outcry over 2,4,5-T in Oregon. Those are only the most notorious of incidents that occur almost monthly and that require the OPP to divert resources to contending with current emergencies. Since OPP's resources are strictly limited, these frequent diversions, imposed by scare publicity and often enforced by court orders, severely limit its ability to follow a systematic plan of review based on reasoned judgments of the importance and dangerousness of different pesticides.

The other great obstacle, though less irritating, is more fundamental. The regulation of pesticides is analogous to the solution of a huge system of simultaneous equations. The restrictions that are appropriate for any pesticide depend on the availability and effectiveness of substitutes. If, for example, the use of chlorobenzilate is restricted, the farmers can resort to any of three alternative methods of mite control at some increase in cost and a small decrease in effectiveness. What one does not know without investigation is whether or not those alternatives are any less hazardous than chlorobenzilate. Thus the benefits of regulating any one pesticide cannot be assessed without thorough study of a number of others. The same is true of the costs, since the cost of restricting the use of any pesticide is magnified if the best alternatives to it are also restricted. This consideration dictates that whole groups of pesticides should be considered simultaneously, and the members of such a group are not necessarily chemically related.

To summarize the situation thus far, the task of regulating pesticides is so immense that some systematic way to approach the problem is essential, but formidable obstacles stand in the way of devising and implementing one. I turn now to the task of reaching decisions about a particular pesticide once it has arrived at the top of the agenda. As a preface, let me recall the nature of the decision that must be made. Most pesticides are used on a variety of crops by a variety of methods in a number of different geographic regions. A few of them, like DDT and Kepone, are so very hazardous that the law clearly forbids virtually all their uses. Fortunately, few pesticides are so comprehensively hazardous. Consequently, the regulatory decision concerns which uses in which circumstances and in which geographic regions should be allowed. There is therefore a large number of alternatives to be considered rather than a simple yes or no decision. In choosing among these alternatives the risks and the benefits of each have to be compared with those of the others. This can be resolved into the usual three-fold task: estimating the risks entailed by each kind of use of the pesticide, estimating the benefits of each kind of use, and finally comparing the two.

18   REFORM OF ENVIRONMENTAL REGULATION

EVALUATION OF RISKS

In practice, the risks that must be taken into account are predominantly risks to the health of both the general public and the people who come into close contact with the pesticide at various stages of its manufacture and use. The menace of primary concern is the danger of inducing cancers or of causing harmful genetic mutations.

EPA is not expected to do any original scientific research in reaching its decisions, but it is expected to be familiar with all the research that has been done that has a bearing on the decision, and to be abreast of the current state of scientific knowledge. Its actual operation on the risk side, then, is to conduct an extensive search of the biological and medical literature and to make a well-reasoned evaluation of the reported findings, which frequently are not consistent with one another. On the other hand, an applicant for registration is required to do a substantial amount of research on the chemical, biological and toxicological properties of the formulation that he wishes to register. The results of the applicant's studies, together with the significant findings from the search of the open literature, form the basis for EPA's estimates of the risks presented by the pesticide in question.

The scientific evidence so acquired is, for all practical purposes, of two sorts: the result of laboratory experiments in which animals are exposed to the pesticide, and epidemiological data on human exposures. In the case of pesticides, epidemiological data are rare and often unsatisfactory. It is easy to see why. New pesticides must be registered before there is any human exposure. For pesticides, there is rarely a record of the extent of exposure and when there is, it is impossible to relate exposure to effects except in the most dramatic instances. This is because carcinogenic and mutagenic effects are typically latent for many years after initial exposure.

Primary reliance, therefore, is placed on the results of animal experiments, but these too are fraught with difficulties. Two difficulties figure especially large in the literature. One is the problem of extrapolating from laboratory animals to human beings. It is frequently asserted that every substance that is carcinogenic in men is also carcinogenic in some animal species. But that is not at issue. The issue is whether or not people can safely be exposed to a substance that has been found to induce malignancies in laboratory animals, or, for that matter, has not been found to do so. This is very tricky. For example, chlorobenzilate has been found to induce tumors, possibly malignant, in male mice but not in female mice and not in rats. Experienced oncologists are not surprised by such selectivity. It is believed that slight differences in the hormonal content of an organism's blood make great differences in its defenses against tumors. This fact makes it perilous to draw inferences from animal experiments though they remain the best indicator we have.

The other difficulty is a different kind of extrapolation. If a pesticide is used, people will be exposed to doses of one or two micrograms a day, and we should regard a substance as dangerous if such a dose induced cancers in perhaps one in a hundred thousand or one in a million of the people so exposed. To detect such tiny probabilities would require experiments in which at least 300,000 animals were exposed to the substance in question, even if there were no background exposure. Such large-scale experiments are out of the question. So in order to attain a probability of inducing cancer that is high enough to be observed in a reasonable sample, enormous doses are given. Typically these doses are several thousand times as great as the doses human populations are expected to experience. Thus arises the problem of how to infer from responses to gigantic doses what the responses to the tiny doses likely to be experienced in practice will be. There seems to be no generally accepted solution.

These are not the only problems with using laboratory experiments to decide whether pesticides or other substances are dangerously carcinogenic. The conduct and evaluation of laboratory experiments are more complex than a nonbiologist would expect. Several hundred animals must be kept alive for more than a year. When any animal dies, and some always do, an autopsy is required to determine whether the death is attributable to the substance being studied. If there should be a contagion—and contagions do occur with laboratory animals just as they do with any living things confined together in a small space—all is lost. At the end of the experiment, each surviving animal is sacrificed. Slides are made of a sample of its tissues and examined for detection of tumors. The interpretation of the slides is so delicate that pathologists often disagree in their interpretations. In short, the conduct of laboratory experiments introduces considerable random error even when the number of animals in the sample is large. Moreover, we are frequently concerned not with a single substance but with comparing the carcinogenic potencies of several substances, for example, a particular pesticide and its alternatives. In such cases, the importance of the various sources of estimation and measurement error is magnified.

To go further, suppose that we had a good and decisive laboratory experiment, a reliable method for extrapolating from animals to people, and a way to extrapolate from high doses to low ones. We should still need estimates of the number of people who would be exposed to different doses and for different periods of time. The people who manufacture, apply, and otherwise handle the pesticide are few, but they are relatively highly exposed. The people who ingest the foods treated with the pesticides are numerous, but they are only slightly exposed. If aerial spraying is used or if rain washes some of the pesticide into public waters, still other population groups are exposed.

There may be many distinguishable population groups, and for each of them the number of the people in the group and the dose that each member is likely to receive should be estimated. The largest group is generally the people who eat the foods treated with pesticide. To estimate the dose that each member of that group might receive, one must estimate, for example, how many people eat, let us say, oranges. One must also estimate how much of the pesticide residue remains on the food at the time it is harvested and how much survives the processing, handling, and cooking that intervenes between the harvest and the ultimate consumption. Consider chlorobenzilate again. It is used on oranges, and the residue remains on the skin of the orange rather than penetrating it. Unless one sucks the orange without washing it thoroughly, one is not likely to receive any of the pesticide. Nor will one receive any by drinking frozen orange juice made from treated fruits. But the skins of the oranges used in freezing plants and by other processers are ground up and used in cattle feed. Thus, people other than vegetarians may ingest chlorobenzilate by that indirect route. Other pesticides are transmitted to people by other routes. In general, so much depends on eating habits and methods of preparation that it is not easy to estimate either the number of people exposed or the amounts to which they are exposed.

So ends my catalogue of the difficulties to be surmounted in assessing the risks imposed by the use of any pesticide. It is a discouraging catalogue. What we should like to obtain as a result of investigation are estimates of the number of people who are likely to contract cancer from exposure to a pesticide when it is used in accordance with any of the available regulatory options. These estimates, if available, would be basic ingredients for making a choice among the alternatives. EPA tries to make those estimates and, indeed, routinely produces figures that purport to convey the desired information. Having inspected a number of such estimates and the methods used to derive them, I believe this practice is misleading and imparts an unwarranted impression of scientific certitude. This opinion is fairly widely shared. The report of the Work Group on Risk Assessment (1979:77) of the Interagency Regulatory Liaison Group asserts: "Given the present state of knowledge, the quantitative assessment of cancer risks provides only a rough estimate of the magnitude of the cancer risks which may be useful in setting priorities among carcinogens and in obtaining a very rough idea of the magnitude of the public health problem posed by a given carcinogen." In other passages it urges extreme caution in using numerical risk estimates for regulatory purposes, and there is much more testimony to the same effect.

The recommendation of the NRC committee on pesticides was to be candid about the limitations of scientific knowledge and to abstain from making extrapolations and estimates for which no sound scientific basis exists. This means, in effect, presenting the results of the laboratory experiments and any other hard data, but not indulging in any guesswork. We felt that the guesswork and the exercise of judgment for which science provides little or no foundation belongs in the province of the administrator and his senior staff, and that scientists and subordinate staff should not substitute their judgments for those of responsible officials.

EVALUATION OF BENEFITS

We turn now to the second major task to be performed in deciding on a regulation, namely, estimating the benefits of using the pesticide. In this context, the word benefits always means the benefits of using the pesticide without regulation as compared with those of using it in accordance with a proposed regulatory restriction—in other words, the benefits foregone by imposing the restriction. The task of estimating these benefits is entirely standard, so I do not have to devote much time to it.

Conceptually, the analysis of benefits rests on the notions of consumers' and producers' surpluses. For each crop on which a pesticide is used there is a demand curve and also a supply curve for each of the regulatory options that might be adopted. Concentrate for the moment on the supply curve corresponding to unregulated use of the pesticide. The point where this supply curve cuts the demand curve marks the equilibrium price and quantity under unregulated conditions. If we imagine a horizontal line drawn at the level of the equilibrium price, the area between it and the demand curve is the consumers' surplus under unregulated conditions. Similarly, the area between the horizontal line and the supply curve is the producers' surplus, and the sum of these two areas is the total social surplus from the unregulated use of the pesticide.

The effect of imposing any regulation is to raise the supply curve, which will then intercept the demand curve at a higher equilibrium price and a lower equilibrium quantity. The consumers' surplus will thereby be reduced and the producers' surplus will usually be reduced also. In some circumstances, though, the increase in price will actually increase the producers' surplus but never by enough to offset entirely the shrinkage in consumers' surplus. Thus the total social surplus will always be reduced. This decrease in the total social benefits is then the social cost of that regulatory alternative.

There is no special difficulty about estimating the demand curves. In fact, they can frequently be taken directly from marketing studies made by the Department of Agriculture. The supply curves do present some problems, for they cannot be observed directly for a number of reasons. One reason is that most agricultural products are not exchanged in freely fluctuating, competitive markets. The supply of many agricultural products is controlled by marketing orders that prevent production from expanding to the point where marginal cost is equal to price. Other agricultural products are subject to other types of output restriction designed to prevent excessive production at the established support price. In these cases, observed market behavior will not reflect the competitive response of supply to price changes.

Besides, most of the supply curves required are hypothetical, that is, they are estimates of the supply that would be forthcoming under various restrictions on the use of pesticides that have not, in fact, been experienced. As a result, the supply curves must be inferred by estimating the marginal cost curves that would correspond to the different alternative regulations under consideration. I have already mentioned that these marginal cost curves require making assumptions about the methods of pest control to which farmers would resort if use of the pesticide in question were restricted. Neither the demand curves nor these marginal cost curves can be estimated with any great precision, but they do not present any peculiar difficulties.

In actual practice, the methods of benefit estimation used by EPA are not even this elaborate. Their standard method is simply to estimate the increase in farm costs per unit of output imposed by a regulation under evaluation and to multiply this by the forecast level of output. Our studies indicate that the error introduced by using this highly simplified procedure can be safely ignored for all practical purposes.

You may have noticed that I have not even mentioned the producers' surplus that accrues to the manufacturers and distributors of the pesticide. This is invariably ignored on the grounds that any reduction in the pesticide manufacturer's profits will be roughly offset by increases in the profits of the manufacturers and distributors of the substitutes that will be used in its place.

The only other aspect of benefit estimation that should be mentioned is the time dimension. The method that I have described is strictly an application of comparative statics and consequently can yield only estimates applicable to a single year. Regulations, however, apply to the use of a pesticide for as long as it will be used if it is permitted or as long as it would have been used if it is banned. With some exceptions, the useful life of a pesticide is not very great. Most become obsolete within ten years of their date of introduction, either because they are superseded by superior formulations or because pests adapt and become immune to them. The cost of regulating a pesticide is therefore the present value, at an appropriate rate of discount, of the costs in each year of its useful life. Those costs will not be uniform but will grow gradually during the early years when it is being introduced and will wane gradually during the later years when it is being phased out. The key difficulty introduced by this consideration is that of forecasting the remaining useful life of a pesticide under review. The cost can be overestimated greatly (as can the risks) by using methods that assume implicitly that the equilibrium corresponding to any regulatory alternative will persist indefinitely.

EVALUATION OF THE OPTIONS

The third major task is to choose the preferred regulatory option in light of the estimates of risks and benefits just described. This is the payoff task and is probably the hardest one of all.

The officials responsible for the decision would like to be provided with estimates of the risks resulting from each option, reduced to monetary terms. These could easily be compared with the estimates of the monetary benefits foregone, and reaching a decision would require little more than subtracting the cost of each option from the value of the risks that it avoids and selecting the option for which the net benefits are greatest. We have already seen several reasons why this cannot easily be done. In addition to the difficulties already reviewed, reducing to monetary terms risks to life and health introduces yet another unsolvable problem: that of assigning explicit monetary values to changes in the probabilities of illness and death. I do not have to dilate upon that familiar problem. These difficulties notwithstanding, EPA's current evaluation procedures call for expressing the risks of alternatives in just those terms. I do not think, however, that the estimates made receive any more credence than they deserve.

Our review of the difficulties of risk estimation has shown that the goal of arriving at monetary estimates of the benefits and costs of a pesticide regulation, which can be compared directly, is more demanding than can be achieved. As much as that achievement would facilitate making regulatory decisions, we have to confront the fact that choosing among regulatory alternatives is a problem in multiobjective decisionmaking. At the simplest, two considerations have to be weighed: the economic costs imposed by a proposed regulation, and the resultant risks to public health. Furthermore, there is generally no reliable way to express those risks in terms of socially meaningful magnitudes such as the probable effect of the regulation on the incidence of cancers. In practice, the most that EPA can control is the amount of a pesticide discharged into different segments of the environment. How many people will then be exposed to the pesticide, how large a dose each will receive, and how many will suffer ill effects are questions to which we have no well-founded answers.

Responsible officials are then presented with impossible questions such as: Is it worthwhile to forego $5 million a year in economic benefits in order to reduce the amount of heptachlor to which a group of ten million people is exposed from an average of 0.6 to 0.4 milligrams per lifetime? The only way that I can answer such a question is to invoke another tenuous form of extrapolation. For example, we have persuasive epidemiological evidence that 2,4,5-T induces spontaneous abortions in people as well as in rats. Therefore, the finding that another pesticide is as effective an abortifacient as 2,4,5-T under laboratory conditions is fair prima facie evidence that that pesticide is unfit for unrestricted use, particularly if it is related chemically to 2,4,5-T. In general terms, the laboratory behavior of substances for which we have confirmatory evidence, epidemiological or other, can be used to calibrate and interpret the results of laboratory tests of chemicals for which there is no outside evidence. This does not make difficult decisions easy, and officials responsible for making regulatory decisions do not welcome the burdens that using such comparative data place on them.

The real decision problem is actually worse than I have portrayed it. We do not know, in fact, what the foregone benefits from any regulatory option will be. All that is available is an estimate known to be subject to a wide margin of error. For comparison with that imprecise estimate, we have an estimate of the amount of a chemical to which people will be exposed that is at least as imprecise, and impressions about the effects of those exposures that are even more vague. Thus, the estimates presented to the officials are merely sample points surrounded by billowing clouds of uncertainty. Furthermore, we have already noted that the alternatives to be compared rarely involve single population groups, which means that an alternative that reduces the amounts to which one group is exposed may increase the dosages received by one or more others. Furthermore, although effects on health are invariably the primary consideration, effects on wildlife and on ecological stability are often severe enough to be significant components of the benefits of restricting the use of a pesticide.

In short, there is nothing peculiar about the ultimate choice of an alternative for regulating a pesticide. It is a tough regulatory decision in which the administrator, subject to very general legislative guidance, must use his judgment to choose among alternatives whose consequences for good and ill differ in a number of incommensurable ways and are only vaguely foreseeable. The staff work that I have been describing tries to lighten this burden, but cannot make it very light. It assists the administrator by assembling a wide range of relevant data and using the relevant scientific disciplines to interpret them. The result is a characterization of the probable consequences of each alternative. We can think of it as a matrix with a column for each alternative, a row for each kind of consequence, and, in each cell, an entry that tells the poorest, the best, and perhaps the most probable results to be anticipated if that alternative is adopted. These are the data on which the decision must be based.

Two questions naturally arise: Is that all the guidance that all that data gathering and analysis can provide? And if so, is that elaborate, expensive and time-consuming enterprise worthwhile? I think the answers to both questions are yes. Social decisions inherently amount to judgments in which such facts as are available are brought into contact with perceptions of value that remain inchoate. The analysis helps in two indispensable ways. It informs the decisionmaker of what values are at stake and to what extent. It also systematizes the decision process by providing the decisionmaker with comparable data in a comparable format on each occasion so that it is not necessary for him to resolve the same issues afresh each time he confronts a new pesticide.

WHAT IS TO BE DONE?

Relatively few pesticides whose dangerous effects have been experienced have been regulated. A systematic review of all pesticides in use or proposed for use has been launched, but has been frustrated by formidable obstacles. The present situation is intolerable. The public is not being protected, the law is not being executed, the agency is bogged down in an impracticable task, and the pesticide industry is burdened with oppressive procedural expenses and delays from which only the lawyers benefit.

There are palliatives, some of which have been adopted already. For several years, EPA has been authorized to review the safety of active ingredients and to issue generic registrations for all pesticides that employ ingredients found to meet acceptable generic standards, and it has begun to operate on that more economical principle.

The protracted and highly legalistic procedure necessary before a registration can be denied or restricted is in urgent need of streamlining, although this will entail some weakening of the protections now provided. To require EPA to devote three or four years of effort to restraining the use of a single pesticide, or even family of pesticides, effectively prevents it from proceeding expeditiously through the long list of chemicals that await inspection. If Congress is serious about its intention that EPA review all pesticides in a reasonable period of time, then it must admit the possibility of mistakes and allow EPA to arrive at decisions with less documentation and review than is now required of it. On the one hand, the administrator should be allowed to rely on short term tests of carcinogenicity, such as the Ames Test, unless there are substantial indications that a chemical is dangerous. On the other hand, when the administrator finds that the use of a pesticide imposes excessive risks in relation to its benefits, he should be authorized to deny that use, and the applicants should be required to assume a heavy burden of proof in any review or appeal from his decision.

The procedure for selecting the chemicals to be reviewed each year should be systematized and simplified. The National Cancer Institute has adopted a useful procedure. They rely on a panel of experts, mostly from outside the institute, which nominates a short list of substances for early attention using little more information than their collective wisdom, and taking into account both the strength of the indications of dangerousness and the practical importance of a chemical as inferred from the extent to which it is likely to be used. EPA should establish such an agenda panel to select pesticides for early review. The panel should use the two criteria adopted by the NCI, plus a third. Since it is difficult to make reasoned decisions about a pesticide if the alternatives to it have not been reviewed, when a chemical is placed on the agenda for early review it should be accompanied by its close substitutes if at all possible. Deviations from the selections of the agenda panel should be rare. Chemicals should be added to their nominations only if there is direct evidence that they are harmful to humans in the dosages normally experienced.

The procedure for estimating risks is in need of simplification. The current procedure is pretentious, and requires much more work and time than the reliability of the results can justify. No more should be attempted than to place a suspect pesticide in one of four or five risk classes, ranging from substances that are known to be highly toxic to those for which no evidence of harmfulness is found. The regulatory decision for any particular pesticide would then resolve into a judgment as to how great the benefits must be in order to justify exposing the estimated number of people to a substance that is located in its risk class. If structured in this way, the difficult regulatory judgments would be greatly facilitated and could be routinized as precedents accumulate.

The foregoing suggestions are merely stopgaps intended to render an unwieldy task more manageable. They do not attack the fundamental problem, which is that in the present state of understanding, the only way to ascertain whether or not a chemical is dangerous is to try it out. The available methods for trying a chemical are inordinately expensive and time consuming, and produce results that are far from decisive. Using such methods to inspect thousands of chemicals one-by-one constitutes a task that will extend beyond any reasonable time horizon and will cost hundreds of millions of dollars. The only real solutions are either to devise a quick and simple test that is reasonably reliable or, even better, to learn how to predict from a chemical's formula how it will act in the human body. I suppose that a Nobel Prize is waiting for any organic chemist or molecular biologist who makes substantial progress in either of those directions. Certainly, it is of primary importance that EPA actively stimulate and support the basic research that must be performed before thousands of new pesticides and other toxic substances can safely be broadcast throughout the environment.

Those critical scientific breakthroughs appear to be far off. Meanwhile, we must manage. How? An economist's thoughts turn naturally to economic expedients. The one that I shall suggest follows from my previous suggestion that pesticides be classified into risk classes based upon judgmental assessment of the available evidence about them. The notion is to assess fees on the use of pesticides according to the risk classes in which the pesticides are located. The highest risk class should be reserved for pesticides that have been demonstrated to be so risky that no conceivable benefits would justify exposing any substantial population to their effects. Any member of this class should be strictly forbidden. The fee for pesticides in the next highest risk class should be high enough to preclude their use in all but the most urgent circumstances. And so on down the line to the lowest risk class, for which no fee should be charged. It would then be the user's decision whether or not the benefits of a pesticide in a high risk class were great enough to outweigh the social costs as indicated to him by the fee that he would be required to pay. Thus the present detailed evaluation of the benefits and costs of regulatory alternatives would become otiose.

The administrative problems of the plan described above would be minimal since the fees could be collected at the manufacturing level. There is one great difficulty, but it is a concentrated one. Four or five fees would have to be established, and these fees would represent those difficult value judgments that I mentioned above. Each one would be, in effect, a judgment of how great an economic benefit our society would be wise to forego in order to spare its members the risks of exposure to the pesticides in a particular class. In principle, there is no formula that can produce such numbers, and I am sure that many people would be dissatisfied with whatever numbers might be proposed. There is the saving grace that fees could be revised easily from time to time as experience accumulates. But there are surely more difficulties that have not occurred to me. At the moment, I am not prepared to advocate this device though I do recommend it as worthy of study.

I said at the outset that I am not particularly interested in pesticides, though in the course of this study I came to understand much about their importance and the importance of their dangers. I undertook the work in order to learn about the problems that arise in using regulatory methods to protect the environment and to promote other social ends. My study and discussion of pesticide regulation are intended to apply much more broadly. As far as I can make out, pesticides are an entirely typical instance of regulatory problems. The efforts of EPA and the other regulatory agencies are confounded repeatedly by lack of fundamental understanding of the mechanisms they are charged with controlling, by the need to resort to awkward and unsatisfactory expedients to establish their regulations, and by the interminable litigation to which these circumstances give rise. All of the protective legislation that I know of encounters obstacles that are identical in principle to the ones that arise in regulating pesticides. The lessons that emerge from the instance of pesticides are thus widely applicable.

REFERENCES

Work Group on Risk Assessment. 1979. "Scientific Bases for Identifying Potential Carcinogens and Estimating their Risks." Report to the Interagency Regulatory Liaison Group, Executive Office of the President (February).

5   *Ethics, Economics, and the Environment*

ROBERT DORFMAN

The Environmental Protection Agency (EPA) was very much in the news in 1983 because of widespread charges of favoritism in administering funds, of paper shredders where they shouldn't be, of laxity in supervising the disposal of toxic wastes, and assorted other misconduct. A chapter about these and other juicy scandals at EPA would be pleasanter than this one because it is always more agreeable to consider other people's lax moral standards than to scrutinize our own. Nevertheless, I plan to discuss not the EPA's but the public's moral standards and how they have contributed to confusion and ineffectiveness in the national effort to protect and improve the environment.

It has been said, probably too often, that a nation gets the government it deserves. Whether that is true, the characteristics of a nation do have a profound and far-reaching effect on its government. When I look at our attempts to attain a safe and pleasant environment in this country, I am appalled at how indecisive, confused, and wasteful they have been, and I try to understand why. There is never a single, simple explanation of a complicated social state of affairs. It is altogether too easy when contemplating unsatisfactory social performance to say that some people wear white hats and some wear black, that the mean and selfish people in the black hats are frustrating the noble ones in white for their own nefarious purposes. In other words, somebody else's morals are at fault. I reject that easy kind of explanation. On the contrary, I look for an explanation grounded in the nature of the problem.

The government's environmental programs, like all its programs, are responses to public pressures and demands.

65

In the case of environmental protection, we have been demanding two contradictory things, and whenever the government attempts to provide one of them, the contrary goal
interferes. Hence the indecisiveness and confusion. I
will try to clarify that thought, give a few instances of
the interplay between contradictory demands in the environmental area, and discuss how those demands can be reconciled (to the extent they can be).

The contradictory demands arise from two conflicting
ethical principles deeply embedded in the American tradition: the doctrine of natural rights and utilitarianism.
It is not a case of some people adhering to one ethical
principle and other people adhering to the other one. I,
for one, believe in both, and I think that most people do,
and since these principles are contradictory, they con-
fuse us.

THE DOCTRINE OF NATURAL RIGHTS

The doctrine of natural rights (and of its close relative, natural laws) goes back at least to Roman times.
Given its most influential modern formulation by John
Locke in seventeenth century England, it states that every
man has certain inherent, inviolable rights that cannot
legitimately be invaded and that the actions of every government are circumscribed by certain natural laws that it
cannot legitimately violate. This doctrine was influential in America from the very beginning, such as justifying the Declaration of Independence: "We hold these
truths to be self-evident, that all men are created equal,
that they are endowed by their Creator with certain inalienable rights, and that among these are life, liberty,
and the pursuit of happiness. . . ." It was incorporated
in the U.S. Constitution most expressly in the Bill of
Rights and later in the Fourteenth Amendment and has been
reiterated countless times since. And these are not merely empty words; we believe them and many of our laws are
intended to implement them.

Since we all share this system of beliefs we should
all be aware that it has some shortcomings. There is no
generally agreed on list of the rights that are held to be
inalienable and no guidance about what should be done when
one of those rights conflicts with another one or when the
rights of one individual conflict with the rights of others. Rights and wrongs are complicated things, and we
should not expect any clear and simple principle to resolve all issues.

I have cited ancient sources and inarticulate feelings. But I want to remind you that there are eloquent spokesmen for this doctrine today. Milton Friedman (1982), Robert Nozick (1981), and the whole libertarian school argue effectively that it is wrong for a government to invade any citizen's natural rights for the benefit of other citizens. Of course, all governments do that habitually, as when they implement various welfare programs, and it is against such practices that the libertarians levy their diatribes.

As mentioned earlier, there is no accepted catalog of natural rights. In particular, the usual list makes no explicit mention of the environment. But it does include the right of every person that his life and health not be sacrificed or endangered for the benefit of others. Releasing harmful pollutants into the environment falls under these bans, and most of our environmental regulations are intended to protect those natural rights. Furthermore (but I am not sure of this) the doctrine of natural law may enjoin every nation to preserve its environment and to keep the creatures in it in a healthy state. The preamble to the Clean Water Act appears to accept this responsibility. It reads, "The objective of the Act is to restore and maintain the chemical, physical, and biological integrity of the nation's waters. In order to achieve this objective it is hereby declared that consistent with the provisions of the Act it is the national goal that the discharge of pollutants into the navigable waters be eliminated by 1985." In short, the doctrine of natural rights is deeply embedded in the American tradition, and Americans look to their government to help effect those rights in the environmental sphere as well as elsewhere.

UTILITARIANISM

Utilitarianism is equally deeply embedded in the American tradition. The word was coined in the nineteenth century, but the idea was prominent even in Epicurean philosophy, and Socrates espoused it in at least one of the dialogues. The central thrust is conveyed by the eighteenth century expression, "the greatest good for the greatest number." Taken literally the words don't make much sense, but the main idea does. It holds that the sole criterion of whether a government should undertake any action is the effect of that action on the public welfare, somehow defined. According to utilitarian principles it is right and proper for a government to undertake

any action that enhances public welfare and correspondingly wrong and improper for it to refrain from such an
action or to undertake one that reduces public welfare.
Notice that this doctrine is in flagrant contradiction to
the natural rights ethic. Natural rights holds that at
least some actions are inherently right or wrong, regardless of their consequences; utilitarianism holds that the
rightness or wrongness of an action depends only on its
consequences.

In the United States, utilitarianism was enunciated
in the preamble to the Constitution, as one of the purposes of the new government was stated to be promoting the
general welfare. Further on in the Constitution, providing for the general welfare of the United States was specifically included among the powers of Congress. That power was put to work almost immediately in Alexander Hamil-
ton's "Report on Manufactures" and has been exercised ever
since. Skipping over more than a hundred years, the utilitarian foundation of the general welfare concept was af-
firmed in a passage that is especially dear to my heart
and that has had widespread consequences. In the Water
Resources Act of 1936 the Corps of Engineers was instructed to build reservoirs or other improvements only if "the
benefits exceed the costs to whomsoever they may accrue."
This is out-and-out utilitarianism, and naive utilitarianism at that. The same concept has been repeated many
times since, most recently in an order by President Reagan
requiring all agencies of the federal government to estimate and take account of the benefits and costs of the decisions that they propose.

The definition of the general welfare formulated in
the Water Resources Act has been a powerful precedent and
has influenced both congressional and executive decisions
ever since. Under its influence, the conscious weighing
of costs and benefits has become such a conspicuous feature of government decision making in Congress and agencies that we all regard it simply as common sense. A whole
discipline has grown up composed of people who are skilled, or at least specialized, in making such estimates and
who have developed a substantial literature.

The assertion that there is a fundamental contradiction between the natural rights tradition, with its emphasis on inherent rightness and wrongness, and the utilitarian tradition, with its emphasis on results, has been
questioned. A redoubtable opponent, John Stuart Mill
(1963), argued that natural rights are derivative from the
utilitarian ethic because everyone recognizes that

whenever anyone's natural rights are violated, everyone's
life, liberty and security of property are endangered and
the general welfare is severely diminished. If the utilitarian tradition is so construed the conflict is resolved, at least verbally. But then it ceases to be an applicable standard for any practical purpose. When Congress
instructed the Corps of Engineers to take account of the
benefits and costs to whomever they may accrue, they
clearly did not expect the Corps to estimate the feelings
of insecurity that might be generated when any piece of
property is condemned; in fact, such considerations never
do enter official estimates of benefits and costs, though
they are sometimes raised in the course of public debate.
I do not maintain that any utilitarian--and I am one, as
well as a believer in natural rights--has thought through
such subtleties. If we had there might be no confusion.
I do maintain that when the Congress instructed the Corps
of Engineers to take account of benefits and costs, the
Congress was speaking in the main line of the utilitarian
tradition and intended the Corps to compare concrete, observable benefits to some people with concrete, observable
costs to others. The general welfare would be considered
served if the benefits outweighed the costs. It is implicit in this approach that when the stated criterion is
applied consistently some people will be helped and some
harmed on each occasion, but on balance everyone will be
helped more than harmed. Therefore this rule unambiguously promotes the general welfare by promoting the welfare
of each member of the community. Subtle considerations
such as the one advanced by Mill have no place in it.
President Reagan's order (and a similar presidential order
by his predecessor, President Carter) were clearly intended in the same pragmatic spirit and have been obeyed in
that spirit.

THREE ILLUSTRATIONS OF CONFLICTING GOALS

     Thus we have inherited a pair of conflicting ethical
principles, to both of which we are deeply committed. In
our environmental affairs, as elsewhere, we try to implement both of them. The result, inevitably, is confusion.
EPA, which bears the major responsibility for administering environmental laws, is instructed to move in two different directions at the same time, which it cannot do.
How it manages to live with such instructions is an interesting story. Following are three brief illustrations of
the agency's struggle to contend, one from the Clean Water
Act, one from the Clean Air Act, and one from the Toxic

Substances Control Act, all of which in different ways
direct EPA to regulate intrusions on the environment so as
to prevent violations of citizens' rights and simultaneously promote the general welfare.

The Clean Water Act

The inspiring statement of objectives with which the
Clean Water Act begins has already been quoted. It af-
firms that the national goal is to eliminate the discharge
of all pollutants into navigable waters by 1985. In 1983,
as far as acts of Congress are concerned, that was still
the national goal. Needless to say, there is no possibility of achieving it, and I cannot believe that any of the
senators and representatives who voted for that act were
naive enough to believe polluting discharges could be
eliminated completely in thirteen years, if ever. They
voted for it nevertheless, enough of them to override a
presidential veto, because that was the year of the presidential election that immediatley followed Earth Day
(1972) and public concern about the state of the environment was at its height. Congress heard a loud public demand that the waters be cleaned up; and without too much
niggling over the wording of the act, it passed, was ve-
toed, and three weeks before the election passed again.
Congress does listen.

The goals are just words, of course, but words written into law have consequences. The consequence of these
words is that the EPA could not, and cannot, direct its
effort toward cleaning up the lakes and rivers where the
pollution is most damaging. Instead it must implement a
program called the National Pollution Elimination System,
which attempts to reduce discharges of pollutants everywhere, whether damaging or not. Even without further complication this compels the agency to squander billions of
dollars (from a utilitarian point of view), for example,
in financing the construction of waste treatment plants in
places where natural processes would purify the water before anyone was inconvenienced.

There are further complications. Utilitarian considerations were not forgotten in writing the body of the
act. It was clear that restricting polluting discharges
--not to mention eliminating them--would impose heavy
costs on food-processing plants, steel mills, and many
other industries that use large amounts of water and
return it, polluted, to lakes and rivers. The law, therefore, imposes restrictions on what EPA can order such
plants to do. A five-year transition period was allowed,

after which EPA could (and should) require all plants in
the country to reduce their polluting discharges by the
amount achievable by applying "the best practicable control technology currently available." Beginning in 1983
EPA was told to require "the best available technology
economically achievable." Congress was careful not to
define those words in the act, leaving that delicate task
to EPA. EPA has given definitions and has changed them
several times, always with careful attention to the quali-
fication "economically achievable," which it enforced in
such a way that none but the most marginal plants could be
rendered unprofitable by the clean-up requirements.

Needless to say, the enforcement of this restriction
left room for a great deal of pollution. Unintentionally
another large loophole was left. Farms generate a vast a-
mount of pollution; unless precautions are taken, rains
wash fertilizers and pesticide residues into nearby lakes
and streams. The animal wastes generated on livestock
feedlots also end up in public waters in large quantities.
EPA was not given any authority to control those sources
of pollution.

In these and other ways the text of the act undercut
thoroughly the announced objective but still did not allow
EPA to undertake the measures needed to reduce water pollution in proportion to the damage it caused. Neither the
natural rights nor the utilitarian objective was served.

The Clean Air Act

In one of the major provisions of the Clean Air Act
the shoe is on the other foot. The announced purpose of
the act, "to protect and enhance the quality of the nation's air resources so as to promote the public health
and welfare and the productive capacity of its population," is as utilitarian as anybody could want, but the
operating provisions go the other way. In particular they
require EPA to establish and enforce requirements (called
national primary ambient air quality standards) defined as
"ambient air quality standards the attainment and maintenance of which in the judgment of the administrator and
allowing an adequate margin of safety are requisite to
protect the public health." This sounds like a perfectly
reasonable and humane provision, but it contains at least
three pitfalls that have caused unending difficulty since
the law was enacted.

The first pitfall was the Senate's explanation of
what they meant by "protecting the public health." They
meant protecting the health of all persons exposed to

outdoor air, including--and the example is the Senate's--
persons who suffer from emphysema. So EPA was instructed
to identify the population group that was most vulnerable
to the effects of any air pollutant and to set a standard
strict enough to protect them though they might be a few
in number. A standard set in accordance with this criterion would inevitably be much stricter, and correspondingly
more expensive to attain, than one that would suffice to
protect the great bulk of the population.

That requirement might not have caused so much trouble except for the other two pitfalls. The second one is
scientific. The law, as interpreted by the Senate, presumes that there is some level of a pollutant in the air
that will do no harm to even the most sensitive individuals. Whether there is any such level is a scientific
question; epidemiologists and toxicologists refer to it as
the question of the existence of a threshold. No source
that I have consulted answers that question with great
confidence, but the weight of opinion with respect to most
air pollutants is that there is no threshold below which a
pollutant does no harm to anyone. If there is no such
threshold, EPA would have to require that all man-made
discharges of pollution be stopped--exactly the same unat-
tainable level of aspiration encountered when discussing
the Clean Water Act.

The third pitfall is one that, so far as I know, is
unique to the air quality provisions of this act. The requirement that the air quality standards should be strict
enough to protect the health of all individuals makes no
mention of costs, and there is no qualifying provision
that permits EPA to take costs into account in establishing air quality standards. Taken literally, this in-
structs EPA to pay no heed to costs in setting standards
strict enough to protect the most susceptible person in
the population. This might well require forbidding all
emissions of some pollutants. It surely conflicts with
the announced purpose of promoting public welfare and the
productive capacity of the population.

Naturally, EPA has done no such thing. Instead it
has assumed that for every pollutant there is a threshold
concentration below which no one would be harmed, despite
the weight of scientific opinion. The agency has established the threshold at a level that is attainable in
practice and at the same time appears not to harm susceptible individuals noticeably more than a lower practical
level, being careful, all the while, not to mention costs.

My favorite example is carbon monoxide (CO). The
current standard permits 9 parts CO per million parts air.
Now it happens that there is no evidence that CO at that
level of concentration or anywhere near it harms anybody
except people who suffer from severe angina pectoris. They
are few in number and, besides, it doesn't affect them
much. The situation is that an angina patient has a very
marginal supply of oxygen to the heart muscle. Anything
that increases the heart's need for oxygen, such as exercise, can bring on a terribly painful attack. The CO in
the air reduces the blood's ability to supply oxygen. The
result is that if an angina patient engages in exercise
that would bring on an attack in 3 minutes in pure air,
the attack will be induced in about 2 1/2 minutes if the
air contains 10 to 12 parts per million CO. There are no
aftereffects. The ambient standard for CO has been set
primarily with this effect in mind and is low enough so
that stricter but still attainable standards would not
noticeably reduce the amount of exercise the patient could
take before experiencing an attack.

No one knows how much money could be saved without
significant harm by relaxing this standard or others set
by similar considerations, because EPA is not allowed to
look into that. My impression is that it is substantial.

Of course, these strict standards are not met universally. The latest data I have show that in 1978 the CO
standard was violated on ten or more days in more than
half the communities in New England, the Pacific North-
west, and the Mountain States, and by large proportions in
nearly all parts of the country.

In short, in the case of the Clean Air Act, the public gave mixed signals and EPA received confusing instructions. It was told to "promote public health and welfare," but to pay no attention to the effects on the general welfare when setting the national ambient air quality
standards. Air quality in most cities has improved, but
the drain on other aspects of general welfare, as measured
by the dollar cost, has been enormous--about $25 billion a
year. Much of the drain was probably unnecessary.

The Toxic Substances Control Act

The final example concerns a currently notorious
function of EPA: regulation of the use and disposal of
toxic substances. No law is proof against malfeasance and
nonfeasance, though a law can facilitate those things by
being confused and indecisive. The current furor over

toxic substances concerns their proper final interment;
this example deals with the other end of their biography,
their creation. That aspect of control may some day be in
the news because the provisions of the act that regulate
the introduction of new toxic substances have not been implemented seven years after their enactment.

To understand this seven years of effective paralysis, we have to look at the act itself and its context.
Though the Toxic Substances Control Act was passed in
1976, it was conceived about six years earlier, at the
crest of the wave of environmental awareness. People were
frightened, and properly frightened, at the dangerousness
of injecting new and untried substances into their environment, homes, diets--everywhere. The ingenuity of chemists is vast. Roughly a thousand new chemicals are invented and introduced commercially every year. Nearly all
are harmless, maybe 990 out of 1,000, but a few--such as
dioxin--are terrible. The problem is how to detect in
time the handful of dangerous ones without shutting off
the flow of beneficial ones.

Congress wrestled with this problem for about six
years before emerging with a program known as Premanufac-
turing Notification. It requires everyone who wishes to
introduce a new chemical into the United States to inform
EPA in advance and to provide enough information about it
so that the agency can judge whether to permit it, to permit it under certain restrictions, or to forbid it. And
that is where the blockage, extending for six years before
enactment and since then, arose. Just what informtion
should the prospective manufacturers and importers be required to provide?

Providing information about hazards is expensive.
Moderately thorough testing of a new chemical for carcinogenicity and mutagenicity takes two years and costs from a
half million to a million dollars. To demand such tests
for all new substances--about most of which there are no
grounds for suspicion--would stop chemical innovation in
its tracks. Besides, chemical innovators are normally
very reluctant to divulge information about their new products that would be likely to give valuable clues to their
competitiors.

So some compromise with the goal of absolute protection is necessary if the chemical industry is to survive.
The Congress wrestled long and hard with this problem, and
in the end fudged it. It set forth rather vague requirements for information and gave EPA the power to require
more information if it had good grounds for doing so. In

addition, it inserted numerous safeguards into the act to prevent EPA from making onerous demands when they were not necessary. For example, EPA must demonstrate its need for anything beyond such minimal information as the name and chemical formula of the new substance; a manufacturer not satisfied with EPA's demonstration may appeal to the courts for permission to proceed without providing the data requested.

So the act contains an internal tension. On the one hand, EPA has the responsibility for regulating the introduction of new toxic substances; on the other, it was left with the task of determining specifically what information it needs in order to discharge that responsibility and its authority to require information was severely restricted. And, to cut short a long and discouraging story, from that day on, EPA has not been able to propose a schedule of information to be provided that the chemical manufacturers would accept. In the absence of such a schedule, manufacturers just give EPA the information about new products that they think proper and EPA makes do with it. The result is just what you would expect. About 60 percent of the notifications received contain no data on safety testing, and the data in the rest tend to be skimpy. No one regards this as a satisfactory state of affairs, so the effort to devise a useful set of information requirements acceptable to the manufacturers continues.

The interplay of ethical and other considerations in the case of this act is more intricate than in the preceding two. Remember that the toxic substances act was conceived at the peak of the zeal for environmental protection, in an assertion of the public's right to be safe from harmful chemicals. There was also a utilitarian tinge, since the sickness, suffering, and property loss that toxic chemicals can cause are catastrophic reductions in the welfare of the victims (as the Love Canal and Times Beach episodes remind us). On the utilitarian side, there was a concern to retain the benefits the many new synthetics confer on all of us, and, especially after the act was passed, there was the crass utilitarian interest of the chemical manufacturers.

Before you shrug your shoulders and say, "Aha, that's the answer; why drag in all this philosophic stuff," I must mention that a sister act, the Federal Insecticide, Fungicide, and Rodenticide Act, has had quite a different fate. There are three differences: the insecticide act is much older; it is much more severe, since a half-million-dollar biological test is required for all

pesticides; and, most importantly, it deals only with
pesticides that even the manufacturers acknowledge are
dangerous poisons. Because of the latter, the pesticide
act includes none of the elaborate restrictions on EPA's
authority that complicate the toxic substances act, and
the pesticide manufacturers--including many of the very
same firms that have frustrated the toxic substances act
--have acquiesced almost cheerfully. But in the case of
the toxic substances act it is hard not to have reservations about requiring manufacturers to spend large sums to
gather information on the dangers of chemicals that almost
certainly are not dangerous. Such reasonable reservations
not only explain why the chemical manufacturers have resisted but also explain why their resistance has been
tolerated and, thus far, successful. This confusion about
what we really want to do about new chemicals, a few of
which are possibly toxic, has led to half-hearted support
and to paralysis in implementaiton.

PROPOSED SOLUTIONS
    There are many other examples of fundamental con-
flicts in these and in the other environmental protection
programs, but I'll rest my case with these three. They
illustrate the pervasive indecisiveness that places the
administrators in the predicament of having to strive for
two inconsistent goals at the same time. Generally speaking, neither goal is attained.
    This moral predicament is not an easy one to get out
of, nor is it the only obstacle that stands between us and
the safe and pleasant environment we all desire. But it
would make progress easier if we could resolve it.
    Most economists, but not I, are addicted to an easy
method for solving all such goal conflicts. It consists
of establishing a scale, nearly always money, for measuring the importance of the different goals and then advocating the decisions that make the sum of all these values
as great as possible. This is a sweeping version of utilitarianism that subsumes respect for human rights under
the broad umbrella of general welfare. It is a spurious
solution, however. The economists who advocate it are
deluding themselves, since they also believe in the sanc-
tity of our fundamental rights and immunities.
    There is, in fact, no way to place a monetary value
on a violation of somebody's rights. That does not mean
that societies and governments never violate individual
rights; on the contrary, they do so routinely. But each
violation is a serious matter and can be justified only by

advancing some goal of commanding social importance. So
this easy way out is only make-believe, one that cannot
be, and is not, used in practice.

The only clue to a solution that I know of is in the
work of American philosopher (naturally) John Rawls
(1971), who squarely confronted the inconsistency in the
ethical principles he had inherited. I suggest a revised
version of his solution, but he mustn't be blamed for my
revision.

Rawls's idea is to divide all social goals affected
by a decision into two classes, which I shall call primary
values and secondary values. The primary values are those
that concern the respect for natural rights; the secondary
values are those included in the general welfare in the
ordinary sense of the term. The effect of a decision on
the secondary values is measured most conveniently by the
benefit-cost calculus already discussed. But those are
only the secondary values. The primary values are primary
in importance and must be considered separately. They
concern losses, suffering, and even death inflicted on
people through no fault of their own.

Here is where I diverge from Rawls's own position.
He maintains that no diminution in the respect for primary
values can be justified by any increase in the attainment
of the secondary, utilitarian values--in effect, that no
one should legitimately be harmed, not even one angina patient, for example, no matter how great the resultant improvement in the general welfare. I believe that such an
extremely fastidious society could not survive. Although
such violations are not to be taken lightly, neither can
we hope to avoid them completely.

The situation we now confront is this. We must
choose between two decisions, such as two different levels
for the CO ambient standard, Decision A and Decision B.
Suppose Decision A contributes more to the general welfare
than does Decision B. That would be enough for a thor-
oughgoing utilitarian, but it is not enough for us. We
have to check to see whether Decision A invades any of the
basic human rights more than does Decision B. If not, all
is well and Decision A is the preferable alternative. But
if Decision A does violate some people's rights more seriously than does Decision B, we are likely to be confronted with what Calabresi (1978) has aptly called a tragic
choice.

Circumstances differ vastly, so there seems to be no
possibility of a formula analogous to the one that can be
applied to the secondary benefits for deciding whether the

violations are justified in any particular instance. But,
though he does not believe in making such choices, Rawls
has proposed a standard by which they can be made. Each
of us would have to ask himself or herself earnestly the
following hypothetical question: If I did not know how
the decision would apply to me, would I prefer to live in
a society that chose Decision A or one that chose Decision
B? Let us consider an example. The chances are about one
in ten thousand that I will suffer from angina pectoris.
Would I prefer to live in a society that permitted a pollution level that would accelerate my attacks (in order to
increase the general welfare, including my own, by $100
million a year) to living in one that would not?

That is not an easy question to answer, and it is not
the same as the standard economist's question, "If I were
an angina sufferer, how much would I be willing to pay to
have the onset of an attack deferred by half a minute?"
The answer to the economist's question, if it can be ascertained, belongs in the ordinary account of benefits and
costs. The answer to the Rawlsian question relates to the
kind of ethical standards an individual would like a society to maintain, with special attention to its reluctance to infringe on individual rights. I do not think
that our preferences in this regard can be described in
general terms, at least not until we have gained a great
deal of experience in answering the kinds of specific
questions that I have proposed. So such questions must be
posed again and again.

One more example will illustrate how hard, or how
easy, those questions can be. Suppose you did not know in
which country you were going to live after this year but
you did know that if the United States continues to use
synthetic chemicals, two toxic waste depositories will
have to be established in each state, regardless of the
wishes of the people living nearby. Would you prefer to
live in a country that permitted chemical production generating toxic wastes or in one that banned it?

One last matter. I propose this approach as a solution to the problem of releasing EPA, and other agencies
as well, from the contradictory mandates that they now receive. Could it really do so? Obviously, I think it
could. The agency would have to perform the ordinary benefit-cost analysis that it now is required to go through,
at the same time and using the same data keeping track of
the extent to which human rights are invaded under the
various options. Finally in most instances, it would have

to form a considered judgment as to whether a decent and
humane society would consider the more advantageous economic choice to be advantageous enough to justify the
accompanying infringements of individual rights.

I am sure this approach is possible in the kind of
society that prefers such a procedure to the current one
of espousing infeasible or contradictory goals.

REFERENCES

Calabresi, Guido. 1978. Tragic Choices. New York:
    Norton.
Friedman, Milton, 1982. Capitalism and Freedom.
    Chicago: University of Chicago Press.
Mill, John Stuart. 1963. Collected Works. Toronto:
    University of Toronto Press.
Nozick, Robert. 1981. Philosophical Explanations.
    Cambridge, Mass.: Harvard University Press, Belknap.
Rawls, John. 1971. A Theory of Justice. Cambridge:
    Harvard Univerity Press, Belknap.

25

Why benefit-cost analysis is widely disregarded and what to do about it

For reasons that are not entirely clear, the 104th Congress has awarded benefit-cost analysis a prominent place on its agenda. Two contradictory explanations have been proposed. They are: (1) The Congress, in order to increase economic efficiency in general and the Federal government's efficiency in particular, wants to establish more objective and reliable procedures for appraising proposed governmental regulations, projects and programmes and (2) The Congress, in order to reduce the size and intrusiveness of the Federal government, wants to impede initiating new regulations, projects and programmes, and even implementing existing regulations and programmes.

I have not done the research that would be needed to evaluate these hypotheses, and therefore shall not take any position on their relative merits. Instead, my principal concern will be to take advantage of the interest they have aroused to discuss some deficiencies in the usual applications of benefit-cost analysis that impair its reliability and usefulness and, thereby, public and official confidence in it.

I shall discuss several characteristics of the current practice of benefit-cost analysis that contribute to the low esteem in which it is frequently held. The first is the stubborn attempt to do something that long experience as well as a little theorizing shows to be impossible. This impossible aspiration is to measure the social value of all the consequences of a governmental policy or undertaking by a sum of dollars and cents. Benefit-cost analysis has struggled to attain this goal ever since it was injected into Federal project evaluation by the Flood Control Act of 1936, and persists in the current flurry of Congressional revisions of benefit-cost procedures. For example, a proposal before the Senate (Senate bill S. 343, Sec. 623) requires that

(a) No final rule subject to this subchapter shall be promulgated unless the agency finds that –

    (1) the potential benefits to society from the rule outweigh the potential costs of the rule to society . . . and

    (2) the rule will provide greater net benefits to society than any of the reasonable alternatives identified . . . .

This provision, and other similar ones in both the Senate and the House bills, does not explicitly require that all benefits and costs be expressed in a common metric, presumably dollars and cents, but it is hard to see how it can be obeyed otherwise.

Rather than cite the long string of failed attempts to reduce all the beneficial and costly consequences of governmental undertakings to a common metric, I will sketch some *a priori* reasons for maintaining that it cannot be done. Basically, this mandate would require answers to such questions as 'What is the value of a human life?' and 'How much is an endangered species worth?' and 'What is the proper trade-off between jobs and wetland preservation?' and so on. These are not questions of fact that might admit expert answers, but questions about social values and public preferences, that only the elaborate and clumsy procedures of democratic decision-making can answer. Such answers are not data to be fed into decision-making processes but, rather, outputs of those processes.

But economists have not been daunted. Over the decades we have expended enormous efforts and admirable ingenuity in a vain attempt to answer those questions. We economists should have known better. Consider the first of my illustrative questions and, probably, the most important one. Juries have placed values on lives in scores of specific cases, but their valuations are spread over such a wide range and are influenced by so many adventitious circumstances that no useful generalizations can be inferred from them. One formerly prevalent answer to the value of a human life was to equate it to the value of the individual's future contributions to social welfare, as measured by the present value of his or her expected earnings. But this device was soon seen to be inapplicable to the values of the lives of young children, or of homemakers, or of retired persons, as well as in conflict with the principle of equal protection of the laws and with the moral standard that the value of a human life is inherent in humanness rather than derived from a person's productive abilities. Attempts to infer the value of human life from wage premiums earned in hazardous occupations, or from public and private expenditures on safety devices, or from decisions about life insurance have never carried much conviction; they have all been seen to reflect extraneous and irrelevant considerations.

The pages of economic journals are strewn with ingenious attempts to find 'objective' answers to my other illustrative questions and to similar ones (e.g. Hotelling's travel-cost method for measuring the values of scenic and recreational sites, or 'hedonic' correlations of housing prices with local environmental conditions to estimate willingness-to-pay for environmental amenities). None of them have yielded compelling or authoritative answers.

Probably the leading contender at present is 'contingent valuation' (CV). CV is just an adaptation of commercial market surveys to the valuation of the non-marketed benefits of governmental projects and programmes. In it an appropriately randomized sample is asked questions like, 'Would you be willing to be assessed $x a year to have the quality of the water in the Y river raised to a swimmable standard?'. This approach has the unique advantage that the answers to such questions can reflect the values of the programme to non-users as well as users of the facility being valued. But there are many obvious grounds for doubting the validity of answers to such iffy questions. Empirical verification of the findings of CV studies is difficult and expensive. The scattering of tests that have been made have yielded inconclusive results.

So I hold that there is, and can be, no way to represent the diverse results of governmental undertakings by scalar measures; the results have to be regarded as vector rather than scalar magnitudes. Comparing vectors can be a lot trickier than comparing scalars. If one of the vectors is preferable to the other(s), component by component, then the programme that corresponds to the inferior one is 'dominated' and should not be adopted unless some special, extraneous circumstance requires it. But public choices are rarely that clear cut. More generally, when the result vectors of two plans are compared, one is found to be superior in some respects and the other in others. Then a choice between the plans will depend on the relative importance assigned, explicitly or implicitly, to each component of the vectors, and these relative importance weights, being expressions of community standards or values, are ascertainable only by a political process of some sort.

Benefit-cost analysis does, however, have an essential rôle to play in reaching public decisions. It is far and away the most effective tool for assembling the data relevant to decisions and quantifying the pros and cons to the extent that they can be quantified.

There are several ways to use benefit-cost analysis as a tool for informing public decisions. A typical application would begin by estimating the amounts of resources used, other costs, and all beneficial results in each year of the economic life of the programme in natural units, and to convert to monetary units all the effects for which meaningful market prices are available. If the total of the present values of the monetized benefits exceeds that of the monetized costs, the project promises a net monetized benefit and to that extent is acceptable. No firm decision can be made, however, without considering the non-monetized benefits and costs. Similarly, if the monetized costs exceed the monetized benefits, there is a net monetized cost. Again, that finding is not enough to rule the project out.

Political preferences must now be confronted. For each kind of non-monetized benefit or cost there will be a net gain or loss. For example, a highway improvement project may be expected to reduce the average number of fatalities per year that the highway is used, but it is likely to incur some fatalities while under construction.

Now focus attention on one kind of non-monetized result, say a benefit. Although there is no way to assign a dollar and cents value to each unit of that type of benefit, it is likely to be possible to agree on extreme bounds that bracket that value. For example, there is likely to be general agreement that it is worth while to spend $100,000 to avert an accidental death of a healthy adult but that a policy that costs $5 million for each such death averted would be unduly extravagant. A somewhat narrower range might be possible and would be more informative.

Agreeing on these ranges is the hardest part of the decision process. Once it has been accomplished, an upper bound on the aggregate net value of the project's non-monetized results follows readily. Any proposal for which the net monetized cost is greater than the upper bound of its non-monetized value can be ruled out forthwith. If the lower bound of its non-monetized values exceeds its net monetized cost, the proposal can be accepted unless there is an alternative use of the required resources that promises a greater excess benefit.

The list of admissible undertakings can be narrowed to those for which the anticipated benefits, monetized and non-monetized together, are large enough to justify the costs. Selecting the most preferred project from this list still requires some discriminating comparisons and judgments, but we have gotten about as far as broad objective principles will take us.

The second egregious shortcoming in the current practice of benefit-cost analysis is that it suppresses the information that is most critical for democratic decision-making. The fact that the benefits and costs of governmental undertakings are not spread evenly over the affected populations, but that some affected persons benefit at the cost of others, is the basic fact that politics is all about. Yet the distribution of benefits and costs is sedulously concealed in the standard benefit-cost study, which concentrates on comparing the aggregate of benefits with the aggregate of costs 'to whomsoever they may accrue'.

Since this omitted information is of primary interest to legislators and responsible government officials, they must find it elsewhere, and are likely to base their decisions on the sources that provide it rather than on the benefit-cost analysis. Thus benefit-cost analysis becomes a largely irrelevant exercise in paper-shuffling while decisions are based on estimates and analyses that are provided often by self-seeking interested parties.

The corrective is obvious. I can well understand that, especially in politics, there are some things about which it does not pay to be too explicit. Who enjoys the benefits of governmental activities and who pays for them are among the things about which discretion is the better part of candour. Nevertheless, it is rarely possible to conceal who the beneficiaries of governmental actions are, and at whose expense. The coyness of government agencies about gainers and losers helps the agencies to avoid authenticating assertions about distributive effects, for which the agencies may be grateful, but it impedes candid and constructive discussion of those effects, which is of essence for well-informed political decisions.

It is therefore highly desirable for benefit-cost analyses to enumerate the prospective gainers and losers from proposed government undertakings, and to estimate the extents of the gains and losses incurred by members of each group.

When a number of alternatives are being weighed, a useful technique, sometimes called Paretoan analysis, is to rank the alternatives according to the preferences of each relevant political group. If there is any alternative that all the groups rank higher than some particular other alternative or alternatives, those lower ranked alternatives are said to be 'dominated', and can be dropped from further consideration. The remaining, undominated, alternatives can then be compared with each other. Each pairwise comparison will usually take into account (1) the size of the group that prefers each alternative, (2) any special considerations that pertain to each group, such as veteran status or minority status, and (3) the strength of the preference. The strength of preference can be judged by inspecting the individual components of the two vectors being compared. Some of the components may be numerical, e.g., the effect of the alternatives on family incomes or on incidence of particular ailments. For them, it will be easy to perceive how significant the choice is. Other components may be qualitative. For them the comparison will be cruder. In any case, some judgment will have to be made of the relative weight that each population group considered gives to each component of the vectors being compared.

Such a systematic examination of the attitudes of relevant population groups can help sort the issues out, evaluate their relative importance, and identify the alternative that is preferable, all things considered. It cannot be performed without information from the benefit-cost study or other sources about the effects of each alternative on the various population segments that are affected.

The third serious flaw in current benefit-cost analyses is another kind of concealment. Though benefit and cost estimates can never be precise, reports are generally written as if they were. No one is fooled, of course. But the users of the reports are thereby deprived of information about how great the errors in the published estimates are likely to be.

Fortunately, both the House and the Senate proposals for revising procedures for Federal benefit-cost analysis recognize this problem. Since a Senate version is the most concise, I quote it:

> A description of the benefits and costs of a proposed and a final rule required under this section shall include, to the extent feasible, a quantification or numerical estimate of the quantifiable benefits and costs. Such quantification or numerical estimate shall be made in the most appropriate unit of measurement, using comparable assumptions, including time periods, and *shall specify the ranges of predictions and shall explain the margins of error involved in the quantification methods and in the estimates used.* (104th Congress, First Session, S. 343, Sec. 622, italics added.)

Amen.

Finally, and at a somewhat more technical level, it is important to recognize that in considering most governmental proposals, the question of how much to do is likely to be as significant as the question of just what. When the options being considered include a continuum of sizes (e.g., height of dam, maximum speed limit, etc.), marginal analysis becomes available and even mandatory. In any event, if there is some choice about size, whether continuous or discrete, benefit-cost calculations should be applied to marginal increments. When the criteria are multi-dimensional, the marginal increments should be inspected, and the project enlarged until the vector of results of the final increment is no longer preferred to that of the preceding increment.

Remember that the fundamental economic criterion, from which all other practical criteria are derived, is always: the total excess of the value of social benefits over total costs should be at least as great for the option chosen as for any other option available. Generally speaking, the ratio of benefits to costs does not measure contribution to social welfare; the excess of benefits over costs does. Beware of relying on ratios!

August 29, 1995
Harvard University

PART SIX

HISTORY OF ECONOMICS

[26]

WASSILY LEONTIEF'S CONTRIBUTION TO ECONOMICS

Robert Dorfman

Harvard University, Cambridge, Mass., USA

Whoever thinks of Wassily Leontief thinks of input-output, and vice versa. A review of Leontief's writings and career shows, however, that he cannot be summed up in a single accomplishment, no matter how stellar. To be sure, the discovery of input-output was his outstanding accomplishment, as it was one of the two or three outstanding achievements of a whole generation of economists. But Leontief is not a one idea, one gadget economist. On the contrary, the discovery of input-output might well be regarded as the almost inevitable result of the kind of economist that he is.

There is a dominant theme that runs through Leontief's four decades of professional work, from his earliest papers to his presidential address to the American Economic Association. It is that economics is an empirical and applied science, and that fancy theoretical apparatus can sometimes be helpful but is more likely to seduce students and scholars into intriguing but sterile bypaths. The only valid test of economic research is its empirical significance and its practical implications. This theme recurs again and again in his writings, in many guises. It is the basis of his famous attack on the Cambridge economists who surrounded Keynes,[1] it lies behind his profound paper on the structure of functional relationships,[2] it motivated the complaint in his presidential address against the disproportion between abstruse theorizing and factual digging in contemporary American economics.[3] But most important of all, it is the clue to his discovery of input-output economics.

Input-output economics is that *rara avis* in economics, a genuinely new and original idea. It was not without precursors and Leontief has always been at least adequately generous in acknowledging them. The idea of material balances connecting the levels of activity in different segments of the economy goes back to Quesnay and is deeply embedded in Marxist theory. The notion of a closed system of functional relationships connecting the activity levels of all components of an economy goes back to Walras at least. Nor did Leontief invent the mathematics of input-output analysis. What economists call "Leon-

---

[1] In "Implicit theorizing: a methodological criticism of the neo-Cambridge school." See bibliography.
[2] "A note on the interrelation of subsets of independent variables ..."
[3] Eighty-third meeting of the American Economic Association, December 29, 1970.

tief matrices" have long been known to mathematicians as "Frobenius matrices", and the main theorems concerning them were well worked out by the time Leontief was born, and were developed further over the years by a long succession of mathematicians. I still remember Leontief's gleeful excitement when he came across the work of Remak, who proposed a theoretical input-output formulation of an economy seven years before Leontief's earliest paper on the subject. A mathematician, H. E. Bray, had written in similar vein seven years before that.

But all of these are merely precursors who lacked the vital idea, so characteristic of Leontief, that formulas are mere playthings while real economics begins with operational concepts and, above all, actual numbers. It was Leontief, who first saw the practical potentiality of an input-output *table* and who learned how to really put one together. Next to this achievement the algebraic properties of input-output matrices—long known to mathematicians and for the most part rediscovered by economists other than Leontief—are only theoretical refinements. The fundamental discovery that distinguished Leontief's work from that of all his predecessors is that it was practical to calculate the input-output coefficients from recorded data, to perform the necessary algebraic manipulations, and to use the results to answer a wide variety of practical economic questions. The magnitude of the obstacles in the path of this achievement can be appreciated by remembering that it occurred ten years before the first electronic computer.[1]

One precondition for the discovery of input-output was the proper mental set, already described. The other was a strong mathematical background, needed both to grapple with the algebraic technicalities involved and to dispel the awe that neophytes sometimes feel when confronting elaborate algebra. Leontief satisfied this requirement, too, having been thoroughly trained in mathematics as a student. In short, the discovery of input-output was the accomplishment of a well-prepared mind confronting a problem for which it was ideally suited.

In the sequel, we shall first survey the intellectual development of this mind, and then revert to the discovery and development of input-output analysis.

Leontief's Career

Leontief was born in Leningrad in 1906. The externals of his career give only a faint suggestion of its intellectual quality. He studied first at the University of Leningrad and then at Berlin, earning his doctoral degree at the age of 22.

---

[1] It is recorded that the first input-output solutions on an automatic computing machine required fifty-six hours on the primitive Harvard Mark II computer, for a 42 sector table. I do not know the times required for the previous computations, which were performed by an ingenious application of punchcard machines, but they must have been far greater. It took remarkable vision to perceive that the results could justify such enormously tedious calculations.

He engaged in economic research at the University of Berlin and then served for a short time as an economic advisor to the government of China. In 1931 he came to the United States, and after a brief period at the National Bureau for Economic Research he was appointed an instructor at Harvard University. There he has remained ever since, though not long as an instructor. He is now Henry Lee Professor of Economics at Harvard. During World War II he served as head of the Russian Economic Subdivision of the Office of Strategic Services. His honors include two Guggenheim Fellowships, an honorary degree from the University of Brussels, and the presidency of the American Economic Association.

In the course of his studies Leontief received a thorough mathematical training. Though, as I mentioned, Leontief has consistently been skeptical of applications of higher mathematics to economics, this fact has colored his entire career. In spite of all his protestations he thinks mathematically and quantitatively. Virtually all his research papers deal with the economic interpretation, application, and misapplication of some mathematical formulation used in economic theory or statistics. This is preeminently true of his contribution to input-output analysis. In most of these papers he displays phenomenal ingenuity in translating mathematical concepts into illuminating graphs and words—his papers are peppered with strikingly vivid and original graphic presentations that bring out the central idea of the argument, stripped of obscuring technicalities.

Leontief has not been particularly prolific. He has only one full-length monograph, *The Structure of American Economy, 1919–1929: An Empirical Application of Equilibrium Analysis* (Cambridge, Mass.: Harvard University Press, 1941, later editions by Oxford University Press, New York). He edited, directed, and contributed to a collaborative volume, *Studies in the Structure of the American Economy: Theoretical and Empirical Explorations in Input-Output Analysis*, with H. B. Chenery and others (New York: Oxford University Press, 1953). He has also published two volumes of collected essays, drawing upon his accumulation of some five dozen scientific papers. In addition to the usual scholarly contributions, he has published a number of lively expositions of his work in the *Scientific American* and elsewhere.

His earliest papers, beginning in the early 1930's, were those to be expected of a brilliant young economist whose interests had not yet congealed. There was a series of papers on the statistical estimation of demand and supply curves, foreshadowing his continuing concern with adapting theoretical constructs to empirical reality. There were expository and evaluative papers on a variety of subjects, including indifference curves (then quite novel), the interpretation of index numbers, and the theory of production.

Reread from a perspective of forty years, none of these are decisive and some are noticeably dated, but the reviewer is struck by repeated shafts of sheer brilliance and ingenuity. The 1933 paper on "The use of indifference curves in the analysis of foreign trade" is typical. As an exposition of the use and interpretation of indifference curves, it is unexcelled. Some diagrams of striking ingenuity are devised to show how the community indifference curves and production possibilities curves of two countries interact to determine their trading relationships. But, there is no hint that the author has perceived the really fundamental problems in the construction and use of community indifference curves for the analysis for international trade, problems that were pointed out a few years later by Samuelson, Scitovsky, and others. In this case Leontief was clearly intrigued by the conceptual potential of the indifference curve apparatus but was not close enough to the problem to encounter the fundamental operational difficulties lying just below the surface. In short, this paper is extremely clever and technically adroit, but does not pierce to the substantive conceptual issues on which the whole analysis rests.

A few years later he published another paper of the same general quality, "Composite commodities and the problem of index numbers" (1936). This paper, more than the preceding one, exemplifies his life-long concern with the operational significance of economic concepts. The concept here in question is that of a general price level, purportedly measured by a price index. He takes it for granted, without discussion, that the correct measure of the price change between two periods is the change in the cost of attaining a given indifference curve. This is the modern standpoint but, as Leontief was well aware, it is inherently ambiguous. The ambiguity lies in the fact that the measured change in price depends upon the level of the indifference curve that is chosen as the basis of comparison, and this choice is necessarily arbitrary. The heart of the paper is an ingenious geometricl analysis that shows that none of the index numbers in use resolve this ambiguity or give estimates of the change in price that correspond to the correct one.

Although Leontief perceived the issue and demonstrated the inadequacy of all practical price index formulas, he did not push the analysis as far or as fruitfully as was done a few years later by Hicks and Samuelson who based their treatments much more explicitly than he did on the welfare significance of the different index number formulas. To the reader equipped with the hindsight provided by subsequent literature, it is apparent that Leontief grasped the basic issues in the construction and interpretation of price indices, but not quite firmly enough to advance our understanding of the problem.

These two examples will convey the general spirit and quality of Leontief's early work. It displays thorough technical mastery and a profound concern with the substantive meaning of the technical concepts, a concern that enabled him to perceive difficulties that he was not always able to resolve. His interests were as wide as economic theory and his critical acumen was sharp and effective. He continued to think and write in this vein even after he entered his middle period.

Leontief's middle period and major work began in 1936 when his first paper on input-output appeared. This was "Quantitative input and output relations in the economic system of the United States". It is highly significant and characteristic that this paper, while based upon a novel and important contribution to economic theory, lays its major emphasis on the numerical description of the American economic structure.

From this point on, Leontief's work shows a decisiveness, authoritativeness, and focus not previously evident. He has, so to speak, hit his stride and his writings, whether dealing with input-output or other topics, display the assurance that comes from having discovered his own creative touchstone. It is no longer the work of a clever young man, but that of an experienced scholar who knows what he is doing, and therefore, what others should be doing.

From about 1934 on, Leontief's major efforts were devoted to the development of input-output and its applications, and to the direction of the Harvard Economic Research Project, which he founded and headed. At the same time his interest in other aspects of economics continued and even broadened. He published papers on the theory of international trade, the theory of noncompetitive markets, Marxian theory, the estimation of demand curves, aggregative economics, and other topics. A few of the papers from this period deserve special mention. The paper on "Implicit theorizing: a methodological criticism of the Neo-Cambridge school" (1937) was more than an attack on some of the presuppositions invoked by Keynes' followers. It was, at root, an exposé of the dangers of constructing definitions for theoretical argumentation in such a way as to build in the conclusions to be established, an insidious form of begging the question that is very likely to arise when theoretical arguments are divorced from empirical observations. This danger has nowhere else been so clearly exposed and this paper has stood as a warning to a whole generation of economists.

The papers on the internal structure of functional relationships have already been mentioned. The paper in *Bulletin of the American Mathematical Society* developed the mathematical theory of functions of several variables in which some of the arguments were separable—that is, in which some of the arguments entered the function only through some implicit subsidiary functional relationships. The paper in *Econometrica* explored the economic applications of such functions. In the theory of consumption these include utility functions, since the variables for the quantities consumed of different commodities can be grouped according to the purposes that those commodities serve. This insight was later developed further by Strotz (in his theory of utility trees) and by Lancaster. In the theory of production, which was Leontief's particular interest, separable variables arise when different primary inputs are used in different stages of an integrated production process to produce, in effect, different intermediate goods that are used in the final production process. Furthermore, this analysis resumes in a more fruitful way the problem of index numbers and composite commodities that Leontief essayed some ten years previously.

The connection is that an index number is essentially a subsidiary functional relationship that incorporates the effects of a group of primary variables on some functional relationship that is being studied. These papers brought out the fundamental logical theory that underlies a wide variety of economic theories and concepts. Their full implications have yet to be exhausted.

As time went on, Leontief's interests evolved beyond the development of economic theory and moved toward its applications and even to broad problems of economic criticism. Especially in the 1960's he became increasingly sensitive to the limitations of automatic market adjustments and began to question seriously some of the assumptions on which orthodox economic theory is based. These new concerns are reflected most clearly in his articles in the *New York Review of Books* in which he reported his sympathetic impressions of the Cuban economic experiment, derived during a brief visit to that country. His publications then became widely scattered, including contributions to *Daedulus, Foregin Affairs*, the *Bulletin of the Atomic Scientists*, the *Harvard Law Review*, the *Harvard Business Review, Peace Research*, and repeatedly the *Scientific American*. In all of these articles he reached out to inform the general public of the fruits of his years of study of economic problems, again reflecting his rejection of the concept of economics as a pure, ivory-tower science. These articles reflect also increasing disquiet over fundamental inadequacies in orthodox economics. Leontief has clearly travelled a long way since his early defense of traditional economic analysis against the Keynesian attack. Where these most recent concerns will take him is still to be seen.

Leontief and Input-Output Analysis

The discovery and development of input-output analysis is undoubtedly Leontief's major life work. I have already emphasized that although Leontief discovered the theory and essential mathematical properties of input-output analysis, he had been anticipated in this and it was by no means his main interest or contribution. He saw little purpose in laying out some algebraic relationships that other people might or might not implement. In his view the contribution of any economic theory lay in the light it threw on real economies and their problems, and the test of the significance of a theory lay in its ability to shed such light. The task of the theorist then only began with promulgating a new concept. The crucial task was to verify the empirical significance of the concept and the validity of its predictions, and this could be done only by practical, empirical observation. In so thinking, Leontief was following in the tradition of Newton who withheld publication of his theory of gravitation for twenty years, until he was able to show that the orbit of the moon conformed to it. Fortunately, Leontief did not have to wait for twenty years. In spite of severe obstacles he was able to construct numerical input-output tables for the United States in the middle 1930's. These first input-output tables were exceedingly crude by modern standards—hardly more advanced, comparatively, than the Wright Brothers' first airplane—but they did provide the needed empirical verification. They established that even at that time statistical resources and computational facilities were adequate to make the construction of input-output tables a practical enterprise. They also provided encouraging, though not decisive, evidence in favor of the fundamental empirical postulate of input-output analysis, the postulate that the structural input-output coefficients were relatively stable over time and over a reasonable range of changes in economic circumstances. With this evidence in hand, Leontief was confident that he had discovered a significant and useful tool of economic analysis. Indeed, he had.

Leontief's first, preliminary papers announcing his discovery appeared in 1936 and 1937. His definitive monograph, *The Structure of American Economy, 1919–1929*, was published in 1941. The monograph deserves our particular attention.

The Structure of American Economy, first edition, contained both theoretical and numerical discussions. The theoretical analysis was inspired, quite explicitly, by Walras' vision of a fully determinate general equilibrium system. Indeed, it was largely a severe simplification of Walras' equations, designed to make them empirically implementable. This simplification consisted in going back to Walras' original presentation of his system in which the inputs required for the production of each commodity were assumed to be simply proportional to the level of output of that commodity. But Leontief's reformulation included a significant, in fact decisive, innovation. Whereas Walras had subordinated the whole question of intermediate goods, the purchases of the various industries from each other emerged as the central set of equations in Leontief's system. What began as a bold simplification ended as a basic shift in the emphasis of the whole system.

In this first version of input-output analysis the reorientation was not complete. Leontief retained Walras' concept of an entirely self-contained, self-determining system of economic relationships. This was the "closed" input-output system, and the requirements for closing it not only introduced some technical complications that were later eliminated, but rendered the system inappropriate for studying the impact of external events and disturbances on the level of economic activity. However, only a minor shift in emphasis and abandonment of the goal of complete internal determination were required to put the system into its modern, "open" form. These changes were accomplished three years later, in "Output, employment, consumption, and investment", and incorporated in the second edition (1951).

The numerical analysis was correspondingly primitive, by subsequent standards, but correspondingly path-breaking. It consisted of the construction of two ten-sector input-output tables, one for 1919 and one for 1929, both based primarily on data from the Census of Manufactures.[1] A ten-sector table is nowadays considered to be more like a pilot-model than a usable instrument of analysis, but all the essential conceptual and statistical difficulties had to be overcome to construct the first two, and tables of this size strained the computational facilities available in the 1930's. These tables, however limited for purposes of practical analysis, confirmed the empirical validity of the method and constituted the fundamental break-through. All the rest has been development and explication.

It is hard, now, to revive the excitement created by these first developments. The Walrasian general equilibrium theory was a scheme of economic interconnections in principle, which might be implemented in some future, visionary stage of the development of the science. With Leontief's papers that higher, more competent stage arrived abruptly. The time-honored theory was lifted suddenly out of the textbooks and treatises and placed in the arena of applied economic analysis.

There was a brief lag between the announcement and the effect, because nearly all economic research was in abeyance during World War II, but immediately after the war the ferment boiled over. The time was ripe. Statistical resources in the United States and other economically advanced countries were adequate or almost so. The electronic computer was clearly visible on the horizon, which meant that huge masses of data could be handled and appalling computations could be performed without difficulty. A new interest in quantitative methods was gaining ground in all branches of economic theory and practice.

Leontief published "Output, employment, consumption, and investment" while the war was still in progress. In it he introduced the modern "open" version of input-output and showed how it could be used to estimate the effect of postwar reconversion on the pattern of economic activity and employment. This was the first of his long series of applications of the technique to pressing economic problems.

Almost immediately after the war, the United States Bureau of Labor Statistics adopted the input-output method for its projections of manpower needs and employment opportunities. Leontief, of course, played a central role in this work. The resources of a major statistical agency made it possible to undertake very large and detailed input-output tables; eventually a table with more than 400 sectors was constructed.

Simultaneously, input-output analysis became a major field of economic research. The Harvard Economic Research Project, which is devoted to it, was founded in 1948 with Leontief as director. The first international conference on the subject was held in 1950. By 1955 an extensive bibliographic

---

[1] Input-Output coefficients for a 44-sector table were compiled, but were consolidated into ten sectors for analysis, 44 sectors being far beyond the capacity of the computational facilities of the time.

compilation of research on input-output was in order; several others have followed. Three major international conferences on input-output have been held, and countless local and subsidiary ones. Several textbooks have appeared. Input-output tables of varying degrees of elaborateness have been constructed for at least 50 countries and for several subnational regional economies. The steady flow of work on input-output—theoretical empirical, and policy-oriented—is so great that it merits its own category in the American Economic Association's current bibliographies of research in economics.

Leontief has remained in the forefront of these developments. For the past twenty-five years he has been applying the input-output approach to a succession of the most pressing economic problems of the day.

I have already mentioned "Output, employment, consumption, and investment" (1944). This paper developed the application of input-output analysis to the tasks of estimating the effect of post-war reconversion on the levels of employment and activity in different economic sectors. The problem has remained important ever since, and Leontief has published on it repeatedly, as in "The economic effects of disarmament" (1961) and "The economic impact, industrial and regional, of an arms cut" (1965). These papers have established input-output as a primary tool for assessing hard-headedly in some detail the importance of military procurement for maintaining the levels of economic activity and employment in the United States.

He first applied input-output analysis to the problems of international trade in "Exports, imports, domestic output, and employment" (1946). He returned to this application in 1954–56, in a pair of remarkable papers: "Domestic production and foreign trade: the American capital position re-examined" (1954) and "Factor proportions and the structure of American trade: further theoretical and empirical analysis" (1956). In these papers he used the input-output technique to estimate the relative capital and labor contents of American imports and exports, and was led to the surprising conclusion that American exports are more labor-intensive than American imports, a flat contradiction of received doctrines and current beliefs. This finding, though open to some question, brushed aside much superficial thinking about trading relationships and introduced a potent new method for studying them. The analysis was far from straightforward; the limitations of the data forced him to resort to highly ingenious, indirect methods of estimation and inference.

In 1946 also, Leontief initiated the input-output analysis of inflationary processes, in "Wages, profits, and prices". This paper showed how wage and price increases originating in different sectors of the economy are diffused throughout the price structure, and included quantitative estimates of the differential impacts of increases in different sectors. This, too, remains a current and important problem and the methods introduced by Leontief are among the most powerful ones we have for analyzing it.

Most recently, the impact of economic activity on the quality of the environment has become a prominent source of social concern. Input-output analysis is a natural tool for studying the burden imposed on the environment by different forms of economic activity. Leontief has contributed a significant paper to this field of application, "Environmental repercussions and the economic structure: an input-output approach" (1970).

Other applications of input-output analysis to practical economic problems are too numerous, varied, and well-known to be listed here, but one additional area of application is too fundamental to be ignored. Input-output analysis has proved to be an indispensible component of economic development planning. It is for this reason that input-output tables have been compiled for so many of the nations of the world—at least fifty—and for many subnational regions. These tables serve many purposes, such as indicating appropriate relationships among economic sectors and permitting estimates of import requirements.

These last two applications have coalesced in Leontief's current work. He is now directing a large study under the auspices of the United Nations, in which he is using the input-output technique to examine the environmental implications of the United Nation's strategy for promoting the development of the less developed countries. This study is likely to result in recommendations for altering that strategy in the interest of protecting and preserving the world environment, and for encouraging the less-developed countries to give more weight to local environmental impacts in designing their own development policies.

This recital of applications and Leontief's role in them makes clear that input-output has had a larger impact on economic analysis than any innovation since the development of national income accounting and the Keynesian mode of aggregative analysis. It did not add any fresh, substantive insights to economic theory. On the contrary, its contribution lay in demonstrating that for many important purposes some of the time-hallowed insights, particularly those concerned with optimizing behavior, could be ignored, leading to a greatly simplified and practicable set of economic relationships. In short, input-output is a bold simplification of economic theory. Its substantive content, which required statistical and empirical confirmation, is that this austerely simplified model still conforms well enough to observed economic relationships to be informative for many purposes. This could not have been foreseen a priori, and the discovery that it was so, constituted one of the great economic discoveries of our generation.

Although Leontief's preponderant interest has been in pioneering in the application of input-output to practical issues, he has been deeply concerned also to extend the theory and thereby widen its practical potential. Two extensions have preoccupied him especially. One is temporal or dynamic, the study of the level of investment in different sectors from the input-output point of view. Leontief has devoted great effort to this extension, including the compilation of a detailed table of capital coefficients for the United States and the publication of a series of papers on the theory of dynamic input-output models. But, for a number of statistical and theoretical reasons that do not have to be reviewed here, this effort has not proved to be nearly as fruitful as the basic, static theory. It appears that the simplifications that make static input-output analysis so useful—in particular fixed input-output coefficients, a single producing sector for every commodity, and a single commodity for every sector—are not appropriate for dynamic analyses, in which a wider scope for economic choice is of the essence. For this reason dynamic input-output analysis has remained, largely, a textbook theory. In studies of economic development, where it has been applied faut de mieux, it has not proved very reliable.

The other urgent extension to which Leontief has devoted himself is spatial, the study of interregional and international trading relationships. This effort has been greeted with somewhat greater success. Interregional trading relationships, however, do violate the basic assumption of "one commodity, one source" and no fully satisfactory substitute for this postulate has been discovered for this context. This field also, therefore, cannot be counted among the most successful applications of input-output analysis.

In spite of these evident limitations,it is clear that input-output analysis has been one of the most fundamental and fruitful innovations in economic analysis in recent decades. It is not an advance in economic theory proper— in some respects it is a retreat—as much as in the art of applying economics to practical problems. The exact nature of the contribution is illuminated by fortuitous coincidence. In 1960 Piero Sraffa published *Production of Commodities by Means of Commodities: a Prelude to a Critique of Economic Theory.* In it he presents a very elegant independent discovery of the theoretical basis of input-output analysis. But, in contrast to Leontief's work, there are no numbers; only the closely-reasoned, logical underpinnings. And therein lies all the difference between an insightful contribution to economic theorizing and the discovery of a practical new tool of analysis. Sraffa was content to present some interesting and important logical relationships; Leontief was not content until he had showed how they could be measured and confirmed empirically, and applied to practical problems. It is the implementation that makes the discovery significant.

Concluding Remarks

I have reviewed above Leontief's contributions to economics in general and to input-output analysis, his outstanding achievement. This review reveals him as having an extraordinarily keen mind with a strong critical and empirical bent. He has, in addition, great technical and logical skill. Oddly enough, though he has contributed a major innovation, novelty and originality are not what Leontief seems to strive for in his work. It seems, rather, that he was driven to his innovation by his sharp critical acumen and his dissatisfaction with conceptual abstractions devoid of empirical counterparts. In input-output analysis and elsewhere he made his discoveries by starting with a traditional concept that dissatisfied him and striving to bridge the gap between that concept and the observable phenomena that it purported to describe.

Now this is nothing but the heart of "scientific method", as contrasted with "philosophic method". It is analogous to, say, Einstein's recognition that astronomical positions and velocities could not be observed absolutely but only relatively to one another, so that absolute position and velocity have no empirical referent. The ability to perceive the flaws in concepts that have long been taken for granted is a precious and rare one in all sciences, and especially so in economics where the "philosophic" (or a priori) and "scientific" (or empirical) approaches exist side by side. Leontief has this ability to a superlative degree. We have seen several examples, particularly input-output analysis and the study of index numbers. It is especially instructive that the record of his work contains not only the finally-perfected, highly-polished result of his researches, but, in both these instances, rough-hewn, indecisive way-stations along his road to clear understanding. It is almost as if were privileged to participate with him in the slow, vexatious drama of discovery. It is even illuminating that in some instances—one has been cited above—he failed to ask quite the right questions and to make his characteristic contribution.

Thus, Leontief stands, near the end of his career, as the model of the scientific method in economics. I cannot think of anyone who excels him in this regard among living economists. He is not a polemicist (as, say, Keynes was), though deeply motivated by social concerns. He is not an abstract theorist (like, say, Samuelson, whose scientific studies are nearly devoid of empirical verification and have little to do with his applied policy-oriented writing). He is not a descriptive empiricist (like, say, Kuznets). He, rather, combines all three orientations. He refines and revises theoretical models and concepts to render them empirically meaningful, and confirms them. He is preoccupied, hard-headedly, with the meaning and meaningfulness of the technical words and concepts that he uses and with interpreting economics in practical terms. To resort to a faddish word, he is and always has been concerned with the "relevance" of economics and with its application to "relevant" problems.

Herein lies his preeminence. The student of economics, of any age or stage, could do far worse then review Leontief's work on any topic to see scientific economics exemplified at its best. The discovery of input-output is a fitting capstone to his combination of scientific soundness and technical brilliance.

442 *Robert Dorfman*

BIBLIOGRAPHY

Books by Wassily Leontief

The Structure of American Economy, 1919–1929; an Empirical Application of Equilibrium Analysis. Cambridge, Mass.: Harvard University Press, 1941. Second edition, New York: Oxford University Press, 1951.

Studies in the Structure of the American Economy: Theoretical and Empirical Explorations in Input-Output Analysis, with H. B. Chenery and others. New York: Oxford University Press, 1953.

Essays in Economics, Theories and Theorizing. New York: Oxford University Press, 1966.

Input-Output Economics. New York: Oxford University Press, 1966.

Scholarly Papers by Wassily Leontief

"Die Bilanz der Russischen Volkswirtschaft—Eine methodologische Untersuchung", *Weltwirtschaftliches Archiv*, Vol. 22, No. 2, Oct. 1925, pp. 338–44, and *Weltwirtschaftliches Archiv—Chronik und Archivalien*, Vol. 22, (1925 II), pp. 265–69. Russ. transl. "Balans narodnogo khoziaistva SSSR—metodologicheskii razbor rabotii TSSU", *Planovoe Khoziaistvo*, Moscow, 1925, No. 12, pp. 254–58. Engl. transl. "The Balance of the Economy of the USSR", in: Spulber, N. (ed.), *Foundations of Soviet Strategy for Economic Growth, Selected Short Soviet Essays 1924–1930*. Indiana University Press, Bloomington, Indiana, 1964, pp. 89–94.

"Über Theorie und Statistik der Konzentration", *Jahrbücher für Nationalökonomie und Statistik*, Vol. 126, March 1927, pp. 301–11.

"Die Wirtschaft als Kreislauf", *Archiv für Sozialwissenschaft und Sozialpolitik*, 1928, Vol. 60, No. 3, pp. 577–623.

"Ein Versuch zur statistischen Analyse von Angebot und Nachfrage", *Weltwirtschaftliches Archiv — Chronik und Archivalien*, Vol. 30, No. 1, July 1929, pp. 1–53.

Review of: Marschak, J., "Elastizität der Nachfrage", *Archiv für Sozialwissenschaft und Sozialpolitik*, 1931, Vol. 66, No. 2, pp. 420–23.

"Studien über die Elastizität des Angebots", *Weltwirtschaftliches Archiv*, Vol. 35, No. 1, Jan. 1932, pp. 66–115.

Reivew of: Egner, E., "Der Sinn des Monopols in der gegenwärtigen Wirtschaftsordnung", *Journal of Political Economy*, Vol. 40, No. 5, Oct. 1932, pp. 714–16.

"The Use of Indifference Curves in the Analysis of Foreign Trade", *Quarterly Journal of Economics*, Vol. 47, No. 2, May 1933, pp. 493–503. Reprint in: Ellis, H. S., Metzler, L. A., *Readings in the Theory of International Trade*, The Blakiston Co., 1949, pp. 229–38.

"Pitfalls in the Construction of Demand and Supply Curves: A Reply", *Quarterly Journal of Economics*, Vol. 48, No. 1, Feb. 1934, pp. 355–61.

Review of: Kuznets, S., "Seasonal Variations in Industry and Trade", *Weltwirtschaftliches Archiv*, Vol. 39, No. 2, March 1934, p. 105.

"More Pitfalls in Demand and Supply Curve Analysis: A Final Word", *Quarterly Journal of Economics*, Vol. 48, No. 3, Aug. 1934, pp. 755–59.

"Verzögerte Angebotsanpassung und Partielles Gleichgewicht", *Zeitschrift für Nationalökonomie*, Vol. 5, No. 5, 1934, pp. 670–76. English transl. (Taskier, C. E.), "Delayed Adjustment of Supply and Partial Equilibrium", in *Essays in Economics*, see, item no. 103.

"Interest on Capital and Distribution: A Problem in the Theory of Marginal Productivity", *Quarterly Journal of Economics*, Vol. 48, No. 4, Nov. 1934, pp. 147–61.

"Helping the Farmer" in: Brown, D. V. & others, *The Economics of the Recovery Program*, McGraw-Hill, 1934, pp. 139–59.

"Price-Quantity Variations in the Business Cycles", *The Review of Economic Statistics*, Vol. 17, No. 4, May 1935, pp. 21–27.

"Composite Commodities and the Problem of Index Numbers", *Econometrica* Vol. 4, No. 1, Jan. 1936, pp. 39–59.

"Quantitative Input and Output Relations in the Economic System of the United States", *Review of Economic Statistics*, Vol. 18, No. 3, Aug. 1936, pp. 105–25.

"Stackelberg on Monopolistic Competition", *Journal of Political Economy*, Vol. 44, No. 4, Aug. 1936, pp. 554–59.

"The Fundamental Assumptions of Mr. Keynes' Monetary Theory of Unemployment", *Quarterly Journal of Economics*, Vol. 51, No. 1, Nov. 1936, pp. 192–97. Reprint in: *Memorandum*, Universitetets Socialøkonomiske Institutt, Oslo Norway, May 13, 1954.

"Note on the Pure Theory of Capital Transfer", Chapter VIII in: *Explorations in Economics, Notes and Essays Contributed in Honor of F. W. Taussig*, McGraw-Hill, 1937, pp. 84–91.

"Implicit Theorizing: A Methodological Criticism of the Neo-Cambridge School", *Quarterly Journal of Economics*, Vol. 51, No. 1, Feb. 1937, pp. 337–51.

"Interrelation of Prices, Output, Savings and Investment: A Study in Empirical Application of Economic Theory of General Interdependence", *Review of Economic Statistics*, Vol. 19, No. 3, Aug. 1937, pp. 109–32.

Review of: Pigou, A. C., "Socialism vs. Capitalism", *American Economic Review*, Vol. 28, No. 2, June 1938, pp. 410–11.

"The Significance of Marxian Economics for Present-Day Economic Theory", *American Economic Review*, Vol. 28, No. 1, Supplement, March 1938, pp. 1–9.

"Empirical Application of the Economic Theory of General Interdependence", *Econometrica*, Apr. 1938, Vol. 6, No. 2, pp. 190–91.

"The Theory of Limited and Unlimited Discrimination", *Quarterly Journal of Economics*, Vol. 54, No. 3, May 1940, pp. 490–501.

"Elasticity of Demand Computed from Cost Data", *American Economic Review*, Vol. 30, No. 4, Dec. 1940, pp. 814–17.

The Structure of American Economy, 1919–1929. Harvard University Press, 1941. (1st edition), 181 pages + 2 tables in jacket.

"Economic Statistics and Postwar Policies", Chapter IX, in: Harris, S. (ed), *Postwar Economic Problems*, McGraw-Hill, 1943, pp. 159–68.

"Output, Employment, Consumption, and Investment", *Quarterly Journal of Economics*, Vol. 58, No. 2, Febr. 1944, pp. 290–313. Spanish transl. "Producción, consumo e inversión", *Trimestre Económico*, Vol. 12, No. 2, July–Sept. 1945, pp. 252–82.

Review of: Bienstock, G., Schwartz, S. M. & Yugow, A., "Management in Russian Industry", *Review of Economic Statistics*, Vol. 26, No. 3, Aug. 1944, pp. 161–62.

"A new Approach to the Problem of Market Analysis", *American Management Association*, Marketing Series No. 59, 1945, pp. 3–16.

"The Pure Theory of the Guaranteed Annual Wage Contract", *Journal of Political Economy*, Vol. 54, No. 1, Febr. 1946, pp. 76–79.

"Exports, Imports, Domestic Output, and Employment", *Quarterly Journal of Economics*, Vol. 60, No. 1, Febr. 1946, pp. 171–93. Spanish transl. "Expor-

444   *Robert Dorfman*

taciones, importaciones, producción nacional y occupación", *Trimestre Económico*, Vol. 14, No. 1, Apr.–June 1947, pp. 106–30.

"The Economics of Industrial Interdependence", *Dun's Review*, Vol. 54, Feb. 1946, pp. 22–26, 42–54.

"Wages, Profits, and Prices", *Quarterly Journal of Economics*, Vol. 61, No. 1, Nov. 1946, pp. 26–39.

"A Note on the Interrelation of Subsets of Independent Variables of a Continuous Function with Continuous First Derivatives", *Bulletin of the American Mathematical Society*, Vol. 53, No. 4, April 1947, pp. 343–50.

"Introduction to a Theory of the Internal Structure of Functional Relationships", *Econometrica*, Vol. 15, No. 4, Oct. 1947, pp. 361–73.

"Structural Matrices of National Economies", *Proceedings of the International Statistical Conferences*, 1947, Vol. V, pp. 273–82 Reprint in: *Econometrica*, Vol. 17, Supplement, July 1949, pp. 273–282.

"Comments on: Patinkin, D., 'Multiple Plant Firms'", *Quarterly Journal of Economics*, Vol. 61, No. 3, Aug. 1947, pp. 650–51.

"Postulates: Keynes' General Theory and the Classists" Chapter 19 in: Harris, S. (ed.), *The New Economics*, A. Knopf, New York, 1948, pp. 232–42.

"Note on the Pluralistic Interpretation of History and the Problem of Interdisciplinary Cooperation", *The Journal of Philosophy*, Vol. 45, No. 23, Nov. 1948, pp. 617–24.

"Computational Problems Arising in Connection with Economic Analysis of Interindustrial Relationships", *Proceedings of a Symposium on Large-scale Digital Calculating Machinery*, Harvard University Press, 1948, pp. 169–75.

"Econometrics", Chapter 11 in: Ellis, H. S. (ed.), *A Survey of Contemporary Economics*, The Blakiston Co., 1948, pp. 388–411.

"Recent Development in the Study of Interindustrial Relations", Papers and Proceedings, *American Economic Review*, Vol. 39, No. 3, May 1949, pp. 211–25.

"Comment to: Scott, I. O., re "Postulates: Keynes' General Theory", *Quarterly Journal of Economics*, Vol. 63, No. 4, Nov. 1949, pp. 567–69.

"Dynamic Analysis of Economic Equilibrium", *A Symposium on Largescale Digital Calculating Machinery*, Computation Laboratory, Sept. 1949, Harvard University Press, 1951, pp. 333–37.

"Comments on: Klein, L. R., 'Studies in Investment Behavior'", National Bureau of Economic Research, *Conference on Business Cycles* (Nov. 1949), New York, 1951, pp. 310–313.

"The Consistency of the Classical Theory of Money and Prices", *Econometrica*, Vol. 18, No. 1, Jan. 1950, pp. 21–24.

"Joseph A. Schumpeter (1883–1950)", *Econometrica*, Vol. 18, No. 2, April 1950, pp. 103–110.

"Les tendances future éventuelles des relations économiques internationales des États-Unis", *Revue Economique*, No. 3, May 1951, pp. 271–278.

"Some Basic Problems of Structural Analysis", *Review of Economics and Statistics*, Vol. 34, No. 1, Feb. 1952, pp. 1–9.

Review of: Stone, R., "The Role of Measurement in Economics", *Journal of Political Economy*, Vol. 60, No. 2, April 1952, pp. 168–69.

"The Input-Output Approach in Economic Analysis", in: *Input-Output Relations Proceedings of a Conference on Inter-Industrial Relations, Held at Driebergen, Holland, 1953* (H. E. Stenfert & N. V. Kroese, Leyden, Holland), pp. 1–23.

"The Forest Economy in Relation to Other Branches of the Economy" in: Duers, W. & Vaux, H. (eds.), *Research in the Economics of Forestry*, The Waverly

Press, Baltimore, Md., 1953 (Charles Lathrop Pack Forestry Foundation), pp. 60–64.

Comments on Grossman, G., "National Income", in: Bergson, A. (ed.), *Soviet Economic Growth*, Row, Peterson & Co., 1953, pp. 32–33.

Review of: Diebold, J., "Automation: The Advent of the Automatic Factory", *The Management Review*, July 1953, p. 425.

"Domestic Production and Foreign Trade: The American Capital Position Re-Examined", Proceedings of the *American Philosophical Society*, Vol. 97, No. 4, Sept. 1953. 1953, pp. 332–49. Reprint in: *Economia Internazionale*, Geneva, Vol. 7, No. 1, 1954, pp. 9–45 (with French, German, Spanish resumés).

"Mathematics in Economics" (The Josia Willard Gibbs Lecture for 1953), *Bulletin of the American Mathematical Society*, Vol. 60 No. 3, May 1954, pp. 215–33. Italian transl. "La matematica in economica", *L'Industria*, Rivista di Economia Politica, No. 2, 1955, pp. 3–23. Spanish transl. "Las Matematicas en la Economia", *Direcciones Contemporáneas del Pensiamento Económico, Aspectos de su Problematica*, Universidad Nacional de La Plata, Instituto de Filosofia, Historia y Sociologia de la Economia, 1961, Vol. 2, pp. 17–45.

"National Economic Problems", *Naval War College Review*, Vol. 7, No. 5, Jan. 1955, pp. 51–66.

"Some Basic Problems of Empirical Input-Output Analysis", in: *Input-Output Analysis: An Appraisal*, Studies in Income and Wealth, Vol. 18, National Bureau of Economic Research, New York, 1955, pp. 9–51. Italian transl. "Problemi fondamentali dell'analisi empirica per le interdipendenze strutturali di un sistema economico", *L'Industria*, Rivista di Economia Politica, No. 4, 1952, pp. 3–17.

Review of: Walras, L. (transl. by Jaffé, W.), "Elements of Pure Economics or the Theory of Social Wealth", *Southern Economic Journal*, Vol. 22, No. 2, October 1955, pp. 249–50.

"Prefatory Note" pp. 1–2, "Input-Output Analysis and the General Equilibrium Theory", pp. 41–49, in: *The Structural Interdependence of the Economy, Proceedings of an International Conference on Input-Output Analysis*, Varenna, June 27 – July 10, 1954. John Wiley & Sons, Inc., N. Y. A. Giuffrè (Ed.) Milano, 1956.

"Factor Proportions and the Structure of American Trade: Further Theoretical and Empirical Analysis", *Review of Economics and Statistics*, Vol. 38, No. 4, Nov. 1956, pp. 386–407.

Comments on: Copeland, M., "Feasibility of a Standard Comprehensive System of Social Accounts", in: *Problems in the International Comparison of Economic Accounts*, Studies in Income and Wealth, National Bureau of Economic Research, Vol. 20, N. Y., 1957, pp. 95–100.

"Theoretical Note on Time-Preference, Productivity of Capital, Stagnation, and Economic Growth", *American Economic Review* Vol. 48, No. 1, March 1958, pp. 105–111. Reprint in: *Contribuicões a Análise do Desenvolvimento*, Economico, Livraria Agir, Rio de Janeiro, 1957, pp. 207–216. Reprint in: Morgan, T. et al., (eds.), *Readings in Economic Development*, Wadsworth Publishing Co., 1963, pp. 113–119. Spanish transl. "Nota teorética sobre preferencia en el tiempo, productividad del capital, estanciamiento y crecimiento económico", *El Trimestre Económico*, México, Vol. 25, No. 3, July–Sept. 1958, pp. 454–61.

Reply to: Valavanis, S., "Comment on 'Factor Proportions and the Structure of American Trade: Further Theoretical and Empirical Analysis'", *Review of Economics and Statistics*, Vol. 40, No. 1, Part 2, Supplement, Feb. 1958, pp. 119–22.

446   Robert Dorfman

"The State of Economic Science", *Review of Economics and Statistics*, Vol. 40, No. 2, May 1958, pp. 103–6. (A review of: Koopmans, T. C., "Three Essays on the State of Economic Science".)

"Die Analyse der volkswirtschaftlichen Struktur", *Arbeitsgemeinschaft für Rationalisierung des Landes Nordrhein-Westfalen*, Heft 36, 1958, pp. 13–18.

"Hommage au Docteur François Quesnay", *Bi-centenaire du "Tableau Economique" de François Quesnay (1758–1958)*, Organisé par l'Association française de Science Economique, 1–3 June, 1958, Méré et Paris, pp. 37–38.

"Interregionale Beziehungen wirtschaftlicher Aktivitäten", in: *Probleme des räumlichen Gleichgewichts in der Wirtschaftswissenschaft*, Verhandlungen auf der Tagung des Vereins für Sozialpolitik Gesellschaft für Wirtschafts- und Sozialwissenschaften in Göttingen, 1958, Duncker & Humblot, Berlin 1959, pp. 46–55.

"The Problem of Quality and Quantity in Economics", *Daedalus*, Journal of the American Academy of Arts and Sciences, Fall 1959, Vol. 88, No. 4, pp. 622–32.

"Time Preference and Economic Growth", A Reply to: Westfield, F. M., Comments, *American Economic Review*, Vol. 49, No. 5, Dec. 1959, pp. 1041–43.

"The Decline and Rise of Soviet Economic Science", *Foreign Affairs*, Vol. 38, No. 2, Jan. 1960, pp. 261–72. Reprints in: Leeman, W. A. (ed.), *Capitalism, Market Socialism, and Central Planning*, Houghton-Mifflin Co., 1963, pp. 91–101. Shaffer, H. (ed.), *The Soviet Economy*, A Collection of Western and Soviet Views, Appleton-Century-Crofts, 1963, pp. 367–77. Japanese transl. summary (Kuratani, Y.,) *The Economist*, Tokyo 1960. Japanese transl. (Kaizuka, K.,), *The Kezai Seminar*, Tokyo, 1960. Italian transl. "Il nuovo corso della scienza economica sovietica", *Mercurio*, Anno III, No. 11, Nov. 1960, pp. 11–18. German transl. "Niedergang und Aufstieg der sowjetischen Wirtschaftswissenschaft", *Hamburger Jahrbuch für Wirtschafts- und Gesellschaftspolitik*, Vol. V, J. C. B. Mohr (Paul Siebeck), Tübingen, 1960, pp. 33–43.

"Einsatz-Ausstoss-Analyse", *Handwörterbuch der Sozialwissenschaften* (German Encyclopedia of Social Sciences), Göttingen, Germany, 1960, pp. 83–91. English transl. in: Kapp, K. W. & others (eds.), *History of Economic Thought*, A Book of Readings, College Outlines Series, 2nd ed., Barnes & Nobles, Inc., New York, 1963, pp. 373–78.

Preface to: Paretti, V., Cao-Pinna, V., Cugia, L., and Righi, C., *Struttura e Prospettive dell'economia energetica italiana*, Edizioni Scientifiche Einaudi, Torino, 1960, pp. XIII–XVI.

Introduction to: Silk, L., *The Research Revolution*, McGraw-Hill, New York, 1960, pp. 1–8. German transl. "Das wirtschaftliche Problem der organisierten Forschung", *Hamburger Jahrbuch für Wirtschafts- und Gesellschaftspolitik*, Vol. VI, J. C. B. Mohr (Paul Siebeck), Tübingen, 1961, pp. 74–78. Italian transl. "Il problema economico della 'ricerca organizzata'", *Rivista di Politica Economica*, Anno 51, III Serie, fasc. XII, Dec. 1961, pp. 3–8.

"The Economic Effects of Disarmament" (with Hoffenberg, M.), *Scientific American*, Vol. 204, No. 4, April 1961, pp. 47–55. Reprints in: Berkowitz, M. & Bock, P. G. (eds.), *American National Security*, Free Press, New York, 1964, pp. 398–408.

"Lags and the Stability of Dynamic Systems: A Rejoinder" (to Sargan, J. D., "Lags and the Stability of Dynamic Systems: A Reply", *Econometrica*, Vol. 29/4, Oct. 1961, pp. 659–69, 674–75.

"Greater Efficiency in the Western World", in: Good, I. J. (ed.), *The Scientist Speculates*, William Heinemann Ltd., London, 1962, pp. 216–17.

"Multiregional Input-Output Analysis" (in collaboration with Strout, A.), in: Baroa, T. (ed.), *Structural Interdependence and Economic Development*, Proceedings of an International Conference on Input-Output Techniques, Geneva, 1961, MacMillan-St. Martin's Press, 1963, pp. 119–50. German transl. "Die multiregionale Input-Output Analyse", *Arbeitsgemeinschaft für Forschung des Landes Nordrhein-Westfalen*, Vol. 123, Westdeutscher Verlag, 1963, pp. 7–53 (English and French summaries).

"Statement" in: *Economic Aspects of Government Patent Policies*, Hearings before a Subcommittee on Monopoly of the Select Committee on Small Business, United States Senate, 88th Congress, 1st Session, March 7, 8, 13 & 14, 1963. Government Printing Office, Washington, 1963, pp. 231–37, 250–55.

"The Anatomy of Planning" (Address delivered at the Canadian Manufacturers' Association's Annual General Meeting, Toronto June 3, 1963), *Industrial Canada*, July 1963, pp. 94–96. German transl. "Anatomie der Planung", *Hamburger Jahrbuch für Wirtschafts und Gesellschaftspolitik*, Vol. 9, 1964, J. C. B. Mohr (P. Siebeck), Tübingen, pp. 53–60.

"Discussion du Rapport du Professeur F. Perroux" (Perroux's report "Les industries motrices et la croissance d'une économie nationale", Colloque franco-canadien sur la planification, Montréal, Nov. 1963), *L'Actualité Economique*, Vol. 39, Nos. 3–4, Oct. 1963 – March 1964, pp. 419–25.

"The Structure of Development", *Scientific American*, Vol. 209, No. 3, Sept. 1963, pp. 148–66. Reprints in: *Technology and Economic Development*, A Scientific American Book, A. Knopf, New York, 1963, pp. 105–25, and *Technology and Economic Development*, Penguin Books, Harmondsworth, Middlesex, 1965. Italian transl. "La struttura dello sviluppo", *L'Industria*, Rivista di Economia Politica, No. 4, Oct.–Dec. 1964, pp. 532–46. Spanish transl. "La Estructura dell desarrollo", *Información Commercial Española*, Ministerio de Comercio, Servicio de Estudios, Madrid, Jan. 1967, No. 401, pp. 59–70.

"When Should History be Written Backwards?", *The Economic History Review*, Second Series, Vol. 16, No. 1, 1963, pp. 1–8 (translation of a French lecture presented at the College de France, March 1962). Spanish transl. "Cuando debe escribirse la historia hacia atrás?", *Desarrollo Económico*, Buenos Aires, Vol. 4, No. 13, April–June 1964, pp. 11–20.

"Tecniche moderne per la pianificazione e la previsione economica", *La Scuola in Azione*, Ente Nazionale Idrocarburi—ENI, Scuola Enrico Mattei di Studi Superiori Sugli Idrocarburi, Anno di Studi 1963–64, No. 23, pp. 5–16. English version, "Modern Techniques for Economic Planning and Projection," in *Essays in Economics*.

"On Assignment of Patent Rights on Inventions Made Under Government Research Contracts", *Harvard Law Review*, Vol. 77, No. 3, Jan. 1964, pp. 491–97.

"Alternatives to Armament Expenditures", *Bulletin of the Atomic Scientists*, Vol. 20, No. 6, June 1964, pp. 19–21.

"An International Comparison of Factor Costs and Factor Use: A Review Article", *American Economic Review*, Vol. 54, No. 4 Part I, June 1964, pp. 335–45.

"Proposal for the Establishment by the United Nations of an International Scientific Agency for Technical Economics", *Proceedings of the Fourteenth Pugwash Conference on Science and World Affairs*, "International Cooperation for Science and Disarmament", Venice, April 11–16, 1965, pp. 153–55. Reprint: "An Institute for Technical Economics", *Bulletin of the Atomic Scientists*, Vol. 21, No. 9., Sept. 1965, p. 46.

448 *Robert Dorfman*

"The Economic Impact—Industrial and Regional—of an Arms Cut" (with others), *Review of Economics and Statistics*, Vol. 47, No. 3, Aug. 1965, pp. 217–41. Reprint in: *Economic Effect of Vietnam Spending*, Hearings before the Joint Economic Committee, Congress of the United States, 90th Congress, 1st Session, Vol. II, "The Military Impact on the American Economy: Now and After Vietnam, A Compendium of Statements, Articles and Papers, compiled as background material, Government Printing Office, Washington, 1967, pp. 687–724. Reprint (abbreviated version) entitled: "The Impact of an Arms Cut Employment", *Labor Today*, Vol. 4, No. 4, Sept. 1965, pp. 3–7. Japanese transl. (abridged) of a lecture presented at the Japan Economic Research Center, Tokyo, Nov. 1966, in: *Bulletin of the Japan Economic Research Center*, Jan. 1, 1967, pp. 2–7.

"The Rates of Long-Run Economic Growth and Capital Transfer from Developed to Underdeveloped Areas", Paper presented at the Study Week on the Econometric Approach to Development Planning, Pontifical Adacemy of Sciences, Vatican, Rome, Oct. 1963. Included in: *Semaine D'étude sur le rôle de l'analyse économétrique dans la formulation de plans de développement*, Oct. 7–13, 1963, Pontificia Academia Scientiarum, Vatican, Rome, 1965, vol. 2, pp. 1039–68; also in: *Study Week on the Econometric Approach to Development Planning*, North-Holland Publishing Co.—Rand McNally & Co., 1965, pp. 1039–56. Spanish transl. "Las transferencias de capital de las zonas desarrolladas a las subdesarrolladas y sus tasas futuras de crecimiento económico", in Benard, J.; Kaldor, N. et al., *Programacion del desarrollo economico*, Fondo de Cultura Económica, México-Buenos Aires, 1965, pp. 131–54.

"Primer for the Great Society", A review article of *Technology and the American Economy*, Report of the National Commission on Technology, Automation and Economic Progress, Government Printing Office, Washington, D. C., 1966, in: *The New York Review of Books*, Vol. 7, No. 10, Dec. 15, 1966, pp. 20–24.

"Changements technologiques, consommation, épargne et emploi dans le cadre de la croissance économique", Paper presented at Congrès du Centennaire de la Caisse d'Epargne et de Retraite, Bruxelles, Belgique, Nov. 16–19, 1965, in: *L'épargne dans la recherche économique contemporaine*, Bruxelles, 1966, pp. 127–37. English version: "Technological Change, Consumption, Saving and Employment in Economic Growth", in *Saving in Contemporary Economic Research*, Brussels, 1966, pp. 123–32. German transl. "Technologische Verändrungen, Verbrauch, Sparen und Beschäftigung im Prozess des wirtschaftlichen Wachstums", in: *Das Sparen in der gegenwartigen Wirtschaftsforschung*, Brüssel, 1966. pp. 127–37. Dutch transl. "Technologische wijzigingen, verbruik, sparen en Tewerkstelling in de economische groei", in: *Het sparen in het hedendaags economisch onderzoek*, Brussel, 1966, pp. 131–41.

"La posición de las industrias metalúrgicas en la estructura de una economia en proceso de industrialización" (with Carter, A. P.), Spanish translation of "The Position of Metalworking Industries in the Structure of an Industrializing Economy", Paper presented at the Interregional Symposium on the Development of Metalworking Industries in Developing Countries, United Nations, Center for Industrial Development, Moscow, Sept. Oct. 1966; in: *Economia Industrial*, Ministerio de Industria, Madrid, No. 36, December 1966, pp. 9–37.

"The New Outlook in Economics", University of York, Sir Ellis Hunter Memorial Lectures, 3, July 1967, University of York, 8 pages.

"An Alternative to Aggregation in Input-Output Analysis and National Accounts", *Review of Economics and Statistics*, Vol. 49, No. 3, Aug. 1967, pp. 412–419.

"Input-Output Analysis", *International Encyclopedia of the Social Sciences*, The Macmillan Co. and the Free Press, Vol. 7, pp. 345–53.

Struktureller Ansatz zur Analyse internationaler ökonomischer Interdependenzen, Institut für Weltwirtschaft an der Universität Kiel, Bernhard-Harms-Vorlesungen, herausgegeben von Professor Dr. Herbert Giersch.

"Environmental Repercussions and the Economic Structure—An Input-Output Approach, *Review of Economics and Statistics*, August 1970, Vol. LII, No. 3, pp. 262–271. German transl. "Theoretische Annahmen und nicht beobachtete Fakten", *Fortschrittliche Betriebsführung, Zeitschrift für die* Unternehmensleitung, March 1972.

Comments on John Chipman's "Induced Technical Change and Patterns of International Trade", in *The Technology Factor in International Trade*, editor Raymond Vernon, Universities-National Bureau Conference Series, No. 22, 1970, pp. 132–138, 141–2.

"Theoretical Assumptions and Nonobserved Facts", *American Economic Review*, March 1971, pp. 1–7.

Other Literature Cited

H. E. Bray, "Rates of exchange", *American Mathematical Monthly*, vol. 29 (1922), 365–371.

R. Remak, "Kann die Volkswirtschaftslehre eine exakte Wissenschaft werden?", *Jahrbücher für Nationalökonomie und Statistik, Band 76* (1929), 703–735.

Piero Sraffa, *Production of Commodities by Means of Commodities.* Cambridge: Cambridge University Press, 1960.

A Nobel quest for the invisible hand

The award of the Nobel Memorial Prize in Economic Science to Gerard Debreu of the University of California at Berkeley was a welcome affirmation of the value of basic research in that subject. Professor Debreu is the purest of pure economists. He has left it to others to deal with the pressing problems of inflation, poverty, developing less-developed countries, and the rest. Instead, he has devoted his career to the enduring problems at the foundation of economics.

In large part, he was attracted by the intellectual challenge those problems present. But he was also motivated by the conviction that the solutions to the pressing problems depend sooner or later on solving the fundamental ones.

It is not easy for a noneconomist to appreciate what those fundamental problems are or what Professor Debreu has contributed to our grasp of them. I shall explain only one of them – the one where he made his most notable contribution.

This problem is a legacy of Adam Smith. Compared with Gerard Debreu, Adam Smith was an intensely practical man. One of Smith's principal purposes in writing "The Wealth of Nations" was to attack the tangle of mercantilist regulations and restrictions that then hobbled the economy of England.

In the course of this attack, he wrote his most famous passage:

"As every individual, therefore, endeavours as much as he can both to employ his capital in the support of domestic industry, and so to direct that industry that its produce may be of greatest value; every individual necessarily labors to render the annual revenue of the society as great as he can. He generally, indeed, neither intends to promote the public interest, nor knows how much he is promoting it ... and he is in this, as in many other cases, led by an invisible hand to promote an end which has no part of his intention."

Those words carry immediate conviction, and they have served as the unifying principle of economics ever since they were written. But they do not bear close inspection. Where is the assurance, for example, that a host of businessmen flocking to an industry that promises high profits will not so flood the market that their products sell for less than they cost? How, in general, could Adam Smith be so sure that without any coordination millions of businessmen would produce just the amounts of millions of commodities that the smooth working of the economy requires? Smith's explanation of the invisible hand – occupying barely a page – does little to answer such questions.

The first big step toward spelling out the workings of the invisible hand carefully enough to answer those questions was taken nearly 100 years later by Leon Walras. Walras, like all his successors in this enterprise, was a trained mathematician. He visualized the economy as a huge system of supply and demand equations. In free markets, businessmen would strive to maximize their profits and consumers would seek to get as much satisfaction as they could from spending their incomes, and both would haggle and adjust the quantities they were willing to buy and sell until they arrived at a price equilibrium, i.e., the point at which the amount of each commodity that consumers wanted to buy was equal to the amount that businesses wanted to produce and sell. It was later shown that at the equilibrium the total revenue generated by the economy and the satisfaction afforded to consumers would be as great as the available resources and technology permitted.

This might have settled the questions about the invisible hand except that the demonstration was defective and the supply-demand equations proposed could produce nonsensical results. In particular, the supply and demand equations for the equilibrium could require negative prices for some commodities and resources (to prevent unemployment, for example) and such high prices for other commodities that negative amounts were purchased.

Walras's formulation was a great advance, but the nonsensical possibilities, naturally, bothered economists. Sixty years elapsed before Abraham Wald devised a sound argument that showed that there was an equilibrium at which no price or quantities were negative. To do so, however, he had to make some very restrictive assumptions about the nature of the economy. His demonstration, therefore, provided only modest comfort: the invisible hand might work as alleged in the Waldian economy, but whether it could do so in any real economy remained an open question.

The next breakthrough was a stroke of serendipity. In an apparently unrelated area of research, Leonid V. Kantorovich (Nobel Laureate, 1975) and Geroge B. Dantzig, working independently and a few years apart, invented linear programming to facilitate the calculation of production plans for productive enterprises. Almost at once, Tjalling C. Koopmans (Nobel Laureate, 1975) perceived the implications of this arithmetic device for the gigantic enterprise called an economy, and introduced a new way of looking at the Smithian problem that avoided the complexities of dealing with all of Walras's supply and demand equations.

Taking this point of view, Kenneth J. Arrow (Noble Laureate, 1972) and Gerard Debreu published a brief paper that showed that the equilibrium conditions could be satisfied under much less unrealistic conditions than Wald's. This paper contained the essence of Professor Debreu's classic monograph, published a few years later, in 1959.

To summarize this history, Adam Smith proclaimed his conjecture in his effort to rid England of mercantilist restrictions. Thereafter, a long sequence of economists struggled to confirm it, or, at least, to ascertain the kind of economy for which it could be confirmed. At first these efforts were crude, but as more and more powerful methods of analysis were brought to bear it became possible to justify much of Smith's claim under increasingly realistic conditions. The Debreu formulation is a culmination thus far, of this prolonged effort.

While economists were trying to understand how much truth there is in the invisible hand thesis, the thesis became a slogan in the mouth of everyone who wanted the restrictions to be lifted, and in due course became an article of faith to the general public. It is the justification, for example, of antitrust policy. Indeed, it underlies all policies that rest on the belief that economic decisions are best left to the operation of free markets. By now, Adam Smith's role in spreading this doctrine has become a pious memory, and it is generally supported by asserting that economists have proved that unrestricted competition leads the economy to the best possible performance. The best way to check on the truth of that assertion is to summarize what this year's Nobel Prize winner in economics actually proved.

Professor Debreu showed that unrestricted competition could lead to the highest attainable level of consumer satisfaction in an economy that is very similar to ours but differs in a number of important respects. I'll mention two of the critical differences.

In Professor Debreu's theoretical economy, large size is of no advantage to a corporation, so that, for instance, an automobile company with 100 employees can produce cars as cheaply as General Motors. Ignoring the advantage of large size might have been acceptable in Smith's day, but clearly is not now. Second, in the Debreu economy either there is no uncertainty about what the future will bring or, what amounts to the same thing, there is such a rich array of futures markets for all commodities (including labour) that an investor can protect himself completely against uncertainty.

In such a world, one of the main sources of economic instability would be eliminated since all productive investments would be completely safe. That, too, is far different from our economy.

Besides, while Professor Debreu established that under his conditions the invisible hand could work effectively, he did not show that it would. To show "would" requires a plausible description of how the economy behaves when it is not in Walras's equilibrium, and a demonstration that that behaviour will lead it to equilibrium. He did not consider that problem. Nor did he tackle more long-range problems such as the effect that perfect freedom to compete would have on technological progress if it included abolition of patent protection.

In brief, Professor Debreu's achievement, though the most advanced yet, falls far short of showing that reliance on the invisible hand is the ideal economic policy in any feasible economy. But there is every reason to think that the invisible hand is more powerful and subtle than it has yet been proved to be. So the work of trying to define its limits goes on. Since the Debreu monograph was published, new methods, introduced largely by him and Stephen Smale, also of Berkeley, have somewhat diminished the importance of the assumption that large companies can be no more efficient than small ones. Some progress has been made toward analysing the behaviour of economies that are not in equilibrium. And the other limiting assumptions are under attack.

Is it likely that Adam Smith's brilliant conjecture will be confirmed in the end? I say no. In the first place, there is not going to be any end, inquiries into the foundations of a science never reach an end. Besides, the progress made so far supports the common-sense view that no such simple dictum can be relied on in all circumstances. What we shall gain from the work is a deeper understanding of how a market-guided economy operates, and a sharper view of which economic problems free markets can contend with and which ones should be dealt with by other means.

[28]

The Discovery of Linear Programming

ROBERT DORFMAN

*Around 1940, linear programming was an idea whose time had come.
Accordingly, it was discovered three times, independently, between 1939 and
1947, but each time in a somewhat different form dictated by the special
circumstances of that discovery. The first discovery was by L. V. Kantorovich,
a Soviet citizen, the second was by T. C. Koopmans, Dutch, and the third by
G. B. Dantzig, American. The third discovery turned out to be the most general
and convenient form, and led to the theory of linear programming as we know
it today.*

*Categories and Subject Descriptors: G.1.6 [**Numerical Analysis**]:
    Optimization—linear programming; K.2 [**History of Computing**]—people,
    software*
General Terms: Economics, Management
*Additional Key Words and Phrases: L. V. Kantorovich, T. C. Koopmans,
    G. B. Dantzig*

Foreword

Robert Dorfman in this interesting story of the "discovery" leaves out the important role that he himself played in linear programming's early development. Dorfman, like Tjalling Koopmans, foresaw the fundamental role that linear programming would play in economic theory. He pioneered the development of quadratic programming and was the first to use the term "mathematical programming." His 1958 book (with Samuelson and Solow) on "Linear Programming and Economic Analy-

© 1984 by the American Federation of Information Processing
Societies, Inc. Permission to copy without fee all or part of this
material is granted provided that the copies are not made or distributed for direct commercial advantage, the AFIPS copyright notice
and the title of the publication and its date appear, and notice is
given that the copying is by permission of the American Federation
of Information Processing Societies, Inc. To copy otherwise, or to
republish, requires specific permission.
Author's Address: Department of Economics, Harvard University,
Cambridge, MA 02138.
© 1984 AFIPS 0164-1239/84/030283–295$01.00/00

sis" remains today one of the great classics. I am personally indebted to him for the many stimulating discussions that we had on LP in the early days when we were both at the Pentagon.

George B. Dantzig
Departments of Operations Research
  and Computer Science
Stanford University
Stanford, CA 94305

This report will recount the story of the discovery of linear programming and the roles of the principal contributors. It is not an especially complicated story, as histories of scientific discoveries go, but neither is it entirely straightforward. The complications arise from one general reason and from three special circumstances.

The general reason is that it must be very rare in the case of scientific discoveries to be able to point to some particular instant and say: "Before this moment the facts discovered were not even dimly envisaged; after it they were known and substantially understood." In the case of linear programming, several

Robert Dorfman received his B.A. and M.A. (economics, 1937) from Columbia University and worked as a statistician and then operations analyst during World War II. In 1950 he earned a Ph.D. in economics from the University of California at Berkeley, where he taught until 1955. Since then he has been a professor at Harvard University, now as David A. Wells Professor of Political Economy. He has written many books and papers on economics and on environmental problems, and has been a consultant to numerous federal and private organizations. He has been a member of National Research Council boards, White House committees, and other advisory groups.

papers were published long before the dates that I shall assign to the discovery, each of which perceived some aspect of linear programming almost clearly enough to be called a "discovery." On the other hand, some of the early papers that contained the discovery are so obscure that the reader has to say, "No. He doesn't have it yet." It is on these grounds, indeed, that at least two scholars (Charnes and Cooper 1962) have cast doubt on Kantorovich's claim to codiscovery. There were, in short, several tentative forays followed by at least two great breakthroughs, and the [283] problem of attribution is to judge whether each early development was a sufficient break with the past to be called a discovery, or was so continuous with the past that it should be classed as an antecedent.

One of the special circumstances surrounding the discovery of linear programming is that it seems to have occurred at least twice: first by Leonid V. Kantorovich in 1939, and entirely independently by George B. Dantzig (and several colleagues) in 1947. In the interim, sometime during World War II, Tjalling C. Koopmans developed some of the essential principles of linear programming while working on a problem that is now recognized as an important special case. Like any good mathematician grappling with a practical problem, Koopmans took advantage of the special structure of the problem that confronted him. He had no reason to investigate whether his principles would help solve a much wider class of problems, and did not do so. Dantzig did not know of Koopmans's work until 1947, when his own formulation was already well advanced.

This brings us to the second complicating special circumstance: each of the instances of discovery was stimulated, not by theoretical considerations, but by a particular practical context whose special characteristics diverted attention from the essential logic of the problem. Kantorovich undertook to solve a problem whose form was dictated by the peculiarities of Soviet economic planning. In that environment, the primary responsibility of an enterprise is to fulfill its production quotas, which include a prescribed mix or proportionality among the commodities produced by the enterprise. Maximum profitability and minimum cost of production are subsidiary considerations. Accordingly, constraints on the mix of products produced are a central feature of Kantorovich's formulation; cost and profitability play no role at all. It is obvious now that Kantorovich's problem is an instance of linear programming. It is true, but not at all obvious even now, that his formulation includes the general problem of linear programming.[1]

Koopmans confronted quite a different practical problem. During World War II, he was on the staff of the Combined Shipping Adjustment Board, an agency formed by the Allied governments to coordinate the use of their merchant fleets. Koopmans's task was to plan the assignment of ships to convoys so as to accomplish prescribed deliveries of supplies with the smallest possible amount of travel in ballast. We now recognize that this is a special case of linear programming called, in fact, the Hitchcock-Koopmans transportation problem (see Hitchcock 1941). Because of its special features it is much the easiest kind of linear programming problem to solve—virtually the only kind that can be solved for large-scale problems without using an electronic computer. Despite its computational simplicity, the logic of the solution is identical with the logic of the most general case. Koopmans discovered that logic sometime in 1943.[2] Just because the application of that logic to Koopmans's problem is so very simple, the fact that it can be generalized to a wider range of problems is not at all apparent. Koopmans had no cause to generalize it, and did not.

Dantzig's work, which resulted in the definitive formulation of linear programming, arose out of still a third kind of problem. Shortly after World War II, Dantzig was brought into the headquarters of the U.S. Army Air Force as a mathematician with responsibility for devising improved methods for planning air force activities. The central problem in planning the activities of a military organization in peacetime is to decide on the amounts and timing of procurement, training, and transportation so that the materiel and trained men required for combat operations are on hand when and where needed. Timing is of the essence in this problem. People have to be recruited and

---

[1] The paradox is real. Kantorovich-type problems are a proper subset of Dantzig-type on one interpretation; the reverse inclusion holds on another, equally legitimate, interpretation.

[2] Because of wartime security restrictions, Koopmans's findings were not published until 1947.

aircraft ordered more than a year before they can be used in combat. When budgets are restricted, economy is important, too, but even then the dominant consideration is to plan support activities so as to achieve prescribed levels of combat readiness at specified [284] dates. Accordingly, when Dantzig began his work late in 1946, he concentrated his attention on determining the time sequence in which various activities had to be undertaken—and that turned out to be just the wrong center of attention.

He worked on the problem from this point of view for most of a year, obtaining results that were useful in systematizing the planning of air force programs, but that contained only peripheral hints of what was to become linear programming. The trouble was that the requirements that an operationally practical time sequence of air force operations must meet lead to such an elaborate set of equations that it was not clear how to inject cost minimization or any other objective into the system. There was a transitional stage in Dantzig's thinking, in early 1947, when he was simultaneously developing time-sequenced models of air force operations and thinking about how to minimize costs in simpler, and more abstract, contexts. Both problems, the practical one and the theoretical one, were solved abruptly when they fused—when he saw consciously that in spite of superficial appearances, the time-sequenced problem and the cost-minimizing problem were really the same. (He must have seen this before, subconsciously, or else he would not have been thinking about them both.) This was Dantzig's central achievement: he was the first to free himself from the adventitious particulars of the problem with which he began, and to perceive that it was a special case of linear programming in its purest and most general form.[3]

In summary, linear programming was discovered as a result of solving a number of special, practical prob-

---

[3] Twenty-five years after the discovery, Dantzig wrote, "Nevertheless, in a very short while (June 1947), I decided to introduce formally an objective function in place of the ground rules.... If anyone were to ask me what my greatest achievement was, I would say it was the realization that the planning problem (for all its complicated ground rules, apparent exceptions and variety of ways of stating the technology and the interrelations between activities and items) could for the most part be encompassed into one simple system—namely the linear program." (Dantzig 1972, pp. 8–9)

lems (one of which is, in fact, equivalent to the general problem) that led, painfully, to the perception of the general, inclusive formulation. As we have seen, fragments of the eventual theory were discovered, and rediscovered in disguised contexts, along the way. At what stage, then, was linear programming discovered?

There is still another circumstance that makes this question hard to answer: It isn't easy to say just what linear programming is. It can be regarded as a mathematical technique, and in that spirit Dantzig has defined it as "the maximization of a linear function subject to linear inequality constraints" (Dantzig 1951*a*). As accurately, and only slightly more obscurely, one could say that linear programming is the solution of systems of linear inequalities. Such highly mathematical definitions miss the point. The principal theorems about linear inequalities were known in the nineteenth century; linear programming surely was not. Linear programming is not a branch of mathematics. It lies in the domains of economics (both applied and theoretical) and management, and we must define it accordingly. For the purpose of distinguishing between precursors and discoverers, I shall regard linear programming as a body of theorems and methods in economics and management science that is characterized by formulating problems in those subjects in terms of linear inequalities and solving the problems or deducing theorems about them through the application of the algebra of linear inequalities. In applying this test, I shall not regard it as "discovery" merely to describe a problem by a set of linear inequalities. (That has been done many times; see, for example, Remak 1929, Wald 1936, and Souto 1941.) The true discoverer must also either propose a practical method of solution (Kantorovich and Dantzig both did that; so did Koopmans for his special case) or attain some fresh and significant insights into the economic and managerial properties of the problem (Koopmans and Dantzig did that clearly, and Kantorovich obscurely).

In studying the origins of linear programming, I have had the benefit of invaluable assistance by the principal American contributors, including Dantzig, Koopmans, and Albert W. Tucker. Dantzig went to the trouble of preparing a 30-page memoir of his recollections for my benefit and provided me with photocopies of several hundred memoranda, letters, and notes. Koopmans also wrote an extensive letter and supplied copies of a number of significant documents. I am most grateful for their generous assistance. The discussion of Kantorovich's contributions is based entirely on published material, in translation, including historical papers by G. Sh. Rubinshtein (1959) and L. Weinstein (1964).

Kantorovich's Discovery

Kantorovich's results were first published in *Matematicheskie Metody Organizatsii i Planirovaniya* (1939). This monograph became known to the outside world, largely through the efforts of Koopmans, around 1956, and an English translation was published in *Management Science* in July 1960.

The work arose out of consultations for the Plywood Trust, which, like many other Soviet enterprises, encountered production planning problems of the following sort: There are n different types of machine available, typified by machines of type i. The plant uses [285] these machines to produce m different parts or components, a typical part being designated as part k. The completed product or assortment contains one part of each type. A machine of type i can produce α_{ik} parts of type k per hour (or day or week). The problem is to determine the number of parts of each type to be produced by machines of each type so as to maximize the rate of output of completed products. Nowadays we would recognize this as a typical "assignment problem," a subclass of linear programming problems. Kantorovich appears to have been the first to formulate this kind of problem with mathematical precision.

His formulation goes as follows. Denote by h_{ik} the proportion of available time of machine type i devoted to the production of part type k. Then $\Sigma_k h_{ik} = 1$. Further, the total rate of output of part type k will be

$$z_k = \Sigma_i \alpha_{ik} h_{ik}$$

The time allocations h_{ik} have to be chosen so as to respect these relationships and also so that the production rates of the individual parts, z_k, are equal to each other, and their common value is as great as possible.

This is not exactly how one would set up an assignment problem today; one would use inequalities where Kantorovich used equations; in effect, Kantorovich did this in his analytic restatement of the problem (see "Problem C" in the next paragraph). The essence of the assignment problem is contained in this formulation; as we shall see later, Kantorovich's method of solution is close to the one now used.

Kantorovich went far beyond formulating and solving that problem. He called the assignment problem "Problem A" and formulated two generalizations, of which the more interesting is "Problem C."[4] Problem C goes thus: Each of the machines of Problem A can be used in accordance with a number of different methods or techniques, the typical one being the lth. When a machine of type i is used according to method l, it produces γ_{ikl} units of part type k per hour. Then if h_{il} denotes the proportion of the time that machine i is used according to method l, the total rate of output of part k will be

$$z_k = \Sigma_i \Sigma_l \gamma_{ikl} h_{il}$$

The problem of maximizing the rate of output of complete products now becomes the problem of choosing the machine-time allocations h_{il}, subject to $\Sigma_l h_{il} = 1$, so as to make z_k the same for all parts k and so as to make their common value as great as possible.

This is a powerful generalization of Problem A because it admits the possibility that a single machine may be producing several different parts in preassigned proportions simultaneously. In fact, a set of coefficients $\gamma_{i1l}, \gamma_{i2l}, \ldots, \gamma_{iml}$ for given values of i and l is similar in import to an activity vector in modern activity analysis. A particularly important special case, which I shall call Problem C_1, arises when $n = 1$; that is, when there is only one type of machine. In this case the subscript i can be omitted, since it takes only one value, and Problem C_1 can be stated as: Find values h_l, $l = 1, 2, \ldots$, and z so as to make z as great as possible subject to the conditions

$$h_l \geq 0$$

$$\Sigma_l h_l = 1$$

$$\Sigma_l \gamma_{kl} h_l - z \geq 0, \quad k = 1, 2, \ldots$$

---

[4] "Problem B" is a slight variant of Problem A, which soon dropped from sight. It will not be discussed here.

Written this way, Problem C_1 is seen to be identical with the problem of the maximizing player in a two-person matrix game. By solving Problem C (which includes Problem C_1), Kantorovich proposed a method for solving matrix games long before anyone else did. Even more is true. Any of the problems that we now call linear programming problems can be converted into a matrix game by straightforward and well-known procedures. So Kantorovich's method for solving his Problem C can be applied to any of this broad class of problems, even to ones that in their original form do not seem to resemble Problem C_1. This possibility is of theoretical interest only, however, since much better methods are now known (all descended from Dantzig's original simplex method) for solving matrix games, problems of type C_1, and all other kinds of linear programming problems.

The claim that Kantorovich discovered linear programming rests chiefly on his formulation of Problem C and on his solution to that problem. Is, then, Problem C equivalent to "linear programming"? That is a semantic question, and accordingly hard to answer. We should distinguish between Kantorovich-type linear programming problems, typified by Problem C, and Dantzig-type linear programming problems, which dominate the non-Russian literature. They are different, and the differences reflect differing cultural milieus and illustrate Marx's dictum that the objective relations of production determine the ideological superstructure. Kantorovich-type linear programming is the basic maximization problem in an economy where economic effort is coordinated by the maintenance of socially and technically appropriate material balances. In that context, Problem C was the correct and fundamental problem for Kantorovich to formulate and solve.   [286]

On the other hand, Dantzig-type linear programming[5] is the appropriate form of maximization in an economy in which effort is coordinated by com-

---

[5] The term *linear programming* was coined by Koopmans in 1948 to denote the body of methods that was then emerging for using the principles of linear algebra to construct efficient operating programs for businesses, economies, and organizations of all kinds. He suggested the term to Dantzig in the summer, and it was first used at the Colloquium on Planning held at the Rand Corporation in June–July 1948, according to Dantzig.

parisons of relative value and the individual profitability of decentralized enterprises. This type of programming is virtually a mathematical simulation of profit-maximizing enterprise and price-guided economic decisions—which is why it has been such a potent method of economic analysis in its own institutional context.

Thus it appears that the two formulations are different in substance, though very closely related mathematically. Neither can be assigned primacy over the other, each being appropriate in its own setting. To the westerner, Kantorovich's form may appear awkward and inflexible and, worse still, conceals or confuses fundamental relationships among values. By the same token, a socialist can complain that Dantzig's form obscures the proper proportioning among different kinds of output that is essential to coherent economic planning.

We have already noted that as a formal matter a Dantzig-type problem can always be converted to a Kantorovich-type problem and so solved. That is only a contrived and formal possibility. On the other hand, a Kantorovich-type problem is a Dantzig-type problem, quite naturally, with a certain selection of coefficients. (For example, taking the coefficient of z to be -1 in all the constraints of Problem C_1.) It therefore is probably more than mere cultural bias and habit that leads to the feeling that Dantzig's formulation is the more inclusive and profound expression of the universal problem of economizing. Indeed, in a later publication (*The Best Use of Economic Resources*, 1965, p. 273), Kantorovich set forth a more general problem, which includes Problems A and C as special cases, and which is a Dantzig-type linear programming problem with the exception that the quantity to be maximized is a vector instead of a scalar. Of course, by that time Kantorovich was familiar with the work of Dantzig and his followers in the United States.[6] Thus even in the context of socialist planning, the Dantzig-type formulation is recognized as being inclusive and fundamental. This is not to gainsay that Kantorovich's original formulation, in Problem C, was

---

[6] Dantzig's work is mentioned in the preface to *The Best Use of Economic Resources* (Kantorovich 1965).

general enough to express the key maximizing problem for socialist enterprises.

In addition to formulating this problem, Kantorovich proposed a method for solving it. The method of solution and the mathematical proof that justifies it are strikingly similar to the method of proof later used by Dantzig and co-workers. But they are not identical, and here too it appears that cultural factors were at work. Kantorovich's method depends on the introduction of "resolving multipliers," which play the same role as the "simplex multipliers" in Dantzig-type formulations. He worked in a cultural context in which attention centered on physical quantities—where each enterprise was responsible for producing the quantities of each of its products called for in its plan, and for doing so by using amounts of materials and labor in accordance with its assigned norms. Values, such as prices and profits, played a distinctly subsidiary role. Thus Kantorovich formulated his problems entirely in terms of physical results, and it was not natural for him to conceive of his resolving multipliers as a system of values or "shadow prices."[7]

Kantorovich stated his concept of resolving multipliers succinctly.

> This method is the method of resolving multipliers. Let us indicate its idea. For preciseness, let us consider Problem A. The method is based on the fact that there exist multipliers $\lambda_1, \lambda_2, \ldots, \lambda_m$ corresponding to each (manufactured) part such that finding them leads almost immediately to the solution of the problem. Namely, if for each given i one examines the products $\lambda_1 \alpha_{i,1}, \lambda_2 \alpha_{i,2}, \ldots, \lambda_m \alpha_{i,m}$ and selects those k for which the product is a maximum, then for all the other k one can take $h_{i,k} = 0$. With respect to the few selected values of $h_{i,k}$, they can easily be determined to satisfy the conditions $\Sigma_{k=1}^m h_{i,k} = 1$, and $z_1 = z_2 = \ldots = z_m$. The $h_{i,k}$ found in this way also give the maximum z, which is the solution of the problem. Thus, instead of finding the large number, $n \cdot m$, of the unknowns $h_{i,k}$, it turns out to be possible to solve altogether for only the m unknowns λ_k. (Kantorovich 1960, p. 373)

Moreover, Kantorovich perceived the economic significance of his resolving multipliers. In Problem A there is one multiplier for each of the m different parts

---

[7] Later, as in Kantorovich (1965), he called the resolving multipliers "objectively determined valuations."

produced. Kantorovich recognized that the resolving multiplier that corresponds to each part is proportional to the marginal cost of that part. (In this problem, marginal costs are measured in terms of the attainable rate of output of completed products so that the marginal cost of any part is the reduction in the attainable rate that would result if one more part of that type were required each day.) In addition, he saw [287] that the resolving multipliers imply certain coefficients that correspond to each of the kinds of machine and that those coefficients are proportional to the marginal values of the machines measured in the same units.

In short, he discovered most of the interpretation of the dual problem and the dual variables. Although he came breathtakingly close to discovering the complete analysis as we now understand it, he missed one essential clue: that the absolute values of the resolving multipliers are significant, and not simply their values relative to each other. We can only conjecture why he missed it. In the first place, to compute the economically significant absolute values for the resolving multipliers, you have to impose a scaling constraint on them, which would complicate (though only slightly) the method of calculation that Kantorovich used. For his method of calculation, only the relative values were significant, and it is convenient to change their sum arbitrarily in the course of the computation. More fundamentally, as we have already noted, it was not part of Kantorovich's conceptual background to conceive of problems in terms of costs and prices so that he was not sensitive to the advantages of interpreting the mathematical concepts that arose from his analysis in those terms. At any rate, because he perceived the economic significance of the allocation variables $h_{i,k}$, but not the corresponding significance of the resolving multipliers, he failed to see the complete symmetry between the problem of finding the allocation variables and that of finding the resolving multipliers, and thereby missed the complete primal-dual formation. It was a near miss, and the method of solution that he discovered bears a close resemblance to the primal-dual variant of the simplex algorithm that is now used (Dantzig et al. 1956). In short, Kantorovich must be awarded credit for the discovery of most of the economic interpretation of linear programming as well as for formulating the problem and proposing a suggestive method of solution. His achievement, however, was not known outside the U.S.S.R. until the early 1950s.

Although the method of resolving multipliers is based on sound and incisive theoretical insights, it does not appear to be a practical method for numerical solution, except for problems of very small scale. (The largest problem discussed by Kantorovich in his 1939 paper (see Kantorovich 1960) had about a dozen constraints.) Kantorovich was aware of this limitation of his algorithm and included an approximative method for solving large problems in Kantorovich (1960). He could not reasonably have done more since linear programming problems of useful size require so much arithmetic that only some very special types can be solved without resort to electronic computers. In 1939 there was no way for Kantorovich, or anyone else, to foresee that such machines were only a few years away. The method proposed by Kantorovich is probably as efficient a method as can be devised for solving programming problems with the aid of mechanical desk calculators. Its practical defect is that the resolving multipliers have to be found by an iterative procedure, each step of which requires a subsidiary linear programming problem to be solved. In the early iterations, these subsidiary problems are trivial, but as the calculation proceeds, they become increasingly complex, eventually approaching the complexity of the original problem. In small-scale problems a mathematician's sound judgment can cope, but larger-scale problems, which Kantorovich may not have contemplated, soon outrun that possibility.

Kantorovich also discovered the essential mathematical properties of linear programming problems. He saw that such a problem amounts formally to finding the maximum of a linear function defined on a convex polygonal region. He invoked the Farkas-Minkowski lemma[8] about the existence and properties of supporting planes for such regions just as we do now, and used the fact that the coefficients of those supporting planes are proportional to the resolving multipliers that his method requires or, in western

---

[8] Proved in J. Farkas (1902), but conjectured by H. Minkowski several years earlier. A variant of this theorem is used in Kantorovich (1960), Appendix 3.

vocabulary, to the dual variables of the problem. Indeed, his mathematical analysis was as modern and powerful as any now employed.

In conclusion, there is no room to doubt that Kantorovich discovered linear programming and did so some eight years before any other claimant to this distinction. For reasons already discussed, his formulation and analysis were given a twist that nowadays seems peculiar, although they were entirely appropriate to his cultural situation. He perceived and established most of the significant mathematical properties of linear programming formulations and understood their economic implications. He also proposed what is probably as good a method of numerical solution as is possible without using some kind of electronic computing machine.

Dantzig's Discovery

Kantorovich's work remained completely unknown outside Russia until it came to Koopmans's attention in the middle 1950s. In the interim, Koopmans made his partial discovery, and, more important, Dantzig undertook the work that led to his complete discovery. [288]

Dantzig began his work on programming late in 1946. He announced the discovery of the simplex method at a poorly attended lecture to the American Statistical Association on December 29, 1947. About a week later he circulated a paper (Dantzig 1948—still unpublished in 1984) that contains the essence of the duality properties of linear programming.

The appraisal of Dantzig's work presents very different issues from those just confronted for Kantorovich. Linear programming in its definitive form, with all the principal theorems and the interpretations now given them, emerged from it directly. Throughout the critical stage of the research, the fall–winter of 1947–1948, Dantzig was in close communication with a number of distinguished contributors—Leonid Hurwicz, Koopmans, John von Neumann, Marshall K. Wood, and others. The significant historical question is which aspects of the discovery were made by Dantzig himself and which by other people with whom he was in contact. To answer this question, I was fortunate to have access to several collections of manuscript documents and to the reminiscences of most of the people involved.

The work that led Dantzig to his discovery of linear programming began late in 1946. During World War II, he had been a member of the section of the Air Force staff that developed logistic plans. The methods used were slow and expensive. There was a conscious effort to improve them, to which Dantzig contributed, but they remained essentially laborious hand calculations depending on crude planning factors and the repeated exercise of subjective judgments.

At the conclusion of the war, Dantzig returned to the University of California to complete his doctoral degree under the supervision of Jerzy Neyman.[9] When this had been accomplished, he was persuaded to return to the Air Force headquarters as mathematical advisor to the comptroller, General E. W. Rawlings. His major responsibility was to resume the work on simplifying and expediting methods used for logistic and personnel planning.

Many exploratory discussions ensued between Dantzig and Marshall K. Wood, who had been instrumental in attracting Dantzig back to the Air Force. At first their ideas about how to proceed were confined to the possibilities of using the punch-card machines and analog devices that were then available. But early in 1946 they visited Howard Aiken's Mark I computer at Harvard University, learned about electronic computers, and foresaw the potentialities of such machines (Dantzig 1976, pp. 7–8). Then Dantzig's imagination took flight.

He focused his attention on two tasks. The first was to construct a system of equations that was rich enough to express all the data and relationships needed to formulate a logistic and personnel plan for the Air Force, and still simple enough to be solved on the kind of electronic computer that he envisaged.

---

[9] Dantzig's doctoral thesis is suggestive of the way that certain themes tend to recur in a scholar's work, although in different guises. The thesis contained an extension of the "Neyman-Pearson Fundamental Lemma," which is the basis of much of the statistical theory of hypothesis testing (see Neyman and Pearson 1936). This lemma concerns the maximum of an integral of an unknown function, subject to constraints that involve other integrals of the same function. Its affinity to linear programming can be seen, at least with the benefit of hindsight (see Dantzig 1946 and Dantzig and Wald 1951).

The scale of this undertaking can be appreciated by recalling that the planning system then used required the labors of hundreds of highly trained staff officers extended over most of a year. The second was to establish detailed specifications for a computer to carry out these calculations. After those tasks, of course, a computer that met the specifications would have to be designed and built, but he had no doubt that electronic engineers could produce a machine to meet any reasonable specifications. Note that at that stage the goal was simply to calculate plans that would satisfy some prescribed requirements; no maximization or minimization was yet in view.

In the winter of 1946–1947 and the spring of 1947, Dantzig's major effort was to develop a system of linear equations for determining the amounts of various forms of procurement and training required at different dates in order to achieve a stated level of combat readiness on a preassigned date. The formulation was strongly influenced by Leontief's input-output system (Leontief 1936) with which Dantzig was fully familiar. Dantzig, however, felt that Leontief's model was too rigid to represent the Air Force's problem adequately. In that model, the number of variables to be determined, called the number of activity levels, is precisely equal to the number of requirements or constraints that have to be satisfied. The model therefore determines all the activity levels without any room for choice. But in the Air Force's problem there *is* room—for example, instead of training 1000 pilots simultaneously, they can be trained in two classes of 500, which would require more lead time but a much smaller training establishment—and that scope for choice can be used to reduce the cost of meeting the requirements. Meeting requirements at minimum cost was an important consideration, and Dantzig was not satisfied that there was a way to take account of it within the framework he was using. In spite of his reservations, Dantzig used a variant of Leontief's approach to formulate a time-sequenced model of procurement and training. By early summer [289] he had a clear enough view of the problem that he could prepare requirements for an electronic computer that would solve it, thus completing the second aspect of his assignment (Dantzig 1947*a*). The specifications called for a machine that seemed visionary at the time, but would be regarded as primitive a few years later. It was designed to manipulate matrices of the order of 100×100. It was to have a speed of 1000 multiplications per second, an internal memory of 200K bits, an external memory of 1 million K bits, and an input-output speed of 500 to 1000 words per second.

By May or June of 1947, Dantzig's attention turned increasingly to the question of cost minimization. It was at this time that he consulted Koopmans at the University of Chicago. Koopmans had already completed his work on transportation planning and saw that there must be some connection between his problem and the more elaborate one with which Dantzig was coping. He saw also that Dantzig's problem, although conceived in the context of air force planning, had important ramifications for general economic planning and theory. From then on Koopmans took a deep and lively interest in the work. In particular, he was instrumental in arranging for Leonid Hurwicz, a distinguished mathematical economist at Iowa State University, to consult with Dantzig during August 1947.

Out of these consultations and conversations there emerged an approach referred to as "climbing the beanpole." Since this idea remains the basic strategy of the simplex method and all its variants, it is worthwhile to give a brief sketch of it. Any plan for operating an air force consists of a large number of different elementary activities such as recruiting people, training them, procuring aircraft, constructing bases, etc., etc. They are interrelated: the number of bases constructed and the number of persons recruited must be sufficient for the number of personnel to be trained, and so on. Thus a plan consists of the levels at which a large number of activities are to be conducted, and these levels must be chosen so that they fit together, produce an air force of the desired size and composition, and cost as little as possible in the aggregate.

That describes the concrete problem Dantzig faced. About a year after the concept evolved, Dantzig described the beanpole approach to the problem in abstract terms.

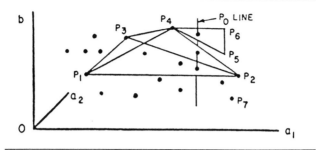

Figure 1.   From Dantzig 1951*b*.

We shall discuss the techniques of maximization in
terms of a more general mathematical problem:
maximize a linear form of nonnegative variables
$X_1, X_2, \ldots, X_n$, i.e.

$$X_1 b_1 + X_2 b_2 + \ldots + X_n b_n = \text{max}, \qquad (X > 0)$$

where X_j satisfy a system of m equations, in vector form

$$X_1 P_1 + X_2 P_2 + \ldots + X_n P_n = P_0,$$

where P_j has coordinates $(a_{1j}, a_{2j}, \ldots, a_{mj})$.

In order to arrive at an intuitive geometrical picture,
let us suppose that it is known that the sum of the X's is
equal to unity. We could then think of the X's as
nonnegative weights assigned to a set of points in say m
dimensional space and form a linear combination of
these points to produce a given point P_0. In other words,
the point P_0 is a center of gravity of known points P_1,
$P_2, \ldots, P_n$ with unknown weights $X_1, X_2, \ldots, X_n$. If we
now add a b-coordinate to each of the points, $P_1, P_2, \ldots$
where $b_1, b_2, \ldots$ is taken from the maximizing form, then
our problem is to create a center of gravity lying on a
given line, P_0, parallel to the b-axis whose b-coordinate is
maximum. [This line is the "beanpole"; watch how it is
used.]

To illustrate, let us examine figure 1: If we think of
these points as spanned by a convex, then we are looking
for a point where this line pierces an "upper" face of the
convex. In the diagram (P_4, P_5, P_6) represents the top
face.

It can be shown that the solution will embody the
following characteristics: That all points (activities) will
be given a weight of zero except m out of the n of them,
where m equals the number of equations. The remaining
m will be given nonnegative weights corresponding
directly to the level of activity. One method of solving
the problem might be as follows: Assume that we have
some kind of a program that means we have found some

combination of points that generates P_0 with
nonnegative weights, e.g., P_1, P_2, P_3 in the diagram. Now
we wish to improve the "program," i.e., find a triangle
that cuts P_0 in a higher point. To do this, we consider
any point P_i that lies above the plane of the triangle P_1,
P_2, P_3, for example P_4. We join such a point to P_1, P_2, P_3
forming a simplex in space. The line P_0 pierces the
simplex in two points. One point represents the b of the
solution involving P_1, P_2, P_3, the other point is higher,
since all points in the simplex lie above the face P_1, P_2,
P_3. Thus a solution involving just P_2, P_3, P_4, represents
an improvement over P_1, P_2, P_3. (Dantzig 1951b)

Thus Dantzig described the basic step in climbing
the beanpole in the summer of 1948: one proposed
activity, P_1, was dropped and replaced by a different [290]
one that completed a triangle along with P_2 and P_3,
and the replacement activity was chosen so that the
new triangle cut the beanpole at a higher point than
the old. He went on to say, "It is clear that by iterating
this procedure one will eventually obtain the best
program in a finite number of iterations," but that
was by no means clear the previous summer, when
this way of looking at the problem was first envisaged.
At that time no one knew how to find a superior point
to introduce in problems of more than two or three
dimensions, nor how to perform the basic replacement
step, nor even whether a finite sequence of such steps
would be sure to lead to the maximizing program.
When climbing the beanpole was first conceived, it
was a goal rather than a calculation that could be
performed since there was no systematic way to carry
out the basic step and no way to tell when the maximum had been attained.

The obstacle that stood in the way of implementing
the beanpole strategy was one that occurs frequently
in the history of scientific discovery; we can call it
"premature rejection." Dantzig notes in his memoirs
that the successful approach occurred to him immediately, and that, in fact, it had been used over 100
years previously by Fourier when he encountered a
similar problem.[10] When Dantzig first considered the

---

[10] In Dantzig's words: "The first idea that comes to a trained
mathematician, as a solution technique for solving linear programs,
is that of moving from one vertex to the next along the edges of the
convex polyhedral set of feasible solutions.... Up to 1947, no one
seems to have formulated the general linear program as a general

task of trying out modifications of an initial cluster of plans to see which variants helped in climbing the beanpole, however, the number of variants that had to be explored seemed so enormous that the whole concept appeared out of the question. Instead of trying this method of attack, Dantzig sought alternatives to it. (In fact, he remained unpersuaded of the efficiency of the simplex method for more than a year after its discovery and first successes.) So for a short period of time Dantzig almost deliberately tried to avoid discovering the simplex method that made him famous.

Logic triumphed over doubt sometime in September 1947. Dantzig's files contain an undated handwritten set of notes, which appear to have been written during that month, in which a linear programming problem with five activities and two constraints is set forth and a feasible (but not optimal) solution is determined by the classic strategy of starting with an arbitrary simplex, which naturally is not feasible, and improving it by inspecting neighboring simplexes.[11] The work is not carried through to the determination of an optimal solution but only far enough to be sure that the strategy was working. Dantzig identified this set of notes much later as "the first solution of a problem using the simplex method" (Dantzig 1972?).

This small test assured Dantzig that the simplex method would work in principle, but it appeared to be too laborious to be feasible for solving the Air Force's problem or other problems large enough to be useful. Nevertheless, he continued to explore it. During October 1947 he arranged for the Mathematical Tables Project of the National Bureau of Standards (NBS) to make two tests of the method on a more realistic scale. One test was a schematic planning problem with 46 constraints. The other was based on a paper by George J. Stigler (1945) in which Stigler had sought to ascertain the least expensive diet that would satisfy

---

problem of importance. If they had, they would have probably (as I did initially) quickly discarded, as a solution procedure, any movement along edges. It appeared obvious (at least to me) that there would be, in general, simply too many vertices and edges to wander over in higher dimensional space for such a method to be efficient" (Dantzig 1976, pp. 14–15).

[11] Notes dated in the summer of 1947 show no indication of the insight; on October 1, Dantzig was able to discuss the new approach with von Neumann at the Institute for Advanced Study.

an adult's daily requirements for nine nutrients. Stigler had obtained only an approximate solution to this problem, but Dantzig sought to find an exact solution by expressing it as a linear programming problem with 77 activities (i.e., foods) and 9 constraints.

Neither of these was a practical calculation at the time since all computations had to be performed with mechanical desk calculators. The solution of the diet problem required nearly 17,000 multiplications and divisions, which were carried out by five statistical clerks using desk calculators in 21 working days (105 man-days). The test was carried out successfully and may be considered to be the first life-sized computation to be performed by the simplex method. It established that the method would be practical, for moderate-size problems at least, once the projected electronic computers became available.

While the testing of the simplex method was in progress, Dantzig met with John von Neumann for the first time. This turned to be a remarkably fruitful meeting and is best described in Dantzig's own words.

On October 1, 1947, I visited von Neumann for the first time at the School [*sic*] for Advanced Study at Princeton. I remember trying to describe to von Neumann the Air Force problem. I began with the formulation of the linear programming model in terms of activities and items, etc. Von Neumann did something which (I believe) was not characteristic of him. "Get to the point," he said impatiently. Having a somewhat low kindling-point myself at times, I said to myself, "O.K., if he wants a quick version of the problem, then that's what he will get." In under one minute I slapped the [291] geometric and the algebraic version of the problem on the board. Von Neumann stood up and said, "Oh that!" He then proceeded for the next hour and a half to lecture to me on the mathematical theory of linear programs (as it later came to be called). At one point seeing me sitting there with my eyes popping and my mouth open (after all I had searched the literature and found nothing), von Neumann said something like this: "I don't want you to think I am generating all this out of my head on the spur of the moment. I have just recently completed a book with Oskar Morgenstern on the Theory of Games. What I am doing is conjecturing that the two problems are equivalent. The theory that I am outlining to you is really an analogue of the one that we have developed for the Theory of Games." Thus I learned about Farkas' Lemma, and about duality for the first time. (Dantzig 1976, p. 18)

At the meeting Dantzig and von Neumann agreed to put their ideas in writing, and there followed an exchange of three highly significant memoranda. On November 13, 1947, Dantzig sent von Neumann a description of the simplex algorithm as it then stood (Dantzig 1947*b*). This memorandum appears to be the earliest comprehensive statement and justification of the algorithm. It is a somewhat polished version of the method used in the desk-size trial problem, and although it goes through the computational steps that have since become standard, the logical underpinnings of the simplex method were still not clearly perceived. A footnote gives credit to Koopmans for making suggestions on which the procedure for moving from one simplex to a better one is based.

A few days later von Neumann replied with a memorandum entitled "Discussion of a Maximum Problem," which presumably contains most of the ideas that excited Dantzig at their meeting (von Neumann 1963). In this paper von Neumann proposes an alternative method of calculation that is much more similar to the extreme methods of the calculus than the simplex method. Von Neumann's proposal does not appear to have ever been implemented. The significant feature of this paper is that in the course of expounding his proposal von Neumann derived some necessary conditions for a solution to a linear programming problem that are, in effect, the basic equations of the duality theorems. Von Neuman did not dwell on these equations long—he derived them almost in passing— nor did he notice that they amounted to the solution of a linear programming problem that was symmetrical to the one that he was trying to solve.

On the following January 5, 1948, Dantzig wrote the third paper in the sequence, "A Theorem on Linear Inequalities" (unpublished). There he presented a careful proof of the relationships derived by von Neumann (von Neumann's own proof was terse and sketchy). He went further, taking the critical step of noticing and labeling the dual problem that was implicit in the original problem. The theorem in this paper, together with a few side results, includes most of the duality properties that make linear programming interesting to mathematicians and economic theorists. Their first clear statement in English was in Dantzig's memorandum. It should be remembered, however, that Kantorovich's "resolving multipliers" are very much like the dual variables of modern linear programming, and Kantorovich had established their essential properties some eight years previously.

While the work of arithmetic testing was going forward at NBS, and the theoretical aspects of linear programming were being formulated in correspondence with von Neumann, Dantzig made arrangements for the first public announcement of his discovery. This took the form of a 20-minute paper at one of the sessions of the joint annual meeting of the American Statistical Association–Institute of Mathematical Statistics on the afternoon of December 29, 1947. Three other papers were presented at the same session, all dealing with ephemeral topics, and there is no evidence that Dantzig's paper attracted any particular interest or notice. Because of the severe time constraint, the ASA–IMS paper was so sketchy that a listener who was not already familiar with the background would not be likely to perceive the importance and the difficulty of the problem whose solution was announced. This paper was never published.

With the successful completion of the computational tests by NBS, the theoretical discoveries in the correspondence with von Neumann, and the announcement of the new (and still unnamed) theory, Dantzig's hectic period of discovery came to an end. The importance of the problem of "maximizing a linear function subject to linear inequalities" was recognized (and this formulation was established as standard), the simplex method for solving such a problem was described clearly and fully tested, and the main theoretical aspects of linear programming were perceived. The year 1948 was devoted to spreading word of the new discoveries, to searching for more efficient methods of solution (apart from variants that facilitate computer operations, none have ever been found), and to more extensive exploration of the theoretical aspects of linear programming, largely in conjunction with Albert W. Tucker of Princeton and his students.

Subsequent years carried the work still further, but the main lines were all developed in the short period

between the undated, trivial test calculation attributed
to September 1947 and the second memorandum sent [292]
to von Neumann on January 5, 1948. The discoveries
of this period included all the main features of linear
programming except the appreciation of the dual variables as economists' "shadow prices" or businessmen's "accounting or costing prices." In the period
1947–1948, this interpretation of the dual variables
and the simplex criteria did not appear natural or
helpful to Dantzig, and he consistently conceptualized
those data in terms of the geometry of n-dimensional
space.

Koopmans's Contributions

The name of Tjalling C. Koopmans has occurred
repeatedly in the preceding narratives. He played several roles at different stages in the history of linear
programming, first as an independent discoverer, then
as a catalyzer on several occasions, and finally as the
central figure in the incorporation of linear programming into economic theory. These roles will be
sketched more or less in sequence.

Koopmans's most distinctive independent discovery
arose out of his work with the Combined Shipping
Adjustment Board during World War II. That board
confronted the classic transportation problem: specified total supplies at points of origin had to be routed
so as to meet specified total requirements at destinations, and it was important that the shipping schedule
be constructed so as to use the available ships as
economically as possible. One of the important decisions they had to make concerned the return voyages
of the empty ships: to which new points of origin
should the ships unloaded at each destination be sent
in order to provide sufficient shipping at each originating port with the smallest possible expenditure of
transit time for empty ships? Koopmans perceived
that the conditions of this problem could, and should,
be expressed as a system of linear inequalities that
happen, in this case, to have a peculiarly simple form.
This much of Koopmans's work had been anticipated
by Hitchcock (1941) in a paper I shall mention below.
The significant contribution of Koopmans's analysis
was that instead of dealing with the inequalities
straightforwardly, he focused on shadow prices (which

he called "potentials") that express the potential value of an empty ship in any port. Koopmans's method of solution consisted of computing a schedule of empty ship movements and a schedule of "potentials" in such a way that the difference in potential between any two ports was equal to the cost of moving a ship from one to the other if any empty ship moved over that route— and so that no empty ships moved between any pair of ports if the difference in potential was less than the cost of moving an empty ship over that route.

The significance of Koopmans's discovery is not only that he found an efficient way to solve a special class of problems, but also that he was the first to perceive the usefulness of "pricing out" choices in terms of shadow prices. The simplex method in all its variants is based on this very same idea—namely, the idea of determining a shadow price for each of the resources used in a program and searching, by iteration, for a set of activities each of which "costs" no more, in terms of the shadow prices, than it contributes to the objectives of the program. Kantorovich saw vaguely that his resolving multipliers amounted to such shadow prices. But Koopmans was the first to solve a practical problem by the explicit application of this insight. By coincidence, Koopmans's first public presentation of his method was made at the International Statistical Conference in Washington in September 1947, the month in which Dantzig discovered the general form of the simplex method. He had solved the problem, of course, several years before. The audience at the conference did not perceive the broad significance of Koopmans's report.

In the formulation of the transportation problem Koopmans was anticipated by Frank L. Hitchcock, who published the problem and a solution in the *Journal of Mathematics and Physics* in 1941. Hitchcock arrived at essentially the same inequalities that Koopmans found, and showed how to solve them directly, at least in small-scale problems. The simplicity of the equation structure of the transportation problem led him to a solution procedure that is far more difficult in general circumstances and that amounts to a special case of the simplex method. Hitchcock's formulation and method of analysis, unfortunately, rested so heavily on the special features of this problem that they blocked the possibility of generalization, so the general simplex method had to be rediscovered afresh, by an entirely different route.

As a result of working on the transportation problem, Koopmans was well prepared and receptive when Dantzig sought him out in June of 1947 at the suggestion of John Curtiss and Albert Cahn, mutual acquaintances at NBS. Dantzig's formulation of a general problem of resource allocation in terms of linear inequalities came to Koopmans as an exciting "broadening of horizon," in his own words (Koopmans 1972). At the time, Dantzig was working with Leonid Hurwicz on the beanpole conceptualization of the problem. Koopmans saw that a geometric argument he had used in his transportation problem could be applied to prove that the replacements used in the beanpole algorithm led to improved programs. He suggested that proof to Dantzig and remained in close touch with him from then on. [293]

Fundamentally Koopmans was not greatly interested in practical methods for solving linear programming problems. He was excited by the implications of linear programming for the whole theory of resource allocation, which is the fundamental problem of economics. He perceived clearly that an entire economy could be thought of as solving a vast linear programming problem in which the prices that emerged from competitive markets played the same role as the dual variables in Dantzig's theory of linear programming. This implied that the theory of linear programming could serve as a basis for rigorous formulation of the theory of general economic equilibrium. Koopmans expounded this approach in "Analysis of Production as an Efficient Combination of Activities," presented at the Cowles Commission conference on activity analysis (organized largely by Koopmans) in 1949 (Koopmans 1951).

Koopmans's perception of the importance of linear programming for economic theory has proved accurate, and all modern treatments of general equilibrium theory follow the lines that Koopmans laid out in that paper.

Concluding Remarks

We have now recounted the emergence of the main ideas that together constitute linear programming.

What is striking is that linear programming is a confluence of influences instead of a single distinctive insight. I suspect that this is typical of radical innovations. To take a simple analog, the invention of the bicycle required more than the realization that a two-wheeled vehicle was stable and maneuverable. The two-wheeled vehicle remained an awkward and virtually useless toy until the pneumatic tire, the wire wheel, and the steel frame became available. So it was with linear programming. It would have been stillborn without the electronic computer; indeed, Kantorovich's work was almost overlooked because of the difficulties of implementation. But when Dantzig set to work, the social and technical preconditions for this new mode of analysis had been achieved. The electronic computer was far enough along that he could design an algorithm that depended on its capabilities for arithmetic, logic, and storage. Leontief's input-output analysis, von Neumann and Morgenstern's formulation of game theory, and Koopmans's work on the transportation problem had all been accomplished, and although they were fundamentally related, the relationship remained to be discovered. All of these developments, indeed, reflected a common mental preconception that had become widespread—that problems in the realms of management, business, economics, and practical affairs generally were amenable to mathematical analysis and solution.

Thus the ground was well prepared for Dantzig, as it was not for Kantorovich. In a few months of brilliant, concentrated effort in the latter half of 1947 he conceived the inclusive framework into which the scattered pieces fitted and added a critical missing piece, the simplex method of solution. With that, linear programming was born.

REFERENCES

Charnes, A., and W. W. Cooper. April 1962. On some works of Kantorovich, Koopmans, and others. *Management Science 8,* 246–263.

Dantzig, G. B. 1946. "I. Complete Form Neyman-Pearson Fundamental Lemma, II. On the Non-Existence of Tests of 'Student's' Hypothesis having Power Functions Independent of Sigma." Ph.D. thesis, University of California, Berkeley (unpublished).

Dantzig, G. B. June 1947a. "Prospectus for the AAF Electronic Computer." Unpublished.

Dantzig, G. B. November 10, 1947b. "Recommended Procedure for Finding Feasible and Maximum Feasible Solutions." Unpublished.

Dantzig, G. B. January 5, 1948. "A Theorem on Linear Inequalities." Unpublished.

Dantzig, G. B. 1951a. "Maximization of a Linear Function of Variables Subject to Linear Inequalities." In T. C. Koopmans (ed.), *Activity Analysis of Production and Alloction*, New York, Wiley, pp. 339–347.

Dantzig, G. B. June 1951b. "Linear Programming." In U.S. National Bureau of Standards, *Problems for the Numerical Analysis of the Future*, Applied Mathematics Series No. 15, pp. 18–21. (Paper presented to the Symposium on Modern Calculating Machinery and Numerical Methods, UCLA, July 1948.)

Dantzig, G. B. November 25, 1972. "Memoirs about Linear Programming." Privately circulated.

Dantzig, G. B. 1972? Personal communication to author. (Possibly 1973.)

Dantzig, G. B. January 1976. "Memoirs About my Own Contributions to Linear Programming and Extensions." Privately circulated.

Dantzig, G. B., and A. Wald. March 1951. On the fundamental lemma of Neyman and Pearson. *Annals of Mathematical Statistics 22*, 87–93.

Dantzig, G. B., L. R. Ford, Jr., and D. R. Fulkerson. 1956. "A Primal-Dual Algorithm for Linear Programs." In H. W. Kuhn and A. W. Tucker (eds.), *Linear Inequalities and Related Systems*, Princeton, Princeton University Press, pp. 171–181.

Farkas, J. 1902. Uber die Theorie der einfachen Ungleichungen. *Journal für die Reine und Angewandte Mathematik 124*, 1–27.

Hitchcock, Frank L. 1941. The distribution of a product from several sources to numerous localities. *Journal of Mathematics and Physics 20*, 224–230.

Kantorovich, L. V. 1939. *Matematicheskie Metody Organizatsii i Planirovaniya.* Leningrad, Leningrad State University Press. (See Kantorovich 1960.)   [294]

Kantorovich, L. V. July 1960. Mathematical methods of organizing and planning production. *Management Science 6*, 363–422. (Translation of Kantorovich (1939) by Robert W. Campbell and W. H. Marlow.)

Kantorovich, L. V. 1965. *The Best Use of Economic Resources.* Cambridge, Harvard University Press. (Translated by P. F. Knightsfield from *Ekonomicheskii Raschot Nailuchshego Ispol' Zovaniia Resursov*, Moscow, AN SSR, 1959.)

Koopmans, T. C. July 1947. Optimum utilization of the transportation system. *Econometrica 17, Supplement*, 136–146.

Koopmans, T. C. 1951. "Analysis of Production as an Efficient Combination of Activities." In *Activity Analysis of*

Production and Allocation, New York, Wiley, pp. 33–97.

Koopmans, T. C. October 31, 1972. Letter to author.

Leontief, W. W. August 1936. Quantitative input and output relations in the economic system of the United States. *Review of Economic Statistics 18*, 105–125.

Neyman, J., and E. S. Pearson. 1936. Contributions to the theory of testing statistical hypotheses. *Statistical Research Memoirs 1*, 1–37.

Remak, Robert. 1929. Kenn die Volkwirtschaftslehre eine exakte Wissenschaft werden? *Jahr b. für Nationalökonomie und Statistik, Band 131*, 703–735.

Rubinshtein, G. Sh. 1959. O razvitii i primeneniiakh linein-ogo programmirovaniia v SSR. In L. V. Kantorovich and V. V. Novozhilov (eds.), *Linear Inequalities and Related Questions*, Moscow. Translated as "On the Development and Applications of Linear Programming in the USSR" by W. H. Marlow and Moses Richardson, George Washington University, Logistics Research Project, Serial T-124/60, August 15, 1960.

Souto, José Barral. 1941. Principios fundamentales de la division del trabajo. *Cuadernos de Trabajo 10*, Buenos Aires, Universidad de Buenos Aires, Facultad de Ciencias Economicas, Instituto de Biometria. Translated as: The fundamental principles of the division of labour, by José Dagnino-Pastore, *International Economic Papers 12*, London, Macmillan, 1967, pp. 31–62.

Stigler, G. J. May 1945. The cost of subsistence. *Journal of Farm Economics 27*, 303–314.

von Neumann, J. 1963. "Discussion of a Maximum Problem." In A. H. Taub (ed.), *Collected Works*, New York, Pergamon, 1963, Vol. 6, pp. 89–95.

Wald, Abraham. December 1936. Uber einige Gleichungssysteme der mathematischen Ökonomie. *Zeitschrift für Nationalökonomie.*

Weinstein, L. 1964. "The Origin and Development of the Application of Linear Programming in the USSR." Translated by Judy Forrester. Unpublished. Based on lecture at Plenary Session of Scientific Soviet of AN USSR on the Application of Mathematical and Computational Techniques to Economic Analysis and Planning, 1964.   [295]

29

Journal of Economic Literature
Vol. XXIV (December 1986), pp. 1773–1785

Communications

Comment: P. A. Samuelson, "Thünen at Two Hundred"*

By ROBERT DORFMAN

Harvard University

All admirers of Heinrich von Thünen should be grateful to Professor Samuelson for his paper (1983) commemorating the two hundredth anniversary of Thünen's birth. This paper makes Thünen's achievements accessible to a much wider audience than ever before. For English-speaking economists, it will surely be the principal source of information about Thünen and his work for many years to come.

Just because Samuelson's paper is such a judicious and valuable contribution, it seems necessary to point out a misleading misstatement in his discussion of the equation for the "natural wage," which Thünen regarded as one of his major accomplishments. The slip occurs in equation (A15) on page 1486, which Samuelson writes:

$$(W/P_q)^* \neq \sqrt{aF[K/L, 1]}. \qquad \text{(A15)}$$

In this equation the $\neq$ sign should be $=$, as Thünen asserted.

So much that is obfuscating or downright misleading has been written about Thünen's "natural wage," that it is important to be clear from the outset about just where I dissent from Samuelson and the critics who preceded him. Nearly every reader, including Samuelson and me, finds the social welfare function that Thünen invoked to derive his formula uncongenial, to say the least. It is a peculiar welfare function, as we shall see. I cannot defend it, though I can excuse it as the effort of a first pioneer who had neither precedent nor experi-

ence to guide him. My sole purpose is to set the record straight by demonstrating that Thünen's welfare function and other assumptions entail his natural wage formula as a matter of logical necessity. Those who reject the formula must do so on grounds other than the claim that it rests upon a logical fallacy.

Life is often more complicated and subtle than is desirable. In the present instance, Thünen did commit logical fallacies, repeatedly. He did so, however, after he had attained the insight on which his formula rests, and presented the fallacious arguments in three unfortunate attempts (Chs. 15, 16, and 18) to clarify and justify the relationship that he had perceived by a different route in Chapter 11. Even in the error-free Chapter 11, it must be conceded, the chain of reasoning is not entirely explicit.

I shall try to clear things up by demonstrating Thünen's equation for the natural wage, using the reasoning of Chapter 11, with improved notation, completed to the point where the natural wage formula emerges.

Thünen imagines a world in which there are two commodities: rye, which serves as numeraire, and "capital," which assists workers in growing the rye. The production function, which we (not Thünen) will denote by $f(q)$, gives the number of bushels of rye that can be produced in a year on rent-free land by a worker assisted by q units of capital. The unit of capital is the amount that can be produced in one work-year. There is no explicit allowance for depreciation, on the presumption that sufficient labor is devoted continually to repair

* Paul A. Samuelson. "Thünen at Two Hundred," *J. Econ. Lit.*, Dec. 1983, *21*(4), pp. 1468–88.

and replacement so that capital goods, once installed, endure forever. Only labor is required to produce capital, so that the cost of producing a unit of capital is simply the annual wage. a denotes the subsistence amount of rye per year and $a + y$ denotes the annual wage.

With that set of definitions we can follow Thünen's derivation step by step. If a worker is helped by q units of capital the marginal productivity of one unit of capital will be $f'(q)$ bushels of rye per year and that will also be the annual rent that a unit of capital will command. A worker's annual wage, $a + y$, will be equal to his annual product less the rent on the q units of capital he uses. We thus have the basic relationship $a + y = f(q) - qf'(q)$. (That appears to be the first appearance in the literature of that familiar mainstay of two-factor, linear homogeneous production theory.) We have already noted that a unit of capital costs $a + y$. In the stationary state, with which Thünen is concerned, the interest rate, z, is the ratio of the annual earnings of a unit of capital to its cost. Thus, $z = f'(q)/(a + y)$.

At this point Thünen introduces the "natural wage," which he regards as highly desirable though not "natural" in the sense of resulting from automatic equilibrating forces. The excess of a worker's annual wage over his subsistence needs, a, is y bushels of rye. If he invested that disposable income in capital at the rate of interest z, he would receive a perpetuity of zy bushels per year. The natural wage is the value of $a + y$ that makes this perpetuity (not its present value, which is always y) as great as possible, recognizing that the values of y and z depend on the choice of q. What's so good about that? Only that this perpetuity is the real income that a worker can purchase by investing the disposable portion of his wages. The optimizing task is thus to find the value of q that induces the values of y and z that maximize zy, a fact on which Thünen insists at length although Samuelson accuses him of ignoring it.

We have now encountered the welfare function that a long procession of readers finds objectionable. No defense will be entered here, but attention will be called to some extenuating circumstances. One is that this is probably the first occurrence in the literature of a model in which important theorems are deduced by maximizing an explicit, quantitative welfare function. More pertinently, one component of this welfare function, z, has been called "the internal rate of return" in more recent literature, and, under that designation is quite frequently regarded as an appropriate objective for maximization. Thünen's objective function, zy, is a bit more sophisticated than that. The excess of the wage over the subsistence level can be regarded as a measure of the painfulness of saving and investing: the larger y, the easier it is for the worker to put some of her wage aside for the sake of future returns. Thus zy can be considered to be a better measure than z itself of the future return to a unit of psychological sacrifice of current satisfactions. This extenuation, however, is a substantial extrapolation from the justification offered by Thünen himself. He says merely that zy is the perpetuity that a worker can obtain by saving and investing all the wage she can spare above subsistence requirements.

It must not be thought that Thünen laid out this derivation in so many words, as I have done. It is much easier to know where you are going if someone has been there before and given you a map. Thünen had to slog his way through, experiencing the struggle and delight of discovery at each step. In this first presentation he did not use the neat algebraic notation used above,[1] but worked through arithmetic examples based on linear homogeneous production functions of proper curvature. From them he perceived the relationships among productivity, the rental of capital, interest rates, and wages. He also noticed that as the amount of capital used by a worker increased, the size of the perpetuity she could purchase with her supplementary earnings, denoted above by zy, at first increased until it reached an interior maximum, and then decreased. It was this interior maximum, experimentally derived, that caught his attention, and the corresponding wage rate that became the natural wage.

That is where the presentation of Chapter 11 leaves off and the defective mathematics of the later chapters begins. Thünen reached a true relationship in those later chapters by an erroneous argument and accepted it, I sus-

---

[1] My notation is taken mostly from Chapter 13.

pect, because he was already persuaded of the correct theorem. But we do not have to follow him in that.

By using the formula for the interest rate, z, and the equation for the distribution of value, $f(q) = a + y + qf'(q)$, zy can be written as an explicit function of q:

$$zy = f'(q) - a \frac{f'(q)}{f(q) - qf'(q)}.$$

Notation apart, this maximand is closely related to the one derived by Samuelson in his equation (A14) (1983, p. 1486). In fact, the two are identical in the stationary condition envisaged by Thünen (but not Samuelson), in which the capital stock is constant over time. Samuelson's attempt to generalize Thünen's argument is probably what led him to deny Thünen's formula.

At any rate, carrying out the maximization by differentiating zy with respect to q and setting the derivative equal to zero yields a necessary condition for an interior maximum:

$$f''(q)\{[f(q) - qf'(q)]^2 - af(q)\} = 0.$$

Thünen writes p for $f(q)$. Using this notation, reintroducing $a + y$, transposing, and taking the square root:

$$a + y = \sqrt{ap},$$

the formula whose elegance and simplicity thrilled Thünen to the core.

That formula remains valid if, in the spirit of twentieth century capital theory, the assumption that capital lasts forever is dropped, and replaced by assuming that the good used as capital depreciates exponentially at $100D$ percent per year. The demonstration is a straightforward extension of Thünen's argument just sketched.[2]

In the steady state, the capital that depreciates each year has to be replaced. If there are K units of capital depreciating at $100D$ percent per year, DK work-years of labor are required to maintain the stock, and, with a total work force denoted by L, only $L - DK$ workers are available to grow rye. Then the rate

of production of rye, as a function of K and L can be written:

$$Y = F(K,L) = (L - DK)f\left(\frac{K}{L - DK}\right).$$

Each farmer worker in these circumstances is assisted by $q = K/(L - DK)$ units of capital.

With these stipulations, we can write at once that the annual wage is:

$$w = F_2(K,L) = f(q) - qf'(q),$$

and the annual rental of a unit of capital is

$$\begin{aligned} R &= F_1(K,L) \\ &= -Df(q) + (L - DK)f'(q)L/(L - DK)^2 \\ &= f'(q) - Dw \end{aligned}$$

after some simplification using the relation $K/L = q/(1 + Dq)$.

Because a unit of capital can be obtained by foregoing w bushels of rye and yields a perpetuity of R bu./yr., rye's own-rate of interest is $z = R/w = (f'(q)/w) - D$. Thus the function that is maximized at Thünen's natural wage and the corresponding values of q and R is

$$\begin{aligned} V &= [(f'(q)/w) - D](w - a) \\ &= f'(q) + aD - (af'(q)/w) - Dw. \end{aligned}$$

Note that $dw/dq = -qf''(q)$. Then

$$\frac{dV}{dq} = f''(q) - a\frac{wf''(q) + qf'(q)f''(q)}{w^2} + Dqf''(q).$$

A necessary condition for V to be maximized is $dV/dq = 0$, which requires

$$1 - af(q)/w^2 + Dq = 0,$$

using $w + qf'(q) = f(q)$ and assuming $f''(q) \neq 0$. Now clear of fractions and solve for w^2 to find $w^2 = af(q)/(1 + Dq)$. At this stage, recall the definition of q, from which $1 + Dq = L/(L - DK)$ and $Y = (L - DK)f(q)$. Then $w^2 = aY/L$. But Y/L is the average product per member of the work force. Call it p. And once again,

$$w = \sqrt{ap}.$$

Samuelson undertook to vindicate Thünen despite the alleged incorrectness of his final formula. I hope that I have completed the vindication by showing that the formula is correct and the reservation is unnecessary.

[2] I want to thank Professor Samuelson for a perceptive remark that is incorporated in the proof that follows.

I have derived Thünen's formula using his first, and most explicit, formulation. A. H. Leigh, in his article on Thünen in the *International Encyclopedia of the Social Sciences* (1968), gave brief and accurate digests of the (defective) versions in the later chapters of *Der isolierte Staat.*

REFERENCES

DEMPSEY, BERNARD W. *The frontier wage. The economic organization of free agents.* With the text of the second part of *The Isolated State.* Chicago: Loyola U. Press, 1960.

LEIGH, ARTHUR H. "J. H. von Thuenen," in *International Encyclopedia of the Social Sciences.* Vol. 16. NY: Macmillan and Free Press, 1968, pp. 16–20.

SAMUELSON, PAUL A. "Thünen at Two Hundred," *J. Econ. Lit.,* Dec. 1983, *21,* pp. 1468–88.

THÜNEN, JOHANN HEINRICH VON. *Der isolierte Staat in Beziehung auf Landwirtschaft und Nationalökonomie. Zweiter Teil. Der naturgemässe Arbeitslohn und dessen Verhältnis zun Zinsfuss und zur Landrente.* Rostock, 1850. Republished: Jena: Gustav Fischer, 1921.

30

Journal of Economic Perspectives— Volume 3, Number 3 —Summer 1989— pages 153–164

Thomas Robert Malthus and David Ricardo

Robert Dorfman

Malthus and Ricardo first met in 1811, in circumstances that might be considered unpromising. By then, Malthus was recognized as the leading economist in England, and Ricardo was an established man of property who had recently gained recognition as the most effective of the critics who blamed the Bank of England for the inflation then in progress. Malthus had reviewed the controversy over the causes of the inflation[1] objecting to some of Ricardo's arguments, though not to his basic position. Ricardo had published a rejoinder.[2] Whereupon Malthus wrote a letter to Ricardo that began:

> East India College Hertford
> June 16th 1811.

Dear Sir:
  One of my principal reasons for taking the liberty of introducing myself to you, next to the pleasure of making your acquaintance, was, that as we are mainly on the same side of the question, we might supersede the necessity of a long controversy in print respecting the points in which we differ, by an amicable discussion in private. (*Works*,[3] vol. VI, p. 21.)

They met for their "amicable discussion" about a week later, but did not resolve their

---

[1]"Publications on the depreciation of paper currency," *Edinburgh Review*, vol. XVII, Feb. 1811.

[2]*The High Price of Bullion*, 4th edition., Appendix. Included in *Works*, vol. III.

[3]"*Works* " will denote David Ricardo, *Works and Correspondence*, edited by P. Sraffa with the collaboration of M. H. Dobb.

■ *Robert Dorfman is Professor Emeritus of Political Economy, Harvard University, Cambridge, MA.*

disagreements. In fact, they were still disagreeing when Ricardo died twelve years later.

This article will describe the enduring relationship that Malthus' letter initiated. It was, very likely, the most remarkable and most fruitful collaboration in the history of economics.[4]

Malthus' Background

Their backgrounds are an essential part of the story. Malthus was the older of the two. He was born in 1766, that is, in the midst of that troubled but gloriously optimistic period, the Age of Enlightenment, on a "small but beautiful"[5] estate about 20 miles south of London. He was the second son of one Daniel Malthus, a cultivated landed gentleman of good family and connections but no great distinctions, not even wealth. Daniel had some intellectual stature. He corresponded with Rousseau and was friendly, though not intimate, with Hume.

So Malthus was born into the English country gentry, a highly privileged status in life. But he was born with two disadvantages. First, he was a *second* son. By English law and custom he could not inherit even a share of his father's estate (which was not very great in any event), and therefore had to support himself by engaging in one of the few professions that were considered proper for a member of his privileged caste. Second, he was born with a cleft palate that somewhat disfigured his face and caused a marked stammer throughout his life.

Between these two disadvantages, Malthus' choice of career was narrowly constricted. Service as an officer in the army or Royal Navy was highly respected, but not open to someone with his stammer. A career as a barrister was ruled out for the same reason. A life as a businessman was unthinkable for the son of an ancient country family. In fact, about the only possibility was the church (for which the stammer was apparently not considered so disabling a limitation). Accordingly, Malthus prepared to take orders.

As a boy, Malthus was an excellent student, the pride of his masters. He won scholarships, went on to Cambridge, and performed there with such distinction that immediately upon graduation he was elected a fellow of Trinity College and was appointed to an adequate living in a country parish.

Malthus lived the placid life of a Cambridge don and country cleric until he was about thirty years old. Then an abrupt change occurred in his circumstances. William Godwin, a minister turned author, published his *Enquiry Concerning Political Justice.*[6]

---

[4]The only other collaboration that bears comparison is the one between Karl Marx and Friedrich Engels, but Marx-Engels' relationship was predominantly one of master and disciple, while Malthus-Ricardo's relationship was more complex, as we shall see.

[5]The phrase is Bishop W. Otter's, in his "Memoir on the life of Malthus," published in the London School of Economics reprint of Malthus' *Principles.*

[6]As an instance of how tight the "tight little isle" was, it is worth noting that Godwin was the father of Mary Wollstonecraft, the author of *Frankenstein* and wife of Percy Bysshe Shelley.

Thomas Robert Malthus

David Ricardo

Portrait after Linnell of Thomas Malthus reproduced by courtesy of the Trustees of the British
Museum.

Portrait of David Ricardo by T. Hodgetts from
the National Portrait Gallery, London.

This volume was an immediate sensation, and remains one of the fundamental
statements of belief in human perfectibility and of philosophic anarchism. In it,
Godwin taught that men and women could learn to live entirely rationally, and that
when that had been accomplished, there would be no need for laws, property rights,
or other constraints on perfect freedom, and all people would live in peace, plenty,
and harmony.

Malthus' father, Daniel, was greatly impressed by these doctrines, and expounded them to his son. Whereupon a contentious streak in Malthus' nature revealed
itself: he could not abide such unbridled, unsubstantiated optimism. Father and son
wrangled night after night. Finally, the son was driven to write down his objections to
Godwin's utopian vision in the form of an extended memorandum to his father. The
father was not persuaded, but was so impressed by the passionate eloquence of the
manuscript that he urged Robert to publish it.

He did, under the title *Essay on the Principle of Population*. That was 1798. Though
the first edition was anonymous, it made Malthus famous at the age of 32. It also
made him odious to many people for deriding the hopes for human progress and
arguing that charity to the poor was futile. A couple of quotations will remind you of
the vivid eloquence that made this tract so effective when it was published, and still
effective nearly two centuries later.

First, a passage that describes the fate that befalls a nation when its population
becomes "excessive":

The vices of mankind are active and able ministers of depopulation. They are
the precursors of the army of destruction; and often finish the dreadful work

themselves. But should they fail in this war of extermination, sickly seasons, epidemics, pestilence, and plague advance in terrific array, and sweep off their thousands and ten thousands. Should success be still incomplete, gigantic inevitable famine stalks in the rear, and with one mighty blow, levels the population with the food of the world.[7]

Thus Malthus made clear the evils of overpopulation. And, as to Godwin's faith in the ability of the rule of rationality to supplant the principle of population, he had this to say:

No move towards the extinction of the passion between the sexes has taken place in the five or six thousand years the world has existed. Men in the decline of life have in all ages declaimed a passion which they have ceased to feel, but with as little reason as success. Those who from coldness of constitutional temperament have never felt what love is, will surely be allowed to be very incompetent judges with regard to the power of this passion to contribute to the sum of pleasurable sensations in life.[8]

Ricardo's Background

David Ricardo was born six years after Malthus and to a very different station in life. His father was a stockbroker who had migrated from Amsterdam to London a few years before David was born. In London the father joined the community of Jewish merchants and stockbrokers, who were reasonably prosperous and formed a small island of Jewish culture and tradition in the great metropolis of London. They stood at the periphery of English life, because of both their religion and their profession, just as the landed gentry stood at the center.

When David became old enough, he was sent back to Amsterdam to get a proper education in the much larger Jewish community there, and returned to London at the age of fourteen. There he went to work in his father's countinghouse to learn the trade of stockbroking. All might have been well except that four years later he fell in love with a Quaker, and informed his horrified parents that he planned to marry her. He was disowned, and expelled from the countinghouse. Nothing to do but to go into business for himself in the only trade he knew. He quickly proved himself to be the Boy Wonder of Threadneedle Street. Before he was thirty he had become rich enough to buy a country estate, to become bored with merely making money, and to turn his mind to other things.

One of the principal things he turned his mind to was economics. Somehow, in 1799, he came across *The Wealth of Nations*, devoured it, and was so thrilled by the insights he found in it that he continued to read and think about economics. When,

[7]Malthus, *Essay on the Principle of Population*, Modern Library edn., Ch. VII, p. 52.
[8]Malthus, *ibid.*, Modern Library edition, Ch. XI, p. 77.

around 1810, a controversy broke out in Parliament and in the press about the cause of the wartime inflation then in progress, Ricardo, as an experienced financier with a background in economics, was ready for his first publication: a series of letters to the *Morning Chronicle* tracing the inflation to the Bank of England's excessive issue of banknotes. These letters brought Ricardo to the attention of James Mill, who was prominent in London literary circles. Mill introduced Ricardo to his circle of economists and other intellectuals.

The letters plus Ricardo's pamphlet, *The High Price of Bullion, a Proof of the Depreciation of Banknotes,*[9] led to the first meeting between Malthus and Ricardo, as related above. Though they were brought together by some disagreements, they became close friends almost immediately. From their first meeting until Ricardo's death in 1823 they saw each other frequently, often several times a week, exchanged some eighty letters each way, stayed frequently at each other's homes, and were never long out of each other's minds.

The "Corn Laws" Controversy

Their extraordinary method of collaboration emerged just a few years later. The occasion was the controversy over the Corn Laws. The English Corn Laws were a scheme of variable tariffs and export subsidies, dating back to Elizabethan times, intended to protect and promote English agriculture. During the Napoleonic Wars, a coincidence of wartime demand and moderate harvests generated farm prices that were satisfactorily high. But as the war waned, the normal war-end economic disorganization, aggravated by some bumper crops, broke the agricultural markets. Wheat prices fell by about 50 percent between 1812 and 1815.[10] The agricultural interests demanded stiffened tariff protection, thereby precipitating lively debates in Parliament and the press. Malthus and Ricardo entered the public debate on opposite sides.

This debate is important for the history of economics, since in the course of it Malthus formulated his theory of rent and Ricardo elaborated that theory and embedded it in an argument that forms the kernel of his *Principles of Political Economy and Taxation*.

The earliest recorded discussions between Malthus and Ricardo that relate to the Corn Laws occurred in the summer of 1813. (The date is not important except to help keep the sequence of developments straight.) A letter from Ricardo to Malthus in August of that year mentions oral discussions between them concerning a thesis that was to become a centerpiece of Ricardian theory.[11] The thesis was that as a country's population grew and its capital accumulated, the rate of profit in farming would fall because farmers would have to resort to less and less productive land, and, moreover,

---

[9] Reprinted in *Works*, vol. III.
[10] B. R. Mitchell, 1962, p. 486.
[11] Letter dated August 17, 1813, *Works*, vol. VI, pp. 94–95. A letter from Ricardo to Hutches Trower, dated March 8, 1814, is somewhat more explicit. See *Works*, vol. VI, p. 104.

the general rate of profits in the country also would fall, since the rate of profits in other sectors tended to be equal to that in farming. Malthus, apparently, disagreed with this conclusion. Later letters dated in 1813 and 1814 mention more discussions of farm profits and profits in general, but do not inform us of the reasoning of either participant.

The first publication to emerge from these discussions was Malthus' pamphlet, *Observations on the Corn Laws*, published the following year, 1814. It was an even-handed review of the advantages and drawbacks of imposing a high tariff on imported grain. The intensive exchange occurred the following February, when Parliamentary action on corn imports was imminent and a heated public debate on the Corn Laws was in progress. Malthus contributed to this debate by publishing two pamphlets a week apart. The first was *An Inquiry into the Nature and Progress of Rent*, in which he presented the Malthusian-Ricardian theory of rent for the first time.[12] Toward the end of the pamphlet, Malthus expressed his preference for retaining the high tariffs on corn in order to protect the prosperity of the farmers and the rural population in general. A week later he took a stronger stand. In *Grounds of an Opinion on the Policy of Restricting the Importation of Foreign Corn*, his original diffident endorsement of the Corn Laws was replaced by forthright advocacy. He there argued that the protection afforded by the Corn Laws was essential to the continued health of English agriculture, and that the vitality of English ways and institutions, as well as national security, was rooted in the prosperity of her farms and villages.

Ricardo responded within two weeks with his *Essay on the Influence of a Low Price of Corn on the Profits of Stock*. This pamphlet announced his theory, which had been germinating for the previous two years, of the adverse effect of population growth and capital accumulation on the rate profit. In developing his argument, Ricardo relied repeatedly on the theory of rent that Malthus had just published. This fact did not deter him from drawing policy conclusions diametrically opposed to those advocated by Malthus, or, indeed, from rebutting explicitly some of Malthus' contentions. He argued vehemently that England's future depended on the progress of her industries, which was being stifled by the Corn Laws. On the other hand, Ricardo concluded,

> If, then, the prosperity of the commercial classes will most certainly lead to accumulation of capital, and the encouragement of productive industry; these can by no means be so surely obtained as by a fall in the price of corn. (*Works*, vol. IV, p. 37.)

Thus the policy issue between the two friends was clearly and openly joined.

Though they could not reach agreement about policy, their efforts to explain their views, first to each other and then to the public, led them to their comprehensive theory of the distribution of national income among the three great classes of claimants: the workers, the merchants, and the landed gentry. They both contributed

---

[12] Neither Malthus nor Ricardo was aware that Edward West was publishing the same ideas at virtually the same time, and apparently none of the three knew that James Anderson had anticipated them all in 1777. See Anderson's *Enquiry*, footnote beginning on p. 45, or his *Observations*, p. 376.

to this effort and to each other's argumentation. Both relied on Malthusian population theory to explain the level of real wages. Both used Malthus' theory of rent. Both recognized that the rate of profit in agriculture was determined by the productivity of the marginal land cultivated, thereby injecting marginal considerations into economic thought, albeit in a limited application. And they agreed that the rate of profit had to be the same in all industries where competition prevailed. Thus all the ingredients of Ricardian distribution and growth theory were in place and agreed upon.

Their debate over the Corn Laws was now over. Its effect on economic policy was modest. Parliament voted to retain, and even strengthen, the laws, and they remained in force for another 30 years. But its effect on economic thought was enormous and enduring.

Ricardo's and Malthus' *Principles of Political Economy*

At this point, developments took on a momentum of their own. James Mill reentered the story. He appreciated, and was enormously impressed by, the clear and comprehensive theory sketched in the *Influence of a Low Price of Corn*, and urged Ricardo to expand his pamphlet of thirty-odd pages into a fully developed treatise on the principles of economics. Ricardo demurred; he did not feel competent to compose a full-fledged treatise. Somewhat later, he said of himself, "I am but a poor master of language."[13] Mill persisted, and Ricardo was persuaded and published his *Principles of Political Economy and Taxation* two years later, in 1817. It was an expansion, and in some respects a revision, of the *Influence of a Low Price of Corn*, but its basic argument was the same. It was an immediate success. In fact, it was the most authoritative and influential text on economics published in the 75-year span between Smith's *Wealth of Nations* and John Stuart Mill's *Principles of Political Economy*. Nor did its influence end even then since Mill's *Principles* was based on Ricardo's doctrines. In short, the friendly but intense debate between Malthus and Ricardo during the Corn Laws controversy set the course that English economics followed for the rest of the nineteenth century.

The letters that they exchanged during the public controversy and during the preceding year indicate what was going on behind the pamphlets. They labored together to understand the economic consequences of the Corn Laws. Their discussions led them to a deeper understanding of economics than anyone had attained before. But they could not agree on the substantive matter of policy. So, having failed to persuade each other by argument or by letter, they laid their individual conclusions before the public. Indeed, their correspondence shows that each encouraged the other to make his views public. In so doing neither moderated his criticisms of his friend's arguments. Neither ever wavered from the conviction that the other was striving as earnestly and honestly as himself to attain a true and objective understanding of the principles at work.

[13]*Works*, vol. VIII, p. 20, letter dated Oct. 9, 1820.

The termination of their controversy over the Corn Laws did not, by any means, terminate their joint efforts to understand how the economy works. It is significant that Ricardo devoted the last chapter of his *Principles* to criticizing some aspects of Malthus' pamphlet, *On the Nature and Progress of Rent*. Shortly after seeing the *Principles* Malthus wrote to Ricardo, "I am mediating a volume as I believe I have told you, and I want to answer you, without giving my work a controversial air."[14] The answer was Malthus' *Principles of Political Economy*, published in 1820. This is so much a point-by-point response to Ricardo's *Principles* that it can hardly be read with comprehension unless the earlier work is clearly in mind.

The "Gluts" Controversy

The exchange was not yet over but, with the publication of Malthus' *Principles*, it shifted to a new topic, or rather a long smoldering topic that flared up: "gluts." With the return of peace after Waterloo, the English economy had sagged into a postwar depression or, as they called it, "glut." What should be done about it? Ricardo held that a condition of general overproduction was impossible except transiently. An oversupply of one commodity would have to be counterbalanced automatically by a shortage of some other. Ricardo explained this, in effect Say's Law, to Malthus, painstakingly in letter after letter, but Malthus could not see it. Malthus, for his part, explained to Ricardo repeatedly that total demand might be smaller than the total output that the working population and other resources could produce if fully employed. The working population could not afford to buy much more than bare subsistence. If the well-off classes were too abstemious, the prices of luxuries could fall to the point where there was no profit in producing them, and glut would ensue. In the extreme, Malthus pointed out, if everyone lived on a subsistence scale there would have to be a vast oversupply of commodities since each worker could produce much more than bare subsistence for himself and his family. To no avail. Ricardo couldn't see it.

Keynes revived this debate a hundred years after the principals had died, and claimed Malthus as his predecessor in appreciating the possibility of underemployment equilibrium. At any rate, when Malthus wrote his *Principles*, he devoted the final chapters to the problem of gluts and to the need for a class of "unproductive consumers" who would provide the demand that would keep the rest of the economy employed profitably. He pointed out that the English landed gentry were exceptionally well equipped to fulfill this function. To this notion, Ricardo could only respond, "I can see no soundness in the reasons you give for the usefulness of demand on the part of unproductive consumers. How their consuming, without reproducing, can be beneficial to a country, in any possible state of it, I confess I cannot discover."[15] One can almost see him shaking his head as he wrote those words.

---

[14]*Works*, vol. VII, p. 215, letter dated Jan. 3, 1817
[15]*Works*, vol. VIII, p. 301, letter dated Nov. 24, 1820.

Of course, Malthus did not have the last word. When Ricardo received Malthus' book, he went through it meticulously, recording his disagreements with Malthus' contentions paragraph by paragraph. The result was a book-length manuscript which Ricardo decided not to publish.[16] He did circulate it among his friends, including Malthus, however.

As a result of being withheld from publication, the manuscript was very nearly lost. No one knew where it was when Ricardo died, and its whereabouts remained a mystery for 89 years until one of his great-grandsons came across it when cleaning out the lumber room of a country house that had been in the Ricardo family. Thanks to that stroke of luck, we know Ricardo's responses to the book that Malthus wrote to answer his own. We also know Malthus' rejoinders to those responses; the second edition of Malthus' *Principles* includes many changes and allusions in response to Ricardo's criticisms. But that is where the exchange ends. Ricardo died before Malthus revised his *Principles*.

The "Value" Controversy

All the while that Malthus and Ricardo were arguing about the Corn Laws and the nature of gluts, they were conducting a third interminable dispute. This one concerned the definition, measurement, and cause of "value." From our perspective, the concern over value, which extended from Adam Smith to Stanley Jevons at least, was a great waste of words and time. But Malthus, Ricardo, and their contemporaries took it very seriously, and with some reason. They had enough experience with inflations, crop failures and bumper crops, and other economic disturbances to recognize that money prices fluctuated too erratically to indicate long-run relationships or to reveal underlying trends. They believed that each commodity had a property that, following Adam Smith, they called its "natural value," which explained the ratio of its money price to the prices of other commodities. About that they agreed, but when they attempted to define this natural value, explain its level and changes, and devise ways to measure it in practice (since money prices were not reliable indicators), they became engaged in endless debate. Their final debate concerned the practical measurement of commodities' values.

Ricardo held that there was no accurate measure of natural value, but that a commodity's price in terms of gold was the best practical approximation, because the costs of labor and capital contributed to the total cost of gold production in proportions that were about the average for all commodities. (Notice that this reasoning conflicts with the common impression that Ricardo explained commodities' values by a "labor theory of value"; in fact, he held a cost-of-production theory much like Adam Smith's.) Malthus advocated using the cost of labor—that is, wages—as the standard for measuring the values of other commodities, on the ground that "a

---

[16]The manuscript was entitled "Notes on Mr. Malthus' work 'Principles of Political Economy, considered with a view to their practical application.'" It was published after long delay in 1928 under the editorship of J. H. Hollander and T. E. Gregory, It is included in *Works* as vol. II.

given quantity of labor must always be of the same natural and absolute value,"[17] a presumption that Ricardo denied.

As I said, Ricardo and Malthus tirelessly and fruitlessly expounded to each other their contradictory convictions about the meaning and measurement of value throughout the time they knew each other. They were still at it on August 31, 1823, when Ricardo was beginning to suffer severe headaches from an abscess on his brain. On that day, Ricardo wrote Malthus a long letter, which began, "I have only a few words more to say on the subject of value, and I have done." After about two pages of careful reasoning, he concluded, "And now, my dear Malthus, I have done. Like other disputants, after much discussion we each retain our own opinions. These discussions, however, never influence our friendship; I could not like you more than I do if you agreed in opinion with me. Pray give Mrs. Ricardo's and my kind regards to Mrs. Malthus. Yours truly ..."[18]

Two weeks later, Ricardo was dead. At his funeral, Malthus is reported to have said, "I never loved anybody out of my own family so much. Our interchange of opinions was so unreserved, and the object after which we were both enquiring was so entirely the truth and nothing else, that I cannot but think we sooner or later must have agreed."[19]

Envoi

So ends the story of Thomas Robert Malthus and David Ricardo, the two great friends in the history of economics. I cannot help dissenting from Malthus' affectionate and hopeful remark at the funeral. I believe that if there is a corner in heaven where good economists go, they are there to this very day getting no closer to agreement about the meaning and proper measurement of value.

There were good reasons why they could never agree. We have already seen that they were born and bred in two subcultures that were as disparate as could be found in England. They came to economics, therefore, with differing preconceptions, particularly with respect to the roles of the gentry and the entrepreneurial class in the British economy and society. Inevitably, these commitments colored their thinking; witness their positions in the Corn Laws and gluts controversies.

Besides, their minds operated in entirely different modes. Ricardo's style was quick, brilliant, concise, syllogistic. Malthus' mode was slower, and seemed motivated by deep common-sensical convictions that he had difficulty articulating precisely enough to serve as a basis for rigorous argument. Ricardo was the archetypical theorist; Malthus the typical practical economist. Ricardo loved the clean, simple case where conclusion followed inexorably from hypothesis; Malthus could not avert his gaze from the rich complication of real economic life. Ricardo recognized this source

[17]A. Smith, *Wealth of Nations*, Modern Library edn., p. 30.
[18]*Works*, IX, pp. 380–382.
[19]Reported in *Letters of David Ricardo to Thomas Robert Malthus, 1810–1823*, edited by James Bonar, p. 240.

of misunderstanding, and wrote to Malthus:

> Our differences may in some respects, I think, be ascribed to your considering my book as more practical than I intended it to be. My object was to elucidate principles, and to do this I imagined strong cases that I might shew the operation of those.[20]

The miracle is not that they disagreed, but that they could stand each other. It appears, though, that their long and intimate collaboration, and their friendship as well, thrived on their continual disputations. It is as though each served as the anvil for the other's hammer, and their ideas were hammered out in their efforts to persuade each other. They were two men obsessed by a common enthusiasm, tirelessly pursuing a common goal: to understand the economy. But they did not share a common vision of the good society and thus were condemned to wrestle interminably, though remarkably fruitfully, over the roles of the social classes.

Their struggles to convey to each other their views of the forces that drove their economy are an inspiring case study in both the difficulty and the possibility of human communication. These two friends, sustained by enormous affection and respect for one another, never could nullify the differences in preconception and mental style that separated them, but still could help each other attain a deeper understanding of their economy than anyone had achieved before. To do this required invincible faith in each other's candor and open-mindedness, great patience, inexhaustible good will, and unflagging civility.[21] These qualities, that made possible their twelve years of fruitful collaboration, remain essential to scientific discourse, particularly in economics. Malthus and Ricardo show that with sufficient good will we, too, can communicate with and perhaps persuade each other.

[20]*Works*, vol. VIII, p. 184, letter dated May 4, 1820.

[21]To be sure, like every long relationship, theirs was not exempt from occasional strains. There are a few letters from Ricardo (to correspondents other than Malthus) expressing impatience with Malthus. Examples are a letter to Hutches Trower dated March 2, 1821 (*Works*, vol. VIII, p. 349) and one to J. R. McCulloch dated April 25, 1821 (*Works*, vol. VIII, p. 373).

References

Anderson, James, *An Enquiry Into the Nature of the Corn Laws*. Edinburgh, 1777.

Anderson, James, *Observations on the Means of Exciting a Spirit of National Industry*. Edinburgh, 1777.

Bonar, James, ed., *Letters of David Ricardo to T. R. Malthus, 1810–1832*. Oxford: The Clarendon Press, 1887.

Keynes, J. M., "Robert Malthus: The First of the Cambridge Economists." In *Essays in Biography*. New York: Horizon Press, 1951.

Malthus, T. R., *An Essay on the Principles of Population, as it Affects the Future Improvement of Society*. London: 1798. Reprinted many times.

Malthus, T. R., "Publications on the Depreciation of Paper Currency," *Edinburgh Review, XVII*, February 1811.

Malthus, T. R., *An Inquiry into the Nature and Progress of Rent, and the Principles by which it is Regulated*. London: 1815. (Reprinted by the Johns Hopkins Press, Baltimore, 1903, J. H. Hollander, ed.)

Malthus, T. R., *The Grounds of an Opinion on the Policy of Restricting the Importation of Foreign Corn*. London: John Murray, 1815.

Malthus, T. R., *Principles of Political Economy Considered with a View to their Practical Application*. London: 1820. (2nd edn., 1836, reprinted by the London School of Economics, London: 1936.)

Mitchell, B. R., *Abstract of British Historical Statistics*. Cambridge: Cambridge University Press, 1962.

Ricardo, David, *Works and Correspondence*, vols, I–XI, edited by P. Sraffa with the collaboration of M. H. Dobb. Cambridge: Cambridge University Press, 1951–1973. Referred to above as *Works*.

Smith, Adam, *An Inquiry into the Nature and Causes of the Wealth of Nations*. London: 1776. Republished many times.

[31]

AUSTRIAN AND AMERICAN CAPITAL THEORIES: A CONTRAST OF CULTURES

BY

ROBERT DORFMAN

I. INTRODUCTION

Controversies about capital, its role in the economy, and its claims for reward are still very much with us. Though the exchanges are often heated, all the contestants[1] are descended from either of two monumental works of about a century ago: Eugen von Böhm-Bawerk's *Positive Theory of Capital* (1889) and Irving Fisher's *The Rate of Interest*[2] (1907). This essay inquires: in what respects are these two theories the same? In what respects do they differ? And why?

Since suspense has no proper place in a journal article, I will state my conclusions forthwith. Böhm-Bawerk and Fisher confronted precisely the same questions, to wit: how to define capital, how to explain the existence and the amount of capital so defined, and how to explain the existence and level of the rate of interest, which is the payment or return for the use of capital. Their answers, I shall contend, are very much the same when stripped down to bare essentials, but differ greatly in the social contexts that inspired them and that they take for granted. Both, indeed, are rediscoveries of insights that go back to John Rae's *Statement of Some New Principles on the Subject of Political Economy* (1834). Apparently, though, Böhm-Bawerk was not aware of Rae's work until after he published his own,[3] while Fisher dedicated his first

---

Harvard University.

1. Except for some Marxists.

2. Usually read in its somewhat revised version, *The Theory of Interest* (1930).

3. As we shall see, Böhm-Bawerk denied that John Rae anticipated important aspects of his own theory, while praising the importance of Rae's contribution to capital theory.

Journal of the History of Economic Thought, 17, Spring 1995.
©1995 by the History of Economics Society.

book on interest theory to the memory of John Rae.[4]

It is relevant and important that Fisher and Böhm-Bawerk were the products of two strikingly different cultures. Böhm-Bawerk, whose full name and title was Eugen, Ritter von Böhm von Bawerk, lived and worked in Vienna,[5] the capital and cultural center of the Hapsburg Austro-Hungarian empire. He was educated at, and closely associated with, the Universität Wien (founded 1365), and, in addition to attaining a distinguished professorship there, had an equally distinguished career in the Austrian Ministry of Finance, serving as Minister several times. As might be expected, his outlook on the world was that of a member of the elite establishment of a Central European monarchy.

Irving Fisher, in contrast, was quintessentially a Connecticut Yankee. His father was Congregational minister in a number of communities, mostly in New England. Fisher spent most of his life in New Haven, a provincial center somewhat under the shadow of the nearby metropolises of Boston and New York. He studied at Yale, which was still called Yale College at the time he enrolled, and was connected with Yale most of his life. His outlook, as might be expected, was pragmatic, democratic, optimistic, and more concerned with the prospects and tasks of human betterment and social improvement than with cultural achievements and social stability.

Their professional training also differed widely. Böhm-Bawerk was trained originally in the law, at the University of Vienna. After graduation, he went to Germany to study economics with Karl Knies and other leaders of the German Historical School. His professional background was therefore heavily literary and legalistic. Fisher, on the other hand, was undecided about his career plans during his undergraduate years at Yale. He was the outstanding mathematics student during his studies there, and was greatly influenced by Willard Gibbs, perhaps the leading mathematical physicist in America at the time. But mathematics was too remote from the advancement of human welfare for his tastes, and he shifted to economics for his graduate study. As it turned out, his career combined these two interests.

The two thus came to economics and to their common destination, capital theory, by very different routes. Even within economics, they

---

4. He added Böhm-Bawerk's name to the dedication of the revised edition. In the interval between the editions, Fisher and Böhm-Bawerk engaged in some controversies and Böhm-Bawerk died.

5. Except for nine years as a professor at the University of Innsbruck, during which he completed his magnum opus. I thank Professor Robert Dimand of Brock University for pointing this out to me.

came to concentrate on capital theory from contrasting points of view. Capital theory has a much broader scope than its name suggests. Any explanation of the share of a product's value claimed by capital (or, more exactly, by suppliers of capital) is necessarily also an explanation of the share going to the other main claimant, labor. Thus, capital theory can be no less than a theory of the functional distribution of income. In the latter half of the nineteenth century, the disturbances of 1848 and the spread of Marxist and socialist doctrine[6] pushed the functional distribution of income, which was effectively the class distribution, to the top of the political agenda. Several of Böhm-Bawerk's professors in Vienna and, later, in Germany, urged him to tackle this topic to provide a cogent theoretical response to Karl Marx's exploitation theory of wages. Böhm-Bawerk undertook this task with a will when he embarked on his academic career in 1880.

Fisher approached the topic less directly. His doctoral dissertation, *Mathematical Investigations in the Theory of Value and Prices* (1892), was essentially an independent rediscovery of Léon Walras's theory of the determination of relative prices in a competitive economy in static equilibrium.[7] It is distinguished from Walras's *Elements of Pure Economics* less in substance than in its greater clarity and brevity and in its decreased attention to the psychology of economic choices, the neoclassical revolution having already been achieved.

Fisher's second major publication was *Appreciation and Interest* (1896a), a work stimulated by the bimetallism controversy then raging. "Appreciation" in this context meant appreciation in the value of the currency, or decrease in general level of prices. Here Fisher introduced the distinction between real and nominal rates of interest and the classic formula: Real interest rate = Nominal interest rate + rate per annum of appreciation.[8] In this monograph, Fisher again displayed his mathematical skills. In short, from the beginning of his career, Fisher was a skilled, technically adept, professional economist.[9]

6. The first volume of *Kapital* was published in 1867.

7. If Fisher's examiners had been better versed in European economic literature than they were, a promising career might have been blighted at its inception. Professor Dimand has pointed out, though, that Fisher recognized Walras's priority in the preface to his dissertation without jeopardizing its acceptance.

8. The formula in the text is the conventional approximation to the exact formula that Fisher presented.

9. In mid-career, Fisher's major interests turned to promoting a variety of causes ranging from opposing both drinking and amending the Constitution to suppress it, improved dietary habits, adherence to the League of Nations, and adjusting the gold con-

Fisher was already disturbed by the vagueness of the concept of capital when he published *Appreciation*. In the same year, he published a paper, "What is capital?" in the *Economic Journal* roundly criticizing the use of "capital" by practically all economists beginning with A. R. J. Turgot and Adam Smith, and explicitly including Böhm-Bawerk. Fisher's own view was that capital was essentially synonymous with wealth and that income was roughly the same thing as consumption.[10] He argued this position in a string of papers from 1896 (1896b) until 1907, culminating in his treatise, *The Nature of Capital and Income*.

Fisher's definitions have never become prevalent, and may seem strange, though it is sometimes hard to keep a straight face when defending the conventional and Böhm-Bawerkian concepts according to which a loaf of bread on a baker's shelves is part of the nation's capital while that same loaf, having been purchased and transported to a consumer's bread box, is not. Fisher (and John Rae) staunchly maintained that the bread remains a component of national capital until it gives rise to a flow of psychic income (part of national income according to Fisher's definitions) by being eaten. It is hard to find a flaw in this logic.

While wrestling with these concepts, Fisher kept his eye on the relationship between the stock of capital and the flow of income to which it gives rise, i.e., the rate of interest. Böhm-Bawerk's treatment in *The Positive Theory of Capital* had already become authoritative. Fisher was well acquainted with it, was impressed by it, and accepted it in large part. But many of his own convictions diverged from Böhm-Bawerk's theory enough to justify a full-fledged presentation. They received it in *The Rate of Interest* (1907).

There is an important difference in expository style also. The same mathematical turn of mind that Fisher displayed in the *Mathematical Investigations* and *Appreciation and Interest* is an essential feature of *The Rate of Interest*. Fisher's mathematical facility contrasts strikingly with Böhm-Bawerk's limitations. Böhm-Bawerk knew as little mathematics as an intelligent person possibly could. Though he had an essentially mathematical thesis to advance, he could express it only by means of arithmetic examples, which can be misleading (and Böhm-Bawerk

---

tent of the dollar in order to damp price fluctuations.

10. Incidentally, Rae defined his concept of capital in essentially the same way. As far as I know, these two were the only economists to use so broad a definition of capital.

was misled, as Fisher, Bortkiewicz, and others pointed out), and are exceedingly constraining.[11]

II. THEIR DOCTRINES

The foregoing recital of contrasts leads one to expect that Böhm-Bawerk and Fisher would emphasize different aspects of their joint topic. They surely did; they described it like the blind men stationed at opposite corners of the elephant. Böhm-Bawerk based his theory on social considerations, in particular on the balance between propertied people's search for profitable investments and working people's search for jobs. Contrasting social classes play no role in Fisher's theory, which rests on the maximizing behavior of undifferentiated, symmetrically placed individuals.

Böhm-Bawerk's contribution came first, announced sketchily in 1884 and published in full in 1889. His *Positive Theory of Capital* is a frankly polemic work. It is volume II in a two volume set, of which the first volume, *History and Critique of Interest Theories*, is a scholarly and acute appraisal of all previous interest theories known to Böhm-Bawerk.[12] He found serious flaws in them all, particularly in the labor theories of value expounded by Marx and his predecessor, Johann Karl Rodbertus.

The *Positive Theory of Interest* is designed to establish that a positive rate of interest is inevitable, and therefore justified, in a capital-using economy.[13] It presumes a society divided into a property-owning class and a propertyless, wage-earning class, as in Marx. Each property owner invests his property so as to earn the highest possible rate of profit per annum, taking the wage rate as a datum beyond his control. Böhm-Bawerk used an extended arithmetic example to show that this situation leads to a positive rate of interest, but I shall follow a different route.

The fulcrum of the argument is the concept of "the average period of

11. For example, Böhm-Bawerk had to present his argument for the superiority of currently available resources over deferred ones in terms of a point-input, point-output technology, which is an excessively simplified special case.

12. As was mentioned above, Böhm-Bawerk did not know of Rae's theory, until after the first edition of the *History and Critique of Interest Theories* was published, but he devoted an entire chapter to Rae in the second edition. It was largely laudatory, but pointed out several places where Rae had gone seriously astray, in Böhm-Bawerk's opinion.

13. This is not exactly the same thing as justifying the existence of a propertied class of individuals who own the capital and claim the interest that accrues to it.

production" (APP), introduced by Böhm-Bawerk. The name describes the concept. The average period of production is simply the length of time, measured perhaps in months, that elapses between the moment when some factor of production is invested in a specific product and the moment when that product is ready to be consumed.[14]

The APP is essentially an extension of the notion of a wages fund. In classical economic theory, a wages fund was a stock of subsistence goods available to an economy (or an enterprise) to support its work force for a period generally considered to be one harvest cycle.[15]   It determined the average wage in the economy, which could not exceed the size of the fund divided by the size of the work force. The APP operated similarly but more flexibly. It conceived of a flow of consumables in various stages of completion. The stock in the pipeline was sufficient to support the work force, not for one year, but for a length of time equal to roughly twice the average time that each unit of effort remained in work-in-process. The APP was more flexible than the wages fund because the period for which the fund had to suffice was determined endogenously by investors when they chose the technologies they employed. The investors had to choose between lengthening the APP, which would permit using technologies with greater output per work-year, and employing more workers using the current APP. Thereby it reflected one of the most significant kinds of choice made in an industrialized economy.

The average period of production was a particularly appealing concept. It promised to solve the perennially vexatious problem of how to measure the quantity of capital in terms distinct from its monetary value. This problem, still awaiting definitive solution, lies at the heart of the "paradoxes" of capital theory. The basic paradox is the fact that the capital value of a specific capital good can change while the good itself remains unaltered. Consequently, the amount of capital in a firm or an economy can change without any change in the physical composition of its stock of capital goods, its inventories, etc. These changes in the amount of capital occur because the amount of capital represented by a capital good, i.e., its value, is defined to be the present value of the services the good will render during its useful life, discounted at an appropriate rate of interest. Value, so defined, changes when the inter-

---

14. Friedrich Hayek remarked perceptively that the "average period of investment" would have been a more appropriate label.

15. The wages fund was especially relevant, therefore, to an eighteenth-century agricultural economy.

est rate used does.[16]

This behavior is the source of the "monetary Wicksell effect," of Joan Robinson's famous diatribe (1954) against aggregative productive functions, and the subsequent capital theory controversy, and of many additional confusions which could all be annihilated by a purely physical definition of capital such as Böhm-Bawerk's APP. Böhm-Bawerk was particularly proud of having invented this concept. But Fisher rejected it and so, in the end, did practically everyone else.

One of Fisher's objections to Böhm-Bawerks's theory was its reliance on the APP. In his opinion, Böhm-Bawerk's definition, a weighted arithmetic mean of the times for which units of effort remain invested, was arbitrary (Why not use a harmonic mean? How should the weights of the components be chosen?) and was merely an arithmetic concoction without substantive significance. He rejected it,[17] instead advocating valuing income flows according to their present values (PVs) computed at the market rate of interest. An income stream's PV has the substantive and motivational significance that Fisher wanted, but it lacks the direct definitional connection with the demand for labor that the APP has in Böhm-Bawerk's theory of interest and wage determination.

The relationship between the APP and the demand for labor follows from Böhm-Bawerk's concept of "roundaboutness." The APP measures the roundaboutness of a production process, and Böhm-Bawerk argued that a technological change that increased a process's output per worker per year generally entailed an increase in roundaboutness, i.e. the average time that a unit of effort had to remain invested before the resulting product could be consumed. In Böhm-Bawerk's model of production, increases in output per work-year of effort could be achieved only by increasing the APP, but each unit increase in the APP resulted in a smaller increase in output per work-year than the preceding one.[18]

---

16. Changes in the prices of products or factors of production also affect the quantity of capital according to this definition, but the effect of changes in the interest rate is of most concern theoretically. The difficulty is that the theory holds that the quantity of capital is one of the main determinants of the interest rate, but the quantity of capital is not well defined until the interest rate has been determined.

17. As did Ladislaus von Bortkiewicz and several other early critics. Fisher's objection to the use of the APP as defined by Böhm-Bawerk was not entirely justified. If the equilibrium rate of interest is zero, which is the case that Böhm-Bawerk rather inconsistently considered, Böhm-Bawerk's definition corresponds to the value of goods-in-process per worker required to sustain a steady flow of output. For an economy in equilibrium, this ratio would be called nowadays the capital-labor ratio.

18. This last clause amounts to the conventional assumption of diminishing marginal productivity of capital.

Eventually, the APP would reach a length at which any further increase in roundaboutness would increase the value of output per year less than the same sum used to hire additional workers. The value of the APP at that point is the one that would maximize the rate of profit earned by resources invested in that process. Investors seeking the maximum attainable rate of profit would allocate the economy's resources among products and processes so that all attained the same, maximum, rate of profit, which would also be the market rate of interest in the economy. So goes the gist of Böhm-Bawerk's theory.[19]

It would have been nice if the average period of production concept had solved the problem of quantifying the amount of capital, just as it would have been nice if planetary orbits were as simple as Copernicus initially believed, but the world isn't built that way. Böhm-Bawerk defended his concept indomitably, although, in fact, the principal conclusions require only the assumption, made by Fisher and most of his successors, that the marginal returns to successive equal investments in any type of capital good decrease and eventually approach zero as the stock of that good grows, together with the argument that investors distribute their investments among types of capital goods so that the marginal rates of return to all types remain equal. Böhm-Bawerk actually made the necessary assumption in the course of explaining the relationship between the APP and the rate of output per work-year. Thus the sometimes furious debates about the validity of the APP concept were logically beside the point, but the inflexible determination with which Böhm-Bawerk defended it suggests that it was psychologically indispensable to him.

We have already noted that Fisher thought that Böhm-Bawerk's APP device was arbitrary and technically defective. He felt also that the two-class characterization of economic participants, by Marx and Böhm-Bawerk, though perhaps applicable in Central Europe, was not a useful way to view economic relationships in the United States or in general. Instead, his theory is based on an economy populated by utility-maximizing actors, distinguished only by their individual tastes and preferences and by their differing degrees of access to economic opportunities.

Although Fisher built his theory on the foundation of Böhm-Bawerk's, the major exceptions just noted, plus a few minor ones,

---

19. In addition, Böhm-Bawerk adduced his two psychological grounds of interest to help account for the total amount of capital per worker in the economy, which is needed to determine the equilibrium wage.

make the connection almost undetectable. He retained Böhm-Bawerk's basic insight that interest was not a monetary phenomenon, but rather a price that arose primarily from choices by investors seeking the most profitable investments. He replaced Böhm-Bawerk's concern with capital's and labor's competing claims to shares of the national output by a disinterested, scientific interest in clarifying the economic significance and function of the interest rate. Thus, he dropped the worker-owner distinction and the special role of the labor market in favor of an economy populated by symmetrically placed, depersonalized economic agents. He eliminated the class struggle aspect from the theories of capital and interest, and treated the determination of factor shares of national income as simply an instance of the general theory of price determination.

Fisher also dropped Böhm-Bawerk's preoccupation with the psychological underpinnings of time preference, expressed in Böhm-Bawerk's two psychological grounds of interest, preferring to leave such matters to psychologists. Instead, he posited that each individual, capitalist or worker, disposed of his capital or labor in the way available to him that had the greatest possible present value.

What then remained? What remained was Böhm-Bawerk's basic concept that interest arises from a tension between the urgency of consumption at present or soon and the technological advantages of time-consuming production methods, in Böhm-Bawerk's formulation, or between "impatience to consume and opportunity to invest," in Fisher's (Fisher 1930, title page). The major difference between the two approaches is that Böhm-Bawerk conceived of the tension as existing between two social classes, workers and owners of capital, while Fisher saw it as an internal psychological conflict experienced by individual economic actors.

In Fisher's conception, each economic actor had two kinds of choices to make concerning the timing of his income and consumption.[20] One kind concerned borrowing and lending. On the assumptions of complete certainty and perfect capital markets, each actor could borrow and lend so as to modify his stream of expected incomes into any time-shape he chose, just so long as the present value of the chosen time-stream, computed at the market rate of interest, did not exceed that of the original time-stream. So, given any time-stream of income expected with certainty, the actor would use it to finance the most desirable time-

---

20. We here use the words in their conventional rather than their Fisherian meanings.

stream of consumption that the anticipated income would buy. This implies, among other things, that when the rates of consumption at any two dates along an optimal time stream are compared, the marginal rate of substitution of consumption at the later date for consumption at the earlier one must equal the market rate of interest between the two dates.

The other kind of choice concerned the use that the actor made of his economic assets, including his ability to perform useful work. The range of these choices was depicted by the actor's "opportunity curve," which specified all the time-streams of income that the actor could realize by choosing how to use those assets. Fisher illustrated this range of choice by the example of a landowner who could use his land as a farm which would yield a steady stream of income indefinitely, or as a mine that would yield an income stream that grew smaller gradually as the vein became exhausted, or as a wood lot that produced no income for a considerable period and then, when harvested, yielded a sudden substantial burst of salable timber.

In making this second type of choice, the consumer-investor is concerned only with maximizing the present value of his anticipated income-stream, since doing so will give him access to the widest range of choice of consumption-streams. An important property of an optimal income stream is that if it be changed into an alternative attainable income stream by a marginal reduction in the flow of income at any date compensated by an increase at a later date, the resultant increase could not exceed the initial reduction plus the interest accumulated between the two dates, calculated at the market rate. A similar statement holds between an initiating increase at some date and the compensating decrease that would be necessary at the later date.

The two sorts of choice interact to produce Fisher's "separation theorem," which holds that consumption decisions are made separately from the production decisions, and that saving-investment plans depend on the market rate of interest rather than on the investor's personal rate of time preference.

The market rate of interest applicable to any interval of time is determined in the financial markets so as to equate the value of loans demanded for that interval to the amount of credit offered for the same interval. We have already noted that in equilibrium, the value of loans demanded to finance any type of investment will be just enough to assure that the marginal rate of return to investments of that type equals the market rate of interest and that each consumer-investor invests to the point where his marginal rate of substitution between consumption expenditures at any two dates equals the market rate of interest applicable to loans between those dates, because otherwise he could move to a preferable consumption path by either saving more (if the interest rate was higher than the marginal rate of substitution) or less (if the interest rate was lower). In this manner, all relevant marginal rates are brought into equilibrium.

To summarize Fisher's doctrine: Investment choices are basic. Each investor invests his capital in undertakings that promise the highest available rate of return. In equilibrium, they all succeed, thus allocating the economy's capital in the most productive way possible, as measured by the present value of the resulting flows of final products, computed at the resulting rates of discount. In this allocation, the capital invested in all industries and enterprises has the same marginal productivity (measured in present value terms) when this common marginal productivity of invested capital is calculated by discounting the anticipated cash flows in accordance with the time structure of the market rates of interest.

The explicit market for borrowing and lending operates in close correspondence with allocation of capital among investment opportunities, and permits each participant, investor, worker, or pensioner, to allocate his expenditures over time in the way that suits him best within the constraint that the present value of his expenditure plan cannot exceed that of his anticipated receipts. The result, again, is that for all pairs of time periods, each consumer's marginal rate of substitution between expenditures in those time periods is the same as all the others' because everyone's marginal rate of substitution between consumption expenditures at those times equals the market rate of interest applicable to the interval between them.

All this is a theory of remarkable subtlety, elegance, and ingenuity. Of course, these sophisticated conclusions rest on strong assumptions of which Fisher was well aware. They assume perfectly functioning, frictionless, competitive markets, and perfect information and complete, unerring foresight on the part of every economic actor. Fisher was particularly chagrined that he could not take account of the uncertainty of life and of investment results. But subsequent economists, in spite of vast efforts, have not done very well at that either.

The Rate of Interest, where these theses were first expounded, met a cool reception. Böhm-Bawerk's theory was the reigning doctrine at the time, and in America there was a lively controversy between two schools of thought. One attributed the existence of positive interest rates primarily to the physical productiveness of capital-using methods of production, as did Böhm-Bawerk himself. The other emphasized the psychological factors, i.e. time preference. Fisher's theory, being eclectic, drew fire from both.

Advocates of the productivity explanation of interest complained that if capital-using methods of production were no more productive than hand methods, most of the motivation for borrowing would vanish along with the ability to pay positive interest for loans. Besides, they pointed out, even the psychological preference for early receipt of income depends ultimately on recognizing that currently available income can be used to produce a larger product at any later time than deferred income can produce at that same time. They concluded therefore that Fisher paid undue attention to the psychological grounds for time preference. Adherents to the time-preference school insisted, on the other hand, that unless present goods were preferred to deferred goods in like kind and number, capital would become so abundant that the interest rate would be driven down to near zero. Therefore, they argued, Fisher's analysis of investment is unnecessary for explaining why the rate of interest is normally positive, and obscures the true explanation.

Fisher argued in vain that his theory did justice to both considerations, and showed that both were essential to the existence of a positive rate of interest in equilibrium. He wrote several papers to defend his theory,[21] but felt that his position continued to be misunderstood widely. His textbook, *Elementary Principles of Economics* (1912) made matters worse because it omitted virtually all mention of the relation of interest rates to technological choices, apparently because Fisher felt that the necessary explanation would be too complicated for beginning students.

After twenty-three years, Fisher undertook such a thorough revision of *The Rate of Interest* that he gave the new edition a new name: *The Theory of Interest*. The substance of the theory was not changed, indeed many of the examples and explanations of the 1907 version were repeated verbatim, but the ideas were presented in a completely new and greatly clarified order. Of course, by that time the old controversies were all but forgotten.

One further contrast should be mentioned. Recall that from the outset Böhm-Bawerk undertook to demonstrate that interest was an inevitable and justifiable cost of capital-using methods of production. One of his basic assumptions in arguing to this conclusion was that increases in the APP or, what is essentially the same thing, the capital-labor ratio, were always subject to decreasing returns. Böhm-Bawerk defended this assertion inflexibly on several occasions when it was challenged, and

21. For example, in the *Quarterly Journal of Economics*, May 1909, and the *American Economic Review*, September 1913.

never conceded that the criticisms had merit.

Fisher was one of the economists who doubted it. In the context of his own theory, the analogous assumption would be that the income streams available to any economic actor formed a convex set. This assumption also would amount to assuming decreasing returns, or at least non-increasing returns, to increases in the capital-labor ratio, and would lead to a positive rate of interest in equilibrium. But Fisher did not make it. He used the assumption in some of his diagrams and expositions, but he also showed examples of circumstances in which the equilibrium rate of interest could be zero or less. Thus, he concluded, an equilibrium with a negative rate of interest is a logical possibility. Though he recognized that the conditions in which this possibility would be realized are highly unlikely, he could not accept Böhm-Bawerk's conclusion that the interest rate in a capital-using economy would have to be positive.

III. CONCLUDING COMMENTS

It is now more than a century since Böhm-Bawerk published *The Positive Theory of Capital* and nearly a century since Fisher's *The Rate of Interest*. It is hard to appreciate how different from now the world was when these two books were written, and how fast it was changing even then. Though *The Positive Theory of Capital* treats all capital as work-in-process, its basic theme is the advantages of roundabout methods of production, i.e., those that employ substantial amounts of fixed capital. Yet when it was published, 1889, such methods were only beginning to be used. Daimler drove his first automobile that same year; large-scale oil and petrochemical industries were still in the future. Edison's first power plant lit up part of New York in 1882, only seven years before; other cities were still in the coal-gaslight era or in the dark in 1889. Water power was still prevalent in the textile industries then and for many years to come. The steam engine and the steel industry represented the outer frontier of high-tech. Ford began mass-producing automobiles around the year that *The Rate of Interest* was published.

No more examples are needed to make the point that twentieth century industry was bursting out while Böhm-Bawerk and Fisher were laying out the economic theory of capital-using production. The contrast between the two books, including the shift from a social to a technological point of view, reflects the transformation that went on during the eighteen years that separated them as well as the contrasting social milieu's in which they were conceived. The remarkable thing is that the theory as it left Fisher's hands remains pertinent and helpful eighty-seven years later.

REFERENCES

Allen, Robert Loring, *Irving Fisher: A Biography*, Blackwell Publisher, Cambridge, Mass., 1993.

Böhm-Bawerk, Eugen von. 1884. *Geschichte und Kritik der Kapitalzinstheorien*; English translation: *Capital and Interest, I, History and Critique of Interest Theories*, translated by G. D. Huncke and H. F. Sennholz, Libertarian Press, South Holland, 1959.

_____. 1889. *Positive Theorie des Kapitales*; English translation: *Capital and Interest, II, Positive Theory of Capital*; translated by G. D. Huncke, H. F. Sennholz, consultant, Libertarian Press, South Holland, 1959.

Eatwell, John, Murray Milgate, and Peter Newman, eds. 1987. *The New Palgrave Dictionary of Economics,* Macmillan Press, London; entries "Böhm-Bawerk, Eugen von," by K. Hennings, and "Fisher, Irving," by J. Tobin.

Fisher, Irving, *Mathematical Investigations in the Theory of Value and Prices, Transactions of the Connecticut Academy, 9*, July 1892

_____. 1896a. *Appreciation and Interest*, Macmillan, New York.

_____. 1896b. "What Is Capital?," *Economic Journal, 6*, December, 509-34.

_____. 1906. *The Nature of Capital and Income*, Macmillan, New York.

_____. 1907. *The Rate of Interest*, Macmillan, New York.

_____. 1909. "A Reply to Critics," *Quarterly Journal of Economics, 23*, May, 536-41.

_____. 1912. *Elementary Principles of Economics*, Macmillan, New York.

_____. 1913. "The Impatience Theory of Interest," *American Economic Review, 3*, September, 610-18.

_____. 1930. *The Theory of Interest*, Macmillan, New York.

Fisher, Irving Norton. 1956. *My Father Irving Fisher*, Comet Press Books, New York.

Rae, John. 1834. *Statement of Some New Principles on the Subject of Political Economy*, Hilliard, Gray, Boston; reprinted in R. W. James, *John Rae, Political Economist, II*, University of Toronto Press, Toronto, 1965.

Robinson, Joan. 1954. "The Production Function and the Theory of Capital," *Review of Economic Studies, 21*, 81-106.

Name index

Abbot, Lawrence 103, 112–13
Achilles 320
Ackoff, Russell 82
Aiken, Howard 416
Alchian, A.A. 154
Ames 354
Anderson, F.J. 184, 186, 194
Anderson, James 440
Arrow, Kenneth J. 93, 98, 100, 121, 155, 266–7, 400
Atkinson, Anthony B. 150

Barnard, Chester 121
Barnett, H.J. 54
Baumol, William J. 62, 65, 120, 123
Bellman, R. 86
Bentley, Arthur 268
Bergson 181
Black, Duncan 121
Blackett, P.M.S. 77, 79
Böhm-Bawerk, E. von 86, 114–16, 118–20, 154, 447–55, 457–9
Bonar, James 444
Bonsor, N.C. 184, 186, 194
Borden, Neil H. 107
Bortkiewicz, Ladislaus von 451, 453
Boulding, K.E. 162
Bowen, Howard 122, 140–45
Bray, H.E. 380
Buechley, R.W. 310

Cahn, Albert 427
Calabresi, Guido 369
Camp, Glen 75–6, 82
Carter, Jimmy 361
Cassels, J.M. 22
Charnes, A. 34–5, 63, 404
Chenery, H.B. 49, 52, 381
Cheung, Steven N.S. 286
Chipman, John S. 47, 53, 155, 162
Clark 120
Clark, J.B. 40
Clark, P.G. 52
Coase, Ronald 281, 293
Cobb 47
Coleman 265
Cooper, W.W. 34–5, 63, 404
Copernicus 454

Cordes, Joseph 165
Cournot 42
Cowles 45, 427
Curtiss, John 427

Daimler, Gottlieb 459
Dantzig, George B. 36, 400, 402–7, 410–13, 415–28
Dasgupta, Partha 150
De Viti de Marco 131
Debreu, Gerard 125, 399–401
Diamond, P.A. 182
Dimand, Robert 448–9
Dobb, M.H. 435
Dorfman, Robert 62, 165, 402–3
Douglas 47
Downs, Anthony 121, 128
Duesenberry, J.S. 51–2, 56
Dupuit 143, 182
Durkheim, Emile 264

Eckstein, O. 155
Edelson, N.M. 192
Edison, Thomas 459
Einstein, Albert 390
Engel 239
Engels, Friedrich 435
Evans, W.D. 49

Farkas, J. 414, 423
Farr, Donald 34
Fechner 58
Fei, John C.H. 150
Fellner, W. 22
Ferguson, A.R. 49
Fisher, Irving 15, 154–5, 330, 447–51, 453–60
Fleming, J.S. 154
Foley, Duncan K. 126
Foley, Eugene P. 265
Ford, Henry 459
Ford, L.R. 66
Fourier 420
Frank Robert 165
Freeman, A.M. 190
Friedland, Robert 165
Friedman, Milton 359
Frobenius 380

Economists of the Twentieth Century

Monetarism and Macroeconomic
Policy
Thomas Mayer

Studies in Fiscal Federalism
Wallace E. Oates

The World Economy in Perspective
Essays in International Trade and European
Integration
Herbert Giersch

Towards a New Economics
Critical Essays on Ecology, Distribution and
Other Themes
Kenneth E. Boulding

Studies in Positive and Normative
Economics
Martin J. Bailey

The Collected Essays of Richard E.
Quandt (2 volumes)
Richard E. Quandt

International Trade Theory and Policy
Selected Essays of W. Max Corden
W. Max Corden

Organization and Technology in Capitalist
Development
William Lazonick

Studies in Human Capital
Collected Essays of Jacob Mincer, Volume 1
Jacob Mincer

Studies in Labor Supply
Collected Essays of Jacob Mincer, Volume 2
Jacob Mincer

Macroeconomics and Economic Policy
The Selected Essays of Assar Lindbeck
Volume I
Assar Lindbeck

The Welfare State
The Selected Essays of Assar Lindbeck
Volume II
Assar Lindbeck

Classical Economics, Public Expenditure
and Growth
Walter Eltis

Money, Interest Rates and Inflation
Frederic S. Mishkin

The Public Choice Approach to Politics
Dennis C. Mueller

The Liberal Economic Order
Volume I Essays on International Economics
Volume II Money, Cycles and Related Themes
Gottfried Haberler
Edited by Anthony Y.C. Koo

Economic Growth and Business Cycles
Prices and the Process of Cyclical Development
Paolo Sylos Labini

International Adjustment, Money and
Trade
Theory and Measurement for Economic Policy
Volume I
Herbert G. Grubel

International Capital and Service Flows
Theory and Measurement for Economic Policy
Volume II
Herbert G. Grubel

Unintended Effects of Government
Policies
Theory and Measurement for Economic Policy
Volume III
Herbert G. Grubel

The Economics of Competitive Enterprise
Selected Essays of P.W.S. Andrews
*Edited by Frederic S. Lee
and Peter E. Earl*

The Repressed Economy
Causes, Consequences, Reform
Deepak Lal

Economic Theory and Market Socialism
Selected Essays of Oskar Lange
Edited by Tadeusz Kowalik

Trade, Development and Political
Economy
Selected Essays of Ronald Findlay
Ronald Findlay

General Equilibrium Theory
The Collected Essays of Takashi Negishi
Volume I
Takashi Negishi

The History of Economics
The Collected Essays of Takashi Negishi
Volume II
Takashi Negishi

Studies in Econometric Theory
The Collected Essays of Takeshi Amemiya
Takeshi Amemiya